Canadian Criminology Today

Canadian Criminology Today

THEORIES AND APPLICATIONS

THIRD EDITION

FRANK SCHMALLEGER

Professor Emeritus,

The University of North Carolina at Pembroke

REBECCA VOLK

Algonquin College

PEARSON
Prentice
Hall

Toronto

Library and Archives Canada Cataloguing in Publication

Schmalleger, Frank
    Canadian criminology today : theories and applications / Frank
Schmalleger, Rebecca Volk. — 3rd ed.

Includes bibliographical references and index.
ISBN 978-0-13-205028-9

    1. Criminology—Textbooks.   2. Criminology—Canada—Textbooks.
I. Volk, Rebecca   II. Title.

HV6025.S34 2008364C2007-902369-X

ISBN-13: 978-0-13-205028-9
ISBN-10: 0-13-205028-5

Vice President, Editorial Director: Gary Bennett
Senior Acquisitions Editor: Laura Paterson Forbes
Marketing Manager: Sally Aspinall
Developmental Editor: Patti Altridge
Production Editor: Amanda Wesson
Copy Editor: Lenore Latta
Proofreader: Camille Isaacs
Production Coordinator: Janis Raisen
Composition: Debbie Kumpf
Photo and Permissions Research: Sandy Cooke
Art Director: Julia Hall
Cover Design: Julia Hall
Interior Design: Gail Ferriera Ng-A-Kien
Cover Image: Getty Images

1 2 3 4 5   11 10 09 08 07

Printed and bound in the United States of America.

Brief Contents

Contents

Preface

More than a quarter century ago, the criminologist Austin Turk began the preface to his book *Criminality and Legal Order* with these words:

> *Embarrassment provided much of the initial push that led to the writing of this book. I was embarrassed at my lack of good answers when confronted by students who wondered, somewhat irreverently, why criminology is "such a confused mish-mash."... Some of these students were especially bothered by the "unreality" of criminological studies, by which they meant the lack of sustained attention to connections between the theories and statistics about crime, and what they heard every day about relations among social conflicts, political manoeuvers, and law violation and enforcement.*[1]

Much has changed since Turk's time, yet much remains the same. Crime is still with us in the 21st century and is becoming more complex and difficult to understand. The events of 2001 have changed the world and how we think about crime and criminality. In addition to the realities of conventional crime, we are now faced with transnational and international activities. More criminological studies have been proposed and conducted, and all levels of government—federal, provincial/territorial, and municipal—have placed crime near the top of their political agendas.

The complexity of crime and criminal behaviour is fascinating. The challenge to prevent and control crime has seemingly become more complex as the face of crime changes, and continues to daunt criminologists and policy-makers alike. For the student of crime and criminal behaviour, the crucial question to be answered remains, *why*? Why, despite all the theorizing and studies, can we not "solve" the crime puzzle? Do some people behave violently because they are "born violent"? Or, is their exposure to violence in childhood responsible? Why does the affluent CEO engage in insider trading while the young person living in a high-crime neighbourhood remains crime-free? What is it that motivates one person and not another to violate social norms? And, does this motivation vary according to the type of law broken?

This third edition of *Canadian Criminology Today: Theories and Applications* continues to examine these questions by building on the preceding editions. Other special features making this book substantially different from comparable texts include the following:

- *Canadian Criminology Today* meets the needs of students preparing for careers in the Canadian criminal justice system. Its applied focus on the explanations of crime and deviance and their application to real-life examples of criminal behaviour reflects the learning outcomes of introductory criminology courses.
- *Canadian Criminology Today* emphasizes the wide variety of interdisciplinary academic perspectives that contribute to a thorough understanding of the crime problem. The text is thematic, building on the divergence between the social problems viewpoint and the social responsibility perspective. In so doing, it highlights the central issue facing criminologists today: whether crime should be addressed as a matter of individual responsibility and accountability or treated as a symptom of a dysfunctional society.

1. Austin Turk, *Criminality and Legal Order* (Chicago: Rand McNally, 1969), p. vii.

- *Canadian Criminology Today* is up-to-date. It addresses the latest social issues and discusses innovative criminological perspectives within a well-grounded and traditional theoretical framework. Socially relevant, it contrasts contemporary issues of crime and social order with existing and proposed crime-prevention policies.
- *Canadian Criminology Today* makes use of the most recent instructional technologies and offers students the opportunity to learn from the internet and print media.
- *Canadian Criminology Today* is interesting and easy to read. It is written for today's student and makes use of attention-getting stories, news briefs, images, charts, and graphs. Study tools such as learning outcomes, marginal definitions, and a glossary serve to reinforce student learning.

The thematic approach of *Canadian Criminology Today* is dualistic. On the one hand, it presents a social problems framework, which holds that crime may be a manifestation of underlying cultural issues such as poverty, discrimination, and the breakdown of traditional social institutions. On the other, it contrasts the social problems approach with a social responsibility perspective, which claims that individuals are fundamentally responsible for their own behaviour and maintains that they choose crime over other, more law-abiding, courses of action. The thematic contrast is an important one, for it provides students with a useful framework for integrating the voluminous material contained within the field of criminology. Contrasting the two perspectives, as this book does, provides fertile ground for discussion and debate, allowing students to better understand the central issues defining contemporary criminology and to reach their own conclusions about the value of criminology theory.

The hope is that today's students will find *Canadian Criminology Today* relevant, interesting, informative, and useful. It is designed to assist them in understanding the reasons and motivations behind criminal and deviant behaviour, to allow them to draw their own conclusions about the most effective ways to treat such behaviour and, ultimately, to prepare them for their future careers within the criminal justice system. After all, it is only by understanding the reality of crime and criminal behaviour that we can ever hope to come close to solving and preventing it.

Canadian Criminology Today: Theories and Applications retains a number of the organizational features of the US Fourth Edition, *Criminology Today: An Integrative Introduction*, which have made it one of the most popular and accessible introductory criminology texts.

New to this Edition

The major changes to this third Canadian edition are

- a new final chapter: Chapter 12, "Future Directions and Emerging Trends." This chapter addresses changes in crime and criminal activity and highlights a number of emerging trends which are defined by the realities of globalization and the transnational nature of crime, including the trafficking of humans and cyber-crime. It concludes with a discussion of the resurgence of comparative criminology.
- expanded discussion of the differences between psychopathy and anti-social personality disorder.
- updated analysis of various legislation including the *Youth Criminal Justice Act*, the *Firearms Act*, and the *National Crime Prevention Strategy*.

- updated chapters examining crime statistics and patterns of crime with expanded use of Canadian and international examples and case studies.
- the streamlining of material from Chapter 4, "Research Theories and Development" into Chapter 1, "What is Criminology?"

Features

Learning features for the third edition of *Canadian Criminology Today* build on those found in the second edition. They include the following:

- Learning outcomes that help to organize key concepts
- Important names and terms highlighted at the beginning of each chapter that assist with recall
- Current crime stories opening each chapter that pique interest and alert students to key topics
- Boxes that relate theory to actual cases by highlighting crime theory versus reality
- Updated news stories that provide students with reality-based studies
- Updated tables, graphs, charts, and figures that reflect the current trends in the field
- Marginal definitions that provide students with immediate comprehension and application of terms
- End-of-chapter summaries that reinforce important concepts and issues discussed within the chapter
- Discussion questions that encourage students to apply the knowledge they have gained
- Updated weblinks for each chapter that allow students to explore the internet for more chapter-related material

A variety of instructor and student supplements enhance the teaching and learning experience provided by the text.

Student Supplement

Updated Companion Website (ISBN 978-0-13-206287-9). The extensive Companion Website has been updated for this new edition at **www.pearsoned.ca/schmalleger**. Features of the Companion Website include chapter learning outcomes, brief chapter summaries for review, practise tests (online quizzing through multiple-choice and discussion questions with immediate grading), Web Destinations, PowerPoint® slides, and Resources on the Net.

Instructor Supplements

- The Instructor's Manual (ISBN 978-0-13-206253-4) includes learning objectives for each chapter, a brief topic outline, and detailed lecture outlines with teaching tips. Issued on the Instructor's Resource CD-ROM, the Instructor's Manual is in PDF format. This supplement can also be downloaded by instructors from a password-protected location on Pearson Education Canada's online catalogue (**vig.pearsoned.ca**).

Simply search for the text, then click on "Instructor" under "Resources" in the left-hand menu. Contact your local sales representative for further information.

- The Test Item File (ISBN 978-0-13-206286-2) is a comprehensive test bank featuring multiple-choice and true-false questions with references to text page numbers, level of difficulty, and skill level. The Test Item File is in Word format located on the Instructor's Resource CD-ROM or can be downloaded by instructors from a password-protected location on Pearson Education Canada's online catalogue (**vig.pearsoned.ca**).
- MyTest (ISBN 978-0-13-206255-8) from Pearson Education Canada is a powerful assessment generation program that helps instructors easily create and print quizzes, tests, exams, as well as homework or practice handouts. Questions and tests can all be authored online, allowing instructors ultimate flexibility and the ability to efficiently manage assessments at anytime, from anywhere.
- The **new** Image Library (ISBN 978-0-13206403-3) is available on the Instructor's Resource CD-ROM. This library includes the tables and figures from the text. Instructors can make us of these images in their handouts and in-class presentations.
- The PowerPoint Presentations (ISBN 978-0-13-206256-5) are located on the Instructor's Resource CD-ROM and the Companion Website.
- The Instructor's Resource CD-ROM (ISBN 978-0-13-206254-1) features all of the instructor supplements in a convenient format, along with the appropriate viewers to read and use these materials.

Acknowledgments

The third edition of *Canadian Criminology Today: Theories and Applications* would not have been possible without the support from the team at Pearson Education Canada. Special thanks again to Patti Altridge for her patient guidance, encouragement, and insight. Thanks to Lenore Latta and Camille Isaacs whose editorial talents and feedback have ensured that this book is accessible and easy to read. Amanda Wesson, Kathleen McGill, and Ky Pruesse helped to keep everything in order, for which I am grateful.

Reviews and comments from colleagues have helped me make this book relevant and up-to-date. Special thanks are due to Melanie Gates of Algonquin College and Oliver Stoetzer of Fanshawe College for their ongoing support and for sharing their understanding of the field with me. Thanks also to Julian Hermida of Dalhousie University, Myrna Dawson of the University of Guelph, Dale Dearden of Kwantlen University College, Darryl Davies of Carleton University and Elaine DeCuhna of Fleming College for all their feedback. Research assistance from Monica Thornell meant that I was able to come close to meeting deadlines!

Finally, thank you again to Martin, Monica, and Aaron for your unwavering support, understanding, and patience.

I continue to be indebted to my students whose desire to learn continues to stimulate my passion for the field of criminology. I salute them and encourage them to take up the challenges presented by the realities of crime and criminality, always with the goal of bettering the lives of all those affected.

Rebecca Volk

About the Authors

Frank Schmalleger, Ph.D., Director, The Justice Research Association

Frank Schmalleger, Ph.D., is director of the Justice Research Association, a consulting firm focusing on issues of crime and justice. Schmalleger is also founder and co-director of the Criminal Justice Distance Learning Consortium (**cjcentral.com/cjdlc**). He holds degrees from Notre Dame and Ohio State, having earned both a master's (1970) and doctorate in sociology (1974) from Ohio State University with a special emphasis in criminology. From 1976 to 1994 he taught criminal justice courses at the University of North Carolina at Pembroke. For the last 16 of those years, he chaired the University's Department of Sociology, Social Work, and Criminal Justice. Schmalleger has also taught in the New School for Social Research's online graduate program. His numerous articles and books include *Criminology Today, Criminal Law Today, Criminal and Justice System in America: An Encyclopedia, Computers in Criminal Justice, Criminal Justice Ethics, Finding Criminal Justice in the Library, A History of Corrections*, and *The Social Basis of Criminal Justice.*

Rebecca Volk, M.A., professor at Algonquin College of Applied Arts and Technology

Rebecca Volk is a coordinator and professor in the Police Foundations Program at Algonquin College in Ottawa, Ontario. She holds a bachelor's degree in political science from Queen's University in Kingston, Ontario and an applied master's degree in criminology from the University of Ottawa.

In addition to teaching, Volk's professional experience has included involvement with a variety of offender aftercare and advocacy agencies, federal and provincial correctional institutions and residential centres, legal aid services, and various police agencies. She serves on the boards of several organizations devoted to promoting social justice for the most vulnerable among us.

CHAPTER 1

What Is Criminology?

Rather than attributing crime and all that is evil to a relatively small group of people, I am saying that crime and socially harmful behaviour is widely (although not evenly) dispersed in society.

—THOMAS GABOR[1]

Criminological research is most frequently concerned with the discovery of the causes of crime and the effect of various methods of treatment.

—HERMAN MANNHEIM[2]

LEARNING OUTCOMES

After reading this chapter, you should be able to

● understand what criminology is and what criminologists do

● recognize the difference between criminal and deviant acts, and appreciate the complexity of this distinction

● distinguish between the three perspectives of theoretical criminology

● appreciate the relevance of criminology theory to the study of crime and criminals

● understand the distinction between the social problems and social responsibility perspectives of crime causation

CP/The Guelph Mercury.

IMPORTANT TERMS

crime	general theory	survey research
civil law	unicausal	case sudy
criminal law	integrated theory	participant observation
indictable offence	consensus model	self-reports
summary conviction offence	pluralistic perspective	secondary analysis
hybrid offence	social conflict perspective	quantitative methods
administrative law	research	qualitative methods
statute	applied research	data confidentiality
criminalize	pure research	informed consent
common law	primary research	social policies
statutory law	secondary research	V-chip
deviance	hypothesis	social problems perspective
criminologist	variable	social responsibility perspective
criminology	research design	social relativity
criminality	confounding effects	criminal justice system
criminal justice	controlled experiments	socialization
theory	quasi-experimental designs	

Introduction

Senseless murder is the kind of crime that everyone fears. On November 14, 1997, this fear became a reality for Reena Virk, 14, when she joined a group of friends to "hang out" on a Friday night at a park in Victoria, British Columbia, known as The Gorge, overlooking a saltwater inlet. She called her parents from a convenience store at 9:45 p.m. to say she was on her way home; her parents never saw her again. The next day, Reena Virk's body was found half-submerged in the water at the base of The Gorge. Several days later, police received a tip that Virk had been murdered, and they rounded up and arrested eight teens. Six girls were charged with aggravated assault. Kelly Ellard and Warren Glowatski were charged with second-degree murder. All the accused were between 14 and 16 years of age.[3]

From her birth on March 10, 1983, Reena Virk had been the darling of an extended family within the 5000-strong Indo-Canadian community in Victoria. As she approached adolescence, Virk felt the tight-knit extended family beginning to stifle her; she wanted friends her own age and of her own choosing. She became frustrated and angry with her family when they disapproved of the friends she began associating with. Virk disliked her parents' strict rules, such as a 9:00 p.m. curfew. She rebelled and left home. She drifted from her grandparents' house to various shelters and group homes. Although she kept in touch with her mother by telephone, at the time of her death Virk had gone from a strictly supervised situation to one in which she set her own limits. One of her pastimes included spending hours with friends at The Gorge.

According to media accounts, seven girls and one boy surrounded Virk at the park as she sat on a stone wall. Kelly Ellard stubbed her cigarette on Virk's forehead, accusing her of taking her address book and spreading rumours about her. Virk tried to run away, but the group caught her as she attempted to climb the stairs leading to a bridge spanning the gorge; they bent her over the rail and beat her. Warren Glowatski repeatedly kicked her in the head. Virk broke free and stumbled across the bridge, where she was again attacked by the group of teens. Pulled down to the water's edge, Virk was repeatedly punched and kicked; Ellard rammed Virk's head into a tree with such force that Virk eventually fell on her face, unconscious. Ellard then grabbed Virk's hair, pulled her head backward, and administered a karate chop to her windpipe. Ellard smoked a cigarette and held Virk's head under the water with her foot until she drowned. Pathologist Dr. Laurel Gray stated that the injuries to Virk's brain, head, liver, and other vital organs were similar to those suffered by victims of motor vehicle accidents.

As the profiles of Warren Glowatski and Kelly Ellard emerged, it became clear that they did not really seem to appreciate the seriousness of their actions. Glowatski was described as a typical "98-pound weakling" who insisted that he had played only a minor role in Virk's death. He claimed that he thought Ellard was going to rob Virk and that his participation in the beating was to that end. Testifying that he left before Virk drowned, he stated, "I didn't know she was going to die."

When police arrested Kelly Ellard for the murder of Reena Virk, her immediate response was, "Oh, my God," and then she laughed. While she appeared cold and calculating at times, Ellard frequently lapsed into childlike behaviour, promising to stay in her room for the rest of her life if she was allowed to go home. She admitted pushing Virk, whom she had just met for the first time, but insisted that other girls were responsible for her death. Amazingly, Ellard claimed later that the last time she saw Virk she appeared drunk, because she couldn't walk straight. She suggested that Virk probably fell into the water and drowned as a result of her intoxicated state.

The six girls charged with aggravated assault were found guilty and received sentences ranging from sixty days to one year in jail. Both Ellard and Glowatski were tried as adults and were convicted of second-degree murder and sentenced to life imprisonment. Ellard is eligible for parole after five years, while Glowatski can be considered for parole after seven years.

Glowatski and Ellard both appealed their convictions. While the appeal court upheld Glowatski's conviction, in February 2003 it overturned the jury's second-degree murder conviction of Ellard, and ordered a new trial because of improper questioning by the Crown. Her second trial in June 2004 ended in a hung jury. At her third trial in April 2005, Ellard was found guilty of second-degree murder and sentenced to life in prison with no chance of parole for seven years.

Fourteen-year-old Reena Virk was punched, kicked, and eventually drowned by a group of teenage peers. What do murders like this have to say about the condition of Canadian society today?
The Canadian Press/Chuck Stoody.

The troubling thing about Reena Virk's death, however, is not so much *how* she was killed, but *why* she died. Reena Virk's mother, Suman Virk, expressed rage and sorrow that some of the youths stood around and watched her daughter being attacked and did nothing to help her.

What Is Crime?

Canadians and the Canadian mass media display a penchant for closely following gruesome and spectacular crimes, such as the murder of Reena Virk, and for thoroughly documenting crimes and transgressions of celebrities and other well-known individuals. The serial killings committed by Clifford Olson and the mass murder of 14 female students in Montreal in the 1980s, the heinous murders of Leslie Mahaffy and Kristen French at the hands of Paul Bernardo and Karla Homolka in the 1990s, and the ambush and murder of four RCMP officers on an Alberta farm in 2005 all received national coverage. Gillian Guess became somewhat of a celebrity in 1996 when she was charged with obstruction of justice. As a juror in a 1995 murder trial in British Columbia, Ms. Guess had established a sexual relationship with one of the accused—the latter was subsequently acquitted. It was the first time in North America or the Commonwealth that this had ever happened!

Easy accessibility to the US mass media also means that Canadians are inundated with news of criminal activities south of the border, which seem to occur more frequently and sensationally than similar events in Canada. For example, the murders of the wife of actor Robert Blake, fashion designer Gianni Versace, Ennis Cosby (son of entertainer Bill Cosby), 6-year-old starlet JonBenet Ramsey, and basketball great Michael Jordan's father (James Jordan) on a North Carolina roadside all received much press coverage. The alleged misdeeds of other celebrities such as Martha Stewart, O.J. Simpson, Michael Jackson, Robert Downey Jr., and Winona Ryder seemed to attract even more attention. Of course, not all misdeeds are crimes. Seen from a legalistic perspective, **crime** is human conduct in violation of the criminal laws of a jurisdiction that has the power to make such laws. Without a law that circumscribes a particular form of behaviour, there can be no crime, no matter how deviant or socially repugnant the behaviour in question may be.

A recent case from Australia well illustrates the principle that without a law to define an activity as illegal, there can be no crime. A few years ago, an Australian court acquitted Aboriginal activist John Kelly of "making a demand with menaces"—an offence under Australian law that is similar to the crime of extortion. Kelly was charged by prosecutors with trying to extort $10 000 (Australian) by threatening to "point the bone," or place a death curse, on a well-known Australian comedian. Northern Territory Supreme Court Judge Steven Bailey directed a jury to acquit Kelly after a three-day trial, saying that "there was no evidence of unlawful conduct" in the Aboriginal activity of "pointing the bone" and that any threat made on the basis of such activity was essentially meaningless.[4] Had Kelly threatened to kill the comedian with a gun, the judge would probably have found otherwise. As in this case, however, the laws of most states would make it difficult or impossible to convict someone of assault charges for putting a voodoo curse on another person, or for burning an effigy of the person in a "black magic" ritual.

The notion of crime as behaviour[5] that violates the law derives from earlier work by criminologists who defined crime as "an intentional act in violation of the criminal law... committed without defence or excuse, and penalized by the state as a felony or mis-

Crime human conduct in violation of the criminal laws of a jurisdiction that has the power to make such laws, and for which there is some form of authorized sanction.

demeanor."[6] Edwin Sutherland, one of the best-known criminologists of the last century, said of crime that its "essential characteristic . . . is that it is behavior which is prohibited by the State as an injury to the State and against which the State may react . . . by punishment."[7]

In the study of criminology, three major forms of the law must be distinguished: civil, criminal, and administrative. **Civil law** deals with arrangements between individuals, such as contracts and claims to property. It exists primarily for the purpose of enforcing private rights. In contrast, **criminal law** regulates actions that have the potential to harm interests of the state. Because the state is made up of citizens, acts that are harmful to citizens of the state are fundamentally criminal in nature. Hence, although serious crimes with identifiable victims—such as murder and sexual assault—are clearly criminal, offences that have no obvious victims, such as drug use, gambling, and prostitution, may also be regulated by the criminal law because they detract from the quality of life of citizens or decrease social order.

Serious criminal offences are referred to as **indictable offences** and include murder, robbery, sexual assault, hostage taking, perjury, and passing counterfeit money, among others. Less serious crimes or misdemeanours, such as making indecent telephone calls, being found in a common bawdy house, causing a disturbance in or near a public place, and loitering on private property at night, are known as **summary conviction offences**. **Hybrid offences** (dual-procedure offences) constitute a third category of criminal offence and include pointing a firearm, driving while disqualified, and uttering death threats. They may be tried as either indictable or summary conviction offences. The decision on how to treat a hybrid offence is made by the Crown Attorney and is based on the circumstances surrounding the offence and the accused.

Administrative law regulates many daily business activities. Violation of such regulations generally results in warnings or fines, depending on their adjudged severity. For example, decisions of the British Columbia Crime Victim Assistance Program or the Ontario Workplace Safety and Insurance Board constitute part of administrative case law.

Although the legalistic approach to crime—which sees crime solely as conduct in violation of the criminal law—is useful in the study of criminology, it is also limiting. Many times, those who adhere to a legalistic perspective insist that the nature of crime cannot be separated from the nature of law, as the one explicitly defines the other. Not easily recognized by any legalistic definition of crime, however, is the social, moral, and individual significance of fundamentally immoral forms of behaviour. Simply put, some activities not contravened by **statute** nonetheless call out for a societal response, sometimes leading commentators to proclaim "that ought to be a crime!" or "there ought to be a law against that!"

Another serious shortcoming of the legalistic approach to crime is that it yields the moral high ground to powerful individuals who are able to influence the making of laws and the imposition of criminal definitions on lawbreakers. By making their own laws, powerful but immoral individuals may escape the criminal label. Although democratic societies such as Canada would seem to be immune from such abuses of the legislative process, history demonstrates otherwise. In Chapter 10, we will explore this issue further and focus on the process of criminalization, the method used to **criminalize** some forms of behaviour—or make them illegal—while other forms remain legitimate.

The legalistic definition of crime also suffers from its seeming lack of recognition of the fact that formalized laws have not always existed. Undoubtedly, much immoral behaviour occurred in the distant past, and contemporary laws probably now regulate most such

Civil law body of law that regulates arrangements between individuals, such as contracts and claims to property.

Criminal law body of law that regulates actions that have the potential to harm interests of the state.

Indictable offence a serious criminal offence; specifically, one that carries a prison sentence of 14 years or longer.

Summary conviction offence a criminal offence that is less serious than an indictable offence; one that carries a maximum penalty of six months in jail.

Hybrid offence a criminal offence that can be classified as indictable or as a summary conviction; the classification is usually made by the Crown Attorney.

Administrative law regulates many daily business activities. Violation of such regulations generally results in warnings or fines, depending upon their adjudged severity.

Statute a formal written enactment of a legislative body.

Criminalize to make illegal.

Common law law
originating from usage
and custom rather than
from written statutes.
The term refers to non-
statutory customs,
traditions, and precedents
that help guide judicial
decision making.

Statutory law law in the
form of statutes or
formal written strictures,
made by a legislature or
governing body with the
power to make law.

behaviour. English **common law**, for example, upon which much Canadian **statutory law** is based, judged behaviour in terms of usage and custom rather than against written statutes. Although Canada has enacted a comprehensive federal legal code, it still adheres to the common-law tradition. The exception to this is Quebec provincial law, which operates under the civil-law system used in many continental European countries. Dating back to the law of the Romans, the modern civil-law system is based on the Napoleonic Code of the early 19th century. Common law is discussed in more detail in Chapter 5.

Changes in the law will undoubtedly continue to occur, perhaps even legitimizing former so-called crimes or recognizing that fundamentally moral forms of behaviour have been unduly criminalized. For over a decade, for example, the federal government, along with members of the general public, have debated the virtues of euthanasia. In 1993, Sue Rodriguez, a 42-year-old British Columbia woman, challenged before the Supreme Court of Canada the statute that criminalizes the act of assisted suicide (see Box 1.1). Suffering a slow and painful death from amyotrophic lateral sclerosis (ALS), also known as "Lou Gehrig's disease," Ms. Rodriguez felt that the law forbidding a third party to assist in her death violated her rights under the *Canadian Charter of Rights and Freedoms*. She lost her bid and committed suicide two years later.

Until recently, US Dr. Jack Kevorkian, perhaps the best-known pro-euthanasia activist of modern times, had been waging a crusade to legalize doctor-assisted suicide for terminally ill individuals. Kevorkian admitted assisting many seriously ill people who took their own lives, mostly in the state of Michigan. In the mid-1990s, tried under Michigan common law, Kevorkian was acquitted. In 1999, however, after Michigan enacted statutory provisions outlawing physician-assisted suicide, he was rearrested, tried, and convicted of a number of crimes and sentenced to ten to fifteen years in prison. Evidence against Kevorkian came mostly from a videotape aired on CBS showing the doctor giving a lethal injection to 52-year-old Thomas Youk, who suffered from Lou Gehrig's disease.

Practical considerations can also force re-evaluation of existing laws. A report prepared in 2002 by a Special Senate Committee on Illegal Drugs and a House of Commons Special

The debate over assisted suicide highlights the changing nature of criminal activity. Sue Rodriguez used her personal situation to attempt to get the Supreme Court to strike down section 241(b) of the *Criminal Code of Canada*, which makes it illegal to assist someone in committing suicide. She was unsuccessful and the law stands.
The Canadian Press/Chuck Stoody.

Committee on the Non-Medical Use of Drugs contends that marijuana should be treated like tobacco or alcohol rather than like harder drugs. The committees argued that the current criminal penalties for possession and use of small amounts of cannabis are disproportionately harsh and they went on to recommend that the Canadian ministers of justice and of health come up with a strategy to decriminalize the possession and cultivation of not more than 30 grams (roughly an ounce) of cannabis for personal use. While the use and possession of small amounts of marijuana would remain illegal, jail sentences and criminal records would be replaced with fines. Others argue that continued criminalization of marijuana unnecessarily puts a lucrative trade into the hands of organized crime, since it is the criminal status of drugs, not drugs themselves, that causes the crime. Further, proponents of the legalization of drugs argue that valuable enforcement resources are diverted away from the attack on other more serious forms of crime.[8] The current Canadian government, under Prime Minister Stephen Harper, has publicly stated that it will not be introducing a marijuana decriminalization plan prosed by the previous administration.

Box 1.1

Should Assisted Suicide Remain Illegal?

On September 30, 1993, in a 5 to 4 decision, the Supreme Court of Canada upheld the constitutionality of the law banning assisted suicide (section 241(b) of the *Criminal Code of Canada*). In *Rodriguez v British Columbia (Attorney General)*, lawyers for Sue Rodriguez argued that the law violated the right to equal benefit of the law (section 15) and the right to life, liberty, and security of the person (section 7) protected in the *Canadian Charter of Rights and Freedoms*. In essence, Ms. Rodriguez argued that the law prohibiting assisted suicide violated her right to equality, since it prevents persons who are physically unable to end their lives unassisted from choosing suicide when that option is available to other members of the public (attempted suicide was decriminalized in Canada in 1972). She also argued that the assisted suicide law infringed on her personal autonomy, or the protection of the dignity and privacy of individuals with respect to decisions concerning their own bodies.

The Supreme Court disagreed. The majority judgment advanced the following argument:

> Assisted suicide, outlawed under the common law, has been prohibited by Parliament since the adoption of Canada's first *Criminal Code*. The long-standing blanket prohibition in section 241(b), which fulfills the government's objective of protecting the vulnerable, is grounded in the state interest in protecting life and reflects the state policy that human life should not be depreciated by allowing human life to be taken.

The dissenting minority held that

> Section 7 of the Charter, which grants Canadians a constitutional right to life, liberty and the security of the person, is a provision which emphasizes the innate dignity of human existence. Dying is an integral part of living and, as a part of life, is entitled to the protection of s. 7. It follows that the right to die with dignity should be as well protected as any other aspect of the right to life. State prohibitions that would force a dreadful, painful death on a rational but incapacitated terminally ill patient are an affront to human dignity.

Similarly, in 1997 the US Supreme Court upheld the constitutionality of two laws prohibiting assisted suicide. Although the court ruled that terminally ill people do not have a constitutionally protected right to assisted suicide, it did nothing to bar the individual states from legalizing the process. Some jurisdictions, led by the state of Oregon, have legalized doctor-assisted suicide under prescribed conditions.[9]

DISCUSSION QUESTIONS

1. What is crime? Is assisted suicide a crime? What about doctor-assisted suicide? Why or why not?
2. Who is Dr. Jack Kevorkian? Is he a criminal? Why or why not?
3. Are there any activities that are not against the law that you think should be criminal? If so, what are they?
4. Are there any activities that are against the law that you think should not be illegal? If so, what are they?

Another perspective on crime is the political one. From a political point of view, crime is a result of criteria that have been built into the law by powerful groups and that are then used to label selected undesirable forms of behaviour as illegal. Those who adhere to this point of view say that crime is a definition of human conduct that is created by authorized agents in a politically organized society. Seen this way, laws serve the interests of the politically powerful, and crimes are merely forms of behaviour that are perceived by those in power as direct or indirect threats to their interests. Thus the political perspective defines crime in terms of the power structures that exist in society and asserts that criminal laws do not necessarily bear any inherent relationship to popular notions of right and wrong.

Crime and Deviance

Deviance behaviour that violates social norms or is statistically different from the average.

Sociologically speaking, most crimes can be regarded as deviant forms of behaviour—that is, as behaviours that are in some way abnormal. Abnormality, **deviance**, and crime, however, are concepts that do not always easily mesh. Some forms of deviance are not criminal, and the reverse is equally true (see Figure 1.1). Deviant styles of dress, for example, although perhaps outlandish to the majority, are not circumscribed by criminal law, unless (perhaps) decency statutes are violated by a lack of clothing. Even in such cases, laws are

Figure 1.1

The Overlap between Deviance and Crime

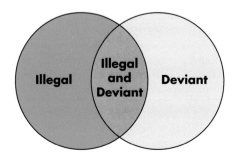

Illegal   Illegal and Deviant   Deviant

Deviance is relevant to the social context within which it occurs, as these licensed sex workers in Amsterdam show. Why is sex for hire against the law in most Canadian jurisdictions?
Todd Haimann/Corbis.

subject to interpretation and may be modified as social norms change over time. A little over a decade ago, for example, the Court of Appeal in Ontario overturned the conviction of Gwen Jacob, who had been charged with committing an indecent act after she walked topless down a city street on a hot summer's day. The three judges on the panel ruled that there had to be a sexual connotation for the act to be considered indecent, and they found that Jacob had no such motivation. The topfree movement that has emerged across Canada and the United States highlights the role that societal interpretation plays in defining a criminal offence.

Some forms of behaviour are motivated by religious beliefs, such as the case highlighted in Box 1.2. Other forms of behaviour are quite common but are still against the law. Speeding on provincial highways, for example, although probably something that most motorists engage in occasionally, is illegal. Complicating matters further is the fact that some forms of behaviour are illegal in some jurisdictions but not in others. Panhandling and the activities of "squeegie kids," for example, violate provincial statutes in some provinces but not in others.

What Do Criminologists Do?

A typical dictionary definition of a **criminologist** is "one who studies crime, criminals, and criminal behaviour."[10] Occasionally, the term *criminologist* is used broadly to describe almost anyone who works in the criminal justice field. There is a growing tendency,

Criminologist one who is trained in the field of criminology; also, one who studies crime, criminals, and criminal behaviour.

Box 1.2

Parents Guilty of Lesser Charge in Son's Death

Do parents have the right to deny medical treatment for their children because of their religious beliefs? As the following story shows, religious beliefs are not a defence when a child dies.

Parents whose religious beliefs kept them from seeking treatment for their gravely ill 14-year-old son were found not guilty Wednesday of criminal negligence causing death.

But Steven Shippy, 44, and his wife, Ruth, 36, were convicted of failing to provide the necessities of life.

Calahan Shippy died at home Dec. 30, 1998, from complications of diabetes. The parents said they didn't know he had diabetes and thought he had the flu.

The Shippys belong to the Followers of Christ based in Oregon City, Oregon. The sect believes illness is cured by prayer and anointing oil.

After the verdict, the boy's father said he believes he has the right not to seek medical help for his eight children.

The parents will be sentenced June 26 in Red Deer Court of Queen's Bench.

Crown prosecutor Ian Fraser told Justice Douglas Sirrs he will not seek a jail term.

Sirrs said he was troubled by the case.

He said the family and other sect members in the area showed a wilful blindness and an ignorance of medical issues.

"I have little doubt they are caring and responsible parents with their children," he said.

"Calahan was emaciated to the point where he looked like a starving victim from the Holocaust."

Harold Grinde, a supporter of the family, said it was a case of religious discrimination.

The Shippys on their family homestead northwest of Red Deer, Alberta.

The Alberta Report.

▶ **DISCUSSION QUESTIONS**

1. The parents in this story each received a three-year suspended sentence for failing to provide the necessities of life. Do you think this sentence is justified? Why or why not?
2. Should a person's religious beliefs be controlled by law? If so, what limits should the law specify?

Source: *Edmonton Journal*, Thursday, June 8, 2000, p. A8. Reprinted with permission of the Canadian Press.

however, to reserve application of the term *criminologist* to academics, researchers, and policy analysts with advanced degrees who are involved in the study of crime and crime trends and in the analysis of societal reactions to crime. Hence, specially skilled investigators, crime-laboratory technicians, fingerprint experts, crime-scene photographers, ballistics experts, and others who work to solve particular crimes are often referred to as *criminalists*. Police officers, corrections professionals, probation and parole officers, judges, Crown Attorneys, defence counsel, and others who do the day-to-day work of the criminal justice system are often referred to as *criminal justice professionals.*

Academic criminologists and research criminologists generally hold doctoral or master's degrees in the field of criminology or criminal justice from an accredited university. Some criminologists hold degrees in related fields such as sociology and political science and have specialized in the study and control of crime and deviance. Many academic criminologists teach either criminology or criminology-related subjects in institutions of higher learning, including universities and community colleges. Many criminology professors are involved in research or writing projects, by which they strive to advance criminological knowledge. Other criminologists are strictly researchers and work for federal agencies such as the Department of Justice Canada, Public Safety Canada, or the Canadian Centre for Justice Statistics.

The results of criminological research in Canada and the United States are generally published in journals such as the *Canadian Journal of Criminology and Criminal Justice* (the official publication of the Canadian Criminal Justice Association), the *Canadian Journal of Law and Society*, the *Canadian Journal of Women and the Law, Criminology* (the official publication of the American Society of Criminology), *Theoretical Criminology, Crime and Delinquency, Social Problems,* and *Victimology.*[11] International English-language journals are numerous and include the *Australian and New Zealand Journal of Criminology* and the *British Journal of Criminology* (see Box 1.3).

The term *criminologist* may also be applied to persons who have earned undergraduate degrees in the field. These degrees may provide entry into police investigative or support work, probation and parole agencies, court-support activities, and correctional (prison) work. Criminologists also work for government agencies interested in the development of effective social policies intended to deter or combat crime.

Private security provides another career track for individuals interested in criminology. The number of personnel employed by private security agencies today is one-third greater than that by public law enforcement agencies, and the gap is widening.[12] Many upper- and mid-level managers working for private security firms hold criminology or criminal-justice degrees.

A similar trend is emerging in the field of public policing. While most Canadian police services require applicants to have a minimum education of grade 12, a majority of recent

Professional Journals Publishing Criminological Research   Box 1.3

Criminologists often seek to publish the results of their research to share them with others working in the field. A wide range of professional journals publishes the work of criminologists, some of which are listed below. Most of these journals are available through community college or university libraries, and a number of them can be accessed through the internet.

American Journal of Criminal Justice

*Australian and New Zealand Journal of
    Criminology*

British Journal of Criminology

*Canadian Journal of Criminology and
    Criminal Justice* (formerly
    Canadian Journal of Criminology)

Canadian Journal of Law and Society

Canadian Journal of Women and the Law

Corrections Today

Crime and Delinquency

Crime and Social Justice

Criminal Justice Ethics

Criminal Justice Review

Criminology

Federal Probation

*International Journal of Comparative and
    Applied Criminal Justice*

International Journal of Victimology

Journal of Contemporary Criminal Justice

Journal of Crime and Justice

Journal of Criminal Justice Education

Journal of Criminal Law and Criminology

Journal of Interpersonal Violence

*Journal of Police Science and
    Administration*

Journal of Quantitative Criminology

*Journal of Research in Crime and
    Delinquency*

Justice Professional

Justice Quarterly

Law and Society Review

Law Now Magazine

RCMP Gazette

Social Forces

Social Problems

Sociology of Criminal Law

The Prison Journal

Theoretical Criminology

Violence and Victims

Victimology

new recruits to the profession have attained levels of education greater than this minimum. Of these, 36 percent had a community college diploma, while 19 percent had a university degree. The remainder had attended some type of post-secondary institution.[13]

Anyone trained in criminology has various alternatives. Some with undergraduate degrees in criminology or criminal justice go on to law school. Some teach high school, while others become private investigators. Many criminologists provide civic organizations (such as victims' assistance and justice advocacy groups) with much-needed expertise, a few work for politicians and legislative bodies, and some appear on talk shows to debate the pros and cons of various kinds of social policies designed to "fight" crime. Some criminologists even write books such as this one!

What Is Criminology?

The attempt to understand crime predates written history. Prehistoric evidence, including skeletal remains showing signs of primitive cranial surgery, seems to indicate that preliterate people explained deviant behaviour in terms of spirit possession. Primitive "surgery" was an attempt to release unwanted spiritual influences. In the thousands of years since, many other theoretical perspectives on crime have been advanced. This book describes various criminological theories and covers some of the more popular ones in detail.

Before beginning any earnest discussion, however, it is necessary to define the term *criminology.* As our earlier discussion of the nature of crime and deviance indicates, criminologists must not only deal with a complex subject matter—consisting of a broad range of illegal behaviours committed by frequently unknown or uncooperative individuals—they must also manage their work under changing conditions mandated by ongoing revisions of the law and fluctuating social policy. In addition, as we have already seen, a wide variety of perspectives on the nature of crime exists. All this leads to considerable difficulties in defining the subject matter under study.

There is some evidence that the term *criminology* was coined in 1889[14] by a Frenchman, Paul Topinard, who used it to differentiate the study of criminal body types within the field of anthropology from other biometric pursuits.[15] Topinard, while he may have coined the term, did little to help define it. As with the concept of crime, various definitions of *criminology* can be found in the literature today.

One straightforward definition can be had from a linguistic analysis of the word *criminology.* As most people know, *ology* means "the study of something," and the word *crimen* comes from the Latin, meaning "accusation," "charge," or "guilt." Hence, linguistically speaking, the term *criminology* literally means "the study of crime." In addition to this fundamental kind of linguistic definition, three other important types of definitions exist. They are (1) disciplinary, (2) causative, and (3) scientific. Each type of definition is distinguished by its focus. Disciplinary definitions are those that, as the name implies, focus on criminology as a discipline. Seen from this viewpoint, criminology is a field of study or a body of knowledge. Causative definitions emphasize criminology's role in uncovering the underlying causes of crime. Finally, there are those who point to the scientific nature of contemporary criminology as its distinguishing characteristic.

Edwin H. Sutherland, a leader in the field, suggests that criminology consists of three "principal divisions": (1) the sociology of law, (2) scientific analysis of the causes of crime, and (3) crime control.[16] Another well-known criminologist similarly sees three components of the field: (1) detection (of the offender), (2) treatment, and (3) explaining crime and criminal behaviour.[17] Criminology can also be defined as "an interdisciplinary study of the various bodies of knowledge, which focuses on the etiology of crime [or the construction of theories to describe, explain, or predict criminal behaviour], the behavior of criminals, and the policies and practices of crime control."[18]

For our purposes, we will use a definition that brings together the works of previous writers but that also recognizes the increasingly professional status of the criminological enterprise. Throughout this book, then, we will view **criminology** as an interdisciplinary profession built around the scientific study of crime and criminal behaviour, including their manifestations, causes, legal aspects, and control. As this definition indicates, criminology includes consideration of possible solutions to the problem of crime. Hence, this text (in later chapters) describes prevention and treatment strategies and social policy initiatives that have grown out of the existing array of theoretical explanations for crime.

Our definition is in keeping with the work of another outstanding criminologist of the 20th century, who has written that the purpose of criminology is to offer well-researched and objective answers to four basic questions: (1) "Why do crime rates vary?" (2) "Why do individuals differ as to **criminality**?" (3) "Why is there variation in reactions to crime?" and (4) "What are the possible means of controlling criminality?"[19]

Criminology an interdisciplinary profession built around the scientific study of crime and criminal behaviour, including their form, causes, legal aspects, and control.

Criminality a behavioural predisposition that disproportionately favours criminal activity.

As a field of study, criminology in its present form is primarily a social scientific discipline. Contemporary criminologists generally recognize, however, that their field is interdisciplinary; that is, it draws upon other disciplines to provide an integrated approach to understanding the problem of crime in contemporary society and to advancing solutions to the problems crime creates. Hence, biology, sociology, political science, psychology, economics, medicine, psychiatry, law, philosophy, and numerous other fields all have something to offer the student of criminology, as do the tools provided by statistics, computer science, and other forms of scientific and data analysis.

It is important, however, to note that although criminology may be interdisciplinary in its approach to the subject matter of crime, few existing explanations for criminal behaviour have been successfully integrated into one comprehensive explanation or theory. Just as physicists today are seeking a unified field theory to explain the wide variety of observable forms of matter and energy, criminologists have yet to develop a generally accepted, integrated approach to crime and criminal behaviour that can explain the many diverse forms of criminality while also leading to effective social policies in the area of crime prevention and control. The attempt to construct criminological theories of relevance is made all the more difficult because, as discussed earlier, the phenomenon under study—crime— is subject to arbitrary and sometimes unpredictable legalistic and definitional changes.

Not only must a successfully integrated criminology bring together the contributions of various theoretical perspectives and disciplines, it must also—if it is to have any relevance—blend the practical requirements of our nation's judicial system with emotional and rational calls for morality and justice. Should capital punishment, for example, be

Criminology examines the causes of crime and seeks ways to prevent or control it. Criminal justice examines the criminal justice system, including police, courts, and corrections. How do the two disciplines complement one another?

D. Greco/The Image Works.

reinstated? If so, on what basis? Is it because it is a type of vengeance, and therefore deserved? Or can we continue to say that it is unjustified because many sociological studies have shown that it does little to reduce the rate of serious crime such as murder? Just what do we mean by *justice*, and what can criminological studies tell us—if anything—about what is just and what is unjust?

The editors of the relatively new journal *Theoretical Criminology*,[20] which began publication in 1997, tell us in their inaugural issue that "criminology has always been somewhat of a haphazardly assembled, umbrella-like structure which nevertheless usefully shelters a variety of theoretical interests that are espoused and employed by different disciplinary, methodological, and political traditions." In other words, while the field of criminology can benefit from the wide variety of ideas available from a multiplicity of perspectives, all of which seek to understand the phenomenon we call "crime," cross-discipline collaboration can be quite difficult.

As the earlier definition of *criminology* indicates, however, it is more than a field of study or a collection of theories—it is also a profession.[21] Notably, criminology also contributes to the discipline of **criminal justice**, which emphasizes application of the criminal law and study of the components of the justice system, especially the police, courts, and corrections. As one author stated, "criminology gives prominence to questions about the *causes of criminality*, while the *control of lawbreaking* is at the heart of criminal justice."[22]

> **Criminal justice** the scientific study of crime, the criminal law, and components of the criminal justice system, including the police, courts, and corrections.

Theoretical Criminology

Theoretical criminology, a subfield of general criminology, is the type of criminology most often found in community colleges and universities. Theoretical criminology, rather than simply describing crime and its occurrence, posits explanations for criminal behaviour. As Edwin Sutherland stated, "[t]he problem in criminology is to explain the criminality of behavior . . . . However, an explanation of criminal behavior should be a specific part of [a] general theory of behavior and its task should be to differentiate criminal from non-criminal behavior."[23]

To explain and understand crime, criminologists have developed many theories. A **theory**, at least in its ideal form, is made up of clearly stated propositions that posit relationships, often of a causal sort, between events and things under study. An old Roman theory, for example, proposed that insanity is caused by the influence of the moon, and may even follow its cycles—hence the term *lunacy*.

Theories attempt to provide us with explanatory power and help us to understand a phenomenon under study. The more applicable a theory is found to be, the more generalizable it is from one specific instance to others—that is, the more it can be applied to other situations. A **general theory** of crime is one that attempts to explain all (or at least most) forms of criminal conduct through a single, overarching approach. Unfortunately, often "[t]heories in criminology tend to be unclear and lacking in justifiable generality."[24] When we consider the wide range of behaviours regarded as criminal—from murder, through drug use, to white-collar and computer crime—it seems difficult to imagine one theory that can explain them all, or which might even explain the same type of behaviour under varying circumstances. Still, many past theoretical approaches to crime causation were **unicausal** while attempting to be all-inclusive. In other words, the approaches posited a single, identifiable source for all serious deviant and criminal behaviour.

> **Theory** a series of interrelated propositions that attempt to describe, explain, predict, and ultimately to control some class of events. A theory gains explanatory power from inherent logical consistency and is "tested" by how well it describes and predicts reality.

> **General theory** one that attempts to explain all (or at least most) forms of criminal conduct through a single, overarching approach.

> **Unicausal** having one cause. Unicausal theories posit only one source for all that they attempt to explain.

An **integrated theory**, in contrast to a general theory, does not necessarily attempt to explain all criminality but is distinguishable by the fact that it merges (or attempts to merge) concepts drawn from different sources. Put another way, "An integrative criminology . . . seeks to bring together the diverse bodies of knowledge that represent the full array of disciplines that study crime."[25] Hence, integrated theories provide potentially wider explanatory power than narrower formulations. Recognizing that no one theory can explain all criminal behaviour, it has been noted that "the basic idea of theoretical integration is straightforward; it concerns the combinations of single theories or elements of those theories into a more comprehensive argument. At the same time, it would be well to note that in practice, integration is a matter of degree: some theorists have combined or integrated more concepts or theoretical elements than have others."[26]

> Integrated theory an explanatory perspective that merges (or attempts to merge) concepts drawn from different sources.

Both theoretical integration and the general applicability of criminological theories to a wide variety of law-violating behaviours are intuitively appealing concepts. Even far more limited attempts at criminological theorizing, however, often face daunting challenges. To date, "criminologists have not managed to articulate a large collection of relatively formalized arguments in a general or integrated form."[27] Hence, although we will use the word *theory* in describing the many explanations for crime covered by this book, it should be recognized that the word is only loosely applicable to some of the perspectives we will discuss.

As we shall learn later in this chapter, many social scientists insist that to be considered *theories*, explanations must consist of sets of clearly stated, logically interrelated, and measurable propositions. The fact that only a few of the theories described in this book rise above the level of organized conjecture—and those offer only limited generalizability and have rarely been integrated—is one of the greatest challenges facing criminology today.

Theoretical Perspectives in Criminology

What starting point do criminologists use when developing their theories? Does the way in which a criminologist views the social order have any impact on the theory of crime and criminal behaviour she posits? There are three generally accepted perspectives within criminology, each of which maintains its own view of what constitutes crime and, by definition, criminal behaviour. Known as the *consensus perspective*, the *pluralistic perspective*, and the *social conflict perspective*, each sees the relationship between the law and the social order somewhat differently. A criminologist's choice of perspective can influence his or her approach in explaining the causes of crime and criminal behaviour and, in turn, his or her suggestions for their prevention or control.

> Consensus model an analytical perspective on social organization holding that most members of society agree as to what is right and wrong and that the various elements of society work together in unison toward a common and shared vision of the greater good.

The Consensus Perspective
The **consensus model** of social organization is built around the notion that most members of society agree on what is right and wrong, and that the various elements of society—including institutions such as churches, schools, government agencies, and businesses—work together toward a common and shared vision of the greater good. According to Raymond J. Michalowski, whose excellent analytical work is used to describe each of the three major approaches discussed in this section, the consensus perspective is characterized by four principles:[28]

- A belief in the existence of core values. The consensus perspective holds that commonly shared notions of right and wrong characterize the majority of society's members.
- The notion that laws reflect the collective will of the people. Law is seen as the result of a consensus, achieved through legislative action, and represents a kind of social conscience.
- The assumption that the law serves all people equally. From the consensus point of view, the law not only embodies a shared view of justice, but is itself perceived to be just in its application.
- The idea that those who violate the law represent a unique subgroup with some distinguishing features. The consensus approach holds that law violators must somehow be improperly socialized, psychologically defective, or suffer from some other lapse which leaves them unable to participate in what is otherwise widespread agreement on values and behaviour.

The Pluralistic Perspective

Contrary to the assumptions made by consensus thinkers, however, it has become quite plain to most observers of the contemporary social scene that not everyone agrees on what the law should say. Society today is rife with examples of conflicting values and ideals. Consensus is hard to find. Modern debates centre on issues such as abortion, euthanasia, the death penalty, the purpose of criminal justice agencies in a diverse society, social justice, the rights and responsibilities of minorities and other under-represented groups, women's issues, the proper role of education, economic policy, social welfare, the function of the military in a changing world, environmental concerns, and appropriate uses of high technology. As many contemporary public forums would indicate, there exists within Canada today a great diversity of social groups, each with its own point of view regarding what is right and what is wrong, and each with its own agenda.

Such a situation is described by some writers as pluralistic. A **pluralistic perspective** mirrors the thought that a multiplicity of values and beliefs exists in any complex society and that different social groups will have their own respective sets of beliefs, interests, and values. A crucial element of this perspective, however, is the assumption that although different viewpoints exist, most individuals agree on the usefulness of law as a formal means of dispute resolution. Hence, from a pluralistic perspective the law, rather than reflecting common values, exists as a peacekeeping tool that allows officials and agencies within the government to settle disputes effectively between individuals and among groups. It also assumes that whatever settlement is reached will be acceptable to all parties because of their agreement on the fundamental role of law in dispute settlement. The basic principles of the pluralistic perspective include the following notions:[29]

Pluralistic perspective an analytical approach to social organization holding that a multiplicity of values and beliefs exists in any complex society but that most social actors agree on the usefulness of law as a formal means of dispute resolution.

- Society consists of many and diverse social groups. Differences in age, gender, sexual preference, ethnicity, and the like often provide the basis for much naturally occurring diversity.
- Each group has its own characteristic set of values, beliefs, and interests. Variety in gender, sexual orientation, economic status, ethnicity, and other forms of diversity produces interests that may unite like-minded individuals but that may also place them in natural opposition to other social groups.

- A general agreement exists on the usefulness of formalized laws as a mechanism for dispute resolution. People and groups accept the role of law in the settlement of disputes and accord decisions reached within the legal framework at least a modicum of respect.
- The legal system is value-neutral. That is, the legal system is itself thought to be free of petty disputes or above the level of general contentiousness that may characterize relationships between groups.
- The legal system is concerned with the best interests of society. Legislators, judges, prosecutors, attorneys, police officers, and correctional officials are assumed to perform idealized functions that are beyond the reach of interest groups. Hence, such official functionaries can be trusted to act in accordance with the greater good, to remain unbiased, and to maintain a value-free system for the enforcement of laws.

According to the pluralistic perspective, conflict is essentially resolved through the peace-keeping activities of unbiased government officials exercising objective legal authority.

The Social Conflict Perspective A third point of view, the **social conflict perspective**, maintains that conflict is a fundamental aspect of social life itself that can never be fully resolved. At best, according to this perspective, formal agencies of social control merely coerce the unempowered or the disenfranchised to comply with the rules established by those in power. From the conflict point of view, laws become a tool of the powerful, useful in keeping others from wresting control over important social institutions. Social order, rather than being the result of any consensus or process of dispute resolution, rests upon the exercise of power through law. Those in power must work ceaselessly to remain there, although the structure they impose on society—including patterns of wealth building that they define as acceptable and circumstances under which they authorize the exercise of legal power and military might—gives them all the advantages they are likely to need. The conflict perspective can be described in terms of the following key elements:[30]

Social conflict perspective an analytical perspective on social organization holding that conflict is a fundamental aspect of social life itself and can never be fully resolved.

- Society is made up of diverse social groups. As in the pluralistic perspective, diversity is thought to be based on distinctions that people hold to be significant, such as gender, sexual orientation, social class, and the like.
- Each group holds to differing definitions of right and wrong. Moralistic conceptions and behavioural standards vary from group to group.
- Conflict between groups is unavoidable. Conflict is based on differences held to be socially significant (such as ethnicity, gender, and social class) and is unavoidable because groups defined on the basis of these characteristics compete for power, wealth, and other forms of recognition.
- The fundamental nature of group conflict centres on the exercise of political power. Political power is the key to the accumulation of wealth and to other forms of power.
- Law is a tool of power and furthers the interests of those powerful enough to make it. Laws allow those in control to gain what they define (through the law) as legitimate access to scarce resources and to deny (through the law) such access to the politically disenfranchised.
- Those in power are inevitably interested in maintaining their power against those who would usurp it. The powerful strive to keep their power.

The Science of Criminology

The theoretical perspectives adopted by criminologists provide the underpinning for the direction of their research and the development of their theories. Indeed, over the past century, criminologists have undertaken the task of building a "scientific criminology," as distinguished from what had been the "armchair criminology" of earlier years. Armchair criminologists offered their ideas to one another as conjecture—fascinating "theories" that could be debated (and sometimes were) *ad nauseam*. The ruminations of armchair criminologists achieved a considerable degree of popular acclaim through the involvement of distinguished lecturers, the association of such ideas with celebrated bastions of higher learning, and their publication in prestigious forums, but they were rarely founded on anything other than mere speculation.

Present-day criminology is decidedly more scientific, however, than its intellectual predecessor—which means that it is amenable to objective scrutiny and systematic testing. In fact, the drive to make criminology "scientific" has been a conscious one, beginning with many of the approaches discussed in Chapter 5.

A variety of criteria has been advanced for declaring any endeavour "scientific." Among them are[31]

- the systematic collection of related facts (as in the building of a database)
- an emphasis on the availability and application of the scientific method
- "the existence of general laws, a field for experiment or observation . . . and control of academic discourse by practical application"
- "the fact that it has been . . . accepted into the scientific tradition"
- an "emphasis on a worthwhile subject in need of independent study even if adequate techniques of study are not yet available" (as in the investigation of paranormal phenomena).

Probably all the foregoing could be said of criminology. For one thing, criminologists do gather facts. The mere gathering of facts, however, although it may lead to a descriptive criminology, falls short of offering satisfactory explanations for crime. Hence, most contemporary criminologists are concerned with identifying relationships among the facts they observe, and with attempting to understand the many and diverse causes of crime. This emphasis on unveiling causality moves criminology beyond the merely descriptive into the realm of conjecture and theory building.

Theory Building

Ultimately, the goal of research within criminology is the construction of theories or models that allow for a better understanding of criminal behaviour and that permit the development of strategies intended to address the problem of crime. A theory consists of a set of interrelated propositions that provide a relatively complete form of understanding. Hence, even if we find that crime is higher when the moon is full, we must still ask, "Why?" Is it because the light from full moons makes it possible for those interested in committing crime to see better at night? If so, then we would expect crime to be higher on full moon nights in areas where there is no cloud cover than in areas where clouds obliterate the moon's light. Likewise, cities should show less of a rise in crime during full moons than do rural areas and small towns, as city lights effectively minimize the impact of the light of the moon. In any event, a complete lunar theory of crime causation would contain specific propositions about the causal nature of the phenomena involved.

While there are many ways to define the word *theory,* for our purposes, a theory consists of a series of interrelated propositions that attempt to describe, explain, predict, and ultimately control some class of events. Theories gain explanatory power from inherent logical consistency and are "tested" by how well they describe and predict reality. In other words, a good theory provides relatively complete understanding, is supported by observations, and stands up to continued scrutiny.

Theories serve a number of purposes. For one thing, they give meaning to observations. They explain what we see in a particular setting by relating those observations to other things already understood. Hence, a simple example of a theory of physics explains the behaviour of light by saying that light has the properties of both waves and particles. Such a theory is immediately useful, for although we may have trouble conceptualizing the light's essence, we can easily grasp ideas such as "wave" and "particle," both of which we experience in everyday living.

Theories within criminology serve the same purpose as those in the physical sciences, although they are often more difficult to test. Few people, for example, can intuitively understand the motivation of "lust murderers" (a term developed by the Federal Bureau of Investigation in the United States and popularized by some recent movies) or men who sexually abuse and kill women, often sadistically. Most people, after all, are not lust murderers, and therefore lack an intellectual starting point in striving to understand what goes on in the minds of those who are. Some psychiatric theories (discussed in Chapter 7) suggest that lust murderers kill because of a deep-seated hatred of women. Hate is something that most minds can grasp, and a vision of lust murder as an extreme example of the age-old battle between the sexes provides an intellectual "handle" that many can appreciate. Hence, theory building dispenses of the old adage that "it takes one to know one," instead bringing at least the possibility of understanding within the reach of all. Note, however, that although such limited explanations as the one discussed here may provide a degree of understanding, they must still be tested to determine whether they are true.

The Role of Research

More important than the claims made by theories and by the theorists who create them are findings of fact that either support those claims or leave them without foundation. Hence, theories, once proposed, need to be tested against the real world through a variety of research strategies, including experimentation and case studies. This is equally true whether the proposed theory is relatively simple or complex.

In the late 1990s, for example, Kim Rossmo, Ph.D., an inspector with the Vancouver Police Department, used a simple hypothesis that he had developed through years of experience to help police capture a serial rapist.[32] The rapist had attacked 11 women and had eluded officials for years. Rossmo's hypothesis involved geographic profiling, which extended the belief that most humans—offenders included—are inherently creatures of habit who tend to live and work in specific familiar areas and that most of their daily activities are limited to these areas. Offenders then, are more likely to commit crimes close to where they live and work. Based on this simple assumption, Rossmo created a computer simulation designed to estimate the location of a suspect's residence by assessing the areas where crimes attributable to him or her had occurred. When Canadian authorities compared probable locations identified by the computer with suspects whom they had already identified as possible rapists, only one name stood out. A comparison of that man's DNA with DNA found in semen recovered from the victims convinced them that he was the person they were looking for. (See Chapter 5 for a more detailed look at the work of Kim Rossmo.)

Knowledge is inevitably built on experience and observation. Hence, the crux of scientific research is data collection. Data collection occurs through a variety of techniques, including direct observation, the use of surveys and interviews, participant observation, and the analysis of existing data sets—all of which will be discussed shortly.

Research can be defined as the use of standardized, systematic procedures in the search for knowledge.[33] Some researchers distinguish between applied research and non-applied or pure research. **Applied research** "consists of scientific inquiry that is designed and carried out with practical application in mind."[34] In applied research, the researcher is working toward some more or less practical goal. It may be the reduction of crime, the efficient compensation of victims of crime, or an evaluation of the effectiveness of policies

Research the use of standardized, systematic procedures in the search for knowledge.

Applied research scientific inquiry that is designed and carried out with practical application in mind.

Former Vancouver Police Service detective Kim Rossmo (centre) used the hypothesis that humans—offenders included—are creatures of habit as the basis for his geographic profiling tool. How do hypotheses presented by researchers gain credibility?
CP/AP/Nick Wass.

implemented to solve some specific aspect of the crime problem. **Pure research**, on the other hand, is undertaken simply for the sake of advancing scientific knowledge and is not expected to be immediately relevant.

Another type of research is called secondary research or secondary analysis.[35] It is distinguished from **primary research** in that the latter is characterized by original and direct investigation.[36] **Secondary research**, on the other hand, consists of new evaluations of existing information collected by other researchers.

Scientific research generally proceeds in stages, which can be divided conceptually among (1) problem identification, (2) the development of a research design, (3) a choice of data-gathering techniques, and (4) a review of findings, which often includes statistical analysis. These four techniques will be briefly discussed here.

Problem Identification

Problem identification, the first step in any research, consists of the naming of a problem or choice of an issue to be studied. Topics may be selected for a variety of reasons. It may be that private foundation monies have become available to support studies in a specific area, perhaps the researcher has a personal interest in a particular issue and wants to learn more, or maybe a professor or teacher has assigned a research project as part of the requirements for successful class completion. Whatever the reason for beginning research, however, the way in which a research problem is stated will help narrow the research focus and serve as a guide to the formulation of data-gathering strategies.

Although some criminological research undertaken today is purely descriptive, the bulk of such research is intended to explore issues of causality—especially the claims made by theories purporting to explain criminal behaviour. As such, much contemporary research in criminology is involved with the testing of hypotheses.

Within the modern scientific tradition, a **hypothesis** serves two purposes: it is an explanation that accounts for a set of facts and that can be tested by further investigation, and it is something that is taken to be true for the purpose of argument or investigation. Some criminologists, as mentioned earlier, have observed what appears to be a correlation, or relationship, between phases of the moon and the rate of crime commission. Such observers may propose the following hypothesis: "the moon causes crime." Although this is a useful starting hypothesis, it needs to be further refined before it can be tested. Specifically, the concepts contained within the hypothesis must be translated into measurable variables. A **variable** is simply a concept that can undergo measurable changes.

Research Designs

Research designs structure the research process. They provide a kind of road map to the logic inherent in one's approach to a research problem. They also serve as guides to the systematic collection of data. **Research designs** consist of the logic and structure inherent in any particular approach to data gathering.

A simple study, for example, might be designed to test the assertion that the consumption of refined white sugar promotes aggressive or violent tendencies among men. One could imagine researchers approaching prison officials with the proposal that inmate diets should be altered to exclude all refined sugar. Likewise the prison canteen would be prohibited from selling items containing sugar for the duration of the experiment.

To determine whether the forced reduction in sugar consumption actually affected inmates' behaviour, researchers might look at the recorded frequency of aggressive incidents occurring within the confines of the prison before the experiment was initiated and

Pure research research undertaken simply for the sake of advancing scientific knowledge.

Primary research research characterized by original and direct investigation.

Secondary research new evaluations of existing information collected by other researchers.

Hypothesis 1. an explanation that accounts for a set of facts and that can be tested by further investigation. 2. something that is taken to be true for the purpose of argument or investigation.

Variable a concept that can undergo measurable changes.

Research design the logic and structure inherent in an approach to data gathering.

compare such data with similar information on such incidents following the introduction of dietary changes.

Although this basic research design well illustrates the logic behind naive experiments, it does not lend good structure to a research undertaking, because it does not eliminate other possible explanations of behavioural change. For example, during the time between the first and second observations, inmates may have been exposed to some other influence that reduced their level of aggression. A new minister may have begun preaching effective sermons filled with messages of love and peace to the prison congregation; television cable service to the prison may have been disrupted, lowering the exposure inmates received to violent programming; a new warden may have taken control of the facility, relaxing prison rules and reducing tensions; or a transfer or release of especially troublesome inmates may have occurred. In fact, the possibilities for rival explanations (i.e., those that rival the explanatory power of the hypothesis under study) are nearly limitless. Rival explanations such as these, called "competing hypotheses" by some researchers and **confounding effects** by others, make the results of any single series of observations uncertain.

To amass greater confidence that the changes intentionally introduced into a situation are the real cause of observed variations, it is necessary to achieve some degree of control over factors that threaten the certainty that experimental interventions did indeed cause the changes observed in the study group. **Controlled experiments** are those that attempt to hold conditions (other than the intentionally introduced experimental intervention) constant. In fact, some researchers have defined the word *experiment* simply as controlled observation.

Whereas constancy of conditions may be possible to achieve within laboratory settings, it is far more difficult to come by in the social world—which by its very nature is in an ongoing state of flux. Therefore, **quasi-experimental designs** are especially valuable when aspects of the social setting are beyond the control of the researcher. The crucial defining feature of quasi-experimental designs is that they give researchers control over the *when and to whom of measurement*, even though others decide the "when and to whom" of exposure to the experimental intervention.

Sometimes, for example, legislators enact new laws intended to address some aspect of the crime problem, specifying the kinds of crime preventative measures to be employed and what segment of the population is to receive them. Midnight basketball, intended to keep young people off the streets at night, is an example of such legislatively sponsored intervention. The question, of course, is whether money spent in support of such an activity would actually reduce the incidence of street crime committed by youth. Unfortunately, good research data that could answer the question ahead of time are often unavailable. However, once the programs are in place, researchers can study them. Hence, although criminologists were not politically situated so as to be able to enact midnight basketball legislation, they are able to study the effects of such legislation after it has been enacted.

Techniques of Data Collection
Once a research problem has been identified, concepts have been made measurable, and a design for the conduct of the research has been selected, investigators must decide on the type of data to be gathered and the techniques of data gathering they wish to employ. Ultimately, all research depends on the use of techniques to gather information, or data, for eventual analysis. The most important question to consider, however, when beginning to gather information is *whether the data-gathering strategy selected will produce information in a form usable by the researcher.* The kind of

Confounding effects
rival explanations, also called competing hypotheses, which are threats to the internal or external validity of any research design.

Controlled experiments
those that attempt to hold conditions (other than the intentionally introduced experimental intervention) constant.

Quasi-experimental designs approaches to research that, although less powerful than experimental designs, are deemed worthy of use when better designs are not feasible.

information needed depends, of course, on the questions to be answered. Surveys of public opinion as to the desirability of the death penalty, for example, cannot address issues of the punishment's effectiveness as a crime control strategy.

Five major data-gathering strategies typify research in the field of criminology:

Survey research a social science data-gathering technique involving the use of questionnaires.

SURVEYS: **Survey research** typically involves the use of questionnaires. Respondents may be interviewed in person, over the telephone, or queried via email or fax. Mail surveys are common, although they tend to have a lower response rate than other types of social surveys. The information produced through the use of questionnaires is referred to as *survey data*. Similarly, Statistics Canada data, for example, are gathered by survey-takers who are trained periodically for that purpose. Survey data also inform the Canadian Urban Victimization Survey and result in such publications as *Violence Committed by Strangers, Risk of Personal and Household Victimization,* and other Statistics Canada–related reports produced by the Canadian Centre for Justice Statistics. Surveys have also been used in criminology to assess fear of crime and attitudes toward the police and to discover the extent of unreported crime.

Case study an investigation into an individual case.

CASE STUDIES: The **case study** is built around an in-depth investigation into an individual case. The study of one (perhaps notorious) offender, scrutiny of a particular criminal organization, analysis of a prison boot camp, and others may all qualify as case studies. Case studies are useful for what they can tell us to expect about other, similar cases. If study of a street gang, for example, reveals the central role of a few leaders, then we would expect to find a similar organizational style among other gangs of the same kind.

Participant observation a variety of strategies in data gathering in which the researcher observes a group by participating, to varying degrees, in the activities of the group.

PARTICIPANT OBSERVATION: **Participant observation** "involves a variety of strategies in data gathering in which the researcher observes a group by participating, to varying degrees, in the activities of the group."[37] Some participant researchers operate undercover, without revealing their identity as researchers to those whom they are studying, whereas others make their identity and purpose known from the outset of the research endeavour.

It is possible to distinguish between at least two additional kinds of participant observation: (1) the participant as observer and (2) the observer as complete participant. When researchers make their presence known to those whom they are observing, without attempting to influence the outcome of their observations or the activities of the group, they fit the category of participants who are observers. When they become complete participants in the group they are observing, however, researchers run the risk of influencing the group's direction.

Self-reports research investigations of subjects in order to record and report their behaviours.

SELF-REPORTING: Another subjective data-gathering technique is one that uses **self-reports** to investigate aspects of a problem not otherwise amenable to study. When official records are lacking, for example, research subjects may be asked to record and report rates of otherwise secretive behaviour. Self-reports may prove especially valuable in providing checks on official reports consisting of statistical tabulations gathered through channels such as police departments, hospitals, and social services agencies.

Many self-reporting techniques require the maintenance of a diary or personal journal and request vigilant and ongoing observations of one's own behaviour by the subject under study. Hence, sex researchers may ask subjects to maintain an ongoing record of their frequency of intercourse, the variety of sexual techniques employed, and their preference in partners—items of information that are not easy to come by through other means or that cannot be accurately reconstructed from memory.

SECONDARY ANALYSIS: Not all data-gathering techniques are intended to generate new information. **Secondary analysis** entails the reanalysis of existing data, that is, second-hand analysis of data that were gathered for another purpose. Secondary analysis of existing data and using previously acquired information can save researchers a considerable amount of time and expense.

> **Secondary analysis** the reanalysis of existing data.

One important source of data for secondary analysis is the Canadian Centre for Justice Statistics, created through the National Justice Statistics Initiative (NJSI) of the federal government. The mandate of the NJSI is "to provide information to the justice community and the public on the nature and extent of crime and the administration of criminal justice in Canada."[38] Through the Canadian Centre for Justice Statistics, the NJSI is meant to ensure the production of useful information to support legislative, policy, management, and research agendas, and to inform the public. Access to Canadian Centre for Justice Statistics data is open to the public, and data sets are available for sale to individual researchers. (A more detailed look at the Canadian Centre for Justice Statistics is found in Chapter 2.)

Quantitative versus Qualitative Methods

There are some who feel that there has been a tendency in criminology research over the past half century to overemphasize **quantitative methods** or techniques—that is, those that produce measurable results that can be analyzed statistically. To be sure, as such critics would be quick to admit, a considerable degree of intellectual comfort must be achieved in feeling that one is able to reduce complex forms of behaviour and interaction to something countable (as, say, the frequency of an offence). Intellectual comfort of this sort derives from the notion that anything expressible in numbers must somehow be more meaningful than that which is not.

> **Quantitative methods** research techniques that produce measurable results.

It is crucial to realize, however, that numerical expression is mostly a result of how researchers structure their approach to the subject matter and is rarely inherent in the subject matter itself. Such is especially true in the social sciences, where attitudes, feelings, behaviours, and perceptions of all sorts are subject to quantification by researchers, who impose upon such subjective phenomena artificial techniques for their quantification.

Qualitative methods, in contrast to those that are quantitative, produce subjective results or results that are difficult to quantify. Even though their findings are not expressed numerically, qualitative methods provide yet another set of potentially useful criminological research tools. Qualitative methods are important for the insight they provide into the subjective workings of the criminal mind and the processes by which meaning is accorded to human experience. Introspection, life histories, case studies, and participant observation all contain the potential to yield highly qualitative data.[39]

> **Qualitative methods** research techniques that produce subjective results or results that are difficult to quantify.

Consider, for example, how the following personal account of the motivation needed to rob banks provides subjective insights into the life of a young offender that would otherwise be difficult to express:[40]

> *I rob banks for the money. I like the excitement and thrills, but I do it for the money. The danger is exciting, but I don't do it for that. I spend my money on drugs—a lot on coke. It really does fly. I don't know where half of it goes. I had an apartment when I was sixteen and I was really proud of it. I bought a bed, a T.V., a 13-foot-long couch worth $1600. I was proud of myself. I was doing well. I was living with a chick who was 18, but she was just a friend. I'd also spend a lot of money on my family. I'd give some to my sisters. I'd spend a lot on taxis. I'd take them everywhere. On movies and amusement parks. Money is important to me. I never have enough, I always want more. If I was to*

get a big score, I would want another big score. After a while you start getting bigger ideas. I've thought about doing an armoured vehicle and I've watched them make deliveries.

It's only a fluke or a set-up that gets you caught. You either get caught cold-cock or you don't get caught at all. If they don't catch us in the first couple of hours, then forget it. They don't have a very good chance. This was the first time I got caught, but I think I learned a lot. Next time it will not be so easy. Once you get caught, everyone goes through a process where they don't want to do it anymore. Then after a couple of months, you're willing to do it again. I'm supposed to have a job when I hit the street, but if I have no job and no money I would do a bank for sure. It's your only means of survival. If I have no job and nowhere to stay, of course I'm going to do a bank. It's what I know. I've been trained to do that.

This passage is taken from an interview with Jules, aged 17. From a French-Canadian family of 8 brothers and 8 sisters, Jules started robbing banks at 15. His 5 older brothers have all been convicted of robbing banks and armoured vehicles. At the time of the interview, Jules was serving an 18-month prison sentence for 2 counts of robbery. He was arrested 5 years later at 22, again for bank robbery, and was sentenced to 15 years in prison.

Although the preceding is a purely personal account, and may hold questions of generalizability for researchers, imagine the difficulties inherent in acquiring this kind of data through the use of survey instruments or other traditional research techniques. Autobiographical accounts, introspection, and many forms of participant observation amount to a kind of phenomenological reporting, in which description leads to understanding and intuition is a better guide to theory building than are volumes of quantifiable data. A growing number of criminologists believe that qualitative data-gathering strategies represent the future of criminological research.

An 18-year-old gang member. Some researchers doubt that quantitative methods can adequately assess the subjective experiences of certain kinds of offenders. What is the nature of such "subjective experiences"?
Jim Tynan/Impact Visuals Photo & Graphics, Inc.

Values and Ethics in the Conduct of Research

Research, especially that conducted within the social sciences, does not occur in a vacuum. Values enter into all stages of the research process, from the selection of the problem to be studied to the choice of strategies to address it. In short, research is never entirely free from preconceptions and biases, although much can be done to limit the impact such biases have on the results of research.

The most effective way of controlling the effects of biases is to be aware of them at the outset of the research. If, for example, researchers know that the project they are working on elicits strong personal feelings but necessitates the use of interviewers, then it would be beneficial to strive to hire interviewers who are relatively free of biases or can control the expression of their feelings. Potential data gatherers might themselves be interviewed to determine their values and the likelihood that they might be tempted to interpret the data they gather or report it in ways that are biased. Similarly, data gatherers who are prejudiced against subgroups of potential respondents can represent a threat to the validity of the research results. The use of such interviewers may "turn off" some respondents, perhaps through racial innuendo, personal style, mannerisms, and so forth.

Of similar importance are ethical issues that, although they may not affect the validity of research results, can have a significant impact on the lives of both researchers and research subjects. The protection of human subjects, privacy, and **data confidentiality**— in which research data are not shared outside of the research environment—are the most important ethical issues facing researchers today. **Informed consent** is a strategy used by researchers to overcome many of the ethical issues inherent in criminological research. Informed consent means that research subjects will be informed as to the nature of the research about to be conducted, their anticipated role in it, and the uses that will be made of the data they provide. Ethics may also require that data derived from personal interviews or the testing of research subjects be anonymous (not associated with the names of individual subjects) and that raw (unanalyzed) data be destroyed after a specified time interval (often at the completion of the research project).

Federal regulations require a plan for the protection of sensitive information as part of grant proposals submitted to federal agencies. Some universities, research organizations, and government agencies have established institutional review boards tasked with examining research proposals before they are submitted to funding organizations to determine whether expectations of ethical conduct have been met. Institutional review boards often consist of other researchers with special knowledge of the kinds of ethical issues involved in criminological research.

Participant observation sometimes entails an especially thorny ethical issue. In other words, should researchers themselves violate the law if their research participation appears to require it? The very nature of participant observation is such that researchers of adult criminal activity may at times find themselves placed in situations where they are expected to "go along with the group" in violating the law. Those researching gang activity, for example, have sometimes been asked to transmit potentially incriminating information to other gang members, to act as drug couriers, and even to commit crimes of violence to help establish territorial claims important to members of the gang. Researchers who refuse may endanger not only their research but also themselves.

Data confidentiality an ethical requirement of social scientific research that stipulates that research data not be shared outside of the research environment.

Informed consent an ethical requirement of social scientific research that specifies that research subjects will be informed as to the nature of the research about to be conducted, their anticipated role in it, and the uses to which the data they provide will be put.

Compliance with the expectations of criminal groups, of course, evokes other kinds of dangers, including the danger of apprehension and prosecution for violations of the criminal law.

Although the dilemma of a participant observer, especially one secretly engaged in research, is a difficult one, some of the best advice on the subject is offered by Frank E. Hagan, who writes: "In self-mediating the potential conflicting roles of the criminal justice researcher, it is incumbent on the investigator to enter the setting with eyes wide open. A decision must be made beforehand on the level of commitment to the research endeavor and the analyst's ability to negotiate the likely role conflicts. Although there are no hard and fast rules . . . *the researcher's primary role is that of a scientist.*"

Hagan also suggests that a code of ethics should guide all professional criminologists in their research undertakings. This code, says Hagan, would require the researcher to assume the following personal responsibilities:[41]

- Avoid procedures that may harm respondents.
- Honour commitments to respondents and respect reciprocity.
- Exercise objectivity and professional integrity in performing and reporting research.
- Protect confidentiality and privacy of respondents.

Criminology and Social Policy

Professional criminologists are themselves acutely aware of the need to link sound social policy to the objective findings of well-conducted criminological research. At a recent meeting of North American criminologists, the need to forge just such a link was emphasized. At the meeting, criminologists were told that they are crucial to "the generation of knowledge that is useful in dealing with crime and the operation of the criminal justice system, and then helping public officials to use that knowledge intelligently and effectively. . . . [S]o little is known about the causes of crime and about the effects of criminal justice policy on crime that new insights about the criminal justice system can often be extremely revealing and can eventually change the way people think about the crime problem or about the criminal justice system."[42]

.Social policies
government initiatives, programs, and plans intended to address problems in society. The National Crime Prevention Strategy, for example, is a kind of generic, large-scale social policy—one consisting of many smaller programs.

Examples of the development of **social policies** as a result of criminological research are evident. In a document entitled *Safer Communities* by the Departments of Justice and the Solicitor General of Canada, for example, the role of the mass media in encouraging violence among young people is examined. High-profile cases have caused many to blame the media for creating a current culture of violence. The television series *Mighty Morphin' Power Rangers* was dropped from a number of television networks in Canada in the 1990s after a five-year-old girl in Norway was beaten senseless by three young boys and left to freeze to death. In the United States, a mother claimed that the MTV cartoon *Beavis and Butt-Head* had prompted her five-year-old son to set a fire that killed his two-year-old sister.[43] Experts on research into violence on television claim that scenes of violence occur six times per hour on average in prime-time evening shows, while children's programming averages between 20 and 25 violent scenes per hour.[44]

The Canadian Radio-Television and Telecommunications Commission (CRTC) has tackled the issue of violence on television and has approved guidelines that forbid the broadcasting of shows with violence that is gratuitous or made to look glamorous. It has also stipulated that scenes of violence intended for adult audiences cannot be telecast between 6:00 a.m. and 9:00 p.m.[45]

The creation of the **V-chip** by Canadian electrical engineering professor Tim Collins allows parents to block certain television programs or scenes. While hundreds of thousands of televisions manufactured annually are equipped with a V-chip, Canada has yet to introduce legislation that would require all new television sets to have V-chips built in.

Copycat violence has also been attributed to films. Touchstone Pictures, for example, re-edited the movie *The Program*, cutting scenes in which drunken football players test their nerve by lying end to end in the middle of a highway. Of the several young men who apparently copied the stunt, some were killed and some critically injured. Commenting on the incidents, a Touchstone spokesperson said, "[w]hile the scene in the movie in no way advocates this irresponsible activity, it is impossible for us to ignore that someone may have recklessly chosen to imitate it. . . ."[46] The *Safer Communities* document bemoans the fact that television doesn't do more to influence public opinion in positive ways. "This medium has the most powerful ability to shape our perceptions," it states. "It can educate its audience, combat stereotypes, provide models of pro-social behaviour and attitudes. But for the most part television, and other media too, have not picked up the challenge."[47]

Nevertheless, despite the evidence that research in the area of criminology has much to offer policy makers, too often publicly elected officials either remain ignorant of current research or simply pay lip service to the advice of professional criminologists, seeking instead to create politically expedient policies. Nowhere is this reality more evident than in the area of Aboriginal justice initiatives in Canada. In an article entitled "The Impact of Aboriginal Justice Research on Policy: A Marginal Past and an Even More Uncertain Future," Carol La Prairie writes,

> the benefits of research for Aboriginal criminal justice in Canada have scarcely been tapped. There have been some issue-specific activities. . . over the past 25 years but research has not systematically been designed and integrated into policy, practice, and project development. Because research is often negatively perceived by Aboriginal people and is of sporadic interest to government, its history of shaping justice projects and influencing policy decision-making has been marginal at best.[48]

La Prairie concludes that this apparent lack of research impact and integration results from the fact that government legislators equate Aboriginal justice issues with the self-government movement, which has largely served to portray Aboriginal justice problems (such as the over-representation of Aboriginals as offenders in the criminal justice system) as conflicts over race and culture, rooted in a colonial history of conflict and discrimination. She claims that the emphasis of research on the race/cultural issue has failed to consider other possible explanations for problems faced by Aboriginal people, such as "community marginalization, inequity of distribution of community resources, and family breakdown and dysfunction."[49]

Even when excellent research is available to guide policy creation, a realistic appraisal must recognize that criminologists are sometimes as much to blame for counterproductive policies as anyone. The American experience with the "three-strikes" laws provides an example of the kind of dilemma facing criminologists who would influence social policy on the basis of statistical evidence.

V-chip a device that enables viewers to program their televisions to block out content with a common rating. It is intended for use against violent or sexually explicit programming.

Three-strikes laws, which became popular with legislatures across the United States over the last decade, require that three-time felons receive lengthy prison sentences (often life without the possibility of parole) following their third conviction. Such laws are built on the notion that "getting tough" with repeat offenders by putting them in prison for long periods should reduce the crime rate. Logic seems to say that lengthy prison sentences for recidivists will reduce crime by removing the most active offenders from society.

A recent study of the three-strikes laws in 22 states, however, concluded that such legislation typically results in clogged court systems and crowded correctional facilities and encourages three-time felons to take dramatic risks to avoid capture.[50] A wider-based study,[51] dubbed "the most comprehensive study ever of crime prevention,"[52] found that "much of the research on prisons was inadequate or flawed, making it impossible to measure how much crime was actually prevented or deterred by locking up more criminals." More significantly, the central finding of this massive study was that current government-sponsored crime prevention initiatives are often poorly evaluated, leading to uncertainty over whether funded programs actually "work." Hence, although the three-strikes laws remain popular with the American voting public, and lawmakers have been quick to seize upon get-tough crime prevention policies in the interest of winning votes, solid and consistent research support showing the efficacy of such laws continues to be elusive.

The Media and Public Crime Concerns

"If it bleeds it leads" is a phrase often used by the mass media to determine how much attention and coverage is given to a news story. Indeed, the news media, both print and television, seem to be preoccupied with delivering stories about war, disease, and incidents of violent crime. Many argue that the media are simply giving the public what it wants; in turn, others argue that the public's perception about threats to its safety and protection is skewed. A report by Julian Roberts identifies a number of ways that the mass media influence public attitudes and belief about crime.[53] He contends that (1) the media tend not to report or to emphasize declining crime rates; (2) national crime figures (which for the past decade have been reporting declining crime rates) are published only once a year, allowing the media the remainder of each year to concentrate on extreme, violent cases; and (3) crime stories reported by the media are rarely put in a statistical context, and the electronic and print news outlets neglect to comment on trends in crime rates over time.

A recent example of the role of the media in the development of social policy, and crime control policy in particular, is apparent in the announcement by the Canadian federal government in 2006 of a bill that will make it easier for the justice system to label offenders as dangerous after a third serious conviction.[54] A dangerous offender designation carries with it an indeterminate sentence with no ability to apply for parole for seven years. The Federal Minister of Justice introducing the bill is quoted as saying that the attention was generated around a specific case involving convicted pedophile Peter Whitmore. Released after serving his sentence, Whitmore was arrested after an intensive manhunt near Kipling, Saskatchewan, where he had been living with a 14-year-old boy from Winnipeg and a 10-year-old boy from Saskatchewan. The media coverage of the case was extensive and served to galvanize public sentiment about the sentencing of repeat offenders.[55] Detractors of this approach to sentencing point to research that indicates that similar legislation in the United States (the three-strikes law) has not had the desired effect.

According to pollsters, fear of crime is a persistent concern among Canadians. Given recent statistics showing falling crime rates, is such fear realistic? What role does the media play in the perception of crime among Canadians?
H. Darr Beisner/USA Today.

While crime is still a concern in contemporary Canada, recent surveys indicate that it may not be as pressing an issue as are health and education. Surveys by the Earnscliffe Strategy Group indicate that the percentage of Canadians identifying crime as a "high priority" is declining.[56] Despite a softening concern for crime, most Canadians believe that crime has been on the increase in their communities.[57] A recent Angus Reid/CTV News poll indicates that, of those polled, 59 percent perceived an increase in crime over the past 5 years. This concern was especially marked in Western Canada, where 30 percent of British Columbians perceived a "great increase" in crime. The same poll found that 21 percent of Canadians surveyed feared being a victim of crime in their own community, with 5 percent harbouring a "great deal" of fear and 16 percent a "fair amount" of fear. When asked to name the most important problems in their community, 22 percent of the respondents named crime and related issues as "top of mind." This figure ranged from 10 percent in Atlantic Canada and Quebec to 42 percent in British Columbia.

This poll also examined public confidence in the Canadian justice system, finding that 86 percent of respondents are at least "somewhat confident" in their local police (37 percent are "very confident"). Canadians were less pleased with the courts—52 percent expressed "overall confidence" compared to 47 percent who were "not very confident" or "not at all confident" in the operation of the courts. A modest majority surveyed expressed a lack of faith in the prison system (54 percent "not very/not at all confident"), while 72 percent expressed "little/no confidence" in the parole system.

Fear of crime is not necessarily related to the actual incidence of crime. A recent Department of Justice report concluded that "despite an increasing concern for crime, the public's fears remain unrelated to actual crime rates and potential for victimization, as perceptions of criminal activity and violence are not in tune with reality."[58] Even if fear of crime has reached "unreasonable" levels when objectively compared with the actual incidence of criminal activity, however, fear remains an important determinant of public policy. Hence, government agendas that promise to lower crime rates, and that call for changes in the conditions that produce crime, can be quite successful politically for those who promote them in an environment where fear of crime is high.[59]

**Social problems
perspective** the belief
that crime is a
manifestation of
underlying social
problems such as poverty,
discrimination, pervasive
family violence,
inadequate socialization
practices, and the
breakdown of traditional
social institutions.

The Theme of This Book

This book builds on a social policy theme by contrasting two popular perspectives (see Figure 1.2). One point of view, termed the **social problems perspective**, holds that crime is a manifestation of underlying social problems such as poverty, discrimination, the breakdown of traditional social institutions, the poor quality of formal education available to some, pervasive family violence experienced during the formative years, and inadequate socialization practices that leave young people without the fundamental values necessary to contribute meaningfully to the society in which they live. Advocates of the social problems perspective advance solutions based on what is, in effect, a public health model, which says that crime needs to be addressed much like a public health concern.

Proponents of this perspective typically foresee solutions to the crime problem as coming in the form of government expenditures in support of social programs designed to address the issues that lie at the root of crime. Government-funded initiatives, designed to enhance social, educational, occupational, and other opportunities, are perceived as offering programmatic solutions to ameliorate most causes of crime. The social problems approach to crime is characteristic of what social scientists term a *macro* approach. Instances of individual behaviour (crimes) are portrayed as arising out of widespread and contributory social conditions that enmesh unwitting individuals in a causal nexus of uncontrollable social forces.

In the early nineties, the Solicitor General and the Parliamentary Standing Committee on Justice produced a report entitled *Crime Prevention in Canada: Toward a National Strategy*. The report recommended the implementation of a "National Strategy on Community Safety and Crime Prevention" (now known as the National Crime Prevention Strategy) focused on developing new plans to look at the causes of crime and to develop

---

Figure 1.2

The Theme of This Book
Social Problems versus Social Responsibility

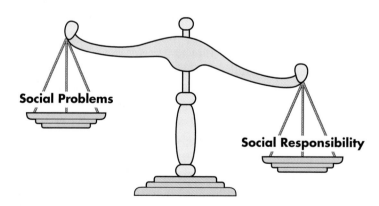

At the core of today's thinking about crime exists a crucial distinction between those who believe that *crime is a matter of individual responsibility* (the social responsibility perspective) and those who emphasize that *crime is a manifestation of underlying social problems* beyond the control of individuals (the social problems perspective).

partnerships with communities across the country to carry out crime-prevention activities. Phase I of the National Strategy (1994–1997) saw the creation of the National Crime Prevention Council (NCPC), whose mandate was the promotion of crime prevention through social development, with particular emphasis on early-prevention programs targeting children and youth. The NCPC identified a number of factors that place children and youth at risk of engaging in criminal behaviour. These included child poverty, inadequate living conditions, inconsistent and uncaring parenting, childhood traumas such as physical and sexual abuse, family breakdown, racism, and other forms of discrimination, difficulties in school, delinquent friends, and living situations where there is alcohol, drug, and other kinds of substance abuse. Phase II (since 1997) is building on the work done by the NCPC and focuses on helping communities develop programs and partnerships to reduce crime and victimization. In addition to focusing on children and youth, this phase places priority on Aboriginal people and women's personal safety.[60] A detailed examination of the National Crime Prevention Strategy can be found in Chapter 11.

A contrasting perspective lays the cause of crime squarely at the feet of individual perpetrators. This point of view holds that individuals are fundamentally responsible for their own behaviour and maintains that they choose crime over other, more law-abiding courses of action. Perpetrators may choose crime, advocates of this perspective say, because it is exciting, it offers illicit pleasures and the companionship of like-minded thrill-seekers, or because it is simply less demanding than conformity. This viewpoint, which we shall call the **social responsibility perspective**, tends to become increasingly popular in times when the fear of crime rises. Advocates of the social responsibility perspective, with their emphasis on individual choice, tend to believe that social programs do little to solve the problem of crime because, they say, a certain number of crime-prone individuals, for a variety of personalized reasons, will always make irresponsible choices. Hence, advocates of the social responsibility approach suggest crime prevention and reduction strategies based on firm punishments, imprisonment, individualized rehabilitation, increased security, and a wider use of police powers. The social responsibility perspective characteristically emphasizes a form of *micro*-analysis that tends to focus on individual offenders and their unique biology, psychology, background, and immediate life experiences. A note about wording is in order: although this perspective might also be termed the *individual responsibility perspective*, because it stresses individual responsibility above all else, we've chosen to use the term *social responsibility perspective* instead, as it holds that individuals must be ultimately responsible to the social group of which they are a part, and that they should be held accountable by group standards if they are not. In short, this perspective is one characterized by societal demands for the exercise of individual responsibility.

In Canada, the social problems perspective remains in the forefront of national thinking. A recent Environics survey indicates that 64 percent of respondents attribute crime to poor parenting and broken homes, another 52 percent cite poverty, 51 percent cite low moral standards, 50 percent cite unemployment, 49 percent cite violence on television, and 49 percent cite lack of discipline in schools.[61] An Angus Reid/CTV News poll done about the same time indicates that Canadians attach the greatest weight to the "social-development" approach for crime prevention. A total of 84 percent of those polled indicated that a "much higher/somewhat higher priority" should be given to social development as a means of crime prevention. Forty-one percent placed a "much higher priority" on enhanced law and order efforts, while 36 percent wanted a "much higher priority" given to community crime prevention programs.[62]

Social responsibility perspective the belief that individuals are fundamentally responsible for their own behaviour and that they choose crime over other, more law-abiding courses of action.

The social responsibility perspective is most evident in the approach to crime prevention and control adopted by our US neighbours to the south. With the introduction of the *Violent Crime Control and Law Enforcement Act* in 1994, the United States has been waging a "war on crime." This legislation has expanded the number of capital crimes under federal law from a handful of offences to 52.[63] It has also made billions of dollars available to municipalities to put 100 000 new police officers on the streets, and allocated billions more for states to build and operate prisons and incarceration alternatives such as boot camps. A subchapter of the 1994 *Violent Crime Control and Law Enforcement Act* created a federal "Three Strikes and You're Out" law (mentioned previously in this chapter), mandating life imprisonment for criminals convicted of three violent federal felonies or drug offences. Similarly, the law increased or created new penalties for over 70 federal criminal offences, primarily covering violent crimes, drug trafficking, and gun crimes.

Some segments of Canadian society have echoed the US call for a get-tough approach to crime. Pressure on legislators has resulted in proceeds-of-crime legislation that increases police authority to seize goods suspected of being purchased with the proceeds of crime, and firearms legislation that attempts to restrict the circulation of illegal firearms and their use in the commission of crimes, and the *Anti-Terrorist Act* expands police powers of arrest and electronic surveillance in instances where terrorist activity is suspected. Individual provinces have also "gotten tough" on crime and criminals. Some provinces have opened US-model boot camps for young offenders, and Manitoba and Ontario recently passed parental responsibility legislation that holds parents of children under 18 financially responsible for property damage committed by their children.

The contrast between the social problems and social responsibility perspectives was spotlighted in the 1997 US trial of Jesse Timmendequas, a previously convicted sex offender and admitted killer of 7-year-old Megan Kanka.[64] The defence for Timmendequas centred on his claims of repeated sexual abuse by his father as he was growing up—an experience his attorneys said left him helplessly attracted sexually to young children. The jury hearing the case rejected Timmendequas's abuse defence, found him guilty of killing Kanka, and recommended that he be sentenced to die. In summing up the feelings of many of those present, prosecutor Kathryn Flicker noted that "Timmendequas's childhood was not a bed of roses." But, she asked, "where does individual responsibility fit into the whole scheme? He was responsible as an adult, as we all are."[65]

The Social Context of Crime

Crime does not occur in a vacuum. Every crime has a quasi-unique set of causes, consequences, and participants. Crime affects some people more than others, having a special impact on those who are direct participants in the act itself—offenders, victims, police officers, bystanders, and so on. Crime, in general, provokes reactions from the individuals it victimizes, from concerned groups of citizens, from the criminal justice system, and sometimes from society as a whole, which manifests its concerns through the creation of social policy. Reactions to crime, from the everyday to the precedent-setting, may colour the course of future criminal events.[66]

In this book, we shall attempt to identify and examine some of the many social, psychological, economic, biological, and other causes of crime while simultaneously expounding on the many differing perspectives that have been advanced to explain both crime and criminality. An example of differing perspectives can be found in Box 1.4 in this chapter entitled, "The Murder of John Lennon." The article provides insight into the motivation of Mark David Chapman (Lennon's killer) and shows that the assumptions we, as outsiders to the event itself, make about the genesis of criminal purpose are not always correct. As "The Murder of John Lennon" reveals, popular conceptions of criminal motivation are typically shaped by media portrayals of offender motivation, which often fail to take into consideration the felt experiences of the law violator. By identifying and studying this diversity of perspectives on criminality, we will discover the characteristic disjuncture among victims, offenders, the justice system, and society as to the significance each assigns to the behaviour in question—and, often, to its motivation. It will not be unusual to find, for example, that sociological or psychological initiatives with which the offenders themselves do not identify are assigned by theorists and others.

Another example of misattribution can be seen in the case of Damian Williams, the African-American sentenced in December 1993 to 10 years in prison for beating Caucasian truck driver Reginald Denny during the Los Angeles riots. Most reporters and many attorneys assumed that Williams was motivated during the beating by his knowledge of verdicts of innocence that had been returned earlier that same day in the state trial of California police officers accused of beating African-American motorist Rodney King—an incident whose capture on videotape galvanized the United States and Canada. An infuriated Williams, the media supposed (and reported), attacked Denny in response to frustrations he felt at a justice system that seemed to protect Caucasians at the expense of African-Americans. Williams, however, told a reporter at his sentencing that he knew nothing about the verdicts and was just caught up in the riots. "Maybe other people knew about [the King verdict], but I wasn't aware of it until later . . . I was just caught up in the rapture," Williams said.[67]

Box 1.4

The Murder of John Lennon

At 10:50 p.m. on December 8, 1980, Mark David Chapman, 25, killed famous musician and former Beatle John Lennon. Lennon, who was returning home from a recording session with his wife, Yoko Ono, died in a hail of bullets fired from Chapman's .38-calibre pistol. As a musical luminary, John Lennon was well known to the world. Even his private life—from his residence in the exclusive Dakota Apartments in New York City to his dietary preferences and investment portfolios—was the subject of popular news stories and media exposés.

Following Lennon's death, the public generally assumed that Chapman had chosen his murderous course of action due to innate, albeit perverted, needs fed by a twisted rationale—specifically, to become famous by killing a celebrity. In similar assassination attempts involving Gerald Ford, Ronald Reagan, and others, the media has assumed much the same type of motivation. News stories have communicated to the public the image of would-be assassins sparked by the desire to make headlines and see their names become household words. To assign such motivation to the killers of famous people is understandable from the media perspective. Many of the people encountered by newscasters and writers in daily work have an obvious interest in seeing their names in print. Constant experiences with such people do much to convince byline authors and narrators that the drive for glory is a major motivator of human behaviour.

Such "pop psychology," however, probably does not provide an accurate assessment of the motivation of most assassins. We know from recent conversations with Chapman that he, at least, was driven by a different mindset. In an interview 10 years after the killing (the first one he gave since the shooting), Chapman related a story of twisted emotions and evil whisperings inside his own head. Just before the shooting, the unemployed Chapman, living in Hawaii, had gotten married. Faced with a difficult financial situation and rising debts, he became enraged by what he perceived as Lennon's "phoniness." Lennon, he reasoned, had become rich singing about the virtues of the common person, yet Lennon himself lived in luxury made possible by wealth far beyond the reach of Chapman and others like him. According to Chapman, "He [Lennon] had told us to imagine . . . He had told us not to be greedy. And I had believed!" In effect, Chapman shifted responsibility for his own failure onto Lennon. For that, he reasoned, Lennon must pay. In preparation for the killing, Chapman would record his own voice over Lennon's songs, screaming such things as, "John Lennon must die! John Lennon is a phony." Once a born-again Christian, Chapman turned to Satanism and prayed for demons to enter his body so that he could have the strength to carry out the mission he had set for himself.

Today, says Chapman, he has changed. Much of his time behind bars is spent writing religious tracts and other stories, with inspiration drawn from verses Lennon made famous. Chapman became eligible for parole in the year 2000, but his request to be released was turned down.

DISCUSSION QUESTIONS

1. Why did Chapman kill Lennon? Will we ever be sure of his true motivation? How can we be certain we have uncovered it?
2. Was Chapman insane at the time of the killing? What does *insanity* mean in this context? How can it be determined?
3. Should Chapman be released from custody? Why or why not?

Source: Jack Jones, "Decade Later, Killer Prays to be Forgiven," *USA Today*, December 3, 1990, p. 1A.

Making Sense of Crime: The Causes and Consequences of the Criminal Event

This book recognizes that criminal activity is diversely created and variously interpreted. In other words, this book depicts crime not as an isolated individual activity, but as a *social event*.[68] Like other social events, crime is fundamentally a social construction.[69] To say that crime is a social construction is not to lessen the impact of the victimization experiences which all too many people undergo in our society every day. Nor does such a statement trivialize the significance of crime prevention efforts or the activities of members of the criminal justice system. Likewise, it does not underplay the costs of crime to individual victims and to society as a whole. It does, however, recognize that although a given instance of criminal behaviour may have many causes, it also carries with it many different kinds of meanings—at least one for offenders, another (generally quite different meaning, of course) for victims, and still another for agents of the criminal justice system. Similarly, a wide range of social interest groups, from victims' advocates to prisoner rights and gun control organizations, all interpret the significance of lawbreaking behaviour from unique points of view—and each arrives at different conclusions as to what should be done about the so-called crime problem.

For these reasons, we have chosen to apply the concept of **social relativity** to the study of criminality.[70] Social relativity refers to the fact that social events are differently interpreted according to the cultural experiences and personal interests of the initiator, the observer, or the recipient of that behaviour. Hence, as a social phenomenon, crime means different things to the offender, to the criminologist who studies it, to the police officer who investigates it, and to the victim who experiences it first-hand.

Figure 1.3 illustrates the causes and consequences of crime in rudimentary diagrammatic form. In keeping with the theme of this book, it depicts crime as a social event. The figure consists of a foreground, describing those features that immediately determine the nature of the criminal event (including responses to the event as it is transpiring), and a background, in which generic contributions to crime can be seen with interpretations of the event after it has taken place. We call the background causes of crime *contributions* and use the word *inputs* to signify the more immediate propensities and predispositions of the actors involved in the situation. Inputs also include the physical features of the setting in which a specific crime takes place. Both background contributions and immediate inputs contribute to and shape the criminal event. The more or less immediate results or consequences of crime are termed *outputs*, while the term *interpretations* appears in the diagram to indicate that any crime has a lasting impact both on surviving participants and on society.

As Figure 1.3 shows, the criminal event is ultimately a result of the coming together of inputs provided by the offender, the victim, society, and the justice system.

Social relativity the notion that social events are differently interpreted according to the cultural experiences and personal interests of the initiator, the observer, or the recipient of that behaviour.

Figure 1.3

The Causes and Consequences of Crime

Offenders bring with them certain background features, such as personal life experiences, a peculiar biology (insofar as they are unique organisms), a distinct personality, personal values and beliefs, and various kinds of skills and knowledge (some of which may be useful in the commission of crime). Background contributions to crime can be vitally important. Recent research, for example, tends to cement the existence of a link between child-rearing practices and criminality in later life. Joan McCord,[71] reporting on a 30-year study of family relationships and crime, found that self-confident, non-punitive, and affectionate mothers tend to insulate their male children from delinquency and, consequently, later criminal activity. Difficulties associated with the birthing process have also been linked to crime in adulthood.[72] Birth trauma and negative familial relationships are but two of the literally thousands of different kinds of experiences individuals may have. Whether individuals who undergo trauma at birth and are deprived of positive maternal experiences will turn to crime depends on many other things, including their own mixture of other experiences and characteristics, the appearance of a suitable victim, failure of the justice system to prevent crime, and the evolution of a social environment in which criminal behaviour is somehow encouraged or valued.

Each of the parties identified in Figure 1.3 contributes immediate inputs to the criminal event. Foreground contributions by the offender may consist of a particular motivation, a specific intent (in many cases), or a drug-induced state of mind.

Criminal justice system
the various agencies of justice, especially police, courts, and corrections, whose goal it is to apprehend, convict, sanction, and rehabilitate law violators.

Like the offender, the **criminal justice system** also contributes to the criminal event, albeit unwillingly, through its failure to (1) prevent criminal activity, (2) adequately identify specific offenders prior to their involvement in crime, and (3) prevent the early release of convicted criminals who later become repeat offenders. Such background contributions can be seen in prisons (a central component of the justice system) that serve as "schools for crime," fostering anger against society and building a propensity for continued criminality in inmates who have been "turned out." Similarly, the failure of system-sponsored crime prevention programs—ranging from the patrol activities of local police departments to educational and diversionary programs intended to redirect budding offenders—helps to set the stage for the criminal event.

On the other hand, proper system response may reduce crime. A recent study found that police response (especially arrest) could, under certain demographic conditions, dramatically reduce the incidence of criminal behaviour.[73] Additionally, the study found that arrest "constitutes communication to criminals in general," further supporting the notion that inputs provided by the justice system have the power to either enhance or reduce the likelihood of criminal occurrences. Immediate inputs provided by the justice system typically consist of features of the situation such as the presence or absence of police officers, the ready availability (or lack thereof) of official assistance, the willingness of police officers to intervene in pre-crime situations, and the response time required for officers to arrive at a crime scene.

Few crimes can occur without a victim. Sometimes the victim is a passive participant in the crime, such as an innocent person killed by an impaired driver. In such cases, the victim is simply in the wrong place at the wrong time. Even then, however, merely by being present the victim contributes his person to the event, thereby increasing the severity of the incident (i.e., the impaired driver who injures no one may still be breaking the law but is committing a far less serious crime than if somebody is killed). Sometimes, however, victims more actively contribute to their own victimization through the appearance of defencelessness (perhaps because of old age, drunkenness, or disability), by failing to take

Some crimes are especially difficult to understand. In 2004, Michael Briere, a computer software programmer, confessed to the sexual assault, murder, and dismemberment of 10-year-old Holly Jones, whom he abducted off a downtown Toronto street as she walked home from a friend's house. Former Toronto Police Chief Julian Fantino is shown here holding a photograph of Briere at a news conference.
CP/J.P. Moczulski.

appropriate defensive measures (leaving doors unlocked or forgetting to remove keys from a car's ignition), through an unwise display of wealth (flashing large-denomination bills in a public place), or simply by making other unwise choices (walking down a dark alley in a dangerous section of the city at 2:00 or 3:00 a.m., for example). In a study of Canadian victimization, Leslie W. Kennedy and David R. Forde found that violent personal victimization ". . . is contingent on the exposure that comes from following certain lifestyles."[74] This was especially true, they found, "for certain demographic groups, particularly young males." See Chapter 4 for a further discussion on victims of crime.

Although lifestyles may provide the background that fosters victimization, a more active form of victimization characterizes "victims" who initiate criminal activity—such as the barroom brawler who picks a fight but ends up on the receiving end of the ensuing physical violence. Victim-precipitated offences are those that involve active victim participation in the initial stages of a criminal event and that take place when the soon-to-be victim instigates the chain of events that ultimately results in the victimization.

Finally, the general public (termed *society* in Figure 1.3) contributes to the criminal event both formally and informally. Society's formal contributions sometimes take the form of legislation, whereby crime itself is defined. Hence, as we shall discuss in considerable detail in Chapter 11, society structures the criminal event in a most fundamental way by delineating (through legislation and statute) what forms of activity are to be thought of as criminal.

Society's less formal contributions to crime arise out of generic social practices and conditions such as poverty, poor and informal education, various forms of discrimination by which pathways to success are blocked, and the **socialization** process. The process of socialization has an especially important impact on crime causation because it provides

Socialization the lifelong process of social experience whereby individuals acquire the cultural patterns of their society.

the interpretative foundation used to define and understand the significance of particular situations in which we find ourselves, and it is upon those interpretations that we may (or may not) decide to act. Date rape, for example, can occur when a man concludes that his date "owes" him something for the money he has spent on her. That feeling, however inappropriate from the point of view of the victim and the justice system, probably has its roots in early-learned experiences—including values communicated from television, the movies, and popular music—about gender-related roles under such circumstances. In other words, society, through the divergent values and expectations it places upon people, property, and behaviour under particular conditions, may provide the motivational basis for many offences.

The contributions society makes to the backgrounds of both offender and victim and to the structure of the justice system, and the influences each in turn have upon the general social order, provide for a kind of "feedback loop" in our vision of crime (the loop is not shown in Figure 1.3 for fear of unnecessarily complicating it). Through socialization, for example, individuals learn about the dangers of criminal victimization; but when victimization occurs and is publicized, it reinforces the socialization process, leading to an increased wariness of others, and so on. An example can be seen in the fact that children throughout Canada are routinely taught to avoid strangers and to be suspicious of people they do not know. A few decades ago, avoiding strangers was not ordinarily communicated to children, but entered cultural awareness following a number of horrendous and well-publicized crimes involving child victims. It is now a shared part of the socialization process experienced by countless children every day throughout Canada.

The contributions made by society to crime are complex and far-reaching. Some say that the content of the mass media (movies, television, popular music, etc.) can lead to crime by exposing young people to inappropriate role models and to the kinds of activity—violence and unbridled sexuality, for example—that encourage criminality.

Society's foreground contributions to crime largely emanate from the distribution of resources and the accessibility of services, which are often the direct result of economic conditions. A study of the availability of medical resources (especially quality hospital emergency services) found that serious assaults may "become" homicides when such resources are lacking but that homicides can be prevented through the effective utilization of capable medical technology.[75] Hence, societal decisions leading to the distribution and placement of advanced medical support equipment and personnel can effectively lower homicide rates in selected geographic areas. Of course, homicide rates will be higher in areas where such equipment is not readily available. According to the study, "the causes of homicide transcend the mere social world of the combatants."[76]

The moments immediately preceding any crime are ripe with possibilities. When all the inputs brought to the situation by all those present coalesce into activity that violates the criminal law, a crime occurs. Together, the elements, experiences, and propensities brought to the situation by the offender and the victim, and those contributed to the pending event by society and the justice system, precipitate and decide the nature, course, and eventual outcome of the criminal event. While we focus on the criminal event as it unfolds, however, it is important to note that some of the inputs brought to the situation may be inhibiting; that is, they may tend to reduce the likelihood or severity of criminal behaviour.

As mentioned earlier, the causes of crime, however well documented, tell only half the criminological story. Each and every crime has consequences. Although the immediate consequences of crime may be relatively obvious for those parties directly involved (e.g., the offender and the victim), crime also has an indirect impact on society and the justice system. Figure 1.3 terms the immediate effects of crime *outputs*. As with the causes of crime, however, the real impact of such outputs is mediated by perceptual filters, resulting in what the figure terms *interpretations*. After a crime has taken place, each party to the event must make sense of what has transpired. Such interpretations consist of cognitive, emotional, and (ultimately) behavioural reactions to the criminal event.

Interpretations are ongoing. They happen before, during, and after the criminal event, and are undertaken by all those associated with it. An interesting and detailed study of the interpretive activity of personnel in the criminal justice system documents what happens when callers reach the 911 dispatcher on police emergency lines.[77] Because many prank calls and calls for information are made to 911 operators, the operator must judge the seriousness of every call that comes through. In the study, what the caller says was found to be only a small part of the informational cues that the dispatcher seeks to interpret prior to assigning the call to a particular response (or non-response) category. Honest calls for help may go unanswered if the operator misinterprets the call. Hence, quite early on in the criminal event, the potential exists for a crucial representative of the justice system to misinterpret important cues and conclude that no crime is taking place.

Other interpretative activities may occur long after the crime has transpired, but they are at least as significant. The justice system, taken as a whole, must decide guilt or innocence and attempt to deal effectively with convicted offenders. Victims must attempt to make sense of their victimizations in such a way as to allow them to testify in court (if need be) and to pick up the pieces of their crime-shattered lives. Offenders must come to terms with themselves and decide whether to avoid prosecution (if escape, for example, is possible), accept blame, or deny responsibility. Whatever the outcome of these more narrowly focused interpretative activities, society—because of the cumulative impact of individual instances of criminal behaviour—will also face tough decisions through its courts and lawmaking agencies. Societal-level decision making may revolve around the implementation of policies designed to stem future instances of criminal behaviour, the revision of criminal codes, or the elimination of unpopular laws.

Our perspective takes a three-dimensional integrative view of the social event called *crime*. We will (1) attempt to identify and understand the multiple causes giving rise to criminal behaviour, (2) highlight the processes involved in the criminal event as it unfolds, and (3) analyze the interpretation of the crime phenomenon, including societal responses to it. From this perspective, crime can be viewed along a temporal continuum as an emergent activity that (1) arises out of past complex causes; (2) assumes a course that builds upon immediate relationships between victim, offender, and the social order that exist at the time of the offence; and, after it has occurred, (3) elicits a formal response from the justice system, shapes public perceptions, and (possibly) gives rise to changes in social policy.

The advantages of an integrative perspective can be found in the completeness of the picture that it provides. The integrative point of view results in a comprehensive and inclusive view of crime because it emphasizes the personal and social underpinnings as well as the consequences of the crime. The chapters that follow employ the integrative perspective advocated here to analyze criminal events and to show how various theoretical approaches can be woven into a consistent perspective on crime.

The Primacy of Sociology

This book recognizes the contributions made by numerous disciplines to the study of crime and crime causation, including biology, psychology, and political science. It is important to recognize, however, that the primary perspective from which most contemporary criminologists operate is a sociological one. Today's dominant theoretical understandings of criminal behaviour are routinely couched in the language of social science, and fall within the framework of sociological theory. The social problems versus social responsibility theme, around which this book is built, is in keeping with such a tradition.

Some, however, would disagree with those who claim that the sociological perspective should be accorded heightened importance in today's criminological enterprise. Those who argue for the primacy of the sociological perspective emphasize the fact that crime, as a subject of study, is a social phenomenon. Central to any study of crime must be the social context of the criminal event, which brings victims and criminals together.[78] Moreover, much of contemporary criminology rests upon a sound tradition of social scientific investigation into the nature of crime and criminal behaviour that is rooted in European and North American sociological traditions that are now well over 200 years old.[79]

One of the criticisms of the sociological perspective is its seeming reluctance to accept the significance of findings from other fields, as well as its frequent inability to integrate such findings into existing sociological understandings of crime. Another has been its seeming difficulty in conclusively demonstrating effective means of controlling violent (as well as other forms of) crime.

While sociological theories continue to develop, new and emerging perspectives ask to be recognized. The role of biology in explaining criminal tendencies, for example, appears to be gaining strength as investigations into the mapping of human DNA increase.

Nonetheless, whatever new insights may develop over the coming years, it is likely that the sociological perspective will continue to dominate the field of criminology for some time to come. Such dominance is rooted in the fact that crime—regardless of all the causative nuances that may be identified in its development—occurs within the context of the social world. As such, the primary significance of crime and of criminal behaviour is fundamentally social in nature, and any control over crime must stem from effective social policy.

Summary

At the start of this chapter, the term *crime* was simply defined as a violation of criminal law. Near the end of this chapter, we recognized the complexity of crime. In the process, crime was effectively redefined as a lawbreaking event whose significance arises out of an intricate social nexus involving a rather wide variety of participants. As we enter the 21st century, contemporary criminologists face the daunting task of reconciling an extensive and diverse collection of theoretical explanations for criminal behaviour. All these perspectives aim to assist in understanding the social phenomenon of crime—a phenomenon that is itself open to interpretation and that runs the gamut from petty offences to major infractions of criminal law. At the very least, we should recognize that explanations for criminal behaviour rest on shaky ground, insofar as the subject matter they seek to interpret contains many different forms of behaviour, each of which is subject to personal, political, and definitional vagaries.

Discussion Questions

1. This book emphasizes a social problems versus social responsibility theme. Describe both perspectives. How might social policy decisions based upon these perspectives vary?

2. What is *crime*? What is the difference between crime and deviance? How might the notion of crime change over time? What impact does the changing nature of crime hold for criminology?

3. Do you believe that assisted suicide should be legalized? Why or why not? What do such crimes as assisted suicide have to tell us about the nature of the law and about crime in general?

4. Do you think that policy makers should address crime as a matter of individual responsibility and accountability, or do you think that crime is truly a symptom of a dysfunctional society? Why?

5. Describe the various participants in a criminal event. How does each contribute to an understanding of the event?

6. What is a *theory*? Why is the task of criminological theory construction so demanding? How do we know if a theory is any good?

7. This chapter recognizes the primacy of the sociological perspective in today's criminological thought. Why is the sociological perspective especially important in studying crime? What other perspectives might be relevant? Why?

Weblinks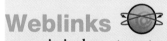

www.criminology.utoronto.ca
The University of Toronto Centre of Criminology. Research and instruction on a broad range of crime, order, and social control issues.

www.acjnet.org/splash/default.aspx
Access to Justice Network. The Access to Justice Network (ACJNet) is an electronic community that brings together people, information, and educational resources on Canadian justice and legal issues.

www.ccja-acjp.ca
Canadian Criminal Justice Association (CCJA). The CCJA is a national membership organization dedicated to improving the criminal justice system in Canada.

www.icclr.law.ubc.ca
International Centre for Criminal Law Reform & Criminal Justice Policy. A non-profit institute located in Vancouver, British Columbia. Affiliated with the United Nations, its goal is to contribute to national and international efforts to reduce crime and improve justice. Provides an extensive list of research publications.

www.ciaj-icaj.ca
Canadian Institute for the Administration of Justice (CIAJ). The CIAJ is a national, non-profit organization that seeks to foster improvements in the administration of justice in Canada through discussion and program development.

www.sfu.ca/criminology/
www.socialsciences.uottawa.ca/crm/eng/index.asp
www.crim.umontreal.ca/
Simon Fraser University, School of Criminology; University of Ottawa, Department of Criminology; Université de Montréal, École de Criminologie. All offer undergraduate and graduate programs in criminology.

CHAPTER 2

Crime Statistics

Who does what? When? How often? These are the perennial questions about crime. There is no scarcity of answers. Indeed, there is a surplus. The problem is that the answers seldom satisfy. Dissatisfaction follows from the fact that our measures of crime are of doubtful accuracy.

—JOHN HAGEN[1]

LEARNING OUTCOMES

After reading this chapter, you should be able to

- understand the usefulness and limitations of crime data

- recognize the various methods used to collect and disseminate crime data

- identify the predominant social dimensions of crime

- assess various explanations for the correlation between specific social dimensions and criminal behaviour

Simon Hayter, Ottawa Citizen.

IMPORTANT NAMES

Thomas Robert Malthus   Adolphe Quételet
André-Michel Guerry   John Braithwaite

IMPORTANT TERMS

demographics   Victimization Survey   self-report study
statistical school   crime rate   correlation
Uniform Crime Report (UCR) dark figure of crime   correlates of crime

Introduction

Ninety-eight-year-old Wesley "Pop" Honeywood, knows little about statistics, but he is familiar with crime. Honeywood, who lives in the United States, has been arrested 46 times and has been imprisoned on 8 occasions since 1946.

Honeywood's troubles with the law began at the close of World War II, when he and a couple of friends stole a bomber and flew it over Italy for fun. After landing, Honeywood was arrested by military police, did a brief stint in jail, and received a dishonourable discharge from the army.

Not long ago, the geriatric career criminal stood before a criminal-court judge, awaiting sentencing after pleading guilty to charges of armed assault and possession of a firearm. The incident grew out of Honeywood's liking for grapes, which he had watched ripen in his neighbour's yard at the end of the summer. Finally, unable to resist the temptation any longer, Honeywood helped himself to bunches of the fruit. When confronted by the neighbour, Honeywood pulled a gun and threatened the man.

Because of all the crimes he's committed, Honeywood faced sentencing as a habitual offender and could have been sent to prison for 60 years. Worse, Honeywood was on probation for the attempted sexual assault of a 7-year-old girl when he was arrested for the grape theft. And age hasn't mellowed him. Honeywood admits to shooting a man in the buttocks in 1989, but claims self-defence. The case never went to trial.

Honeywood says he is not afraid of a prison sentence. "I can do it," he smiles. "I've been locked up a whole lot of times here, but they turn me loose every time."

As things turned out, the judge sentenced him to three years in prison. Honeywood survived the time behind bars and returned to his home upon release. It may be, however, that we haven't heard the last from Pop Honeywood. His father lived to be 113.

A History of Crime Statistics

Pop Honeywood is a statistical anomaly. Few people are involved in crime past middle age. Fewer still are involved in crime at Honeywood's age. Data from the Canadian Centre for Justice Statistics show that the likelihood of someone committing a crime declines with age. People 65 years of age and older, for example, commit fewer than 1 percent of all crimes, and the proportion of crimes committed by those over the age of 90 is so small that it cannot be meaningfully expressed as a percentage of total crime.

Although the gathering of crime statistics is a relatively new phenomenon, population statistics have been collected periodically since pre-Roman times. Old Testament accounts of enumerations of the Hebrews, for example, provide evidence of Middle Eastern census taking thousands of years ago. In like manner, the New Testament describes how the family of Jesus had to return home to be counted during an official census—providing evidence of routine census taking during the time of Christ. The *lustrum*, which was a ceremonial purification of the entire ancient Roman population after census taking, leads historians to conclude that Roman population counts were made every five years. Centuries later, the *Doomsday Book*, created by the order of William the Conqueror in 1085–1086, provided a written survey of English landowners and their property. Other evidence shows that primitive societies around the world also took periodic counts of their members. The Incas, for example, a pre-Columbian indigenous empire in western South America, required successive census reports to be recorded on knotted strings called *quipas*.

Although census taking has occurred throughout history, inferences based on statistical **demographics** appear to be a product of the last 200 years. In 1798, the English economist **Thomas Robert Malthus** (1766–1834) published his *Essay on the Principle of Population as It Affects the Future Improvement of Society*, in which he described a worldwide future of warfare, crime, and starvation. The human population, Malthus predicted, would grow exponentially over the following decades or centuries, leading to a shortage of needed resources, especially food. Conflict on both interpersonal and international levels would be the result, Malthus claimed, as individuals and groups competed for survival.

Demographics the characteristics of population groups, usually expressed in statistical form.

André-Michel Guerry and Adolphe Quételet

As a direct result of Malthusian thought, investigators throughout Europe began to gather "moral statistics," or social enumerations, which they thought might prove useful in measuring the degree to which crime and conflict existed in societies of the period. Such statistics were scrutinized in hopes of gauging "the moral health of nations"—a phrase commonly used throughout the period. One of the first such investigators was **André-Michel Guerry** (1802–1866), who calculated per capita crime rates throughout various French provinces in the early 19th century.

In 1835, the Belgian astronomer and mathematician **Adolphe Quételet** (1796–1864) published a statistical analysis of crime in a number of European countries, including Belgium, France, and Holland. Quételet set for himself the goal of assessing the degree to which crime rates varied according to climate and people's sex and age. He noticed what is still obvious to criminal statisticians today—that crime changes with the seasons, with many violent crimes showing an increase during the hot summer months and property crimes increasing in frequency during colder parts of the year. As a consequence of these observations, Quételet proposed what he called the "thermic law." According to thermic law, Quételet claimed, morality undergoes seasonal variation—a proposal that stimulated widespread debate in its day.[2]

The first officially published crime statistics appeared in London's *Gazette* beginning in 1828 and France's 1825 *Compte generale*. Soon, comparisons (or what contemporary statisticians call *correlations*) began to be calculated between economic conditions and the rates of various types of crime. From a study of English statistical data covering the years

1810 to 1847, Joseph Fletcher concluded that prison commitments increased as the price of wheat rose. In like fashion, the German writer Georg von Mayr, whose data covered the years 1836 to 1861, discovered that the rate of theft increased with the price of rye in Bavaria.

The work of statisticians such as Guerry and Quételet formed the historical basis for what has been called the **statistical school** of criminology. The statistical school anticipated the development of both sociological criminology and the ecological school, perspectives that are discussed in considerable detail later in this book.

Statistical school a criminological perspective with roots in the early 19th century that seeks to uncover correlations between crime rates and other types of demographic data.

Usefulness of Crime Statistics

How many assaults were committed last year in Canada? Who committed them? Who were the most likely to be victims? What part of the country had the highest rate of assault? Why?

These are the types of questions frequently asked, not only by those with a particular interest in the study of crime and criminals, but also by members of the general public. Crime statistics help provide answers to these and other questions and paint a picture of the reality of crime in this country. Often the first step toward solving a problem is understanding it, and this certainly applies to the problem of crime. Criminologists, students of criminology, and interested members of the public must understand the crime problem before any serious attempts at controlling or preventing it can be made. Crime statistics and data can be useful toward this end, in a number of ways.

Crime data assist in describing the nature and extent of crime, which is necessary to develop effective crime-prevention policies. These policies, in turn, are usually responses to public pressure. Since it is the public that is the major player in reporting crime, the types of crime it reports reflect those issues most concerning it. By providing descriptive information about criminal activity, crime data serve as a gauge of the community's well-being.

Chapter 1 provides a brief discussion of the usefulness of theory development in the study of crime and criminals. Crime data provide the empirical support for the hypotheses developed by criminologists, who attempt to explain the phenomenon of crime and criminals. Crime data ultimately provide the test for theoretical assertions.

Just as crime statistics are used as a basis for developing social policy, they are also crucial in evaluating that policy. Whether or not young offender "boot camps" will reduce the amount of youth crime or federal firearms registration legislation will reduce the amount of violent crime committed with a firearm will ultimately be assessed through an analysis of the data (see Chapter 11 for an in-depth look at these and other crime-prevention initiatives). Program evaluation is often difficult to do well, and many such evaluations fall prey to the cost factor. Some programs are introduced largely because they are more cost-effective than conventional approaches, yet they may not achieve the desired result of reducing crime. Likewise, some programs that successfully reduce crime are shelved because they are seen as too expensive.

Most criminologists agree that the prevention of crime is generally considered preferable to its punishment. Prevention, in turn, is largely based on prediction. What types of people are most likely to commit what types of crime and why? Where will they commit them?

Canadians are especially fearful of violent crime. Here police investigate the scene of a fatal shooting of a bank teller during an armed robbery. Is the public's perception of the amounts and types of crime borne out by official statistics?

The Canadian Press/Toronto Star/Ron Bull.

Criminologists and others use crime data to help provide answers to these questions. The Canadian Crime Prevention Through Environmental Design model (CPTED) is based on the theory that the proper design and effective use of a physical space can help reduce the incidence of crime in that area. This theory, in turn, is based on crime data showing that crime occurs more often in areas where the opportunities for criminal activity are greatest (see Chapters 8 and 11 for a further description of the CPTED model).

It is important to note that predicting criminal activity and behaviour is an inexact science open to numerous pitfalls. In the early part of the 20th century, for example, Cesare Lombroso believed he could predict future criminal behaviour based on an individual's physical characteristics such as the size of his ears or the shape of his nose. In the search for a quick fix to the crime problem, some people subscribed to such predictors. For others, prediction models for crime and criminal behaviour seem about as accurate as flipping a coin.[3]

Finally, crime data are useful in providing a picture of risk. Public perceptions of the amount and types of crime are often inconsistent with reality. Crime statistics are useful in assessing the risk to various segments of the population. For example, does one's sex, age, or social class have any bearing on his or her risk of becoming a victim of crime or of becoming involved in criminal behaviour? The study of risk assessment, with crime data used as its basis, is a growing area of interest within criminology.

Sources of Crime Statistics

**Uniform Crime Report
(UCR)** a summation of
crime statistics tallied
annually by the Canadian
Centre for Justice
Statistics (CCJS) and
consisting primarily of
data on crimes reported
to the police.

Victimization Survey
first conducted as the
Canadian Urban
Victimization Survey in
1981 by Statistics Canada
and then every five years
since 1988 as part of the
General Social Survey. It
provides data on
surveyed households
reporting that they had
been affected by crime.

Compilation of crime statistics has continued apace ever since crime-related data began to be gathered over a century ago. Crime statistics in Canada are reported in two major surveys: the **Uniform Crime Reporting** (UCR) system and the **Victimization Survey**, conducted through the General Social Surveys. Both fall under the auspices of Canada's national statistics department, Statistics Canada. In 1981, the Canadian Centre for Justice Statistics was created as a satellite of Statistics Canada, through the cooperation of the federal and provincial governments. See Box 2.1 for an overview of the Canadian Centre for Justice Statistics.

It is important to realize at the outset that these two types of data differ. Because of the differences in methodology and crime coverage, the two approaches examine the nation's crime reality from unique perspectives, and results are not strictly comparable. Nevertheless, the two surveys can complement one another, and each is certainly useful in providing an overall picture of criminal activity. The two surveys are compared in detail later in the chapter. See Box 2.2 for information about sources of crime and justice statistics and research.

The Canadian Centre for Justice Statistics (CCJS)

Box 2.1

As the collection of crime data became more formalized through the introduction of the uniform crime reports in the 1960s and victimization and self-report surveys in the 1970s, it became apparent that Canada needed a national centre for the collection, collation, and dissemination of these data. The creation of the Canadian Centre for Justice Statistics (CCJS) in 1981 was a result of a decade of numerous task forces and ongoing federal–provincial negotiations around this issue. By 1985, the CCJS had evolved as the administrative arm of Canada's National Justice Statistics Initiative (NJSI), whose mandate is to "provide information to the justice community and the public on the nature and extent of crime and the administration of justice in Canada."[4] It is through the CCJS that the NJSI produces statistical information to be used to support the legislative, policy, management, and research agenda of the Canadian government and also to inform the public.

As such, the CCJS is subdivided into program areas, including law enforcement, courts, legal aid, corrections, and juvenile justice. Each of these program areas collect and collate data to examine the incidence of crime and criminal activity in Canada in areas such as homicide, street prostitution, criminal harassment, weapons and violent crime, motor vehicle crimes and impaired driving, and violent youth crime. The work of the CCJS also includes compiling information on other aspects of the criminal justice system, including justice-system expenditures, prisons and corrections data, probation and parole populations, inmate profiles, public perceptions and fear of crime, criminal justice system personnel figures, and information on the activities of adult and youth courts. This information is made available to the public through a service bulletin known as *Juristat*, which is published periodically throughout the year. *Juristat* and other CCJS reports are made available through the centre in Ottawa or through a number of Statistics Canada Regional Reference Centres throughout the country. Most public, community college, and university libraries also carry this information in reference departments. Publications of the CCJS can also be obtained by telephone at 1-800-267-6677, by email at infostat@statcan.ca, or through the Statistics Canada website at **www.statcan.ca**. Some statistical information is also available through this website.

Crime and Justice Information on the World Wide Web

Box 2.2

A rich repository of crime and justice information can be found on the World Wide Web. One place to start is the Network for Research on Crime and Justice (RCJ-NET), at **www.qsilver. queensu.ca/rcjnet**. The RCJ-NET is a network of academics and senior government officials set up in 1996 to "develop, conduct, and communicate superior quality research on crime and justice, and to provide policy-relevant advice." This website maintains, among other things, a comprehensive list of links, including

- Access to Justice Network
- Canadian Association of Chiefs of Police
- Correctional Service of Canada
- Criminal Intelligence Service of Canada
- Department of Justice Canada
- Department of the Solicitor General of Canada
- International Centre for the Prevention of Crime
- Law Commission of Canada
- National Clearinghouse on Family Violence
- National Crime Prevention Centre
- Police Futures Group
- Royal Canadian Mounted Police
- Social Sciences and Humanities Research Council of Canada

Many of these sites provide statistics and research on crime, criminals, and victims.

Websites of criminology departments at various Canadian universities are another good starting point for collecting crime information. Many of these sites provide information on crime, or good links to it.

You might also be interested in information found at the Justice Information Center (JIC), a service of the National Criminal Justice Reference Service (NCJRS) in the United States. Located at **www.ncjrs.gov**, the NCJRS maintains an extensive source of information on crime statistics, crime prevention, and research and evaluation in the area of crime control.

The Uniform Crime Reporting System

The Uniform Crime Reporting (UCR) system was initiated in 1961 through the efforts of Statistics Canada and the Canadian Association of Chiefs of Police. The purpose of the system is twofold. It provides a standardized procedure by which police departments across the country can collect information about crimes that come to their attention and then report this information to Statistics Canada, specifically to the Canadian Centre for Justice Statistics (CCJS). The CCJS then collates the raw data and makes them available to the public.

Initial UCR data are structured in terms of six major categories of crime. These include crimes of violence, property crimes, other criminal code offences, federal statute violations, provincial statute violations, and municipal bylaw violations. Police record crimes according to these categories and a set of rules specified by Statistics Canada and the Canadian Association of Chiefs of Police—the records are contained in the *Uniform Crime Reporting Manual*. Between 1962 and 1988, the official crime statistics generated from the UCR were based on summarized monthly police reports from police departments across the country. These police reports included the number of incidents and offences reported to police, the number of actual offences, the number of offences cleared, the number of adults charged, the number of youths charged, and the sex of those charged. Known as the Aggregate Uniform Crime Reporting Survey, this system has been criticized on the grounds that aggregated statistics are "less useful for analytical purposes than information based on characteristics of individual crimes."[5]

Changes to the Uniform Crime Reporting System

Changes in the UCR after 1988 shifted the emphasis of data collection away from summary or aggregate collection to incident-based collection. The new system, known as the Revised UCR Survey or Incident-Based UCR, included changes in the following areas:

- *information on victims:* age, sex, victim/accused relationship, level of injury, type of weapon causing injury, drug and/or alcohol use;
- *information on the accused:* age, sex, type of charges laid or recommended, drug and/or alcohol use; and
- *information on the circumstances of the incident:* type of violation (or crime), target of violation, types of property stolen, dollar value of property affected, dollar value of drugs confiscated, type of weapon present, time and type of location of the incident.[6]

The Revised UCR or UCR2 was fully implemented in 1992 but to date only includes data from 127 police services in 9 provinces, or 62 percent of the national volume of reported substantiated Criminal Code crimes. The incidents recorded in the most recent UCR are distributed as follows: 41 percent from Ontario, 29 percent from Quebec, 11 percent from Alberta, 6 percent from British Columbia, 5 percent from Manitoba, and 4 percent from Saskatchewan, 2 percent from Nova Scotia, and less than 1 percent each from New Brunswick and Newfoundland/Labrador. Other than Ontario and Quebec, the data are primarily from urban police services.[7]

An arson fire. Arson causes millions of dollars' worth of property damage yearly. Are UCR statistics on arson accurate?
Lester Sloan/Woodfin Camp & Associates.

The UCR also records offences cleared by charge or otherwise and rates of crime. The phrase *offence cleared by charge* refers to an offence that is closed when police have formally charged a person or when there is sufficient evidence to lay a charge against an identified person, even if that person has not been apprehended by police. *Offence cleared otherwise* refers to a case in which police cannot or do not charge a person even if they have identified a suspect and have enough evidence to support the laying of a charge. Examples include cases of diplomatic immunity, instances in which the complainant declines to proceed with charges against the accused, cases in which police have opted not to lay a charge (e.g., the uses of extra judicial measures for youth), or cases where the alleged offender dies before being formally charged.[8] The *clearance rate* indicates the proportion of incidents that are cleared by charge or otherwise for different types of offences, compared to the total number of actual incidents.

The **crime rate** used in the UCR is based on a population of 100 000. By taking into account population, the crime picture is standardized across the country in any given year. For example, in 2005, the total number of recorded violent crimes was 304 274. The rate of crimes of violence was 943, based on a 2005 Canadian total population of 32 270 507. This crime rate was calculated as follows:

Crime rate crime per capita based on the number of recorded crimes calculated per 100 000 population.

$$\frac{\text{\# of reported violent crimes}}{\text{total population}} \times 100\ 000$$

$$\frac{304\ 274\ \text{violent crimes reported}}{32\ 270\ 507\ \text{total population}} \times 100\ 000 = 943$$

Thus, we see that there were 943 violent crime incidents per 100 000 population in Canada in 2005. If we consider a specific type of violent crime, such as homicide, and apply the same procedure, the equation would look like this:

$$\frac{658\ \text{homicides reported}}{32\ 270\ 507\ \text{total population}} \times 100\ 000 = 2.0$$

This tells us that there were approximately 2 homicides for every 100 000 Canadians in 2005.[9] A summary of the UCR findings for 2005 is reproduced in Box 2.3.

Programmatic Problems with Available Data The most significant methodological feature of the Uniform Crime Reporting system is indicated by its name. It is a "reporting" system. In other words, only crimes that are reported to the police (or that are discovered by them, or by someone else who then reports them) are included in the statistics compiled by the system. Unless someone complains to the police about a criminal incident, it will go unreported and will not appear in the UCR. Most complaints, of course, are made by victims.

Because UCR data are based on *reported* crime, the system has been criticized for underestimating the true incidence of criminal activity within Canada—a measurement that would also include unreported crimes. Unreported and under-reported criminal activity has been called the **dark figure of crime**. Some experts say, for example, that sexual assault is the most under-reported crime in the UCR. Reasons for not reporting a crime

Dark figure of crime refers to that portion of criminal activity that goes unreported and/or undetected by official sources.

Highlights of the 2005 UCR   Box 2.3

- The overall crime rate dropped 5% in 2005. Decreases were seen in most crimes, with the exception of the serious crimes of homicide, attempted murder, assault with a weapon, aggravated assault, and robbery.
- The national crime rate had increased during the 1960s, 70s, and 80s, peaking in 1991. Crime rates then fell throughout the rest of the 1990s, stabilizing somewhat in the early 2000s.
- The overall decrease was driven by declines in non-violent crimes, with property crime falling 6% and other *Criminal Code* offences falling 5%. In particular, large drops were reported for break-ins (-7%), motor vehicle thefts (-7%), counterfeiting (-20%) and thefts under $5,000 (-6%).
- Declines in crime rates were observed in all provinces and territories. The largest provincial drops were reported in Manitoba (-8%), New Brunswick (-8%), and Saskatchewan (-6%).
- After increasing 13% in 2004, the homicide rate increased by 4% in 2005. There were 658 homicides in 2005, 34 more than in 2004. The 2005 homicide rate was the highest since 1996. Attempted murders were also on the rise, up 14% from the previous year.
- In 2005, police reported the first decrease in counterfeiting in 5 years. The 20% drop may be attributed to the recent introduction of enhanced security features to the most common denominations, such as the $20 bill, which make it more difficult to illegally produce paper currency.
- Drug offences decreased for the second time in three years, dropping 6%. Cannabis offences accounted for the majority of drug offences, and fell 12%.
- The youth crime rate, as measured by the number of youths formally charged plus youths cleared by means other than the laying of a charge, dropped 6%. Youth violent crime dropped 2%, while youth property crime was down 12%.
- Since the introduction of the *Youth Criminal Justice Act* (YCJA) in 2003, the proportion of apprehended youths who are formally charged by police has dropped from 56% in 2002 (pre-YCJA) to 43% in 2005 (post-YCJA).

Source: Adapted from the Statistics Canada publication "Juristat," Catalogue 85-002, vol. 26, no. 4. Released July 20, 2006. http://www.statcan.ca/bsolc/english/bsolc?catno=85-002-XIE.

such as sexual assault are numerous and include (1) the victim's fear of the perpetrator; (2) the victim's shame, which may carry over from traditional attitudes about sexual behaviour and a woman's role in sexual encounters; (3) fears the victim may have of not being believed; and (4) the victim's fear of further participation in the justice system (such as the possibility of the victim being required to go to court and testify against the offender, thereby exposing herself to potentially embarrassing cross-examination and public scrutiny). Other general reasons cited by victims for failure to report a crime include "fear of revenge," "nothing can be done," "the crime was too minor," or the incident was a "private matter."

Many other crimes are under-reported as well. Although sexual assault is indeed seriously under-reported (a conclusion drawn from comparison of UCR and Victimization Survey sexual assault statistics), the most seriously under-reported crime may in fact be theft $5000 and under, because the theft of small items may never make it into official police reports and may even be forgotten by victims during interviews with victimization surveyors.

It is interesting to note that changes in public attitude about certain types of crime such as child abuse have resulted in the public's inclination to report these crimes more readily.

Does an increase in the number of reported child abuse cases mean that there are more incidents of child abuse occurring or simply that more cases are being reported?

Another concern raised about the accuracy of UCR numbers lies with the way in which police services record and report the criminal activity that is detected. The UCR receives crime data from municipal police departments across Canada as well as from the RCMP, the Ontario Provincial Police, and the Sûreté du Québec (Quebec's provincial police force). To expect that all these police services are recording their crime statistics in a uniform manner is unrealistic, although the CCJS does work with police agencies on an ongoing basis to detect and resolve any difficulties in the reporting or transmission of data. Nevertheless, there are variations in how the police count crime, resulting from a number of factors. Changes in the number of police services and police officers will most certainly affect the number of detected crimes. Enforcement practices or mandates often vary from police department to police department. If commercial break and enters are a problem in one community, for example, local police will be more vigilant toward this type of criminal activity, which will be reflected in the crime report.

Related to police recording and reporting are methodological concerns with the way the UCR "counts" crime, especially in an incident involving multiple offences. The UCR counts only the most serious offence in the incident. For example, if someone breaks into a store, severely assaults the security personnel, and steals a stereo, only the assault is recorded. The most serious offence is determined by the maximum sentence length; in the scenario just mentioned, although the break and enter and assault both carry a maximum life sentence, the crime against the person is considered more serious and takes precedence over the crime against property. As a result, less serious offences tend to be under-represented by the UCR survey.

Even though for the purposes of counting, crimes against the person take precedence over crimes against property, this is not the case when the crime rate is calculated. Recall that the crime rate is the total number of reported crimes in a given year per 100 000 population. This total includes all categories of crime including federal and provincial statute violations. For example, the number of reported motor vehicle thefts might skyrocket in a given year, while the number of assaults might fall. The resulting overall crime rate for that year would be higher than for the year before because both classifications of crime are assigned the same weight.

Finally, for violent crime, the UCR records the number of incidents in terms of number of victims. If one person assaults two people, two incidents are recorded. But if two people assault one person, only one incident is recorded. The exception to this scoring rule for violent crime is robbery: one occurrence of robbery is counted as one incident regardless of the number of victims. Since robbery can involve many people who could be considered victims (for example, in the case of a bank robbery), to count each one would seriously overstate the occurrence of robbery. Thus, the total number of incidents recorded in the UCR is actually equal to the number of victims of violent crimes (other than robbery) plus the number of individual occurrences of non-violent crimes and robbery.[10]

A final concern with the accuracy of the UCR centres around the legal definition of crime. A case in point: the renaming and redefinition of rape to sexual assault in 1983 means that the types of behaviour constituting sexual assault have been more clearly defined to include those behaviours from unwanted sexual touching to aggravated sexual assault that endangers the life of the victim. Similarly, amendments to the definition of arson in 1990 now include mischief fires as arson. Both of these redefinitions have broadened the scope of these criminal activities and have resulted in a corresponding increase in the statistical incidence of these crimes.

The consistency of definition is also a concern. Part of the difficulty in measuring child abuse, for example, arises from the fact that there is no apparent consensus as to what constitutes child abuse across Canada at the provincial and territorial level, where child-welfare services are organized and delivered. For example, the maximum age of the child to be protected (under 16 in Newfoundland to under 19 in British Columbia) and the policies underlying child protection vary across the country. It is estimated that cases of child abuse would double if threats and acts of indecent exposure were added to the definition. As well, the distinction between corporal punishment and physical abuse is not clear, which further thwarts the accurate accounting of child abuse. For the purposes of recording, the CCJS defines child abuse as incidents of physical and sexual assault and homicide where the victim is under 18 years of age.[11]

Data Gathering Using Victimization Surveys

Victimization Surveys differ from the UCR in one especially significant way: rather than depending on reports of crimes to the police, the data contained in Victimization Surveys consist of information elicited through interviews with members of randomly selected households throughout the country. Hence, these surveys uncover a large number of crimes that may not have been reported, and are therefore regarded by many researchers as a more accurate measure of the actual incidence of crime in Canada than is the UCR.

A number of significant Victimization Surveys have been undertaken in Canada. The first, and perhaps the most comprehensive, was the *Canadian Urban Victimization Survey* (CUVS) conducted in 1981 under the auspices of the solicitor general of Canada. It randomly sampled roughly 60 000 Canadians over the age of 16 in 7 major cities. In telephone interviews, respondents were asked to describe any victimization experiences they had suffered in the preceding calendar year. Eight categories of crime were included in the survey: sexual assault, robbery, assault, break and enter, motor vehicle theft, theft of household property, theft of personal property, and vandalism. The survey uncovered over 700 000 personal victimizations and almost 900 000 household victimizations for the calendar year of 1981. It also revealed that fewer than 42 percent of these victimizations had been reported to the police or had otherwise come to police attention.[12] (The highlights from the CUVS are found in Box 2.4.)

Beginning in 1988, Statistics Canada has conducted a Victimization Survey every five years, as part of the General Social Survey (GSS). The 2004 GSS (the latest one from which victimization data are available) sampled a national target population of roughly 24 000 Canadians, aged 15 and over, in the 10 provinces, excluding full-time residents of institutions. For the first time, as part of a pilot study, the 2004 survey interviewed Canadians in the Northwest Territories, the Yukon, and Nunavut. Interestingly, the data collected are not included in the analysis. Interviews were conducted by telephone from January to December 2004, using random-digit dialling techniques. In an interview lasting 30 minutes on average, respondents were asked about their experiences with the criminal justice system in the previous 12 months and specifically about 8 types of criminal victimization: sexual assault, robbery (and attempted robbery), physical assault, theft of personal property, break and enter (and attempted break and enter), motor vehicle/parts theft (and

Highlights of the Canadian Urban Victimization Survey (CUVS)

Box 2.4

- Fewer than 42% of all crimes are reported to the police: 62% of all sexual assaults go unreported, 55% of robberies, 66% of assaults, 36% of break and enters, 3% of motor vehicle thefts, 56% of household thefts, 22% of personal thefts, and 65% of incidents of vandalism go unreported.
- Of the respondents, 66% said they did not report the crime because they thought it was "too minor," 61% because they felt the "police couldn't do anything," and 24% because they felt reporting was an "inconvenience."
- Of the respondents, 40% felt unsafe in their own neighbourhoods during the evenings, while 5% felt unsafe there during the day.
- Those who reported spending more time outdoors in the evening also reported a greater incidence of victimization.
- Thirty percent of offences against the person occur in the summer months, while 18% occur in the winter months.
- The major determinants of fear are being older, being female, living in an urban setting, and having a lower income.
- Thirty-five percent of personal violent crimes involve the use of a weapon (13% involve guns).

Source: Compiled from Ministry of Solicitor General, *Canadian Urban Victimization Survey* (Ottawa: Ministry of Supply and Services, 1982).

attempts), attempts at—and theft of—household property, and vandalism. Respondents who had been victims of a crime were asked for detailed information about each incident including when and where it occurred, whether the incident had been reported to the police, and how they had been affected by the experience. Respondents were also questioned about their perceptions and fear of crime and their knowledge and perceptions of the criminal justice system. Demographic information about the respondents was also gathered, including age, sex, marital status, as well as educational, occupational, and income levels. Highlights of the findings of the survey are presented in Box 2.5.

Generally, the summary indicates a slight increase in household victimization rates in the five-year period between 1999 and 2004. A significant proportion of Canadians (roughly 28 percent) were affected by one or more of the crimes covered in the 2004 GSS as compared to 26 percent in the 1999 survey. It is interesting to compare these rates of victimization with the concerns about fear of crime among Canadians, discussed in Chapter 1.

While the CUVS and subsequent GSS have helped to provide a picture of the amounts and types of crime generally in Canada, other surveys have been conducted to look at specific types of crime victims. Most notable among these is the first-ever national Violence Against Women Survey (VAWS), undertaken by Statistics Canada in 1993. Over 12 000 women 18 years of age and older were interviewed by telephone about their experiences of physical and sexual violence since the age of 16 and their perceptions of their personal safety. The findings of the survey indicated significantly more incidents of violence against women than had ever been previously indicated in official UCR numbers. One-half of all Canadian women reported having experienced at least one incident of violence since age 16, and almost one-half reported that this violence had been perpetrated by men known to them. A summary of the findings from the VAWS is outlined in Box 2.6.

Criminal Victimization in Canada, 2004

Box 2.5

- Results from the 2004 General Social Survey (GSS) indicate that 28% of Canadians aged 15 years and older reported being victimized one or more times in the 12 months preceding the survey. This is up slightly from 26% in 1999, when the victimization survey was last conducted.

- Increases in victimization rates were recorded for three of the eight offence types measured by the GSS: theft of personal property, theft of household property, and vandalism. There were no significant changes in rates of sexual assault, robbery, physical assault, and motor vehicle theft. A decrease was observed in the rate of break and enter.

- Household victimization offences were the most frequently occurring criminal incidents (34%), followed by violent victimization (29%) and thefts of personal property (25%). About 12% of incidents could not be classified within the eight offence types.

- Residents of western provinces generally reported higher rates of victimization than residents living east of the Manitoba-Ontario border. However, there were two exceptions to this regional pattern. Nova Scotia had the second highest rate of violent victimization, while Ontario's rate of personal property theft was comparable to rates recorded in the West.

- The risk of violent victimization (based on the number of incidents per 1,000 population) was highest among young Canadians (aged 15 to 24 years). Other factors, such as being single, living in an urban area, and having a low household income (under $15,000) also increased the likelihood of violent victimization.

- For household victimization, rates per 1,000 households were highest among renters, those living in semi-detached, row, or duplex homes, and urban dwellers. For both household victimization and personal property theft, higher household income made households and individuals more attractive targets for victimization.

- The GSS reveals that a large proportion of Canadians never reported criminal incidents to police. In all, only about 34% of criminal incidents came to the attention of police in 2004, down from 37% in 1999. Household victimization incidents were most likely to be reported (37%), while thefts of personal property were the least likely (31%).

- In 4% of all incidents, victims believed the act was hate-motivated. This is the same as the figure recorded in 1999. In 2004, among hate-motivated incidents, about two-thirds (65%) were believed to be motivated by the victim's race or ethnicity, 26% by the victim's sex, 14% by their religion, and 12% by their sexual orientation.

- Canadians who self-identified as being Aboriginal were three times as likely as the non-Aboriginal population to report being victims of violent victimization. There was no significant difference between rates for visible minorities and non-visible minorities, while rates were lower among immigrants than non-immigrants (68 versus 116 per 1,000 population).

- Although the presence of weapons in violent incidents has remained relatively stable since 1999 (69% in 2004 and 72% in 1999), violent incidents resulting in injury increased. In 2004, 25% of violent offences resulted in injury to the victim, compared to 18% in 1999.

- Most often, violent incidents took place in a commercial establishment or public institution (38%). Some form of workplace violence represented 43% of the incidents occurring in a commercial establishment or public institution.

Source: "Criminal Victimization in Canada, 2004," adapted from the Statistics Canada publication "Juristat," Catalogue 85-002, vol. 25, no. 7. Released November 24, 2005. http://www.statcan.ca/bsolc/english/bsolc?catno=85-002-XIE.

Highlights of the Violence Against Women Survey (VAWS)

Box 2.6

- Fifty percent of all Canadian women have experienced at least one incident of violence since the age of 16.
- Almost 50% of women reported violence by men known to them, and 25% reported violence by a stranger.
- Twenty-five percent of all women have experienced violence at the hands of a current or past marital partner (includes common-law unions).
- Roughly 15% of currently married women reported violence by their spouses; 50% of women with previous marriages reported violence by a previous spouse.
- More than 10% of women who reported violence in a current marriage have at some point felt their lives were in danger.
- Sixty percent of Canadian women who walk alone in their own area after dark feel "very" or "somewhat" worried doing so.
- Women with violent fathers-in-law are at three times the risk of assault by their partners than are women with non-violent fathers-in-law.

Source: *The Daily*, Catalogue No. 11-001, Nov. 18, 1993, page 1.

There have been a number of initiatives undertaken at the international level to compare victimization rates from country to country. The International Crime Victimization Survey (ICVS) is one such initiative. Since first being implemented in 1989, the ICVS has been conducted three times—in 1992, 1996, and 2000. The 2000 survey was coordinated by the Netherlands Institute for the Study of Criminality, the United Nations Interregional Crime and Justice Research Institute, the United Nations Centre for International Crime Prevention, and the British Home Office. Canada was one of 17 countries participating in this survey that set out to provide comparable information on the incidence of victimization around the world. People aged 16 years and older were asked through random telephone sampling for information on 11 offences (robbery/attempted robbery, sexual assault, assaults/threats, theft of personal property, burglary of residence, attempted burglary of residence, theft of car, theft from car, car vandalism, theft of motorcycle, theft of bicycle). Respondents were asked when, where, and how often offences had occurred during the previous year and the previous five years; whether offences were reported to police; and whether victimization experiences were considered serious. Respondents were also asked for their opinion on public safety, policing, and sentencing. An average of 1000 to 5000 persons were interviewed per country. Despite some recognized methodological shortcomings, such as the likelihood of fairly large sampling errors, the findings of the survey are interesting. Twenty-four percent of Canadians reported having been victimized within the previous year, which was slightly above the average of 21 percent when compared to 10 other Western industrialized countries. A summary of the highlights of this survey can be found in Box 2.7.

Critique of Victimization Surveys
Just as the UCR has been criticized for under-representing the actual incidence of criminal activity in Canada, Victimization Surveys in general, and the GSS in particular, can be criticized for possible over-reporting of some crimes. It is beyond the purview of a Victimization Survey to verify the actual occurrence of any of the crimes reported to the interviewers. Hence, no measure exists as to the number of crimes that might be under-reported. Victimization Surveys are dependent upon

Highlights of the International Crime Victimization Survey (ICVS)

Box 2.7

- On average for 13 of the industrialized countries that participated in the 2000 International Crime Victimization Survey (ICVS), 22% of the population aged 16 and older in those countries were victims of at least 1 of 11 offences in the previous year. Canada's figure was near the average, at 24%.

- Between 1996, the previous time the ICVS was conducted, and 2000, victimization rates were fairly stable. Of the ten countries that participated in both survey cycles, six, including Canada, did not experience any significant change in victimization rates. The remaining four countries experienced decreases in their overall victimization rates.

- Of the 11 crimes measured by the ICVS, the most prevalent in 2000 was car vandalism. On average for the 13 countries, 7% of the population was a victim of this crime. The next most common crime was theft from car, at 5%.

- On average for the 11 crimes, just over one-half of incidents were reported to police in 2000. The figures ranged from a high of 65% for Scotland to a low of 39% for Japan, with Canada's figure near the lower end at 49%. Many incidents were not reported because the victims did not believe they were serious.

- In 2000, a majority of people in each of the 13 countries felt very or fairly safe when walking alone in their area after dark. Figures were highest for Sweden (85% of the population), followed by Canada (83%), and the United States (83%). People in Australia and Poland were least likely to feel safe (64% for each). In four countries, including Canada, there has been an increase in the proportion of the population that feels safe when walking alone at night.

- Satisfaction with police performance is quite high, particularly in the United States and Canada. In 2000, 89% of Americans and 87% of Canadians felt that the police were doing a very or fairly good job at controlling crime in their area, the highest figures among the 13 countries. Canadians and Americans were also most likely to believe that police do everything they can to help people and be of service.

- When asked to decide on a sentence for a burglar convicted for a second time, the majority of people in eight countries, including Canada, preferred a non-prison sanction. Leading the way were France, where 84% of the population preferred a non-prison sanction, and Finland with a figure of 79%. Canada's figure was 52%.

- Canadians do appear to have grown more punitive in their attitudes toward sentencing. In 1989, less than one-third (32%) of the population felt that prison would be an appropriate sentence for a recidivist burglar. This figure climbed to 39% in 1992, 43% in 1996, and 45% in 2000. People in seven other countries also appear to have become harsher in their attitudes.

- In 2000, a majority of households in 11 of the countries used at least one type of security measure, including a burglar alarm, special door locks, special window/door grills, a dog, a high fence, a neighbourhood watch scheme or a caretaker/security guard. The one exception was Poland, where 40% of households used one of these devices.

Source: "Criminal Victimization in Canada, 2004," adapted from the Statistics Canada publication "Juristat," Catalogue 85-002, vol. 22, no. 4. Released November 24, 2005. http://www.statcan.ca/bsolc/english/bsolc?catno=85-002-XIE.

the ability of the respondent to not only recall incidents and their details but also accurately place them in time. Some respondents provide more detailed and accurate accounts of their victimization experiences, which may, in turn, skew the data. As well, by their nature, Victimization Surveys exclude data on homicide, kidnapping, so-called "victimless crimes" (public intoxication, prostitution, and gambling), impaired driving, drug offences, crimes such as vandalism and theft committed against commercial or public property, and crimes committed against children under the age of 15.

Comparing Uniform Crime Reporting Surveys and Victimization Surveys

The data generated by the UCR and Victimization Surveys, while based on the same categories of crime, reveal very different pictures. Findings from the UCR are the reports of crimes recorded by the police, who are generally alerted to the crime as a result of a call from a victim. The type and frequency of calls to police change over time and vary according to location. For example, as the community tolerance for sexual assault and family violence declines, victims or witnesses of these crimes may be more willing to report them to authorities, and authorities will be more likely to treat them as crimes.

Victimization Surveys, on the other hand, were developed to provide a way of looking at crime from the perspective of individual victims. They describe what has happened to individual Canadians and the way in which these individuals respond to their victimization experiences. Without a doubt, these surveys reveal that many Canadians do not report personal victimizations and suggest the reasons for this.

Despite their divergent focuses, UCR and Victimization Surveys can complement one another. Victimization data can help place UCR findings in context. For instance, how much change in official crime data for family violence can be attributed to changes in reporting patterns or police practices? (Police in Ontario and some other provinces are mandated to lay charges against the perpetrator in a domestic assault situation if sufficient evidence exists, regardless of the victim's willingness to concur.) How are crime trends a reflection of people's attitudes toward crime and the criminal justice system? While neither UCR nor victimization data can provide comprehensive information about crime, when considered together they are useful in providing a picture of crime and criminal activity in Canada. See Table 2.1 for a comparison of the UCR and GSS.

Data Gathering Using Self-Report Studies

Another approach to the production of data on the amount and types of crime is the **self-report study**. Within the field of criminology, there is a widely held belief that to understand crime, it is important to ask people about their involvement with it. There have been countless self-report studies conducted with various groups of individuals, most notably with youth. The results of the groundbreaking work by Short and Nye[13] led many to believe that traditional police data have the potential to be biased toward certain segments of society, in particular the lower socio-economic classes. Other gaps between official sources of data and self-report data have been found in the age, sex, and race of the offender. One of the most notable Canadian self-report studies was conducted by LeBlanc and Fréchette.[14] Using a list of 39 questions, these researchers questioned a large group of high-risk Montreal youth on a variety of behaviours (the list of questions is reproduced in Table 2.2). LeBlanc and Fréchette hoped to use the results of their surveys to describe delinquent patterns for all high-risk Canadian male youth. Despite methodological shortcomings, including the failure to consider cultural differences between French- and English-speaking Canadians and the failure to consider delinquency rates among females, the study was important in its contribution to a general understanding of the crime picture among youth in Canada.

Self-report study a data collection method requiring subjects to reveal their own participation in criminal behaviour.

Table 2.1

Differences between the UCR and GSS

UCR	GSS
Data Collection Methods:	
Administrative police records	Personal reports from individual citizens
Census	Sample survey
100% coverage of all police agencies	Sample of approximately 10 000 persons using random digit dialling sampling technique
Data submitted on paper or in machine-readable format	Computer Assisted Telephone Interviewing (CATI); excludes households without telephones
National in scope	Excludes Yukon, Northwest Territories, and Nunavut
Continuous historical file: 1962 onwards	Periodic survey: 1988, 1993, 2000, 2004
All recorded criminal incidents regardless of victims' age	Target population: persons aged 15 and over, excluding full-time residents of institutions
Counts only those incidents reported to and recorded by police	Collects crimes reported and not reported to police
Scope and Definitions:	
Primary unit of count is the criminal incident	Primary unit of count is criminal victimization (at personal and household levels)
Nearly 100 crime categories	Eight crime categories
"Most Serious Offence" rule results in an undercount of less serious crimes	Statistics are usually reported on a "most serious offence" basis, but counts for every crime type are possible, depending on statistical reliability
Includes attempts	Includes attempts
Sources of Error:	
Reporting by the public	Sampling error
Processing error, edit failure, non-responding police department	Non-sampling error related to the following: coverage, respondent error (e.g., recall error), non-response, coding, edit and imputation, estimation
Police discretion, changes in policy and procedures	
Legislative change	

Source: Adapted from the Statistics Canada publication "An Overview of the Differences Between Police-Reported and Victim-Reported Crime," Catalogue 85-542, no. 01. Released May 14, 1997. http://www.statcan.ca/bsolc/english/bsolc?catno=85-542-XIE.

In general, self-report studies are recognized within the field of criminology as one means of counting crime and criminals. When considered in conjunction with other methods of information gathering, self-report studies help provide a more clear and complete picture of crime and who commits it. They are considered to be particularly useful in highlighting the relationship between social class and crime and in uncovering much crime that goes undetected.[15]

Limitations of Self-Report Studies
Since their acceptance as a legitimate means of examining the reality of crime and criminals, self-report studies have consistently become more sound. Nevertheless, a number of shortcomings continues to exist, largely methodological. For example, the accuracy of this research approach is largely predicated on the honesty and forthrightness of the respondent. Inaccurate answers may result from

Table 2.2

Self-Report Questions from the Montreal Youth Study by LeBlanc and Fréchette

During the past 12 months, did you

1. ... purposely damage or destroy musical instruments, sports supplies, or other school equipment?
2. ... purposely damage or destroy public or private property that did not belong to you?
3. ... take some school property worth $5.00 or more?
4. ... purposely damage school building (windows, walls,...)?
5. ... take a motorcycle and go for a ride without the owner's permission?
6. ... take a car and go for a ride without the owner's permission?
7. ... purposely destroy a radio antenna, tires, or other parts of a car?
8. ... "beat up" someone who hadn't done anything to you?
9. ... take something from a store without paying?
10. ... threaten to beat up someone to make him do something he didn't want to do?
11. ... get into a place (a movie, a game, or a performance) without paying the admission price?
12. ... use a weapon (stick, knife, gun, rock,...) while fighting another person?
13. ... use stimulants (speed, pep pills, etc....) or hallucinogens (LSD, STP, THC, etc....)?
14. ... have a fist fight with another person?
15. ... take something of large value (worth $50.00 or more) that did not belong to you?
16. ... gamble for money with persons other than your family members?
17. ... sell any kind of drugs?
18. ... break into and enter somewhere to take something?
19. ... carry a weapon (chain, knife, gun, etc....)?
20. ... take something of some value (between $2.00 and $50.00) that did not belong to you?
21. ... purposely set a fire in a building or in any other place?
22. ... take and keep a bicycle that did not belong to you?
23. ... take something of little value (worth less than $2.00) that did not belong to you?
24. ... trespass anywhere you were not supposed to go (vacant house, railroad tracks, lumber yard, etc....)?
25. ... use marijuana or hashish?
26. ... make anonymous phone calls (not say who you were)?
27. ... use opiates (heroin, morphine, opium)?
28. ... send in a false alarm?
29. ... buy, use, or sell something that you knew to be stolen?
30. ... drive a car without a driver's licence?
31. ... have sexual relations (other than kissing) with a person of the same sex?
32. ... skip school without a legitimate excuse?
33. ... have sexual relations (other than kissing) with a person of the opposite sex?
34. ... take part in a gang fight between adolescents?
35. ... run away from home for more than 24 hours?
36. ... tell your parents (or those who replace them) that you would not do what they ordered you to do?
37. ... take money from home without permission and with no intention of returning it?
38. ... get drunk on beer, wine, or other alcoholic beverages?
39. ... "fool around" at night when you were supposed to be at home?

Source: M. LeBlanc and M. Fréchette, *Male Criminal Activity from Childhood through Youth: Multilevel and Developmental Perspectives* (New York: Springer-Verlag, 1989), pp. 195–196, cited in M.A. Jackson and C.T. Griffiths (eds.), *Canadian Criminology: Perspectives on Crime and Criminality* (Toronto: Harcourt, Brace & Company, Canada, 1995), p. 193. Reprinted with permission.

a number of factors, including the respondent's failure to disclose behaviour or, conversely, to exaggerate behaviour, or the respondent's failure to remember. Often respondents are concerned about confidentiality and anonymity, which is understandable given the information they are being asked to reveal. This, in turn, may affect the way they answer or indeed whether they even participate in the survey. Analyses of self-report studies indicate, for example, that the more offences a respondent has committed, the fewer he is likely to admit to. Conversely, a respondent who has committed a lesser number of offences is more likely to admit to them in a self-report survey.

Other methodological limitations include a lack of standardized data collection methods, such as comparable questions, time frames, or geographic areas. In general, however, there seems to be agreement that self-report studies are useful in providing a more rounded picture of the criminal, especially when compared with the picture that is often captured in official statistics based on police reports. While the official statistics provide information on tangibles such as the age and sex of an offender, self-report studies serve to reveal characteristics such as education levels, home life, peer group, and general socio-economic realities of the offender. It has been suggested that this approach could be used to include an examination of those biological and psychological factors that contribute to criminal behaviour, thereby complementing the environmental realities they already help to illuminate. Whether the findings of these self-report studies that target a specific group in a specific time and place can be used to deduce general assumptions about criminals and the crimes they commit is still open to debate.

The Social Dimensions of Crime

What Are Social Dimensions?

Crime does not occur in a vacuum. It involves real people—human perpetrators and victims. Because society defines certain personal characteristics as especially important, however, it is possible to speak of the "social dimensions of crime," that is, aspects of crime and victimization as they relate to socially significant attributes by which groups are defined, and according to which individuals are assigned group membership. Socially significant attributes include gender, ethnicity or race, age, income or wealth, profession, and social class or standing within society. Such personal characteristics provide criteria by which individuals can be assigned to groups such as "the rich," "the poor," "male," "female," "young," "old," "Black," "White," "white-collar worker," "manual labourer," and so on.[16]

We have already alluded briefly to the fact that the UCR, GSS or Victimization Surveys, and self-report studies structure the data they gather in ways that reflect socially significant characteristics. The UCR, for example, provides information on reported crimes, which reveals the sex and age of perpetrators. Victimization statistics document the age and sex of crime victims and the educational, occupational, and income levels of households reporting victimizations. Self-report studies provide some insight into the age, sex, ethnic background, education levels, social habits, and socio-economic status of those engaged in delinquent or criminal behaviour.

Correlation a causal, complementary, or reciprocal relationship between two measurable variables.

The social dimensions of crime are said by statisticians to reveal relationships or correlations. A **correlation** is simply a connection or association observed to exist between two measurable variables. Correlations are of two types: positive and negative. If one measurement increases when its correlate does the same, then a positive correlation or positive relationship is said to exist between the two. When one measurement decreases in value as another rises, a negative or inverse correlation has been discovered. Victimization data, for example, show a negative relationship between age and victimization. As people age, victimization rates decline. Hence, although some elderly people do become crime victims, older people as a group tend to be less victimized than younger people. Uniform Crime Report data, on the other hand, show a positive relationship between youth and likelihood of arrest—specifically, between young adulthood and arrest. Young adults, it appears, commit most crimes. Hence, as people age, they tend to be both less likely to be victimized and less likely to become involved in criminal activity.

A word of caution is in order, however. Correlation does not necessarily imply causation. Because two variables appear to be correlated does not mean that they have any influence on one another, or that one causes another either to increase or to decrease. Correlations that involve no causal relationship are said to be *spurious*. A study of crime rates, for example, shows that many crimes seem to occur with greater frequency in the summer. Similarly, industry groups tell us that food retailers sell more ice cream in the summer than at any other time. Are we to conclude, then, from the observed correlation between crime rates and ice cream sales, that one in some way causes the other? To do so on the basis of an observed correlation alone would obviously be foolish.

Some observed correlations do appear to shed at least some light on either the root causes of crime or the nature of criminal activity, often referred to as **correlates of crime**. Our discussion now turns to these.

Correlates of crime
those variables observed to be related to criminal activity such as age, gender, ethnicity, and social class.

Age and Crime

If records of persons accused are any guide, criminal activity is associated more with youth than any other stage of life. Year after year, Uniform Crime Reports consistently show that younger people, from their mid- to late teens to their early and mid-twenties, account for

---

Figure 2.1

Persons Accused of Property Crimes and Violent Crimes by Age, Canada

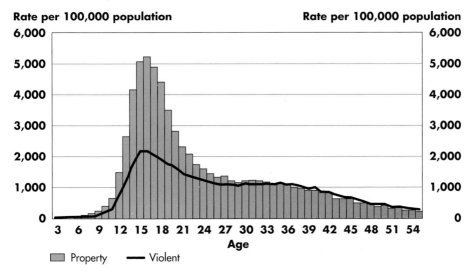

Source: Adapted from the Statistics Canada publication "Exploring Crime Patterns in Canada," Crime and Justice Research Paper Series, Catalogue 85-561, no. 05. Released June 29, 2005.
http://www.statcan.ca/english/research/11-621-MIE/11-621-MIE2004013.htm.

the bulk of the crime reported in this country. Indeed, age is one of the strongest correlates of criminal behaviour.

A recent Statistics Canada report indicates that persons aged 15 to 24 represented 14 percent of the total population but accounted for 45 percent of those charged with property crimes and 32 percent of those charged with violent crimes.[17] It is interesting to note when considering Figure 2.1 that "age-specific" crime rates were calculated using census information as it relates to age distribution. Prior to 1998, the age distribution of accused persons was based on the actual number of people accused by the police, which did not take into account the age distribution of the entire population.

Recent cautions raised by some US criminologists that an impending demographic shift will result in a substantial increase in crime, and especially violent crime,[18–21] have proven to be misguided. A look at the demographic reality in Canada paints a somewhat different picture. Figures 2.2a and 2.2b show that crime rates in Canada have followed population shifts, with somewhat of a time lag. According to Statistics Canada, most of the baby boomers were 15 years of age between 1960 and 1980, a time that witnessed steady increases in violent and property crime rates. Property crime rates levelled out in the 1980s as the percentage of 15- to 24-year-olds began to drop, and increased slightly in the early 1990s before declining sharply (as the percentage of 25- to 34-year-olds began to decline). Note that violent crimes do not parallel as closely the demographic shift; the violent crime rate continued to increase steadily until 1993. The decline in the violent crime rate began several years after the start of the decline in the 15-24 age group.[22] Other studies suggest that our crime rates have steadily declined due to positive changes in economic and employment opportunities for youth today as compared with the realities of the recession years of the 1980s, which negatively affected the cohort of those born in the 1960s.[23] Further explanations for the correlation between youth and crime are raised in Box 2.8.

Figure 2.2a

Comparison over Time in Rates of Property Crime and Population Accounted for by Age Groups, 1962 to 2003

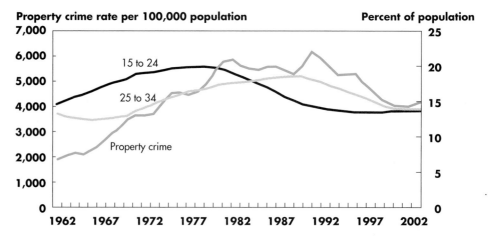

Source: Adapted from the Statistics Canada publication "Exploring Crime Patterns in Canada," Crime and Justice Research Paper Series, Catalogue 85-561, no. 05. Released June 29, 2005.
http://www.statcan.ca/english/research/11-621-MIE/11-621-MIE2004013.htm.

Figure 2.2b

Comparison over Time in Rates of Violent Crime and Population Accounted for by Age Groups, 1962 to 2003

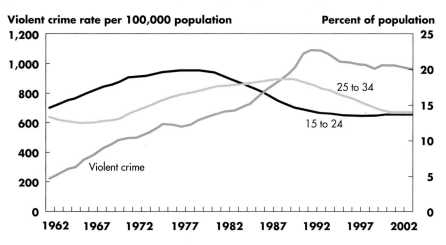

Source: Adapted from the Statistics Canada publication "Exploring Crime Patterns in Canada," Crime and Justice Research Paper Series, Catalogue 85-561, no. 05. Released June 29, 2005. http://www.statcan.ca/english/research/11-621-MIE/11-621-MIE2004013.htm.

When considering the correlation between age and victimization, statistics from 2004 show that Canadians between the ages of 15 and 24 years experienced personal victimization at rates 1.5 to 19 times greater than the rate for other groups. The risk of violent victimization steadily declined as age increased. For example, those 25 to 34 years of age had a rate of 157 per 1000 compared to a rate of 115 per 1000 for the group aged 35 to 44. Rates of violent victimization were lowest among those aged 65 and older. These Canadians had a rate of 12 violent incidents per 1000 population.[24] Statistics show that

Correlation between Age and Crime

Box 2.8

Why is there such a strong correlation between age and crime? Explanations range from the biological, which look at hormonal variables such as higher levels of testosterone in males, to an examination of the social and personal realities existing at various stages of life. Do offenders "grow out of crime" as they mature? Do they develop significant attachments to people, such as spouses and children, or to jobs that they do not want to risk losing through continued involvement in crime? Do they settle down and no longer see criminal or deviant behaviour as fun or as a means to attain immediate gratification or peer approval? Does the age at which a youth becomes involved in criminal behaviour and is labelled by the criminal justice system as an offender have any bearing on how long his or her criminal career will last? Do some offenders simply grow too tired and physically unable to continue in a criminal lifestyle? There is no simple explanation as to why age and crime are correlated. Keep these questions in mind as you consider the theories of criminal behaviour presented in Chapters 6 to 10. Can the age of the offender be factored into any or all of these theories?

children are over-represented as victims of certain types of crimes. While Victimization Surveys only poll Canadians over 15 years of age, UCR statistics indicate that for offences such as sexual assault and other sexual offences (sexual interference, invitation to sexual touching, sexual exploitation, and incest), children under 13 years of age represent 15 percent and 29 percent respectively.[25]

Gender and Crime

Gender appears so closely linked to most forms of criminal activity that it has been called "the best single predictor of criminality...."[26] The most recent data available indicate that males account for over 80 percent of those adults accused of a criminal offence. This is particularly true when considering violent crimes; adult males make up over 90 percent of accusations for homicide, sexual assault, and robbery. With property crimes, adult males constitute 78 percent of overall accusations, weighing in at 98 percent, 91 percent, and 82 percent for break and enter, motor vehicle theft, and theft over $5000 respectively. Indeed, prostitution-related offences are the only ones where any parity between the sexes appears to exist; statistics show males accused of 51 percent of all incidents.[27] The apparently low rate of female criminality has been explained by some as primarily due to cultural factors, including early socialization, role expectations, and a reluctance among criminal justice officials to arrest and prosecute women. Others have assumed a biological propensity toward crime and aggression among men that may be lacking in women. These and other issues are addressed in Chapters 6 to 10.

It is important to note, however, that the rate of female criminality, especially relating to property crimes, has increased substantially in Canada since the 1960s. A comparison of the rates of males and females involved in property offences such as serious theft, fraud, and minor theft since 1968 shows that women have become twice as involved in these types of offences in the 2000s. Some criminologists cite *role convergence*, or the adaptation of the role of women to more closely resemble that of men, as an explanation for this. Others see the significant increases in female involvement in offences such as shoplifting, credit card fraud, and passing bad cheques as a manifestation of the *feminization of poverty*, rather than the convergence of male and female roles.[28] As the number of poor, female single parents grows, their marginalization may be reflected in increases in certain types of female property crimes.

When women commit crime, they are more often followers than leaders. A recent study of women in correctional settings, for example, found that women are far more likely to assume "secondary follower rules during criminal events" than "dominant leadership roles."[29]

Concerning victimization, there is very little difference in the overall risk of personal victimization for women and men. The General Social Survey (GSS) indicates that the rate of personal violent victimization in 2004 was 102 incidents per 1000 population for women as compared to 112 per 1000 for men. While men reported higher rates for assault (91 per 1000 population for men, 59 for women) and for robbery (13 for men, 8 for women), women are still much more likely to be victims of sexual assault at a rate of 35 per 1000 population as compared to 7 per 1000 for men.[30] (Table 2.3 looks at adult victims of violent crime based on gender for selected categories of crime.) The Violence Against Women Survey (VAWS) indicates that up to one-half of all Canadian women have

Female gang members fighting. Although much female criminality has long been overlooked, criminologists are now increasingly aware of gender issues. How does the criminality of men and women appear to differ?
Copaken/Gamma-Liaison, Inc.

experienced at least one incident of violence since the age of 16. Specifically, the VAWS findings indicate that 34 percent of women surveyed reported having experienced a physical assault, 39 percent reported having been sexually assaulted, and 15 percent had experienced unwanted sexual touching. Almost one-half of the women surveyed experienced violence by men known to them (boyfriends, dates, marital partners, friends, family, neighbours).[31] A more detailed examination of some of the current Canadian legislation aimed at assisting victims of crime, and female victims in particular, can be found in Chapter 4.

Table 2.3

Adult Victims of Violent Crime by Gender: Selected Incidents

	Males	Females
Total violent	51%	49%
Assault (levels 1, 2, 3)	60%	40%
Sexual assault (levels 1, 2, 3)	16%	84%
Robbery	62%	38%

Source: Adapted from M. Gannon and K. Mihorean, "Criminal Victimization in Canada, 2004," Statistics Canada, *Juristat*, Catalogue No. 85-002, vol. 25, no. 7, 2005, p. 23.

Ethnicity and Crime

Unlike data from the United States, Canadian crime statistics do not routinely report on the racial and ethnic makeup of offenders. The only official Canadian statistics that report on the correlation between ethnicity and crime derive from studies that consider incarcerated offender or inmate profiles. The number of inmates, while accurate, is not representative of the actual number of offenders and offences detected by police. Nevertheless, correctional statistics can be useful in shedding light on the reality of ethnicity and crime in Canada, especially with respect to the representation of Aboriginal Canadians. Figure 2.3 shows the representation of the adult offender population in federal custody (serving a custody sentence of two years or more) by race.

The reality of Aboriginal over-representation in the Canadian criminal justice system has been studied for some time. Correctional Service of Canada statistics indicate that in 2005, Aboriginal peoples represented approximately 16 percent of the federal adult inmate population (27 percent of the female inmate population, 18 percent of the male inmate population) while representing less than 3 percent of the total Canadian adult population.[32]

A number of reasons are cited for the disproportionate number of Aboriginal peoples in the Canadian criminal justice system. Some maintain that this reality is a result of the discriminatory treatment of Aboriginals by the criminal justice system. A number of studies have concluded that "biased discretion" or selective enforcement by criminal justice officials translates into the over-represented numbers of Aboriginals in the system.[33] While there may exist instances when discrimination has played a role in a police officer's

---

Figure 2.3

Percentage of Federal Offender Population (by Race, Canada)

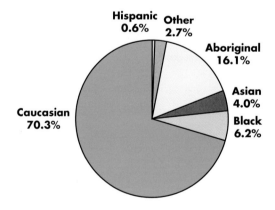

- The federal offender population is diverse; however, 70.3% of offenders identify themselves as Caucasian.
- These proportions have changed little since 2002.

Source: *Corrections and Conditional Release Statistical Overview*, Figure C8, p. 11, Solicitor General Canada, 2003. Reproduced with the permission of the Minister of Public Works and Government Services, 2007.

decision to arrest an Aboriginal person or in the decision of a justice of the peace to deny bail to an Aboriginal offender, there is limited research evidence to support the claim of active, systemic discrimination against Aboriginal peoples by the Canadian criminal justice system. A recent report by the federal correctional investigator criticized the federal correctional system for its "routine" discrimination of Aboriginal offenders. See Box 2.9 for one overview of the correctional investigator's report.

Jail Conditions for Canadian Aboriginals a "Disgrace": Ombudsman

Box 2.9

Aboriginal offenders are routinely discriminated against by the corrections system and are far less likely to get parole or be rehabilitated by their experiences in jail, the ombudsman for federal prisons says.

Releasing his annual report into conditions in federal prisons, correctional investigator Howard Sapers said the challenges faced by Aboriginal people in Canadian jails amounts to "a national disgrace."

"Despite years of task force reports, internal reviews, national strategies, partnership agreements and action plans, there has been no measurable improvements in the conditions for Aboriginal offenders during the last 20 years," said Sapers at a news conference in Ottawa.

He said the overall incarceration rate for Aboriginal Canadians was nine times higher than for the population at large and the situation was even worse for Aboriginal women.

One in three inmates in federally run women's prisons were Aboriginal, he said, with almost half of them in maximum security institutions.

Aboriginals often sent to maximum security prison

He said there was "routine overclassification" of Native prisoners, who were far more likely to be sent to maximum security prison than offenders from other backgrounds.

"That means they [Aboriginal offenders] often serve their sentences away from family, community, their friends and elders," Sapers said, "They are sent into segregation more often . . . severely limiting access to rehabilitative programs and services that are intended to prepare them for their release."

Parole is routinely denied or revoked, often on technical grounds, he said.

Sapers called on the federal government to address the situation urgently with new programs, more resources and consultations with Aboriginal leaders and communities.

Angus Toulouse, of the Ontario Regional Council of the Assembly of First Nations, said poverty, inadequate educational and employment opportunities, alcoholism, and domestic abuse were among the reasons for overrepresentation.

"Where disadvantaged socio-economic factors lead to overrepresentation of First Nations peoples in the criminal justice system, this is systemic discrimination," said Toulouse.

Public Safety Minister Stockwell Day has said he will consider the findings of Sapers's report but there is no evidence of systemic discrimination against Native offenders in the prison system.

The president of the Native Women's Association of Canada said the alarming rise in the number of Aboriginal women who are incarcerated affects all Canadians.

"If this was the case for non-Aboriginal people, I'm almost certain that Canadians would react and demand that something be done," said Beverly Jacobs.

Source: CBC News, www.cbc.ca, October 16, 2006.

Other explanations look to the socio-economic realities of many Aboriginal peoples. The role of social and economic inequality and the realities of past and current living conditions for many Aboriginals are more often cited as causes contributing to criminality among Native peoples.[34] A recent work by Carol La Prairie explores the contribution that certain large Canadian cities may make to the over-representation of Aboriginal peoples in the system. She concludes that a disproportionate number of Aboriginals living in urban centres (and most notably Thunder Bay, Winnipeg, Regina, and Saskatoon) experience the social realities of low income, unemployment, lack of education, unstable housing, and single-parent families. For La Prairie, what explains an Aboriginal person's likelihood of involvement in the criminal justice system is "... the concentration of poor, single-parent, and poorly educated Aboriginal people in the inner core of their large cities."[35] In addition to the social realities identified by La Prairie, the role of alcohol and substance abuse in the offences committed by Aboriginals cannot be overlooked. A review of a number of Canadian studies concludes that alcohol is a major contributor to the crimes committed by Native peoples.[36] Furthermore, a significant number of Aboriginals serving provincial terms of incarceration are doing so for default of an original fine sentence. Some studies indicate that almost two-thirds of the Aboriginals in some provincial institutions are serving sentences for such defaults.[37] It is most likely that socio-economic conditions have more to do with the inability to meet fine payments than a wilful refusal to pay.

As victims of crime, 40% of Aboriginal Canadians report having been victimized as compared to 28% of non-Aboriginal Canadians. In particular, Aboriginal peoples experience violent victimization at a rate of 319 incidents per 1000 population as compared to 101 incidents, a rate about three times as great. This difference is largely a result of the rate of physical assault, which is the most frequently occurring violent offence. The rate of violence for Aboriginal females is 3.5 times higher that that for non-Aboriginal females (343 versus 96 incidents per 1000 females), while for Aboriginal males, the pattern is similar with a rate of violent victimization that is almost 3 times higher than that of non-Aboriginal males (292 versus 107 incidents per 1000 males).[38]

Social Class and Crime

Prior to 1960, criminologists generally assumed that a correlation existed between social class and crime. They believed that members of lower social classes were more prone to commit crime, and they thought that this propensity applied to all types of criminal activity. In the early 1960s, however, studies of the relationship between social class and crime, which made use of offender self-reports, seemed to show that the relationship between social class and criminality was an artefact of discretionary practices within the criminal justice system.[39] Such studies, especially of teenagers, found that rates of self-reported delinquency and criminality were fairly consistent across various social classes within North American society. Similar studies of white-collar criminality seemed to show that, although the nature of criminal activity may vary between classes, members of all social classes had nearly equal tendencies toward criminality. Hence, the apparent penchant for crime among members of the lower social classes was explained partially by the fact that the types of crime traditionally committed by these groups were those most likely to come to the attention of law enforcement officials and be fully prosecuted by the criminal justice system. While there is no doubt that people from all social classes commit crimes, a number of studies point to a significant correlation between lower socio-economic status and criminal activity, as we shall see below.

In 1978, a comprehensive re-evaluation of 35 previous studies of the relationship between social class and crime concluded that previously claimed links were non-existent.[40] Publication of the report fuelled further study of the relationship between social class and crime, and in 1981 a seminal article by Australian criminologist **John Braithwaite**—which summarized the results of 224 previous studies on the subject—concluded convincingly that members of lower social classes were indeed more prone to commit crime.[41] In contrast to earlier studies, Braithwaite found that "socio-economic status is one of the very few correlates of criminality which can be taken, on balance, as persuasively supported by a large body of empirical evidence."

Many of the difficulties surrounding research into the relationship between social class and crime appear to stem from a lack of definitional clarity. In the many different studies evaluated by Braithwaite, for example, neither *crime* nor *class* was uniformly defined. Some researchers have similarly suggested that earlier studies may have been seriously flawed by their near-exclusive focus on young people and by their conceptualization of crime in terms of relatively minor offences (truancy, vandalism, etc.).[42] Hence, a lack of concise definitions of the subject matter, combined with inadequate measurement techniques, may have led to misleading results.

Recent Canadian studies of street youth in Toronto and Edmonton found that many came from lower-class families and were on the street because of poor relationships at home and at school. The struggle for survival often resulted in involvement in delinquency and crime.[43]

Figure 2.4a

Comparison over Time in Rates of Property Crime and Unemployment, 1962 to 2003

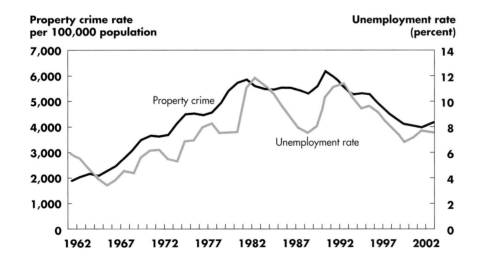

Source: Adapted from the Statistics Canada publication "Exploring Crime Patterns in Canada," Crime and Justice Research Paper Series, Catalogue 85-561, no. 05. Released June 29, 2005.
http://www.statcan.ca/english/research/11-621-MIE/11-621-MIE2004013.htm.

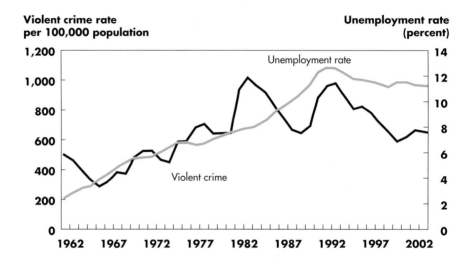

Figure 2.4b

*Comparison over Time in Rates of Violent Crime
and Unemployment, 1962 to 2003*

Source: Adapted from the Statistics Canada publication "Exploring Crime Patterns in Canada," Crime and Justice Research Paper Series, Catalogue 85-561, no. 05. Released June 29, 2005. http://www.statcan.ca/english/research/11-621-MIE/11-621-MIE2004013.htm.

Unemployment and measures of poverty and income inequality are often cited as risk factors for criminal activity. Inasmuch as these factors can be used as indicators of social class, statistical trends indicate that unemployment rates in Canada were relatively high in the 1980s and 1990s. Similarly, overall trends in property crime were also high in the same time periods. Interestingly, rates of violent crime do not seem to follow these patterns.[44] A comparison of unemployment and crime rates is found in Figures 2.4a and 2.4b.

Are those from the lowest socio-economic classes also most likely to be victims of crime? Victimization Survey data from the GSS indicate that those households with incomes below $15 000 have the highest violent victimization rate at 156 per 1000 population, significantly higher than the rate of those in other income categories. People with household incomes of more than $60 000 had the highest rate of household victimization (including break and enter, motor vehicle theft, theft of household property, and vandalism) at 300 incidents per 1000 population.[45]

Summary

Crime statistics have been gathered in one form or another for at least 150 years. Although early data about crime may have been used to assess the moral health of nations, modern-day criminal statistics programs provide a fairly objective picture of crime in Canada and elsewhere. Statistics often form the basis for social policy.

Today, two large-scale government programs collect crime data in Canada. One, the Uniform Crime Reporting system, is administered by Statistics Canada and annually collects information on crimes reported to the police and on charges laid throughout the country. The other, Victimization Surveys conducted as part of the General Social Survey every five years, is also run by Statistics Canada. These surveys provide reports on the criminal victimization of households and individuals.

As discussed, the social correlates of crime in Canada include age, sex, race, and social class. Although crime statistics do not tell the whole story and other forms of crime need to be recognized, it appears from the best information available that young men are especially over-represented in Canadian crime statistics. Among these men, Aboriginals account for a proportion that is vastly over-representative of their numbers in our population. Recognizing the reality of such involvement should help our society secure a safer future for all its citizens and enhance effective crime prevention efforts.

Other than gender, age, and ethnicity, social class can be a significant indicator of the likelihood of criminal involvement. Suffice it here to say that crimes are committed by members of all social classes. As we will recognize in later chapters, however, powerful classes make the laws and are therefore less apt to have need of breaking them and are probably more committed to preservation of the status quo. Hence, many offenders, especially those arrested for street, property, and crimes of violence, come from the lower social classes.

Some people argue that crime statistics do not justify the degree of fear Canadians express about crime. Others suggest that statistics are misleading and that they do not provide a true picture of crime in Canada. Even though the actual incidence of crime is difficult to measure, crime statistics do provide us with an appreciation for the extent of the challenges facing victims of crime, social policy makers, and law enforcement personnel today.

Discussion Questions

1. This book emphasizes a social problems versus social responsibility theme. Which perspective, if any, is best supported by a realistic appraisal of the "social dimensions" of crime discussed in this chapter?

2. What are the major differences between the UCR and the Victimization Surveys? Can useful comparisons be made between these two crime indices? If so, what might comprise such comparisons?

3. What is a crime rate? How are rates useful?

4. What is the dark figure of crime? Why is it important to be aware of this when considering official crime statistics?

5. What are the reasons victims don't report crimes to the police? Which crimes appear to be the most under-reported? Why are those crimes so infrequently reported? Which crimes appear to be the most frequently reported? Why are they so often reported?

6. This chapter implies that if you are young, male, Aboriginal, and unemployed, you have a greater likelihood of being represented in Canadian criminal justice statistics. What are some of the reasons for this "reality"?

Weblinks

www.statcan.ca

Statistics Canada. Current Canadian statistics including those on crime, victims, suspects, the police, and the courts.

www.canada.justice.gc.ca

Department of Justice, Canada. Numerous links to current news and events, programs and services, and general information about Canada's criminal justice system.

www.csc-scc.gc.ca

Correctional Service of Canada. Information on Canadian correctional policy, legislation, research, basic facts and statistics, and publications. Good links to provincial/territorial sites.

www.npb-cnlc.gc.ca

National Parole Board, Canada. Provides useful information on all aspects of parole as well as links to related legislation and statutes.

www.scc-csc.gc.ca

Supreme Court of Canada. History of the Supreme Court, overview of the Canadian judicial system, judgments, information on cases, and frequently asked questions.

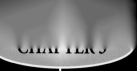

CHAPTER 3

Patterns of Crime

Crime has a thousand roots ... but a single outcome. It stems from fear and hatred, greed and corruption, deprivation and suffering. But it always ends with one thing: victims.

—PETER KENT[1]

There may be lies, damned lies, and statistics, but study after study tells the same, consistent story. Crime is down ... across Canada.

—MICHELE MANDEL[2]

LEARNING OUTCOMES

After reading this chapter, you should be able to

- analyze the amounts and types of crime in Canada

- distinguish between the myths and the reality of patterns of Canadian crime

- recognize the usefulness of criminological theory in explaining crime

- apply various theories to different classifications of crime

IMPORTANT TERMS

typologies of crime	serial murder	hate crime
homicide	mass murder	breaking and entering
murder	sexual assault	theft
first-degree murder	date rape	motor-vehicle theft
second-degree murder	criminal harassment	impaired driving
manslaughter	robbery	counterfeiting
infanticide	assault	prostitution

Introduction

It was a crime spree that was as cunning as it was insidious. After six years and ill-gotten gains of over $1 million in stolen money and property, Ken Crawford was eventually apprehended in the late 1990s by police in Ottawa, Ontario. Known as the "Locker Room Bandit," Crawford had the look of a respectable, middle-aged businessman. Throughout the 1990s, however, his "business" involved the theft of wallets, jewellery, and other personal possessions from health-club locker rooms across the country.

His crime spree began when Crawford, an out-of-work tool and die maker, tried to go back to school for retraining but was denied a student loan and was unable to get a part-time job to help pay for his tuition. Instead, he devised a plan that would get him the money he needed.

His scheme was simple and it worked hundreds of times over the six years that he was actively involved in crime. He would approach a health club and ask to try out the facilities, saying that he was interested in a membership. Once inside the locker room, he would select a wealthy-looking patron and wait until he went to work out. Out of his gym bag Crawford would produce a set of bolt cutters and a combination lock. After snapping the lock off the victim's locker and emptying it of the wallet and other valuable personal items, Crawford would re-lock the locker using the combination lock he had brought. When the unsuspecting victim returned, Crawford was long gone, buying himself valuable time as the victim struggled with his lock in vain. Using the personal identification in the wallet, Crawford emptied the victims' bank accounts and took cash advances using the credit cards. Police estimated he averaged about $5000 cash for each job. When Crawford was apprehended, police found bolt cutters, 103 wallets, watches, jewellery, and thousands of dollars in cash in his home.

In return for pleading guilty to defrauding the public, possession of property obtained by crime, and possession of stolen credit cards, Crawford received a three and one-half year sentence. As he handed down his sentence, Judge Paul Bélanger told Crawford, "If you have talent, it is as a talented crook. But not that talented bearing in mind where you currently sit."[3]

Classifications of Crime

A significant portion of this book is devoted to examining a variety of explanations for why people commit crime. Chapter 2 provides an overview of the ways in which crime statistics are collected so that a picture of the incidence of crime and the number and types of criminals in a given period will emerge.

But what *types* of crime are committed in Canada? How many of each type occur annually? Typically, crimes are organized into categories, or **typologies of crime**. The Uniform Crime Reporting (UCR) system classifies crimes into the following categories: violent crime, property crime, other crime, traffic offences (as defined in the *Criminal Code of Canada*), federal drug legislation offences, and other federal statute violations. Categorization helps to identify patterns that may exist within these groupings and to focus discussion concerning motivation of the offender. For example, does the person who commits murder do it for reasons distinct from those of the person who breaks into someone's home and robs it?

This chapter examines three categories of crime: violent crime, property crime, and crimes against the public order such as prostitution and drug abuse. In addition to providing a snapshot of the incidence of crime committed in Canada for each of these categories, this chapter makes the link to theoretical explanations discussed in later chapters that might explain why these crimes are committed. Unless otherwise noted, all the 2005 statistics cited in this chapter are taken from 2005 UCR crime statistics.[4] Table 3.1 provides a statistical snapshot of the crime picture in Canada in 2005.

Typologies of crime classifications of crime useful in identifying patterns of criminal activity and motivations for criminal behaviour.

Violent Crime

Violent crime incidents include homicide, attempted murder, assault, sexual assault, other assaults, other sexual offences, robbery, and abduction. The 2005 UCR reports that the violent crime rate in Canada has been falling since the mid-1990s and had remained largely unchanged from the previous year. At a rate of 943 incidents per 100 000 population in 2005, however, the violent crime rate has declined by 7 percent in the last decade. Interestingly, within the categories of offences classified as violent crime, common assault accounts for 60 percent of the total number. Across the regions of the country, violent crime rates fell in most provinces with the most notable declines in New Brunswick (−11 percent) and Nunavut (−11 percent). The only provinces reporting increases between 2004 and 2005 were Quebec (+2 percent), Ontario (less than 1 percent increase), and British Columbia (+1 percent). For the eighth year in a row, Saskatchewan reported the highest violent crime rate among the provinces (1983 per 100 000), which was 24 percent higher than the next highest province, Manitoba (1600 per 100 000). Both were lower than all three territories, however. Quebec continued to record the lowest rate of violent crime at 739, with Ontario having the second lowest rate at 748 per 100 000.

Homicide In the late 1990s, James Blum pled guilty to second-degree murder in the death of his grandmother, Emma Blum. Blum, who was unemployed at the time and $715 behind in the rent for the Kitchener, Ontario, apartment he shared with his common-law wife and their young son, claimed that he killed his grandmother as an act of mercy. He said he hit the 90-year-old woman two or three times on the temple with a magazine rack in the hope that this would be painless. Blum, who weighed 240 pounds, then stomped on her back, strangled her, and stabbed her in the neck to make sure she was dead. Marks on Emma Blum's hands, shoulders, and forearms indicated that she tried to fend off her grandson. James Blum claimed that, even though he deposited $228 taken from his grandmother just hours after the murder, he did not go to his grandmother's home to kill and rob her. Blum received a life sentence with eligibility for parole in ten years.[5]

Table 3.1

Federal Statute Incidents Reported to Police, by Most Serious Offence, Canada, 2001–2005

	2001 Number	2001 Rate[1]	2002 Number	2002 Rate[1]	2003 Number	2003 Rate[1]	2004[r] Number	2004[r] Rate[1]	2005 Number	2005 Rate[1]	Percent change in rate* 2004-2005	Percent change in rate* 1995-2005
Population	**31,021,251**		**31,372,587**		**31,669,150**		**31,974,363**		**32,270,507**			
Homicide[2]	553	1.8	582	1.9	549	1.7	624	2.0	658	2.0	4	2
Attempted murder	725	2.3	678	2.2	707	2.2	671	2.1	772	2.4	14	-20
Assault - Total	**236,957**	**764**	**235,710**	**751**	**236,802**	**748**	**234,259**	**733**	**234,729**	**727**	**-1**	**-2**
Level 1	191,147	616	189,185	603	188,667	596	184,883	578	182,049	564	-2	-8
Level 2 - Weapon	43,094	139	43,793	140	45,222	143	46,643	146	49,653	154	5	25
Level 3 - Aggravated	2,716	9	2,732	9	2,913	9	2,733	9	3,027	9	10	4
Other assaults	12,260	40	12,454	40	12,534	40	12,811	40	12,818	40	-1	-14
Sexual assault - Total	**24,044**	**78**	**24,499**	**78**	**23,514**	**74**	**23,036**	**72**	**23,303**	**72**	**0**	**-25**
Level 1	23,563	76	23,973	76	22,983	73	22,449	70	22,736	70	0	-24
Level 2 - Weapon	320	1	373	1	359	1	397	1	396	1	-1	-39
Level 3 - Aggravated	161	1	153	0	172	1	190	1	171	1	-11	-47
Other sexual offences	2,689	9	2,756	9	2,565	8	2,614	8	2,741	8	4	-29
Abduction	674	2	605	2	559	2	637	2	584	2	-9	-55
Robbery - Total	**27,284**	**88**	**26,662**	**85**	**28,437**	**90**	**27,495**	**86**	**28,669**	**89**	**3**	**-15**
Firearms	3,818	12	3,483	11	3,856	12	3,645	11	3,505	11	-5	-53
Other Weapons	10,280	33	10,104	32	10,057	32	8,362	26	8,558	27	1	-24
No Weapons	13,186	43	13,075	42	14,524	46	15,488	48	16,606	51	6	12
Violent crime - Total	**305,186**	**984**	**303,946**	**969**	**305,667**	**965**	**302,147**	**945**	**304,274**	**943**	**0**	**-7**
Breaking & entering - Total	**279,461**	**901**	**275,573**	**878**	**284,925**	**900**	**275,869**	**863**	**259,521**	**804**	**-7**	**-40**
Residential	166,500	537	163,156	520	161,494	510	153,223	479	148,270	459	-4	-43
Business	80,264	259	81,162	259	86,842	274	86,226	270	79,722	247	-8	-33
Other	32,697	105	31,255	100	36,589	116	36,420	114	31,529	98	-14	-39
Motor vehicle theft	168,595	543	161,912	516	174,208	550	169,977	532	160,100	496	-7	-10
Theft over $5,000	20,845	67	19,816	63	19,416	61	16,968	53	17,491	54	2	-62
Theft $5,000 and under	659,589	2,126	667,312	2,127	700,605	2,212	673,999	2,108	640,714	1,985	-6	-29
Possession of stolen goods	26,960	87	30,056	96	33,151	105	35,743	112	33,848	105	-6	-2
Fraud	86,486	279	91,812	293	92,924	293	97,443	305	94,468	293	-4	-18
Property crime - Total	**1,241,936**	**4,004**	**1,246,481**	**3,973**	**1,305,229**	**4,121**	**1,269,999**	**3,972**	**1,206,142**	**3,738**	**-6**	**-29**
Mischief	333,136	1,074	333,334	1,063	357,568	1,129	353,518	1,106	353,955	1,097	-1	-15
Counterfeiting currency[3]	38,674	125	79,970	255	139,267	440	201,108	629	163,323	506	-20	623
Bail violations	90,545	292	96,206	307	101,095	319	106,664	334	100,334	311	-7	36
Disturbing the peace	89,971	290	89,354	285	102,803	325	117,389	367	122,803	381	4	117
Offensive weapons	15,876	51	15,930	51	17,621	56	18,202	57	19,337	60	5	0
Prostitution	5,087	16	5,770	18	5,688	18	6,452	20	5,793	18	-11	-25
Arson	14,484	47	13,131	42	13,875	44	13,150	41	13,315	41	0	-8
Other	239,916	773	233,322	744	230,253	727	222,342	695	215,283	667	-4	-17
Other *Criminal Code* offences - Total	**827,689**	**2,668**	**867,017**	**2,764**	**968,276**	**3,057**	**1,038,825**	**3,249**	**994,143**	**3,081**	**-5**	**14**

Table 3.1 continued

Federal Statute Incidents Reported to Police, by Most Serious Offence, Canada, 2001–2005

	2001		2002		2003		2004[r]		2005		Percent change in rate* 2004-2005	Percent change in rate* 1995-2005
	Number	Rate[1]	Number	Rate[1]	Number	Rate[1]	Number	Rate[1]	Number	Rate[1]		
***Criminal Code* without traffic - Total (crime rate)**	**2,374,811**	**7,655**	**2,417,444**	**7,706**	**2,579,172**	**8,144**	**2,610,971**	**8,166**	**2,504,559**	**7,761**	**-5**	**-14**
Impaired driving[4]	82,718	267	80,045	255	77,645	245	80,339	251	75,613	234	-7	-33
Fail to stop/remain	22,538	73	22,040	70	23,336	74	24,022	75	27,217	84	12	-54
Other - *Criminal Code* Traffic[5]	14,978	48	15,486	49	16,138	51	16,276	51	15,908	49	-3	-17
Criminal Code Traffic - Total	**120,234**	**388**	**117,571**	**375**	**117,119**	**370**	**120,637**	**377**	**118,738**	**368**	**-2**	**-38**
***Criminal Code* - Total (incl. traffic)**	**2,495,045**	**8,043**	**2,535,015**	**8,080**	**2,696,291**	**8,514**	**2,731,608**	**8,543**	**2,623,297**	**8,129**	**-5**	**-15**
Drugs	**89,395**	**288**	**92,781**	**296**	**86,791**	**274**	**97,630**	**305**	**92,255**	**286**	**-6**	**36**
Cannabis	67,921	219	69,687	222	61,087	193	67,895	212	59,973	186	-12	24
Cocaine	12,145	39	12,737	41	14,225	45	16,974	53	18,951	59	11	51
Heroin	951	3	786	3	657	2	799	2	803	2	0	-38
Other drugs	8,378	27	9,571	31	10,822	34	11,962	37	12,528	39	4	253
Other federal statutes	**38,013**	**123**	**40,122**	**128**	**36,264**	**115**	**34,017**	**106**	**31,501**	**98**	**-8**	**-21**
Total federal statutes (incl. C.c.)	**2,622,453**	**8,454**	**2,667,918**	**8,504**	**2,819,346**	**8,902**	**2,863,255**	**8,955**	**2,747,053**	**8,513**	**-5**	**-14**

* Percent change based on unrounded rates.
[r] Revised figures.
1. Rates are calculated on the basis of 100,000 population. The population estimates come from the Annual Demographic Statistics, 2005 report, produced by Statistics Canada, Demography Division. Populations as of July 1st: final postcensal estimates for 2001 and 2002, updated postcensal estimates for 2003 and 2004, and preliminary postcensal estimates for 2005.
2. As a result of ongoing investigations in Port Coquitlam, B.C. there were 15 homicides in 2002, 7 homicides in 2003 and 5 homicides in 2004 that occurred in previous years. Homicide are counted according to the year in which police file the report.
3. Due to an improved data collection methodology for counterfeiting introduced in 2005, numbers for certain police services, primarily in Ontario, were revised for 2004. Therefore, please use caution when comparing these data with prior years.
4. Includes impaired operation of a vehicle causing death, causing bodily harm, alcohol rate over 80mg, failure/refusal to provide a breath/blood sample. In 2001, the RCMP began reporting incidents in which a roadside suspension was issued, rather than a charge laid, to the CCJS. In 2002, most other police services began reporting this way as well. Previous to 2004, Vancouver Police only reported incidents of impaired driving when a charge had been laid. As of 2004, their data also include incidents where the driver was tested to be over .08 and received a road-side suspension. This resulted in 1,900 more impaired driving incidents being reported in 2004 than 2003.
5. Includes dangerous operation offences and driving a motor vehicle while prohibited.
Source: "Federal Statute Incidents Reported to Police, by Most Serious Offence, Canada, 2001 to 2005," adapted from the Statistics Canada publication "Juristat", Catalogue 85-002, vol. 26, no. 4. Released July 20, 2006. http://www.statcan.ca/bsolc/english/bsolc?catno=85-002-XIE.

Homicide when a person, directly or indirectly, by any means, causes the death of a human being. Homicide can be culpable or non-culpable.

Murder when a person intentionally causes the death of another human being or intends to cause bodily harm likely to result in death.

First-degree murder culpable homicide that is planned and deliberate.

Second-degree murder all murder that is not first-degree murder.

Manslaughter all non-intentional homicide.

Infanticide when a female considered disturbed from the effects of giving birth causes the death of her newborn child (under age 1).

Serial murder culpable homicide that involves the killing of several victims in three or more separate events.

The terms "homicide" and "murder" are often used interchangeably, but they are not synonymous. **Homicide** occurs when a person, directly or indirectly, by any means, causes the death of a human being. Homicide, therefore, can be either culpable or non-culpable. *Culpable homicide* is considered an offence under the *Criminal Code of Canada* and includes murder, manslaughter, and infanticide. *Non-culpable homicide* consists of justifiable and/or excusable homicide. Justifiable homicide includes legally authorized acts such as a police officer killing someone in the course of duty, while excusable homicide includes acts of self-defence, defence of others, or defence of property.

Murder (s. 229) occurs when a person intentionally causes the death of another human being or intends to cause bodily harm likely to result in death. Murder is further classified into first-degree murder and second-degree murder. **First-degree murder** (defined in s. 231) describes culpable homicide that is planned and deliberate; or involves the killing of a peace officer such as a police officer or correctional worker; or occurs during the commission of another serious offence such as sexual assault, kidnapping, or hijacking. **Second-degree murder** (defined in s. 231) includes all murder that is not first degree. In other words, it is intentional and unlawful but not planned. **Manslaughter** (s. 234) is considered to be a non-intentional homicide committed in response to sudden provocation, as a result of impaired judgment due to alcohol or drug consumption, or as a result of recklessness or carelessness. **Infanticide** (s. 233) occurs when a female causes the death of her newborn child (under age 1) if her mind is considered disturbed from the effects of giving birth.

Serial murder and mass murder are two varieties of what is usually termed first-degree murder. Although most murderers kill only once in their lives, serial and mass murderers kill more than one person. **Serial murder** has been defined as culpable homicide that "involves the killing of several victims in three or more separate events."[6] These separate events are sometimes spread out over years. Infamous Canadian serial killers include Clifford Olson, who killed at least 11 young people aged 9 to 18 over a 9-month period in 1980–1981 in British Columbia. Between 1987 and 1990, Paul Bernardo committed at least 18 violent sexual assaults in Toronto and later went on to abduct, sexually assault, and

Convicted murderer Paul Bernardo enters court in Kingston under heavy security. Bernardo was appealing his convictions in the deaths of two Ontario teenagers.

The Canadian Press/The Whig-Standard/Ian MacAlpine.

strangle two teenaged girls in 1991 and 1992 in St. Catharines, Ontario. He was assisted in these murders by his wife, Karla Homolka, who subsequently testified against her husband. Allan Legère killed a grocery store owner in 1987 and went on to kill four other people in Miramichi, New Brunswick, terrorizing the rural community between 1987 and 1989, and earning for himself the nickname "The Monster of the Miramichi." Robert Picton currently stands accused of 27 charges of first-degree murder for the deaths of sex-trade workers who went missing between 1995 and 2002. Other notorious serial killers include Jeffrey Dahmer, who killed and dismembered 15 young men in the 1980s; David Berkowitz, better known as "Son of Sam," who killed young men and women in New York City in the 1970s; Charles Manson, who ordered his followers to kill seven people in California; Ted Bundy, who killed many college-aged women; and the female serial killer Aileen Carol Wuornos, who killed six men who had picked her up as she hitchhiked through Florida.[7] Internationally infamous killers include Dr. Harold Shipman of Britain, who was convicted of killing 15 female patients and suspected in the deaths of 23 more; and Javed Iqbal, convicted of sexually assaulting and killing 100 street children in Pakistan and sentenced to die in the same way his victims died—by strangulation.

Similar to the serial killer is the spree killer, who kills a number of victims over a relatively short period. Andrew Cunanan, who killed fashion designer Gianni Versace and others in 1997, is an example. Cunanan's killing spree lasted three months and claimed five victims.

Mass murder is different from serial murder in that it entails "the killing of four or more victims at one location, within one event."[8] On December 6, 1989, in what has become known as the "Montreal Massacre," Marc Lepine shot and killed 14 female students at Montreal's École Polytechnique. Other mass murderers in Canada include Victor Hoffman, who, at age 19, killed 9 members of a family as they slept in their Saskatchewan farmhouse in 1967. Mark Chahal, a Vancouver accountant who shot dead his ex-wife and eight other members of her family at a home in Vernon, British Columbia, in 1996; Kevin Vermette, who shot three young men at a deserted campground in Kitimat, British Columbia, in 1997; and James Roszko, who ambushed and then killed four RCMP officers on his Alberta farm in 2005. Other infamous mass murders include the 31 people killed in 1991 when a man smashed his pickup truck through a cafeteria window in Texas and shot lunch-goers to death; 21 killed at a McDonald's restaurant in San Ysidro, California, in 1984 by an out-of-work security guard; 16 school-aged children and their teacher killed in Dunblane, Scotland, in 1995; and, in 1999, 12 high school students and a teacher killed by 2 fellow students who marched through the halls of Columbine High School in Colorado targeting specific individuals.

In 2005, homicides (658) and attempted murders (772) accounted for less than half of 1 percent of all violent crimes committed. The rate of homicide increased by 4 percent nationally in 2005, following an increase in 2004. Rates of attempted murder increased as well, up 14 percent from the previous year.

Geographically, homicide rates increased from east to west in Canada. The lowest rates were reported in Prince Edward Island where no homicides were recorded, followed by New Brunswick (1.2 homicides per 100 000 population) and Quebec (1.3). The highest homicide rates per 100 000 were found in Saskatchewan (4.3), Manitoba (4.2), and Alberta (3.3). In absolute numbers, Ontario and Alberta led the country in 2005, with 218 and 109 homicides respectively, although Ontario's rate, at 1.7 per 100 000, is at about the national average. Among the largest metropolitan areas in the country, six recorded a greater number of homicides in 2005 compared to 2004. Edmonton recorded the largest increase from 34 to 44 homicides (an increased rate of 4.3 per 100 000). With 26 recorded homicides,

Mass murder the illegal killing of four or more victims at one location, within one event.

Winnipeg's rate increased by 3.7 percent from the previous year, followed by Vancouver with an increased rate of 2.9 per 100 000 (62 homicides). The lowest rates per 100 000 population were reported in Quebec City (0.7), Ottawa (1.3), and Montreal (1.3).

Sixty-five youth (aged 12 to 17 years) were accused of homicide in 2005, an increase of 21 from the previous year. This increase is in contrast to findings for youth crime overall which decreased by 6 percent from 2004.

Statistics reveal additional information about murder in Canada.[9] Of the solved homicides in 2005, 36 percent of victims were killed by a spouse or other family member, and 49 percent were killed by an acquaintance; about 20 percent of murders were committed by strangers. Spousal homicides (spouses being defined as persons in legal marriages, common-law relationships, including same-sex spouses, and separated or divorced persons) accounted for 16 percent of all solved homicides. In 2005, 74 people were killed by a spouse. Other family-related homicides in 2005 included 20 victims killed by a parent (12 by a father, 8 by a mother), 27 by one of the children in the family, 14 by a sibling, and 21 by another family relation. Of the 20 children killed by a parent, 13 were under the age of 12, a number substantially lower than the previous 10-year average of 34, and the lowest total since 1964.

Since 1992, firearms have been used in roughly one-third of all homicides each year. Statistics for 2005 indicate this proportion to be 34 percent, a slight increase from the previous year. Of the 222 homicides involving firearms in 2005, 128 (58 percent) were committed with a handgun, 55 (25 percent) with a rifle/shotgun, 11 (5 percent) with a sawed-off rifle/shotgun, 7 (3 percent) with a fully automatic firearm, and 5 (2 percent) with other types of firearms. Relatively strict gun-control laws in Canada compared with the United States may be partially responsible for the relatively low number of homicides involving a firearm (see Chapter 11 for a detailed look at Canada's firearm legislation). By comparison, American statistics indicate that 66 percent of all homicides involve the use of a firearm.[10] Of the remaining 66 percent of homicides in Canada in 2005, stabbings accounted for 30 percent (198); beatings, 22 percent (145); strangulation/suffocation, 7 percent (45); shaken-baby syndrome, 2 percent (12); fire/burns, 1 percent (7); poisoning, 0.8 percent (5); and injuries caused by a vehicle, 0.6 percent (4).

Various circumstances are associated with homicide in Canada. In 2005, police reported that 73 percent of those accused of homicide and 57 percent of all homicide victims had consumed alcohol and/or drugs at the time of the offence. As well, almost half (45 percent) of all homicide incidents in 2005 (224) occurred during the commission of another criminal offence. Of these 224 incidents, 73 percent (164) were committed at the same time as another violent offence: 43 percent (97) of these were committed during an assault and 17 percent (38) during a robbery. Official statistics for 2005 also indicated that 13 percent of all persons accused of homicide were suspected by police of having mental or developmental disorders. Consistent with previous years, police suspect the presence of mental disorders among females accused of homicide more often than among males. These numbers may, in fact, be underestimated, since police officers may not feel qualified to make such assessments (refer to Chapter 7 for a discussion of mental illness and crime).

Sexual Assault In 2004, friends and fans of NBA star Kobe Bryant were relieved when prosecutors dropped rape charges that they had filed against him a year earlier.[11] Bryant had been accused of sexually assaulting a 19-year-old concierge in Colorado while he was preparing to undergo knee surgery. The dramatic turn in the case came in the middle of a jury selection and less than a week before opening statements were to begin. Bryant admitted to having sexual intercourse with the woman, but claimed that the sex was consensual. He had been facing four years to life in prison.

At-risk Occupations

Box 3.1

Since 1997, Statistics Canada has conducted an annual Homicide Survey that collects a wide range of information on homicides, including information related to a victim's occupation, either legal or illegal. Findings indicate that here has been an average of 17 victims killed each year while "on-the-job."

Since 1961, 125 police officers have been killed in the line of duty, including five in 2005. In the same year, 55 police officers were feloniously killed in the United States, a nation with a population about eight times greater than Canada's.

Statistics for 2005 also indicate that ten other homicides occurred as a result of the victim's legal employment, including taxi drivers, convenience store clerks, and gas station attendants.

Homicides can also be associated with a victim's involvement in illegal activities. In 2005, police reported an increase in the number of gang-related homicides, or those that occur as a consequence of activities involving an organized crime group or street gang. Up from 72 confirmed gang homicides in 2004, there were 107 gang-related homicides (or 16 percent of all homicides) recorded in 2005. Most of these homicides occurred in Toronto (23), Edmonton (16), Montreal (15), and Calgary (9). Almost two-thirds of these homicides were motivated by a "settling of accounts." Innocent bystanders killed as a result of gang-related activity are also included in the count for gang-related homicides.

The number of sex trade workers killed in 2005 was reported at nine, similar to the average number reported annually before the discovery of the homicides in Port Coquitlam, British Columbia, in 2004, 2003, and 2002.

Source: Adapted from the Statistics Canada publication "Juristat," Catalogue 85-002, vol. 26, no. 6. Released November 8, 2006. http://www.statcan.ca/bsolc/english/bsolc?catno=85-002-XIE.

The *Criminal Code of Canada* distinguishes between three levels of sexual assault, according to the seriousness of the incident. These levels reflect amendments made to the *Criminal Code* in 1983. Prior to that year, section 143 of the *Criminal Code* defined rape to have occurred when "a male person has sexual intercourse with a female person who is not his wife (a) without her consent, or (b) with her consent if the consent (i) is extorted by threats or fear of bodily harm, (ii) is obtained by impersonating her husband, or (iii) is obtained by false or fraudulent representations as to the nature and quality of the act." Under this definition, the act was largely defined as one of sexual penetration, and the offender was presumed to be a male and the victim female. As well, under the legislation husbands could not be charged with raping their wives.

Currently, sexual assault legislation focuses on the violent nature of the act, rather than its sexual nature. **Sexual assault** is considered to be an assault committed in circumstances of a sexual nature such that the sexual integrity of the victim is violated. The current laws allow for the accused (including husbands) to be charged with sexual assault regardless of whether or not penetration occurred. As well, the offence has been "degenderized" such that perpetrators can be either male or female, as can victims. Critics charge, however, that it is overwhelmingly men who sexually assault women and that it has now been left to the discretion of the courts to determine what constitutes sexual assault, as opposed to common assault.[12] *Level 1 sexual assault* (s. 271) is the classification of least physical injury to the victim and can include unwanted sexual touching; *level 2 sexual assault* (s. 272) involves the use of a weapon or threats to use a weapon, or results in bodily harm; *level 3 sexual assault* (s. 273) is aggravated sexual assault, resulting in wounding, maiming, or disfiguring the victim, or endangering his or her life.[13]

Sexual assault an assault committed in circumstances of a sexual nature such that the sexual integrity of the victim is violated. The degree of violence used determines whether the sexual assault is level 1, level 2, or level 3.

Date rape sexual assault
that occurs within the
context of a dating
relationship.

Date rape is a term used to define sexual assault that occurs within the context of a dating relationship. It has received much attention recently, although it has undoubtedly occurred as long as there has been dating. According to recent studies, date rape is much more common than previously believed. Some authors suggest that date rape may occur when a male concludes that his date "owes" him something for the money he has spent on her.[14] A current factor in the date rape phenomenon is the presence of the "date rape pill," generally known as "rohypnol" and referred to on the street as "roofies," "roach," "ruffies," or "R2." These small white tablets have no taste or odour and, when dropped into an unsuspecting victim's drink, make that person feel dizzy, disoriented, and nauseated until finally rendered unconscious. This state can last from two to eight hours, and the victim often has little or no memory of what has happened in that interval.[15]

The Violence Against Women Survey (VAWS) conducted in 1993 revealed that only 6 percent of all sexual assaults were reported, and results of the 2004 General Social Survey found that about 8 percent of incidents were reported.[16] The reasons for victims' hesitancy were varied. Some victims feel they are responsible for some aspect of their social relationship that led to the sexual assault, some are ashamed or embarrassed, and in some cases victims may feel some concern for the offender and not wish to have him become the target of criminal prosecution—even if deserved.[17] Educational campaigns against date rape, found largely on college and university campuses, cite the slogan "No Means No" in an attempt to combat the notion that the dating game is one where the women hold the "prize" that men attempt to "win" and that when a woman says "No" she really means "Yes."

Statistics on sexual assault collected by the UCR are delineated according to the three levels of sexual assault. In 2005, 23 303 sexual assaults were reported nationwide under the UCR program—97 percent of those were classified as level 1. In 2005, the rates for all three levels of sexual assault remained largely unchanged from the previous year—level 1 sexual assault at 70 per 100 000 population, level 2 at 1 per 100 000, and level 3 at 1 per 100 000. While the rate of level 1 sexual assaults has decreased by 8 percent in the past decade, the rates of levels 2 and 3 have increased by 25 and 4 percent respectively. Despite these increases, the overall rate of sexual assault at 72 per 100 000 population is 25 percent lower than a decade earlier, but still close to twice the rate in 1983 when the new definition of the offence was introduced (41 per 100 000). Refer to Chapter 2 for a discussion of the impact of crime definitions on crime rates. It is interesting to note that the sexual assault rate for females is effectively twice that indicated by the official figures, since any realistic tally of such crimes should compare the number of female victims assaulted with the number of females in the overall population (rather than to a count of the entire population, which includes males).

Data from the most recent UCR indicate that 84 percent of victims of sexual assault were female compared to 49 percent of victims of all other violent crimes.[18] Male victims account for about 16 percent of victims of sexual offences overall. Most had been victimized by a friend or acquaintance, and the remainder by a family member or stranger. Forty-four percent of all sexual assault victims reported to the police were between the ages of 15 and 24.

The sexual assault laws are applicable to all victims regardless of the age of the victim. In 1988, however, several new offences were created to deal with cases of sexual abuse involving children younger than 18 years of age. These new offences, referred to in the UCR as "other sexual offences," include sexual interference, invitation to sexual touching, sexual exploitation, incest, anal intercourse, and bestiality. Statistics from the UCR for

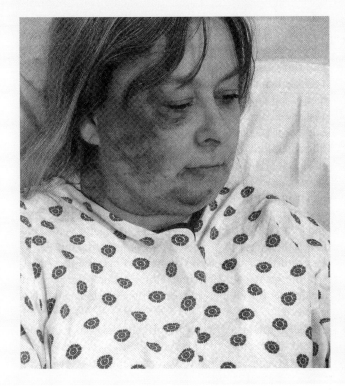

An assaulted woman in an emergency shelter. Why do you think sexual assault is one of the most under-reported crimes in Canada?

2005 show that 2741 incidents of child sexual abuse came to the attention of police, a rate of 8 cases per 100 000 population.

Related to the offence of sexual assault is the offence of criminal harassment, often referred to as *stalking*. Legislation regarding this offence was first enacted in Canada in 1993. **Criminal harassment** (s. 264) is generally defined as "repeated following, watching or communicating with a person or someone known to them in a way that causes them to fear for their safety or for the safety of someone known to them."[19] Before the enactment of the criminal harassment legislation, stalkers could be charged with uttering threats, intimidation, trespassing, indecent or harassing phone calls, or assault by threatening. Those fearing injury to themselves, their families, or their property could also have a *peace bond* laid against the accused. These measures, however, failed to adequately protect victims, since the accused usually had to threaten or physically harm someone before action could be taken. There also existed no means to deal with non-violent harassing behaviour such as following or watching.

The increased use of the internet by Canadians has also led to an increase in the incidence of *cyberstalking*, or online harassment. Closely related to real-life stalking, individuals use chat rooms, message boards, and emails to threaten or post obscene messages about the victim. It is possible for cyberstalking to extend to real life as the stalker may use the internet or obtain information about the target and then use it in a conventional stalking incident. While online stalkers can be charged under the criminal harassment provision of the *Criminal Code*, the nature of the activity makes it difficult to identify stalkers. There are rarely any witnesses, and jurisdictional problems arise if the stalker is located in a city or country different from that of the victim. The limited evidence that does exist about cyberstalking indicates that the majority of the victims are women.[20] See Chapter 12 for a more in-depth look at cyber-crimes.

Criminal harassment also known as stalking, is the repeated following, watching, or communicating with a person or someone known to the person in a way that causes that person to fear for his/her safety or for the safety of someone known to him/her.

Statistics from the UCR on criminal harassment show 5382 reported incidents, or a rate of 18 per 100 000 population, in recent years.[21] Seventy-seven percent of all reported victims of criminal harassment are female, while 84 percent of those accused of criminal harassment are males. In most cases, the offender is known to the victim; 37 percent of all female victims were stalked by ex-spouses, 25 percent by a casual acquaintance, and 16 percent by a current or ex-boyfriend. Other offenders include strangers (7 percent), business relations (5 percent), current spouses (3 percent), and other family members (3 percent). Male victims of criminal harassment are most commonly stalked by casual acquaintances (44 percent), business acquaintances (12 percent), strangers (12 percent), ex-spouses (11 percent), other family members (7 percent), and current or ex-girlfriends (6 percent).

Twenty-five percent of criminal harassment incidents involved other offences. Some of these included uttering threats (20 percent), breach of probation or other court orders (14 percent), threatening/harassing phone calls (12 percent), common assault (11 percent), mischief (10 percent), other *Criminal Code* offences (8 percent), and breaking and entering (6 percent).[22]

Robbery The crime of **robbery** (s. 343) is regarded as a violent personal crime because it is committed in the presence of a victim and involves threatened or actual use of force or violence in the commission of a theft or attempted theft from another person. Although some individuals mistakenly use the terms "robbery" and "break and enter" interchangeably (as in the phrase "my house was robbed"), it should be remembered that robbery is a personal crime and that individuals are robbed, not houses.

The 2005 UCR reports that 28 669 robberies came to the attention of the authorities across the nation that year, meaning that the robbery rate was 89 for every 100 000 people in Canada. This was an increase of 3 percent from the previous year but 15 percent lower than a decade ago.

Over half of these robberies were committed without a weapon (58 percent). A further 12 percent were committed with a firearm, while robberies using other weapons were roughly 30 percent of the total. Most robberies occurred against commercial establishments such as convenience stores, banks and financial institutions, gas stations, and other establishments such as restaurants and liquor stores.

In recent years, robberies of private residences have attracted attention. Commonly referred to as *home invasions*, this type of robbery is characterized by a forced entry into a private residence while the occupants are home and usually includes violence and extortion against the occupants.[23] While there is no specific offence in the *Criminal Code of Canada* called "home invasion," a 2002 amendment to the *Criminal Code* made "home invasion" an aggravating circumstance at sentencing. And, even though there are no officially recorded statistics, some police services are reporting it specifically. Major metropolitan police departments, including those in Calgary, Toronto, and Vancouver, report that while home invasions constitute only a small percentage of the total number of robberies, they evoke a disproportionate amount of fear among victims and communities because they violate the safety and sanctity of one's home.[24]

Assault **Assault** (defined in s. 265) involves the intentional or threatened application of force on another person without consent. The *Criminal Code of Canada* includes several categories of assault: *level 1 assault* (s. 266), or common assault, which is the least serious type of assault and includes behaviours such as punching, pushing, slapping, shoving, or threats

Robbery the unlawful taking or attempted taking of property that is in the immediate possession of another, by threatened or actual use of force or violence.

Assault the intentional or threatened application of force on another person without consent. The categories of assault include level 1—assault or common assault; level 2—assault involving the use of a weapon or that causes bodily harm; and level 3—assault that results in wounding or endangering the life of the victim.

by act or gesture; *level 2 assault* (s. 267), which involves the use of a weapon or results in bodily harm; *level 3 assault* (s. 268), which includes assaults that wound, maim, disfigure, or endanger the life of the victim; and *other assaults*, which involve use of force against a peace officer, unlawfully causing bodily harm, and discharge of a firearm with intent.

Of the 234 729 incidents of recorded assaults at levels 1, 2, and 3 in 2005, level 1 accounted for 78 percent of all assaults and for 60 percent of all reported violent incidences. Overall, the rate of assault for 2005 (727 per 100 000 population) decreased by 1 percent from the previous year (733 in 2004).

The majority of assaults continue to be perpetrated by adult males, yet among youth aged 12 to 17, about a third of assaults are committed by females. Unlike sexual assaults, victims of assault are as likely to be female as male.

Hate crime The definition of **hate crime** has evolved out of the sections of the *Criminal Code* that address hate propaganda and the *Purpose and Principles of Sentencing*. Sections 318 and 319 of the *Criminal Code* refer to "advocating genocide, public incitement of hatred, or the wilful promotion of hatred against an identifiable group, including those distinguished by colour, race, religion, ethnic origin, or sexual orientation." Section 718.2 of the *Criminal Code*, which addresses sentencing principles, allows the courts to take into consideration whether an offence was "motivated by bias, prejudice, or hate based on race, national or ethnic origin, language, colour, religion, sex, age, mental or physical disability, sexual orientation, or any other similar factor."[25] In other words, courts now consider hate motivation as an aggravating circumstance.

Two methods are used to measure incidents of hate crime in Canada. Victimization Surveys (as part of the General Social Survey) ask a random sampling of the population whether they feel they have been a recent victim of crime and whether they believe the incident was motivated by hate.[26] If they indicate a hate motivation, they are asked to specify the motive. (Refer to Chapter 2 for a more detailed look at the methodology of Victimization Surveys.) Results from the most recent Victimization Survey indicate that about 4 percent of the reported criminal incidents (273 000) were considered by victims to be motivated by hate and race/ethnicity was reported in 43 percent of these incidents. Seventy-seven percent of hate crimes recorded in the GSS involved offences against the person (49 percent were assaults) compared to 58 percent of non-hate-related incidents, supporting research that shows that hate-motivated crimes are more likely to involve offences against the person and are more likely to involve excessive violence. While the most recent Victimization Survey showed little difference in the overall rates of hate victimization by sex, results did show that younger individuals, aged 15 to 25, were twice as likely to report having experienced a hate crime, compared to those aged 25 to 34 (22 per 1000 versus 11 per 1000 population). Among visible minorities, the reported rate of hate crime was almost three times greater (19 per 1000) than for non-visible minorities (7 per 1000 population).

Corroborating the GSS, a Statistics Canada Ethnic Diversity Survey (EDS) undertaken in 2002 polled 42 500 people aged 15 years and older to inquire whether any recent criminal victimization was motivated by hatred. Not unlike the findings of the GSS, the EDS concluded that visible minorities were over-represented among hate crime victims; visible minority individuals were more than one and a half times more likely to have suffered a hate crime (13 per 1000 population compared to 20 per 1000 population).

The other official source of hate crime statistics is police-reported data. A pilot survey undertaken in 2002 and involving 12 metropolitan police services across the country

Hate crime a criminal act directed toward a person or group because of race, national or ethnic origin, religion, language, colour, sex, age, sexual orientation, mental or physical disability. Also referred to as hate-motivated crime, or bias crime.

collected information on criminal events, including whether or not the motivation for the event involved hate.[27] Findings indicated that the majority of the 928 hate crime incidents recorded were offences against the person (52 percent), followed by property offences (31 percent). The most common types of hate crime incidents involved mischief/vandalism (26 percent), assault (25 percent), uttering threats (20 percent), and hate propaganda (13 percent). Substantiating the findings of the GSS and EDS, police-reported findings indicate that race/ethnicity was the motivating factor in 57 percent of all recorded hate crime, followed by religion (43 percent), and sexual orientation (10 percent). Three percent were motivated by language, sex, age, or disability. Further, while race/ethnicity was cited as the most frequent motive, Jewish people and/or institutions were identified as the largest single targeted group. Two hundred and twenty-nine of the 928 reported incidents (25 percent) were anti-Semitic in nature. The next most victimized groups were Blacks (17 percent), Muslims (11 percent), South Asians (10 percent), and gays and lesbians (9 percent). See Box 3.2 for a summary of the findings for all three surveys.

Highlights of Hate Crime in Canada | Box 3.2

- According to the 1999 General Social Survey (GSS), Canadians indicated that about 4% (273,000) of all self-reported criminal victimization incidents were believed by the victims to be motivated by hate.
- Data collected in the 2002 Ethnic Diversity Survey suggest that 5% of Canadians are worried or very worried about becoming the victim of a crime because of their race, ethnicity, language, and/or religion. This figure increases to 11% when only visible minorities are considered.
- Of the 928 hate crime incidents recorded in a pilot survey of 12 major police forces in Canada in 2001 and 2002, the majority were motivated by race/ethnicity (57%), followed by religion (43%), and sexual orientation (10%).
- Of those hate crimes reported to police, the majority involved offences against the person (52%) followed by property offences (31%) and other offences (17%), such as hate propaganda.
- One-quarter of the hate crime incidents reported by the police services participating in the pilot survey were anti-Semitic in nature involving Jewish people or institutions.
- Incidents motivated by the victim's sexual orientation were the most likely to be violent in nature (65%). Six in ten of these incidents involved assault (63%), followed by uttering threats (21%).
- About one in five victims of violent hate crime had a weapon used against them. Fewer than one in ten of these victims had a knife or cutting instrument used against them, and less than 1% involved a firearm. One-quarter of victims of a violent crime suffered an injury. Gays and lesbians were almost twice as likely as hate crime victims in general to suffer an injury.
- The pilot survey found that in cases where the relationship of the accused to the victim was identified, the majority of victims did not know their perpetrator (83%). A further 15% of victims stated that the accused was a casual acquaintance or a business relationship.
- The pilot survey data indicate that there was a significant, but short lived, impact on the number of hate crimes reported to police following the September 11th terrorist attacks in the United States. Fifteen percent of the hate crime incidents recorded by police following this event were associated with the terrorist attacks, three-quarters of these incidents occurring within the two months following the attack.

Source: Adapted from the Statistics Canada publication "Juristat," Catalogue 85-002, vol. 24, no. 4. Released June 1, 2004. http://www.statcan.ca/bsolc/english/bsolc?catno=85-002-XIE.

Theoretical Explanations of Violent Crime Why do people commit acts of violence? What compels a man to sexually assault a woman or a youth to pick up a knife and force a convenience store clerk to hand over the money in the till? While there are no easy answers to these questions, there are certainly a number of theoretical explanations commonly accepted within the field of criminology that might provide answers.

Cases of mass or serial murder, such as the 14 women killed by Marc Lepine in Montreal on December 6, 1989, or the 11 children killed by Clifford Olson between 1980 and 1981, often tempt us to examine the individual offender for clues. Surely people who kill others must have "something wrong with them" that compels them to commit these heinous acts. Chapters 6 and 7 examine a number of biological and psychological explanations of crime that can be applied to violent offenders. The biological theories found in Chapter 6 question whether certain individuals are predisposed to violence. Is the male sex drive, which has been developed through evolution to perpetuate the species, an explanation for man's sexual aggression toward women? Can naturally occurring levels of the male hormone testosterone be seen as a reason why males commit close to 90 percent of all violent crime in Canada? Chapter 7 outlines a number of psychological or neurological dysfunctions such as abnormal electroencephalograms, low intelligence, Attention Deficit Disorder (ADD), or Attention Deficit Hyperactivity Disorder (ADHD), as well as psychotic symptoms such as hallucinations, paranoia, and distorted views of reality that may account for criminal behaviour. Various personality disorders, including anti-social personality disorder—psychopathy in particular—are considered as possible causes for deviant sexual behaviour. Psychological theories emphasizing personality types look to Freudian analysis and contend that it is the *id*, or that aspect of personality from which drives, wishes, urges, and desires emanate, that causes the behaviour of rapists, for example. The hostile and sadistic feelings toward women many rapists tend to display are often considered to be rooted in psychotic or personality disorders.

Mass murderer Marc Lepine killed 14 female students at L'École Polytechnique in Montreal. Which theories do you think work best to explain such violent criminal behaviour: those from the social responsibility perspective or those from the social problems perspective?

The Gazette (Montreal).

An inability to deal with frustration is considered by some to contribute to aggressive behaviour. Chapter 7 recounts the case of Pierre Lebrun, who killed four fellow employees after years of taunting because of a speech impediment; this apparently caused him to "snap." Donald Lauzon, 19, who killed his 2-year-old daughter Samantha in August 1996 by repeatedly banging her head against the arm of a sofa, was at a loss to explain the anger that welled inside him and surfaced whenever he became frustrated. "The kid would do something and I would hit her," he is quoted as saying. "I wouldn't mean to actually use full force, but that's what would happen. I hit her. Kid would go flying. When it happened I'd freak out, I'd go 'Oh God. What did I do? I'm never going to do this again.'"[28]

Social learning theories assume that people learn how to behave by modelling themselves after others whom they have the opportunity to observe. Does a young boy's exposure to violence in the home account for his future violent behaviour? Violence on television and in the movies has been cited as the cause of violence in some instances, most notably in the tragic 1993 case of James Bulger, aged 2, of Liverpool, England, who was abducted from a shopping mall, beaten to death, and dumped on a railway track by two 10-year-old boys, who claimed they got the idea after watching the same violent video several times the previous day. The individual responsibility perspective contends that it is the psychological makeup of each person that determines the way in which observed behaviour is absorbed, processed, and acted upon. Some individuals may be exposed to violence in the home and never become violent themselves, while others are compelled to model their behaviour on the actions, and even deviant actions, of others.

The same issues can be examined in the debate over whether or not those children who are abused physically or sexually in the home later go on to inflict harm on others. The link between family violence and future criminality is not a direct one, and there appear to be numerous other factors that need to be taken into consideration. Some criminologists argue that, while being abused as a child may increase the risk of future violence or criminality, there are many people who are victims of childhood violence who do not become violent adult offenders.[29]

In contrast to the individual responsibility perspective are those theories that fall under the social problems perspective. Discussed in Chapters 8, 9, and 10, these theories look to socialization and cultural factors as explanations for acts of violence. Are males raised to behave more aggressively? Are our cultural values responsible for sending a message to young males that the way to deal with stress and frustration is through the use of aggression? Well-known accounts of drivers who assault others as a result of what is known as *road rage* suggest that perhaps societal tolerance for the use of violence to solve disputes has increased.

The subculture of violence theory in Chapter 8 is frequently cited as an explanation for acts of violence perpetrated by individuals from a certain subculture that promotes certain values or codes of conduct. For example, the expectation that young males defend their honour and reputation at all costs naturally leads to the use of violence, if that is what is necessary to achieve this end. Therefore, it is conformity to this set of values that leads to violence; violence is not seen in these subcultural settings as the result of deviant behaviour. This argument is used further to explain why victims of violence in these groups are usually members of the group and not outsiders. The account in Chapter 8 of the murder of Sylvain Leduc helps to illustrate this point.

The feminist criminology perspective discussed in Chapter 10 would explain violence against women as resulting from societal inequalities due primarily to gender. The physical

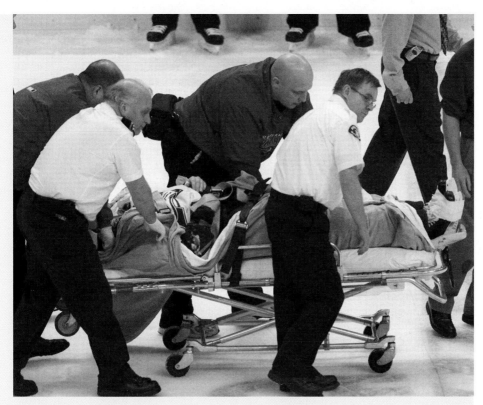

Professional hockey player Steve Moore is wheeled to an ambulance after being hit from behind during a 2004 game by Vancouver Canucks hockey star Todd Bertuzzi. Moore suffered broken neck vertebrae, a concussion, and nerve damage in the incident, ending his hockey career. Bertuzzi was suspended by the National Hockey League and prevented from finishing the season. In a controversial decision, he was also charged with assault causing bodily harm and subsequently pled guilty to assault. Do you think Bertuzzi should have been criminally charged for his actions?

AP Wide World Photos.

and sexual assault of women is a means by which males are able to maintain their dominance over women. Thus, the sexual victimization of girls is a behaviour learned by young males in a patriarchal society.

Property Crime

Property crimes are comprised of those unlawful acts perpetrated with the intent of gaining property, but do not involve the use or threat of violence. Included in this category are breaking and entering, theft, fraud, crime involving motor vehicles, arson, and possession of stolen goods.

The 2005 UCR reports 1.2 million incidents of property crime, or a rate of 3738 per 100 000 population in that year, which represents a 6 percent drop from the previous year and the lowest recorded number in over 30 years. The rates of property crime declined in every province in 2005. The most significant drops were recorded in both Manitoba and Saskatchewan where the rates declined by 12 percent. Newfoundland and Labrador had

Breaking and entering
the unlawful entry of a
place to commit an
indictable offence.

the lowest rate in the country at 2535 per 100 000 population. Overall, for 2005, the western provinces recorded the highest property crime rates, with the highest in British Columbia (6234 per 100 000).

Breaking and Entering

Breaking and entering (s. 348) is one of the most common and serious of property offences. This crime constitutes an invasion of personal territory or a workspace and often results in the theft or destruction of property. While most break and enters are, strictly speaking, property crimes, the potential for personal violence is inherent. Breaking and entering a dwelling house carries a maximum penalty of life imprisonment (as compared with 10 years for breaking and entering of a place other than a dwelling house), reflecting the possibility of violent confrontations between the offender and the homeowner. In the UCR, police-reported breaking and entering is categorized into three different types: (1) residential—the breaking and entering of a private residence, including single homes as well as attached garages, garden homes, apartments, cottages, mobile homes, rooming houses, etc.; (2) business—the breaking and entering of a facility used for commercial or public affairs, including, for example, financial institutions, stores, and non-commercial enterprises such as government buildings, schools, churches, and non-profit agencies; (3) other—the breaking and entering of private property structures such as sheds, detached garages, or storage and transportation facilities. The UCR statistics include attempted as well as completed break and enters.

In 2005, 259 521 incidents of breaking and entering were recorded, representing a rate of 804 per 100 000 population. This is a decrease of 7 percent from the previous year, in keeping with the consistent decreases since 1991. Fifty-seven percent of all break and enters were residential (for a rate of 459 per 100 000), while business break and enters accounted for 31 percent (or a rate of 247 per 100 000). The remaining 12 percent included other locations such as sheds and storage facilities (for a rate of 98 per 100 000).

Figure 3.1

Beaking and Entering, Canada, 1985–2005

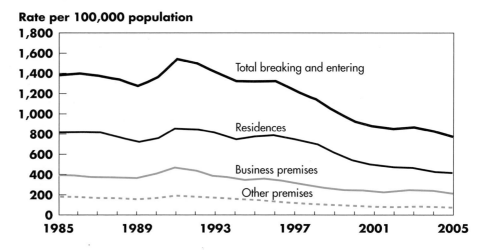

Source: Adapted from the Statistics Canada publication "Juristat," Catalogue 85-002, vol. 26, no. 4. Released July 20, 2006. http://www.statcan.ca/bsolc/english/bsolc?catno=85-002-XIE.

The type of property stolen from residences is quite different from that stolen from businesses. Audio/video equipment such as televisions, stereos, and VCRs typify the property stolen from residences. Other types of property frequently stolen from residences include jewellery, money, cheques or bonds, personal accessories, machinery and tools, photographic equipment, office equipment, and bicycles. In comparison, thefts from break and enters into businesses include money, cheques or bonds, office equipment, consumable goods (alcohol, cigarettes), audio/video equipment, machinery and tools, and personal accessories. Firearms were more frequently stolen from homes during break and enters than from businesses. The majority of these were rifles and shotguns, while the minority consisted of restricted weapons.[30] Data from the UCR suggest break and enters involving violence occur in fewer than 5 percent of cases. Of these, the majority involved an assault, while others involved robbery, sexual assault, abduction, and criminal harassment. Almost all violent break and enters occurred at a place of residence.[31]

Of those charged with breaking and entering in 2005, 69 percent were adults and 31 percent were youths aged 12 to 17. Within both these age groups, almost all of those charged were males.

The highest rates of breaking and entering were recorded by Saskatchewan (1468 per 100 000) despite a 14 percent decrease from 2004. Ontario and Prince Edward Island recorded the lowest rates at 545 and 612 respectively.

Theft

Theft (s. 322) is defined as the act of dishonestly taking property belonging to another person with the intention of depriving its owner of it either permanently or temporarily.[32] Specific categories of theft included in the *Criminal Code of Canada* are *theft of gas, electricity, or telecommunications* (cable television) (s. 326), and *theft of credit card* (s. 342). The severity of the theft is determined largely by the monetary value placed on the property taken. In 1995, the *Criminal Code* was amended to include *theft over $5000* and *theft $5000 and under* (prior to 1995, this amount was $1000; prior to 1986, it was $200). Not included in the category are motor-vehicle theft, fraud, or possession of stolen property. While the *Criminal Code* does include a section prohibiting the unauthorized use of computer services, the area of theft perpetrated using computers, such as theft of software or information obtained through online access, is one that will require further amendments. See Chapter 12 for a more in-depth discussion of computer-related crime trends.

In 2005, 818 311 incidents of theft accounted for about 30 percent of all *Criminal Code* incidents and 68 percent of all property crimes. Of these, 78 percent were classified as theft $5000 and under. This figure most likely under-represents the amount of theft that occurs: theft under $5000 remains one of the crimes most under-reported by victims. Official statistics indicate that it constitutes a rate of 1985 incidents per 100 000 population, while the rate for theft over $5000 stood at 54 per 100 000 for 2005. The overall theft rate was 5 percent lower than for the previous year and has been declining since 1991.

Compared with different types of offences, the number of females charged with theft $5000 and under is quite high—females constitute about a third of both adults and youth aged 12 to 17. The majority of these females were charged with shoplifting (see Chapter 2 for a discussion on the correlation between females and criminal behaviour and the *feminization of poverty*).

Motor-Vehicle Theft

Motor-vehicle theft is defined as the taking of a vehicle without the owner's authorization. A motor vehicle is defined as a car, truck, van, bus, recreational vehicle, semi-trailer truck, motorcycle, construction machinery, agricultural

Theft the act of dishonestly taking property belonging to another person with the intention of depriving its owner of it either permanently or temporarily.

Motor-vehicle theft the taking of a vehicle without the owner's authorization. A motor vehicle is defined as a car, truck, van, bus, recreational vehicle, semi-trailer truck, motorcycle, construction machinery, agricultural machinery, or other land-based motor vehicle (such as a go-kart, snowmobile, all-terrain vehicle, or dune buggy).

machinery, or other land-based motor vehicle (such as a go-kart, snowmobile, all-terrain vehicle, or dune buggy).[33] Excluded from the category of motor-vehicle theft is theft of airplanes, boats, trains, and spacecraft, which are counted as thefts over $5000.

In 2005, 160 100 incidents of motor-vehicle theft accounted for slightly less than 20 percent of all property crimes. At a rate of 496 per 100 000 population, this constitutes a 7 percent decrease from the previous year. Cars were the most commonly stolen vehicles in 2005, accounting for 56 percent of all vehicle thefts. Thirty-three percent of all vehicles stolen were trucks, including minivans and sport-utility vehicles. The growing popularity of sport-utility vehicles and trucks among consumers has been reflected in the 12 percent increase in the theft of these vehicles (as compared to the 21 percent decrease in car thefts) from a decade earlier.

Motor-vehicle theft is a crime often associated with youth. Statistics from 2002 show that over 40 percent of people charged with motor-vehicle theft were youth aged 12 to 17. Of these, the vast majority were male.

The rate of motor-vehicle theft decreased between 2004 and 2005 in every province and territory with the exception of Alberta, where the rate remained unchanged. Newfoundland and Labrador and Prince Edward Island reported the lowest rates of motor-vehicle theft, at 150 and 166 per 100 000 respectively, while Manitoba (1206) and British Columbia (818) reported the highest rates. Explanations for such varied provincial rates could include extra high rates of motor-vehicle theft in Winnipeg (1712 per 100 000) and Vancouver (990 per 100 000). Prevailing social or economic issues, such as youth gang activity in Winnipeg and Vancouver that is conducive to the operation of car-theft rings, may provide a partial explanation for the very high rates.

Car-theft rings have become a reality in Canada in recent years as markets for stolen cars have expanded overseas. To be resold, the stolen vehicles must be made difficult to trace. This is usually done by altering or removing the Vehicle Identification Number (VIN). Altered VIN plates are sanded down and a new number etched in, or VIN plates are replaced with those matching cars considered "write-offs." Many of these accident wrecks are auctioned off by auto-insurance companies. The cars are auctioned with the valid VINs still attached and bought by those involved in stolen-car rings. Lax regulations regarding the handling of wrecked cars in some provinces have meant that they have become virtual havens for illegal car-ring operators.[34]

For a number of decades now, another form of motor-vehicle theft has captured the attention of the public. Known as *carjacking*, this violent form of motor-vehicle theft involves the forced abdication of the vehicle by its owner to the felon. Usually armed with a weapon, the perpetrator will confront a car owner as he returns to his parked car, demanding the keys. Others who unwittingly leave their car running as they go into a store for a couple of minutes come out to find it gone. Still other victims are forced out of their cars as they wait at an intersection for a light to change. Another variation of carjacking involves "bumping" the victim's car from behind to get her to pull over in the belief there has been a traffic accident. Once out of the car, the perpetrator robs the victim of his vehicle and its contents. Currently in Canada, official statistics do not record carjackings as a separate category; there is no *Criminal Code* section dealing with this offence. Most incidents of carjacking are dealt with as a robbery, since force or fear are typically used to steal the vehicle directly from the owner.

Offences Involving Motor Vehicles

It is generally the responsibility of the provincial governments to regulate the use of roads and waterways within their jurisdictions. For example, speed limits, regulations regarding turns, and general rules of the road fall under the authority of each province. However, for those actions in which the use of a motor vehicle creates a risk of injury or death, the federal government uses its authority to make a federal law. The *Criminal Code* includes a number of offences addressing the use of motor vehicles, including dangerous operation of a motor vehicle (s. 249); failure to stop at the scene of an accident (s. 252); operating while impaired (s. 253); and driving while disqualified (s. 259). Many of these *Criminal Code* offences are similar to offences outlined in provincial statutes; however, the *Criminal Code* offence is always considered a more serious one. The UCR records include only reported incidents that violate traffic offences identified in the *Criminal Code*.

In 2005, police reported 118 738 incidents involving *Criminal Code* traffic crimes, resulting in a rate 2 percent below that of the previous year (368 per 100 000 population compared with 377 in 2004). Impaired driving accounted for 64 percent of these incidents, while failure to stop or remain at the scene of an accident accounted for 23 percent, and incidents of dangerous driving and driving while prohibited made up 13 percent.

The rate of **impaired driving** charges has been declining steadily since 1981. In that year, the rate was 859 per 100 000, while the 2005 rate was 234 per 100 000 (75 613 incidents), or a drop of over 70 percent. These changes are a result of a number of factors, including changes in public attitudes, trends in police enforcement measures such as R.I.D.E. programs (Reduce Impaired Driving Everywhere), and introduction of legislation.[35]

Counterfeiting

Counterfeiting (s. 448) is considered to include any unauthorized reproduction of a thing with the intention that it be accepted as genuine. Counterfeiting can thus refer to any thing that is capable of reproduction, including things that are subjects of rights of private property, such as art, or things that are subject to protection as intellectual property. It most commonly refers to the reproduction of currency (s. 449), forging of credit cards or debit cards (s. 342), documents for identification, such as passports (s. 57), or any paper that represents value (e.g., stamps, travellers' cheques or negotiable instruments, ss. 370, 376).[36] The penalties for these activities range from a maximum penalty of 14 years' imprisonment for counterfeiting currency and forging a passport to 10 years for fraudulent credit cards.

Based on reporting from police services, counterfeiting has grown in proportion to other *Criminal Code* offences from 5 percent in 2000 to 17 percent in 2005. Nevertheless, all provinces recorded a decrease in these offences in 2005 with Saskatchewan (59 percent) and Alberta (57 percent) recording the largest drops. Quebec, Ontario, and British Columbia had the highest rates of counterfeiting offences at 777, 590, and 473 per 100 000 population respectively. Newfoundland and Labrador had the lowest rate at 27 per 100 000.

The Royal Canadian Mounted Police Bureau for Counterfeit and Document Examinations is another source of information on trends in counterfeiting. The RCMP identifies counterfeit currency as bank notes (bills) that have been successfully passed without detection and seized notes that are intercepted by law enforcement officials. According to RCMP statistics (which are not part of the UCR), there was a 35 percent drop in counterfeit bills from 2004 to 2005, with a total of 422 447 bills, for a value of 9.4 million dollars, passed or seized. Nevertheless, this number is still substantially higher than the number of 55 951 passed or seized bills in 1995. Using RCMP data, Ontario had the highest rate of passed counterfeit bills in 2005, followed by British Columbia and Quebec. Prince Edward Island recorded the lowest rate.[37]

Impaired driving the operation of a motor vehicle by a person whose ability to operate it is impaired by alcohol or a drug. In the case of alcohol, impairment is said to occur when the concentration of alcohol in the person's blood exceeds 80 milligrams in 100 millilitres of blood.

Counterfeiting any unauthorized reproduction of a thing with the intention that it be accepted as genuine. It can thus refer to any thing that is capable of reproduction, including things that are subjects of rights of private property. It also includes the reproduction of documents for identification, such as passports, or any paper that represents value (e.g., stamps, travellers' cheques, or negotiable instruments).

Figure 3.2

Counterfeit Canada Bank Notes Passed, By Denomination, 2005

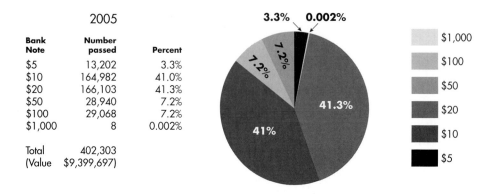

2005		
Bank Note	**Number passed**	**Percent**
$5	13,202	3.3%
$10	164,982	41.0%
$20	166,103	41.3%
$50	28,940	7.2%
$100	29,068	7.2%
$1,000	8	0.002%
Total	402,303	
(Value	$9,399,697)	

Source: Royal Canadian Mounted Police, "Currency Counterfeiting Statistics," http://www.rcmp-grc.gc.ca/scams/counter_e.htm (Accessed February 27, 2007) Reprinted with the permission of the RCMP.

Access to sophisticated computer devices and software and to high-quality colour photocopiers have been among the reasons for the prevalence of counterfeiting currency. The RCMP also indicates that organized crime groups have become increasingly involved in the production and distribution of counterfeit bank notes and documents. Chapter 12 takes another look at the extent of the involvement of organized crime groups in a number of criminal activities.

A number of organizations are involved in prevention, detection, and awareness-raising around the growing activity of counterfeiting, including the Bank of Canada and coalitions such as the Anti-Counterfeiting Network. The Bank of Canada, for example, continues to issue bank notes with added security features (see Box 3.3). The 54 percent drop between 2004 and 2005 in counterfeit activity of $20 bills may have been due to the introduction of a new $20 bill in 2004. A new security-enhanced $10 bill introduced in 2005 and a new $5 bill in 2006 may result in similar recorded drops in illegal activity involving those denominations as well.

Theoretical Explanations for Property Crime
The realities surrounding property crime are complex and belie the ability to pinpoint a simple explanation. Does the person who breaks into someone's home and steals the television and DVD player do this for the same reason that someone else breaks into a car and rides around in it at high speeds?

The most obvious motivating factor in many cases of property crime appears to be greed, and many criminological theories have used this notion as a starting point. These theories fall under the social problems perspective heading, because they largely assume that property crime is the manifestation of a variety of underlying social problems, not the least of which is poverty. Theories such as the strain theory (discussed in Chapter 8) and the routine activity theory (Chapter 5) suggest that there is a desire to achieve a universal goal, which is defined in terms of money and the goods, services, privileges, and prestige it can buy. The opportunity to achieve this goal through legitimate means such as schooling and employment is restricted for some people, who then turn to illegitimate or criminal opportunities to do so. If the illegitimate opportunities outnumber the legitimate

Bank of Canada Currency Security Features

Box 3.3

The Bank of Canada has included a number of security features in recent releases of $5 and $10 bills including

- **Iridescent maple leaves:** A patch of three maple leaves located near the centre of the bill should become more or less visible as the bill is tilted from side to side.
- **Hidden number:** Held at eye level, the bill should reveal a hidden number (either a 5 or a 10) near the bottom left of the bill.
- **Raised ink:** The words "Bank of Canada, Banque du Canada" are printed vertically along the left edge of these bills with raised ink. This text feels different from the rest of the bill. The large 5 or 10 in the bottom right-hand corner is also raised.
- **Ultraviolet graphic:** When the bill is placed under ultraviolet light, the value of the bill in writing, the Canadian coat of arms, and the words "Bank of Canada, Banque du Canada" should all glow a fluorescent blue behind the face on the bill.
- **Micro printing:** Lines to the left of the portrait have the miniature text "FIVE 5 CINQ" or "TEN 10 DIX" printed repeatedly along the lines.

© Bank of Canada / Banque du Canada

❶ Holographic Stripe
Tilt the note, and brightly coloured numerals (5) and maple leaves will "move" within the shiny, metallic stripe. There is a colour-split within each maple leaf.

❷ Watermark Portrait
Hold the note to the light and a small, ghost-like image of the portrait appears to the left of the large numeral (5).

❸ Windowed Colour-Shifting Thread
Hold the note to the light, and a continuous, solid line appears. From the back of the note, the thread resembles a series of exposed metallic dashes (windows) that shift from gold to green when the note is tilted.

❹ See-Through Number
Hold the note to the light and, just like two pieces of jigsaw puzzle, the irregular marks on the front and back will form a complete and perfectly aligned numeral **5** .

Source: The Bank of Canada.

ones, the temptation for some to seek this "easy route" may become too great to resist. The increase in the amount of fraud being committed using credit cards over cheques may be explained using this theory, for example.

Still other theories contend that the commission of property crimes, including motor-vehicle theft, breaking and entering, and shoplifting, all satisfy a need for excitement. The subcultural theories discussed in Chapter 8 maintain that material needs are often insufficient to explain the fascination with theft some people have. These theories suggest that crime is fun and is done to achieve a sense of status and belonging within a peer group.

The social process theories outlined in Chapter 9 look to the interaction between individuals as an explanation for criminal behaviour. What role, for example, does peer pressure and group behaviour have on the behaviour of some individuals? Can association with delinquent peers promote the learning of crimes such as theft and joyriding in stolen cars? The differential association theory suggests this is so. The social control theory outlined in Chapter 9 looks to the individual's attachment to positive role models, commitment to realistic goals, involvement in recreational and school activities, and belief in conventional values as a means of decreasing the likelihood of criminal behaviour. This theory suggests that those people, especially youth, who are bored and have no positive direction in life run a much greater risk of being attracted to crimes such as theft, shoplifting, arson, and vandalism.

Crimes against the Public Order

Included in the *Criminal Code of Canada* are a number of activities often referred to as *public order crimes* or *victimless crimes*. While it is debatable whether these activities do or do not victimize, it is generally agreed that though they violate prevailing morality, social policy, and public opinion, it *is* open to debate whether they should be classified as criminal. Such crimes against the public order traditionally refer to activities and behaviours involving sex (such as commercial sex, pornography, and erotic materials), activities involving the use, abuse, and sale of drugs and alcohol, and behaviours involving individual lifestyle choices, such as gambling and assisted suicide.

Prostitution most commonly used to refer to the illegal activities of publicly communicating with another person for the purposes of buying or selling sexual services, running a bawdy house, or living on the avails of the prostitution of another person.

Prostitution   **Prostitution**, or the exchange of money for sex, is not illegal in Canada. What is illegal are the associated activities such as publicly communicating with another person for the purposes of buying or selling sexual services (s. 213) or running a bawdy house (s. 210) or living on the avails of a prostitution of another person (s. 212(2)).

Prostitution is a controversial issue and there seems to be little consensus as to the best means of dealing with it. While it is generally considered to be a voluntary activity and is therefore often classified as a victimless crime, there are serious health, social, legal, and community issues associated with it. Other forms of activity such as drug trafficking and use are often linked to it. Those neighbourhoods in which prostitutes ply their trade constantly struggle with the health and safety risks associated with discarded needles and condoms. Health concerns, such as the spread of sexually transmitted diseases, affect the prostitutes, their customers, and the families of customers.

Statistics on prostitution are very closely tied to the law enforcement practices of any given police service and therefore vary across provinces and municipalities. In 2005, the rate of prostitution incidents reported to the police decreased by 11 percent from the previous year. This decrease is most probably a reflection of police enforcement practices.

Over half of the 5793 individuals charged with prostitution-related crimes are females. Of the males charged, it can be assumed that most were clients, although some

Police round up women in a prostitute sweep. Do you think prostitution is a victimless crime? Why or why not?
The Canadian Press/Welland Tribune/Aaron Beaudoin.

were prostitutes themselves or were living on the avails of prostitution. Of those charged in 2005, official statistics indicate that less than 1 percent were youth aged 12 to 17. It is generally believed that this number vastly under-represents the actual number of youths involved in prostitution, since many in this age group are diverted by police to social services rather than charged.

Recent public concerns have been raised about the ever-decreasing age of prostitutes. Incidents of children being recruited and sold into a life of prostitution in Asian countries such as Thailand, Japan, India, and the Philippines are well documented.[38] The alarmingly increasing activity in the trafficking of persons for sexual exploitation is discussed in detail in Chapter 12. Of equal concern to law enforcement officials is the increased practice of what is known as "sex tourism," which involves the promotion to Canadians of travel packages designed for the purpose of illegal sexual encounters, often with minors. Box 3.4 outlines the recently amended sections of the *Criminal Code of Canada* that target this illegal activity.

Illicit Drugs   There is a correlation between illicit drug use and criminal activity, albeit a complex one. This examination of illicit drugs considers those related criminal activities contained in the *Controlled Drugs and Substances Act* (CDSA). Essentially, the drug law is made up of two categories of offences: *supply offences*, which include the growing and distribution (trafficking and importing) of illegal and prohibited drugs, and *possession offences*, which include the purchase and use of illegal and prohibited drugs. The official number of recorded offences is obviously sensitive to enforcement and detection practices. An increase in the number of arrests and seizures does not necessarily indicate an increase in the population's use of illicit drugs, but rather may indicate an increased circulation of drugs or stepped up enforcement at national or international levels. Canadian government estimates indicate that the illegal drug market in Canada generates billions of dollars annually.[39]

Canada's "Sex Tourism" Law

Box 3.4

The recent case of Donald Bakker was the first involving charges under Canada's sex tourism law. In 2005, Bakker was charged with 22 counts of assault involving adult prostitutes and 16 counts related to children in a foreign country. His case did not proceed to trial when he subsequently pled guilty to 10 counts of sexual assault, three of which involved attacks on women in British Columbia, and the rest involving children in Asian countries. A 1997 amendment to the Criminal Code introduced section 7.4(1)* or what has come to be known as the sex tourism law. Section 7.4(1) reads:

> Notwithstanding anything in this Act or any other Act, every one who, outside Canada, commits an act or omission that if committed in Canada would be an offence against section 151, 152, 153, 155, or 159, subsection 160(2) or (3), section 163.1, 170, 171 or 173 or subsection 212(4) shall be deemed to commit that act or omission in Canada if the person who commits the act or omission is a Canadian citizen or permanent resident within the meaning of subsection 2(1) of the *Immigration and Refugee Protection Act* who is ordinarily resident in Canada.

*The offences listed in section 7.4(1) are
s.151 sexual interference;
s.152 invitation to sexual touching;
s.153 sexual exploitation;
s.155 incest;
s.159 anal intercourse;
s.160(2) compelling the commission of bestiality;
s.160(3) bestiality in the presence of a child under 14/inciting child under 14 to commit;
s.163(1) making, distributing, selling, or possessing child pornography
s.170 parent or guardian procuring sexual activity;
s.171 householder permitting sexual activity;
s.173 indecent acts/exposure;
s.212(4) prostitution of a person under 18.

Do you agree that Canadian citizens should be subject to prosecution if they sexually abuse children, including engaging in child prostitution, while outside Canada?

There were 92 255 incidents (or a rate of 286 per 100 000) related to the CDSA reported in 2005, representing an overall decrease of 6 percent from 2004. Cannabis offences made up 65 percent of the recorded incidents, representing a 12 percent decrease from the previous year. Declines in the possession of cannabis (−11 percent), trafficking and importation (−14 percent), and cultivation (−17 percent) were also recorded. No change occurred in the rate of heroin offences; however, increases were noted for cocaine offences (+11 percent) and other drug offences, such as those related to PCP, LSD, ecstasy, amphetamines ("crystal meth"), barbiturates, and anabolic steroids (+4 percent). Increases in the rates for other drugs may be a result of growing popularity of drugs such as ecstasy and crystal methamphetamines. Manufactured in labs using ingredients found in drug stores, methamphetamines are relatively inexpensive and produce a prolonged sense of euphoria as well as episodes of violent behaviour, paranoia, and anxiety.[40]

The considerable variation in trends and rates of drug offences between provinces is due in large part to differences in local enforcement policies and practices. Every province recorded a decrease in drug crimes with the exception of Newfoundland and Labrador, where the overall rate increased by 3 percent from the previous year. The most significant declines were recorded in New Brunswick and Prince Edward Island at 33 percent each. British Columbia recorded the highest rate of drug offences at 607 incidents per 100 000 population, with Saskatchewan recoding the next highest rate at 310. The lowest provincial rates were seen in Prince Edward Island (135), Manitoba (163), and Newfoundland and Labrador (164).

Theoretical Explanations of Crimes against the Public Order

The radical criminology perspectives outlined in Chapter 10 contend that behaviours are deemed to be deviant or criminal by definition. Crimes against the public order are seen by many as examples of *conflict crimes*, or those behaviours around which there is much controversy within society as to their acceptance. Social conflict criminology would contend that laws against behaviours such as prostitution and substance abuse are made by the powerful segment of society to ensure the subordination of those who engage in these activities. Feminist criminology, for example, would propose that, in the case of prostitution, women are conditioned to be subservient to men and are transformed into commodities to be bought and sold.

Many of the other social problem theories are useful to explain public order crimes. Refer to the differential association theory in Chapter 9; how can the crimes of prostitution and drug use be explained in terms of learned behaviour brought on through peer pressure? Similarly, social control theory, with its emphasis on strong bonds between the individual and the social order, might be applicable when explaining the criminal behaviour of bored and unfocused youth. Weak attachments to the family early on in life because of dysfunction within the home can compel many youth to flee and find refuge in the street, where prostitution and drug abuse are available options.

Individual responsibility theories can be seen to apply to public order crimes as well. For example, is it possible that dependency on alcohol and drugs has a genetic basis? Are addictive personality types passed on from generation to generation? Chapter 6 looks at some genetic roots of crime, while Chapter 7 examines theories of personality and asks whether there are certain personality types that are predisposed to certain types of criminal behaviour. For example, does low self-esteem, poor self-image, and anxiety result in a personality that is prone to addiction?

Summary

Canada's overall police-reported crime rate dropped 5 percent in 2005. Overall, the crime rate in Canada has been declining since the early 1990s, stabilizing in the 2000s. Declines in crime rates were observed in all provinces and territories. Manitoba (-8 percent), New Brunswick (–8 percent), and Saskatchewan (–6 percent) recorded the largest provincial drops. Of the 2.7 million *Criminal Code* incidents reported, violent crimes constituted 11 percent, property crimes 44 percent, and other offences such as prostitution, gaming and betting, and disturbing the peace 36 percent.[41]

Given this look at the incidence of crime reported and counted in Canada, the question that remains, especially for criminologists, is why? Why do people feel compelled to violate our laws? How can this understanding of the root causes of criminal and deviant behaviour assist those who design and implement policies to combat crime? Should their efforts be focused on targeting the individual offender, seeking to "cure" him of his criminal "sickness"? Or should they look instead to the challenging social realities that so many offenders seem to have experienced and attempt to rectify them? Chapter 11 examines some recent legislative and policy initiatives undertaken in Canada to address crime. Nevertheless, there are no simple answers, and, despite the current downward trend, it is certain that crime and criminals will always be with us.

Discussion Questions

1. This book emphasizes a social problems versus social responsibility theme. Which perspective best explains the reality of crime in this country? Is one perspective more appropriate when considering violent crime? Property crime? Crime against the public order?

2. How are typologies of crime useful in understanding patterns of crime? What are the categories used by the Canadian Uniform Crime Reporting (UCR) system?

3. Which of the categories of crime discussed in this chapter do you think has the most accurate crime count? Why?

4. From a study of the incidence of crime and of crime rates discussed in this chapter, do you feel that Canadians should fear the spread of crime? Why or why not?

5. How does the definition of a crime affect the counting of it? How do police enforcement activities affect the count?

6. Canada's crime rate has remained relatively stable in recent years after a steady decline throughout the 1990s. What do you think has contributed to this reality?

Weblinks

www.statcan.ca
Statistics Canada. National statistics on crime, victims, suspects, criminals, police, and the courts.

www.canada.justice.gc.ca
Department of Justice Canada. Research reports, statistical reports, and fact sheets on a variety of criminal justice issues.

www.ps-sp.gc.ca
Public Safety Canada (formerly known as Public Safety and Emergency Preparedness Canada) offers national statistics on corrections, policing, and parole.

www.acjnet.org/
Access to Justice Network (ACJNet). ACJNet is an electronic community that brings together people, information, statistics, and educational resources surrounding Canadian justice and legal issues.

www.cisc.gc.ca
Criminal Intelligence Service Canada (CISC). Unites the criminal intelligence units of law enforcement agencies in their integrated efforts to detect, prevent and reduce organized and serious crime affecting Canada.

CHAPTER 4

Victimology: The Study of the Victim

The problem of crime always gets reduced to, "What can be done about criminals?" Nobody asks, "What can be done about victims?"

—ROBERT REIFF[1]

Victims' rights have become far too important to relegate them to mere abstract statements of principle and the time has come to translate symbolic recognition into a practical and meaningful law reform agenda.

—ALAN YOUNG[2]

LEARNING OUTCOMES

After reading this chapter, you should be able to

- recognize the factors contributing to victimization and the realities of being a victim of crime

- discuss the development of the field of victimology and the emergence of the rights of victims of crime

- identify the current services available to victims of crime

- assess future directions in the field of victimology

Allan Tannenbaum, Corbis/Sygma.

IMPORTANT NAMES

Hans von Hentig	Marvin E. Wolfgang	Margaret Fry
Benjamin Mendelsohn	Ezzat Fattah	Irvin Waller
International Review of Victimology	Herbert Packer	
	Kent Roach	

IMPORTANT TERMS

victimology	routine activity approach	Victim/Witness Assistance
victim-proneness	opportunity model	Program
penal couple	post-crime victimization	victim impact statement
victimogenesis	secondary victimization	restitution
lifestyle model	Code of Hammurabi	victim surcharge
	Canadian Statement of Basic Principles of Justice for Victims of Crime	

Introduction

In March 2003, the grief-stricken family of Andy Moffitt left an Ottawa courtroom unable to believe or understand the five-year prison sentence just handed down to the man who had killed their son.

Several years earlier, Moffitt, a computer engineering student at the University of Ottawa, was celebrating the end of his exams with some friends at a neighbourhood bar and grill. Just after midnight, Moffitt and his friends witnessed a scuffle between a man and the bar manager. One of Moffitt's companions ran to the aid of the manager but was immediately attacked. Moffitt rushed to help his friend and was stabbed once in the chest by the assailant. He was pronounced dead later at the hospital. "This guy was a great kid and he was trying to be a Good Samaritan by smoothing out the fight," Detective Dale Hayes said. "For trying to help, he got shanked."[3]

Several hours later, a man telephoned 911, asking police to come and pick him up. Henry Danninger, a 26-year-old student also attending the University of Ottawa, was apprehended and charged with second-degree murder. Danninger had gone to the restaurant that evening looking for a roommate whom he believed had taken some drugs belonging to him. The bar manager was trying to remove Danninger from the establishment when Moffitt tried to help. Danninger and Moffitt had never met before. Moffitt was simply in the wrong place at the wrong time.

The five-year sentence of incarceration was a shock to Moffitt's family. They had hoped for a much stiffer penalty, but a plea-bargain arrangement reduced the charge from second-degree murder to manslaughter. That, in conjunction with the time Danninger had spent in pretrial custody and the fact that he had no prior criminal record, compelled Justice Roydon Kealey to impose the sentence. "I'm speechless," said the victim's mother, Paulette Moffitt of Brockville, who'd been hoping for a sentence twice as long. "I hope for the remainder of his life that he thinks about what he did to Andy," she railed before walking away from the courthouse one final time.[4] "I will never forget having to phone Andy's older brother to tell him his brother was dead," said Ms. Moffitt. "I was the one (who) broke his heart, telling him the most dreadful news imaginable. To witness the pain that Andy's two brothers and my husband have endured because of Henry Danninger is like his knife is slowly piercing my heart."[5]

The governor general of Canada honoured Andy Moffitt in 2003 with a Medal of Bravery for the heroic deed that cost him his life.

The Dynamics of Victimization

Just as criminals have been studied to determine what kinds of social and personal experiences they have, so, too, have criminologists advocated close scrutiny of victims. The development of the field of **victimology**, or the study of victims, has closely paralleled the development of criminology. As was characteristic of the wider body of criminological theory, early victimologists stressed constitutional factors that propelled the victim toward victimization. The adjudged degree of an individual's potential for victimization was termed **victim-proneness**.

One of the earliest writers in the field, **Hans von Hentig,** depicted crime poetically as a duet played by two.[6] "In a sense," wrote von Hentig, "the victim shapes and moulds the criminal."[7] Comparing the criminal and victim to carnivore and prey, he argued, "In a certain sense, the animals which devour and those that are devoured complement each other ... To know one we must be acquainted with the complementary partner."[8]

Von Hentig created a typology, or classificatory scheme, of victims based on what he saw as biological or situational weaknesses. Weaknesses could be physically, socially, psychologically, or environmentally based. Anything that puts the potential victim at a disadvantage relative to the criminal predator, constituting "easy prey," so to speak, found a place in his typology.

Von Hentig also wrote of "victim areas," or parts of the country to which tourists and others with money are drawn. Similarly attracted are the criminals who prey upon them. Recent incidents involving Canadian and other foreign tourists in destinations such as Mexico and Florida were presaged by this kind of thinking. Likewise, inner-city areas rich in crime were seen as creating a special relationship between victim and criminal.

Von Hentig used colloquial information and pre-existing statistical data, and documented individual experiences and personal observations to support his concepts. Although he did not undertake any empirical research of his own, von Hentig's ideas helped propel the importance of the victim into the forefront of criminological thinking during the 1950s and 1960s.

Some criminologists trace the development of the field of victimology to even earlier writings, including those of **Benjamin Mendelsohn**. In 1937, Mendelsohn, a European defence attorney, published a paper advocating the study of victims.[9] Like von Hentig, Mendelsohn created his own classification of victim types. Mendelsohn's typology was based on the degree of guilt that the victim brought to the criminal event.

Mendelsohn is generally credited with coining the term *victimology* and developing the concept of the **penal couple**, which describes the relationship between victim and criminal. He also coined the term *victimal* to describe the victim counterpart of the criminal and the word *victimity*, which signified the opposite of criminality. In his writings, Mendelsohn called for the development of victimology as a field of study independent from criminology. He foresaw the creation of an international institute for victimological research as part of

Victimology the study of victims and their contributory role, if any, in the criminal event.

Victim-proneness the degree of an individual's likelihood of victimization.

Penal couple a term that describes the relationship between victim and criminal. Also, the two individuals most involved in the criminal act—the offender and the victim.

Victimogenesis the
contributory
background of a victim
as a result of which he or
she becomes prone to
victimization.

the United Nations and called for the creation of an international society of victimology with its own journal (see the *International Review of Victimology*).

In 1954, Henry Ellenberger introduced the concept of **victimogenesis**[10] to explain how people can undergo life experiences that eventually place them in circumstances that contribute to their future victimization. Just as a criminal experiences events in life that lead to criminality, Ellenberger argued that many victims undergo a process of socialization that results in less caution, a proclivity to associate with possible offenders, an increased likelihood of frequenting places associated with criminal activity, and a generally higher risk of criminal victimization.

In 1964, writing in collaboration with Thorsten Sellin, **Marvin E. Wolfgang** introduced a typology of victims based on victim–offender relationships.[11] They described

1. primary victimization—in which an individual falls victim to crime
2. secondary victimization—in which an impersonal agency such as a business is victimized
3. tertiary victimization—in which the government or public order is offended, perhaps through regulatory violations
4. mutual victimization—in which the participants in an offence (such as drug sales, gambling, or prostitution) willingly involve themselves
5. no victimization—a category reserved for offences committed by youth that could not be committed by an adult, such as the buying of cigarettes by an underage person

The advent of routine, state-sponsored, nationwide victimization surveys such as the Canadian Urban Victimization Survey, first conducted in Canada in 1982, led to the further development of theoretical models of victimizations. Experts attempted to explain why certain groups of individuals and locations were especially prone to victimization, but also new theories were developed to offer explanations for the variations in the rates of victimization and for the phenomenon of repeat victimization.

Purse-snatchers in action. How could a victim's lifestyle be a factor in a crime such as this one?
Buu-Turpin/Gamma-Liaison, Inc.

One of the first and most important theories was tabled by Michael Hindelang, Michael R. Gottfredson, and James Garofalo in 1978.[12] Known as the **lifestyle model** and based on empirical data collected from an eight-city survey by the United States Bureau of Census in 1972, the theory holds that the likelihood that an individual will suffer a personal victimization depends heavily on the concept of lifestyle. Lifestyle, in turn, is influenced by social roles played by people, the position one occupies in the social structure, and how one chooses to process options based on life experiences.[13]

Lawrence E. Cohen and Marcus Felson put forth the **routine activity approach** in 1979, arguing that occurrences of personal victimization are dependent upon the "routine" or "daily activities" of people and are the outcome of three elements: the motivated offender, a suitable target, and the absence of a capable guardian. Central to this approach are opportunity, proximity/exposure, and facilitating factors. The risk of criminal victimization, therefore, will vary in keeping with the circumstances and locations in which people place themselves and their property.[14]

The **opportunity model** posited by Lawrence E. Cohen, J.R. Kluegel, and Kenneth Land in 1981 incorporates elements from the lifestyle and routine activity theories, contending that the risk of criminal victimization depends largely on people's lifestyle and daily activities that bring them and their property into direct contact with potential offenders in the absence of capable guardians.[15]

Ezzat Fattah, a Canadian criminologist recognized as one of the leading thinkers in the field of victimology, has attempted to integrate the various lifestyle/opportunity theories into a comprehensive scheme. He contends that this scheme is comprised of ten different components,[16] which he identifies as

1. *Opportunities* that are closely linked to the characteristics of potential targets and to the activities and behaviour of these targets
2. *Risk factors* and particularly those related to socio-demographic realities such as age, sex, area of residence, etc.
3. *Motivated offenders* who do not choose their victims/targets at random but select them according to specific criteria
4. *Exposure* of the victim to potential offenders and to high-risk situations that increase the risk of criminal victimization
5. *Associations* between offenders and victims so that those who are in close personal, professional, or social contact with offenders run a greater risk of being victimized
6. *Dangerous times and dangerous places* include evenings, early evening hours, weekends, and places of public entertainment
7. *Dangerous behaviours* such as provocation increase the risk especially of violent victimization, while other behaviours, such as negligence and carelessness, enhance chances of property victimization
8. *High-risk activities* increase the potential for victimization and can include deviant and illegal activities
9. *Defensive/avoidance behaviours* tend to contribute to the reduction in the risk of victimization. Those who take precautions are less likely to be victimized than those who are risk-takers
10. *Structural/cultural proneness* of people means that those who are powerless and culturally stigmatized and marginalized are more likely to be criminally victimized

Lifestyle model holds that the likelihood that an individual will suffer a personal victimization depends heavily on the concept of lifestyle.

Routine activity approach holds that occurrences of personal victimization are dependent upon the "routine" or "daily activities" of people and are the outcome of three elements: the motivated offender, a suitable target, and the absence of a capable guardian.

Opportunity model contends that the risk of criminal victimization depends largely on people's lifestyle and daily activities that bring them and their property into direct contact with potential offenders in the absence of capable guardians.

It is interesting to note that the findings of the 2004 General Social Survey in Canada indicate that the risk of victimization is greatest for those who are 15 to 24 years of age, who are single, whose main activity is classified as "student," who occupy the lowest household income categories, who live in an urban setting, and who participate in evening activities outside the home more than 30 times per month (that last number reflecting the fact that youths partake in more than one activity per evening).[17]

Realities of Being a Victim

Some authors have identified a number of procedural models that can be applied to a study of the victimization process, the experience the victim undergoes during and following victimization.[18] The "victims of crime model" developed by Bard and Sangrey[19] postulates that three stages are involved in any victimization: (1) the stage of impact and disorganization, during and immediately following the criminal event; (2) recoil, during which the victim formulates psychological defences and deals with conflicting emotions of guilt, anger, acceptance, and desire for revenge (the state of recoil is said to last from three to eight months); and (3) the reorganizational stage, during which the victim puts his life back together and gets on with daily living in a more or less normal fashion. Some victims do not successfully adapt to the victimization experience, and a maladaptive reorganizational stage may last for many years.

Another model with applicability to the victimization experience is the "disaster victim's model," originally developed to explain the coping behaviour of victims of natural disasters. This model outlines four stages in the victimization process: (1) pre-impact, which describes the state of the victim prior to being victimized; (2) impact, or the stage at which victimization occurs; (3) post-impact, which entails the degree and duration of personal and social disorganization that follows victimization; and (4) behavioural outcome, which describes the victim's adjustment, or lack thereof, to the victimization experience.

The model developed by Elizabeth Kübler-Ross to describe the stages that dying persons go through has some applicability to the victimization process. Kübler-Ross described a five-part transitional process of denial, anger, bargaining, depression, and acceptance.[20] Victims often either deny the likelihood of their own victimization or believe that "this can't be happening to me." After the victimizing event, many victims feel anger, and some express rage toward their victimizers. Bargaining occurs when victims negotiate with themselves as well as with family members, representatives of the criminal justice community, and social-service providers over how the victimization experience should be personally interpreted and officially handled. Acceptance occurs when the victim finally acknowledges that victimization has occurred, and the victim makes the adjustments necessary to go on with life. Of course, as in the case of other models, the Kübler-Ross model allows for maladjustment in the final phase as some victims never successfully integrate the victimization experience into their psyches in a way that avoids reduction in the quality of their lives.

Countless studies examining the psychological well-being of victims[21] have concluded that criminal victimization

- can leave psychological scars that last as long as or longer than any physical or financial loss

- can result in anxiety disorders, depression, drug and alcohol abuse, fear, flashbacks, lowered self-esteem, sexual dysfunction, thoughts of suicide, suspiciousness, and a feeling of social isolation
- can result in the development of Post-Traumatic Stress Disorder (PTSD)
- can result in feelings of guilt, with victims of violence experiencing the greatest level of guilt
- can result in a decreased sense of satisfaction with life and a perception that the world is less caring

In addition to the literature examining the psychological realities of criminal victimization, there has been much discussion about the **post-crime victimization** or **secondary victimization** created by the criminal justice system in its treatment of victims during the criminal process. In an often-cited article, Dean Kilpatrick and Randy Otto contend that "promising victims' rights that are not delivered may involve a certain danger: providing rights without remedies would result in the worst of consequences, such as feelings of helplessness, lack of control and further victimization. . . . Ultimately, with the victims' best interests in mind, it is better to confer no rights than 'rights' without remedies."[22]

A study into victim alienation with 200 American crime victims concluded that criminal justice officials, and most specifically the police, contribute to the victim's heightened or lessened sense of alienation.[23] Other examinations have concluded that victim distress is largely due to the type of offence, the victim's perception of the severity of the criminal sentence, and whether restitution was received by the victim.[24] Anoter study of more than 500 victims found that over 90 percent felt that the criminal justice system should be responsible for providing a range of victim services including case status information, legal assistance, assistance dealing with police and courts, psychological counselling, and personal protection. The study also reports that access to such services fell below the expectations of the victims surveyed.[25]

Two Canadian studies concluded that victims of rape and child sexual abuse suffer from psychological distress years after victimization, but the studies were less conclusive about the psychological ill effects of non-sexual offences. They conclude by highlighting a lack of coordination among social psychologists, clinical psychologists, social support providers, and criminologists in the study of the impact of criminal victimization on victims.[26] A growing body of literature has emerged examining the role of social workers and other health-care professionals in dealing with victims of crime. Much of this literature has been critical of the role of these individuals, noting that they are often ill-equipped and improperly trained.

Post-crime victimization or **secondary victimization** refers to problems in living that tend to follow from initial victimization, some of which may be related to the victim's interaction with the criminal justice system.

Emergence of Victims' Rights

Fuelled largely by the expansion of theoretical study within the field of criminology of the victim as a participant in the criminal event, a focus on the role of the victim in the formal criminal justice process took hold in Canada in the late 1980s and early 1990s. The emergence of victims' advocacy and support organizations served to further highlight the need to critically examine the role and rights of victims within the criminal justice system.

A Historical Overview of Victim Responses to Crime

Code of Hammurabi an
early set of laws
established by the
Babylonian King
Hammurabi, who ruled
the ancient city from
1792 to 1750 BC.

In early times, victims took the law into their own hands. If they were able to apprehend their victimizers, they enacted their own form of revenge and imposed some form of personal retaliation. The **Code of Hammurabi** (circa 1750 BC), one of the earliest known legal codes, required that many offenders make restitution. If the offender could not be found, however, the victim's family was duty bound to care for the needs of the victim. This early period in history has been called the Golden Age of the Victim, because victims not only were well cared for but also had considerable say in imposing punishments upon apprehended offenders.

Eventually, however, crimes came to be understood as offences against society, and the victim was forgotten. By the late Middle Ages, the concept of "King's Peace" had emerged, wherein all offences were seen as violations of imperial law. The notion of private injury became one of public wrong and the law of wrongdoing became the law of crime. It became the duty of local governments to apprehend, try, and punish offenders, effectively removing the victim from any direct involvement in judicial decision making. Victims were expected only to provide evidence of a crime and to testify against those who had offended them. Society's moral responsibility toward making victims "whole again" was forgotten, and victims as a class were moved to the periphery of the justice process. Justice for the victim was forgotten, translated instead into the notion of justice for the state.

It is widely believed that this movement was largely a power play by the state to enhance its own coffers.[27] The previous practice of a compensatory award made to the victim by the offender for a harm done now became a fine for the benefit of the state. In the 13th century, fines levied by the courts constituted one-eighth of all revenue to the king.[28] By the 14th century, the victim was no longer the focus of the criminal process and the notion of an

Commemorative vigils like this one have been held every year on December 6 since the Montreal Massacre in 1989 when 14 women died at the hands of gunman Marc Lepine. Do you think that this type of public memorial helps to raise the awareness of victims' rights?
CP/Peter Power/Toronto Star.

active role for the victim did not re-emerge until the 19th century. Nils Christie sees this as the theft of criminal conflicts from the real parties to the conflict. He states,

> *So, in a modern criminal trial, two important things have happened. First, the parties are being represented. Secondly, the one party that is represented by the state, namely the victim, is so thoroughly represented that she or he for most of the proceedings is pushed completely out of the arena, reduced to the trigger-off of the whole thing. She or he is a sort of double loser; first vis-à-vis the offender, but secondly and often in a more crippling manner by being denied rights of full participation in what might have been one of the most important ritual encounters in life. The victim has lost the case to the state.*[29]

The situation remained largely unchanged until the 20th century, when renewed interest in the plight of victims led to a resurgence of positive sentiments around the world. Discussion of the role of the victim in the formal criminal justice process ensued with supporters and detractors of the victim's right to participate in the process lining up on opposite sides of the argument. Much of the current academic debate continues to centre on the discussion as to whether or not increased protection for victims can be achieved only at the expense of the rights of the accused. Much of this debate is focused on the participatory rights of the victim in the formal court process. For example, some victims' rights advocates recommend that victims be allowed to express an opinion or recommendation as to a convicted offender's sentence at the sentencing portion of the formal court process. Those who caution against the increased participation of victims in the court process argue that this will only serve to whittle away at the accused's right to due process and turn the sentencing into an opportunity for victims to seek revenge.[30]

Within the emerging discipline of study known as victimology, the academic discussion focused on the development of a pedagogical basis for the strengthening victims' rights movement. This discussion centred largely around the two models of criminal justice put forth by **Herbert Packer** in 1968. In *The Limits of the Criminal Sanction*,[31] Packer presents the *crime control model* and the *due process model*. The former model describes an assembly-line approach to justice, focusing on the efficient repression of crime and the safety of the community. The latter model discusses an approach to criminal justice that emphasizes civil liberties and the importance of the verdict rather than the efficiency of the process. For many involved in the victims' rights movement, Packer's time-tested theory failed to provide the underpinning required to support the role of victims in the criminal process. In the late 1990s, **Kent Roach**, then dean of law at the University of Saskatchewan, proposed a third model as a theoretical base for victims' rights. He referred to it as the *victims' rights model* and called for more laws and prosecutions, a greater role for the victim in the trial, and more services and support for victims.[32]

Roach develops his model by distinguishing between what he identifies as the *punitive* victims' rights model and the *non-punitive* victims' rights model. He describes the punitive approach as one resembling the crime control model because it focuses on the enactment of criminal law, prosecution, and punishment as ways to control crime. Under this approach, he says that

> *victim advocacy is often focused on creating new criminal laws in the hope that they will prevent future victimization. Feminist reforms of sexual assault laws and new laws targeting the sexual abuse of children are designed not only to protect the privacy and integrity of the victims, but to make convictions easier to obtain. Victim impact statements*

and victim involvement at sentencing and parole hearings are often directed toward greater punishment. Much more directly than due process, victims' rights can enable and legitimate crime control.[33]

His non-punitive model of victims' rights, on the other hand, looks away from the reliance on criminal sanction and punishment and toward the prevention of crime and restorative justice. He states,

Both the processes of prevention and restoration can be represented by a circle. One manifestation of the circle may be the gated community with its own private police force. Another example would be successful neighbourhood watch or the self-policing of families and communities. Once a crime has occurred, the circle represents the processes of healing, compensation, and restorative justice. Normatively, the circle model stresses the needs of victims more than their rights, and seeks to minimize the pain of both victimization and punishment.[34]

Roach goes on to advocate that the non-punitive approach would seek to shift the focus of importance away from traditional crime-control strategies and agents such as the police, prosecutors, defence lawyers, and judges and toward the victim, the offender, families, and supporters. Victims, in turn, would play the most significant role in determining how the offender should be dealt with.

Current Directions in Victimology and Victims' Rights

Against this backdrop of increasing recognition for victims, a flurry of laws and legislation has been developed, the earliest of which were intended to provide compensation primarily to victims of violent crimes.

Compensation for criminal injury is not unknown throughout history. More than 100 years ago, Jeremy Bentham advocated "mandatory restitution, to be paid by a state compensation system, in cases of property crime."[35] Long before that, the Code of Hammurabi (circa 1775 BC) specified that

If a man has committed robbery ... that man shall be put to death. If the robber is not caught, the man who has been robbed shall formally declare what he has lost ... and the city ... shall replace whatever he has lost for him. If it is the life of the owner that is lost, the city or the mayor shall pay one maneth of silver to his kinfolk.

The first modern victim compensation statute was adopted by New Zealand in 1963. Known as the *Criminal Injuries Compensation Act*, it provided an avenue for claims to be filed by victims of certain specified violent crimes. A three-member board was empowered to make awards to victims. One year later, partially in response to a movement led by the social reformer **Margaret Fry**, Great Britain established a similar board. In 1965, California passed the first piece of US legislation intended to assist victims of crime, and today all 50 states have passed similar legislation.

The first Canadian criminal injuries compensation plan was created in Saskatchewan in 1967. By 1988, a compensation program was available in every province and territory, providing financial compensation for injuries or death resulting from a crime of violence committed by another person. Each provincial compensation program is unique, but all include time limits on the filing of an application and set maximum award amounts per applicant, varying from $5000 to $30 000. In addition, most plans allow surviving relatives of murder victims, and those injured while preventing a crime, to qualify for compensation. Payments are not generally awarded, however, for victims with injuries caused by motor vehicle accidents. In all plans, payments for lost wages, medical expenses, and prescription drugs are commonly made. Some provincial plans compensate victims for general damages, including pain and suffering caused by the offence. Victims who are responsible in some significant way for their own victimization may receive a lower reward or be disqualified completely. Factors such as intoxication, prior knowledge of the offender's criminalistic tendencies, and provocation of the offender can all result in reduced awards.

Although many tout the benefits of victim compensation programs, recent studies of the effectiveness of government-sponsored compensation programs have found that most crime victims are reluctant to seek compensation and that those who do are generally from households with higher incomes. Frustrations with delays, poor information about the programs, and unmet expectations regarding assistance with psychological and support needs as well as financial needs were also cited as limitations.[36]

A 2007 report by the Provincial Ombudsman entitled *Adding Insult to Injury* blasted that province's Criminal Injuries Compensation Board, calling it a "colossal failure that needlessly revictimizes people." In his report, the Ombudsman claims that board has become mired in bureaucratic red tape that serves only to delay or deny compensation to victims. Compared to Quebec and British Columbia, where the average time to process a victim's claim is about four months, it takes an average of three years to do so in Ontario. He details the cases of several victims, including one who was forced to choose between buying food and burying his murdered daughter and another who had his claim returned because he had failed to dot an "i" on his form.[37]

Interestingly, several days later, the government of Ontario announced a 20-billion-dollar infusion into the Criminal Injuries Compensation Board to bolster payments to claimants and hire staff to address backlogs in processing claims.[38]

At the 1979 Federal–Provincial Conference of Ministers Responsible for Criminal Justice, the issue of victims' rights was raised by provincial ministers and subsequently formally brought to the attention of the federal government. A loose coalition of Canadian feminist organizations, Canadian victim assistance programs, and the strengthening US victims' rights movement came together to move the issue into the forefront. A number of grassroots lobby groups were influential in promoting awareness of victims' issues. Most notable of these was Victims of Violence (now known as Victims of Violence, Canadian Centre for Missing Children), founded by Gary and Sharon Rosenfeldt, the parents of one of Clifford Olson's victims, and Canadians Against Violence Everywhere Advocating its Termination (CAVEAT), founded by Priscilla de Villiers, whose daughter was murdered.

This raising of awareness resulted in the creation of the 1983 Federal–Provincial Task Force on Justice for the Victims of Crime. The task force made 79 recommendations addressing the needs of victims and the requirements for effective victim services, many of which are in place today. Among these are provisions for improvements in emotional and practical assistance for victims as well as provisions within the *Criminal Code of Canada* that ensure criminal injuries compensation, the increased use of restitution, and the introduction of the idea of a victim impact statement in the pre-sentence report.

**Canadian Statement of
Basic Principles of
Justice for Victims of
Crime** a 1988 document
promoting access to
justice, fair treatment,
and provision of
assistance for victims of
crime.

International attention to the issue saw a number of nations sign on to the 1985 United Nations' *Declaration of Basic Principles of Justice for Victims of Crime and Abuses of Power*, which is essentially a declaration of general principles. In adopting the Declaration, the General Assembly of the United Nations stated that it was "cognizant that millions of people throughout the world suffer harm as a result of crime and abuse of power, and that the rights of these victims have not been adequately recognized."[39] Despite the lack of concrete details regarding implementation of these rights for victims, the document served as a catalyst for similar documents around the world, not the least of which was the *Canadian Statement of Basic Principles of Justice for Victims of Crime*, endorsed by the provincial and territorial ministers of justice in 1988 (see Box 4.1). These principles have served to guide the development of policy and legislation for the victims of crime at both the federal and the provincial levels. A 1998 report from the House of Commons Standing Committee

Box 4.1

Canadian Statement of Basic Principles of Justice for Victims of Crime

In recognition of the United Nations' *Declaration of Basic Principles of Justice for Victims of Crime and Abuses of Power*, federal and provincial ministers responsible for criminal justice agree that the following principles should guide Canadian society in promoting access to justice, fair treatment, and provision of assistance for victims of crime.

1. Victims should be treated with courtesy, compassion, and respect for their dignity and privacy and should suffer the minimum of necessary inconvenience from their involvement with the criminal justice system.
2. Victims should receive, through formal and informal procedures, prompt and fair redress for the harm that they have suffered.
3. Information regarding remedies and the mechanisms to obtain them should be made available to victims.
4. Information should be made available to victims about their participation in criminal proceedings and the scheduling, process, and ultimate disposition of the proceedings.
5. Where appropriate, the view and concerns of victims should be ascertained and assistance provided throughout the criminal process.
6. Where the personal interests of the victim are affected, the views or concerns of the victim should be brought to the attention of the court, where appropriate and consistent with criminal law and procedure.
7. Measures should be taken when necessary to ensure the safety of victims and their families and to protect them from intimidation and retaliation.
8. Enhanced training should be made available to sensitize criminal justice personnel to the needs and concerns of victims and guidelines developed, where appropriate, for this purpose.
9. Victims should be informed of the availability of health and social services and other relevant assistance so that they might continue to receive the necessary medical, psychological, and social assistance through existing programs and services.
10. Victims should report the crime and cooperate with the law enforcement authorities.

Source: Department of Justice Canada http://canada.justice.gc.ca/en/ps/voc/csbp.html. Reproduced with the permission of the Minister of Public Works and Government of Canada, 2000.

on Justice and Human Rights entitled *Victims' Rights—A Voice, Not a Veto* makes a number of recommendations regarding further amendments to the *Criminal Code* to strengthen the voice of victims of crime. Most provinces and territories in Canada have enacted legislation to promote and protect the interests of victims.

The provincial governments are primarily responsible for the provision of individual welfare rights and, as such, have virtually all enacted legislation to recognize the rights of victims. In 1986, Manitoba was the first province to place principles from the United Nations' Declaration into its own law.[40] Many of these provincial bills emphasize the notion of empowerment for the victim and provide rights of participation and notification. Ontario's legislation, known as *An Act Respecting Victims of Crime—Victims' Bill of Rights*, is emblematic of the rights enshrined in most provincial and territorial legislation. Box 4.2 reproduces the principles for the treatment of victims found in the Act.

An Act Respecting Victims of Crime—Victims' Bill of Rights (Ontario)

Box 4.2

Section 2(1)

The following principles apply to the treatment of victims of crime:

1. Victims should be treated with courtesy, compassion, and respect for their personal dignity and privacy by justice system officials.
2. Victims should have access to information about,
    i. the services and remedies available to victims of crime,
    ii. the provisions of this Act and of the *Compensation for Victims of Crime Act* that might assist them,
    iii. the protection available to victims to prevent unlawful intimidation,
    iv. the progress of investigations that relate to the crime,
    v. the charges laid with respect to the crime and, if no charges are laid, the reasons why no charges are laid,
    vi. the victim's role in the prosecution,
    vii. court procedures that relate to the prosecution,
    viii. the dates and places of all significant proceedings that relate to the prosecution,
    ix. the outcome of all significant proceedings, including any proceedings on appeal,
    x. any pretrial arrangements that are made that relate to a plea that may be entered by the accused at trial,
    xi. the interim release and, in the event of conviction, the sentencing of an accused,
    xii. any disposition made under section 672.54 or 672.58 of the *Criminal Code* (Canada) in respect of an accused who is found unfit to stand trial or who is found not criminally responsible on account of mental disorder, and
    xiii. their right under the *Criminal Code* (Canada) to make representations to the court by way of a victim impact statement.
3. A victim of a prescribed crime should, if he or she so requests, be notified of,
    i. any application for release or any impending release of the convicted person, including release in accordance with a program of temporary absence, on parole or on an unescorted temporary absence pass, and

▶

       ii. any escape of the convicted person from custody.

4. If the person accused of a prescribed crime is found unfit to stand trial or is found not criminally responsible on account of mental disorder, the victim should, if he or she so requests, be notified of,

       i. any hearing held with respect to the accused by the Review Board established or designated for Ontario pursuant to subsection 672.38(1) of the *Criminal Code* (Canada),

       ii. any order of the Review Board directing the absolute or conditional discharge of the accused, and

       iii. any escape of the accused from custody.

5. Victims of sexual assault should, if the victim so requests, be interviewed during the investigation of the crime only by police officers and officials of the same gender as the victim.

6. A victim's property that is in the custody of justice system officials should be returned promptly to the victim, where the property is no longer needed for the purposes of the justice system.

Section 2(2)

The principles set out in subsection (1) are subject to the availability of resources and information, what is reasonable in the circumstances of the case, what is consistent with the law and the public interest, and what is necessary to ensure that the resolution of criminal proceedings is not delayed.

Source: Ontario Statues and Regulations, www.e-laws.gov.on.ca/DBLaws/Statutes/English/95v06_e.htm.

Current Services for Victims

In addition to the development of statements of principles, the movement to recognize the needs and rights of victims has led to the development of a variety of services and programs across the country. These can be found within various components of the criminal justice system and assist and support an individual's involvement with the system as a victim. Most of these were not available as recently as the 1970s. A number of these services are highlighted in Box 4.3.

Police-Based Victim Services Usually located in police departments, these types of programs are designed to help victims as soon as possible after their contact with the criminal justice system begins. These types of services typically include death notification, information about the investigation, assistance with various applications for compensation, and referrals. In order to provide this support to victims, many police services across Canada now have in-house victim services units.[41] Usually staffed by civilians and volunteers, these services are available 24 hours a day for immediate victim support. For example, in the case of a fatal car accident, police officers can call upon their department's victim services unit to provide crisis intervention at the scene of the accident. Such services not only allow police officers to resume their duties but also ensure that the victim is supported by a trained professional. Many victim services units also use volunteers who represent various cultural, ethnic, and linguistic groups to help meet the specific needs of victims.

Provincial/Territorial Victim Services

Box 4.3

Alberta
Edmonton Police Service—Victim Services Unit
www.vfsedm.org
Staffed by trained police officers, civilians, and volunteers, this unit provides crisis response, personal support, follow-up assistance, court preparation, and trauma debriefings for victims of crime.

British Columbia
Ministry of Public Safety and the Solicitor General—Court Prep
www.courtprep.ca
This interactive information site provides an overview of criminal-court procedures including the roles of victims and witnesses of crime.

Newfoundland and Labrador
Department of Justice—Victim Services
www.justice.gov.nl.ca/just/PUBLICPR/victimservices/victim_services.htm
Eleven regional offices throughout the province provide support to victims through information about the justice system, their court cases, pre-court preparation, assistance with victim impact statements, referrals to specialized community resources, and short-term emotional support and counselling.

Ontario
Ministry of the Attorney General—SupportLink
www.attorneygeneral.jus.gov.on.ca/english/about/vw/supportlink.asp
Located in 20 communities across the province, this service provides safety planning, follow-up contact, and, where appropriate, wireless phones pre-programmed to 9-1-1 to people at high risk of sexual assault, domestic violence, and stalking.

Quebec
Justice Québec—Crime Victims Assistance Centres (CAVACs)
www.cavac.qc.ca/english/index.html
Located in most urban centres throughout Quebec, CAVACs provide free and confidential services including post-traumatic shock counselling, and support to victims through the court process.

Yukon
Department of Justice—Domestic Violence Treatment Option Court (DVTO Court)
www.yukoncourts.ca/courts/territorial/dvtoc.html
Specially assigned judiciary, Crown Attorneys, and defence council deal with domestic assault cases only in this court which sits one afternoon a week. Probation officers, counsellors, and victim-services personnel provide assistance to the process as well as the victim. Disposition in this court often involves the offender's participation in the Spousal Assault Program (SAP).

Some provinces have also established and funded independent crisis intervention services that provide victim support through referrals from police. In Ontario, the Victim Crisis Assistance and Referral Service (VCARS) is found in 48 centres across the province. A full-time coordinator and a group of trained volunteers, who are available as support to police at the scene of a crime, staff most VCARS programs. Available 24 hours a day and 7 days a week, VCARS personnel help victims cope with the impact of the crime or tragic circumstance. This may mean helping an elderly woman clean up after her home has been burglarized, or spending time with survivors of a fatal car accident. Follow-up is often provided in the form of referrals for ongoing counselling if required.

Crown/Court-Based Services   Most court-based victims programs are located within the courthouses and work closely with the Crown's office. Most assist those victims whose cases have resulted in prosecution. They emphasize court preparation and are designed to assist the victim through the trial process. One such program is the **Victim/Witness Assistance Program** located throughout Ontario. It provides services such as notification of court dates and adjournments, guided tours through the courtroom, explanations of court proceedings and emotional support throughout the trial, especially on the day(s) of victim testimony.[42] Many provinces also provide specialized court-based support programs for child victims and witnesses.

The recognition of the victim's involvement and the need for support throughout the court process has resulted in a number of provisions outlined in the *Criminal Code of Canada* with special attention to victims of violence. For example, section 722 allows victims to record a statement describing the emotional suffering, trauma, and/or financial hardship experienced as a result of their victimization. Known as a **victim impact statement**, these accounts are introduced into court after conviction and prior to sentencing (see Box 4.4). They are most common in cases of interpersonal victimization, and judges are expected to consider these statements in arriving at an appropriate sanction for the offender. The extent to which victim impact statements affect a judge's sentencing determination is debatable, and most victims do not submit one. Proponents of victim impact statements contend that they allow victims to have their say and feel involved in the criminal justice process, providing, for many, a cathartic emotional outlet.[43]

A number of other *Criminal Code* provisions are aimed at reducing the secondary victimization often experienced by people who appear as witnesses at trials. Section 486(3) states that judges can order "the identity of the complainant or of a witness and any information that could disclose the identity of the complainant or of a witness shall not be published in any document or broadcast in any way." These publication bans can be imposed in specific types of cases only, such as those involving sexual assault, incest, extortion, or a sexual offence involving children. Contravention of a publication ban is a summary-conviction offence.

In some instances, a trial judge may override the fundamental principle of justice that trials be public and issue an order to "exclude all or any members of the public from the courtroom for all or part of the proceedings" (s. 486(1)). Rarely done, this action is meant to allow for the "proper administration of justice" by allowing a victim or witness to testify free from stress or fear. These public-exclusion orders are most often used in cases involving child witnesses.

Other provisions intended to facilitate the participation of witnesses include subsection 486(1.2), which permits a support person to be present in court with a witness under

Victim Impact Statement

Box 4.4

In November 1999, Elaine Rose Cece, 41, and Barbara Taylor, 31, were found guilty of first-degree murder in the August 4, 1998, slaying of Toronto police constable William Hancox. The following is an excerpt from the transcript of the victim impact statement submitted by Kim Hancox, wife of the murdered officer.

I have attempted to write this victim impact statement several times and each time had to give up in fear of returning to a place in my life that I may not be able to escape from again. In order to relate to anyone the experience I have been through and continue to go through on a daily basis requires me to journey into the very depths of my existence, a dark, lonely and truly horrifying place. It has taken me over a year to be able to control, to some degree, the haunting capabilities of that place which eats away at my soul day and night. The images of my husband, my best friend, my soulmate, the father of my children, being savagely attacked with a butcher knife. The very look of horror that I imagine being on his face, a look of sheer terror and helplessness....

What were his thoughts, were they only thoughts of survival or were they thoughts of never seeing his daughter again, never seeing his new baby, never seeing me. Did he struggle in vain to stay alive, knowing that to be left without him would break me into pieces? I walk through these images daily whether I want to or not and even put myself in the passenger's seat of his van so he doesn't have to die alone....

The completely selfish act of two people has not only left my husband dead, it has left me on the brink of insanity, struggling only to survive to the next day. I was in a wonderful spot in my life, married to a man I simply adored, with a beautiful daughter who was a mirror image of her father, and expecting another child. All that was reduced to an existence where I just get up and remember to breathe....

My daughter will never have that golf lesson with her dad. My son will never play that hockey game with his father. I will never be able to fill his shoes. I am learning to live without him, but it requires just settling with what life has dealt me rather than living every moment to the fullest. Nothing is the same.... I am not the same. Bill would be destroyed to know the suffering everyone has had to endure, and that is hard to live with.

I believe Bill was put on this earth just for me and me for him. We truly had a wonderful relationship. I try to appreciate that I was lucky enough to have true love in my life, even if it was for a short time. Some people never get it at all.

Source: Kim Hancox and *The Canadian Police Association Express.* Used with permission.

---

the age of 14 in sexual-offence proceedings, and subsection 486(2.1), which permits a sexual-offence complainant who is under the age of 18 to provide his or her testimony from behind a screen or by closed-circuit television. This provision has recently been expanded to include victims and witnesses in prostitution and assault cases. Subsection 715.1 permits, as evidence, a videotaped version of a witness's testimony in proceedings relating to sexual offences where the victim or witness was under the age of 18 at the time of the offence.

Victims and Corrections Victim involvement with the criminal justice system often continues after the offender is convicted and sentenced. The federal *Corrections and Conditional Release Act* of 1992, for example, outlines the role of the victim in the parole process. In addition to those victims' rights highlighted in Box 4.5, the victim and/or any other interested party may attend a parole hearing, provided a written request has been made in advance of the hearing. Victims must travel to the location of the hearing and

What rights do victims have in parole decisions?

Under the law, victims have a legitimate and essential voice in the parole process. Victims are entitled to three things: (1) to submit a victim impact statement; (2) to attend and read prepared statements at National Parole Board hearings; and, (3) to obtain information about an offender while he is under sentence.

A victim impact statement helps Parole Board members assess whether an offender understands and appreciates the harm inflicted on victims and whether that person is likely to reoffend. The information is equally important in assessing the type of conditions that should be imposed especially if the offender will be living near the victim or is a member of the victim's family.

Victims are also allowed to attend an offender's parole hearing but any victim impact statement must be submitted in written form before the hearing takes place. As of July 1, 2001, victims are permitted to read prepared statements at National Parole Board hearings. Prior to these changes victims could only submit written statements and attend Board hearings as observers, never being permitted to speak directly to the Board. The role of victims in the parole process has increased, providing them with the option to make oral presentations to the Board in relation to their victimization. Also, victims or their families can request and receive basic information about an offender. This information could include when the sentence began and its length; and the eligibility and review dates of the offender for conditional release, including unescorted temporary absences, day and full parole.

Victims can also request to receive additional information about an offender that is not readily disclosed to the public. Such information includes whether or not an offender is in custody, and if not, why; where the offender is being held; the location the offender will be released to and when; the type of release the offender received and any conditions attached to this release.

Can a victim's information be considered in conditional release decisions?

The *Corrections and Conditional Release Act* recognizes that victims have certain rights. The Board considers information from victims, especially that which can help to assess whether an offender's release may pose a risk to society. The Board is interested in information that will assist in assessing the offender's understanding of the effect of the offence and whether that person is likely to reoffend. In cases of statutory release, where the Board must decide whether to detain an offender, information about the harm suffered by victims is critical for the Correctional Service of Canada and the National Parole Board.

Information from victims is also important when it is directly relevant to assessing conditions necessary to manage a particular risk that the offender might present, and to the offender's release plans, especially if the offender will be near the victim or is a member of the victim's family. Victims are encouraged to provide this information as soon as possible after sentencing or before an offender becomes eligible for parole.

Will information from victims be kept confidential?

The National Parole Board and the Correctional Service of Canada are required by law to share with the offender any information that will be considered during the decision-making process. Information cannot be used if it is not shared with the offender. Exceptions to this rule are rare; they include extraordinary situations, such as the safety of a person, the security of a correctional institution, or the possible jeopardy of an ongoing investigation.

Who is a victim?

The *Corrections and Conditional Release Act* defines a victim as someone to whom harm was done or who suffered physical or emotional damage as the result of a crime. The law considered that relatives are victims when the victim has been killed or is unable to be responsible for some reason such as age or illness.

Victims may authorize someone to act for them should they prefer. The Board will recognize someone as an agent for a victim if the victim makes a written statement designating someone to that effect.

How does someone request information about an offender?

Victims may write to request information from either the National Parole Board or the Correctional Service of Canada. If asked, the National Parole Board or the Correctional Service of Canada must release certain information to victims and may release certain other information.

Because the release of certain information about offenders is limited to victims as defined in the law, the request should clearly identify the offender and the crime committed. If guidance is needed, victims are invited to contact any of the offices of the National Parole Board or the Correctional Service of Canada.

A victim, or in some cases a victim's family, can request and will receive basic information about an offender, including

- when the sentence began and the length of the sentence; and
- the eligibility and review dates of the offender for unescorted temporary absences and parole.

More information may be released if the Chairperson of the National Parole Board or the Commissioner of the Correctional Service of Canada determines that the interest of the victim outweighs any invasion of the offender's privacy that could result from the disclosure.

Such information may include

- the location of the penitentiary in which the sentence is being served;
- the date, if any, on which the offender is to be released on unescorted or escorted temporary absence, work release, parole, or statutory release;
- the date of any hearing for the purposes of a review for possible detention;
- any of the conditions attached to the offender's unescorted temporary absence, work release, parole, or statutory release;
- the designation of the offender when released on any temporary absence, work release, parole, or statutory release, and whether the offender will be in the vicinity of the victim while travelling to that destination;
- whether the offender is in custody and, if not, why not; and
- whether or not the offender has appealed a decision of the Board, and the outcome of that appeal.

In addition, when an offender has been transferred from a penitentiary to a provincial correctional facility, the name of the province in which the provincial facility is located may be disclosed.

Is a victim or the family of a victim informed when a person convicted of a crime is granted conditional release?

No, not automatically. This information will be given only upon written request. Some victims prefer to have no further knowledge of the offender. A victim or a victim's family must ask for information.

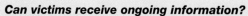

Can victims receive ongoing information?

Yes. Victims must make the request in writing and ensure that the National Parole Board or the Correctional Service of Canada has their current address and telephone number. They may then be informed of changes such as a move from one institution to another or the grant of a conditional release.

Can information be given to anyone other than victims?

The same information that can be released to victims can also be given to certain other people. However, they must satisfy the Chairperson of the National Parole Board or the Commissioner of the Correctional Service of Canada that they suffered harm or physical or emotional damage because of an offender's act, whether or not the offender was prosecuted or convicted for that act. If they have made a complaint to the police or the Crown Attorney, or any information was laid under the *Criminal Code*, then the person will be formally recognized as a victim and given the same information that would be given had the offender been convicted of the offence.

Source: National Parole Board of Canada, Ottawa, "Parole: Balancing Public Safety and Criminal Responsibility," 1996, pp. 126–128.

absorb any associated costs. Written transcripts of the hearing are made available upon request to those victims who cannot attend a hearing. In addition, some provinces have adopted legislation and procedures allowing the victim to remain informed of changes in the status of incarcerated offenders. In British Columbia, the Victim Safety Unit of the Ministry of Public Safety and the Solicitor General operates an automated Victim Notification System. Victims can register to be notified of changes in the custody status of an offender. The notification system provides victims with a personal identification number to access such information about their cases.

System-Based Services This is a relatively new approach to the provision of assistance to victims—it emphasizes a system-based approach instead of one that is police- or Crown/court-based. It allows victims to receive all their services from one location so that they don't have to deal with various components of the system independently. Both Nova Scotia and Prince Edward Island have implemented the system-based model (see Box 4.6).

Victim Restitution

Restitution a criminal sanction, in particular the payment of compensation by the offender to the victim.

The victims' movement has also spawned a rebirth of the concept of **restitution**. Restitution is punishment through imposed responsibility—in particular, the payment of compensation to the victim. Restitution encompasses the notion that criminal offenders should shoulder at least a portion of the financial obligations required to make the victim whole again. Not only does restitution help make the victim whole again, it places responsibility for the process back upon the offender who caused the loss of wholeness initially. Restitution, which works through court-imposed fines and garnishments, has many advocates who claim that it benefits society by leading to an increased sense of social and individual responsibility on the part of convicted offenders.

Nova Scotia Regional Victim Services Program

Box 4.6

Operated by the Nova Scotia Department of Justice, the Regional Victim Services Program provides centralized service to victims of crime through 4 regional offices. Program staff work with victims to provide information and assistance in a variety of areas including

- general information on the criminal justice system (police, courts, prosecution, corrections)
- information about the court case
- contacting police, the Crown Attorney, and the correctional system
- preparation for testifying in court
- explanation and assistance in preparing a victim impact statement
- assistance in applying for restitution
- assistance in applying for Criminal Injuries Counselling
- special help to child victims or witnesses of crime
- referrals to other agencies such as those providing legal and long-term counselling

Specific programs operated as part of the Regional Victim Services Program include the Child Victim/Witness Program, the Criminal Injuries Counselling Program, and the Victim Impact Statement Program.

All services are available to all victims of crime and are free of charge.

Source: Department of Justice, Nova Scotia, www.gov.ns.ca/. Reprinted by permission.

At one time in Canada, the responsibility for requesting restitution lay with the victim. Many who were not aware of this option failed to petition the court and restitution was not ordered. Currently, a judge can unilaterally order restitution or do so at the request of the Crown. Restitution can be so ordered as a stand-alone sentence or as part of another, such as a probation order or a conditional sentence. These types of sentences help ensure that beneficiaries of the restitution order receive payment. Failure to pay in either instance can lead to a breach of the sentence and incarceration. Beneficiaries can also use civil courts to enforce a restitution order.

A recent addition to the *Criminal Code of Canada* has extended the use of restitution to criminal cases involving criminal injury. Subsection 738(1) allows a judge to impose a sentence of restitution to cover expenses to the victim relating to things such as loss of income or support, costly dental work, or physiotherapy expenses. In addition, in the case of an offence causing bodily harm to the offender's spouse or child in instances of family violence, this subsection allows restitution to be ordered for readily ascertainable expenses incurred by the victim as a result of moving out of the offender's household, for temporary housing, child care, food, and transportation.

Section 737 of the *Criminal Code of Canada* requires a **victim surcharge** to be automatically imposed in addition to any other sanction handed down to an offender convicted of an offence in the *Criminal Code* or the *Controlled Drugs and Substances Act*. The revenue raised by this surcharge remains in the province or territory where it is imposed and is to be used specifically to fund programs and initiatives providing assistance to victims of crime. This provision further stipulates that the maximum victim fine surcharge is 15 percent of any fine imposed or, where no fine is imposed, is not to exceed $50 for an offence punishable by summary conviction and $100 in the case of an offence punishable

Victim surcharge a mandatory, judicial imposition of a monetary fine administered in addition to a criminal sentence and used to finance victim services.

The reality of violence against women brings victims and their supporters together in Take Back the Night marches like this one. Do you think that there are currently sufficient services for victims of crime?
CP/Ottawa Sun/Tony Caldwell.

by indictment. The sentencing judge may waive the victim fine surcharge where the imposition of the surcharge would cause undue hardship. Most provinces and territories have also enacted legislation imposing a surcharge on provincial offences such as highway traffic violations. This revenue is also used to fund victim programs and services.

Future Directions in Victimology

Initiatives taken by the federal and provincial governments in Canada in recent decades have done much to emphasize and highlight the rights and role of victims within our criminal justice system. However, despite this recognition, there is still concern that the needs of victims are not being fully met. Results from the General Social Survey conducted in 2004 indicate that, among those Canadians polled about their perceptions of the justice system, only 20 percent felt that the courts were doing a good job at helping the victim.[44] Indeed, some assert that the victims' movement has been adopted by governments to boost ratings and opinion polls and justify a platform of increased penalties for offenders as the primary way of recognizing victims' rights. Ezzat Fattah asserts "Crime victims are not the first group whose cause is exploited by unpopular governments seeking a higher rating in public opinion polls, by opportunistic politicians seeking electoral votes, or by incompetent public officials trying to detract attention from their failure to control crime or reduce its incidence."[45] A year before the implementation of a provincial bill of rights for victims, a government of Ontario Standing Committee warned that "A victim's bill of rights typically sets out the kinds of services a victim may ask for and contains no government commitment to make those remedies and services available ... A close look behind such bills may reveal they're little more than a cover for failure to provide adequate programs and services."[46] With this as the primary concern of governments, it is feared that concessions to victims will remain largely inefficient and do not permit meaningful involvement of victims in the justice process.

Various victims' bills of rights state that victims should have access to information and notification of services, investigation, court progress, and the like, but in fact there exists no means of ensuring compliance with these requirements. Police and prosecutors are not legally obligated to ensure that victims are notified and may violate a bill of rights with impunity. Additionally, even if notification is given, the legislation does not allow a victim's role in the process to override that of the prosecution. In other words, delays or stays of prosecutions and plea bargaining decisions all remain at the discretion of the Crown and can be made without victim notification or involvement. Much of the victims' rights legislation does not include language that mandates the right of victims to participate in the proceedings. The *Victims' Crime Act of British Columbia* and the *Victims' Services Act of New Brunswick*, for example, require that victims' views be heard only insofar as it is "appropriate and consistent with criminal law and procedure."[47] Finally, while victims of crime are now provided with a wide range of legal rights, most legislation does not provide for legal representation to ensure that these rights are exercised.

Groups representing victims of crime continue to advocate and apply pressure. In December 2006, a Victims' Summit Conference held in Ottawa and sponsored by the Ontario Office for Victims of Crime brought together academics, civil servants, law enforcement officials, criminal justice personnel, frontline victim service providers, and victims. The agenda included a critical look at needs and gaps in services to victims at certain key junctures: at the point of crisis (supports and services to victims in the aftermath of a crime), in the criminal justice system (supports and services to victims as they proceed through the criminal justice system), and outside the criminal justice system (supports and services to victims who do not proceed through the criminal justice system). Strong recommendations about ways to address these gaps and needs were generated and will go forward to the Ontario Ministry of the Attorney General for consideration.

Some, such as Kent Roach and others, believe that there needs to be a fundamental, structural change away from an adversarial approach to our criminal justice system and toward a restorative, victims-centred approach before victims' rights can be truly respected. Until that time, any recognition of victims' rights and roles in the criminal process cannot be considered as anything more than "window dressing," and the modern crime victim can be seen only as a participant who is "all dressed up with nowhere to go."[48] **Irvin Waller**, a leading Canadian academic in the field of victimology, poses some fundamental questions which he believes must be definitively answered before we can say that the rights of crime victims are truly entrenched. Some of the questions he asks are[49]

- How are victims informed of the different sources of assistance, of their rights, and of what they have to do to secure these rights?
- What informal mechanisms for the resolution of disputes are supported and encouraged by the law?

- Do victims have the right to start legal proceedings against the offender?
- Do they have the right to legal aid?
- Are victims informed about the progress of their case?
- Are they informed about what role they should play in the proceedings?
- Are they regularly consulted in the scheduling of cases?
- How are their views and concerns taken into consideration by the court?
- How is the right of the victim to privacy and safety protected?
- How is the right of the victim to fair restitution from the offender secured?
- What training is provided to persons who come into contact with victims, for example, the police, justice, health, and social service personnel?
- What is done to help victims of abuse and power?

The struggle to recognize crime victims' needs and rights continues. There is no doubt that victims have been unjustifiably left out of the criminal process for too long. Governments at all levels have formally acknowledged this. How to ensure their effective and balanced involvement in the future is the next challenge.

Summary

The role of the victim in the criminal justice process is one that has developed and expanded over the last few decades. The emergence of the formal study of the dynamics of victimization in the 1950s and 1960s, now known as victimology, has been instrumental in bringing this issue to public attention. Supported and vocalized through the burgeoning, grassroots victims' rights movement of the 1970s and 1980s, there now exists a consensus that victims do deserve recognition and participation in our criminal justice system. To this end, federal and provincial governments in Canada have enacted legislation enshrining rights for victims as well as introducing and funding services and programs that are designed to directly assist the victim throughout the criminal process.

Debate continues in a number of areas. Do we know, for example, what the real needs of crime victims are? What impact does involvement in the criminal process have on the psychological and physical well-being of the victim? And does mere victim participation in the criminal process translate into victim satisfaction? Will we require a significant structural change to the way justice is done before a true participatory role for victims can be ensured?

Discussion Questions

1. This book emphasizes a social problems versus social responsibility theme. Which of the theoretical perspectives of victimology discussed in this chapter (if any) best support the social problems approach? Which (if any) support the social responsibility approach? Why?
2. What are some of the realities of victimization? What is meant by *secondary victimization*? Do you think our criminal justice system addresses these realities well? Why or why not?

3. What is the difference between the *punitive* victims' rights model and the *non-punitive* victims' rights model as described by Roach? Which approach do you believe will facilitate the victim's role in the criminal justice process? Why?

4. Review the *Canadian Statement of Basic Principles of Justice for Victims of Crime*. Do you believe victims in Canada should have more rights? Should the rights of victims be included in the *Canadian Charter of Rights and Freedoms*? Defend your position.

5. What are some of the existing services for victims of crime? Do you think they adequately address the questions posed by Waller? How could they be improved?

6. Should the role of victims in the criminal process be changed from its current status? Can our current adversarial approach to justice ever allow this to happen? Explain your position.

Weblinks

www.crcvc.ca
Canadian Resource Centre for Victims of Crime (CRCVC). The CRCVC is a national, non-profit victims' rights advocacy group. Good links to criminal justice sites and provincial victims' legislation and services.

www.canada.justice.gc.ca/en/ps/voc/index.html
Policy Centre for Victim Issues. This Department of Justice site provides information on federal government initiatives concerning crime victims.

www.phac-aspc.gc.ca/ncfv-cnivf/familyviolence
National Clearinghouse on Family Violence. Federal Department of Health site that provides extensive links to research on victims of violence and abuse. Extensive list of international, national, provincial, and local links.

www.vaonline.org
Victim Assistance Online Resources. This non-profit online organization provides victim-assistance organizations, service providers, and professionals in related fields with an online central directory of information and education resources related to their fields. Good links to academic publications.

www.acjnet.org/victims
ACJNet Canada, Victims of Crime. ACJNet is an electronic community that brings together people, information, and educational resources on justice and legal issues of interest to Canadians. This site deals with victims' issues.

www.victimsofviolence.on.ca
Victims of Violence. Canadian Centre for Missing Children. This non-profit organization is dedicated to assisting victims of violence and to the prevention of missing children.

www.madd.ca
Mothers Against Drunk Driving. This site is dedicated to public education around drinking and driving.

The Classical Thinkers

Nature has placed mankind under the governance of two sovereign masters, pain and pleasure.

— JEREMY BENTHAM[1]

The more promptly and the more closely punishment follows upon the commission of a crime, the more just and useful will it be.

— CESARE BECCARIA[2]

LEARNING OUTCOMES

After reading this chapter, you should be able to

- discuss the relevance of the history of criminology and its early thinkers to current views of crime and criminality

- recognize the primary elements of the classical school

- identify modern-day practices that embody the principles of the classical school

- assess the shortcomings of the classical approach

The Granger Collection.

IMPORTANT NAMES

Thomas Hobbes	Thomas Paine	Marcus Felson
John Locke	Cesare Beccaria	Ronald Clarke
Montesquieu	Jeremy Bentham	Derek Cornish
Jean-Jacques Rousseau	Lawrence E. Cohen	

IMPORTANT TERMS

mores	natural rights	displacement
folkways	classical school	just deserts model
mala in se	hedonistic calculus	deterrence
mala prohibita	(utilitarianism)	specific deterrence
trephination	Panopticon	general deterrence
retribution	neo-classical criminology	recidivism
Twelve Tables	rational choice theory	recidivism rate
common law	routine activity theory	capital punishment
the Enlightenment	lifestyle theory	individual-rights advocates
social contract	situational choice theory	dangerousness
natural law	situational crime prevention	incapacitation
	target hardening	law-and-order advocates

Introduction

On April 10, 1995, Canada Customs officials seized and confiscated computer disks from John Robin Sharpe that contained a text authored by Sharpe and entitled, "Sam Paloc's Flogging, Fun, and Fortitude—A Collection of Kiddiekink Classics." Sharpe was charged with simple possession of child pornography contrary to section 163.1(4) of the *Criminal Code of Canada* and possession of child pornography for the purpose of distribution and sale, contrary to s. 163.1(3). Thirteen months later, on May 13, 1996, police again charged Sharpe under sections 163.1(4) and 163.1(3) after confiscating a collection of books, manuscripts, stories, and photographs depicting child pornography from his home near Surrey, British Columbia.

At trial, Sharpe argued that s. 163.1(4) infringed upon his individual freedoms, especially his freedom of expression guaranteed and protected under section 2(b) of the *Canadian Charter of Rights and Freedoms* since many of the articles seized were written or drawn by him. The trial judge, Justice Duncan Shaw, accepted this submission, finding s. 163.1(4) to be unconstitutional. Sharpe was acquitted on the counts of possession. The Crown appealed the court's ruling to the British Columbia Court of Appeal, where it was dismissed. An appeal to the Supreme Court of Canada was heard in early 2001. In a unanimous decision, the Supreme Court upheld the sections of the *Criminal Code* restricting the possession of child pornography; however, the Court remained split as to whether there should be exceptions based on freedom of expression. In a 6–3 ruling, the Supreme Court ruled that people can't be prosecuted for creating photographic or written material intended solely for their own use as long as real pictures or videos do not show illegal acts.

In 2002, Sharpe returned to court to face the original charges of possession and distribution of child pornography. Sharpe admitted guilt to the possession of pornographic pictures of children but was found not guilty of possessing or distributing written child pornography. He was sentenced to a four-month conditional sentence of house arrest.

The Sharpe case has ignited public controversy across the nation. Those who opposed the courts' decisions protested that the protection of an individual's right to freedom of expression should not come at the expense of public safety, especially that of children. Child advocacy groups such as Alliance for the Rights of Children and Beyond Borders are concerned that the Supreme Court ruling creates a loophole for pedophiles. They argued that literature of the type possessed by Sharpe ignores the rights of children and serves to sexually excite pedophiles and romanticize violent acts against children. Others, like the Canadian Civil Liberties Association (CCLA), believe that the Sharpe case highlights concerns about Canadians' freedom to write, draw, or imagine anything they want. The CCLA cited the case of Toronto artist Eli Langer, who was charged with having created "child pornography" because of a number of drawings he had on display in an art gallery that depicted youngsters in sexual situations. The charges were ultimately withdrawn and Langer's work was deemed by the court to have "artistic merit." In this case, however, as in Sharpe's, the constitutionality of the child pornography law was upheld; the CCLA contends that legitimate artists who deal with such subject matter will continue to risk criminal charges. Indeed, the CCLA points out, those parents who take and keep photographs of their nude babies run a similar risk.

The controversy sparked by the Sharpe case highlights the balancing act the Canadian criminal justice system must play between upholding and protecting the rights of each individual Canadian as enshrined in the *Charter of Rights and Freedoms* and upholding and protecting the collective rights of Canadian society as a whole as embodied in the *Criminal Code* and other statutes. Some argue that an overemphasis on individual rights comes at the expense of the rights of the group. Others fear that the erosion of individual rights may make the state too powerful. This debate has roots in the Enlightenment and the emergence of the classical school of criminology, both of which are discussed in this chapter.

Major Principles of the Classical School

This brief section serves to summarize the central features of the classical school of criminological thought. Each of the points listed in this discussion can be found elsewhere in this chapter, where they are discussed in more detail. The present cursory overview, however, is intended to provide more than a summation—it is meant to be a guide to the rest of this chapter.

Most classical theories of crime causation make the following basic assumptions:

- Human beings are fundamentally rational, and most human behaviour is the result of free will coupled with rational choice.
- Pain and pleasure are the two central determinants of human behaviour.
- Punishment, a necessary evil, is sometimes required to deter law violators and to serve as an example to others who would also violate the law.
- Root principles of right and wrong are inherent in the nature of things and cannot be denied.
- Society exists to provide benefits to individuals that they would not receive in isolation.

- When men and women band together for the protection offered by society, they forfeit some of the benefits that accrue from living in isolation.
- Certain key rights of individuals are inherent in the nature of things, and governments that contravene those rights should be disbanded.
- Crime disparages the quality of the bond that exists between individuals and society and is therefore an immoral form of behaviour.

Forerunners of Classical Thought

The notion of crime as a violation of established law did not exist in the most primitive of preliterate societies. The lack of lawmaking bodies, the paucity of formal written laws, and loose social bonds precluded the concept of crime as law violation. All human societies, however, from the simplest to the most advanced, evidence their own widely held notions of right and wrong. Sociologists term such fundamental concepts of morality and propriety as *mores* and *folkways*. Mores, folkways, and laws were terms used by William Graham Sumner near the start of the 20th century to describe the three basic forms of behavioural strictures imposed by social groups upon their members. According to Sumner, mores and folkways govern behaviour in relatively small primitive societies, whereas in large, complex societies they are reinforced and formalized through written laws.[3]

Mores consist of proscriptions covering potentially serious violations of a group's values. Murder, sexual assault, and robbery, for example, would probably be repugnant to the mores of any social group. **Folkways**, on the other hand, are simply time-honoured customs, and although they carry the force of tradition, their violation is less likely to threaten the survival of the social group. The fact that North American men have traditionally worn little jewellery illustrates a folkway that has given way in recent years to various types of male adornment, including earrings, gold chains, and even makeup. Mores and folkways, although they may be powerful determinants of behaviour, are nonetheless informal, because only laws, from among Sumner's trinity, have been codified into formal strictures wielded by institutions and created specifically for enforcement purposes.

Another method of categorizing socially proscriptive rules is provided by some criminologists who divide crimes into the dual categories of *mala in se* and *mala prohibita*. Acts that are ***mala in se*** are said to be fundamentally wrong, regardless of the time or place in which they occur. Forcing someone to have sex against her will, and the intentional killing of children, are sometimes given as examples of behaviour thought to be *mala in se*. Those who argue for the existence of *mala in se* offences as a useful heuristic category usually point to some fundamental rule, such as religious teachings (the Ten Commandments, the Koran, etc.), to support their belief that some acts are inherently wrong. Such a perspective assumes that uncompromisable standards for human behaviour rest within the very fabric of lived experience.

Mala prohibita offences are those acts that are said to be wrong for the simple reason that they are prohibited. So-called victimless or social order offences such as prostitution, gambling, drug use, and premarital sexual behaviour provide examples of *mala prohibita* offences. The status of such behaviours as *mala prohibita* is further supported by the fact that they are not necessarily crimes in every jurisdiction. Gambling, for example, is legal in parts of Canada, mainly because of the huge revenue potential it holds. Certain types of gambling are being rapidly legalized in many areas while other forms remain illegal. Raffles and games

Mores behavioural proscriptions covering potentially serious violations of a group's values. Examples might include strictures against murder, sexual assault, and robbery.

Folkways time-honoured customs. Although folkways carry the force of tradition, their violation is unlikely to threaten the survival of the social group.

Mala in se acts that are thought to be wrong in and of themselves.

Mala prohibita acts that are wrong only because they are prohibited.

of chance have been legal in Canada since the early 1900s. Government-regulated lotteries were legalized in 1969 and continue to generate huge sums of money. The late 1980s saw the advent of casinos, and they now can be found in most provinces and territories.[4]

The Demonic Era

Humankind has always been preoccupied with what appears to be an ongoing war between good and evil. Evil has often appeared in impersonal guise, as when the great bubonic plague, also known as the Black Death, ravaged Europe and Asia in the 14th century, leaving as much as three-quarters of the population dead in a mere span of 20 years. At other times, evil has seemed to wear a human face, as when the Nazi Holocaust claimed millions of Jewish lives before and during World War II.

Whatever its manifestation, the very presence of evil in the world has begged for interpretation, and sage minds throughout human history have advanced many explanations for the evil conditions that individuals and social groups have at times been forced to endure. Some forms of evil, such as the plague and the Holocaust, appear cosmically based, whereas others—including personal victimization, criminality, and singular instances of deviance—are the undeniable result of individual behaviour. Cosmic-level evil has been explained by ideas as diverse as divine punishment, karma, fate, and the vengeful activities of offended gods. Early explanations of personal deviance ranged from demonic possession to spiritual influences to temptation by fallen angels—and even led to the positing of commerce between humans and supernatural entities such as demons, werewolves, vampires, and ghosts.

Archaeologists have unearthed skeletal remains that provide evidence that some early human societies believed outlandish behaviour among individuals was a consequence of spirit possession. Carefully unearthed skulls, dated by various techniques to approximately 40 000 years ago, show signs of early cranial surgery, or **trephination**, apparently intended to release evil spirits thought to be residing within the heads of offenders. Such surgical interventions were undoubtedly crude, and probably involved fermented anaesthesia along with flint cutting implements.

As discussed in Chapter 1, any theory gains credence if activity based on it produces results in keeping with what that theory would predict. Hence, spirit possession, as an explanation for deviance, probably appeared well validated by positive behavioural changes in those "patients" who submitted to the surgery called for by the theory. The actual cause of such observed reformation, however, might have been brain infections resulting from unsanitary conditions, accidental slips of the stone knife, or the deterrent power of the pain endured by those undergoing the procedure. Nonetheless, to the uncritical observer the theory of spirit possession as a cause of deviance, and cranial surgery as a treatment technique, might have appeared to be supported by the "evidence" of low rates of future crime.

Trephination a form of surgery, typically involving bone and especially the skull. Early instances of cranial trephination have been taken as evidence for primitive beliefs in spirit possession.

Early Sources of the Criminal Law

The Code of Hammurabi
Modern criminal law is the result of a long evolution of legal principles. The Code of Hammurabi is one of the first known bodies of law to survive and be available for study today. King Hammurabi ruled the ancient city of Babylon

from 1792 to 1750 BC and created a legal code consisting of a set of strictures engraved on stone tablets. The Hammurabi laws were originally intended to establish property and other rights and were crucial to the continued growth of Babylon as a significant commercial centre. Hammurabi's laws spoke to issues of theft, property ownership, sexual relationships, and interpersonal violence. As Marvin Wolfgang has observed, "in its day, 1700 BC, the Hammurabi Code, with its emphasis on **retribution**, amounted to a brilliant advance in penal philosophy mainly because it represented an attempt to keep cruelty within bounds."5 Prior to the code, captured offenders often faced the most barbarous of punishments, frequently at the hands of revenge-seeking victims, no matter how minor their transgressions had been.

Retribution the act of taking revenge upon a criminal perpetrator.

Early Roman Law

Of considerable significance for our own legal tradition is early Roman law. Roman legions under Emperor Claudius I (10 BC–AD 54) conquered England in the mid-1st century, and Roman authority over then Britannia was further consolidated by later Roman rulers who built walls and fortifications to keep out the still-hostile Scots. Roman customs, law, and language were forced upon the English population during the succeeding three centuries under the Pax Romana—a peace imposed by the military might of Rome.6

Early Roman law derived from the **Twelve Tables**, which were written circa 450 BC. The tables were a collection of basic rules regulating family, religious, and economic life. They appear to have been based on common and fair practices generally accepted among early tribes which existed prior to the establishment of the Roman Republic. Unfortunately, only fragments of the tables survive today.

Twelve Tables early Roman laws written circa 450 BC that regulated family, religious, and economic life.

The best known legal period in Roman history occurred during the reign of Emperor Justinian I (AD 527–565). By the end of the 6th century, the Roman Empire had declined substantially in size and influence and was near the end of its life. In what may have been an effort to preserve Roman values and traditions, Justinian undertook the laborious process of distilling Roman laws into a set of writings. The Justinian Code, as these writings came to be known, actually consisted of three lengthy legal documents: (1) the Institutes, (2) the Digest, and (3) the Code itself. Justinian's Code distinguished between two major legal categories: public and private laws. Public laws dealt with the organization of the Roman state, its Senate, and governmental offices. Private law concerned itself with contracts, personal possessions, the legal status of various types of persons (citizens, free persons, slaves, freedmen, guardians, husbands and wives, and so forth), and injuries to citizens. It contained elements of our modern civil and criminal law and influenced Western legal thought through the Middle Ages.

Common Law

Common law forms the basis for much of our modern statutory and case law. It has often been called *the* major source of modern criminal law. **Common law** refers to a traditional body of unwritten legal precedents created through everyday practice and supported by court decisions during the Middle Ages in English society. Common law is so called because it was based on shared traditions and standards rather than on those that varied from one locale to another. As novel situations arose, the declarations of British justices on them became the start for any similar future deliberation. These decisions generally incorporated the customs of society as it operated at the time.

Common law a body of unwritten judicial opinion originally based on customary social practices of Anglo-Saxon society during the Middle Ages (also discussed in Chapter 1).

Common law was given considerable legitimacy upon the official declaration by the English King Edward the Confessor (ruled AD 1042–1066) that it was the law of the land. The authority of common law was further reinforced by the decision of William the

Conqueror to use popular customs as the basis for judicial action following his subjugation of Britain in 1066.

Eventually, court decisions were recorded and made available to *barristers* (the British word for trial lawyers) and judges. As Howard Abadinsky wrote, "common law involved the transformation of community rules into a national legal system. The controlling element (was) precedent."[7] Today, common law forms the basis of many of the laws on the books in English-speaking countries around the world.

The Magna Carta

The Magna Carta (literally, "great charter") is another important source of modern laws and legal procedure. The Magna Carta was signed on June 15, 1215, by King John of England at Runnymede, under pressure from British barons who took advantage of John's military defeats at the hands of Pope Innocent III and King Philip Augustus of France. The barons demanded a pledge from the king to respect their traditional rights and forced him to agree to be bound by law.

At the time of its signing, the Magna Carta, although 63 chapters in length, was little more than a feudal document listing specific royal concessions.[8] Its original purpose was to ensure feudal rights and to guarantee that the king could not encroach on the privileges claimed by landowning barons. Additionally, the Magna Carta guaranteed the freedom of the church and ensured respect for the customs of towns. Its wording, however, was later interpreted during a judicial revolt in 1613 to support individual rights and jury trials. Sir Edward Coke, chief justice under James I, held that the Magna Carta guaranteed basic liberties for all British citizens. One section of the Magna Carta states that "no free man shall be arrested and imprisoned ... unless by the lawful judgment of his peers and by the law of the land."[9] Section 7 of the *Canadian Charter of Rights and Freedoms* assures this fundamental right for Canadians today. Similarly, another specific provision of the Magna Carta, designed originally to prohibit the king from prosecuting the barons without just cause, was expanded into the concept of "due process of law," a fundamental cornerstone of modern legal procedure. Because of these later interpretations, the Magna Carta has been called "the foundation stone of our present liberties."[10]

The Magna Carta, an important source of modern Western laws and legal procedure. What are some other important sources of modern criminal law?
© *Bettmann/Corbis.*

The Enlightenment

The Enlightenment, also called the Age of Reason, was a highly significant social movement that occurred during the late-17th and 18th centuries. The Enlightenment built upon ideas developed by 17th-century thinkers such as Francis Bacon (1561–1626), Thomas Hobbes (1588–1679), John Locke (1632–1704), René Descartes (1596–1650), Jean-Jacques Rousseau (1712–1778), Baruch Spinoza (1632–1677), and others. Because of their indirect contributions to classical criminological thought, it will be worthwhile briefly discussing the writings of several of these important historical figures.

Thomas Hobbes (1588–1679) The English philosopher **Thomas Hobbes** developed what many writers regard as an extremely negative view of human nature and social life, which he described in his momentous work, *Leviathan* (1651). Hobbes described the natural state of men and women as one that is "nasty, brutish, and short." Fear of violent death, he said, forces human beings into a **social contract** with one another to create a state. The state, according to Hobbes, demands the surrender of certain natural rights and submission to the absolute authority of a sovereign, while offering protection and succour to its citizens in return. Although the social contract concept significantly influenced many of Hobbes's contemporaries, much of his writing was condemned for assuming an overly pessimistic view of both human nature and existing governments.

John Locke (1632–1704) In 1690, the English philosopher **John Locke** published his *Essay Concerning Human Understanding*, in which he put forth the idea that the natural human condition at birth is akin to that of a blank slate (or *tabula rasa*), upon which interpersonal encounters and other experiences indelibly inscribe the traits of personality. In contrast to earlier thinkers, who assumed that people are born with certain innate propensities and even rudimentary intellectual concepts and ideas, Locke ascribed the bulk of adult human qualities to life experiences.

In the area of social and political thought, Locke further developed the Hobbesian notion of the social contract. Locke contended that human beings, through a social contract, abandon their natural state of individual freedom and lack of interpersonal responsibility to join together and form society. Although individuals surrender some freedoms to society, government, once formed, is obligated to assume responsibilities toward its citizens and to provide for their protection and welfare. According to Locke and other writers, governments should be required to guarantee certain inalienable rights to their citizens, including the right to life, health, liberty, and possessions. A product of his times, during which the dictatorial nature of monarchies and the Roman church were being much disparaged, Locke stressed the duties that governments have toward their citizens, while paying very little attention to the inverse—the responsibilities of individuals to the societies of which they are a part. As a natural consequence of such an emphasis, Locke argued that political revolutions, under some circumstances, might become an obligation incumbent upon citizens.

Locke also developed the notion of checks and balances between divisions of government, a doctrine that was elaborated by the French jurist and political philosopher Charles Louis de Secondat **Montesquieu** (1689–1755). In *The Spirit of Laws* (1748), Montesquieu wove Locke's notions into the concept of a separation of powers between divisions of government. The Canadian parliamentary system is based on these very principles.

The Enlightenment, also known as the Age of Reason. A social movement that arose during the late-17th and 18th centuries and built upon ideas such as empiricism, rationality, free will, humanism, and natural law.

Social contract the Enlightenment-era concept that human beings abandon their natural state of individual freedom to join together and form society. Although in the process of forming a social contract individuals surrender some freedoms to society as a whole, government, once formed, is obligated to assume responsibilities toward its citizens and to provide for their protection and welfare.

Jean-Jacques Rousseau (1712–1778) The Swiss-French philosopher and political theorist **Jean-Jacques Rousseau** further advanced the notion of the social contract in his treatise of that name (*Social Contract*, 1762). According to Rousseau, human beings are basically good and fair in their natural state, but historically were corrupted by the introduction of shared concepts and joint activities such as property, agriculture, science, and commerce. As a result, the social contract emerged when civilized people agreed to establish governments and systems of education to correct the problems and inequalities brought on by the rise of civilization.

Natural law the philosophical perspective that certain immutable laws are fundamental to human nature and can be readily ascertained through reason. Human-made laws, in contrast, are said to derive from human experience and history—both of which are subject to continual change.

Rousseau also contributed to the notion of **natural law**, a concept originally formulated by St. Thomas Aquinas (1225–1274), Baruch Spinoza (1632–1677), and others to provide an intuitive basis for the defence of ethical principles and morality. Natural law was used by early Christian church leaders as a powerful argument in support of their interests. Submissive to the authority of the church, secular rulers were pressed to reinforce church doctrine in any laws they decreed. Thomas Aquinas, a well-known supporter of natural law, wrote in his *Summa Theologica* that any human-made law that contradicts natural law is corrupt in the eyes of God. Religious practice, which strongly reflected natural law conceptions, was central to the life of early British society. Hence, natural law, as it was understood at the time, was incorporated into English common law throughout the Middle Ages.

Rousseau agreed with earlier writers that certain immutable laws are fundamental to human nature and can be readily ascertained through reason. Human-made law, in contrast, he claimed, derives from human experience and history—both of which are subject to continual change. Hence, human-made law, also termed *positive law*, changes from time to time and from epoch to epoch. Rousseau expanded the concept of natural law to support emerging democratic principles and claimed that certain fundamental human and personal rights were inalienable because they were based on the natural order of things.

Natural rights the rights that, according to natural law theorists, individuals retain in the face of government action and interests.

Thomas Paine (1737–1809), the English-American political theorist and author of *The Rights of Man* (1791 and 1792), defended the French Revolution, arguing that only democratic institutions could guarantee the **natural rights** of individuals. For example, commentators have cited the "crimes against humanity" committed by Nazis during World War II as indicative of natural law principles. The chilling testimony of Rudolf Hess,[11] Hitler's deputy, during the 1945 war crimes trial in Nuremberg, Germany, as he recalled the "Fuehrer's" order to exterminate millions of Jews, indicated the extent of the planned "final solution." Hess testified,

> *In the summer of 1941 I was summoned to Berlin to Reichsfuehrer SS Himmler to receive personal orders. He told me something to the effect—I do not remember the exact words—that the Fuehrer had given the order for a final solution of the Jewish question. We, the SS, must carry out that order. If it is not carried out now then the Jews will later on destroy the German people. He had chosen Auschwitz on account of its easy access by rail and also because the extensive site offered space for measures ensuring isolation.*[12]

Who could argue against the premise, natural law supporters ask, that Hitler's final solution to the Jewish "problem" was inherently wrong?

Although the concept of natural law has waned somewhat in influence over the past half century, many people today still maintain that the basis for various existing criminal laws can be found in immutable moral principles, or in some other identifiable aspect of the natural order outside the social group.

The present debate over abortion is an example of modern-day use of natural law arguments to support both sides in the dispute. Those who oppose abortion claim that an unborn fetus is a person and that that being is entitled to all the protection that we would give to any other living human being. Such protection, "pro-life" advocates suggest, is basic and humane and lies in the natural relationship of one human being to another, and within the relationship of a society to its children. Advocates of the present law (which allows abortion upon request under certain conditions) maintain that abortion is a "right" of any pregnant woman because she is the only one who should be in control of her body. Such "pro-choice" groups also claim that the legal system must address the abortion question, but only by way of offering protection to this "natural right" of women.

The Classical School

As many authors have pointed out, the Enlightenment fuelled the fires of social change, leading eventually to the French and American revolutions. The Enlightenment—one of the most powerful intellectual initiatives of the last millennium—also inspired other social movements and freed innovative thinkers from the chains of convention. As a direct consequence of Enlightenment thinking, superstitious beliefs were discarded and men and women began to be perceived, for the first time, as self-determining entities possessing a fundamental freedom of choice. Following the Enlightenment, many supernatural explanations for human behaviour fell by the wayside, and free will and rational thought came to be recognized as the linchpins of all significant human activity. In effect, the Enlightenment inspired the re-examination of existing doctrines of human behaviour from the point of view of rationalism.

Within criminology, the Enlightenment led to the development of the **classical school** of criminological thought. Crime and deviance, which had been previously explained by reference to mythological influences and spiritual shortcomings, took their place in Enlightenment thought alongside other forms of human activity as products of the exercise of free will. Once humankind was seen as self-determining, crime came to be explained as a particularly individualized form of evil, or moral wrongdoing fed by personal choice.

Classical school a criminological perspective operative in the late-18th and early 19th centuries that had its roots in the Enlightenment. It held that men and women are rational beings, that crime is the result of the exercise of free will, and that punishment can be effective in reducing the incidence of crime, as it negates the pleasure to be derived from crime commission.

Cesare Beccaria (1738–1794)

Cesare Beccaria (whose Italian name was Cesare Bonesana, but who held the title Marchese di Beccaria) was born in Milan, Italy. The eldest of four children, he was trained at Catholic schools and earned a doctor of laws degree by the time he was 20.

In 1764, Beccaria published his *Essay on Crimes and Punishments*.[13] Although the work appeared originally in Italian, it was translated into English in London in 1767. Beccaria's *Essay* consisted of 42 short chapters covering only a few major themes. Beccaria's purpose was not to set forth a theory of crime but to communicate his observations on the laws and justice system of his time. In the *Essay*, Beccaria distilled the notion of the social contract into the idea that "[l]aws are the conditions under which independent and isolated men united to form a society." More than anything else, however, his writings consisted of a philosophy of punishment. Beccaria claimed, for example, that although most criminals are punished based on an assessment of their criminal intent, they should be punished instead

Theory in Perspective

The Classical School and Neo-Classical Thinkers

THE CLASSICAL SCHOOL

A criminological perspective operative in the late 1700s and early 1800s centuries that had its roots in the Enlightenment and held that men and women are rational beings, that crime is the result of the exercise of free will, and that punishment can be effective in reducing the incidence of crime because it negates the pleasure to be derived from crime commission.

CLASSICAL CRIMINOLOGY

The application of classical school principles to problems of crime and justice.
Period: 1700s–1880
Theorists: Cesare Beccaria, Jeremy Bentham, others
Concepts: Free will, deterrence through punishment, social contract, natural law, natural rights, due process, Panopticon

---

NEO-CLASSICAL CRIMINOLOGY

The modern-day application of classical principles of crime and crime control in contemporary society, often in the guise of get-tough policies.
Period: 1970s–present
Theorists: Lawrence Cohen, Marcus Felson, Ronald Clarke, Derek Cornish, others
Concepts: Rational choice, routine activities, capable guardians, just deserts, determinant sentencing, specific deterrence, general deterrence, incapacitation, dangerousness

---

based on the degree of injury they cause. The purpose of punishment, he said, should be deterrence rather than retribution, and punishment should be imposed to prevent offenders from committing additional crimes. Beccaria saw punishment as a tool to an end and not an end in itself, and crime prevention was more important to him than revenge.

To help prevent crimes, Beccaria argued, adjudication and punishment should both be swift, and once punishment is decreed, it should be certain. In his words, "the more promptly and the more closely punishment follows upon the commission of a crime, the more just and useful it will be." Punishment that is imposed immediately following crime commission, claimed Beccaria, is connected with the wrongfulness of the offence, both in the mind of the offender and in the minds of others who might see the punishment imposed and thereby learn of the consequences of involvement in criminal activity.

Beccaria concluded that punishment should be only severe enough to outweigh the personal benefits to be derived from crime commission. Any additional punishment, he argued, would be superfluous. Beccaria's concluding words on punishment are telling: "in order for punishment not to be, in every instance, an act of violence of one or of many against a private citizen, it must be essentially public, prompt, necessary, the least possible in the given circumstances, proportionate to the crimes, [and] dictated by the laws."

Beccaria distinguished between three types of crimes—those that threatened the security of the state, those that injured citizens or their property, and those that ran contrary to the social order. Punishment should fit the crime, Beccaria argued, and theft should be punished through fines, personal injury through corporal punishment, and serious crimes against the state (such as inciting revolution) through the death penalty. Beccaria, however, was opposed to the death penalty in most other circumstances, seeing it as a kind of warfare waged by society against its citizens.

Beccaria condemned the torture of suspects, a practice still used in the 18th century, saying that it was a device that ensured that weak suspects would incriminate themselves, while strong ones would be found innocent. Torture, he argued, was also unjust, because it punished individuals before they had been found guilty in a court of law. In Beccaria's words,

> no man can be called guilty before a judge has sentenced him, nor can society deprive him of public protection before it has been decided that he has in fact violated the conditions under which such protection was accorded him. What right is it then, if not simply that of might, which empowers a judge to inflict punishment on a citizen while doubt still remains as to his guilt or innocence?

Beccaria's *Essay* also touched upon a variety of other topics. He distinguished, for example, between two types of proof—that which he called "perfect proof," in which there was no possibility of innocence, and "imperfect proof," where some possibility of innocence remained. Beccaria also believed in the efficacy of a jury of one's peers but recommended that half of any jury panel should consist of acquaintances of the victim, whereas the other half should be made up of those who know the accused. Finally, Beccaria wrote that oaths were useless in a court of law, because accused individuals will naturally deny their guilt even if they know themselves to be fully culpable.

Beccaria's ideas were widely recognized as progressive by his contemporaries. His principles were incorporated into the French penal code of 1791 and significantly influenced the justice-related activities of European leaders such as Catherine the Great of Russia, Frederick the Great of Prussia, the Austrian Emperor Joseph II, and the framers of the American Constitution. Perhaps more than anyone else, Beccaria is responsible for the contemporary belief that criminals have control over their behaviour, that they choose to commit crimes, and that they can be deterred by the threat of punishment.

Jeremy Bentham (1748–1832)

Jeremy Bentham, another founding personality of the classical school, wrote in his *Introduction to the Principles of Morals and Legislation* (1789) that "nature has placed mankind under the governance of two sovereign masters, pain and pleasure."[14] To reduce crime or, as Bentham put it, "to prevent the happening of mischief," the pain of crime commission must outweigh the pleasure to be derived from criminal activity. Bentham's claim rested upon his belief, spawned by Enlightenment thought, that human beings are fundamentally rational and that criminals will weigh in their minds the pain of punishment against any pleasures thought likely to be derived from crime commission.

Bentham advocated neither extreme nor cruel punishment—only punishment sufficiently distasteful to the offender that the discomfort experienced would outweigh the pleasure to be derived from criminal activity. Generally, Bentham argued, the more serious the offence the more reward it holds for its perpetrator and, therefore, the more weighty the official response must be. "Pain and pleasure," said Bentham, "are the instruments the legislator has to work with" in controlling anti-social and criminal behaviour.

Hedonistic calculus or
utilitarianism the belief,
first proposed by Jeremy
Bentham, that behaviour
holds value to any
individual undertaking
it according to the
amount of pleasure or
pain that it can be
expected to produce for
that person.

Bentham's approach has been termed **hedonistic calculus** or **utilitarianism** because of its emphasis on the worth any action holds for an individual undertaking it. As Bentham stated, "[b]y the principle of utility is meant that principle which approves or disapproves of every action whatsoever, according to the tendency which it appears to have to augment or diminish the happiness of the party whose interest is in question; or, what is the same thing ... to promote or to oppose that happiness." In other words, Bentham believed that individuals could be expected to weigh, at least intuitively, the consequences of their behaviour before acting, so as to maximize their own pleasure and minimize pain. The value of any pleasure, or the inhibitory tendency of any pain, according to Bentham, could be calculated by its intensity, duration, certainty, and immediacy (or remoteness in time).

Bentham claimed that nothing was really new in his pleasure–pain perspective. "Nor is this a novel and unwarranted, any more than it is a useless, theory," he wrote.

> *In all this there is nothing but what the practice of mankind, wheresoever they have a clear view of their own interest, is perfectly comfortable to. An article of property, an estate in land, for instance, is valuable, on what account? On account of the pleasures of all kinds which it enables a man to produce, and what comes to the same thing the pains of all kinds which it enables him to avert.*

In fact, Bentham's ideas were not new, but their application to criminology was. In 1739, David Hume distilled the notion of utilitarianism into a philosophical perspective in his book *A Treatise of Human Nature*. Although Hume's central concern was not to explain crime, scholars who followed Hume observed that human behaviour is typically motivated more by self-interest than by anything else.

Like Beccaria, Bentham focused on the potential held by punishment to prevent crime and to act as a deterrent for those considering criminal activity. In any criminal legislation, he wrote, "[t]he evils of punishment must ... be made to exceed the advantage of the offence."

Utilitarianism is a practical philosophy, and Bentham was quite practical in his suggestions about crime prevention. Every citizen, he said, should have their first and last names tattooed on their wrists for the purpose of facilitating police identification. He also recommended creation of a centralized police force focused on crime prevention and control—a recommendation that found life in the English Metropolitan Police Act of 1829, which established London's New Police under the direction of Sir Robert Peel. This model of policing was adopted in the creation of Canada's first national police force, the Dominion Police Force, in 1867.

Panopticon a prison
designed by Jeremy
Bentham that was to
be a circular building
with cells along the
circumference, each
clearly visible from a
central location staffed
by guards.

Bentham's other major contribution to criminology was his suggestion that prisons be designed along the lines of what he called a Panopticon House. The **Panopticon**, as Bentham envisioned it, was to be a circular building with cells along the circumference, each clearly visible from a central location staffed by guards. Bentham recommended that Panopticons should be constructed near or within cities so that they might serve as examples to others of what would happen to them should they commit crimes. He also wrote that prisons should be managed by contractors who could profit from the labour of prisoners, and that the contractor should "be bound to insure the lives and safe custody of those entrusted to him." Although a Panopticon was never built in Bentham's England, French officials funded a modified version of such a prison, which was eventually built at Lyon, and three prisons modelled after the Panopticon concept were constructed in the United States.

Bentham's critics have been quick to point out that punishments seem often not to work. Even punishments as severe as death appear not to have any effect on the incidence of crimes such as murder (a point that we will discuss in greater detail later in this chapter). Such critics forget Bentham's second tenet, however, which is that for punishment to be effective, "it must be swift and certain." For any punishment to have teeth, Bentham said, it must not only mandate a certain degree of displeasure but also follow almost immediately upon its being decided, and there must be no way of avoiding it.

Heritage of the Classical School

The classical school was to influence criminological thinking for a long time. It has been instrumental in moulding the way in which thinkers on the subject of crime have viewed the topic for more than 200 years. The heritage left by the classical school is still operative today in the following five principles, each of which is a fundamental constituent of modern-day perspectives on crime and human behaviour:

- *The principle of rationality:* Human beings have free will and the actions they undertake are the result of choice.
- *The principle of hedonism:* Pleasure and pain, or reward and punishment, are the major determinants of choice.
- *The principle of punishment:* Criminal punishment is a deterrent to unlawful behaviour, and deterrence is the best justification for punishment.
- *The human-rights principle:* Society is made possible by individuals cooperating together. Hence, society owes to its citizens respect for their rights in the face of government action, and for their autonomy insofar as such autonomy can be secured without endangering others or menacing the greater good.
- *The due-process principle:* An accused should be presumed innocent until proven otherwise, and an accused should not be subject to punishment prior to guilt being lawfully established.

Some of these concepts are easily recognizable in the *Canadian Charter of Rights and Freedoms*, the *Criminal Code of Canada*, and the *Youth Criminal Justice Act*.

Neo-Classical Criminology

By the end of the 19th century, classical criminology, with its emphasis on free will and individual choice as the root causes of crime, gave way to another approach known as *positivism*. Positivism, which made use of the scientific method in studying criminality, is discussed in much greater detail in Chapter 6. In essence, positivism, in its original formulation, was based upon the belief that crime results from forces that are beyond the control of the individual. Hence, as we shall see later in this book, the original positivists rejected the notion of free will and turned their attention to the impact of socialization, genetics, economic conditions, peer influences, and other factors that might determine criminality.

The 1970s saw a growing dissatisfaction with many of the assumptions of positivism and a resultant resurgence of the notions of the classical school. At that time, the public was becoming more and more frustrated by increasing crime rates and the apparent ineffectiveness of correctional programs designed to rehabilitate offenders. In addition, government policies designed to rectify social conditions such as unemployment and poverty—which were believed to contribute to criminality—were viewed as failures. Many conservative politicians and some criminologists began calling existing notions of crime prevention and rehabilitation into question amid claims that enhanced job skills, increased opportunities for employment, and lessened punishment did nothing to stem a rising crime rate.

In an often-quoted article entitled, "What Works?" Robert Martinson noted that "[w]ith few and isolated exceptions, the rehabilitative efforts that have been reported so far have had no appreciable effect on recidivism."[15] In his work entitled *Thinking About Crime*, James Q. Wilson wrote that crime is not a result of poverty or social conditions and cannot be affected by social programs.[16] In this atmosphere of frustration, some criminologists turned to a revival of the classical tenets of criminology. This resurgence of classical ideals, referred to as **neo-classical criminology**, focused on the dynamics of character development and the rational choices that people make as they are faced with the opportunities for crime.

Rational Choice Theory

Rational choice theory, a product of the late 1970s and early 1980s, mirrors many of the principles found in classical criminology. The theory rests upon the belief that individuals make a conscious, rational, and at least partially informed choice to commit crime. It uses cost-benefit analysis, akin to similar theories in the field of economics that view human behaviour as the result of personal choice made after weighing both the costs and the benefits of available alternatives. Rational choice theory is noteworthy for its emphasis on the rational and adaptive aspects of criminal offending. It "predicts that individuals choose to commit crime when the benefits outweigh the costs of disobeying the law. Crime will decrease," according to such theories, "when opportunities are limited, benefits are reduced, and costs are increased."[17]

Two varieties of rational choice theory can be identified. One, which builds on an emerging emphasis on victimization, is called "routine activity theory." A second, which is largely an extension of the rational choice perspective, is called "situational choice theory."

Routine activity theory (also called **lifestyle theory**) was proposed by **Lawrence E. Cohen** and **Marcus Felson** in 1979.[18] Cohen and Felson suggested that lifestyles contribute significantly to both the volume and the type of crime found in any society. The two believed that changes in the nature of North American society during the 1960s and 1970s—specifically increased personal affluence and greater involvement in social activities outside the home—brought about increased rates of household theft and personal victimization by strangers. Central to the routine activity approach is the claim that crime is likely to occur when a motivated offender and a suitable victim come together in the absence of preventative measures (which were sometimes termed "capable guardians"). Hence, "the risk of criminal victimization varies dramatically among the circumstances and locations in which people place themselves and their property."[19] For example, a person who routinely uses an automated teller machine late at night in an isolated location is far more likely to be preyed upon by robbers than is someone who stays home after dark. Lifestyles that contribute to criminal opportunities are likely to result in crime because they increase the risk of potential victimization.[20] Although non-criminal lifestyles at a given point in the life course are partly the result of unavoidable social roles and assigned social positions, those who participate in a given lifestyle generally make rational decisions about specific behaviours (such as going to

Neo-classical criminology a contemporary version of classical criminology that emphasizes deterrence and retribution, with reduced emphasis on rehabilitation.

Rational choice theory a perspective that holds that criminality is the result of conscious choice and that predicts that individuals choose to commit crime when the benefits outweigh the costs of disobeying the law.

Routine activity theory (or **lifestyle theory**) a brand of rational choice theory that suggests that lifestyles contribute significantly to both the volume and the type of crime found in any society.

a given automatic teller machine at a certain time). The same is true of criminal lifestyles. Hence, the meshing of choices made by both victims and criminals contributes significantly to both the frequency and the type of criminal activity observed in society. See Box 5.1 for an examination of a Canadian geographic profiling system used to track down criminals that is based on this notion of routine activities.

In a later work, Felson suggested that a number of "situational insights" might combine to elicit a criminal response from individual actors enmeshed in a highly varied social world.[21] Felson pointed out that "individuals vary greatly in their behaviour from one situation to another" and said that criminality might flow from temptation, bad company, idleness, or provocation. Convenience stores, for example, create temptations toward theft when they display their merchandise within easy reach of customers. Other authors have defined the term *situation* to mean "the perceptive field of the individual at a given point in time" and have suggested that it "can be described in terms of who is there, what is going on, and where it is taking place."[22]

Situational choice theory views criminal behaviour "as a function of choices and decisions made within a context of situational constraints and opportunities."[23] It suggests that the probability of criminal activity can be reduced by changing the features of a given social situation or of the surrounding environment. **Ronald Clarke** and **Derek Cornish**, collaborators in the development of the situational choice perspective, analyze the choice-structuring properties of a potentially criminal situation. They define *choice-structuring properties* as "the constellation of opportunities, costs, and benefits attaching to particular kinds of crime."[24] Clarke and Cornish suggest the use of situational strategies, such as "cheque guarantee cards, the control of alcohol sales at football matches, supervision of children's play on public housing estates, vandal resistant materials and designs, 'defensible space' architecture, improved lighting, closed-circuit television surveillance,"[25] and the like, as effective crime-preventative additions to specific situations—all of which might lower the likelihood of criminal victimization in given instances.

In brief, rational choice theorists concentrate on "the decision-making process of offenders confronted with specific contexts" and have shifted "the focus of the effort to prevent crime ... from broad social programs to target hardening, environmental design or any impediment that would [dissuade] a motivated offender from offending."[26]

Although rational choice theory is similar to classical deterrence theory, earlier approaches focused largely on the balance between pleasure and pain as the primary determinant or preventative of criminal behaviour. Rational choice theory tends to place less emphasis on pleasure and emotionality and more upon rationality and cognition. Some rational choice theorists have gone so far as to distinguish among the types of choices offenders make as they move toward criminal involvement. One type of choice, known as "involvement decisions" have been described as "multi-stage" and are said to "include the initial decision to engage in criminal activity as well as subsequent decisions to continue one's involvement or to desist.[27] Another type of choice, "event decisions," relates to particular instances of criminal opportunity such as the decision to rob a particular person or to let the prospective victim pass. Event decisions—in contrast to involvement decisions, which may take months or even years to reach—are usually made quickly.

Situational Crime Control Policy
Building upon the work of rational and situational choice theorists, Israeli criminologist David Weisburd describes the advantages of a situational approach to crime prevention. Weisburd points out that

Situational choice theory a brand of rational choice theory that views criminal behaviour as a function of choices and decisions made within a context of situational constraints and opportunities.

Geographic Profiling Online

Box 5.1

Hot on a Killer's Trail

Rigel is a Canadian-made computer program that uses geographic profiling to hunt serial killers, repeat rapists, bombers, arsonists, and other major miscreants.

Rigel is at the core of an emerging crime-fighting field called geographic profiling. Instead of the traditional police approach of working outward from the crime scene to figure out where a criminal went, geographic profiling works inward to find out where the criminal came from. It has had impressive results.

As a test, Rigel was fed information about convicted serial killer Clifford Olson's 11 child murders. It pointed to a four-block area in Coquitlam, B.C., including his former street.

Late in the Paul Bernardo case, by using the locations of where teens Leslie Mahaffy and Kristen French were abducted and their bodies later found, Rigel pointed to the St. Catharines area town of Port Dalhousie where Mr. Bernardo and his wife Karla Homolka lived. Police were already closing in.

It worked again in the case of the Abbotsford killer wanted for murdering an Abbotsford, B.C. teenage girl and attempting to kill her friend. By giving Rigel the murder-scene location and the positions of telephone booths the killer used to make taunting calls to police, Rigel came incredibly close to pinpointing the home of Terry Driver.

Some day it could even be used to predict where a serial killer might strike next.

Rigel was invented by Kim Rossmo who overnight rose from a Skid Road beat constable to a detective inspector with Vancouver city police by coming up with the unique way to track down the likes of Hannibal Lector and Jeffrey Dahmer.

Named after the star in the constellation of Orion—the hunter—Rigel is a complex computer program that mathematically analyzes the hunting habits of serial criminals and points to where they most probably live.

Detective-Inspector Rossmo, a math whiz, came up with the idea in the late 1980s while working on the beat and beginning studies for his Ph.D. in criminology at Simon Fraser University. He even researched hunting techniques of lions on Africa's Serengeti plains.

In 1995, Vancouver police were the first in the world to open a geographic profiling unit under Rossmo's command. "Canada does not have a whole lot of money by comparison with the United States and Britain," he says. "So we have to be creative and innovative and more effective. To me, that's one of the most exciting parts of it."

Serial crimes, especially homicides and sex attacks, are investigative nightmares for police. Since serial killers often strike at random, there's no victim–killer relationship, which is the basic starting point for most homicide investigations. And because of their random, brutal nature, serial crimes can create intense public fear. That puts big pressure on the police, who then assign considerable resources to the case. And that generates enormous lists of tips, witnesses, and suspects to be checked out. Cases start suffering from information overload. In only 9 months, for example, the Bernardo murder case generated 3200 suspects and 31 000 tips.

Rigel, in the hand of a skilled geographic profiler with a computer, math, and behavioural science background, helps find the needle in that haystack. But it will never replace a seasoned homicide sleuth.

About 20 years ago, Simon Fraser criminologists Patricia and Paul Brantingham came up with the idea of predicting where criminals were most likely to commit crimes based on where they lived, worked, and played.

Investigators walk toward the house that was rented by Paul Bernardo in Port Dalhousie, Ontario, April 30, 1993.
CP Photo/Jeff Chevrier.

Detective-Inspector Rossmo, who studied under the husband and wife team, inverted that theory.

Rigel predicts where criminals are most likely to live, work, or play based on where they commit crimes.

While serial killers and rapists often target victims randomly, where they attack is revealing. "Every time somebody makes a choice about something, we learn something about him," says the inspector.

Like the rest of us, criminals have defined geographic areas in which they go about their daily lives, including key "anchor" points such as home and work. Research into criminal behaviour has found most criminals won't commit crimes near home, for fear of being recognized and apprehended. That crime-free area around their home is called the buffer zone. Just outside of that is an area known as the comfort zone.

"When you leave your house and go to work, you drive the same couple of ways to work and use the same stores to pick up bread and milk, you have the place to go play basketball, whatever, all those things are in your awareness space," explains Ontario Provincial Police sergeant Brad Moore, who in 1998 graduated from extensive training to become one of the world's first geographic profilers.

"Criminals are the same. They're creatures of habit as well. So when they commit crimes, they commit crimes in areas they know, whether it's near their home or near their work. There's a comfort zone."

When a victim or opportunity intersects with a criminal's comfort zone, and at a time when he's ready to strike, a crime will usually occur.

The size of any one serial criminal's buffer and comfort zones is impossible to determine. But there are some clues among the vast body of research on criminal behaviour.

Criminals who carry out acts with a certain level of sophistication and planning, such as bringing a murder weapon and removing it or hiding a body, are classified as "organized." And research shows organized criminals tend to travel farther from home to commit crimes than disorganized offenders.

That means they will have larger buffer zones than those of disorganized criminals.

To get a very basic idea of how Rigel works, place a small X, representing a criminal's home, on a piece of paper and draw a circle around it. The circle represents a 1 kilometre area around the home. Place a dot on a crime scene—somewhere within the circle. Draw another 1 kilometre circle around that dot. Draw a few more dots and circles.

In the end, they will all intersect around the crook's house.

In the case of a serial rapist terrorizing a city, Rigel studies the location of each rape site and, through some mathematical tricks, assesses the probability of every other point in the city being the rapist's home. It can take more than a million calculations.

Once it's done looking at each site, it will display a coloured map on a computer screen, with the highest probability areas marked in red.

If police already have a list of suspects, Rigel can cross-reference their addresses and quickly narrow down which ones live in the red zone so police can prioritize their next moves.

Or, if police have a partial licence plate number of a car used in a serial crime, Rigel's high-probability areas can be cross-referenced with postal codes and car registration databanks to look for a match.

Or, if police only have a description of a suspect, they can use Rigel's high-probability areas to tailor a direct-mail campaign and mail out a composite sketch of the suspect to everyone living in the area.

Or they can target an area for increased patrols, or know where to go door-to-door for leads.

The program does have some limits. It won't be able to track serial criminals who have no "anchor" points, or ones who commit crimes across great distances. And because it's based on probabilities, it needs at least five crime-site locations to have any real precision. But the more locations, the greater its focus.

When police arrested British Columbia serial rapist John Oughton in the mid-1980s, they found coloured pins stuck in maps in his house indicating the locations of his 79 rapes.

Mr. Oughton was trying to make sure he kept his crime locales random so police couldn't pinpoint where he lived.

But when the 79 spots were later put into Rigel, a red, high-probability dot appeared precisely where Oughton's Vancouver apartment had once been.

"The hardest thing to beat is your habits," explains Sgt. Moore. "Even when you're trying to, sometimes unconsciously, you just can't."

DISCUSSION QUESTIONS

1. How is Kim Rossmo's Rigel computer program supported by the routine activity theory?

2. Are there any other theories that would support the Rigel program?

Source: Adapted from Ian MacLeod, "Hot on a Killer's Trail," *Ottawa Citizen*, January 25, 1998, p. B3. Reprinted with permission.

crime prevention research and policy have traditionally been concerned with offenders or potential offenders. Researchers have looked to define strategies that would deter individuals from involvement in crime or rehabilitate them so they would no longer want to commit criminal acts. In recent years crime prevention efforts have often focused on the incapacitation of high-rate or dangerous offenders so they are not free to victimize law-abiding citizens. In the public debate over crime prevention policies, these strategies are usually defined as competing approaches. However, they have in common a central assumption about crime prevention research and policy: that efforts to understand and control crime must begin with the offender. In all of these approaches, the focus of crime prevention is on people and their involvement in criminality.[28]

"Although this assumption continues to dominate crime prevention research and policy," says Weisburd, "it has begun to be challenged by a very different approach that seeks to shift the focus of crime prevention efforts." The new approach developed in large part as a response to the failures of traditional theories and programs. The 1970s, in particular, saw a shattering of traditional assumptions about the effectiveness of crime prevention efforts and led to a re-evaluation of research and policy about crime prevention. For many scholars and policy makers, this meant having to rethink assumptions about criminality and how offenders might be prevented from participating in crime. Others suggested that a more radical reorientation of crime prevention efforts was warranted. They argued that the shift must come not in terms of the specific strategies or theories that were used, but in terms of the unit of analysis that formed the basis of crime prevention efforts. This new crime prevention effort called for a focus not on people who commit crime but on the context in which crime occurs.[29]

This approach, which is often called **situational crime prevention**, looks to develop greater understanding of crime and more effective crime prevention strategies through concern with the physical, organizational, and social environments that make crime possible.[30] The situational approach does not ignore offenders; it merely places them as one part of a broader crime-prevention equation that is centred on the context of crime. It demands a shift in the approach to crime prevention, however, from one that is concerned primarily with why people commit crime to one that looks primarily at why crime occurs in specific settings. It moves the context of crime into central focus and sees the offender as but one of a number of factors that affect it. Situational crime prevention is closely associated with the idea of a "criminology of place," discussed in Box 8.1 in Chapter 8.

Weisburd suggests that a "reorientation of crime prevention research and policy from the causes of criminality to the context of crime provides much promise." Says Weisburd, "at the core of situational prevention is the concept of opportunity ...." In contrast to offender-based approaches to crime prevention that usually focus on the dispositions of criminals, situational crime prevention begins with the opportunity structure of the crime situation. By "opportunity structure," advocates of this perspective are not referring to sociological concepts such as differential opportunity or anomie, but rather to the immediate situational and environmental components of the context of crime. Their approach to crime prevention is to try to reduce the opportunities for crime in specific situations. This may involve efforts as simple and straightforward as **target hardening** or access control.[31]

The value of a situational approach lies in the fact that criminologists have found it difficult to identify who is likely to become a serious offender or to predict the timing and types of future offences that repeat offenders are likely to commit. And, as Weisburd says, "legal and ethical dilemmas make it difficult to base criminal justice policies on models that still include a substantial degree of statistical error." Moreover, Weisburd adds, "if traditional approaches worked well, of course, there would be little pressure to find new forms of crime prevention. If traditional approaches worked well, few people would possess criminal motivation and fewer still would actually commit crimes."

Situational prevention advocates argue that the context of crime provides a promising alternative to traditional offender-based crime prevention policies.[32] They assume that situations provide a more stable and predictable focus for crime prevention efforts than do persons. In part, this assumption develops from common-sense notions of the relationship between opportunities and crime. Shoplifting, for example, is by definition clustered in stores and not residences, and family disputes are unlikely to be a problem outside of the home. High-crime places, in contrast to high-crime people, cannot flee to avoid

Situational crime prevention a social policy approach that looks to develop greater understanding of crime and more effective crime prevention strategies through concern with the physical, organizational, and social environments that make crime possible.

Target hardening the reduction in criminal opportunity for a particular location, generally through the use of physical barriers, architectural design, and improved security measures.

criminal-justice intervention; and crime that develops from the specific characteristics of certain places cannot be easily transferred to other contexts.

Another example can be had in robberies, which are seen as most likely to be found in places where many pedestrians stroll (such as bus stops and business districts), where there are few police or informal guardians (e.g., doormen), and where a supply of motivated offenders can be found nearby or at least within easy public transportation access.[33] Similarly, such places are not likely to be centres for prostitution, which would favour easy access of cars (and little interference by shopkeepers who are likely to object to the obvious nature of street solicitations), nor flashing, which is more likely to be found in the more anonymous environments of public parks.

Situational crime-prevention policy is most clearly manifest in the Crime Prevention Through Environmental Design (CPTED) concept, which is discussed in detail in Chapter 11.

Critique of Rational Choice Theory

Rational and situational choice and routine activity theories have been criticized for their overemphasis on individual choice and their relative disregard for the role of social factors in crime causation such as social and economic inequality of persons and groups, poor home environment, and inadequate socialization. In a recent study, Laura J. Moriarty and James E. Williams found that the routine activity approach explained 28 percent of property crimes committed in socially disorganized (high-crime) areas of a small Virginia city, and explained only 11 percent of offences committed in low-crime areas.[34] In the words of the authors, "this research demonstrates more support for routine activities theory in socially disorganized areas than in socially organized areas." Hence, although one could argue that the kinds of routine activities supportive of criminal activity are more likely to occur in socially disorganized areas, it is also true that the presence (or absence) of certain ecological characteristics (i.e., the level of social disorganization) may either increase (or reduce) the likelihood of criminal victimization. As the authors state,

> those areas characterized by low socio-economic status will have higher unemployment rates, thus creating a larger pool of motivated offenders. Family disruption characterized by more divorced or separated families will result in more unguarded living structures, thus making suitable targets more available. Increased residential mobility will result in more non-occupied housing, which creates a lack of guardianship over the property and increases the number of suitable targets.[35]

Rational choice theory, in particular, seems to assume that everyone is equally capable of making rational decisions when, in fact, such is probably not the case. Some individuals are more logical than others by virtue of temperament, personality, or socialization, whereas others are emotional, hotheaded, and unthinking. Empirical studies of rational choice theory have added scant support for the perspective's underlying assumptions, tending to show instead that criminal offenders are often unrealistic in their appraisals of the relative risks and rewards facing them.[36] Similarly, rational and situational choice theories seem to disregard individual psychology and morality by their emphasis on external situations. Moral individuals, say critics, when faced with easy criminal opportunities, may rein in their desires and turn their backs on temptation.

Displacement a shift of criminal activity from one spatial location to another.

Finally, the emphasis of rational and situational choice theories upon changing aspects of the immediate situation to reduce crime has been criticized for resulting in the **displacement** of crime from one area to another.[37] Target hardening,[38] a key crime-prevention strategy advocated by such theorists, has sometimes caused criminals to find new targets of opportunity in other areas.[39]

Punishment and Neo-Classical Thought

Punishment is a central feature of both classical and neo-classical thought. Whereas punishment served the ends of deterrence in classical thought, its role in neo-classical thinking has been expanded to support the ancient concept of retribution. Those who advocate retribution see the primary utility of punishment as revenge.

If a person is attracted to crime and chooses to violate the law, modern neo-classical thinkers argue, then she *deserves* to be punished because the consequences of the crime were known to the offender before the crime was committed. Moreover, the criminal *must* be punished, such thinkers propose, so that future criminal behaviour can be curtailed.

In 1994, the "caning" of a US teenager in Singapore provided an example of just this kind of thinking. In that year, 18-year-old Michael Fay was ordered to receive six lashes from a four-foot-long, half-inch-thick split-bamboo rod called a *rotan*. Fay's caning was to be his punishment for five charges of vandalism, mischief, and keeping stolen property—crimes committed while he lived in Singapore with his parents and to which he pleaded guilty. Fay, along with other teenagers, had spray-painted and thrown eggs at parked cars. At the time of the offences, Fay was probably unaware that Singapore law mandates caning in cases of vandalism when an indelible substance is used. The law was originally passed in the 1960s to curtail the use of political graffiti. Caning is no simple punishment and has been described as making "pieces of skin and flesh fly at each stroke."[40] Singapore law requires that those who faint be revived by a doctor so that the caning can continue.[41]

Michael Fay, the 18-year-old American teenager who was caned in Singapore in 1994 for spray-painting cars, makes the "sign of the cross" before entering Singapore's High Court. Should Fay have been caned?
Jonathan Drake/Corbis.

Before Fay's caning, his parents begged Singapore's courts for leniency, and pleaded for intervention from the International Red Cross, beseeched Singapore President Ong Teng Cheong for clemency, and asked then US President Clinton for help—all to no avail. Although many around the world expressed dismay at the severity of the punishment, others, such as then Member of Parliament Art Hanger, declared that corporal punishment practices such as caning might work to reduce crime and that Canada should adopt a system of corporal punishment similar to that of Singapore.[42]

Just Deserts

Just deserts model the notion that criminal offenders deserve the punishment they receive at the hands of the law and that punishments should be appropriate to the type and severity of the crime committed.

The old adages "he got what was coming to him" or "she got her due" well summarize the thinking behind the **just deserts model** of criminal sentencing. Just deserts, a concept inherent in the justice model, refers to the concept that criminal offenders deserve the punishment they receive at the hands of the law and that any punishment that is imposed should be appropriate to the type and severity of crime committed. The idea of just deserts has long been a part of Western thought, dating back at least to Old Testament times. Many have cited the Old Testament dictum of "an eye for an eye, and a tooth for a tooth" as divine justification for strict punishments. Some scholars believe, however, that in reality the notion of "an eye for an eye" was intended to reduce the barbarism of existing penalties whereby an aggrieved party might exact the severest of punishments for only minor offences. Even petty offences were often punished by whipping, torture, and sometimes death.

According to the neo-classical perspective, doing justice ultimately comes down to an official meting out of what is deserved. Justice for an individual is nothing more or less than what that individual deserves when all the circumstances surrounding that person's situation and behaviour are taken into account.

Deterrence

Deterrence the prevention of crime.

Specific deterrence a goal of criminal sentencing that seeks to prevent a particular offender from engaging in repeat criminality.

General deterrence a goal of criminal sentencing that seeks to prevent others from committing crimes similar to the one for which a particular offender is being sentenced.

True to its historical roots, **deterrence** is a hallmark of modern neo-classical thought. In contrast to early thinkers, however, today's neo-classical writers distinguish between deterrence that is specific and that which is general. **Specific deterrence** is a goal of criminal sentencing that seeks to prevent a particular offender from engaging in repeat criminality. **General deterrence**, in contrast, works by way of example and seeks to prevent others from committing crimes similar to the one for which a particular offender is being sentenced.

Following their classical counterparts, modern-day advocates of general deterrence frequently stress that for punishment to be an effective impediment to crime it must be swift, certain, and severe enough to outweigh the rewards flowing from criminal activity. Those who advocate punishment as a deterrent are often frustrated by the complexity of today's criminal justice system and the slow and circuitous manner in which cases are handled and punishments are meted out. Punishments today, even when imposed by a court, are rarely swift in their imposition. If they were, they would follow quickly after sentencing. The wheels of modern criminal justice, however, are relatively slow to grind to a conclusion, given the many delays inherent in judicial proceedings. Similarly, certainty of punishment is anything but a reality. Certain punishments are those that cannot be easily avoided. However, even when punishments are ordered, they are often not carried out—at least not fully.

The recommendation that determinant sentencing tactics be adopted in Canada is an attempt to address this concern.[43] Determinant sentencing is a strategy that mandates a specified and fixed amount of time to be served for every category of offence. Under determinant sentencing schemes, for example, judges might be required to impose a seven-year sentence on an offender convicted of armed robbery, but only a one-year sentence on those convicted robbers who use no weapon. Determinant sentencing schemes build upon the classical notion that a fixed amount of punishment necessary for deterrence can be calculated and specified. Proponents contend that determinant sentences may also reduce sentencing bias since disparity based on race or social status would be eliminated. Canadian judges have voiced the concern that determinant sentencing models limit the amount of discretion or personal judgment they can exercise when meting out a sentence. It is unlikely that these sentencing models will be fully adopted in Canada.

If the neo-classicists are correct, ideally, criminal punishments should prevent recidivism. **Recidivism** means, quite simply, the repetition of criminal behaviour by those already involved in crime. Recidivism can also be used to measure the success of a given approach to the problem of crime. When so employed, it is referred to as a **recidivism rate**, expressed as the percentage of convicted offenders who, during a designated period of time after release from a correctional facility, are rearrested for a new crime or a violation of the conditions of their release (known as a "technical violation").

Recidivism the repetition of criminal behaviour.

Recidivism rate the percentage of convicted offenders who have been released from prison and who are later rearrested for a new crime.

While the public perception is that recidivism rates in Canada are high, the reality is somewhat different. A study released by the Canadian federal government in 2003, which tracked released offenders for up to two years after their release into the community, found that reconviction rates for offenders released from federal institutions was 43 percent. Non-violent offences accounted for the majority of reconvictions. The violent reconviction rate was 13 percent while the sexual reconviction rate was very low at 0.7–1.7 percent. The study also indicated that more than half of the reconvictions occurred after the sentence was completed when the offender was no longer under supervision.[44]

The Death Penalty Notions of deterrence, retribution, and just deserts all come together in **capital punishment**. Given the many different philosophies of punishment represented by the death penalty, it is not surprising that so much disagreement exists as to the efficacy of death as a form of criminal sanction. While capital punishment has not been legal in Canada since 1976, there are some Canadians who would like to see its reinstatement. It is practised in many states in the US and other parts of the world, such as Japan, Russia, and China.

Capital punishment the legal imposition of a sentence of death upon a convicted offender. Another term for the death penalty.

The extent to which the death penalty acts as a general deterrent has been widely studied. Some researchers have compared murder rates between US states that have eliminated the death penalty and those that retain it, finding little variation in the rate at which murders are committed.[45] Others have looked at variations in murder rates over time in jurisdictions that have eliminated capital punishment, with similar results.[46] A now classic 1988 Texas study provided a comprehensive review of capital punishment by correlating homicide rates with the rate of executions within the state between 1930 and 1986.[47] The study, which was especially important because Texas has been quite active in the capital punishment arena, failed to find any support for the use of death as a deterrent. Opponents of capital punishment frequently cite such studies to claim that the death penalty is ineffective as a deterrent and should be abolished.

Other abolitionist rationales include claims that (1) the death penalty has, at times, been imposed on innocent people; (2) human life is sacred, and state-imposed death lowers society to the same moral (or amoral) level as the individual murderer; (3) the death penalty has been (and may still be) imposed in haphazard and discriminatory fashion; and (4) the death penalty is imposed disproportionately upon ethnic minorities.

Advocates of capital punishment generally discount each of these claims, countering with the notion that death is *deserved* by those who commit especially heinous acts, and that anything short of capital punishment under certain circumstances is an injustice in itself. Some people, the claim is made, deserve to die for what they have done. Such arguments evolve from a natural law perspective, and are based on the notion of just deserts as discussed earlier.

Public Humiliation The practice of "shaming," or public humiliation, is also a reflection of the notion that offenders must pay. Used widely in the US, convicted offenders can be ordered by the courts to participate in a number of humiliating activities. Examples include those such as the case of an offender ordered to wear a T-shirt in public advertising his crime. Another had to post a sign on his property announcing his offence. Still another was ordered to take out a newspaper ad detailing her crime.[48]

Some feel the merits of these sentences of public humiliation in deterring the offender from further crime are doubtful, since the result is more likely degradation than rehabilitation. Not all proponents of shaming see degradation as the sole outcome, however. Australian John Braithwaite and others advocate a policy of "reintegrative shaming," through which offenders begin to understand and recognize their misdeeds and shame themselves. The actual shaming must be brief and controlled and followed by forgiveness, apology, and repentance.[49] Some of the ideas found in this "restorative justice" approach are discussed in Chapter 9.

Policy Implications of the Classical School

Much of the practice of criminal justice in North America today is built around a conceptual basis provided by the classical school theorists. The social policy position of today's classical school heirs, however, is complex and anything but clear. On the one hand, that school of today's neo-classical thinkers known as **individual-rights advocates** emphasizes individual rights rather than punishment. Individual-rights advocates defend the prerogatives of individuals against potential government excesses inherent in the social contract. Citing correctional overcrowding and increased criminal activity in many areas of society, individual-rights advocates point out that an increasing emphasis on imprisonment has done little to reduce the amount of crime. They call for a renewed recognition of constitutional and personal rights in the face of criminal prosecution and for reduction in the use of imprisonment as a criminal sanction, suggesting that it be employed as a last resort to deal with only the most dangerous offenders. In Canada, the federal government's official stance toward crime and criminals remains tempered by this approach. In 1993, the Standing Committee on Justice and the solicitor general recommended a move away from the use of imprisonment. Instead, the committee proposed the development of a national crime-prevention strategy as an effective way of dealing with crime. As a result, much focus is placed on the use of crime-prevention programs such as the Community Justice Program, initiated under the auspices of the Royal Canadian Mounted Police.

Individual-rights advocates those who seek to protect personal freedoms in the face of criminal prosecution.

Multisystemic Therapy: A New Tactic on Teen Crime

 Box 5.2

Program Focuses on Family of Young Offenders

Can the behaviour of young offenders be changed if intervention comes early enough? Should this process involve strict discipline? Can more innovative programs, such as the one described here, be effective?

In 1997, a committed and energetic group of people in four Ontario communities embarked upon a process that brought a promising intervention for serious young offenders to Canada. Multisystemic Therapy (MST) is an intensive, home-based intervention program for serious young offenders. It had attracted attention in the United States where two randomized studies showed dramatic success in reducing arrests and incarceration.

Supported by Ontario's Ministry of Community and Social Services and the National Crime Prevention Centre, the MST project appeared to be a cost-efficient way of reducing youth crime. Reductions in offending would, in turn, reduce both losses to crime victims and costs associated with youth involvement in the criminal justice system.

MST works from the premise that intervention for youth is more effective within the family home setting. Services are delivered at those youth with the most serious criminal behaviour, are time-limited (one to three months), are flexibly scheduled to meet the family's needs, are delivered in the home, are tailored to the needs of family members (rather than simply the identified youth), are provided in the context of a family's values, beliefs, and culture, and are available 24 hours a day, seven days a week. MST therapists carry small caseloads of four to six families and usually make several visits each week to the family home for an average of 2 to 15 contact hours each week, more in the early weeks and fewer as the case nears closure.

The Ontario project established therapy teams in London, Mississauga, Simcoe County, and Ottawa. About 200 families received MST between 1997 and 2001. At the same time, about 200 families continued with the usual services available through the local youth justice and social service systems. These services most typically took the form of probation supervision with referral to specialized programs, in some cases.

The sample consisted of 409 youth. Seventy-four percent were males. The average age at referral was 14.6, including 27 Ottawa youth who were 10 or 11 years old. Thirteen percent self-identified as Aboriginal. The median family income was $20 000 to $30 000, although 36 percent of families had been supported by welfare in the previous year. Forty-seven percent of the families were lone-parent families.

About one-third (30 percent) of youth had no record of prior criminal convictions at referral although there had to be evidence of past criminal behaviour in order to qualify for MST. Almost one-third (30 percent) had previously served custody sentences, on an average of 47 days.

The key research question was: Will MST be more effective in reducing criminal behaviour in serious young offenders than are the services already available to them in Ontario? The project sought to provide answers to these questions:

1. Are recipients of MST less likely to be convicted of offences than youth who did not receive MST?
2. Do recipients of MST who offend do so after a longer period?

3. Are recipients of MST less likely to be sentenced to youth custody?

4. Do recipients of MST spend less time in custody?

5. Are recipients of MST reconvicted of fewer offences than youths who did not receive MST?

6. Are those who drop out of MST more likely to offend than program completers?

7. Do recipients of MST commit less serious offences?

8. Will the savings to the correctional system outweigh the cost of the MST intervention?

By 2002, 407 of the 409 youth had been tracked at least six months since the termination of treatment or, in the case of the control group, since six months after intake into the project. The majority (89 percent) had been tracked at least one year and 59 percent had been tracked for two years.

While the usual services group had marginally better outcomes on some variables (such as average number of days to first conviction, average number of days to first custody admission, average number of days of open custody sentence, and overall rate of conviction) and the MST group evidenced slightly better outcomes on other variables (such as average number of days in secure custody, average number of offences of conviction, average number of prosecutions, rate of sentencing to custody, average length of adult prison sentence, and rate of open custody sentences), findings to date indicate that there is no significant difference between the overall rates of non-reoffending between the MST group and the usual services group. Looking only at cases with custody sentences, the average cost for MST was $68 826. For the usual services, the average cost is $61 768.

Interim findings of the project have concluded that the usual services group had better outcomes on some variables and the MST group had better measures on others, but in no case did the differences reach the level of statistical significance. Final findings may come to a different conclusion but it is unlikely. As a result, at this time, project supervisors cannot recommend the adoption of Multisystemic Treatment in Canada.

DISCUSSION QUESTIONS

1. What do the interim findings about the effectiveness of the Multisystemic Therapy pilot project say about this approach to intervention with delinquent youth?

2. What type of approach do you think might be more effective? Why?

Sources: Alison Cunnningham, *One Step Forward. Lessons Learned from a Randomized Study of Multisystemic Therapy (MST) in Canada* (London: Centre for Children and Families in the Justice System, 2002); and A.W. Leschied and Alison Cunningham, *Seeking Effective Interventions for Serious Young Offenders: Interim Results of a Four-Year Randomized Study of Multisystemic Therapy in Ontario, Canada* (London: Centre for Children and Families in the Justice System, 2002).

Dangerousness the likelihood that a given individual will later harm society or others; it is often measured in terms of recidivism, or the likelihood of new crime commission or rearrest for a new crime.

Incapacitation the use of imprisonment or other means to reduce the likelihood that an offender will be capable of committing future offences.

Individual-rights advocates argue that **dangerousness**, or the likelihood that a given individual will later harm society or others, should be the major determining criterion for government action against the freedom of its citizens. Dangerousness, they suggest, should form the standard against which any need for incapacitation might be judged. **Incapacitation**, simply put, is the use of imprisonment or other means to reduce the likelihood that an offender will be capable of committing future offences.

Proponents of modern-day incapacitation often distinguish between selective incapacitation, in which crime is controlled via the imprisonment of specific individuals, and collective incapacitation, whereby changes in legislation and/or sentencing patterns lead to the removal from society of entire groups of individuals judged to be dangerous.

Advocates of selective incapacitation as a crime-prevention strategy point to studies showing that the majority of crimes are perpetrated by a small number of hardcore repeat offenders. The most famous of those studies was conducted by Marvin Wolfgang and focused on 9000 male individuals born in Philadelphia in 1945. By the time this cohort of men had reached age 18, Wolfgang was able to determine that 627 "chronic recidivists," or repeat offenders, were responsible for the large majority of all serious violent crimes committed by the group. More recent studies have similarly shown that a small hard core of criminal perpetrators is probably responsible for most criminal activity.[50]

Proponents of collective incapacitation advocate the reformation of sentencing policies to include, for example, mandatory minimum sentences. Such a practice dictates that a sentencing judge must impose a certain minimum penalty at the very least. In Canada, there are very few offences that carry a minimum sanction. Included among them are first- and second-degree murder, the use of a firearm during the commission of an offence, a second conviction for impaired driving, and bookmaking and placing bets on behalf of others (outside a legally sanctioned system).

Such thinking has led to the development of incapacitation as a modern-day treatment philosophy and to the creation of innovative forms of incapacitation that do not require imprisonment—such as home confinement, the use of halfway houses or career training centres for convicted felons, and psychological and/or chemical treatments designed to reduce the likelihood of future crime commissions. Similarly, such thinkers argue, the decriminalization of many offences and the enhancement of social programs designed to combat what they see as the root causes of crime—including poverty, low educational levels, a general lack of skills, and inherent or active discrimination—will lead to a much-reduced incidence of crime in the future, making high rates of imprisonment unnecessary.

The direction of the courts in Canada continues to be that incarceration be used only as a last resort in those cases where it is believed that no other course of action will protect the community. This message was very clearly reflected through the passage of the *Sentencing Reform Bill*, Bill C-41, into law in 1996. Among other amendments to the *Criminal Code of Canada*, this bill created a new disposition, the Conditional Sentence of Imprisonment. This provision (section 742 of the *Criminal Code of Canada*) allows the court to order that an offender sentenced to imprisonment serve her sentence in the community under supervision. The conditional sentence applies only to sentences of up to two years less a day and where there is no mandatory minimum sentence. Bill C-41 was specifically designed to reduce the number of admissions to custody. Official statistics indicate that there were about 32 000 adults incarcerated in 2003–2004 (134 per 100 000), a decrease of 13 percent from a decade earlier.[51] By comparison, the rate of conviction in the United States has increased by over 700 percent in the last 10 years. Currently, over 1 400 000 (600 per 100 000) adults are serving time in correctional facilities there.

Standing in sharp contrast to today's individual-rights advocates are those modern-day heirs of the classical school who see punishment as the central tenet of criminal justice policy and believe it to be a natural and deserved consequence of criminal activity. Such thinkers call for greater prison capacity and new prison construction. They argue that although punishment theoretically prevents crime, in today's society few criminals are ever effectively punished. These proponents of neo-classical theory, often called **law-and-order advocates**, frequently seek stiffer criminal laws and increased penalties for criminal activity. They insist on the importance of individual responsibility and claim that law violators should be held unfailingly responsible for their actions. Law-and-order advocates generally want to ensure that sentences imposed by criminal courts are the sentences served

Law-and-order advocates those who suggest that, under certain circumstances involving criminal threats to public safety, the interests of society should take precedence over individual rights.

by offenders, and they argue against reduced prison time for whatever reason. Many of today's neo-classical thinkers rally around the death penalty because they believe it is either justified as a natural consequence of specific forms of abhorrent behaviour or because they believe that it will deter others from committing similar crimes in the future. They answer critics who claim that evidence does not support a belief in capital punishment as a deterrent by pointing out that death is at least a specific deterrent, if not a general one.

Despite official government proclamations, it would appear that the advocates of law and order are gaining a foothold in today's political arena. Those who fear crime and call for "get-tough-on-crime" policies are often well received by many political constituencies.

Recent Canadian outcries against perceived increases in the amount of violent crime committed by youth have resulted in changes in the legislation used to deal with this group of offenders. The federal government's *Youth Criminal Justice Act* reduces the age of adult sentences from 16 to 14 for those young people convicted of serious crimes such as murder and sexual assault, and for repeat offenders. It also allows for the publication of the names of offenders who receive adult sentences. Despite these apparently "tougher" sanctions for violent youth, the Act also specifies that sentences should reflect the seriousness of the offence. See Chapter 11 for an in-depth look at this Act.

In May 2006, an Act was introduced to amend the conditional sentence of imprisonment provisions of the *Criminal Code* found in section 742. The new amendments would eliminate the conditional sentence as a sentencing option for over 100 offences including, for example, possession of stolen property over $500, uttering a forged document, and possession of drugs for the purpose of trafficking. While the exact impact of Bill C-9 is unknown, it is likely that that the effect will be an increase in the provincially and federally sentenced custody population.[52]

The "get-tough-on-crime" approach has led to the opening of young offender boot camps in some provinces. What are some alternatives to boot camps? *CP/Doug Crawford/Barrie Examiner.*

Other policies that clearly reflect the neo-classical approach of just deserts include the suspension of various inmate privileges in correctional institutions, such as limiting access to television, video players, sports activities, weight rooms, and smoking. As well, pressure is being placed on the federal government to mandate the use of consecutive sentences for those convicted of more than one murder or violent sexual offence. Under such sentencing reform, an offender found guilty of two murders, for example, would be required to serve two life sentences—one after the other rather than at the same time, or concurrently, which is now the practice.

The reality in the United States indicates that advocates of law and order currently have the upper hand. In 1994, the US Congress passed the *Violent Crime Control and Law Enforcement Act*, one of the most far-reaching get-tough-on-crime measures ever seen. The law contains the "three-strikes-and-you're-out" provision that provides for mandatory life sentences after a third felony conviction. It also allocates billions of dollars for new prison construction and mandates long prison sentences for violent offenders and for those who use guns during the commission of crimes. The new law also bans many types of semi-automatic assault weapons and authorizes the hiring of thousands of additional police officers across the country. Typical of the current nationwide resurgence of interest in the death penalty, it expands the federal death penalty to nearly 60 offences.

Critique of Classical Theories

Classical and neo-classical thought represents more a philosophy of justice than it does a theory of crime causation. As some writers have observed, however, "[t]he true test of Beccaria's essay can be judged by the influence it has had over time on our justice system."[53] The influence of Beccaria, the Enlightenment, and classical thinkers remains today in the *Canadian Charter of Rights and Freedoms*, in the get-tough approaches to crime, and in the emphasis on individual rights. The classical school "has left behind a legacy that we see in almost every aspect of our present-day justice system."[54]

Critics charge, however, that the classical school lacks explanatory power over criminal motivation, other than to advance the simple claim that crime is the result of free will and individual choice. Such critics point out that classical theory is bereft of meaningful explanations as to how a choice for or against criminal activity is made. Similarly, classical theory lacks any appreciation for the deeper aspects of personal motivation, including those represented by human biology, psychology, and the social environment. Moreover, the classical school, as originally detailed in the writings of Beccaria and Bentham, lacked any scientific basis for the claims it made. Although neo-classical writers have advanced the scientific foundation of classical claims (through studies such as those showing the effectiveness of particular forms of deterrence), many still defend their way of thinking by reference to philosophical ideals, such as just deserts.

In a world grown accustomed to measuring the success of an idea in terms of its measurable consequences, neo-classical theorists are hard put to defend their philosophies. Citing the fact that boot-camp prisons, for example, have not measured up to the claims of reduced recidivism touted by get-tough neo-classical politicians, some writers have called for a return to programs already shown to work. As a critic of increased funding for boot camps recently stated, "If helping non-violent first offenders get their lives and values together is the goal, then the [funding] for boot camps needs to be redirected to such proven programs as drug counselling, alternative sentences, work furloughs, literacy courses, and well-supervised probation."[55]

Assessing Dangerousness

Dangerousness is a difficult concept to comprehend. Indicators of dangerousness have yet to be well defined in the social scientific literature, and legislators who attempt to codify any assessment of future dangerousness often find themselves frustrated. On the individual level, however, dangerousness might be more easily assessed. What follows is a description of the criteria one judge, Lois G. Forer, used in deciding whether an offender needed to spend a long time away from society:

> I had my own criteria or guidelines—very different from those established by most states and the federal government—for deciding on a punishment. My primary concern was public safety. The most important question I asked myself was whether the offender could be deterred from committing other crimes. No one can predict with certainty who will or will not commit a crime, but there are indicators most sensible people recognize as danger signals:

- First, was this an irrational crime? If an arsonist sets a fire to collect insurance, that is a crime but also a rational act. Such a person can be deterred by being made to pay for the harm done and the costs to the fire department. However, if the arsonist sets fires just because he likes to see them, it is highly unlikely that he can be stopped from setting others, no matter how high the fine. Imprisonment is advisable even though it may be a first offence.
- Second, was there wanton cruelty? If a robber maims or slashes the victim, there is little likelihood that he can safely be left in the community. If a robber simply displays a gun but does not fire it or harm the victim, then one should consider his life history, provocation, and other circumstances in deciding whether probation is appropriate.
- Third, is this a hostile person? Was his crime one of hatred, and does he show any genuine remorse? Most rapes are acts of hostility, and the vast majority of rapists have a record of numerous sexual assaults. I remember one man who raped his mother. I gave him the maximum sentence under the law—20 years—but with good behaviour, he got out fairly quickly. He immediately raped another elderly woman.
- Fourth, is this a person who knows he is doing wrong but cannot control himself? Typical of such offenders are pedophiles. One child abuser who appeared before me had already been convicted of abusing his first wife's child. I got him on the second wife's child and sentenced him to the maximum. Still, he'll get out with good behaviour, and I shudder to think about the children around him when he does. This is one case in which justice is not tough enough.

> By contrast, some people who have committed homicide present very little danger of further violence—although many more do. Once a young man came before me because he had taken aim at a person half a block away and then shot him in the back, killing him. Why did he do it? "I wanted to get me a body." He should never get out.

DISCUSSION QUESTIONS

1. How are public safety and criminal punishment related?
2. Do you agree that the criteria used by Judge Forer to identify dangerousness are useful? Why or why not?
3. Do you believe that offenders who are identified as "dangerous" should be treated differently from other offenders? If so, how?

Source: Lois G. Forer, "Justice by the Numbers; Mandatory Sentencing Drove Me from the Bench," *The Washington Monthly*, April 1992, pp. 12–18. Reprinted with permission from *The Washington Monthly*. Copyright by The Washington Monthly Company, 1611 Connecticut Ave., N.W., Washington, D.C. 20009 (202) 462-0128.

Summary

The Enlightenment, a social and cultural renaissance that occurred throughout the late 17th and early 18th centuries, proved to be a highly liberating force in the Western world. Enlightenment thinkers established many of the democratic principles that formed the conceptual foundations of Canadian society. Their ideas are still alive today, and significantly shape our understanding of human nature and behaviour. The twin conceptual prongs around which this textbook is built—social responsibility and individual rights—both have their roots in Enlightenment thought and the belief in free will it engendered. Notions of deterrence as a goal of justice-system intervention, and of punishment as a worthy consequence of crime, owe much of their contemporary influence to the classical school of criminology. Although we live in the 21st century, we carry with us an intellectual heritage far older than we may realize.

Discussion Questions

1. This book emphasizes a social problems versus social responsibility theme. Which perspective is most supported by classical and neo-classical thought? Why?
2. Name the various pre-classical thinkers identified by this chapter. What ideas did each contribute to Enlightenment philosophy? What form did those ideas take in classical criminological thought?
3. Define *natural law*. Do you believe that natural law exists? If so, what types of behaviour would be contravened by natural law? If they would not be, why not?
4. What were the central concepts that defined the classical school of criminological thought? Which of those concepts are still alive? Where do you see evidence for the survival of those concepts?
5. What are the major differences between individual-rights advocates and law-and-order advocates? Which perspective appeals to you? Why?
6. Define recidivism. What is a recidivism rate?

Weblinks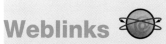

www.crimetheory.com
University of Washington. Good, condensed overview of the predominant criminological theories.

www.ccla.org
Canadian Civil Liberties Association. The CCLA is a lobbying and law reform, non-profit organization dealing with issues of Canadians' fundamental human rights. Good discussions on controversial criminal justice issues provide an individual-rights perspective.

www.lfcc.on.ca
Centre for Children and Families in the Justice System of the London Family Court Clinic. This site provides an excellent overview of MultiSystemic Therapy.

www.geographicprofiling.com
Environmental Criminology Research Inc. Based in Vancouver, B.C., this company develops and supplies software for geographic profiling and serial crime analysis. Good overview of the Rigel system.

CHAPTER 6

Biological Roots of Criminal Behaviour

The evidence is very firm that there is a genetic factor involved in crime.

—SARNOFF A. MEDNICK[1]

Social programs aim to eradicate educational, social, and economic inequities. These efforts can only be undermined by statements stressing the importance of genetic factors in determining criminality.

—JULIAN V. ROBERTS, THOMAS GABOR[2]

LEARNING OUTCOMES

After reading this chapter, you should be able to

- recognize the importance of biological explanations of criminal behaviour

- consider the relationship between human aggression and biological determinants

- be aware of the research linking genetics and crime

- recognize the contribution of sociobiology to the study of criminality

- identify modern-day social policy that reflects the biological approach to crime causation

- assess the shortcomings of the biological theories of criminal behaviour

Ian Turner, Spooner, Liason Agency, Inc.

IMPORTANT NAMES

C. Ray Jeffery	Charles Buckman Goring	Henry H. Goddard
Konrad Lorenz	Earnest A. Hooton	Edward O. Wilson
Charles Darwin	Ernst Kretschmer	James Q. Wilson
Franz Joseph Gall	William H. Sheldon	Richard J. Herrnstein
Johann Gaspar Spurzheim	Richard L. Dugdale	
Cesare Lombroso	Arthur H. Estabrook	

IMPORTANT TERMS

biological theories	somatotyping	testosterone
criminal anthropology	cycloid	Juke family
phrenology	schizoid	Kallikak family
atavism	displastics	eugenics
positivism	endomorph	supermale
criminaloids	mesomorph	monozygotic (MZ) twins
born criminals	ectomorph	sociobiology
constitutional theories	hypoglycemia	paradigm

Introduction

At a recent annual meeting of the American Neurological Association, two neuroscience researchers from the University of Virginia Medical School reported on the case of a man with no history of pedophilia who began molesting children after developing an egg-sized brain tumour.[3] According to the neuroscientists, Russell Swerdlow and Jeffrey Burns, friends of the man told investigators that the 40-year-old married teacher had never previously exhibited abnormal impulses but suddenly started visiting prostitutes, making sexual advances toward children, and spending time on websites selling child pornography. Soon, they reported, his wife left him and he was arrested and convicted on child molestation charges. Although he entered a treatment program for pedophiles, he propositioned women at the facility and was expelled from treatment. About the same time, he began having headaches and went to a hospital emergency room where he reported experiencing strong sexual urges and said that he feared he would rape his landlady. Attending neurologists noticed other symptoms indicative of neurological problems, such as poor balance and the inability to copy simple drawings. An MRI scan conducted at the hospital showed that the man had a large tumour in the right frontal cortex of his brain. The tumour was removed and the man's abnormal urges disappeared. Later, however, they reoccurred, and another scan showed that the tumour had returned. Once again it was removed, and the man's behaviour returned to normal. Swerdlow and Burns reported that the tumour was located in the part of the brain associated with social judgments and self-control, and they speculated that it was the cause of the man's pedophiliac urges. "We're dealing with the neurology of morality here," said Swerdlow.

Can a brain tumour cause crime? We may never be sure; however, many biological theories have been advanced to explain criminality. Abnormalities of the brain, genetic predispositions, vitamin deficiencies, an excess of hormones such as testosterone, hypoglycemia (low blood sugar), fetal alcohol spectrum disorder, a relative lack of neurotransmitters such as serotonin in the brain, and blood abnormalities are among the many current biological explanations of crime.

The field of criminology has been cautious about giving credence to biological theories of human behaviour. One reason for this, as noted in Chapter 1, is that criminology's academic roots are firmly grounded in the social sciences. As the well-known biocriminologist **C. Ray Jeffery**, commenting on the historical development of the field, observes,

> [t]he term criminology was given to a social science approach to crime as developed in sociology. . . . Sutherland's (1924) text Criminology was pure sociology without any biology or psychology; beginning with publication of that text, criminology was offered in sociology departments as a part of sociology separate from biology, psychology, psychiatry, and law. . . . Many of the academicians who call themselves criminologists are sociologists.[4]

As recently as 1992, a National Institutes of Health–sponsored conference in the United States that was intended to focus on the biological roots of crime was cancelled after critics charged that the meeting would, by virtue of its biological focus, be racist and might intentionally exclude sociological perspectives on the subject.[5] Those opposed to the conference argued that "[t]he primary problems that afflict human beings are not due to their bodies or brains, they are due to the environment. Redefining social problems as public health problems is exactly what was done in Nazi Germany."[6] Three years later, when the conference was finally held at a site selected to discourage demonstrations, C. Ray Jeffery pointed out that "[w]hen ideology replaces rational thought there is little hope for a better understanding of human problems."[7]

Society tends to shy away from biological explanations for criminality and disordered behaviour because of concern with concepts such as "genetic determinism" which have come to be seen as synonymous with inevitability, since the physical makeup of a person is hard to change. Open inquiry, as C. Ray Jeffery notes, requires objective consideration of all points of view, and an unbiased examination of each for its ability to shed light upon the subject under study. Hence, for an adequate consideration of biological theories as they may relate to crime and crime causation, we need to turn to literature outside of the sociological and psychological mainstream.

Major Principles of Biological Theories

Biological theories (of criminology) maintain that the basic determinants of human behaviour, including criminality, are constitutionally or physiologically based and often inherited.

This brief section serves to summarize the central features of **biological theories** of crime causation. Each of these points can be found elsewhere in this chapter, where they are discussed in more detail. This cursory overview, however, is intended to provide more than a summary; it is meant to be a guide to the rest of this chapter.

Biological theories of crime causation make certain fundamental assumptions. These include the following:

- The brain is the organ of the mind and the locus of personality. In the words of the biocriminologist C. Ray Jeffery, "The brain is the organ of behavior; no theory of behavior can ignore neurology and neurochemistry."[8]
- The basic determinants of human behaviour, including criminal tendencies, are, to a considerable degree, constitutionally or genetically based.

- Observed gender and racial differences in rates and types of criminality may be at least partially the result of biological differences between the sexes and/or between racially distinct groups.
- The basic determinants of human behaviour, including criminality, may be passed on from generation to generation. In other words, a penchant for crime may be inherited.

Theory in Perspective
Types of Biological Theories

BIOLOGICAL THEORIES

Adhere to the principle that the basic determinants of human behaviour, including criminality, are constitutionally or physiologically based and inherited.

Early Positivism. These biological approaches built upon evolutionary principles and were the first to apply scientific techniques to the study of crime and criminals. Early positivistic theories saw criminals as throwbacks to earlier evolutionary epochs.
Period: 1880s–1930
Theorists: Franz Joseph Gall, Johann Gaspar Spurzheim, Cesare Lombroso, Charles Goring, and Earnest A. Hooton
Concepts: Phrenology, atavism, born criminals, criminaloids

Constitutional Theories. These biological theories explain criminality by reference to offenders' body types, inheritance, genetics, and/or external observable physical characteristics.
Period: Modern constitutional theories, 1960s–present; Classical constitutional theories, 1930s–1940s
Theorists: Ernst Kretschmer, William H. Sheldon, Richard L. Dugdale, Arthur H. Estabrook, Henry H. Goddard
Concepts: Somatotyping, mesomorph, ectomorph, endomorph, XYY supermale, twin studies

Body Chemistry. These biological theories utilize chemical influences, including hormones, food additives, allergies, vitamins, and other chemical substances to explain criminal behaviour.
Period: 1940s–present
Theorists: Various
Concepts: Hypoglycemia, vitamins, food allergies, serotonin, PMS, MAOA

Sociobiology. This theoretical perspective developed by Edward O. Wilson includes "the systematic study of the biological basis of all social behavior," which is "a branch of evolutionary biology and particularly of modern population biology."
Period: 1975–present
Theorists: Edward O. Wilson
Concepts: Altruism, tribalism, survival of the gene pool

- Much of human conduct is fundamentally rooted in instinctive behavioural responses characteristic of biological organisms everywhere. Territoriality and acquisitiveness are but two examples of behaviour that may be instinctual to human beings.
- The biological roots of human conduct have become increasingly disguised, as modern symbolic forms of indirect expressive behaviour have replaced more primitive and direct ones.
- At least some human behaviour is the result of biological propensities inherited from more primitive developmental stages in the evolutionary process. In other words, some human beings may be further along the evolutionary ladder than others, and their behaviour may reflect that fact.
- The interplay between heredity, biology, and the social environment provides the nexus for any realistic consideration of crime causation.

Biological Roots of Human Aggression

In 1966, **Konrad Lorenz** published his now famous work *On Aggression*.[9] It was an English-language translation of a 1963 book entitled *Das Sogenannte Bose: Zur Naturgeschichte der Aggression* (*The Nature of Aggression*) which had originally appeared in German. In his writing, Lorenz described how aggression permeates the animal kingdom and asked, "What is the value of all this fighting?" "In nature," he said, "fighting is such an ever-present process, its behavior mechanisms and weapons are so highly developed and have so obviously arisen under the . . . pressure of a species-preserving function, that it is our duty to ask this . . . question."[10]

Lorenz accepted the evolutionary thesis of the 19th-century biologist **Charles Darwin** that intraspecies aggression favoured the strongest and best animals in the reproductive process, but he concluded that aggression served a variety of other purposes as well.

Charles Darwin (1809–1882), founder of modern evolutionary theory.
Julia Cameron/© Bettman/Corbis.

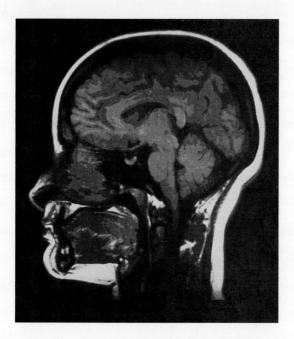

The brain is indeed "the organ of the mind"
as modern researchers are continuing to
discover. Here, a computer-enhanced
image shows areas of activity within the
brain. Do you think biology may play a role
in crime?

Scott Camazsine/Photo Researchers, Inc.

Aggression, said Lorenz, ensures an "even distribution of animals of a particular species over an inhabitable area ..."[11] and provides for a defence of the species from predators. Human aggression, he claimed, meets many of the same purposes but can take on covert forms. The drive to acquire wealth and power, for example, that was so characteristic of Western men at the time of his writing, was described by Lorenz as part of the human mating ritual, whereby a man might "win" a prized woman through displays of more civilized forms of what could otherwise be understood as intraspecies aggression.

In today's enlightened times, such observations may seem to many like mere foolishness. Lorenz's greatest contribution to the study of human behaviour, however, may have been his claim that all human behaviour is, at least to some degree, "adapted instinctive behavior." In other words, much of human conduct, according to Lorenz, is fundamentally rooted in instinctive behavioural responses characteristic of biological organisms everywhere and present within each of us in the form of a biological inheritance from more primitive times. Even rational human thought, claimed Lorenz, derives its motivation and direction from instinctual aspects of human biology. The highest human virtues, such as the value placed on human life, "could not have been achieved without an instinctive appreciation of life and death."[12]

Building upon the root functions of aggression, Lorenz concluded that much of what we today call "crime" is the result of overcrowded living conditions, such as those experienced by city dwellers, combined with a lack of legitimate opportunity for the effective expression of aggression. Crowding, from this perspective, increases the likelihood of aggression, while contemporary socialization simultaneously works to inhibit it. In the words of Lorenz, "... in one sense we are all psychopaths, for each of us suffers from the necessity of self-imposed control for the good of the community."[13] When people break down, argued Lorenz, they become neurotic or delinquent; crime may be the result of stresses that have been found to typically produce aggression throughout the animal kingdom.

At first blush, Lorenz's explanations, like many of the biologically based theories we will encounter in this chapter, appear more applicable to violent crime than to other forms of criminal offence. However, it is important to recognize that modern frustrations and concomitant manifestations of aggression may be symbolically, rather than directly, expressed. Hence, the stockbroker who embezzles a client's money, spurred on by the need to provide material goods for an overly acquisitive family, may be just as criminal as the robber who beats his victim and steals her purse to have money to buy liquor.

Early Biological Theories

Criminal anthropology
the scientific study of
the relationship between
human physical
characteristics and
criminality.

Phrenology the study of
the shape of the head to
determine anatomical
correlates of human
behaviour.

Numerous perspectives on criminal biology predate Lorenz's work. Some of the perspectives fall into the category of criminal anthropology. **Criminal anthropology** is the scientific study of the relationship between human physical characteristics and criminality. One of the earliest criminological anthropologists was **Franz Joseph Gall** (1758–1828). Gall hypothesized in his theory of **phrenology** (also called *craniology*) that the shape of the human skull was indicative of the personality and could be used to predict criminality. Gall's approach contained four themes:

- The brain is the organ of the mind.
- Particular aspects of personality are associated with specific locations in the brain.
- Portions of the brain that are well developed will cause personality characteristics associated with them to be more prominent in the individual under study, whereas poorly developed brain areas lead to a lack of associated personality characteristics.
- The shape of a person's skull corresponds to the shape of the underlying brain and is therefore indicative of the personality.

Gall was one of the first Western writers to firmly locate the roots of personality in the brain. Prior to his time, it was thought that aspects of personality resided in various organs throughout the body—a fact reflected in linguistic anachronisms surviving into the present day (as, for example, when someone is described as being "hard-hearted," as having "a lot of gall," or as thinking with some organ other than the brain). The Greek philosopher Aristotle was said to believe that the brain served no function other than to radiate excess heat from the body. Hence, Gall's perspective, although relatively primitive by today's standards, did much to advance physiological understandings of the mind–body connection in Western thought.

Although Gall never tested his theory, it was widely accepted by many of his contemporaries because it represented something of a shift away from theological perspectives prevalent at the time and a move toward scientific understanding—a trend that was well underway by the time of his writings. Phrenology also provided for systematic evaluation of suspected offenders and was intriguing for its ease of use. One of Gall's students, **Johann Gaspar Spurzheim** (1776–1853), brought phrenological theory to North America and, through a series of lectures and publications on the subject, helped to spread its influence. Phrenology's prestige in North America extended into the 20th century, finding a place in classification schemes used to evaluate newly admitted prisoners. Even Arthur Conan Doyle's fictional character Sherlock Holmes was described as using phrenology to solve a number of crimes.

The Positivist School

One of the best known, early scientific biological theorists—19th-century Italian physician **Cesare Lombroso** (1836–1909)—coined the term *atavism* to suggest that criminality was the result of primitive urges which, in modern-day human throwbacks, survived the evolutionary process. He described "the nature of the criminal" as "an atavistic being who reproduces in his person the ferocious instincts of primitive humanity and the inferior animals."[14]

At roughly this time, Charles Darwin was making a substantial impact on the scientific world with his theory of biological evolution. Darwin proposed that human beings and other contemporary living organisms were the end products of a long evolutionary process governed by rules such as natural selection, survival of the fittest, and so on. Lombroso adapted elements of Darwin's theory to suggest that primitive traits survived in present-day human populations and led to heightened criminal tendencies among individuals who harboured them. Darwin himself had proposed this idea when he wrote, "[w]ith mankind some of the worst dispositions, which occasionally without any assignable cause make their appearance in families, may perhaps be reversions to a savage state, from which we are not removed by very many generations."[15]

The atavistic individual, said Lombroso in his now classic work *L'Uomo delinquente* (1876), was essentially a throwback to a more primitive biological state. According to Lombroso, such an individual, by virtue of possessing a relatively undeveloped brain, is incapable of conforming his behaviour to the rules and expectations of modern complex society. Lombroso has been called the father of modern criminology because he was the first criminologist of note to employ the scientific method—particularly measurement, observation, and attempts at generalization—in his work. Other writers, more specific in their pronouncements, have referred to him as the "father of the Italian School" of criminology, in recognition of the fact that 19th-century positivism began in Italy.

Positivism, as mentioned in Chapter 5, built upon two principles: (1) an unflagging acceptance of social determinism, or the belief that human behaviour is determined not by the exercise of free choice but by causative factors beyond the control of the individual, and (2) application of scientific techniques to the study of crime and criminology. The term *positivism* had its roots in the writings of Auguste Comte (1798–1857), who proposed use of the scientific method in the study of society in his 1851 work *A System of Positive Polity*.[16] Comte believed that a new "positive age" was dawning during which both society and human nature would be perfected, and his writings were an attempt to bring that age to fruition. Positivism holds that social phenomena are observable, explainable, and measurable in quantitative terms. For a strict positivist, reality consists of a world of objectively defined facts, which can be scientifically measured and—ultimately—controlled.[17]

Lombroso's scientific work consisted of postmortem studies of the bodies of executed and deceased offenders, which he conducted with assistants, measuring the bodies in many different ways. The body of one such well-known criminal, named Vilella, provided Lombroso with many of his findings and reinforced his belief that most offenders were genetically predisposed toward criminality. When he examined Vilella's brain, Lombroso found an unusual depression, which he named "the median occipital fossa." Lombroso identified features of Vilella's brain as being similar to those found in lower primates. Study of another offender, an Italian soldier whom Lombroso calls "Misdea" in his writings and who "attacked and killed eight of his superior officers and comrades," supported his conclusions.[18]

In addition to his examinations of Vilella and Misdea, Lombroso conducted autopsies on another 65 executed offenders and examined 832 living prison inmates, comparing

Atavism a concept used by Cesare Lombroso to suggest that criminals are physiological throwbacks to earlier stages of human evolution. The term is derived from the Latin term *atavus*, which means "ancestor."

Positivism the application of scientific techniques to the study of crime and criminals.

physical measurements of their body parts with measurements taken from 390 soldiers. As a result of his work, Lombroso claimed to have found a wide variety of bodily features predictive of criminal behaviour.

Among them were exceptionally long arms, an index finger as long as the middle finger, fleshy pouches in the cheeks "like those in rodents," eyes that were either abnormally close together or too far apart, large teeth, ears that lack lobes, prominent cheekbones, a crooked nose, a large amount of body hair, protruding chin, large lips, a non-standard number of ribs, and eyes of differing colours or hues. Lombroso went so far as to enumerate characteristics of particular types of offenders. Murderers, whom he called "habitual homicides," have, in Lombroso's words, "cold, glassy eyes, immobile and sometimes sanguine and inflamed; the nose, always large, is frequently aquiline or, rather, hooked; the jaws are strong, the cheekbones large, the hair curly, dark, and abundant; the beard is frequently thin, the canine teeth well developed and the lips delicate...."[19]

Atavism implies the notion that criminals are born that way. Lombroso was continuously reassessing his estimates of the proportion, from among all offenders, of the born criminal population. At one point, he asserted that fully 90 percent of offenders committed crimes because of atavistic influences. He later revised the figure downward to 70 percent, admitting that normal individuals might be pulled into lives of crime. In addition to the category of the born criminal, Lombroso described other categories of offenders, including the insane, criminaloids, and criminals incited by passion. The insane were said to include mental and moral degenerates, alcoholics, drug addicts, and so forth. **Criminaloids**, also termed occasional criminals, were described as persons who were pulled into breaking the law by virtue of environmental influences. Nevertheless, most criminaloids were seen by Lombroso as exhibiting some degree of atavism and hence were said to "differ from **born criminals** in degree, not in kind." Those who became criminals by virtue of passion were said to have surrendered to intense emotions, including love, jealousy, hatred, or an injured sense of honour.

Although he focused on physical features, Lombroso was not insensitive to behavioural indicators of criminality. In his later writings, he claimed that criminals exhibited acute sight, hearing abilities that were below the norm, an insensitivity to pain, a lack of moral sensibility, cruelty, vindictiveness, impulsiveness, a love of gambling, and a tendency to be tattooed.

In 1893, Lombroso published *The Female Offender*.[20] In that book, he expressed his belief that women exhibit far less anatomical variation than do men but insisted that criminal behaviour among women, as among men, derived from atavistic foundations. Lombroso saw the quintessential female offender, the prostitute, as "the genuine typical representative of criminality ..."[21] Prostitutes, he said, are acting out atavistic yearnings and returning to a form of behaviour characteristic of humankind's primitive past.

Evaluations of Atavism

Around the turn of the 20th century, the English physician **Charles Buckman Goring** (1870–1919), following in Lombroso's positivistic footsteps, conducted a well-controlled statistical study of Lombroso's thesis of atavism. Using newly developed but advanced mathematical techniques to measure the degree of correlation between physiological features and criminal history, Goring examined nearly 3000 inmates at Turin prison, beginning in 1901. He enlisted the aid of London's Biometric Laboratory to conclude that "the whole fabric of Lombrosian doctrine, judged by the standards of science, is fundamentally unsound."[22] Goring compared the prisoners with students at Oxford and Cambridge universities, British soldiers, and non-criminal hospital

Criminaloids a term used by Cesare Lombroso to describe occasional criminals who were pulled into criminality primarily by environmental influences.

Born criminals individuals who are born with a genetic predilection toward criminality.

patients, and published his findings in 1913 in his lengthy treatise *The English Convict: A Statistical Study.*[23] The foreword to Goring's book was written by Karl Pearson, who praised Goring for having no particular perspective of his own to advance and who could, he said, therefore objectively evaluate the ideas of others such as Lombroso.

Earnest A. Hooton, a professor of anthropology at Harvard University, conducted a similar study between 1927 and 1939. In 1939, Hooton published *Crime and the Man*, in which he reported having evaluated 13 873 inmates from 10 states, comparing them along 107 physiological dimensions with 3203 non-incarcerated individuals who formed a control group.[24] His sample consisted of 10 953 prison inmates, 2004 county jail prisoners, 743 criminally insane, 173 "defective delinquents," 1227 "insane civilians," and 1976 "sane civilians."

Hooton distinguished between regions of the country, arguing that "states have favorite crimes, just as they have favorite sons." He reported finding physiological features characteristic of specific criminal types in individual states. For example, "Massachusetts criminals," he said,

> *are notable for thick beards, red-brown hair, dark brown, green-brown and blue-gray eyes, whites of eyes discolored with yellow or brown pigment flecks, rayed pattern of the iris of the eye, external and median folds of the upper eyelids, broad, high nasal roots and bridges, concave nasal profiles, thick nasal tips, right deflections of the nasal septum, thin integumental lips, thin upper membranous lip and thick lower lip, absence of lip seam, some . . . protrusion of the jaws, pointed or median chins, much dental decay but few teeth lost, small and soldered or attached ear lobes, and right facial asymmetries.*[25]

He went on to say that, through a sufficient degree of statistical manipulation,

> *[w]e finally emerge with differences between the offense groups which are not due to accidents of sampling, are not due to state variations, and are independent of differences between the ages of the offense groups. Thus, in the case of first-degree murder we find the members of that offense group deficient in persons with abundant head hair, deficient in individuals with narrow nasal bridges, presenting an excess of persons with pointed or median chins, and with compressed cheek bones.*[26]

He also found that first-degree murderers were more "square-shouldered" than other criminals and had larger ear lobes. From findings such as these, he was drawn to the conclusion that "crime is not an exclusively sociological phenomenon, but is also biological."[27]

In writing that "It is impossible to improve and correct environment to a point at which these flawed and degenerate human beings will be able to succeed in honest social competition," Hooton made it clear that he did not believe that rehabilitation programs could have much effect upon most offenders and suggested banishing them to a remote location.[28] Hooton concluded that criminals showed an overall physiological inferiority to the general population, and that crime was the result of "the impact of environment upon low grade human organisms."[29]

Hooton, an example of whose work is provided in Figure 6.1, was quickly criticized along a number of dimensions. Stephen Schafer, a contemporary criminologist, says

> *[t]he major criticisms were that his criminal population was not a representative sample of all criminals, that his control group was a fantastic conglomeration of non-criminal civilians, . . . that he emphasized selected characteristics and disregarded*

Figure 6.1

Old American Criminals

Mosaic of Cranial, Facial, Metric, and Morphological Features
MASSACHUSETTS

Narrowest face
Narrowest jaw
Thick beards
Broad, high nasal roots and bridges
Thick nasal tips
Right deflections of nasal septum
Concave profiles ①
External and median eyefolds ②
Small, attached ear lobes ③
Thin integumental lips ④
Membranous lips—upper thin, lower thick
Lip seams absent
Undershot jaw
Facial prognathism ⑤
Right facial asymmetry ⑥
Median chins

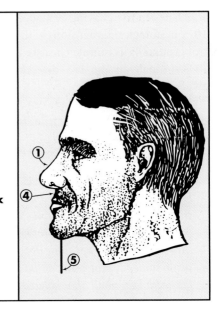

Source: Earnest A. Hooton's "Massachusetts Criminal." Reprinted by permission of the publishers from *Crime and the Man* by Earnest Albert Hooton, Cambridge, Mass: Harvard University Press. Copyright © 1939 by the President and Fellows of Harvard College, renewed 1967 by Mary C. Hooton.

others, that he gave no convincing evidence that the criminal's "inferiority" was inherited, and that he failed to explore other important data that were available.[30]

Perhaps even more significant, Hooton failed to recognize that members of his non-criminal control group may, in fact, have been involved in crime but had managed to elude capture and processing by the criminal justice system. In other words, it may have been that the most successful criminals did not appear in Hooton's study group of inmates because they had eluded the law, thereby making their way into his supposedly non-criminal control group. His study may have simply demonstrated that "inferior" criminal specimens are the ones who get caught and end up in prison.

Nonetheless, claims that physical abnormalities may be linked to crime persist into the present day. In a study of 170 teenage boys reported in 2000, for example, Canadian researchers L. Arseneault and Richard E. Tremblay conducted hormonal, anthropometric, psychophysiological, neuropsychological, and psychiatric evaluations of 1037 boys who had attended kindergarten in 1984 in a socially and economically disadvantaged area of Montreal.[31] Using evaluations provided years later by parents, teachers, classmates, and the children themselves, Arseneault and Tremblay concluded that subtle physical abnormalities, including minor abnormalities in the shape of the ears, tongue, and teeth, were associated with an increased risk of behavioural and psychiatric problems. The researchers suggested that such minor physical abnormalities might have resulted from genetic problems or prenatal insults associated with exposure to toxins. They concluded that "both the total count of minor physical anomalies and the total count of minor physical anomalies of the mouth were significantly associated with an increased risk of violent delinquency in adolescence, beyond the effects of childhood physical aggression and family adversity." Arseneault and Tremblay recognized, however, that abnormalities of the type they identified might be associated with neurological deficits and that abnormalities of the mouth could lead to feeding problems in the first months after birth, which might somehow cause problems in development or socialization.

Body Types

Constitutional theories are those that explain criminality by reference to offenders' body types, genetics, and/or external observable physical characteristics. A constitutional or physiological orientation that found its way into the criminological mainstream during the early and mid-20th century was that of body types. Also called **somatotyping**, this perspective was primarily associated with the work of **Ernst Kretschmer** and **William H. Sheldon**. Kretschmer, a professor of psychiatry at the German University of Tubingen, proposed a relationship between body build and personality type and created a rather detailed "biopsychological constitutional typology." Kretschmer's somatotypology revolved around three basic mental categories: cycloids (also called cyclothymes), schizoids (or schizothymes), and displastics. The **cycloid** personality, which was associated with a heavyset, soft type of body according to Kretschmer, vacillated between normality and abnormality. Cycloids were said to lack spontaneity and sophistication, and were thought to commit mostly non-violent property types of offences. The **schizoid**, who tended to possess an athletic, muscular body but, according to Kretschmer, could also be thin and lean, was seen as more likely to be schizophrenic and to commit violent types of offences. **Displastics** were said to be a mixed group described as highly emotional and often unable to control themselves. Hence, they were thought to commit mostly sexual offences and other crimes of passion.

Influenced by Kretschmer, William H. Sheldon utilized measurement techniques to connect body type with personality.[32] Sheldon felt that Kretschmer had erred in including too large an age range in his work. Therefore, he chose to limit his study to 200 boys between the ages of 15 and 21 at the Hayden Goodwill Institute in Boston. Sheldon concluded that four basic body types characterized the entire group. Each type, described partly in Sheldon's words, is as follows:

- the **endomorph**, who is soft and round and whose "digestive viscera are massive and highly developed" (i.e., the person is overweight and has a large stomach).
- the **mesomorph**, who is athletic and muscular and whose "somatic structures … are in the ascendancy" (i.e., the person has larger bones and considerable muscle mass).
- the **ectomorph**, who is thin and fragile, and who has "long, slender, poorly muscled extremities, with delicate, pipestem bones."
- the balanced type, who is of average build, without overweight, thin, or exceedingly muscular traits (see Figure 6.2).

Individuals were ranked along each of the three major dimensions (the balanced type was excluded) using a seven-point scale. A score of 1–1–7, for example, would indicate that

Constitutional theories those that explain criminality by reference to offenders' body types, genetics, and/or external observable physical characteristics.

Somatotyping the classification of human beings into types according to body build and other physical characteristics.

Cycloid the cycloid personality, which was associated with a heavyset, soft type of body, was said to vacillate between normality and abnormality.

Schizoid a person characterized by a schizoid personality disorder. Such disordered personalities appear to be aloof, withdrawn, unresponsive, humourless, dull, and solitary to an abnormal degree.

Displastics a mixed group of offenders described as highly emotional and often unable to control themselves.

Endomorph a body type originally described as soft and round, or overweight.

Mesomorph a body type originally described as athletic and muscular.

Ectomorph a body type originally described as thin and fragile, with long, slender, poorly muscled extremities, and delicate bones.

a person exhibited few characteristics of endomorphology or mesomorphology but was predominantly ectomorphic. Sheldon claimed that varying types of temperament and personalities were closely associated with each of the body types he identified. Ectomorphs were said to be cerebrotonic, or restrained, shy, and inhibited. Endomorphs were viscerotonic, or relaxed and sociable. The mesomorphic, or muscular, body type, however, he said was most likely to be associated with delinquency or somatotonia, which he described as "a predominance of muscular activity and . . . vigorous bodily assertiveness." William H. Sheldon's work was supported by constitutional studies of juvenile delinquents conducted by Sheldon Glueck and Eleanor Glueck, reported in 1950.[33] The Gluecks compared 500 known delinquents with 500 non-delinquents, and matched both groups on age, general intelligence, ethnical-racial background, and place of residence. Like Sheldon, the Gluecks concluded that mesomorphy was associated with delinquency.

Early biological theorists such as Sheldon, Lombroso, and Gall provide an interesting footnote to the history of criminological thought. Today, however, their work is mostly relegated to the dustbins of academic theorizing. Modern biological theories of crime are far more sophisticated than their early predecessors, and it is to these we now turn.

Figure 6.2

Sheldon's Somatotypes

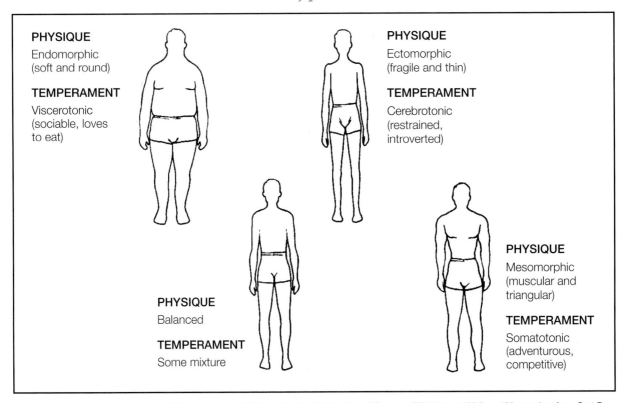

PHYSIQUE
Endomorphic
(soft and round)

TEMPERAMENT
Viscerotonic
(sociable, loves
to eat)

PHYSIQUE
Ectomorphic
(fragile and thin)

TEMPERAMENT
Cerebrotonic
(restrained,
introverted)

PHYSIQUE
Balanced

TEMPERAMENT
Some mixture

PHYSIQUE
Mesomorphic
(muscular and
triangular)

TEMPERAMENT
Somatotonic
(adventurous,
competitive)

Source: V.F. Sacco and L.W. Kennedy, *The Criminal Event* (Toronto: ITP Nelson, 1994), p. 450, as taken from Curt R. Bartol, *Criminal Behaviour: A Psychosocial Approach* (Englewood Cliffs, N.J.: Prentice Hall, 1980).

Chemical and Environmental Precursors of Crime

Recent research in the area of nutrition has produced some limited evidence that the old maxim "You are what you eat!" may contain more than a grain of truth. Biocriminology has made some strides in linking violent or disruptive behaviour to eating habits, vitamin deficiencies, genetics, inheritance, and other conditions that affect the body. Studies of nutrition, endocrinology, and environmental contaminants have all contributed to advances in understanding such behaviour.

One of the first studies to focus on chemical imbalances in the body as a cause of crime was reported in the British medical journal *Lancet* in 1943.[34] Authors of the study linked murder to **hypoglycemia**, or low blood sugar. Low blood sugar, produced by too much insulin in the blood or by near-starvation diets, was said to reduce the mind's capacity to effectively reason or to judge the long-term consequences of behaviour. More recent studies have linked excess consumption of refined white sugar to hyperactivity and aggressiveness. Popular books such as *Sugar Blues* provide guides for individuals seeking to free themselves from the negative effects of excess sugar consumption.[35]

Hypoglycemia a condition characterized by low blood sugar.

To some degree, even courts have accepted the notion that excess sugar consumption may be linked to crime. In the early 1980s, for example, Dan White, a former San Francisco police officer, was given a reduced sentence after his lawyers convinced the court that their defendant's consumption of massive amounts of refined white sugar had increased his excitability and lowered his ability to make reasoned decisions. White had been convicted of murdering San Francisco Mayor George Moscone and City Councillor Harvey Milk during a dispute in the mayor's office. The night before the killings, White stayed awake drinking Coca-Cola and eating many Twinkies.

More than ten years later, however, a well-conducted study reported in the *New England Journal of Medicine* seemed to contradict the notion that sugar may lead to hyperactivity.[36] Similarly, neither sugar nor artificial sweeteners were shown to have any link to an increase in learning disabilities. In the study, researchers at Vanderbilt University and the University of Iowa varied the diets of supposedly sugar-sensitive youngsters from ones that were high in sugar, to one that was low in sugar but contained the artificial sweetener aspartame. A third experimental diet contained very little sugar but had added saccharin. After surveying parents, teachers, and babysitters and testing the study group for changes in memory, concentration, and math skills, the researchers concluded "[w]e couldn't find any difference in terms of their behavior or their learning on any of the three diets."[37] Hence, to date, the evidence concerning sugar's impact on behaviour is less than clear.

Allergic reactions to common foods have been reported as the cause of violence and homicide by a number of investigators.[38] Some foods—including milk, citrus fruit, chocolate, corn, wheat, and eggs—are said to produce allergic reactions in sensitive individuals, leading to a swelling of the brain and the brain stem. Involvement of the central nervous system in such allergies, it has been suggested, reduces the amount of learning that occurs during childhood and may contribute to delinquency as well as to adult criminal behaviour. Such swelling is also thought to impede the higher faculties, reducing one's sense of morality and creating conditions that support impulsive behaviour.

Some studies have implicated food additives, such as the flavour enhancer monosodium glutamate, dyes, and artificial flavourings in producing criminal violence.[39] Other research has found that coffee and sugar may trigger anti-social behaviour.[40] Researchers were led to these conclusions through finding that inmates consumed considerably greater amounts of coffee, sugar, and processed foods than other people did, on average.[41] It is, however, unclear whether inmates drink more coffee because of boredom, or whether "excitable" personalities feel a need for the kind of stimulation available through coffee consumption. On the other hand, habitual coffee drinkers in non-prison populations have not been linked to crime, and other studies show no link between the amount of sugar consumed by inmates and hyperactivity.[42] Nonetheless, some prison programs have been designed to limit intake of dietary stimulants through nutritional management and the substitution of artificial sweeteners for refined sugar. Vitamins have also been examined for their impact on delinquency. At least one researcher found that disruptive children consumed far less than optimal levels of vitamins B_3 and B_6 than did non-problem youths.[43] Some researchers have suggested that the addition of these vitamins to the diets of children who were deficient in them could control unruly behaviour and improve school performance.

The role of food and diet in causing criminal behaviour, however, has not been well established. Some international health associations have concluded that no convincing scientific relationship between crime and diet has yet been demonstrated.[44] Such groups are becoming concerned that poor nutrition may result from programs intended to have behavioural impacts, such as those that reduce or modify diets in prisons or elsewhere.

In 1997, British researchers Roger D. Masters, Brian Hone, and Anil Doshi published a study purporting to show that industrial and other forms of environmental pollution cause people to commit violent crimes.[45] The study used statistics from the FBI's Uniform Crime Reporting Program and data from the US Environmental Protection Agency's Toxic Release Inventory. A comparison between the two data sets showed a significant correlation between juvenile crime and high environmental levels of both lead and manganese. Masters and his colleagues suggested an explanation based on a neurotoxicity hypothesis:

> *According to this approach, toxic pollutants—specifically the toxic metals lead and manganese—cause learning disabilities, an increase in aggressive behavior, and—most importantly—loss of control over impulsive behavior. These traits combine with poverty, social stress, alcohol and drug abuse, individual character, and other social and psychological factors to produce individuals who commit violent crimes.*[46]

According to Masters, the presence of excess manganese lowers levels of serotonin and dopamine in the brain—both of which are neurotransmitters associated with impulse control and planning. Masters notes that low blood levels of serotonin are known to cause mood disturbances, poor impulse control, and increases in aggressive behaviour. Masters claims that children who are raised from birth on infant formula, and who are not breast-fed, will absorb five times as much manganese as do breastfed infants. Calcium deficiency is known to increase the absorption of manganese and, says Masters, "a combination of manganese toxicity and calcium deficiency adds up to 'reverse' Prozac."

In support of his thesis, Masters cites other studies, the largest of which was an examination of 1000 Black children in Philadelphia that showed that levels of exposure to lead was a reliable predictor of the number of juvenile offences among the exposed male population, the seriousness of juvenile offences, and the number of adult offences.

According to Masters, toxic metals affect individuals in complex ways. Because lead diminishes a person's normal ability to detoxify poisons, he says, it may heighten the effects of alcohol and drugs. Industrial pollution, automobile traffic, lead-based paints, and aging

A genome researcher at work. The international Human Genome Project is a research program undertaken to determine the complete nucleotide sequence of human DNA. Do you think this research might assist in identifying whether or not there exists a "criminal gene"? What are some of the ethical, legal, and social implications of such a project?
Durand Trippett, SIPA Press.

water delivery systems are all possible sources of contamination. In a recent interview, Masters said: "The presence of pollution is as big a factor [in crime causation] as poverty... It's the breakdown of the inhibition mechanism that's the key to violent behavior."[47] When brain chemistry is altered by exposure to heavy metal and other toxins, he said, people lose the natural restraint that holds their violent tendencies in check.

In addition to chemical substances likely to be ingested, other environmental features have also been linked to the likelihood of aggressive behaviour. During the early 1980s, for example, Alexander Schauss and his followers[48] were able to show that the use of a specific shade of the colour pink could have a calming effect on people experiencing feelings of anger and agitation. Findings indicated that exposure to pink produced an endocrine change that had a tranquilizing effect on the muscles. This involuntary effect, said researchers, was not subject to conscious control. As a result of such studies, jail cells in some detention centres were painted pink in hopes that aggressive tendencies among inmates might be reduced. Researchers supported such measures, saying that "the use of pink color in reducing aggression and causing muscular relaxation of inmates is humane and requires no medication or physical force."[49]

Hormones and Criminality

Hormones have also come under scrutiny as potential behavioural determinants. The male sex hormone **testosterone**, for example, has been linked to aggression. Most studies

Testosterone the primary male sex hormone; produced in the testes, its function is to control secondary sex characteristics and sexual drive.

on the subject have consistently shown an apparent relationship between high blood testosterone levels and increased aggressiveness in men. More focused studies have unveiled a direct relationship between the amount of the chemical present and the degree of violence used by sex offenders,[50] while other researchers have linked steroid abuse among bodybuilders to destructive urges and psychosis.[51] Contemporary investigations demonstrate a link between testosterone levels and aggression in teenagers,[52] while others show that adolescent problem behaviour and teenage violence rise in proportion to the amount of testosterone levels in the blood of young men.[53] In 1987, for example, a Swedish researcher, Dan Olweus, reported that boys aged 15 to 17 showed levels of both verbal and physical aggression that correlated with the level of testosterone present in their blood.[54] Olweus also found that boys with higher levels of testosterone "tended to be habitually more impatient and irritable than boys with lower testosterone levels." He concluded that high levels of the hormone led to increased frustration and habitual impatience and irritability.

In what may be the definitive work to date on the subject, Alan Booth and D. Wayne Osgood[55] conclude that there is a "moderately strong relationship between testosterone and adult deviance,"[56] but suggest that the relationship "is largely mediated by the influence of testosterone on social integration and on prior involvement in juvenile delinquency."[57] In other words, measurably high levels of testosterone in the blood of young men may have some effect on behaviour, but those effects are likely to be moderated by the social environment.

A few limited studies have attempted to measure the effects of testosterone on women. Women's bodies manufacture roughly 10 percent of the amount of the hormone secreted

Sex hormones, such as testosterone, have been linked to aggressive behaviour. Testosterone also enhances secondary sexual characteristics such as body hair and muscle mass in males. What kinds of crime might be hormonally influenced?
The Kobal Collection.

by men. Even so, subtle changes in testosterone levels in women have been linked to changes in personality and sexual behaviour.[58] Few such studies exist, however, and their findings should therefore be regarded as inconclusive.

Fluctuations in the level of female hormones, however, may also bear some relationship to law violation. In 1980 a British court exonerated Christine English of charges that she murdered her live-in lover, after English admittedly ran him over with her car after an argument. English's defence rested on the fact that she was suffering from premenstrual syndrome (PMS) at the time of the homicide. An expert witness, Dr. Katharina Dalton, testified at the trial that PMS had caused Ms. English to be "irritable, aggressive . . . and confused, with loss of self-control."

Another case involving PMS was decided in 1991 by a Fairfax, Virginia, judge who dismissed drunk driving and other charges against a female orthopaedic surgeon named Dr. Geraldine Richter.[59] Richter allegedly kicked and cursed a Virginia state trooper after being stopped for driving erratically; she also admitted to having consumed four glasses of wine. A Breathalyzer test showed her blood-alcohol level to be nearly 0.13 percent— above the 0.10 percent level Virginia law set for such a violation. Charges against Dr. Richter were dismissed after a gynecologist testified on her behalf, saying that the behaviour she exhibited was likely to have been due primarily to PMS.

Although evidence linking PMS to violent and/or criminal behaviour is far from clear, some researchers believe that a drop in serotonin levels in the female brain just prior to menstruation might explain the agitation and irritability sometimes associated with premenstrual syndrome.[60] Serotonin has been called a "behaviour-regulating chemical," and animal studies have demonstrated a link between low levels of the neurotransmitter present in the brain and aggressive behaviour. Monkeys, for example, with low serotonin levels have been found more likely to bite, slap, and chase others of their kind. Studies at the National Institute on Alcohol Abuse and Alcoholism in Bethesda, Maryland, have linked low serotonin levels in humans to impulsive crimes. Men convicted of premeditated murder, for example, have been found to have normal serotonin levels, whereas those convicted of crimes of passion have lower levels.[61]

Genetics and Crime

Criminal Families

Some scholars suggest that a penchant for crime may be inherited, and that criminal tendencies are genetically based. Early studies of this type often focused on criminal families, or families that appeared to exhibit criminal tendencies through several generations.

In 1877, **Richard L. Dugdale** (1841–1883) published a study of one such clan—the **Juke family**.[62] Dugdale traced the Juke lineage back to a notorious character named Max, a Dutch immigrant who arrived in New York in the early 18th century. Two of Max's sons married into the notorious "Juke family of girls," six sisters, all of whom were said to be illegitimate. Max's male descendants were reputed to be vicious, and one woman named Ada had an especially bad reputation and came to be known as "the mother of criminals." By the time of the study, Dugdale claimed to be able to identify approximately 1200 of Ada's descendants. He included among their numbers 7 murderers, 60 habitual thieves,

Juke family a well-known "criminal family" studied by Richard L. Dugdale.

90 or so other criminals, 50 prostitutes, and 280 paupers. Dugdale compared the crime-prone Jukes with another family, the pure-blooded progeny of Jonathan Edwards, a Puritan preacher and one-time president of Princeton University. Descendants of Edwards included American presidents and vice-presidents and many successful bankers and businesspeople. None identified from among the Edwards lineage had had run-ins with the law. In 1915, **Arthur H. Estabrook** published a follow-up to Dugdale's work, in which he identified an additional 715 Juke descendants, including 378 more prostitutes, 170 additional paupers, and 118 other criminals.[63]

Following in the tradition of family tree researchers, **Henry H. Goddard** (1866–1957) published a study of the **Kallikak family** in 1912.[64] Goddard attempted to place the study of deviant families within an acceptable scientific framework by providing a kind of control group. For comparison purposes, he used two branches of the same family. One branch began as the result of a sexual liaison between Martin Kallikak, a Revolutionary War soldier, and a barmaid whose name is unknown. As a result of this illegitimate union, a son (Martin Jr.) was born. After the war, Martin Sr. returned home and married a righteous Quaker girl, and a second line of descent began. Although the second, legitimate branch produced only a few minor deviants, the illegitimate line resulted in 262 "feeble-minded" births and various other epileptic, alcoholic, and criminal descendants. The term *feeble-minded*, which was much in vogue at the time of Goddard's study, was later recast as *mental retardation*, whereas people exhibiting similar characteristics today might be referred to as mentally handicapped or mentally challenged. Because feeble-mindedness appeared to occur with some predictability in Goddard's study, whereas criminal activity seemed to be only randomly represented among the descendants of either Kallikak line, Goddard concluded that a tendency toward feeble-mindedness was inherited but that criminality was not.

Today, the work of Dugdale and Goddard has been discredited.[65] Nevertheless, studies such as these, which focused on inherited mental degeneration, led to the **eugenics** movement of the 1920s and early 1930s, under which mentally handicapped women were frequently sterilized to prevent their bearing additional offspring. In Canada, sexual sterilization laws in Alberta and British Columbia resulted in the sterilization of almost 3000 citizens between 1928 and 1972. During this period, the legislation targeted not only those with mental illness but also the poor, Aboriginal people, unwed mothers, and non–English-speaking immigrants.[66]

The eugenics movement, as it existed in North America before World War II, was largely discredited by intense worldwide condemnation of Nazi genetic research and mass sterilization and eugenics programs, including those that led to the Holocaust. As a consequence, research attempting to ferret out the biological underpinnings of behavioural traits remains suspect in the minds of many today.

Kallikak family a well-known "criminal family" studied by Henry H. Goddard.

Eugenics the study of hereditary improvement by genetic control.

The XYY "Supermale"

Recent developments in the field of human genetics have led to the study of the role of chromosomes, and sex-linked chromosomes in particular, in crime causation. The first well-known study[67] of this type was undertaken by Patricia A. Jacobs, a British researcher who in 1965 examined 197 Scottish prisoners for chromosomal abnormalities through a relatively simple blood test known as *karyotyping*.[68] Twelve members of the group displayed chromosomes that were unusual, and seven were found to have an XYY chromosome. "Normal" male individuals possess an XY chromosome structure, and "normal" female individuals are XX. Some other unusual combinations might be XXX, wherein a woman's genetic makeup contains an extra X chromosome, or XXY, also called Klinefelter's syndrome, in which a man might carry an extra X, or female, chromosome. Klinefelter's men often are possessed of male genitalia but are frequently sterile and evidence breast enlargement and intellectual retardation. The XYY man, however, whose incidence in the prison population was placed at around 3.5 percent by Jacobs, was quickly identified as potentially violent and termed a **supermale**.

Following introduction of the supermale notion into popular consciousness, a number of offenders attempted to offer a chromosome-based defence. In 1969, for example, Lawrence E. Hannell, who was adjudged a supermale, was acquitted of murder in Australia on the grounds of insanity.[69] Such a defence, however, did not work for Richard Speck, another claimed XYY man, convicted of killing eight Chicago nursing students in 1966. It was later learned that Speck did not carry the extra Y chromosome.

To date, there have been nearly 200 studies of XYY males. Although not all researchers agree, taken as a group these studies tend to show that supermales[70]

- are taller than the average male, often standing 6' 1" or more;
- suffer from acne or skin disorders;
- are of less than average intelligence;
- are over-represented in prisons and mental hospitals; and
- come from families with a lower than average history of crime or mental illness.

The supermale phenomenon, also called the XYY syndrome, was more sensationalism than fact. Little evidence suggests that XYY men actually commit crimes of greater violence than do other men, although they may commit somewhat more crimes overall. A 1976 Danish study of 4000 men, which found precisely that, may have helped put the issue to rest.[71] This survey of men born in Copenhagen between 1944 and 1947 also found that the incidence of XYY men was less than 1 percent in the general male population. Other recent researchers have similarly concluded that "studies done thus far are largely in agreement and demonstrate rather conclusively that males of the XYY type are not predictably aggressive."[72]

Supermale a male individual displaying the XYY chromosomal structure.

Chromosomes and Modern-Day Criminal Families

In 1993, Dutch criminologists caught worldwide attention with their claim that they had uncovered a specific gene with links to criminal behaviour. Geneticist Han G. Brunner, researcher Hans-Hilger Ropers, and collaborators studied what media sources called "the Netherlands' most dysfunctional family."[73] Although the unnamed family displayed IQs in the near normal range, they seemed unable to control their impulses and often ended up being arrested for violations of the criminal law. Arrests, however, were always of men. Tracing the family back five generations, Brunner found fourteen men whom he classified as genetically given to criminality. None of the women in the family displayed criminal tendencies, although they were often victimized by their crime-prone male siblings. One brother raped a sister and later stabbed a mental hospital staffer in the chest with a pitchfork. Another tried to run over his supervisor with his car. Two brothers repeatedly started fires, and were classified as arsonists. Another brother frequently crept into his sisters' rooms and forced them to undress at knifepoint.

According to Brunner and Ropers, because men have only one X chromosome they are especially vulnerable to any defective gene. Women, with two X chromosomes, have a kind of backup system in which one defective gene may be compensated for by another wholesome and correctly functioning gene carried in the second X chromosome. After a decade of study, which involved the laboratory filtering of a huge quantity of genetic material in a search for the defective gene, Brunner and Ropers announced that they had isolated the specific mutation that caused the family's criminality. The gene, they said, is one that is responsible for production of an enzyme called monoamine oxidase A (MAOA). This enzyme is crucially involved in the process by which signals are transmitted within the brain. Specifically, MAOA breaks down the chemicals serotonin and noradrenaline. Both are substances that, when found in excess in the brain, have been linked to aggressive behaviour in human beings. Because men with the mutated gene do not produce the enzyme necessary to break down chemical transmitters, researchers surmise, their brains are overwhelmed with stimuli—a situation that results in uncontrollable urges and, ultimately, criminal behaviour.

Twin Studies

Studies of the criminal tendencies of fraternal and identical twins provide a methodologically sophisticated technique for ferreting out the role of inheritance in crime causation. Fraternal twins (also called dizygotic or DZ twins) develop from different fertilized eggs and share only that genetic material common among siblings. Identical twins (also called **monozygotic or MZ twins**) develop from the same egg and carry virtually the same genetic material.

Monozygotic or MZ twins, as opposed to dizygotic (or DZ) twins, develop from the same egg and carry virtually the same genetic material.

The German physician Johannes Lange published in the 1920s one of the first studies to link MZ twins to criminality.[74] Lange examined only 17 pairs of fraternal and 13 pairs of identical twins, but found that in 10 of the 13 identical pairs both twins were criminal, whereas only 2 of the 17 fraternal pairs exhibited such similarity. Lange's findings drew considerable attention, even though his sample was small and he was unable to adequately separate environmental influences from genetic ones. The title of his book, *Verbrechen als Schicksal*, whose English translation is *Crime as Destiny*, indicates Lange's firm conviction that criminality has a strong genetic component.

A much larger twin study was begun in 1968 by the European researchers Karl Christiansen and Sarnoff Mednick, who analyzed all twins (3586 pairs) born on a selected group of Danish islands between 1881 and 1910.[75] Christiansen and Mednick found significant statistical support for the notion that criminal tendencies are inherited and concluded that 52 percent of identical twins and 22 percent of fraternal siblings displayed the same degree of criminality within the twin pair. Such similarities remained apparent even among twins who had been separated at birth and who were raised in substantially different environments.

Adoption Studies

Adoption studies have shed light on the discussion about the biological roots of criminal behaviour by examining both the genetic factors and environmental contributors to criminal behaviour. One such significant cross-fostering study was carried out by Sarnoff Mednick, W.F. Gabrielli, and B. Hutchings.[76] The study examined 14 427 non-familial adoptions that occurred in Denmark between 1927 and 1947. Mednick, Gabrielli, and Hutchings obtained and examined state records for over 65 000 biological parents, adoptive parents, and adoptive children. Their findings indicated that children of biological parents with criminal records were more likely to have been convicted of one or more criminal offences than those whose parents had no criminal records. This was especially true in cases where these children were also raised by one or both adoptive parents with a criminal record (24.5 percent). Particularly statistically significant was the number of adopted children who had been convicted of one or more criminal offences whose biological parents had criminal records but whose adoptive parents did not (20.0 percent). Children of biological mothers who were criminally convicted were shown to be at greater risk of engaging in criminal behaviour than were the children of biological fathers who were criminal. In cases where children were raised by more than one adoptive, criminal parent, the study found that the risk of criminality for the adoptee did not differ.[77]

Other statistically less significant adoption studies have produced similar findings. In an earlier study, Sarnoff Mednick and B. Hutchings studied male adoptees and their biological and adoptive fathers.[78] Their findings indicated that 36.4 percent of the delinquent adopted boys had biological fathers with criminal records. As well, 23 percent of criminal adoptees had a criminal adoptive father compared to 9 percent who did not. A study of 258 male adoptees conducted in Sweden by M. Bohman found that over 13 percent of the biological fathers or mothers had been charged criminally, compared with 10 percent of the adoptees whose biological parents had no criminal convictions.[79]

Male–Female Differences in Criminality

A number of writers propose that criminologists need to recognize that "the male is much more criminalistic than the female."[80] As Chapter 2 discusses, with the exception of crimes such as prostitution and shoplifting, the number of crimes committed by men routinely far exceeds the number of crimes committed by women in almost any category. The data on the extent of male–female criminality in relation to violent crime show a degree of regularity over time. The proportion of homicides committed by men versus women, for example, has remained more or less constant for decades (see Table 6.1). In fact, as the table shows (and contrary to popular expectations), male perpetrators appear to have been involved in an increasing proportion of murders over most of the 40-year span covered in the table. Similarly, the proportion of men murdered by men versus the proportion of women murdered by women has continuously shown a much larger propensity for men to murder one another.

With the exception of crimes against the person, the gap between male and female crime rates has been narrowing in the past 30 years. Overall, the percentage of *Criminal Code* offences committed by females increased from 9 percent to 17 percent. Increases were seen particularly in offences classified as serious thefts (from 9 to 23 percent), fraud (from 11 to 30 percent), and minor theft (from 22 to 38 percent).[81]

Interestingly, the situation in the United States is somewhat different. Women are arrested for only 18 percent of all violent crimes and 31 percent of property crimes—a proportion that has remained surprisingly constant over the years since the Federal Bureau

Table 6.1

Male and Female Murder Perpetrators as a Percentage of All Homicide Suspects, 1966–2005

1966		1979		1986		1998		2005	
Male	Female	Male	Female	Male	Female	Male	Female	Male	Female
85.6%	14.4%	87.3%	12.7%	85.4%	14.6%	91.5%	8.5%	90%	10%

Sources: Adapted from M.A. Jackson and C.T. Griffiths, *Canadian Criminology: Perspectives on Crime and Criminality* (Toronto: Harcourt Brace, 1995), p.149; Statistics Canada, *Homicide Statistics 1979* (Cat. 85-209) (Ottawa: Minister of Supply and Services, 1980); Statistics Canada, *Homicide in Canada 1986: A Statistical Perspective* (Ottawa: Minister of Supply and Services, 1997); S. Tremblay, "Canadian Crime Statistics, 1988," *Juristat*, vol. 19, no. 9 (Ottawa: Minister of Industry, 1999); and Mia Dauvergne, Geoffrey Li, "Homicide in Canada, 2005," *Juristat*, vol. 26, no. 6 (Ottawa: Minister of Industry, 2003).

of Investigation began gathering crime data more than half a century ago. Such apparent differences not only have existed over time but can also be seen in cross-cultural studies.[82]

In evaluating the criminality of women based on statistics alone, however, there is a danger of misidentifying causal factors operative in the behaviour itself. Although men consistently commit more murders than women, for example, we should not jump to the conclusion that this bit of evidence shows a genetic predisposition toward interpersonal violence in men that is absent in women. To do so would fail to recognize the role of other causal factors. Observable racial variation in crime rates has provided some writers with a basis for claiming that some racial groups are disproportionately criminal—while simultaneously attributing such criminality to a genetic basis. Canadian crime statistics do not routinely report on the racial and ethnic makeup of offenders. Two recent studies of Canadian inmate populations, however, have concluded that offenders from non-Aboriginal, visible, ethnic minorities were under-represented.[83]

The reality for Aboriginal peoples in Canada is quite different. Numerous studies over the years have consistently demonstrated that Aboriginal peoples are over-represented in the criminal justice system. Silverman and Kennedy found that the proportion of Aboriginals involved in homicide is at least five times greater than is their representation in the population.[84] Work by Hyde and La Prairie indicates that Aboriginal peoples are implicated in more offences involving alcohol, in fewer property offences, and in more violent offences.[85] Again, Chapter 2 provides additional statistics of this nature. By comparison, a look at the statistics in the United States shows that African-Americans are six times more likely than Caucasians to commit murder, three times more likely to commit rape, seven times more likely to rob, and twice as likely, on average, to commit any kind of crime.[86]

Such statistics can be inherently misleading because—unlike the undeniable and easily observable biological differences that exist between men and women—racial groupings are defined more by convention than by genetics. In fact, some writers suggest that "pure" racial groups no longer exist, and that even historical racial distinctions were based more on political convention than on significant genetic differences.

The criminality of women (or relative lack thereof) is, in all likelihood, culturally determined to a considerable degree. The consistency of data routinely showing that women are far less likely than men to be involved in most property crimes, however, and less likely still to commit violent crimes, requires recognition. We have already evaluated the role that testosterone may play in increasing the propensity toward violence and aggression among men. A few authors suggest that testosterone is the agent primarily responsible for male criminality and that its relative lack in women leads them to commit fewer crimes. Some evidence supports just such a hypothesis. Studies have shown, for example, that female fetuses exposed to elevated testosterone levels during gestation develop masculine characteristics, including a muscular body build and a demonstrably greater tendency toward aggression later in life.[87] Even so, genetically based behavioural differences between men and women are so overshadowed by aspects of the social environment, including socialization, the learning of culturally prescribed roles, the expectations of others, and so on, that definitive conclusions are difficult to reach.

One recently proposed social-psychological explanation for homicidal behaviour among women, for example, suggests that men who kill tend to do so out of a need to control a situation, whereas women who kill tend to do so because they have lost control over themselves.[88] The theory says that "women as a group are more 'controlled' than men, particularly with respect to their experience and expression of anger." Such control is said to emanate from the fact that "men are always the subjects and women the objects in [a] male-centric universe."[89] As a consequence of our culture's overemphasis on a woman's looks rather than on her performance, the theory says, women internalize a "self-image on the basis of appearance rather than substance of character," resulting in low self-esteem and low self-confidence. Low self-esteem, the argument goes, necessitates greater self-control and results in lower criminality among women. Such a perspective suggests that

Violence Linked to Gene Defect

Box 6.1

Pleasure Deficit May Be the Spark

A gene linked to pleasure-seeking behaviour and addictions also may play a role in murder and violence, new research suggests. This pleasure gene normally is involved in the flow of dopamine, a powerful brain chemical that provides people with their sense of well-being. When defective, the gene diminishes dopamine function, driving a person to drink, take drugs, or engage in other activities that give dopamine a boost.

Studies suggest people who have a variant of the gene, called "DRD2 A1 allele," are prone to becoming smokers, violent alcoholics, gambling addicts, and drug addicts.

"We think they're seeking out ways of fixing the lack of pleasure," says Kenneth Blum, University of Texas Health Science Center, San Antonio. "You might be a pleasure seeker for alcohol, drugs, sex or maybe you get it from violence or murder."

In a study presented Wednesday at an American Psychiatric Association meeting, Blum and 17 researchers found the DRD2 A1 allele in

- six of 11 children in a residential treatment program for pathological violence but only one of 30 normal children.
- half of 109 people diagnosed with "schizoid/avoidant" personality. They are introverted, withdrawn, emotionally cold, and distant.

Other research by psychoanalyst Anneliese Pontius, Harvard Medical School, has tied schizoid/avoidant disorder to more than a dozen bizarre murders. She is testing her subjects for the DRD2 A1 variant.

If the findings are confirmed, Blum says problem children could be screened for the gene and given drugs, special diets, and other treatments known to boost dopamine.

DISCUSSION QUESTIONS

1. How might genes that are linked to pleasure-seeking behaviour lead to crime?
2. Should policies be created to reduce potential criminal activity among persons with the DRD2 A1 allele gene? If so, what might they be?

Source: Tim Friend, "Violence Linked to Gene Defect: Pleasure Deficit May Be the Spark," *USA Today*, May 9, 1996, p. 1D. Copyright 2004, *USA Today*. Reprinted with permission.

women tend to commit homicides only when driven "past the brink" of self-control, thus offering an explanation for why homicides committed by women are generally spontaneous rather than planned, why they usually involve the killing of intimates, and why they generally occur in the home. "Women generally view themselves as part of a collective of relationships around them," says one theorist, "and evaluate their self-worth based on the value and success of these relationships."[90] Hence, when relationships break down, a woman's self-worth may be negated, resulting in a lessening of control—and homicide may ensue.

Sociobiology

Sociobiology the systematic study of the biological basis of all social behaviour.

In the introduction to his article summarizing sociobiology, Arthur Fisher writes, "[e]very so often, in the long course of scientific progress, a new set of ideas appears, illuminating and redefining what has gone before like a flare bursting over a darkened landscape."[91] To some, **sociobiology**—a theoretical synthesis of biology, behaviour, and evolutionary ecology—brought to the scientific community by **Edward O. Wilson** in his seminal 1975 work *Sociobiology: The New Synthesis*, holds the promise of just such a new paradigm.[92] In his book, Wilson defined sociobiology as "the systematic study of the biological basis of all social behavior" and as "a branch of evolutionary biology and particularly of modern population biology." Through his entomological study of social insects, especially ants, Wilson demonstrated that particular forms of behaviour could contribute to the long-term survival of the social group. Wilson focused on altruism (selfless, helping behaviour) and found that, contrary to the beliefs of some evolutionary biologists, helping behaviour facilitates the continuity of the gene pool found among altruistic individuals. Wilson's major focus was to show that the primary determinant of behaviour, including human behaviour, was the need to ensure the survival and continuity of genetic material from one generation to the next.

Territoriality, another primary tenet of Wilson's writings, was said to explain much of the conflict seen between and among human beings, including homicide, warfare, and other forms of aggression. In Wilson's words, "[p]art of man's problem is that his intergroup responses are still crude and primitive, and inadequate for the extended extraterritorial relationships that civilization has thrust upon him." The "unhappy result," as Wilson terms it, may be "tribalism," expressed through the contemporary increase of street gangs and racial tension.

The sad results of territoriality, whatever its cause, can be seen in the deadly adventure of 15-year-old Michael Carter and his companions, who ended up in the proverbial wrong place at the wrong time. On June 18, 1997, Carter, from Highland Township, Michigan, and two of his friends hopped a train headed for the town of Holly. The three were looking for a free ten-mile ride on their way to see friends. But they missed their jump-off point, sailed past the town of Holly, and ended up in a rundown inner-city ghetto in the middle of Flint, Michigan, around midnight. Soon the three were surrounded by gang members, led into a secluded area, and shot. Carter died at the scene, while friend Dustin Kaiser, also 15, survived a gunshot wound to the head. The 14-year-old girl who had accompanied the boys was raped and shot in the face, but lived.[93]

In the view of sociobiologists, the violence and aggressiveness associated with territoriality is often reserved for strangers. The approach of sociobiology may explain intragroup aggression—or the violence that occurs within groups—and that which occurs between groups. Wilson writes that his theory suggests that, within the group, "a particularly severe form of aggressiveness should be reserved for actual or suspected adultery. In many human societies," he observes, "where sexual bonding is close and personal knowledge of the behavior of others detailed, adulterers are harshly treated. The sin," he adds, "is regarded to be even worse when offspring are produced."[94] Hence, territoriality and acquisitiveness extend, from a sociobiological perspective, to location, possessions, and even other people. Human laws, says Wilson, are designed to protect genetically based relationships people have with one another as well as their material possessions and their claimed locations in space. Violations of these intuitive relationships result in crime and in official reactions by the legal system.

Wilson's writing propelled researchers into a flurry of studies intended to test the validity of his assertions. One study, for example, found that Indian adult male Hanuman langurs (a type of monkey) routinely killed the young offspring of female langurs with whom they bonded when those offspring had been sired by other male langurs.[95] A Canadian study by Martin Daly and Margo Wilson of violence in the homes of adoptive children found a human parallel to the langur study, showing that stepchildren run a 70 times greater risk of being killed by their adoptive parent(s) than do children living with their natural parents.[96] Some writers concluded that "murderous behavior, warfare, and even genocide were unavoidable correlates of genetic evolution, controlled by the same genes for territorial behavior that had been selected in primate evolution."[97] Others suggested that biological predispositions developed during earlier stages of human evolution colour contemporary criminal activity. Male criminals, for example, tend toward robbery and burglary—crimes in which they can continue to enact their "hunter instincts" developed long ago. The criminality of women, on the other hand, is more typical of "gatherers" when it involves shoplifting, simple theft, and so on.

Human behavioural predilections can be studied in a variety of ways. In the 1989 book *Evolutionary Jurisprudence*, John H. Beckstrom reports on his examination of over 400 legal documents that, he claimed, showed support for Wilson's contentions that humans tend to act so as to preserve territorial claims, the likelihood of successful reproduction, and the continuation of their own particular genetic material.[98] Beckstrom used legal claims and court decisions in his analysis, spanning over 300 years of judicial activity. Other theorists have gone so far as to imply that, among humans, there may be a gene-based tendency to experience guilt and to develop a conscience. Hence, notions of right and wrong, whether embodied in laws or in social convention, may flow from such a naturalistic origin.

As sociobiology began to receive expanded recognition from investigators, most of whom are American, some social scientists began to treat it as "criminology's anti-discipline."[99] Criticisms were quick to come and included charges that

- sociobiology fails to convey the overwhelming significance of culture, social learning, and individual experiences in shaping the behaviour of individuals and groups.
- sociobiology is fundamentally wrong in its depiction of the basic nature of human beings; there is no credible evidence of genetically based or determined tendencies to act in certain ways.
- sociobiology is just another empirically unsupported rationale for the authoritative labelling and stigmatization of despised, threatening, and powerless minorities.
- human beings are so thoroughly different from other animal species, even other primates, that there is no rational basis for the application to humans of findings from animal studies.

Paradigm an example, model, or theory.

In the words of one observer, "[m]ost criminologists, like most academicians, were wedded to a **paradigm**, and wedded even to the idea of paradigm, the idea that one great problem solution can permit the explanation of nearly all the unexplained variation in the field."[100] In other words, many criminologists were committed to the idea that one theory could explain all that there was to know about crime and its causes. Today, many scholars are beginning to sense the growing need for a new synthesis—for a way to consider the impact of biological theories such as sociobiology along with other long-accepted perspectives such as sociology and psychology.

Crime and Human Nature: A Contemporary Synthesis

In his address at the annual meeting of the American Psychological Association in the mid-1980s, Arnold L. Lieber used the forum to describe his research, which linked phases of the moon to fluctuations in the incidence of violence among human beings.[101] Nights around full moons, according to Lieber, show a significant rise in crime. Although critics found this type of research nonsensical, police officers, hospital personnel, ambulance drivers, and many late-night service providers who heard of Lieber's talk understood what he was describing. Many such individuals, in their own experience, had apparently seen validation of the "full moon thesis."

Shortly after Lieber's presentation, criminologist **James Q. Wilson** and psychologist **Richard J. Herrnstein** teamed up to write *Crime and Human Nature*, a book-length treatise that reiterates many of the arguments proposed by biological criminologists over the past century.[102] Their purpose, at least in part, was to reopen discussion of biological causes of crime. "We want to show," Wilson and Herrnstein said, "that the pendulum is beginning to swing away from a totally sociological explanation of crime."[103] Their avowed goal was "not to state a case just for genetic factors, but to state a comprehensive theory of crime that draws together all the different factors that cause criminal behavior."

Constitutional factors that Wilson and Herrnstein cite as contributing to crime include the following:[104]

- *Gender:* "Crime," the authors say, "has been predominantly male behavior."
- *Age:* "In general, the tendency to break the law declines throughout life."
- *Body Type:* "A disproportionate number of criminals have a mesomorphic build."
- *Intelligence:* Criminality is said to be clearly and consistently associated with low intelligence.
- *Personality:* Criminals are typically aggressive, impulsive, and cruel.

Although personality, behavioural problems, and intelligence may be related to environment, the authors argue that "each involve some genetic inheritance." Wilson and Herrnstein recognize social factors in the development of personality but suggest that constitutional factors predispose a person to specific types of behaviour, and that societal reactions to such predispositions may determine, to a large degree, the form of continued behaviour. Hence, the interplay between heredity, biology, and the social environment may be a key nexus in any consideration of crime causation.

Policy Issues

Biological theories of crime causation present unique challenges to policy makers. According to C. Ray Jeffery, a comprehensive biologically based program of crime prevention and crime control would include

- "pre- and post-natal care for pregnant women and their infants" to monitor and address potentially detrimental developmental conditions that could lead to heightened aggression and crime later in life.
- monitoring of children throughout the early stages of their development to identify "early symptoms of behavioral disorder."
- monitoring of children in their early years to reduce the risk of exposure to violence-inducing experiences such as child abuse and violence committed by other children.
- neurological examinations, including "CAT, PET, and MRI scans . . . given when the need is evident."
- biological research, conducted in prisons and treatment facilities, that might better identify the root causes of aggression and violence. Laws that prevent the experimental use of prison subjects, the analysis of the bodies of executed prisoners, and other similar types of biological investigations must change, says Jeffery.[105]

Jeffery adds that the fundamental orientation of the legal system must change so as to acknowledge contributions of biological criminologists. Such a change would replace or supplement our current "right to punishment" doctrine with a "right to treatment" philosophy. Jeffery concludes his analysis by saying, "[i]f legal and political barriers prevent us from regarding antisocial behavior as a medical problem, and if we do not permit medical research on criminal behavior, how can we ever solve the crime problem?"[106]

The dangers of an overly large dependence on biological approaches to crime, however, raise the spectre of a *1984*-type of Orwellian bogeyman in charge of every aspect of human social life, from conception to the grave—and include the possible abortion of defective fetuses, capital punishment in lieu of rehabilitation, and enforced sterilization. Precedent for such fears can be found in cases such as that of Leilani Muir who, during the 1950s, was placed in Alberta's Provincial Training School for Mental Defectives at the age of 10. Based on a single IQ test, she was labelled a "moron" and, at the age of 14, was sterilized without her consent. The operation was sanctioned under Alberta's *Sexual Sterilization Act*.

Potential links between race and crime, suggested by some researchers, are especially repugnant to many who criticize biological criminology. Canadian criminologists Julian Roberts and Thomas Gabor observe, "People who accept the view that variations in crime rates reflect genetic factors may also embrace an underlying message about crime prevention . . . Social programs aim to eradicate educational, social, and economic inequities. These efforts can only be undermined by statements stressing the importance of genetic factors in determining criminality."[107] Ronald Walters, a political scientist at Howard University, states that, "[s]eeking the biological and genetic aspects of violence is dangerous to African-American youth . . . When you consider the perception that Black people have always been the violent people in this society, it is a short step from this stereotype to using this kind of research for social control."[108] Although biological theories of crime have problems, some criminologists believe that to ignore the potential contributions of biological theorists does a disservice to the science of criminology and denies the opportunity for compassionate and objective researchers to realistically assist in the process of crime prevention and reduction.

In 1997, in an attempt to bring biological theorizing into the criminological mainstream, Lee Ellis and Anthony Walsh expanded on the theme of genetic predispositions, noting that,

> in the case of behavior, nearly all of the effects of genes are quite indirect because they are mediated through complex chains of events occurring in the brain. This means that there are almost certainly no genes for something as complex as criminal behavior. Nevertheless, many genes may affect brain functioning in ways that either increase or reduce the chances of individuals learning various complex behavior patterns, including behavior patterns that happen to be so offensive to others that criminal sanctions have been instituted to minimize their recurrence.[109]

Critique of Biological Theories

A focused critique of biological perspectives on crime causation is provided by Glenn D. Walters and Thomas W. White, who contend that "genetic research on crime has been poorly designed, ambiguously reported, and exceedingly inadequate in addressing the relevant issues."[110] Walters and White highlight the following specific shortcomings of studies in the area:

- Few biological studies adequately conceptualize criminality. "Several studies," they say, "have defined criminality on the basis of a single arrest."
- Twin studies, in particular, have sometimes failed to properly establish "whether a pair of twins is monozygotic (MZ) or dizygotic (DZ)." This is because some MZ twins are not identical in appearance, and only a few twin studies have depended on biological testing rather than on a simple evaluation of appearances.
- Problems in estimating the degree of criminality among sample populations are rife in biological (and in many other) studies of criminality. Interview data are open to interpretation, and existing statistical data on the past criminality of offenders are not always properly appreciated.

- Methodological problems abound in many studies that attempt to evaluate the role of genetics in crime. Walters and White mention, among other things, the lack of control or comparison groups, small sample sizes, the dropping out of subjects from study groups, biased sampling techniques, and the use of inappropriate forms of statistical analysis.
- Results obtained in other countries may not be applicable to the country in question. Twin studies conducted in Sweden and Denmark provide an example of this potential lack of generalizability.

Walters and White nevertheless conclude that "[g]enetic factors are undoubtedly correlated with various measures of criminality," but add that "the large number of methodological flaws and limitations in the research should make one cautious in drawing any causal inferences at this point in time."[111]

Summary

Contemporary criminology has been reluctant to adapt the contributions of biological theories to an understanding of criminality. An objective understanding of any social phenomenon, however, requires clear consideration of all available evidence. Modern proponents of biological perspectives on crime and crime causation point out that the link between the social environment and human behaviour is continuously mediated by the physical brain. Human activity flows from the human mind, and the mind is biologically grounded in the brain. The brain itself is apparently subject to influences from other aspects of the body, such as hormones, neurotransmitters, and the levels of various chemicals in the blood. Such realizations require only a small intellectual leap to the realization that other biological aspects of the human organism may play similar contributory roles in criminal behaviour.

At present, the influence of the environment on human behaviour predominates, and studies purporting to have identified biological determinants of behaviour continue to be thoroughly criticized on methodological and other grounds. For the time being, we must draw the conclusion that while biology provides both a context for and specific precursors to human behaviour, biological predispositions for behaviour in most instances of human interaction are routinely overshadowed by the role of volition, the mechanisms of human thought, and the undeniable influences of socialization and acculturation. Even so, a comprehensive approach to human behaviour must consider the biological precursors of behaviour itself.

Discussion Questions

1. This book emphasizes a social problems versus social responsibility theme. Which perspective would be most supported by biological theories of crime causation? Why?
2. What are the central features of biological theories of crime? How do such theories differ from other perspectives that attempt to explain the same phenomena?
3. Why have biological approaches to crime causation encountered stiff criticism? Do you agree or disagree with those who are critical of such perspectives? Why?

4. Do you agree or disagree with the assertion that "[o]pen inquiry requires objective consideration of all points of view, and an examination of each for their ability to shed light upon the subject under study." Why?

5. What are the social-policy implications of biological theories of crime? What Canadian example discussed in this chapter might presage a type of policy based on such theories?

Weblinks

www.ccja-acjp.ca/en/cjc.html

Canadian Journal of Criminology and Criminal Justice. Provides abstracts of the journal's most current articles.

http://content.nejm.org

New England Journal of Medicine. Cites numerous articles on the biological effects of conditions such as PMS, hypoglycemia and blood sugar levels, etc., on behaviour.

www.crime-times.org

The Crime Times, a non-profit, national publication dedicated to exploring the link between biology and violent crime. Links to numerous discussion papers on a wide range of topics.

www.hypoglycemia.org

The Hypoglycemia Support Foundation. This site provides lots of information on the symptoms and effects of low blood sugar levels.

Psychological and Psychiatric Foundations of Criminal Behaviour

For I have decided to send the feminists, who have always ruined my life, to their maker.

—MARC LEPINE, FROM HIS SUICIDE NOTE
FOUND AFTER THE MONTREAL MASSACRE[1]

Psychopaths are social predators who charm, manipulate, and ruthlessly plow their way though life, leaving a broad trail of broken hearts, shattered expectations, and empty wallets.

—ROBERT HARE[2]

LEARNING OUTCOMES

After reading this chapter, you should be able to

- recognize the contributions of psychology and psychiatry to the understanding of criminal behaviour

- appreciate the relationship between personality and criminal behaviour

- recognize the importance of learning theory to an understanding of criminality

- understand the unique characteristics of those found "not criminally responsible by reason of mental disorder"

- identify current social policy reflecting the psychological approach to criminal behaviour

Canadian Press/Greg Reekie/Toronto Sun.

Introduction

Some crimes defy explanation. In December 2002, Germans were horrified by a story sweeping the nation about a respectable engineer and software specialist who was alleged to have mutilated and eaten a 43-year-old microchip engineer. As police investigators descended upon the home and property of Armin Meiwes on the outskirts of Kassel, Germany, the gruesome details of ritualistic torture and cannibalism unfolded. Frozen human flesh that had been bagged and labelled by body part was found in a freezer, and human bones were discovered discarded in the gardens around the house.

Using advertisements on the internet such as "Wanted: young, well-built 18–30-year-old for slaughter," Meiwes lured scores of men from around the world to his chatroom where he confessed his cannibalistic tendencies. Some of the chat room participants agreed to meet with Meiwes; one 27-year-old conference organizer from London, England, allowed Meiwes to chain him to a bed and stick pins in his body, marking out his liver, a kidney, and other organs to be consumed. Yet another, a 34-year-old cook from southern Germany, allowed Meiwes to string him up on meat hooks in a slaughter parlour in his house. Both men decided that the fantasy had gone far enough and did not proceed to the ultimate conclusion.

One man, Bernd Brandes, did not leave, however. A leading microchip designer who lived in a luxury penthouse suite, Brandes sold his car and other valuables and met with Meiwes at his home in March 2001. Details of their meeting were recorded on a videotape made by Meiwes; together the two men planned a grisly ritual and then executed it as they amputated, fried, and ate part of Brandes' body. Meiwes then stabbed Brandes to death. He sliced his flesh into small chunks which he wrapped and stored in the freezer. He confessed

CHAPTER 7

195

**Psychological and
Psychiatric
Foundations of Criminal
Behaviour**

to eating about 20 kilograms of the flesh in the months between the killing and his arrest.

Armin Meiwes was charged with first-degree murder only, since cannibalism is not legally prohibited in Germany. Thousands of printed emails and internet exchanges were presented as evidence in court. Details of Meiwes' life revealed that he had lived alone with his mother until her death. His father left the family when Meiwes was eight years old and his mother subsequently married and divorced three times. Psychologist Heinrich Wilmer testified at the trial that Meiwes was neither mentally ill nor motivated by sexual gratification. Rather, he lacked male role models, was incredibly lonely, and made up imaginary friends whom he imagined eating so that they would never go away.[3] The defence argued that Meiwes' victim had volunteered for sacrifice; Meiwes was merely assisting Brandes to fulfill his death wish. Prosecutors, on the other hand, argued that Meiwes premeditated the murder of his victim and did it for his own sexual satisfaction.

In one email read at his trial, Meiwes, who became known around the world as the "Cannibal of Rotenburg," writes that cannibalism should be promoted as a form of development aid. "We could solve the problem of over-population and famine at a stroke," he stated. He also told the court that his cannibalism stemmed from an acute sense of loneliness, and that his desperate need for a brother led him to consume a male so he would be "bound to me forever."[4] Meiwes was found guilty of manslaughter in January 2004 and received an eight-and-a-half-year sentence.

In 1989, in a very violent incident that has since heightened the public's awareness of violence against women and has resulted in tougher gun control legislation, 14 female students at L'École Polytechnique in Montreal were shot to death by Marc Lepine, an embittered misogynist. Lepine entered a classroom and shouted, "I want the women," and then, "You're all a bunch of feminists, and I hate feminists."[5] After ordering all the men to leave the room, Lepine shot six women dead. Over the next 20 minutes, the 25-year-old Lepine

Armin Meiwes used the internet to lure victims into his cannibalistic ritual. What explains the public's fascination with bizarre killers?
AP/World Wide Photos.

methodically stalked the cafeteria, the classrooms, and the corridors of the school, leaving 8 other women dead and 13 injured. He finally turned the gun on himself. In the three-page suicide note found in his pocket, Lepine blamed feminists for ruining his life. Lepine's actions were explained by Dr. Renée Fugère, forensic psychiatrist at Montreal's Allan Memorial Institute, as those of a delusional man who repeatedly failed to achieve his ambitions in work—and with women. "Lepine probably did not have the capacity to mourn his failed relationships," she said, "so he kept it inside. Those feelings piled up and finally exploded."[6]

What motivates people to kill or maim—or even to commit other, less serious, offences? How can many killers "seem so normal" before their crimes, giving no hints of the atrocities they are about to commit? Serial killer, mass murderer, sexual mutilator, even book thief—all must wrestle, before and after the criminal event, with their personal demons. For answers to questions such as these, many people turn to psychological theories. Psychologists are the pundits of the modern age of behaviourism—offering explanations rooted in determinants that lie within *individual actors*. Psychological determinants of deviant or criminal behaviour may be couched in terms of exploitive personality characteristics, poor impulse control, emotional arousal, an immature personality, and so on. Canadian criminal psychologists Don Andrews and James Bonta observe, "The major sources of theoretical development in criminology have been—and continue to be—psychological. A theory of criminal conduct is weak indeed if uninformed by a general psychology of human behavior."[7] Other writers go so far as to claim that any criminal behaviour is only a symptom of a more fundamental psychiatric disorder.[8]

What is the fundamental distinguishing feature of psychological approaches as opposed to other attempts to explain behaviour? Two contemporary criminologists offer the following insight: " . . . theories are psychological insofar as they focus on the individual as the unit of analysis. Thus any theory that is concerned with the behavior of individual offenders or which refers to forces or dynamics that motivate individuals to commit crimes would be considered to have a psychological component."[9] Another writer, Curt Bartol, defines psychology as "the science of behavior and mental processes . . . [p]sychological criminology . . . is the science of the behavior and mental processes of the criminal. [P]sychological criminology focuses on individual criminal behavior—how it is acquired, evoked, maintained, and modified."[10]

Major Principles of Psychological Theories

Psychological theories those that are derived from the behavioural sciences and that focus on the individual as the unit of analysis. Psychological theories place the locus of crime causation within the personality of the individual offender.

This brief section serves to summarize the central features of **psychological theories** of crime causation.[11] Each of these points can be found elsewhere in this chapter, where they are discussed in more detail. This cursory overview serves as a guide to the rest of this chapter.

Most psychological theories of crime causation make the following fundamental assumptions:

- The individual is the primary unit of analysis.
- Personality is the major motivational element within individuals, because it is the seat of drives and the source of motives.

Theory in Perspective

Types of Psychological and Psychiatric Theories

PSYCHOLOGICAL AND PSYCHIATRIC THEORIES

Derived from the behavioural sciences and focusing on the *individual* as the unit of analysis.

Psychiatric Criminology, also known as **Forensic Psychiatry.** Envisions a complex set of drives and motives operating from recesses deep within the personality to determine behaviour.
Period: 1930s–present
Theorists: Hervey Cleckley, Robert Hare, and others
Concepts: Psychopath, sociopath, anti-social, asocial personality

Psychoanalytic Criminology. A psychiatric approach developed by the Austrian psychiatrist Sigmund Freud that emphasizes the role of personality in human behaviour, and which sees deviant behaviour as the result of a dysfunctional personality.
Period: 1920s–present
Theorists: Sigmund Freud and others
Concepts: Id, ego, superego, sublimation, psychotherapy, Thanatos, neurosis, psychosis, schizophrenia

Frustration-Aggression Theory. Holds that frustration is a natural consequence of living and a root cause of crime. Criminal behaviour can be a form of adaptation when it results in stress reduction.
Period: 1940s–present
Theorist: J. Dollard, Albert Bandura, Richard H. Walters, S.M. Halleck
Concepts: Frustration, aggression, displacement, catharsis, alloplastic and autoplastic adaptation

Modelling Theory. A psychological perspective that says people learn how to behave by modelling themselves after others whom they have the opportunity to observe.
Period: 1950s–present
Theorists: Albert Bandura and others
Concepts: Interpersonal aggression, modelling, disengagement

Behaviour Theory. A psychological perspective positing that individual behaviour that is rewarded will increase in frequency, while that which is punished will decrease.
Period: 1940s–present
Theorists: B.F. Skinner and others
Concepts: Operant behaviour, conditioning, stimulus-response, reward, punishment

- Crimes result from abnormal, dysfunctional, or inappropriate mental processes within the personality.
- Criminal behaviour, although condemned by the social group, may be purposeful for the individual insofar as it addresses certain felt needs. Behaviour can be judged "inappropriate" only when measured against external criteria purporting to establish normality.
- Normality is generally defined by social consensus—that is, what the majority of people in any social group agree is "real," appropriate, or typical.
- Defective, or abnormal, mental processes may have a variety of causes, including a diseased mind, inappropriate learning or improper conditioning, the emulation of inappropriate role models, and adjustment to inner conflicts.

Early Perspectives

Psychological Perspective

Behavioural conditioning a psychological principle holding that the frequency of any behaviour can be increased or decreased through reward, punishment, and/or association with other stimuli.

Twin threads wove through early psychological theories. One strand emphasized **behavioural conditioning**, the other focused mostly on personality disturbances and diseases of the mind. Together, these two foci constituted the early field of psychological criminology. The concept of conditioned behaviour was popularized through the work of the Russian physiologist Ivan Pavlov (1849–1936), whose work with dogs won the Nobel Prize in physiology and medicine in 1904. The dogs, who salivated when food was presented to them, were always fed in the presence of a ringing bell. Soon, Pavlov found, the dogs would salivate, as if in preparation for eating, when the bell alone was rung—even when no food was present. Hence, salivation, an automatic response to the presence of food, could be conditioned to occur in response to some other stimulus—demonstrating that animal behaviour could be predictably altered through association with external changes arising from the environment surrounding the organism.

Psychopathology the study of pathological mental conditions, that is, mental illness.

The other thread wending its way through early psychological theories was that of mental disease, or **psychopathology**. The concept of psychopathology has been called "one of the most durable, resilient and influential of all criminological ideas."[12] In its original formulation, psychopathology embodied the notion of a diseased mind. It described a particular form of insanity referred to as "moral idiocy," which was thought to have a constitutional, or physiological, basis. The concept is summarized in the words of Nolan Lewis, who wrote during his tenure as director of the New York State Psychiatric Institute and Hospital at Columbia University during World War II that "[t]he criminal, like other people, has lived a life of instinctive drives, of desires, of wishes, of feelings, but one in which his intellect has apparently functioned less effectually as a brake upon certain trends. His constitutional makeup deviates toward the abnormal, leading him into conflicts with the laws of society and its cultural patterns."[13]

Psychiatric criminology theories derived from the medical sciences, including neurology, and that, like other psychological theories, focus on the individual as the unit of analysis. Psychiatric theories form the basis of psychiatric criminology.

Psychiatric Perspective

Psychological criminology, with its traditional dual emphasis on (1) early forces that shape personality and (2) conditioned behaviour, can be distinguished from **psychiatric criminology**, also known as **forensic psychiatry**, which envisions a complex set of drives and motives operating from hidden recesses deep within the personality to determine behaviour. David Abrahamsen, a psychiatrist writing in 1944, explains crime this way: "[a]ntisocial behaviour is a direct expression of an aggression or may be a direct or indirect manifestation of a distorted erotic drive. Crime," said Abrahamsen, "may . . . be considered a product of a person's tendencies and the situation of the moment interacting with his mental resistance."[14] The key questions to be answered by psychiatric criminology, according to Abrahamsen, are "[w]hat creates the criminal impulse? What stimulates and gives it direction?" A later forensic psychiatrist answered the question this way: "every criminal is such by reason of unconscious forces within him . . . ."[15] Forensic psychiatry explains crime as being caused by biological and psychological urges mediated through consciousness. Little significance is placed upon the role of the environment external to the individual after the first few formative years of life. Psychiatric theories are derived from the medical sciences, including neurology, and, like other psychological theories, focus on the individual as the unit of analysis.

Criminal Behaviour as Maladaption

The Psychoanalytic Perspective

Perhaps the best known psychiatrist of all time is **Sigmund Freud** (1856–1939). Freud coined the term **psychoanalysis** in 1896 and based an entire theory of human behaviour on it. From the point of view of psychoanalysis, criminal behaviour is maladaptive, or the product of inadequacies inherent in the offender's personality. Significant inadequacies may result in full-blown mental illness, which in itself can be a direct cause of crime. The psychoanalytic perspective encompasses diverse notions such as personality, neurosis, psychosis, and more specific concepts such as transference, sublimation, and repression. **Psychotherapy**, referred to in its early days as the "talking cure" because it highlighted patient–therapist communication, is the attempt to relieve patients of their mental disorders through the application of psychoanalytical principles and techniques.

According to Freud, the personality is made up of three components—the id, the ego, and the superego—as shown in Figure 7.1. The **id** is that fundamental aspect of the personality from which drives, wishes, urges, and desires emanate. Freud focused primarily on love, aggression, and sex as fundamental drives in any personality. The id is direct and singular in purpose. It operates according to the pleasure principle, seeking full and immediate gratification of its needs. Individuals, however, were said to rarely be fully aware of the urges that percolate up (occasionally into awareness) from the id, because it is a largely unconscious region of the mind. Nonetheless, from the Freudian perspective, each of us carries within our id the prerequisite motivation for criminal behaviour. We are, each one of us, potential murderers, sexual aggressors, and thieves—our drives and urges kept in check only by other, controlling aspects of our personalities.

A second component of the personality, the **ego**, is primarily charged with reality testing. Freud's use of the word *ego* should not be confused with popular practice, whereby a person might talk about an "inflated ego" or an "egotistical person." For Freud, the ego was primarily concerned with how objectives might be best accomplished. The ego tends to effect strategies for the individual that maximize pleasure and minimize pain. It lays out

Forensic psychiatry that branch of psychiatry having to do with the study of crime and criminality.

Psychoanalysis the theory of human psychology founded by Freud and based on the concepts of the unconscious, resistance, repression, sexuality, and the Oedipus complex.[16]

Psychotherapy a form of psychiatric treatment based on psychoanalytical principles and techniques.

Id the aspect of the personality from which drives, wishes, urges, and desires emanate. More formally, it is the division of the psyche associated with instinctual impulses and demands for immediate satisfaction of primitive needs.[17]

Ego the reality-testing part of the personality; also referred to as the reality principle. More formally, it is the personality component that is conscious, most immediately controls behaviour, and is most in touch with external reality.[18]

| Figure 7.1 |

The Psychoanalytic Structure of Personality

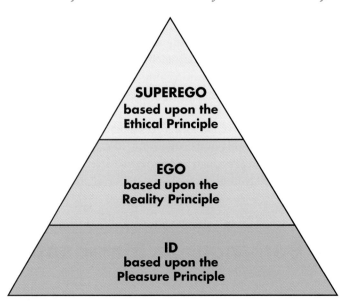

Superego the moral aspect of the personality; much like the conscience. More formally, it is the division of the psyche that develops by the incorporation of the perceived moral standards of the community, is mainly unconscious, and includes the conscience.[19]

the various paths of action that can lead to wish fulfillment. The ego inherently recognizes that it may be necessary to delay gratification to achieve a more fulfilling long-term goal.

The **superego**, the last component of the personality, is much like a moral guide to right and wrong. If properly developed, it assays the ego's plans, dismissing some as morally inappropriate while accepting others as ethically viable. The id of a potential rapist, for example, might be filled with lustful drives, and his ego may develop a variety of alternative plans whereby those drives might be fulfilled, some legal and some illegal. His superego will, however, if the individual's personality is relatively well integrated and the superego is properly developed, turn the individual away from law-violating behaviour based on his sensual desires and guide the ego to select a path of action that is in keeping with social convention. When the dictates of the superego are not followed, feelings of guilt may result. The superego is one of the most misunderstood of Freudian concepts. In addition to elements of conscience, the superego also contains what Freud called the *ego-ideal*, which is a symbolic representation of what society values. The ego-ideal differs from the conscience in that it is less forceful in controlling behaviour in the absence of the likelihood of discovery.

Although Freud wrote little about crime per se, he did spend much of his time attempting to account for a variety of abnormal behaviour, much of which might lead to violations of the criminal law. One way in which a person might be led into crime, according to the perspective of psychoanalysis, is as the result of a poorly developed superego. In the individual without a fully functional superego, the mind is left to fall back on the ego's reality-testing ability. To put it simply, the ego, operating without a moral guide, may select a path of action which, although expedient at the time, violates the law. Individuals suffering from poor superego development are likely to seek immediate gratification without giving a great deal of thought to the long-term consequences of the choices they may make in the moment.

From the Freudian point of view, inadequate sublimation can be another cause of crime. **Sublimation** is the psychological process whereby one item of consciousness comes to be symbolically substituted for another. Sublimation is often a healthy process. Freud held that the many outstanding accomplishments of the human species have been due to sublimation, through which powerful sexual and aggressive drives are channelled into socially constructive activity. However, crime can result from improper sublimation. According to Freud, for example, a man may hate his mother, his hatred being perhaps the faulty by-product of the striving for adult independence. He may, however, be unable to give voice to that hatred directly. Perhaps the mother is too powerful, or the experience of confronting his mother would be too embarrassing for the man. The man may act out his hatred for his mother, however, by attacking other women whom he symbolically substitutes in his mind for the mother figure. Hence, from the Freudian perspective, men who beat their wives, become rapists, sexually harass co-workers, or otherwise abuse women may be enacting feelings derived from early life experiences that they would be unable to otherwise express.

Sublimation, like many other psychoanalytical concepts, is a slippery idea. Mother hatred, for example, although a plausible explanation for acts of violence by men against women, is difficult to demonstrate, and the link between such hidden feelings and adult action is impossible to prove. Even so, should an offender be so diagnosed it would do little good for him to deny the psychoanalytical explanation assigned to him, because doing so would only result in the professional reproach, "Yes, but you have hidden the knowledge about your true feelings from yourself. You are not aware of why you act the way you do!"

Freud also postulated the existence of a death instinct, which he called **Thanatos**. According to Freud, all living things, which he referred to as "animate matter," have a fundamental desire to relax back into an inanimate state, or death. Living, said Freud, takes energy and cunning. Hence death, at least at some level, is an easier choice because it

Sublimation the psychological process whereby one aspect of consciousness comes to be symbolically substituted for another.

Thanatos a death wish.

Sigmund Freud (1856–1939), examining a manuscript in the office of his Vienna home, circa 1930.
Corbis.

releases the organism from the need for continued expenditure of energy. Thanatos was seen as contributing to many of the advances made by the human species and as underlying a large proportion of individual accomplishments. Were it not for a wish to die, operative at some basic instinctual level, said Freud, few people would have the courage to take risks—and without the assumption of risk, precious little progress is possible in any sphere of life. The notion of an innate death wish has been used to explain why some offenders seem to behave in ways that ensure their eventual capture. Serial killers who send taunting messages to the police, terrorists who tell the media of their planned activities or take credit for public attacks, rapists who "accidentally" leave their wallets at the scene, and burglars who break into occupied dwellings may all, for the most part unconsciously, be seeking to be stopped, captured, punished, and even killed.

Neurosis functional disorders of the mind or of the emotions involving anxiety, phobia, or other abnormal behaviour.

From the Freudian perspective, **neurosis**, a minor form of mental illness, may also lead to crime. Neurotic individuals are well in touch with reality but may find themselves anxious, fearful of certain situations, or unable to help themselves or others. Fear of heights, for example, may be a neurosis, as may be compulsive handwashing, or eating disorders. A classic example of the compulsive neurotic can be found in the individual who uses paper towels to open doorknobs, refraining from touching the knob directly for fear of picking up germs. Although such behaviour may be unreasonable from the point of view of others, it is reality based (there *are* germs on doorknobs) and, for the individual demonstrating it, probably unavoidable. Most neuroses do not lead to crime. Some, however, can. A few years ago, for example, a man from Iowa was sentenced to nearly 6 years in prison and fined $200 000 for the theft of more than 21 000 rare books from hundreds of libraries.[20] The offender, whose compulsive interest in rare books began at yard sales and with searches in trash dumpsters, may have seen himself as involved in a messianic mission to preserve recorded history. Compulsive shoplifters may also be manifesting another form of neurosis—one in which a powerful need to steal can drive even well-heeled individuals to risk arrest and jail.

Personality Types and Crime

In 1964, a British psychiatrist named **Hans Eysenck** published *Crime and Personality*, a book-length treatise in which he explained crime as the result of fundamental personality characteristics linked to individual central nervous system characteristics.[21] Eysenck described three personality dimensions, each with links to criminality. Psychoticism, which Eysenck said "is believed to be correlated with criminality at all stages,"[22] is defined by characteristics such as a lack of empathy, creativeness, tough-mindedness, and antisociability. Psychoticism, said Eysenck, is also frequently characterized by hallucinations and delusions. Extroverts were described as carefree, dominant, and venturesome—operating with high levels of energy. "The typical extrovert," Eysenck wrote "is sociable, likes parties, has many friends, needs to have people to talk to, and does not like reading or studying by himself."[23] Neuroticism, the third of the personality characteristics Eysenck described, was said to be typical of people who are irrational, shy, moody, and emotional.

According to Eysenck, of these three personality types, psychotics are the most likely to be criminal because they combine high degrees of emotionalism with similarly high levels of extroversion. Individuals with such characteristics, claimed Eysenck, are especially difficult to socialize and to train. Eysenck cited many studies in which children and others

CHAPTER 7

203

**Psychological and
Psychiatric
Foundations of Criminal
Behaviour**

who harboured characteristics of psychoticism, extroversion, and neuroticism performed poorly on conditioning tests designed to measure how quickly they would respond appropriately to external stimuli. Conscience, said Eysenck, is fundamentally a conditioned reflex. Therefore, an individual who does not take well to conditioning will not fully develop a conscience and will continue to exhibit the asocial behavioural traits of a very young child.

Eysenck's approach might be termed *biopsychology*, because he claimed that personality traits were fundamentally dependent upon physiology—specifically upon the individual's autonomic nervous system, which Eysenck described as "underlying the behavioral trait of emotionality or neuroticism."[24] Some individuals were said to possess nervous systems that could not handle a great deal of stimulation. Such individuals, like the introvert, shun excitement and are easily trained. They rarely become criminal offenders. Those who possess nervous systems that need stimulation, however, seek excitement and are far more likely to turn to crime. As support for his thesis, Eysenck cited studies of twins showing that identical twins were much more likely than fraternal twins to perform similarly on simple behavioural tests. In particular, Eysenck quoted from the work of J.B.S. Haldane, who was reputed to be a "world-famous geneticist." Haldane, having studied the criminality of 13 sets of identical twins, concluded, "[a]n analysis of the thirteen cases shows not the faintest evidence of freedom of the will in the ordinary sense of the word. A man of a certain constitution, put in a certain environment, will be a criminal. Taking the record of any criminal, we could predict the behavior of a monozygotic twin placed in the same environment. Crime is destiny."[25] Up to two-thirds of all behavioural variance, claimed Eysenck, could be attributed to "a strong genetic basis."

The Link between Frustration and Aggression

In his early writings, Freud suggested that aggressive behaviour was a response to frustration. Aggression toward others, Freud said, is a natural response to frustrating limitations imposed upon a person. The frustration-aggression thesis was later developed more fully in the writings of J. Dollard,[26] Albert Bandura, Richard H. Walters, and others. Dollard's frustration-aggression theory held that although frustration can lead to various forms of behaviour—including regression, sublimation, and aggressive fantasy—direct aggression toward others is its most likely consequence. Because everyone suffers some form of frustration throughout life, beginning with weaning and toilet training, Dollard argued, aggression is a natural consequence of living. Dollard pointed out, however, that aggression could be manifested in socially acceptable ways (perhaps through contact sports, military or law enforcement careers, or simple verbal attacks) and that it could be engaged in vicariously by observing others who are acting violently (as in movies, on television, through popular fiction, and so on). Dollard applied the psychoanalytical term "displacement" to the type of violence that is vented on something or someone who is not the source of the original frustration and suggested that satisfying one's aggressive urges through observation was a form of "catharsis."

The story of Pierre Lebrun, a former employee of a public transit company, provides us with an example of the frustration-aggression theory as it applies to real-life crime. In April 1999, the 40-year-old Lebrun entered the maintenance garage at a public transportation company in Ottawa and opened fire with a high-powered .30-06-calibre hunting rifle, killing four people and wounding two others before taking his own life. In his suicide note left at his parents' home, Lebrun expressed his anger toward certain former co-workers whom, he claimed, had teased him for a speech impediment. Ironically, none of the men on his "hit list" were victimized. He had been fired by his company several years earlier but his union fought the dismissal and won. Lebrun had resigned from the company four months before the killing. It appears he was acting out of the frustrations born of his experiences with his co-workers.[27]

Some psychologists have tried to identify what it is that causes some individuals to displace aggression or to experience it vicariously (through catharsis), while others respond violently and directly toward the immediate source of their frustrations. Andrew Henry and James Short, for example, writing in the 1950s, suggested that child-rearing practices are a major determining factor in such a causal nexus.[28] Restrictive parents who both punish and love their children, said Henry and Short, will engender in their children the ability to suppress outward expressions of aggression. When one parent punishes and the other loves, or when both punish but neither show love, children can be expected to show anger directly and perhaps even immediately, because they will not be threatened with the loss of love. Physical punishment, explained Henry and Short, rarely threatens the loss of love, and children so punished cannot be expected to refrain from direct displays of anger.

In 1960, Stewart Palmer studied murderers and their siblings to determine the degree of frustration they had been exposed to as children.[29] He found that male murderers had experienced much more frustration than their brothers—in fact, more than twice as many frustrating experiences, ranging from difficult births to serious illnesses, childhood beatings, severe toilet training, and negative school experiences, were reported by the murderers than by their law-abiding siblings.

The Psychotic Offender

For many of us, extreme forms of criminal behaviour are often difficult to understand, as the gruesome story of Sandy Charles illustrates.[30] At his trial, it was argued that Charles was responding to delusional beliefs that if he consumed the flesh of another human he would acquire supernatural powers. In July 1995, at the age of 14, Charles lured a 7-year-old playmate into a wooded area near his LaRonge, Saskatchewan, home, where he killed and mutilated him. He then cut strips from his victim's flesh and boiled them on a stove. Charged with first-degree murder, Charles pled insanity due to his diagnosed schizophrenia. A jury accepted his defence of insanity and found him not criminally responsible for his actions.

Psychosis a form of mental illness in which sufferers are said to be out of touch with reality.

Some seemingly inexplicable forms of criminality may be the result of **psychosis**. Whereas neurotic individuals often face only relatively minor problems in living, psychotic people, according to psychiatric definitions, are out of touch with reality in some fundamental way. They may suffer from hallucinations, delusions, or other breaks with reality. The classic psychotic thinks he is Napoleon, or sees spiders covering what others see only as a bare wall. Individuals suffering from a psychosis are said to be psychotic. Psychoses may be either organic, that is, caused by physical damage to, or abnormalities in, the brain; or functional, that is, those with no known physical cause. Gwynn Nettler says "[t]hought disorder is the hallmark of psychosis ... people are called crazy when, at some extremity, they cannot 'think straight.'"[31] Nettler identifies three characteristics of psychotic individuals:

CHAPTER 7

205

**Psychological and
Psychiatric
Foundations of Criminal
Behaviour**

Sandy Charles was found not criminally
responsible for the death and mutilation of a
playmate. How are these types of offenders
dealt with by the Canadian criminal justice
system?

Saskatoon StarPhoenix, Richard Marjan.

"(1) a grossly distorted conception of reality, (2) moods, and swings of mood, that seem inappropriate to circumstance, and (3) marked inefficiency in getting along with others and caring for oneself."[32] Psychotic persons have also been classified as schizophrenic or paranoid schizophrenic. **Schizophrenics** are said to be characterized by disordered or disjointed thinking, in which the types of logical associations they make are atypical of other people. **Paranoid schizophrenics** suffer from delusions and hallucinations.

Unfortunately, psychiatrists have not been able to agree on definitive schizophrenic criteria that would allow for convenient application of the term. One prominent psychiatrist writes of "how varying … schizophrenia may appear, ranging from no striking symptoms at all to conspicuous psychotic features …. Thus on the surface," he continues, "the schizophrenic may appear normal and, to some extent, lead a conventional life."[33] The same author later tells us "[s]chizophrenia is not a clearly defined disease …. It is characterized rather by a … kind of alteration of thinking or feeling …."[34] At the very least, then, we can safely say that schizophrenia is a disorganization of the personality. In its most extreme form, it may manifest itself by way of hallucinations, delusions, and seemingly irrational behaviour.

With these caveats in mind, it is fair to say that psychoses may lead to crime in a number of ways. In a highly publicized case in Ottawa, Ontario, Jeffrey Arenburg waited outside a local television station and shot and killed well-known sportscaster Brian Smith as he left work. Arenburg, who had a history of paranoid schizophrenia, believed that radio and television stations were broadcasting his thoughts through the fillings in his teeth. His assault on Smith was his attempt to stop these broadcasts.

Refer to the section of this chapter entitled "Mental Illness and the Law" for an understanding of how our criminal justice system deals with those who are afflicted with a recognized psychosis such as paranoid schizophrenia.

Schizophrenics
mentally ill individuals
who are out of touch
with reality and suffer
from disjointed
thinking.

**Paranoid
schizophrenics**
schizophrenic
individuals who suffer
from delusions and
hallucinations.

The Psychopath

The term *psychopathy* comes from the Greek words *psyche* (meaning "soul" or "mind") and *pathos* ("suffering" or "illness"). The word appears to have been coined by the 19th-century German psychiatrist Richard von Krafft-Ebing (1840–1902),[35] making its way into English psychiatric literature through the writings of Polish-born American psychiatrist Bernard Glueck[36] (1884–1972) and William Healy (1869–1963).[37] The **psychopath**, also called a **sociopath**, was usually viewed as perversely cruel, often without thought or feeling for his victims.[38] By the outbreak of World War II, the role of the psychopathic personality in crime causation had become central to psychological theorizing. In 1944, for example, the well-known psychiatrist David Abrahamsen wrote, "[w]hen we seek to explain the riddle of human conduct in general and of antisocial behavior in particular, the solution must be sought in the personality."[39]

The concept of a psychopathic personality, which by its very definition is asocial, was fully developed by **Hervey Cleckley** in his 1964 book *The Mask of Sanity*.[40] Cleckley described the psychopath as a "moral idiot," or as one who does not feel empathy with others, even though that person may be fully cognizant of what is objectively happening around them. The central defining characteristic of a psychopath is *poverty of affect*, or the inability to accurately imagine how others think and feel. Hence, it becomes possible for a psychopath to inflict pain and engage in acts of cruelty without appreciation for the victim's suffering. Charles Manson, for example, whom some have called a psychopath, once told a television reporter, "I could take this book and beat you to death with it, and I wouldn't feel a thing. It'd be just like walking to the drugstore."

According to Cleckley, psychopathic indicators appear early in life, often in the teenage years. They include lying, fighting, stealing, and vandalism. For a complete list of Checkley's criteria of psychopathy, please see Box 7.1 on page 208. Even earlier signs may be found, according to some authors, in bedwetting, cruelty to animals, sleepwalking, and fire-setting.[41] In a recent report prepared for the Correctional Service of Canada, psychopaths are described as "individuals who display impulsiveness, callousness, insincerity, pathological lying and deception, egocentricity, poor judgment, an impersonal sex life, and an unstable life plan.[42] Cleckley noted that, in the cases he had observed, the behavioural manifestations of psychopathy varied with the person's age, gender, and socioeconomic status.

The terms *psychopath* and *criminal* are not synonymous. Cleckley and others have noted that one can be a psychopath and not a criminal. Individuals manifesting many of the characteristics of a psychopathic personality, however, are likely, sooner or later, to run afoul of the law. As one writer on the topic says, "[t]he impulsivity and aggression, the selfishness in achieving one's own immediate needs, and the disregard for society's rules and laws bring these people to the attention of the criminal justice system."[43] Studies attempting to identify groups of non-criminal psychopaths have been inconclusive.[44]

For the past 40 years or so, researchers have worked on the development of tools and methods for the assessment of the anti-social personality. The leader in this field is **Robert Hare**, from the University of British Columbia. Hare and his colleagues have designed the Psychopathy Checklist—Revised (PCL-R), based on Cleckley's criteria of psychopathy. As

Psychopath or **sociopath** a person with a personality disorder, especially one manifested in aggressively anti-social behaviour, which is often said to be the result of a poorly developed superego.

CHAPTER 7

207

**Psychological and
Psychiatric
Foundations of Criminal
Behaviour**

Clifford Olson has never shown any guilt or remorse for the 11 young people he murdered in British Columbia in the early 1980s. He continues to torment the families of the victims by sending them letters with comments about the murders. Do you think he is the prototypical psychopath?

CP Photo/Regina Leader–Post/Bryan Schlosser.

a diagnostic tool, the PCL-R includes 20 indicators of psychopathy. Individuals are scored from "zero" to "three" for each item, with "zero" indicating not applicable, "one" uncertain, and "two" definitely present. Obviously, the higher the score, the more likely that the individual is a psychopath. Currently, the PCL-R is being used to assess both adult and young offenders in Canada.[45] In an evaluation of the use and misuse of the PCL-R (and the Psychopathy Checklist—Screening Version, PCL-SV) as an assessment tool, Hare contends that they provide a reliable and valid assessment of psychopathy. He concludes that "[t]hey are used widely for research purposes and for making decisions in the mental health and criminal justice systems. They are strong predictors of violence and recidivism in offenders and psychiatric patients, form a key part of current risk assessment procedures, and play an important role in many judicial decisions."[46]

The causes of psychopathology are unclear. Somatogenic causes, or those based on physiological features of the human organism, are said to include a malfunctioning of the central nervous system characterized by a low state of arousal that drives the sufferer to seek excitement, as well as brain abnormalities that may have been present in most anti-social personalities since birth. Work by Hare shows that an **electroencephalogram** (**EEG**) taken of a psychopathic patient is frequently abnormal, reflecting "a malfunction of some . . .

Electroencephalogram (EEG) electrical measurements of brainwave activity.

Cleckley's Criteria of Psychopathy   Box 7.1

Robert Hare's 20 item checklist, which has come to be acknowledged as the standard psycho-diagnostic measurement for assessing psychopathy, is based on the trait list developed by Hervey M. Cleckley in his book, *The Mask of Sanity*. This list includes the following traits:

1. Considerable superficial charm and average or above average intelligence
2. Absence of delusions and other signs of irrational thinking
3. Absence of anxiety or other "neurotic" symptoms; considerable poise, calmness, and verbal facility
4. Unreliability, disregard for obligations, and no sense of responsibility in matters of little and great importance
5. Untruthfulness and insincerity
6. Antisocial behaviour which is inadequately motivated, poorly planned, and seeming to stem from an inexplicable impulsiveness
7. Inadequately motivated antisocial behaviour
8. Poor judgment and failure to learn from experience
9. Pathological egocentricity; total self-centeredness; incapacity for real love and attachment
10. General poverty of deep and lasting emotions
11. Lack of any true insight; inability to see oneself as others do
12. Ingratitude for any special considerations, kindness, and trust
13. Fantastic and objectionable behaviour after drinking and sometimes without drinking, such as vulgarity, rudeness, quick mood shifts, and pranks
14. No history of genuine suicide attempts
15. An impersonal, trivial, and poorly integrated sex life
16. Failure to have a life plan and to live in any ordered way, unless it be a life promoting self-defeat

Source: Permission granted by W.A. Dolan. Used with permission.

inhibitory mechanisms," making it unlikely that persons characterized by anti-social personality disorder will "learn to inhibit behavior that is likely to lead to punishment."[47] It is difficult, however, to diagnose anti-social personalities through physiological measurements, since similar EEG patterns also show up in patients with other types of disorders. Psychogenic causes, or those rooted in early interpersonal experiences, are said to include the inability to form attachments to parents or other caregivers early in life, sudden separation from the mother during the first six months of life, and other early forms of insecurity. In short, a lack of love, or the sensed inability to unconditionally depend on one central loving figure (typically the mother in most psychological literature), immediately following birth is often posited as a major psychogenic factor contributing to the development of anti-social personality disorder. Other psychogenic causes have been identified to include deficiencies in childhood role playing, the inability to identify with one's parents during childhood and adolescence, and severe rejection by others.

Most studies of psychopathy have involved male subjects. Only rarely have researchers focused on women with psychopathic personalities, and it is believed that only a small proportion of those afflicted with the psychopathy disorder are women.[48] What little research there is suggests that psychopathic women exhibit many of the same definitive characteristics as do their male counterparts, and that they assume their anti-social roles at similarly early ages.[49] The lifestyles of female psychopaths, however, appear to emphasize sexual

CHAPTER 7
209
**Psychological and
Psychiatric
Foundations of Criminal
Behaviour**

misconduct, including lifestyles involving abnormally high levels of sexual activity. Such research, however, can be misleading because cultural expectations of female sexual behaviour inherent in early studies may not always have been in keeping with reality. That is, so little may have been accurately known about female sexual activity to early researchers that the behaviour of women judged to possess anti-social personalities may have actually been far closer to the norm than originally believed.

Anti-Social Personality Disorder

In recent years, the terms *sociopath* and *psychopath* have fallen into professional disfavour. In the attempt to identify sociopathic individuals, some psychologists have come to place greater emphasis on the type of *behaviour* exhibited, rather than on the identifiable personality traits. Traditionally, affective and interpersonal traits such as deceit, shallow affect, selfishness, and lack of empathy, guilt, or remorse have been central to the diagnosis of psychopathy. In 1980, the American Psychiatric Association's *Diagnostic and Statistical Manual of Mental Disorders* (DSM-III) had discontinued using the words *sociopath* and *psychopath*, replacing them with the terms *anti-social* and *asocial personality*.[50] The **anti-social (asocial) personality** type was defined as "individuals who are basically unsocialized and whose behavior pattern brings them repeatedly into conflicts with society. They are incapable of significant loyalty to individuals, groups, or social values. They are grossly selfish, callous, irresponsible, impulsive, and unable to feel guilt or to learn from experience and punishment. Frustration tolerance is low. They tend to blame others or offer plausible rationalization for their behavior."[51] The definition of the anti-social personality disorder (sometimes referred to as APD, ASPD, or ANPD) focused on behavioural patterns exemplified by persistent violations of social norms such as lying, stealing, cheating, truancy, and inconsistent work behaviour.[52]

Individuals manifesting characteristics of an anti-social personality have a good likelihood of running afoul of the law. As one writer says, " The impulsivity and aggression, the selfishness in achieving one's own immediate needs, and the disregard for society's rules and laws brings these people to the attention of the criminal justice system."[53] Moreover, studies of individuals who score high on psychological inventories designed to measure the degree of psychopathy have found to exhibit high rates of both criminality and recidivism.[54] A recent Canadian study of penitentiary inmates in Quebec, which attempts to classify criminal offenders by type of mental disorder, determined that anti-social personalities comprise 46.6 percent of all inmates, while schizophrenics account for 6.3 percent, manic-depressives another 1.6 percent, drug-disordered persons 18.6 percent, depressed individuals 8.1 percent, and alcohol abuse–related sufferers another 33.1 percent.[55] A review of 20 such studies found great variation in the degree and type of disorder said to be prevalent among incarcerated offenders.[56] The studies categorized from 0.5 to 26 percent of all inmates as psychotic, 2.4 to 28 percent as mentally subnormal, 5.6 to 70 percent as psychopathic, 2 to 7.9 percent as neurotic, and from 11 to 80 percent of inmates as suffering from mental disorders induced by alcoholism or excessive drinking. Generally, however, such studies conclude that few convicted felons are free from mental *impairment* of one sort or another. It is important to note, however, that the results from studies like these and others are dependent upon the characteristics used in the diagnostic tool. If the diagnostic criteria change, so too will the perceived prevalence of anti-social personality disorder.

anti-social or asocial personality refers to individuals who are basically unsocialized and whose behaviour pattern can bring them into conflict with society.

anti-social personality disorder refers to individuals displaying a personality disorder that includes aggressive, impulsive behaviour and a general disregard for the rights of others.

The shift away from definitions that focused on personality traits and toward those that focused on behavioural traits was due largely to the difficulty in measuring personality traits reliably. It appears easier to agree on the behaviours that typify a disorder rather than to identify the reasons why the behaviours occur. In the opinion of experts in the field of psychopathy, what has resulted is "a diagnostic category with good reliability but dubious validity, a category that lacked congruence with other, well-established conceptions of psychopathy."[57] Essentially, the absence of personality traits in the diagnosis of ASPD means that anti-social persons with completely different personalities, attitudes, and motivations can now share the same diagnosis.

It is important to note that the distinction in definitions between the anti-social personality disorder and the psychopath means that, while most psychopaths meet the criteria for ASPD, most individuals with ASPD are *not* psychopaths. This failure to distinguish between psychopathy and anti-social personality disorder means that offenders are often mistakenly diagnosed as psychopaths rather than individuals with ASPD. Psychopathy is usually considered an aggravating rather than a mitigating circumstance, with the prognosis for treatment being low and the prediction of reoffending being high. Diagnostic confusion about the two disorders has the potential of harming both psychiatric offenders and society as well. There is hope that this situation of diagnostic confusion is addressed with the publication of the *Diagnostic and Statistical Manual of Mental Disorders V* scheduled for 2011.[58]

Crime as Adaptive Behaviour

Some psychiatric perspectives have held that " . . . crime is a compromise, representing for the individual the most satisfactory method of adjustment to inner conflicts which he cannot express otherwise. Thus, his acting out the crime fulfills a certain aim or purpose."[59] One pressing need of many criminals, according to some psychologists, is the need to be punished—which arises, according to psychiatric theory, from a sense of guilt. Psychiatrists who suggest that the need to be punished is a motivating factor in criminal behaviour are quick to point out that such a need may be a closely guarded secret, unknown even to the offender. Hence, from the psychiatric point of view, many drives, motives, and wishes are unconscious or even repressed by people who harbour them. The concept of repression holds that the human mind may choose to keep certain aspects of itself out of consciousness, possibly because of shame, self-loathing, or a simple lack of adequate introspection. The desire for punishment, however, sometimes comes to the fore. In the mid-1990s, for example, Westley Dodd was hanged to death by authorities in the state of Washington for the kidnap, rape, and murder of three little boys four years earlier. Dodd, who said he had molested dozens of children over the course of a decade, sought the death penalty after he was convicted, saying he deserved to die and vowing to sue the American Civil Liberties Union (ACLU) or anyone else who sought to save him.[60]

Crime can be adaptive in other ways as well. Some psychiatrists see it as an adaptation to life's stresses. According to Seymour L. Halleck,[61] turning to crime can provide otherwise disenfranchised individuals with a sense of power and purpose. In Halleck's words, "[d]uring the planning and execution of a criminal act the offender is a free man . . . . The value of this brief taste of freedom cannot be overestimated. Many of the criminal's apparently unreasonable actions are efforts to find a moment of autonomy . . . ."[62] Halleck says

CHAPTER 7

211

**Psychological and
Psychiatric
Foundations of Criminal
Behaviour**

that crime can also provide "excellent rationalizations" for perceived inadequacies—especially for those whose lives have been failures when judged against the benchmarks of the wider society. "The criminal is able to say . . . 'I could have been successful if I had not turned to crime. All my troubles have come to me because I have been bad.'"[63] Hence, crime, according to Halleck, provides "a convenient resource for denying, forgetting or ignoring . . . other inadequacies."

Insofar as the choice of crime reduces stresses that the individual faces by producing changes in the environment (empowerment), it is referred to as an **alloplastic adaptation**. When crime leads to stress reduction as a result of internal changes in beliefs, value systems, and so forth, it is called **autoplastic adaptation**. The offender who is able to deny responsibility for other failures by turning to crime is said to be seeking autoplastic adaptation. Because other forms of behaviour may also meet many of the same needs as does crime, Halleck points out that an individual may select crime over various other behavioural alternatives only when no reasonable alternatives are available or when criminal behaviour has inherent advantages—as might be the case under instances of economic or social oppression. (That is, individuals who are actively discriminated against may find personal and political significance in violating the laws of the oppressing society.)

In any case, from Halleck's point of view, crime "has many advantages even when considered independently of the criminal's conscious or unconscious needs for gratification."[64] In other words, even though crime can be immediately rewarding or intensely pleasureful, says Halleck, such rewards are more "fringe benefits" than anything else. The central significance of criminal behaviour for most offenders is that it "is an action which helps one survive with dignity."[65] Halleck tells us that "[w]e cannot understand the criminal unless we appreciate that his actions are much more than an effort to find a specific gratification."[66] In the final analysis, criminal behaviour is, from Halleck's point of view, a form of adjustment to stress and oppression.

Another approach to stress as a causative agent in crime commission suggests that stress may lead to aggression toward others and toward oneself (i.e., self-destructive behaviour such as suicide, smoking, and abuse of alcohol).[67] This approach attempts to measure stress at the societal level, arguing that although the relationship between stress and aggression has been studied at the individual level, "the neglect of social stress as an explanation for society-to-society differences in aggression may be partially due to a lack of an objective means of comparing the stressfulness of life in different societies . . . ."[68] Concluding that societal stress levels heighten levels of aggression, it is suggested that social policies should be created to reduce the impact of stressful events such as having to stop work, foreclosing on a mortgage, and dropping out of school.

Finally, we should recognize that perceptions vary, and although criminal behaviour may appear to be a valid choice for some individuals who are seeking viable responses to perceived stresses and oppression, their perceptions may not be wholly accurate. In other words, misperceived stress and oppression may still lead to crime, even when far simpler solutions may be found in a more realistic appraisal of one's situation.

Alloplastic adaptation
that form of adjustment resulting from changes in the environment surrounding an individual.

Autoplastic adaptation
that form of adjustment resulting from changes within an individual.

Social Learning Theory

Do violent computer games lead to violent crime? While the jury is still out on that question, the importance of imitation and modelling in shaping behaviour has long been studied. One of the earliest attempts to explain crime and deviance as learned behaviour can be found in the work of Gabriel Tarde (1843–1904), a French social theorist of the late 1800s. Tarde discounted the biological theories of Lombroso and others, which were so prevalent in that day, and suggested that it was possible to infer certain regularities or laws that appeared to govern the social world. The basis of any society, Tarde believed, was imitation—or, more precisely, the tendency of people to pattern their behaviour after the behaviour of others. Tarde developed a theory of human behaviour that built upon three laws of imitation and suggestion.[69] Tarde's first law held that individuals in close intimate contact with one another tend to imitate each other's behaviour. His second law stated that imitation moves from the top down. This means that poor people tend to imitate wealthy people, youngsters tend to emulate those older than themselves, lower-class people tend to imitate members of the upper class, and so on. The third law of imitation is the law of insertion, which says that new acts and behaviours tend to either reinforce or replace old ones. Hence, the music of each generation replaces the music of the one that preceded it, the politics of young people eventually become the politics of the nation, faddish drugs are substituted for traditional ones, and new forms of crime tend to take the place of older ones (as when, for example, computer criminals become a more serious threat to financial institutions than bank robbers do).

Modelling theory
a psychological perspective that says people learn how to behave by modelling themselves after others whom they have the opportunity to observe.

More recently, **Albert Bandura** has attempted to develop a comprehensive **modelling theory** of aggression. Bandura tells us that "[a] complete theory of aggression must explain how aggressive patterns are developed, what provokes people to behave aggressively, and what sustains such actions after they have been initiated."[70] Although everyone is capable of aggression, he says, "[p]eople are not born with . . . repertories of aggressive behavior. They must learn them." He goes on to say, "the specific forms that aggressive behavior takes, the frequency with which it is expressed, the situation in which it is displayed, and the specific targets selected for attack are largely determined by social learning factors." According to Bandura, people learn by observing others. In some of his early work, Bandura experimented with children who observed adult role models striking inflatable cartoon characters. When the children were observed later, they too exhibited similarly aggressive behaviour toward the models. Bandura also studied violence on television and concluded that "[t]elevision is an effective tutor. Both laboratory and controlled field studies in which young children and adolescents are repeatedly shown either violence or non-violent fare, disclose that exposure to film violence shapes the form of aggression and typically increases interpersonal aggressiveness in everyday life." A later study, by other researchers, showed that even after 10 years the level of violence engaged in by young adults was directly related to the degree of violent television they had been exposed to as children.[71]

Modelling theory also shows how people can model the behaviour of others. Bandura explained modelling behaviour by reference to the frequent hijacking of domestic airliners to Cuba that occurred in the United States in the late 1960s and early 1970s. Such hijackings, Bandura found, followed immediately on the heels of similar incidents in Eastern European nations under Soviet domination. American hijackings, he said, were simply modelling those in Europe, and hijackers in the United States were learning from news accounts of their foreign tutors.

Once aggressive patterns of behaviour have been acquired, it becomes necessary to show how they can be activated. Aggression can be provoked, Bandura suggests, through physical assaults and verbal threats and insults, as well as by thwarting a person's hopes or obstructing his or her goal-seeking behaviour. Deprivation and "adverse reductions in the

CHAPTER 7
213
**Psychological and
Psychiatric
Foundations of Criminal
Behaviour**

conditions of life" (a lowered standard of living, the onset of disease, a spouse leaving or caught cheating, etc.) are other potential triggers of aggression. Bandura adds, however, that a human being's ability to foresee the future consequences of present behaviour infuses another dimension into the activation of learned patterns of aggression. That is, aggressive behaviour can be perceived as holding future benefits for individuals exhibiting it. In short, it can be seen as a means to a desired end.

An example of aggression that resulted from thwarted goal seeking, and which may have been seen as holding future benefits for the boy involved, occurred in the early 1990s when Gavin Mandin shot and killed his parents and two sisters.[72] Mandin, who was 15 at the time, waited in the family farmhouse not far from Edmonton, Alberta, for the rest of his family to return from a shopping trip. When the car pulled into the driveway, Mandin sighted through the scope of his pump-action, .22-calibre rifle and fired through a window and screen in the house. A bullet penetrated his father Maurice's temple as he stepped out of the car, killing him instantly. His mother, Susan, still in the car, looked up as another shot crashed through the car's windshield and entered her brain. Mandin then shot his two sisters, Isla, 12, and Janelle, 10, at point-blank range as they sat in the back seat of the car, first in the head and then with the rifle pressed against their chests. Mandin then drove the car with the bodies in it to an area of thick bush nearby. Using ropes and an all-terrain vehicle, Mandin dragged his father's body further into the bush.

By all accounts, Mandin's home life had been normal enough. Mandin was, reportedly, the "apple of his mother's eye" and she would defend him in all circumstances. However, there were signs that Mandin was not as enamoured of his family. Notes found behind Mandin's bed read, "I hate Janelle, I hate Susan, I hate Isla," and "Susan can't make me do anything. I wish she were dead." One particularly disturbing treatise said, "There will come the day when I rule. I will be the leader of the universe. All I love and desire will be mine. I will be the most powerful man on earth. I will have all the world it will be my backyard, all my enemies will die by my hand."[73] During his interrogation by RCMP investigators, Mandin cited many reason for his actions. He stated that he was made to clean his room, carry groceries into the house, and wash dishes. He disliked going to church services with the family, so he put a lock on his door to keep them from disturbing him. Mandin told RCMP investigator Corporal Ted Lachuk,

> sometimes, like, I will have something important to say to my mother and she will be sitting down and eating and I will come up to her and say "mom" and she won't do anything and I'll just keep calling her again and again. One time I called her eight or nine times and she didn't even answer. A couple of times I even tapped her on the shoulder and she ignores me and it really makes me angry.

Shortly after being taken into custody, Mandin declared, "I guess I get the house now, eh?" Later he stated that he intended to use a $1000 bond his mother had saved for him as an investment, to become a "zillionaire."[74]

It is Bandura's contention that individuals sometimes become aggressive because they are rewarded for doing so. The early-20th-century North American concept of a "macho" male figure—virile and masculine—for example, was often associated with the expectation of substantial reward. The macho male figure was the one who won the most respect from his fellows, inevitably came away with the greatest honours (on the playing field, in school, from the community, etc.), and eventually married the most desirable woman. Whether this perception was accurate, it was nonetheless subscribed to by a significant proportion of North American men and, for many decades, served as a guide to daily behaviour.

Another form of reward can flow from aggression. Bandura called it the "reduction of aversive treatment." By this he meant that simply standing up for one's self can improve the way one is treated by others. For example, standing up to a bully is often the most effective way of dealing with the harassment one might otherwise face. Similarly, there is an old saying that "the squeaky wheel gets the grease," and it means, quite simply, that people who are the most demanding will be recognized. Aggressive people often get what they go after.

Bandura recognized that all persons have self-regulatory mechanisms that can ameliorate the tendency toward aggression. People reward or punish themselves, Bandura said, according to internal standards they have for judging their own behaviour. Hence, aggression may be inhibited in people who, for example, value religious, ethical, or moral standards of conduct such as compassion, thoughtfulness, and courtesy. Nonetheless, Bandura concluded, people who devalue aggression may still engage in it through a process he called "disengagement," whereby rationalizations are constructed to overcome internal inhibitions. Disengagement may result from (1) "attributing blame to one's victims," (2) dehumanization through bureaucratization, automation, urbanization, and high social mobility, (3) vindication of aggressive practices by legitimate authorities, and (4) desensitization resulting from repeated exposure to aggression in any of a variety of forms.

Social learning theory has been criticized for lacking comprehensive explanatory power. How, for example, can striking differences in sibling behaviour, when early childhood experiences were likely much the same, be explained? Similarly, why do apparent differences exist between the sexes with regard to degree and type of criminality—irrespective of social background and early learning experiences? More recent versions of social learning theory, sometimes called "cognitive social learning theory," attempt to account for such differences by hypothesizing that reflection and cognition play a significant role in how a person interprets what is observed and then forms responses.[75] Hence, few people are likely to behave precisely as others, because they will have their own ideas about what observed behaviour means and about the consequences of emulation.

Behaviour Theory

Behaviour theory a psychological perspective positing that individual behaviour that is rewarded will increase in frequency, while that which is punished will decrease.

Operant behaviour behaviour that affects the environment in such a way as to produce responses or further behavioural cues.

Behaviour theory has sometimes been called the "stimulus-response approach to human behavior .... At the heart of behavior theory is the notion that behavior is determined by environmental consequences which it produces for the individual concerned."[76] When an individual's behaviour results in rewards, or in the receipt of feedback which the individual, for whatever reason, regards as rewarding, then it is likely that the behaviour will become more frequent. Under such circumstances, the behaviour in question is said to be reinforced. Conversely, when punishment follows behaviour, chances are that the frequency of that type of behaviour will decrease. The individual's responses are termed **operant behaviour**, because behavioural choices effectively operate upon the surrounding environment to produce consequences for the behaving individual. Similarly, stimuli provided by the environment become behavioural cues that serve to elicit conditioned responses from individuals. Responses are said to be conditioned according to the individual's past experiences, wherein behavioural consequences effectively defined some forms of behaviour as desirable and others as undesirable. Behaviour theory is often

CHAPTER 7

215

**Psychological and
Psychiatric
Foundations of Criminal
Behaviour**

Rewards desirable
behavioural
consequences likely to
increase the frequency of
occurrence of that
behaviour.

Punishments
undesirable behavioural
consequences likely to
decrease the frequency
of occurrence of that
behaviour.

employed by parents seeking to control children through a series of **rewards** and **punishments**. Young children may be punished, for example, with spanking, the loss of a favoured toy (at least for a period of time), a turned-off television, and so forth. Older children are often told what rules they are expected to obey and the rewards that they can anticipate receiving from adherence to those rules. They also know that punishments will follow if they do not obey the rules.

Rewards and punishments have been further divided into four conceptual categories: (1) positive rewards, which increase the frequency of approved behaviour by adding something desirable to the situation—as when a "good" child is given a toy; (2) negative rewards, which increase the frequency of approved behaviour by removing something distressful from the situation—as when a "good" child is permitted to skip the morning's chores; (3) positive punishments, which decrease the frequency of unwanted behaviour by adding something undesirable to the situation—as when a "bad" child is spanked; and (4) negative punishments, which decrease the frequency of unwanted behaviour by removing something desirable from the situation—as when a "bad" child's candy is taken away. According to behaviour theory, it is through the application of rewards and punishments that behaviour is shaped.

Behaviour theory differs from other psychological theories in that the major determinants of behaviour are envisioned as residing in the environment surrounding the individual rather than actually in the individual. Perhaps the best known proponent of behaviour theory is Burrhus Frederic Skinner (1904–1990), popularly referred to as **B.F. Skinner**. Skinner rejected unobservable psychological constructs, focusing instead on patterns of responses to external rewards and stimuli. Skinner did extensive animal research involving behavioural concepts and created the notion of programmed instruction, which allows students to work at their own pace and provides immediate rewards for learning accomplishments.

Although behaviour theory has much to say about the reformation of criminal offenders through the imposition of punishment, the approach is equally significant for its contributions to understanding the genesis of such behaviour. As one writer states, "it is the balance of reinforcement and punishment in an individual's learning history which will dictate the presence or absence of criminal behavior."[77] According to the behavioural model, crime results when individuals "receive tangible rewards (positive reinforcement) for engaging in delinquent and criminal behavior, particularly when no other attractive alternative is available."[78]

A number of years ago, for example, Sundahkeh "Ron" Bethune, 15, shot and killed a 26-year-old pizza delivery man who gunned his car motor as Bethune attempted to rob him. Ron, who had been dabbling in the drug trade and who could afford high-priced clothing, jewellery, and other accoutrements of apparent wealth, was esteemed by many other young people in his North Carolina community. When the delivery man tried to run from Ron in front of a group of his friends, Bethune saw no other choice but to kill him. "I just had to show them I wasn't some little punk," he said afterward in a prison interview.[79] Ron Bethune did not think of the long-term consequences of his behaviour on the night of the killing. All he wanted was to earn the approval of those who were watching him. The crowd's anticipated awestruck response to murder was all the reward Ron needed to pull the trigger that night. He was sentenced to a five-year sentence of incarceration for second-degree murder.

Behaviour theory has been criticized for ignoring the role that cognition plays in human behaviour. Martyrs, for example, persist in what may be defined by the wider society as undesirable behaviour, even in the face of severe punishment—including the loss of their own lives. No degree of punishment is likely to deter a martyr who answers to some higher call. Similarly, criminals who are punished for official law violations may find that their immediate social group interprets criminal punishment as status enhancing. From the point of view of behaviour theory, criminal punishments are in danger of losing sway over many forms of human behaviour in today's diverse society. Our society's fragmented value system leads to various interpretations of criminal punishments, thereby changing the significance of experiences such as arrest, conviction, and imprisonment. In times past, criminal offenders were often shunned and became social outcasts. Today, in some circles, those who have been judged criminal may find that their new status holds many rewards.

Mental Illness and the Law

Mental disorder (psychological) disease of the mind including schizophrenia, paranoia, senile dementia, melancholia, various types of epilepsy, and delirium tremens caused by alcohol abuse; **Mental disorder (law)** a legally established inability to understand right from wrong, or to conform one's behaviour to the requirements of the law. Also, a defence allowable in criminal courts.

Mental disorder or insanity is a defence allowable in criminal courts. A criminal defendant may be found not guilty by reason of mental disorder and avoid punitive sanctions even when it is clear that he or she committed a legally circumscribed act. This area of law has been one of endless debate. The *Criminal Code of Canada* defines mental disorder as a "disease of the mind." Whether a specific condition is a disease of the mind, however, is a question of law. While medical evidence is used to assist a judge in deciding whether the accused suffers a disease of the mind, the Supreme Court of Canada has stated that the protection of public safety must also be considered. For example, if the accused suffers from a recurring condition that may continue to present a danger to the public, then, the Court has ruled, the accused's condition should be treated as a mental disorder.[80] A number of mental disorders are recognized by the courts as diseases of the mind. They include schizophrenia, paranoia, senile dementia, melancholia, various types of epilepsy, and delirium tremens caused by alcohol abuse. However, self-induced states caused by alcohol or drugs, and temporary conditions such as hysteria and concussion, are excluded.[81] The burden of proving a claim of "not guilty by reason of mental disorder," however, falls upon the defendant. Just as a person is assumed to be innocent at the start of any criminal trial, so too is the person assumed to be sane.

The McNaughten Rule

McNaughten rule a standard for judging legal insanity that requires that offenders did not know what they were doing, or if they did, that they did not know it was wrong.

Inherent in the discussion of mental disorder and the law is the concept of criminal responsibility. The roots of this notion are found in British tradition and, in particular, in the case of Daniel McNaughten (also spelled "M'Naughton" and "M'Naghton"). This case was one of the first instances within the Western legal tradition where insanity was accepted as a defence to criminal liability. McNaughten was accused of the 1844 killing of Edward Drummond, the secretary of British Prime Minister Sir Robert Peel. By all accounts, McNaughten had intended to kill Peel but, because he was suffering from mental disorganization, shot Drummond instead, mistaking him for Peel. At his trial, the defence presented information to show that McNaughten was suffering from delusions, including the belief that Peel's political party was, in some vague way, persecuting him. The court accepted his lawyer's claims and the defence of insanity was established in Western law. Other jurisdictions were quick to adopt the **McNaughten rule**, as the judge's decision in the case came

CHAPTER 7

217

**Psychological and
Psychiatric
Foundations of Criminal
Behaviour**

to be called. The McNaughten rule holds that individuals cannot be held criminally responsible for their actions if at the time of the offence either (1) they did not know what they were doing, or (2) they did not know that what they were doing was wrong.

Today, the McNaughten rule is still followed in Canada when mental disorder is at issue in criminal cases. Critics of the McNaughten rule say that, although the notion of intent inherent within it appeals well to lawyers, "[i]t is ... so alien to current concepts of human behavior that it has been vigorously attacked by psychiatrists. An obvious difficulty with the McNaughten rule is that practically everyone, regardless of the degree of his criminal disturbance, knows the nature and quality and rightness or wrongness of what he is doing."[82]

Fitness to Stand Trial and Not Criminally Responsible by Reason of Mental Disorder

When the question of mental fitness arises, two standards are assessed. First, is the accused fit to stand trial; that is, does he or she understand the nature of charges against him or her? If a psychiatric assessment, as ordered by the court, determines that the accused is unfit to stand trial (UST), then that individual is usually placed in a psychiatric facility or released under community supervision for ongoing treatment. The individual's case is reviewed annually, and the Crown is responsible for bringing it before the courts every two years. If the individual becomes fit to stand trial, he or she may be put on trial at that time.

The second standard of fitness is the accused's mental state at the time of the offence. If it is determined that the accused was unable, because of mental disorder, to understand the nature and consequences of his or her actions or that the actions were wrong, then the accused will not be held criminally responsible for the act. This finding of **not criminally responsible by reason of mental disorder (NCRMD)** acknowledges that the accused committed the offence but finds that the accused suffered from a mental disorder that made him or her incapable of appreciating the nature and quality of his or her actions or that the actions were wrong. When such a verdict of NCRMD is made, a disposition hearing is ordered to assess whether or not the accused poses any threat to the public or to him or herself. If not, that accused may be released under supervision to the community. Otherwise, the accused may be detained in a custody hospital, under certain conditions.

The length of time in hospital detention has been a subject of controversy in recent years. In 1991, the Supreme Court decision in *R. v. Swain* resulted in an overhaul of the existing legal insanity criteria and practices, most notably automatic and indefinite detention for those found legally insane. In that decision, the Court held not only that "[t]he duty of the trial judge to detain is unqualified by any standard whatsoever" but also that "[i]nsanity acquitees ... should be detained no longer than necessary to determine whether they are currently dangerous due to their insanity."[83] Bill C-30, which contained the amendments to the *Criminal Code* (Mental Disorder), was passed by Parliament in 1992 (see Box 7.2). These amendments reflect the basic principle of Canadian criminal law that to convict someone of a crime, the state must prove not only a wrongful act, but also a guilty mind. In the words of then Minister of Justice Kim Campbell, "The mental disorder provisions of the *Criminal Code* needed to be updated to reflect the evolution of society and the law. These changes will ensure that individuals are not deprived of their *Charter* rights ... At the same time, the amendments offer protection of the public from dangerous mentally disordered persons who come into conflict with the law."[84]

Not criminally responsible by reason of mental disorder (NCRMD) a finding that offenders are responsible for committing the offence that they have committed but, because of their prevailing mental condition, should be sent to a psychiatric hospital for treatment rather than to prison. The maximum length of stay is predetermined.

Interestingly, other countries use a variety of definitions of legal insanity. In the United States, where the issue falls within the jurisdiction of the individual state, there exist a number of alternatives. In addition to the McNaughten rule, the irresistible impulse test is employed in 18 states and holds that a defendant is not guilty of a criminal offence if the person, by virtue of his or her mental state or psychological condition, was not able to resist committing the action in question. Roughly one-quarter of the US states have adopted the "guilty but mentally ill" (GBMI) standard. A GBMI verdict means that a person can be held responsible for a specific criminal act, even though a degree of mental incompetence may be present in his or her personality. Individuals adjudicated GBMI are, in effect, found guilty of the criminal offence with which they are charged but, because of their mental condition, are generally sent to psychiatric hospitals for treatment rather than to prison.[85] Other standards include the Durham rule and the Brawner rule.

Provisions for the Hospitalization of Individuals Found "NCRMD"

Part XX.1 of the *Criminal Code of Canada* makes provisions for the treatment of individuals found NCRMD. The law stipulates that a person found NCRMD must attend a disposition hearing, which can either be held by the trial court, or, as is usually the case, be referred to a provincial review board made up of lawyers, psychiatrists, and other appointees. This disposition hearing must be held within 45 days of the NCRMD finding. The NCRMD person may be present at the disposition, may be represented by counsel, and may cross-examine witnesses. The disposition hearings are public and "may be conducted in as informal a manner as is appropriate in the circumstances."[86] The recommendation of the review board for the treatment of the NCRMD individual is expected to reflect the least intrusive or restrictive option consistent with the protection of society. For example, the court or review board might allow someone who committed a theft, who is not dangerous, and who is willing to submit to psychiatric treatment on an outpatient basis to stay at home rather than be sent to a hospital setting. Such a condition would be subject to the supervision of medical staff giving the treatment and to periodic reviews; changes may be effected as required. The review board in such a case would have the authority to revoke this status and order hospitalization, should the person's condition deteriorate.

Mental Disorder as a Defence   Box 7.2

The *Criminal Code of Canada* permits the defence of insanity, as follows:

Defence of Mental Disorder	**16.** (1)	No person is criminally responsible for an act committed or an omission made while suffering from a mental disorder that rendered the person incapable of appreciating the nature and quality of the act or omission or of knowing that it was wrong.
Presumption	(2)	Every person is presumed not to suffer from a mental disorder so as to be exempt from criminal responsibility by virtue of subsection (1), until the contrary is proved on the balance of probabilities.
Burden of Proof	(3)	The burden of proof that an accused was suffering from a mental disorder so as to be exempt from criminal responsibility is on the party that raises the issue.

Source: *Criminal Code of Canada*, R.S.C. 1985, c. C-46, s.16 [as amended S.C. 1991, c. 43, s. 2].

CHAPTER 7

219

Psychological and
Psychiatric
Foundations of Criminal
Behaviour

André Dallaire, a diagnosed paranoid schizophrenic, was declared not criminally responsible for attempting to kill Prime Minister Chrétien in his home. How does the Canadian criminal justice system deal with dangerous people such as Dallaire?
The Canadian Press/Fred Chartrand.

Bill C-30 further replaces the former practice of indefinite hospitalization under the Warrants of the Lieutenant-Governor with a system of "caps," or maximum periods of deprivation of liberty. The "capping" provides a rough equivalence between the way in which the criminal law treats sane and mentally disordered offenders. For example, in cases of murder the outer limit is life. In cases of offences against the person, the outer limit is 10 years or the maximum penalty stipulated by the *Criminal Code*, whichever is shorter. For all other offences, the "cap" is the lesser of 2 years or the maximum penalty stipulated by the *Criminal Code*. Nevertheless, if at the expiration of the "cap" the NCRMD person is still considered a danger, he or she can be involuntarily committed to a secure hospital under the authority of provincial mental health legislation. The initial length of hospitalization is determined by the review boards. Bill C-30 makes a review board mandatory in each province and stipulates that each NCRMD case be reviewed annually. All decisions rendered by the review boards are binding.

Despite public perception, the defence of mental disorder has not been used successfully in a large number of cases in Canada. There are some who argue, however, that this defence is being used more often since the introduction in 1976 of the 25-year minimum life sentence for first-degree murder.[87] A recent study of mentally accused and the criminal justice system by the Canadian Centre for Justice Statistics indicates that the total number of active cases before review boards in the early 2000s (including UST and NCRMD cases) was fewer than 3000.[88] Some high-profile cases in which the defence of mental disorder was used successfully include those of André Dallaire, the paranoid schizophrenic who tried unsuccessfully to assassinate then Prime Minister Chrétien; Dorothy Joudrie, who attempted to murder her husband with five blasts from a shotgun in Calgary; and Elizabeth Elliott, who stepped in front of a transport truck on a highway near Perth, Ontario, while carrying her five-year-old daughter. Elliott's schizophrenia and bipolar disorder had caused her to have religious delusions that were responsible for her behaviour.[89]

Social Policy and Forensic Psychology

Psychological theories continue to evolve. For example, recent research in the field has shown a stability of aggressiveness over time. That is, children who display early disruptive or aggressive behaviour have been found, through the use of studies that follow the same individuals over time, likely to continue their involvement in such behaviour as adults.[90] Some researchers have found that aggressiveness appears to stabilize over time.[91] Children who demonstrate aggressive traits early in life often evidence increasingly frequent episodes of such behaviour until, finally, it becomes a major component of the adolescent or adult personality. From this research, we can conclude that problem children are likely to become problem adults.

Expanding research of this sort holds considerable significance for those who are attempting to assess dangerousness and identify personal characteristics that would allow for the prediction of dangerousness in individual cases. The ability to accurately predict future dangerousness is of great concern to today's policy makers. In the late 1990s, for example, Jean Gerald Dionne, a convicted sex offender, was charged with the kidnapping, forcible confinement, and sexual assault of a teenaged girl. Dionne at the time had a record of assaulting a 58-year-old woman in 1980, of criminal negligence causing death in the drowning of a 2-year-old boy in 1982, and of sexually assaulting an 8-year-old, wheelchair-bound girl in 1991.[92]

Can past behaviour predict future behaviour? Do former instances of criminality presage additional ones, as appeared to be the case with Gerald Dionne? Are there other identifiable characteristics violent offenders might manifest that could serve as warning signs to criminal justice decision makers faced with the dilemma of whether to release convicted felons? This, like many other areas, is one about which criminologists are still learning. One recent study found a strong relationship between childhood behavioural difficulties and later problem behaviour.[93] According to authors of the study, "early antisocial behavior is the best predictor of later antisocial behavior. It appears that this rule holds even when the antisocial behavior is measured as early as the preschool period." Using children as young as three, researchers were able to predict later delinquency, leading them to conclude that "some antisocial behavioral characteristics may be components of temperament." A second study, which tracked a sample of male offenders for over 20 years, found that stable but as yet "unmeasured individual differences" account for the positive association that exists between past criminal behaviour and the likelihood of future recurrence.[94] A recent analysis of recidivism studies by Canadians Paul Gendreau, Tracy Little, and Claire Goggin found that criminal history, a history of pre-adult anti-social behaviour, and "criminogenic needs," which were defined as measurable anti-social thoughts, values, and behaviour, were all predictors of recidivism.[95]

Prediction, however, requires more than generalities. It is one thing to say, for example, that generally speaking 70 percent of children who evidence aggressive behaviour will similarly show violent tendencies later in life, and quite another to be able to predict which specific individuals will engage in future violations of the criminal law. **Selective incapacitation** is a policy based on the notion of career criminality.[96] Career criminals, also termed *habitual offenders*, are people who repeatedly commit violations of the criminal law. Research has shown that only a small percentage of all offenders account for most crimes reported to the police. Some studies have found that as few as 8 percent of all offenders commit as many as 60 serious crimes per year.[97] The strategy of selective incapacitation, however, which depends on accurately identifying potentially dangerous offenders out of existing criminal populations, has been criticized by some authors for yielding a rate of "false positives" of over

Selective incapacitation a social policy that seeks to protect society by incarcerating those individuals deemed to be the most dangerous.

60 percent.[98] Potentially violent offenders are not easy to identify, even on the basis of past criminal records, and sentencing individuals to long prison terms simply because they are thought likely to commit crimes in the future would no doubt violate their *Charter* rights.

In 1996, as part of what the federal government called the High-Risk Offenders Initiative, Bill C-55 targeted dangerous offenders. Part XXIV of the *Criminal Code of Canada* deals with dangerous and long-term offenders. The Crown Attorney can apply upon conviction (but before sentencing) to have an offender designated as dangerous. The dangerous offender designation brings with it an indefinite or indeterminate sentence of incarceration and a lengthened period of parole ineligibility. One intention of the indeterminate sentence is that these offenders will receive mental and health treatment. Whether or not this happens effectively is debatable. The past decade has seen an increase in the use of the dangerous offender designation to deal with repeat and violent offenders. Currently in Canada there are estimated to be 350 offenders designated as dangerous.[99] Recent studies by James Bonta and his colleagues have revealed that a majority of these offenders were convicted of offences involving sexual aggression.[100]

Definitions of dangerousness are fraught with difficulty because, as some authors have pointed out, "dangerousness is not an objective quality like obesity or brown eyes, rather it is an ascribed quality like trustworthiness." Dangerousness is not necessarily a personality trait that is stable or easily identifiable.[101] Even if it were, recent studies of criminal careers seem to show that involvement in crime decreases with age.[102] Hence, as one author states, if "criminality declines more or less uniformly with age, then many offenders will be 'over the hill' by the time they are old enough to be plausible candidates for preventive incarceration."[103]

No discussion of social policy as it relates to the insights of criminal psychology would be complete without mention of correctional psychology. **Correctional psychology** is concerned with the diagnosis and classification of offenders, the treatment of correctional populations, and the rehabilitation of inmates and other law violators. Perhaps the most commonly used classification instrument in correctional facilities today is the Minnesota Multiphasic Personality Inventory, better known as the MMPI. Based on results of MMPI inventories, offenders may be assigned to various security levels, differing correctional programs, or a variety of treatment programs. Psychological treatment, when employed, typically takes the form of individual or group counselling. Psychotherapy, guided group interaction, cognitive therapy, behavioural modification, and various forms of interpersonal therapy are representative of the range of techniques used.

Correctional psychology that aspect of forensic psychology that is concerned with the diagnosis and classification of offenders, the treatment of correctional populations, and the rehabilitation of inmates and other law violators.

Social Policy and the Psychology of Criminal Conduct

A practical synthesis of psychological approaches to criminal behaviour is offered by Canadians D.A. Andrews and James Bonta in their 1998 book, *The Psychology of Criminal Conduct*.[104] Andrews and Bonta prefer the term "psychology of criminal conduct," or PCC, to distinguish their point of view from what they call "the weak psychology represented in mainstream sociological criminology and clinical/forensic psychology."[105] Any useful synthesis of contemporary criminal psychology, they claim, should be fundamentally objective and empirical. Clearly they dislike many currently well-accepted perspectives, which they say have "placed higher value on social theory and political ideology than [on] rationality and/or respect for evidence."[106] Specifically, say Andrews and Bonta, "[t]he majority of perspectives on criminal conduct that are most favored in mainstream criminology reduce people to hypothetical fictions whose only interesting characteristics are their location in the social system. Almost without exception . . . ," they write, "the causal significance of social location is presumed to reflect inequality in the distribution of social wealth and power." This kind of theorizing, the authors claim, "is a major preoccupation of mainstream textbook criminology, even though such a focus has failed to significantly advance understanding of criminal conduct."[107]

In *The Psychology of Criminal Conduct*, Andrews and Bonta do not attempt to develop a new behavioural theory but rather ask for the objective application of what is now understood about the psychology of crime and criminal behaviour. Their book is a call for practical coalescence of what is already known of the psychology of criminal offenders. Such coalescence is possible, they say, through the application of readily available, high-quality psychological findings. The authors claim, for example, that from the nearly 500 published reports on "controlled evaluations of community and correctional interventions" it is possible to conclude that treatment reduces recidivism "to at least a mild degree." Further, a detailed consideration of published studies finds that, among other things, targeting higher risk cases and using treatments outside of formal correctional settings that extend to an offender's family and peers are all elements of the most effective treatment strategies. Similarly, Andrews and Bonta say, along with objective measures of the success of rehabilitation programs and strategies, effective intervention and treatment services based on the use of psychological assessment instruments that have already demonstrated their validity, empirically established risk factors that can be accurately assessed, and accurately measured community crime rates are all ready and waiting to make a practical psychology of criminal conduct available to today's policy makers. In the words of Andrews and Bonta, "[t]here exists now an empirically defensible general psychology of criminal conduct (PCC) that is of practical value … it should speak to policy advisors, policy makers and legislators who must come to see that … human science is not just [a] relic of a positivistic past."[108] The major remaining issue, say the authors, "on which work is only beginning, is how to make use of what works."[109]

Criminal Psychological Profiling

During World War II, psychologists and psychoanalysts were recruited by the US War Department in an attempt to predict future moves enemy forces might make. Psychological and psychoanalytical techniques were applied to the study of Adolf Hitler, the Italian leader Benito Mussolini, the Japanese general and Prime Minister Hideki Tojo, and other Axis leaders. Such psychological profiling of enemy leaders may have given the Allies the edge in battlefield strategy. Hitler, probably because of his heightened sensitivity to symbols and his strong belief in fate became the central figure analyzed by profilers.

Psychological profiling the attempt to categorize, understand, and predict the behaviour of certain types of offenders based on behavioural clues they provide.

Today, **psychological profiling** is used to assist criminal investigators seeking to better understand individuals wanted for serious offences. Profilers develop a list of typical offender characteristics and other useful principles by analyzing crime scene data in conjunction with interviews and other studies of past offenders. In general, the psychological profiling of criminal offenders is based on the belief that almost any form of conscious behaviour, including each and every behaviour engaged in by the offender during a criminal episode, is symptomatic of an individual's personality. Hence, the way in which a kidnapper approaches his victims, for example, the manner of attack used by a killer, and the specific sexual activities of a rapist might all help paint a picture of the offender's motivations, personal characteristics, and likely future behaviour. Sometimes psychological profiles can provide clues as to what an offender might do following an attack. Some

CHAPTER 7

223

**Psychological and
Psychiatric
Foundations of Criminal
Behaviour**

offenders have been arrested, for example, after returning to the crime scene—a behaviour typically predicted by specific behavioural clues left behind. Remorseful types can be expected to visit the victim's grave, permitting fruitful stakeouts of cemeteries.

In a well-known study of lust murderers (men who kill and often mutilate victims during or following a forced sexual episode), Robert R. Hazelwood and John E. Douglas distinguished between the organized non-social and the disorganized asocial types.[110] The organized non-social lust murderer was described as exhibiting complete indifference to the interests of society, and as being completely self-centred. He was also said to be "methodical and cunning" as well as "fully cognizant of the criminality of his act and its impact on society." His counterpart, the disorganized asocial lust murderer, was described this way: "The disorganized asocial lust murderer exhibits primary characteristics of societal aversion. This individual prefers his own company to that of others and would be typified as a loner. He experiences difficulty in negotiating interpersonal relationships and consequently feels rejected and lonely. He lacks the cunning of the non-social type and commits the crime in a more frenzied and less methodical manner. The crime is likely to be committed in close proximity to his residence or place of employment, where he feels secure and more at ease."[111]

During the 1980s, the Federal Bureau of Investigation (FBI) in the United States led the movement to develop psychological profiling techniques through its concentration on violent sex offenders and arsonists. Today, the behavioural sciences unit at the FBI Training Academy in Quantico, Virginia, continues to focus on serial killers, "lust murderers," domestic terrorists, and the like. The unit's activities were popularized by the 1991 movie *Silence of the Lambs*, starring Jodie Foster and Anthony Hopkins, which portrayed the activities of a serial killer and enforcement activities designed to stop him. Movies, however, may lead the public to put too much stock in behavioural techniques such as psychological profiling. "It's not the magic bullet of investigations," says retired agent Robert Ressler, "[i]t's simply another tool."[112]

Based on training acquired at the FBI Training Academy, Canadian police officials have developed an automated case linkage system that uses some of the behavioural principles of psychological profiling to identify and track violent serial criminals. Through the pioneering work of Inspector Ron MacKay of the Royal Canadian Mounted Police and Sergeant Greg Johnston of the Ontario Provincial Police (OPP), the **Violent Crime Linkage Analysis System (ViCLAS)** was introduced in 1995. ViCLAS is a centralized computer bank containing details of more than 40 000 violent crimes, allowing police to recognize patterns among violent offences. In cases of solved or unsolved homicides and sexual assaults, missing persons, and non-parental abductions, police investigators must respond to 263 questions covering details of all aspects of an incident, including victimology, modus operandi, forensics, and behavioural information. The information is then forwarded to one of the ViCLAS centres throughout the country where trained ViCLAS specialists input it and interpret the results. Most initial operational difficulties have been worked out, and the system has been adopted internationally in countries such as Belgium, Australia, and the United Kingdom. Advocates of ViCLAS believe it is serving to facilitate communication between investigators with the common goal of solving serious serial criminal acts and protecting the public from dangerous repeat offenders.

The Behavioural Sciences Section of the OPP is mandated with providing criminal investigation support services and training of a behavioural nature to the OPP and other criminal justice agencies within the Province of Ontario when requested. It is composed of the Provincial ViCLAS Centre, Criminal Profiling Unit, Geographic Profiling Unit, Threat Assessment Unit, Forensic Psychiatry Unit, Research Unit, Polygraph Unit, and the Ontario Sex Offender Registry.

Violent Crime Linkage Analysis System (ViCLAS) a centralized computer bank containing details of violent crimes that assists police in recognizing patterns among violent offences and offenders.

Summary

Psychological and psychiatric theories of criminal behaviour emphasize the role of individual propensities and characteristics in the genesis of criminality. Whether the emphasis is on conditioned behaviour or on the psychoanalytical foundations of human conduct, such approaches ponder the wellsprings of human motivation, desire, and behavioural choice. Unfortunately, legal strictures have prevented psychology from making the kinds of courtroom contributions of which it appears capable. Even so, some theorists now consider the state of psychological criminology sufficiently advanced to allow for the development of a consistent and dependable social policy in the prediction of dangerousness and in the rehabilitation of offenders. Similarly, psychological profiling may soon facilitate informed criminal investigations as well as the prevention of future crime.

Discussion Questions

1. This book emphasizes a social problems versus social responsibility theme. Which perspective is best supported by psychological theories of crime causation? Why?
2. How do psychological theories of criminal behaviour differ from the other types of theories presented in this book? How do the various psychological and psychiatric approaches presented in this chapter differ from one another?
3. How would the various perspectives discussed in this chapter suggest offenders might be prevented from committing additional offences? How might they be rehabilitated?
4. How can crime be a form of adaptation to one's environment? Why would an individual choose such a form of adaptation over others that might be available?
5. What is the difference between the person diagnosed as a psychopath and the person deemed to be not criminally responsible by reason of mental disorder?
6. How do psychological theories of criminology support the premise behind criminal psychological profiling?

Weblinks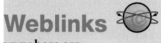

www.hare.org
Webpage of Dr. Robert Hare, international expert on psychopathy and anti-social personality disorder.

www.cmha.ca/bins/index.asp
Canadian Mental Health Association (CMHA). The CMHA is an organization dedicated to the promotion of mental health. A search of this site reveals some interesting commentary on mental illness, crime, and violence.

www.psychiatrictimes.com
Psychiatric Times. This site is a good place to search for topics related to crime and mental illness.

www.rcmp.ca/techops/viclas_e.htm
Violent Crime Linkage Analysis System (ViCLAS). This RCMP site provides an excellent overview of the development, description, and application of ViCLAS.

The Meaning of Crime: Social Structure Perspective

If we would change the amount of crime in the community, we must change the community.

—FRANK TANNENBAUM[1]

It's like it ain't so much what a fellow does, but it's the way the majority of folks is looking at him when he does it.

—WILLIAM FAULKNER[2]

LEARNING OUTCOMES

After reading this chapter, you should be able to

- recognize how the organization, social rules, and structure of society contribute to criminality

- identify the role that the differences in values and culture play in crime causation

- distinguish between a number of social structure theories of criminal behaviour

- identify modern-day social policy that reflects the social-structural approach

- assess the shortcomings of the social-structural approach

IMPORTANT NAMES

Robert Park	Robert Agnew	Marvin Wolfgang
Ernest Burgess	Thorsten Sellin	Richard Cloward
Clifford Shaw	Frederic M. Thrasher	Lloyd Ohlin
Henry McKay	Walter B. Miller	Albert Cohen
Robert K. Merton	Franco Ferracuti	

IMPORTANT TERMS

social structure theories	defensible space	subculture
ecological theory	Crime Prevention Through	subcultural theory
Chicago School of	Environmental Design	focal concerns
Criminology	(CPTED)	opportunity structure
social ecology	anomie	illegitimate opportunity
criminology of place	strain theory	structure
environmental criminology	culture conflict	reaction formation
broken windows thesis	conduct norms	

Introduction

In March 1994, police responded to a 9-1-1 call reporting a collapsed man on a busy street in Ottawa, Ontario. It soon became apparent that the man had been shot through the chest; he died on the sidewalk before he could be taken to hospital. The incident shocked the nation's capital when details of the case revealed that Nicholas Battersby, a 27-year-old, British-born engineer, had been the victim of a so-called drive-by shooting. An employee at a local high-tech firm, Battersby had simply been out for a stroll at 7:30 in the evening when a bullet from a sawed-off .22-calibre rifle shot from within a Jeep hit him in the chest.

After several days of an intensive police manhunt, three local teens, Rubens Henderson, Brian Raymond, and Cory Cyr, were charged with Battersby's murder. All three youths had long records of trouble with the law. Henderson, who had been adopted from a Brazilian orphanage, never really adapted to life in Ottawa. Despite sincere attempts by his mother to provide support, Henderson soon became known as a troublemaker in school. In grade six, he assaulted a student, a teacher, and a vice-principal and was expelled from the school with grades ranging from C to F. He soon acquired a Young Offenders' record, which included break and enter, assault, joyriding in stolen cars, being unlawfully at large, and the use of illicit drugs. His activities brought him into contact with Brian Raymond and Cory Cyr. Raymond was raised by a single mother in a neighbourhood where there was a motorcycle gang clubhouse. Psychologists had used words like "dull" and "borderline" when labelling Raymond's language, math, and reasoning skills. Yet he knew how to hot-wire cars and get his hands on all sorts of drugs. Cory Cyr had spent many of his 16 years in group homes. Two days before the Battersby shooting, he had been released from jail after serving a 30-day sentence for assaulting a youth into unconsciousness after losing a Nintendo game to him. In 1996, Rubens Henderson received a life sentence for second-degree murder, while Cory Cyr and Brian Raymond received five- and four-year sentences, respectively, for manslaughter.[3]

The motivation behind the killing of Nicholas Battersby is not entirely clear. There is no doubt that the three youths were intoxicated on drugs and alcohol as they rode around in the stolen jeep taking random shots at storefronts and people. What is also certain is that all three had socially deprived backgrounds. They lacked educational achievement and the

CHAPTER 8

227
**The Meaning
of Crime:
Social Structure
Perspective**

basic skills needed for success in the modern world. Academic failure, and subcultural values that focused on excitement and greed, dictated the direction their lives were to take—and all but ensured their fateful encounter with Nicholas Battersby.

Sociological Theories

In contrast to more individualized biological and psychological theories, which have what is called a "micro focus" (discussed in Chapters 6 and 7), sociological approaches utilize a "macro focus," stressing behavioural tendencies of group members rather than attempting to predict the behaviour of specific individuals.

Sociological thought has been dominant in behavioural science literature and has influenced criminological theory construction more significantly than any other perspective during the past half century. This emphasis has probably been due, in part, to a widespread North American concern with social issues, including civil rights, the women's movement, issues of poverty, and the changing influence of many traditional social institutions such as government, organized religion, educational institutions, and the family.

Although all sociological perspectives on crime share a common starting point, particular theories give greater or lesser weight to selected components of social life. In this text, we will identify three key sociological explanations for crime:

- Crime is a result of an individual's location within the structure of society. This approach focuses on the social and economic conditions of life, including relative deprivation, differential opportunity, discrimination, social disorganization, personal frustration, alternative means to success, and subcultural values that conflict with conventional values. (These are the primary features of *social structure theories*, which are discussed in this chapter.)
- Crime is the end product of various social processes, especially inappropriate socialization and social learning. This approach stresses the role of interpersonal relationships, the strength of the social bond, and the personal and group consequences of societal reactions to deviance as they contribute to crime. (These are the primary characteristics of the *social process theories* which are discussed in Chapter 9.)
- Crime is the product of class struggle. This perspective emphasizes the nature of the existing power relationships between social groups, the ownership of the means of production, and the economic and social structure of society as it relates to social class and social control. (These are the primary features of the *social conflict theories*, which are discussed in Chapter 10.)

The Social Structure Perspective

The theories in this chapter are termed **social structure theories** because they explain crime by reference to the institutional structure of society. They name the various formal and informal arrangements between social groups as the root causes of crime and deviance. Poverty, lack of education, an absence of salable skills, and subcultural values are all thought to be predicated on the social conditions surrounding early life experiences, and they provide the causal underpinnings of social structure theories. Environmental influences, socialization, and traditional and accepted patterns of behaviour are all used by social structuralists to portray the

Social structure theories explain crime by reference to various aspects of the social fabric. They emphasize relationships among social institutions and describe the types of behaviour that tend to characterize *groups* of people as opposed to *individuals*.

offender as a product of his or her social environment and to depict criminality as a form of acquired behaviour. Social injustice, racism, and feelings of disenfranchisement may play important roles in crime by perpetuating the conditions that cause it.

As this chapter will show, the social structure theories of crime causation are quite diverse; however, most such perspectives build upon the following fundamental assumptions:

- Social groups, social institutions, the arrangements of society, and social roles all provide the focus for criminological study.
- Group dynamics, group organization, and subgroup relationships form the causal nexus out of which crime develops.
- The structure of society and its relative degree of organization or disorganization are important factors contributing to the prevalence of criminal behaviour.

Types of Social Structure Theories

This chapter describes three major types of social structure theories: (1) ecological theory (also known as the "Chicago School of Criminology"), (2) strain theory, and (3) culture conflict theory. All share some elements in common, and the classification of a theory into one subcategory or another is often more a matter of which aspects a writer chooses to emphasize rather than the result of any clear-cut definitional elements inherent in the perspectives themselves.

Ecological Theory

Ecological theory, also called the **Chicago School of Criminology** a type of sociological approach that emphasizes demographics (the characteristics of population groups) and geographics (the mapped location of such groups relative to one another) and sees the social disorganization that characterizes delinquency areas as a major cause of criminality and victimization.

Social ecology an approach to criminological theorizing that attempts to link the structure and organization of any human community to interactions with its localized environment.

The first type of social structure theory discussed in this chapter is the **ecological theory**. Some of the earliest sociological theories to receive widespread recognition can be found in this approach, and specifically in the writings of **Robert Park** and **Ernest Burgess**. In the 1920s and 1930s, Park and Burgess, through their work at the University of Chicago, developed what became known as **social ecology**, or the ecological school of criminology. Social ecology recognizes that crime always shows an uneven geographical distribution. It attempts to explain such variation by the interrelationship between human beings or human groups and their surroundings. As one writer puts it, social ecology is "the attempt to link the structure and organization of any human community to interactions with its localized environment."[4]

The work of Park and Burgess focused on concentric city zones, which were envisioned much like ever-expanding circles on a target (see Figure 8.1), wherein diverse populations and behavioural characteristics predominated. Park and Burgess referred to the central business zone as Zone 1 or the Loop, where retail businesses and light manufacturing were typically located. Zone 2, surrounding the city centre, generally contained areas that were in transition from residential areas to business purposes. Zone 3 contained mostly working-class homes, while Zone 4 was occupied by middle-class citizens. Zone 5, consisting largely of suburbs, was called the commuter zone. Early ecological theories were formed using 1920s Chicago as a model, hence the **Chicago School of Criminology**. Although their applicability to other cities or other time periods may be questionable, such theories

CHAPTER 8
229
The Meaning
of Crime:
Social Structure
Perspective

Theory in Perspective
Types of Social Structure Theories

SOCIAL STRUCTURE THEORIES
Emphasize relationships between social institutions and describe the types of behaviour that tend to characterize *groups* of people as opposed to *individuals*.

Ecological Theory or "Chicago School." Stresses the demographic and geographic aspects of groups and sees the social disorganization that characterizes delinquency areas as a major cause of criminality and of victimization.
Period: 1920s–1930s
Theorists: Robert Park, Ernest Burgess, W.I. Thomas, Florian Znaniecki, Clifford Shaw, Henry McKay
Concepts: Demographics, concentric zones, social disorganization, delinquency areas, criminology of place

---

Strain Theory. Points to a lack of fit between socially approved success goals and the availability of socially approved means to achieve those goals. As a consequence, according to this theory, individuals who are unable to succeed through legitimate means turn to other avenues that promise economic and social recognition.
Period: 1930s–present
Theorists: Robert K. Merton, Richard Cloward, Lloyd Ohlin, Albert Cohen
Concepts: Anomie, goals, means, opportunity structures, differential opportunity, reaction formation, general strain theory

---

Culture Conflict Theory. Sees the root cause of crime as a clash of values between variously socialized groups over what is acceptable as proper behaviour.
Period: 1920s–present
Theorists: Thorsten Sellin, Frederic M. Thrasher, Walter B. Miller, Franco Ferracuti, Marvin Wolfgang, and others
Concepts: Conduct norms, focal concerns, subculture, socialization, subculture of violence

---

pointed out the tendency of criminal activity to be associated with transition zones which, because of the turmoil or social disorganization associated with them, were generally characterized by lower property values, marginal individuals, and a general lack of privacy.

Park and Burgess had been strongly influenced by W.I. Thomas and Florian Znaniecki, who described in their book *The Polish Peasant in Europe and America*[5] the problems Polish immigrants faced in the early 20th century when they left their homeland and moved to the cities of America. Thomas and Znaniecki noted how rates of crime rose among people who had been so displaced, and they hypothesized that the cause was the social disorganization resulting from the immigrants' inability to successfully transplant guiding norms and values from their home culture into their new one.

Clifford Shaw and **Henry McKay**, other early advocates of the ecological approach, conducted empirical studies of delinquency rates in Chicago. One such study, undertaken in

Figure 8.1

Chicago's Concentric Zones

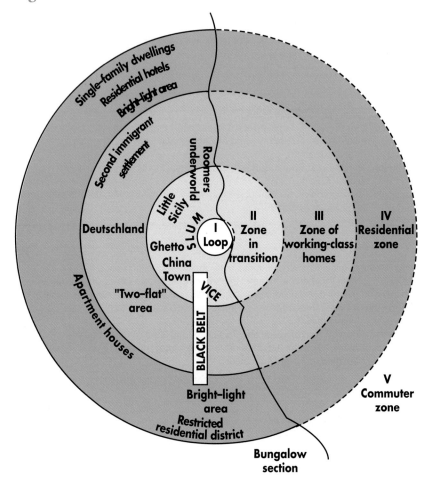

Source: Robert E. Park, Ernest W. Burgess, and R. D. McKenzie, *The City* (Chicago: University of Chicago Press, 1925), p. 55. Copyright © University of Chicago Press. Reprinted with permission.

the late 1920s, found that the rate of delinquency among black youths "on the South Side of Chicago decreases regularly by square mile areas, from 19.4 percent in the area adjoining the center of the city, to 3.5 percent in the area 5 miles from the center of the city."[6]

Even at the height of its popularity, the ecological school recognized that American crime patterns might be different from those found elsewhere in the world and that crime zones might exist in city areas other than those surrounding the core. Early comparisons of American, European, and Asian data, for instance, found higher crime rates at the so-called city gates (near-suburban areas providing access to downtown) in Europe and Asia. The greatest contribution the ecological school made to criminological literature can be found in its claim that society, in the form of the community, wields a major influence on human behaviour.[7]

The work of Canadian Carol La Prairie, which looks at the reality of high crime rates on some First Nations reserves in Canada, is representative of the ecological approach. In

CHAPTER 8

231

**The Meaning
of Crime:
Social Structure
Perspective**

a recent study, La Prairie concludes that those Aboriginal communities that have remained "institutionally complete" have significantly lower rates of crime compared with those reserves that have experienced rapid change due to economic and cultural pressures.[8] Later studies by La Prairie used the concepts of social ecology to help explain the variation in rates of incarceration of Aboriginal peoples between the eastern and western provinces. In her comparison of two eastern and two western urban centres, La Prairie notes significant differences in the degree of integration of the Aboriginal populations. While the eastern centres showed more social integration of inner-city Aboriginal residents, the western cities had displaced most of the Aboriginal population to communities outside the city centres. Not surprisingly, the incarceration rate of Aboriginal peoples is significantly higher in the western centres. La Prairie's findings recognize the importance of social organization from a social-ecological point of view. The author also stresses the additional need for efforts to stabilize Aboriginal populations within urban centres through the provision of, for example, decent, affordable housing.[9]

Similarly, ecological theorists of the Chicago school formalized the use of two sources of information: (1) official crime and population statistics and (2) ethnographic data. Population statistics, also referred to as demographic data, when combined with crime information, provided empirical material that gave scientific weight to ecological investigations. Ethnographic information, gathered in the form of life stories, or ethnographies, described the lives of city inhabitants. By comparing one set of data with the other—demographics with ethnographies—ecological investigators were able to show that life experiences varied from one location to another, and that the possibility of a person's involvement in crime had a strong tendency to be associated with place of residence. See Box 8.1 on the criminology of place.

Critique of Ecological Theory Ecological theory, like many sociological approaches to explaining crime, has been criticized for its tendency to forget the individual. By concentrating on the role social institutions and social disorganization play in crime causation, ecological approaches rarely acknowledge the influence of individual psychology, distinctive biology, or personal choice on criminal activity. This sort of criticism was insightfully advanced by W.S. Robinson in a classic 1950 article.[10] Robinson pointed out the "problematic nature of making individual-level inferences on the basis of aggregate data."[11]

Other authors have suggested that ecological theories give too much credence to the notion that location determines crime and delinquency. The nature of any given location changes over time, and evolutions in land-use patterns, such as a movement away from home ownership and toward rental or low-income housing, may seriously affect the nature of a neighbourhood and the concomitant quality of social organization found there.

Similarly, rates of neighbourhood crime and delinquency may be "an artifact of police decision-making practice" and bear little objective relationship to the actual degree of law violation in an area.[12] Such police bias, should it exist, may seriously mislead researchers into categorizing certain areas as high in crime when, in fact, they may not be.

Another critique of the ecological school can be found in its seeming inability to differentiate between the condition of social disorganization and the things such a condition is said to cause. What, for example, is the difference between social disorganization and high rates of delinquency? Is not delinquency a form of the very thing said to cause it? As Stephen Pfohl has observed, early ecological writers sometimes used the incidence of delinquency as "both an example of disorganization and something caused by disorganization,"[13] making it difficult to gauge the efficacy of their explanatory approach.

Box 8.1

emerging theory

The Criminology of Place

Criminology of place
or **environmental
criminology** an
emerging perspective
that emphasizes the
importance of
geographic location and
architectural features as
they are associated with
the prevalence of
criminal victimization.

Broken windows thesis
a perspective on crime
causation holding that
physical deterioration in
an area leads to
increased concerns for
personal safety among
area residents and to
higher crime rates in
that area. The "broken
windows" metaphor says
that a broken window,
left unattended, invites
other windows to be
broken, which leads to a
sense of disorder that
breeds fear and serious
crime. Hence, by
ignoring minor crimes
we lose opportunities to
repair the first signs of
disorder and to hold
offenders accountable.

Defensible space the
range of mechanisms
that combine to bring an
environment under the
control of its residents.

Ecological approaches to crime causation have found a modern rebirth in what is now called the "criminology of place." The **criminology of place**, also called **environmental criminology**, is an emerging perspective within the contemporary body of criminological theory that emphasizes the importance of geographic location and architectural features as they are associated with the prevalence of victimization. "Hot spots" of crime, including neighbourhoods, specific streets, and even individual houses and business establishments, have been identified by recent writers. Lawrence Sherman, for example, tells of a study that revealed that 3 percent of places (addresses and intersections) in Minneapolis produce 50 percent of all calls to the police.[14] Crime, says Sherman, although relatively rare, is geographically concentrated.

Another researcher, Rodney Stark, asks "[h]ow is it that neighborhoods can remain the site of high crime and deviance rates despite a complete turnover in their populations? ... There must be something about places as such that sustains crime."[15] Stark has developed a theory of deviant neighbourhoods. It consists of 30 propositions, including the following:[16]

- To the extent that neighbourhoods are dense and poor, homes will be crowded.
- Where homes are more crowded, there will be a greater tendency to congregate outside the home in places and circumstances that raise levels of temptation and opportunity to deviate.
- Where homes are more crowded, there will be lower levels of supervision of children.
- Reduced levels of child supervision will result in poor school achievement, with a consequent reduction in stakes in conformity and an increase in deviant behaviour.
- Poor, dense neighbourhoods tend to be mixed-use neighbourhoods.
- Mixed use increases familiarity with and easy access to places offering the opportunity for deviance.

Central to the criminology of place is the **broken windows thesis**, which holds that physical deterioration and an increase in unrepaired buildings leads to increased concerns for personal safety among area residents.[17] Heightened concerns, in turn, lead to further decreases in maintenance and repair and to increased delinquency, vandalism, and crime among local residents—which spawns even further deterioration in both a sense of safety and the physical environment. Offenders from other neighbourhoods are then increasingly attracted by the area's perceived vulnerability.

Even within so-called high-crime neighbourhoods, however, crimes tend to be concentrated at specific locations such as street blocks or multiple-family dwellings. This kind of micro-level analysis has also shown, for example, that some units within specific apartment buildings are much more likely to be the site of criminal occurrences than others. Apartments near complex or building entrances appear to be more criminally dangerous, especially if they are not facing other buildings or apartments. Likewise, pedestrian tunnels, unattended parking lots, and convenience stores with clerks stationed in less visible areas are often targeted by criminal offenders.

The criminology of place employs the concept of **defensible space**, a term that evolved out of a conference in 1964 in St. Louis, Missouri.[18] Defensible space has been defined as "a surrogate term for the range of mechanisms—real and symbolic barriers, strongly defined areas of influence, and improved opportunities for surveillance—that combine to bring an environment under the control of its residents."[19] The St. Louis conference, which brought criminologists, police officers, and architects face to face, focused on crime problems characteristic

▶

CHAPTER 8

233

**The Meaning
of Crime:
Social Structure
Perspective**

of public housing areas. Findings demonstrated that specific architectural changes that improved barriers, defined boundaries, and removed criminal opportunity could do much to reduce the risk of crime—even in the midst of high-crime neighbourhoods.

The criminology of place holds that location can be as predictive of criminal activity as the lifestyles of victimized individuals or the social features of victimized households. (*Place* has been defined by researchers as "a fixed physical environment that can be seen completely and simultaneously, at least on its surface, by one's naked eyes."[20]) Places can be criminogenic due to the routine activities associated with them. On the other hand, some places host crime because they provide the characteristics that facilitate its commission. In Sherman's study, for example, Minneapolis parks drew "flashers" because they provided "opportunities for concealment" up until the moment when the flasher struck. Changes to the parks, such as moving walkways some distance from trees and shrubbery, can reduce criminal opportunity.

Recognizing the criminology of place, the Peel Regional Police Service (Peel region is located just west of Toronto) introduced to the Canadian market in the early 1980s a program of **Crime Prevention Through Environmental Design (CPTED)**. It is based on the theory that the proper design and effective use of a physical environment can help reduce the incidence and fear of crime. The CPTED program revolves around three strategies: (1) natural surveillance (keeping potential intruders under observation); (2) natural access control (decreasing the opportunity for crime); and (3) territorial reinforcement (extending a sphere of influence through physical design to develop a sense of ownership by users). In an example cited by Peel Regional Police, a CPTED review of a restaurant recommended the following changes: (1) improvement of sightlines to the outside by removing unnecessary clutter such as bushy plants and promotional material from the take-out window, (2) improvement of sightlines within the restaurant by removing planters that divided the dining room and waiting area, and (3) improvement of lighting by repairing defective ceiling lamps and increasing the number of light fixtures. These changes resulted in a more intimidating and less private target to would-be offenders while also giving staff the ability to better observe potential offenders before a robbery.[21] (See Chapter 11 for an in-depth look at the CPTED model.)

Sherman points out that

> [n]either capital punishment of places (as in arson of crack houses) nor incapacitation of the routine activities of criminal hot spots (as in revocation of liquor licences) seems likely to eliminate crime. But since the routine activities of places may be regulated far more easily than the routine activities of persons, a criminology of place would seem to offer substantial promise for public policy as well as theory.[22]

Crime Prevention Through Environmental Design (CPTED) a crime prevention strategy based on the premise that the design and effective use of the built environment can lead to a reduction in the incidence and fear of crime.

Finally, many crimes occur outside of geographic areas characterized by social disorganization. Murder, rape, burglary, incidents of drug use, assault, and so on, all occur in affluent "well-established" neighbourhoods as well as in other parts of a community. Likewise, white-collar, computer, environmental, and other types of crime may actually occur with a greater frequency in socially well-established neighbourhoods than elsewhere. Hence, the ecological approach is clearly not an adequate explanation for all crime.

Strain Theory

The second type of social structure theory to be discussed is strain theory. Strain theory depicts delinquency as a form of adaptive, problem-solving behaviour, usually committed in response to problems involving frustrating and undesirable social environments. The classic statement of strain theory was offered in 1938 by **Robert K. Merton**, who developed the concept of anomie.

Anomie, a French word meaning *normlessness*, was popularized by Émile Durkheim in his 1897 book, *Suicide*.[23] Durkheim used the term to explain how a breakdown of predictable social conditions can lead to a feeling of personal loss and dissolution. In Durkheim's writings, anomie was a feeling of not being personally embedded in society. It marked a loss of the sense of belonging.

Merton's use of the term was somewhat different. In Merton's writings, **anomie** came to mean a disjunction between socially approved means to success and legitimate goals.[24] Merton maintained that legitimate goals, involving such things as wealth, status, and personal happiness, are generally defined as desirable for everyone. The widely acceptable means to these goals, however, including education, hard work, financial savings, and so on, are not equally available to all members of society. As a consequence, crime and deviance tend to arise as an alternative means to success when individuals feel the strain to succeed in socially approved ways but find that the tools for such success are unavailable to them. In Merton's words, "[i]t's not how you play the game, it's whether you win."[25] Merton's emphasis on the felt strain resulting from the lack of fit between goals and means led to his approach being called **strain theory**.

Complicating the picture further, Merton maintained, was the fact that not everyone accepted the legitimacy of socially approved goals. Merton diagrammed possible combinations of goals and means as shown in Figure 8.2, referring to each combination as a "mode of adaptation."

The initial row in Figure 8.2 signifies acceptance of the goals that society holds as legitimate for everyone, with ready availability of the means approved for achieving those goals. The mode of adaptation associated with this combination of goals and means is called *conformity* and typifies most middle- and upper-class individuals.

Innovation, the second form of adaptation, arises when an emphasis on approved goal achievement combines with a lack of opportunity to participate fully in socially acceptable means to success. This form of adaptation is experienced by many lower-class individuals who have been socialized to desire traditional success symbols such as expensive cars, large homes, and big bank accounts, but who do not have ready access to approved means of acquiring them, such as educational opportunity. Innovative behavioural responses, including crime, can be expected to develop when individuals find themselves so deprived. However, in Merton's words, "[p]overty as such, and consequent limitation of opportu-

Anomie a social condition in which norms are uncertain or lacking.

Strain or **anomie theory** a sociological approach that posits a disjunction between socially and subculturally sanctioned means and goals as the cause of criminal behaviour.

Figure 8.2

Goals and Means Disjuncture

	Goals	Means
Conformity	+	+
Innovation	+	−
Ritualism	−	+
Retreatism	−	−
Rebellion	±	±

Source: Robert K. Merton, *Social Theory and Social Structure*, 1968 enlarged edition. Copyright 1967, 1968 by Robert K. Merton. Adapted with permission of the Free Press, a division of Macmillan, Inc.

CHAPTER 8
235
**The Meaning
of Crime:
Social Structure
Perspective**

nity, are not sufficient to induce a conspicuously high rate of criminal behavior. Even the often mentioned 'poverty in the midst of plenty' will not necessarily lead to this result." It is only insofar as those who find themselves in poverty are pressured to achieve material success and the acquisition of other associated symbols of status that innovation results.

Third, *ritualism* describes the form of behaviour arising when members of society participate in socially desirable means, but show little interest in goal achievement. A ritualist may get a good education, work every day in an acceptable occupation, and outwardly appear to be leading a solid middle-class lifestyle. Yet that person may care little for the symbols of success, choosing to live an otherwise independent lifestyle.

Retreatism describes the behaviour of those who reject both the socially approved goals and means. They may become dropouts, drug abusers, or homeless, or may participate in alternative lifestyles such as communal living. Such individuals are socially and psychologically often quite separate from the larger society around them.

Merton's last category, *rebellion*, signifies a person, or rebel, who wishes to replace socially approved goals and means with some other system. Political radicals, revolutionaries, and anti-establishment agitators may fit into this category. Merton believed that conformity was the most common mode of adaptation prevalent in society, whereas retreatism was least common.

A contemporary application of Merton's strain theory is offered by Margaret Beare in her examination of the increased involvement of Canadian Mohawks in the smuggling of cigarettes in the early 1990s. High taxes on Canadian cigarettes tempted many smokers to turn to cheaper, contraband US cigarettes. In Ontario and Quebec, residents of some Aboriginal communities along the Canada–US border were the main sources of contraband cigarettes. It is believed that by 1993, more than one-quarter of the cigarettes consumed in Canada had been purchased illegally.[26]

General Strain Theory

In 1992, strain theory was reformulated by **Robert Agnew** and others and changed into a comprehensive perspective called *general strain theory* (GST).[27] General strain theory suggests that delinquent behaviour is a coping mechanism that enables adolescents to deal with the socio-economic problems generated by negative social relations. General strain theory expands on traditional strain theory in several ways. First, it significantly expands the focus of strain theory to include all types of negative relations between an individual and others. Second, GST maintains that strain is likely to have a cumulative effect on delinquency after reaching a certain threshold. Third, GST provides a more comprehensive account of the cognitive, behavioural, and emotional adaptations to strain than do traditional strain approaches. Finally, GST more fully describes the wide variety of factors affecting the choice of delinquent adaptations to strain.

According to GST, strain occurs when others do the following: (1) prevent or threaten to prevent an individual from achieving positively valued goals; (2) remove or threaten to remove positively valued stimuli that a person possesses; or (3) present or threaten to present someone with noxious or negatively valued stimuli. Agnew sees the crime-producing effects of strain as cumulative and concludes that whatever form it takes, "[s]train creates a predisposition for delinquency in those cases in which it is chronic or repetitive."[28] Nonetheless, according to Agnew, several factors determine whether a person will respond to the experience of strain in a criminal or conforming manner. These factors include temperament, intelligence, interpersonal skills, self-efficacy, association with criminal peers, and conventional social support.

An analysis by Agnew of other strain theories found that all such theories share at least two central explanatory features.[29] Strain theories, Agnew said, (1) focus "explicitly on negative relationships with others; relationships in which the individual is not treated as he or she wants to be treated" and (2) argue that "adolescents are pressured into delinquency by the negative affective states—most notably anger and related emotions—that often result from negative relationships."

A 1994 study tested some of the assumptions underlying GST through an analysis of American data.[30] It found partial support for GST and discovered that negative relations with adults, feelings of dissatisfaction with friends and school life, and the experience of stressful events (e.g., family dissolution) were positively related to delinquency, as was living in an unpleasant neighbourhood (one beset by social problems and physical deterioration). When conceived of more broadly as exposure to negative stimuli, the study found general strain to be significantly related to delinquency.

Contrary to Agnew's hypothesis, however, the study found no evidence that the effects of strain were increased when experienced for longer periods of time nor diminished when adolescents classified that part of their life in which they experienced strain as "unimportant." Consistent with earlier findings, the study also found that feelings of general strain were positively related to later delinquency, regardless of the number of delinquent peers, moral beliefs, self-efficacy, and level of conventional social support.[31] Some support was found for the belief that general strain leads to delinquency by weakening the conventional social bond and strengthening the unconventional bond with delinquent peers.

Critique of Strain Theory Merton's original formulation of strain theory, although it has much of value to say about the consequences of unequal opportunity, is probably less applicable to North American society today than it was in the 1930s, because in the last few decades considerable effort has been made toward improving success opportunities for everyone—regardless of ethnic heritage, race, or gender. Hence, it is less likely that individuals today will find themselves without the opportunity for choice, as was the case decades ago. Even so, social programs designed to provide equal opportunity have had little impact on some apparently well-insulated segments of society where even the semblance of participating in "approved means" may be grounds for derision.

General strain theories, like those summarized by Agnew, have more contemporary relevance than Merton's original formulation. As Agnew points out, opportunities for legitimate success may be blocked at many junctures in the life course, resulting in strain, frustration, and anger—all of which may produce law-violating behaviour in those undergoing them.[32]

Travis Hirschi, however, criticizes strain theory for its inability "to locate people suffering from discrepancy" and notes that human beings are naturally optimistic—a fact, he says, that "overrides ... aspiration-expectation disjunction."[33] Hirschi concludes that "[e]xpectations appear to affect delinquency, but they do so regardless of aspirations, and strain notions are neither consistent with nor required by the data."

Culture conflict a sociological perspective on crime that suggests that the root cause of criminality can be found in a clash of values between variously socialized groups over what is acceptable or proper behaviour.

Culture Conflict Theory

The third type of social structure theory discussed in this chapter is the culture conflict approach to explaining crime. **Culture conflict** theory suggests that the root cause of

CHAPTER 8
237
**The Meaning
of Crime:
Social Structure
Perspective**

criminality can be found in a clash of values between differently socialized groups over what is acceptable or proper behaviour. The culture conflict concept is inherent in ecological criminology (discussed earlier in this chapter) and its belief that zones of transition, because they tend to be in flux, harbour groups of people whose values are often at odds with those in the larger, surrounding society.

The culture conflict perspective found its clearest expression in the writings of **Thorsten Sellin** in his 1938 book, *Culture Conflict and Crime*.[34] Sellin maintained that the root cause of crime could be found in different values about what is acceptable or proper behaviour. According to Sellin, **conduct norms**, which provide the valuative basis for human behaviour, are acquired early in life through childhood socialization. It is the clash of norms between variously socialized groups that results in crime. Because crime is a violation of laws established by legislative decree, the criminal event itself, from this point of view, is nothing other than a disagreement over what should be acceptable behaviour. For some social groups, what we tend to call crime is simply part of the landscape—something that can be expected to happen to you unless you take steps to protect yourself. From this point of view, those to whom crime happens are not so much victims as they are simply ill prepared.

Sellin also wrote about culture conflict. Culture conflict suggests that the root cause of criminality can be found in a clash of values between variously socialized groups over what is acceptable or proper behaviour. In 1997, for example, Danish actress Annette Sorensen was arrested in New York after leaving her toddler in a stroller outside a restaurant while she sat inside with the child's father. Sorensen was charged with endangering the welfare of a child. Her 14-month-old daughter, Liv, was placed in temporary foster care. Sorensen, who was in tears following her arrest, could not understand what had happened. "We do this in Denmark all the time," the Copenhagen resident told police.[35] Her daughter was soon ordered returned by a city judge, and Sorensen and the child flew home to Denmark, where children are routinely left in strollers outside of restaurants and other public places.

Sellin described two types of culture conflict. The first type, *primary conflict*, arises when a fundamental clash of cultures occurs. Sellin's classic example was that of an immigrant father who kills his daughter's lover following an old-world tradition that demands that a family's honour be kept intact. In Sellin's words,

> [a] few years ago, a Sicilian father in New Jersey killed the 16-year-old seducer of his daughter, expressing surprise at his arrest since he had merely defended his family honor in a traditional way. In this case … [t]he conflict was external and occurred between cultural codes or norms. We may assume that where such conflicts occur … norms of one cultural group or area migrate to another and that such conflict will continue so long as the acculturation process has not been completed.[36]

The other type of conflict, called *secondary conflict*, arise, according to Sellin, when smaller cultures within the primary one clash. So it is that middle-class values, upon which most criminal laws are based, may find fault with inner-city or lower-class norms, resulting in the social phenomenon we call "crime."

In Sellin's day, prostitution and gambling provided plentiful examples of secondary conflict. Many lower-class inner-city groups accepted gambling and prostitution as a way of life—if not for individual members of those groups, then at least as forms of behaviour that were rarely condemned for those choosing to participate in them. Today, perhaps drug use and abuse provide more readily understandable examples. For some segments of contemporary society, drug sales have become a source of substantial income, and the conduct norms that typify such groups support at least the relative legitimacy of lives built

Conduct norms the shared expectations of a social group relative to personal conduct.

around the drug trade. In other words, in some parts of Canada, drug dealing is an acceptable form of business. To those who make the laws, however, it is not. It is from the clash of these two opposing viewpoints that conflicts, and crime, emerge.

Subcultural Theory

Fundamental to the notion of culture conflict is the idea of subcultures. Like the larger culture of which it is a part, a **subculture** is a collection of values and preferences that is communicated to subcultural participants through a process of socialization. Subcultures differ from the larger culture in that they claim the allegiance of smaller groups of people. Whereas the wider North American culture, for example, may proclaim that hard work and individuality are valuable, a particular subculture may espouse the virtues of deer hunting, male bonding, and recreational alcohol consumption. Although it is fair to say that most subcultures are not at odds with the surrounding culture, some subcultures do not readily conform to the parameters of national culture. Countercultures, which tend to reject and invert the values of the surrounding culture, and criminal subcultures, which may actively espouse deviant activity, represent the other extreme. **Subcultural theory** is a sociological perspective that emphasizes the contribution made by variously socialized cultural groups to the phenomenon of crime.

Some of the earliest writings on subcultures can be found in **Frederic M. Thrasher's** 1927 book, *The Gang*.[37] Thrasher studied 1313 gangs in Chicago. His work, primarily descriptive in nature, led to a typology in which he described different types of gangs. In 1943, William Foote Whyte, drawing on Thrasher, published *Street Corner Society*.[38] Whyte, in describing his three-year study of the Italian slum he called "Cornerville," further developed the subcultural thesis, showing that lower-class residents of a typical slum could achieve success through the opportunities afforded by slum culture—including racketeering and bookmaking.

Focal Concerns   In 1958, **Walter B. Miller** attempted to detail the values that drive members of lower-class subcultures into delinquent pursuits. Miller described *lower-class culture* as "a long established, distinctively patterned tradition with an integrity of its own." In Miller's words,

> [a] large body of systematically interrelated attitudes, practices, behaviors, and values characteristic of lower-class culture are designed to support and maintain the basic features of the lower-class way of life. In areas where these differ from features of middle-class culture, action oriented to the achievement and maintenance of the lower-class system may violate norms of the middle class and be perceived as deliberately nonconforming. ... This does not mean, however, that violation of the middle-class norm is the dominant component of motivation; it is a by-product of action primarily oriented to the lower-class system.[39]

In the same article, entitled "Lower Class Culture as a Generating Milieu of Gang Delinquency," Miller outlined what he termed the **focal concerns** or key values of delinquent subcultures.[40] Such concerns included trouble, toughness, smartness, excitement, fate, and autonomy. Miller concluded that subcultural crime and deviance are not the direct consequences of poverty and lack of opportunity but emanate from specific values characteristic of such subcultures. Just as middle-class concerns with achievement, hard work, and delayed

Subculture a collection of values and preferences that is communicated to subcultural participants through a process of socialization.

Subcultural theory a sociological perspective that emphasizes the contribution made by variously socialized cultural groups to the phenomenon of crime.

Focal concerns the key values of any culture, and especially the key values of a delinquent subculture.

CHAPTER 8

239

**The Meaning
of Crime:
Social Structure
Perspective**

gratification lead to socially acceptable forms of success, said Miller, so too do lower-class concerns provide a path to subculturally recognized success for lower-class youth.

Miller found that trouble is a dominant feature of lower-class culture. Getting into trouble, staying out of trouble, dealing with trouble when it arises become focal points in the lives of many members of lower-class culture. Miller recognized that getting into trouble was not necessarily valued in and of itself, but was seen as an oftentimes necessary means to valued ends. In Miller's words, "[for] men, 'trouble' frequently involves fighting or sexual adventures while drinking; for women, sexual involvement with disadvantageous consequences."[41]

Like many theorists of the time, Miller was primarily concerned with the criminality of men. The lower-class masculine concern with toughness that he identified, Miller admitted, may have been a product of the fact that many men in the groups he examined were raised in female-headed families. Miller's "toughness," then, may reflect an almost obsessive concern with masculinity as a reaction to the perceived threat of over-identification with female role models. In words that sound as applicable today as when they were written, Miller tells us,

> [t]he genesis of the intense concern over "toughness" in lower-class culture is probably related to the fact that a significant proportion of lower-class males are reared in a predominantly female household and lack a consistently present male figure with whom to identify and from whom to learn essential components of a "male" role. Since women serve as a primary object of identification during the pre-adolescent years, the almost obsessive lower-class concern with "masculinity" probably resembles a type of compulsive reaction-formation.[42]

Miller described "smartness" as the "capacity to outsmart, outfox, outwit, dupe, take, [or] con another or others and the concomitant capacity to avoid being outwitted, taken or duped oneself. ... In its essence," said Miller, "smartness involves the capacity to achieve a valued entity—material goods, personal status—through a maximum use of mental agility and a minimum of physical effort."

Excitement was seen as a search for thrills—often necessary to overcome the boredom inherent in lower-class lifestyles. Fights, gambling, picking up women, and making the rounds were all described as derivative aspects of the lower-class concern with excitement. "The quest for excitement," said Miller, "finds ... its most vivid expression in the ... recurrent 'night on the town' ... a patterned set of activities in which alcohol, music, and sexual adventuring are major components."

Fate is related to the quest for excitement and to the concept of luck or of being lucky. As Miller stated, "[m]any lower-class persons feel that their lives are subject to a set of forces over which they have relatively little control. These are not ... supernatural forces or... organized religion ... but relate more to a concept of 'destiny' or man as a pawn. ... This often implicit world view is associated with a conception of the ultimate futility of directed effort toward a goal. ..."

Autonomy, as a focal concern, manifests itself in statements such as "I can take care of myself" or "No one's going to push me around." Autonomy produces behavioural problems from the perspective of middle-class expectations when it surfaces in work environments, public schools, or other social institutions built on expectations of conformity.

Miller's work derived almost entirely from his study of black, inner-city delinquents in the Boston area. As such, it may have less relevance to members of lower-class subcultures at other times, or in other places.

Violent Subcultures

Some subcultures are decidedly violent and are built around violent themes and around values supporting violent activities. In 1967, **Franco Ferracuti** and **Marvin Wolfgang** published their seminal work, *The Subculture of Violence: Toward an Integrated Theory of Criminology*, which drew together many of the sociological perspectives previously advanced to explain delinquency and crime.[43] According to some writers, the work of Ferracuti and Wolfgang "was substantively different from the other subculture theories, perhaps because it was developed almost a decade after delinquent-subculture theories and criminology had developed new concerns."[44] Ferracuti and Wolfgang's main thesis was that violence is a learned form of adaptation to certain problematic life circumstances, and that learning to be violent takes place within the context of a subcultural milieu that emphasizes the advantages of violence over other forms of adaptation. Such subcultures are characterized by songs and stories that glorify violence, by gun ownership, and by rituals tending to stress macho models. They are likely to teach that a quick and decisive response to insults is necessary to preserve one's prestige within the group. Subcultural group members have a proclivity for fighting as a means of settling disputes. Subcultures of violence both expect violence from their members and legitimize it when it occurs. In Wolfgang's words, "the use of violence ... is not necessarily viewed as illicit conduct, and the users do not have to deal with feelings of guilt about their aggression." In other words, for participants in violent subcultures, violence can be a way of life.

Wolfgang and Ferracuti based their conclusions on an analysis of data that showed substantial differences in the rate of homicides between racial groups in the Philadelphia area. At the time of their study, non-Caucasian men had a homicide rate of 41.7 per 100 000, versus only 3.4 for Caucasian men. Statistics on non-Caucasian women showed a homicide rate of 9.3, versus 0.4 for Caucasian women. Explaining these findings, Ferracuti and Wolfgang wrote,

> [h]omicide is most prevalent, or the highest rates of homicide occur, among a relatively homogeneous subcultural group in any large urban community .... The value system of this group, as we are contending, constitutes a subculture of violence. From a psychological viewpoint, we might hypothesize that the greater the degree of integration of the individual into this subculture, the higher the probability that his behavior will be violent in a variety of situations.[45]

Ferracuti and Wolfgang extend their theory of subcultural violence with the following "corollary propositions."[46]

- No subculture can be totally different from or totally in conflict with the society of which it is a part.
- To establish the existence of a subculture of violence does not require that the actors sharing in these basic value elements should express violence in all situations.
- The potential to resort or willingness to resort to violence in a variety of situations emphasizes the penetrating and diffusive character of this culture theme.
- The subcultural ethos of violence may be shared by all ages in a subsociety, but this ethos is most prominent in a limited age group, ranging from late adolescence to middle age.
- The counter-norm is non-violence.

CHAPTER 8
241
**The Meaning
of Crime:
Social Structure
Perspective**

Violent subcultures produce violent acts.
Why are some subcultures "violent" while
others are not?
Bryce Lankard.

- The development of favourable attitudes toward, and the use of, violence in a subculture usually involves learned behaviour and a process of differential learning, association, or identification.
- The use of violence in a subculture is not necessarily viewed as illicit conduct, and the users therefore do not have to deal with feelings of guilt about their aggression.

Canadian researchers have commented on geographical distinctions between violent subcultures in different parts of Canada. National homicide rates have consistently shown a distinct east-to-west/south-to-north upward trend over the last several decades. Homicide rates during this period have been lowest in Newfoundland and Labrador and highest in British Columbia and two to three times higher in the Yukon and the Northwest Territories than in British Columbia. The reasons for these persistent regional differences are difficult to pinpoint. While certain elements of Canada's social structure (age, ethnicity, economic well-being, etc.) are obvious contributing factors, some researchers suggest that cultural differences among regions of Canada also need to be taken into account. Do the accumulated traditions and shared experiences shaping the values and beliefs of people in different regions contribute to varying levels of violence? Many Canadian researchers believe that this cannot be overlooked.[47]

Regional variations are found in other countries as well. In the United States, for example, a body of criminological literature claims that certain forms of criminal violence are more acceptable in the South than in northern portions of the country.[48] Some writers have also referred to variability in the degree to which interpersonal violence has been accepted in the South over time, whereas others have suggested that violence in the South might be a traditional tool in the service of social order.[49]

The wider culture often recognizes, sometimes begrudgingly and sometimes matter-of-factly, a violent subculture's internal rules. Hence, when one member of such a subculture kills another, the wider society may take the killing less "seriously" than if someone outside the subculture had been killed. As a consequence of this realization, Franklin Zimring and his associates described what he called "wholesale" and "retail" costs for homicide, in which killings that are perceived to occur within a subculture of violence (when both the victim and the perpetrator are seen as members of a violent subculture) generally result in a less harsh punishment than do killings that occur outside of the subculture. Punishments, said Zimring, relate to the perceived seriousness of the offence, and if members of the subculture within which a crime occurs accept the offence as part of the landscape, so, too, will members of the wider culture that imposes official sanctions on the perpetrator.

Much of the original research into subcultural theory dates back to the 1950s and 1960s. However, the reality of inner-city gangs and violence, especially in the United States but also in Canada, has brought with it a renewed interest in this approach. In his review of the research literature on gangs, Canadian criminologist John Hagan suggests that subcultural theories continue to have a role to play in understanding the serious problems of largely ethnic, urban youth who see themselves as marginalized.[50]

Differential Opportunity

In 1960, **Richard Cloward** and **Lloyd Ohlin** published *Delinquency and Opportunity*.[51] Their book, a report on the nature and activities of juvenile gangs, blended the subcultural thesis with ideas derived from strain theory. Cloward and Ohlin saw socially structured opportunities for success (**opportunity structures**) as being of two types: illegitimate and legitimate. They observed that whereas legitimate opportunities were generally available to individuals born into middle-class culture, participants in lower-class subcultures were often denied access to them. As a consequence, the choice of an illegitimate avenue to success was often seen as acceptable by participants in so-called illegitimate subcultures.

Cloward and Ohlin used the term **illegitimate opportunity structure** to describe pre-existing subcultural paths to success that are not approved of by the wider culture. Where illegitimate paths to success are not already in place, alienated individuals may undertake a process of ideational evolution through which "a collective delinquent solution" or a "delinquent means of achieving success" may be decided upon by members of a gang. Because the two paths to success, legitimate and illegitimate, differ in their availability to members of society, Cloward and Ohlin's perspective has been termed *differential opportunity*.

According to Cloward and Ohlin, delinquent behaviour may result from the ready availability of illegitimate opportunities with the effective replacement of the norms of the wider culture with expedient subcultural rules. Hence, delinquency and criminality may become "all right" or legitimate in the eyes of gang members and may even form the criteria used by other subcultural participants to judge successful accomplishments. In the words of Cloward and Ohlin, "[a] delinquent subculture is one in which certain forms of delinquent activity are essential requirements for the performance of the dominant roles supported by the subculture."[52] Its "most crucial elements" are the "prescriptions, norms, or rules of conduct that define the activities required of a full-fledged member."[53] "A person attributes legitimacy to a system of rules and corresponding models of behavior," wrote Cloward and Ohlin, "when he accepts them as binding on his conduct."[54] "Delinquents have withdrawn their support from established norms and invested officially forbidden forms of conduct with a claim to legitimacy."[55]

Opportunity structure
a path to success.
Opportunity structures
may be of two types:
legitimate and
illegitimate.

**Illegitimate opportunity
structure** subcultural
pathways to success that
are disapproved of by
the wider society.

CHAPTER 8
243
**The Meaning
of Crime:
Social Structure
Perspective**

Cloward and Ohlin noted that a delinquent act can be "defined by two essential elements: it is behavior that violates basic norms of the society, and, when officially known, it evokes a judgment by agents of criminal justice that such norms have been violated."[56] For Cloward and Ohlin, however, crime and deviance were just as normal as any other form of behaviour supported by group socialization. In their words, "deviance and conformity generally result from the same kinds of social conditions ..." and "deviance ordinarily represents a search for solutions to problems of adjustment." In their view, deviance is just as much an effort to conform, albeit to subcultural norms and expectations, as is conformity to the norms of the wider society. They added, however, that

> [i]t has been our experience that most persons who participate in delinquent subcultures, if not lone offenders, are fully aware of the difference between right and wrong, between conventional behavior and rule-violating behavior. They may not care about the difference, or they may enjoy flouting the rules of the game, or they may have decided that illegitimate practices get them what they want more efficiently than legitimate practices.[57]

Cloward and Ohlin described three types of delinquent subcultures: (1) criminal subcultures, in which criminal role models are readily available for adoption by those being socialized into the subculture; (2) conflict subcultures, in which participants seek status through violence; and (3) retreatist subcultures, where drug use and withdrawal from the wider society predominate. Each subculture was thought to emerge from a larger, all-encompassing "parent" subculture of delinquent values. According to Cloward and Ohlin, delinquent subcultures have at least three identifiable features: (1) "acts of delinquency that reflect subcultural support are likely to recur with great frequency," (2) "access to a successful adult criminal career sometimes results from participation in a delinquent subculture," and (3) "the delinquent subculture imparts to the conduct of its members a high degree of stability and resistance to control or change."[58]

Cloward and Ohlin divided lower-class youth into four types according to their degree of commitment to middle-class values and/or material achievement. Type I youths were said to desire entry to the middle class through improvement in their economic position. Type II youths were seen as desiring entry to the middle class but not improvement in their economic position. Type III youths were portrayed as desiring wealth without entry to the middle class. As a consequence, Type III youths were seen as the most crime prone. Type IV youths were described as dropouts who retreated from the cultural mainstream through drug and alcohol use.

Cloward and Ohlin had a substantial impact on social policy, resulting in government programs designed to change the structures of legitimate opportunities in poor communities. Programs such as Mobilization for Youth (MFY), Job Corps, and Opportunities for Youth created employment and educational opportunities for deprived youths and were largely based on opportunity theory.

Reaction Formation

Another criminologist whose work is often associated with both strain theory and the subcultural perspective is **Albert Cohen.** Like Cloward and Ohlin, Cohen's work focused primarily on the gang behaviour of delinquent youth. In Cohen's words, *[w]hen we speak of a delinquent subculture, we speak of a way of life that has somehow become traditional among certain groups in American society. These groups are the boys' gangs that flourish most conspicuously in the "delinquency neighborhoods" of our larger American cities. The members of these gangs grow up, some to become law-abiding citizens and others to graduate to more professional and adult forms of criminality, but the delinquent tradition is kept alive by the age-groups that succeed them.*[59]

Cohen argued that youngsters from all backgrounds are generally held accountable to the norms of the wider society through a "middle-class measuring rod" of expectations related to such items as school performance, language proficiency, cleanliness, punctuality, neatness, non-violent behaviour, and allegiance to other similar standards. Like strain theorists, Cohen noted that unfortunately not everyone is prepared, by virtue of the circumstances surrounding his or her birth and subsequent socialization, for effectively meeting such expectations.

In an examination of vandalism, Cohen found that "non-utilitarian" delinquency, in which things of value are destroyed rather than stolen or otherwise used for financial gain, is the result of middle-class values being turned upside down.[60] Delinquent youths, argued Cohen, who are often alienated from middle-class values and lifestyles through deprivation and limited opportunities, can achieve status among their subcultural peers through vandalism and other forms of delinquent behaviour.

Children, especially those from deprived backgrounds, turn to delinquency, Cohen claimed, because they experience status-frustration when judged by adults and others according to middle-class standards and goals that they are unable to achieve. Because it is nearly impossible for non-mainstream children to succeed in middle-class terms, they may overcome anxiety through the process of reaction formation, in which hostility toward middle-class values develops. Cohen adapted **reaction formation** from psychiatric perspectives, using it to mean "the process in which a person openly rejects that which he wants, or aspires to, but cannot obtain or achieve."[61]

Cohen discovered the roots of delinquent subcultures in what he termed the "collective solution to the problem of status." When youths who experience the same kind of alienation from middle-class ideals band together, they achieve a collective and independent solution and create a delinquent subculture. Cohen wrote,

[t]he delinquent subculture, we suggest, is a way of dealing with the problems of adjustment .... These problems are chiefly status problems: certain children are denied status in the respectable society because they cannot meet the criteria of the respectable status system. The delinquent subculture deals with these problems by providing criteria of status that these children can *meet.*[62]

Cohen's approach is effectively summarized in a "theoretical scenario" offered by Donald J. Shoemaker, who says that lower-class youths undergo a working-class socialization that combines lower-class values and habits with middle-class success values.[63] Lower-class youths then experience failure in school because they cannot live up to the middle-class norms operative in educational institutions. They suffer a consequent loss of self-esteem and increased feelings of rejection, leading to dropping out of school and "association with delinquent peers." Hostility and resentment toward middle-class standards grow through reaction formation. Finally, such alienated youths achieve status and a sense of improved self-worth through participation in a gang of like-minded peers. Delinquency and crime are the result.

Reaction formation the process in which a person openly rejects that which he or she wants, or aspires to, but cannot obtain or achieve.

CHAPTER 8
245
**The Meaning
of Crime:
Social Structure
Perspective**

Critique of Violent Subcultures Theory Although subcultural approaches are widely accepted within criminology, the notion of a subculture of violence has been questioned. Canadian criminologist Gwynn Nettler criticizes the subculture of violence thesis by insisting that it is tautological, or circular. That is, saying that people fight because they are violent, or that "they are murderous because they live violently" does little to explain their behaviour, according to Nettler. Attributing fighting to "other spheres of violence," he says, may be true, but it is fundamentally "uninformative."[64]

The approach has also been criticized for being racist, because many so-called violent subcultures are said to be populated primarily by minorities. Margaret Anderson says that "[t]he problem with this explanation is that it turns attention away from the relationship

---

Box 8.2

Murder Showed Gang Would Stop at Nothing

On Sept. 6, 1995, John Wartley Richardson walked out of Millhaven penitentiary in Kingston, Ontario. He'd just turned 24, a hardened and violent Ottawa street thug with a previous conviction for robbery. Now, he was free again after serving part of a 30-month prison term for pimping.

National Parole Board file No. 233185C, obtained by the *Citizen*, reveals officials had little doubt Mr. Richardson would strike again. In fact, it took just 50 days.

The crime would be murder. The victim would be Sylvain Leduc.

The file shows Mr. Richardson, now 26, has never held a legitimate job. He's been a pimp and a brute, involved in narcotics and the misery of vulnerable, strung-out young women trapped in Ottawa's street sex trade.

In prison, he was sometimes locked in segregation for "negative behaviour." He showed no remorse for anything. An area woman who helped put him away for procuring was so scared afterwards, the file notes, she had police help her relocate to a new town.

In the fall of 1994, Mr. Richardson was rejected for early parole.

"The board is satisfied that reasonable grounds exist to believe that, if released, you are likely to commit an offence involving violence and directs that you not be released."

But 11 months later, parole officials had little choice but to let him go because of a federal statute that grants all but the most dangerous inmates parole after serving two-thirds of their sentences.

"You remain a high risk to reoffend," officials wrote in his file. "Strict adherence to release conditions (including regularly reporting in to authorities) will be required in order to render that risk manageable."

Mr. Richardson, unmanageable as ever, ignored the conditions. He finally met with authorities Jan. 2, 1996, when heavily armed police in Winnipeg arrested him as an armed-and-dangerous fugitive wanted for the Leduc homicide.

A subsequent parole board document added a grim footnote to the file: "The risk you represent is clearly not manageable and the board orders that your statutory release be revoked."

Yesterday, a judge and jury went further. The jury revoked much of what's left of Mr. Richardson's life by finding him guilty of first-degree murder. Justice Douglas Rutherford then shipped him back to a bleak federal cellblock for life, with no chance of parole for at least 25 years. He

Sylvain Leduc was tortured and killed
by members of the Ace Crew gang
because he had been disrespectful
toward them. Was Sylvain Leduc a
victim of a violent subculture?
The Canadian Press/Ottawa Sun.

also sentenced him to an additional 73 years, to be served concurrently, for various other crimes.

Sylvain Leduc was killed because he innocently strayed into the nasty underworld of urban street gangs, where extreme violence and revenge are rewarded with criminal status and power.

Mr. Leduc, 17, offended a dangerous collection of mostly young, Black men who called themselves Ace Crew and sold $20-hits of crack cocaine on the streets of Lowertown. His death sentence was sealed with one ugly, unfortunate word: he called them "niggers."

Mr. Leduc's timing was particularly bad. In the fall of 1995, the gang's members were feeling threatened on several fronts.

Police, they worried, might be on to them. And at least one of the teenage girls the gang used for drug-running and sex— she was Mr. Leduc's cousin—wanted out, undermining the group's authority and its all-important reputation on the street. As well, rival drug dealers, they suspected, were muscling in on their turf, on their money.

Ace Crew was, at best, disorganized crime. But in late October 1995, it appeared to be losing its grip on even that existence. And that made it potentially lethal.

Enter John Richardson, fresh out of Millhaven. He was a friend of Mark Williams, the then 19-year-old reputed leader of Ace Crew. Mr. Richardson was just the type of crime consultant who could help the outfit rebuild.

If Ace was struggling, perhaps Mr. Richardson and his pal, Kurton Edwards, 28, could teach the gang a thing or two about becoming so bad, so feared, that people would be afraid to walk the streets of Ottawa.

At least that's how it appeared in the hours leading up to the Leduc murder, as Mr. Richardson regaled the group with violent tales about how notorious U.S. Black ghetto gangs ruthlessly maintain their turf. He talked about violence. He talked about retribution. He talked about torture. And he had a gun.

Ace Crew, police believe, has not largely disbanded. Six members and associates have been convicted for various roles in Mr. Leduc's slaying. Another was imprisoned for 11 years for the bold March 1997 shooting of two men inside the crowded Rideau Centre. Five other members and associates, all non-Canadians, have been deported to their native countries because of their criminal activities here.

CHAPTER 8

247

**The Meaning
of Crime:
Social Structure
Perspective**

> ► **DISCUSSION QUESTIONS**
>
> 1. What subcultural elements (beliefs, behaviour patterns, etc.) may have contributed to Sylvain Leduc's death?
> 2. Does the subculture of violence thesis help to explain the behaviour of gang members, such as the named Ace Crew who killed Leduc? If so, how?
> 3. What explanations, other than a subculture of violence thesis, might be offered to explain the death of Leduc?
>
> Source: Ian MacLeod, "The Rise and Fall of the Ace Crew: Murder Showed Gang Would Stop at Nothing," *Ottawa Citizen*, April 15, 1998, p. B1. Reprinted with permission.

of Black communities to the larger society and it recreates dominant stereotypes about Blacks as violent, aggressive, and fearful. Although it may be true that rates of violence are higher in Black communities, this observation does not explain the fact."[65] In sociological jargon, one might say that an observed correlation between race and violence does not necessarily provide a workable explanation for the relationship.

Gangs Today

Street gangs have become a major source of concern in contemporary North American society, particularly in the United States. Although the writings of investigators such as Cohen, Thrasher, and Cloward and Ohlin focused on the illicit activities of juvenile gangs in inner cities, most gang-related crimes of the period involved vandalism, petty theft, and battles over turf. The ethnic distinctions that gave rise to gang culture in the 1920s through the 1950s in the United States are today largely forgotten. Italian, Hungarian, Polish, and Jewish immigrants, whose children made up many of the early gangs, have been, for the most part, successfully integrated into modern society.

Today's gang members appear more violent, involved with drugs, and intransigent than those studied by early researchers. Although the United States is the nation with the most gangs (and has the best information about them), Canada is not exempt from them. One of the challenges in determining accurate amounts of gang activity in Canada stems from issues surrounding the definition of "gang" and "gang member." Law enforcement officials and the media often refer to small groups of offenders as gangs, even though the members of these groups do not see themselves that way. In a recent study of gangs in the Greater Vancouver area, this concern with definition is addressed and distinctions are made between *criminal business organizations*, *street gangs*, and *wannabe groups*. The second phase of the study, known as the Greater Vancouver Gang Study, is concentrating on the emergence, growth, activities, and eventual decline of three Vancouver street gangs.[66]

Bill C-24, known as the Organized Crime Bill, was enacted in February 2002 and includes the current legal definition of an organized crime group such as a gang. See Box 8.3 on page 250 for this definition.

In its 2006 Annual Report on Organized Crime, the Criminal Intelligence Service of Canada (CISC) reports that street gangs are characterized by their involvement in the street-level trafficking of illicit drugs, in addition to their use of specific gang identifiers and paraphernalia. Over 300 street gangs have been identified in Canada, with an estimated 11 000 gang members and associates operating across the country. The gangs are primarily local in scope, with only a limited number having interprovincial and international criminal links. While some Canadian street gangs identify themselves as Crips or Bloods, these gangs are independent from the US-based Crips or Bloods.

In Canada, street gangs are mostly comprised of adults between the ages of 20 and 30 years, though some do have members under 18. Gangs are multicultural and ethnically homogeneous, depending largely on the demographics of the communities where the gangs are located. The structure of street gangs tends to be either family/friendship-based or hierarchical in nature. Ethnically homogenous gangs tend to operate within a fixed area and are generally found in lower-income urban areas. This type of street gang is prevalent in the Prairies, Toronto, and Montreal. CISC reports that the majority of street gangs across Canada are involved in street-level crimes, such as drug trafficking, the sex trade, or theft. Their sex trade involvement nationwide includes street-level prostitution, escort agencies, and exotic dancing establishments. Some gangs recruit women, including minors, into the sex trade and transport them to various locations across Canada—sometimes through intimidation and threats of violence. Street gangs are also active in robberies and home invasions and, to a lesser extent, fraud and the counterfeiting of currency and merchandise. Several gangs are more sophisticated and are involved in the importation or production of illicit commodities such as drugs or counterfeit goods. See Box 8.4 on page 251 for information about street gang activity by province.

While street gang-related violence is not a new phenomenon, a recent increase in gang-related violence is being reported and appears to be related to street gang expansion, recruitment and encroachment on the territory of other criminal groups. The degree of street gang violence differs by region and gang. Violence may be planned—to promote and protect the gang's interests, such as targeting rival gang members or resources—or be spontaneous and opportunistic, resulting in intentional or unintentional harm to the general public from drive-by shootings, street gang cross-fire and mistaken identities. Street gangs use a wide variety of weapons including swords, knives, machetes, hammers, screwdrivers, and firearms. Illicit firearms used by street gangs are typically acquired through residential or commercial thefts, or are smuggled into the country from the United States.[67]

Information about gangs in the United States is much more detailed. A recent national survey estimated that there were 21 500 active gangs accounting for 731 500 gang members in the United States.[68] A large-scale project of the National Gang Crime Research Center, known as Project Gangfact, provides a profile of gangs and gang members throughout the United States. The most recent Gangfact report, based on data collected by 28 researchers in 17 states, presents much detailed information specific to the US, but shows similar characteristics to the Canadian reality:[69]

- The average age for joining a gang, nationally, is 12.8 years of age.
- Over one-half who joined gangs have tried to quit.
- More than two-thirds of gangs have written rules for members to follow.
- Over one-half of all gangs hold regular weekly meetings.
- Nearly 30 percent of gangs require their members to pay dues.
- Approximately 55 percent of gang members have been recruited by other gang members, while the remainder sought out gang membership.
- Most gang members (79 percent) said they would leave the gang if given a "second chance in life."
- Four-fifths of gang members reported that their gangs sold crack cocaine.
- Most gangs (70 percent) are not racially exclusive and consist of members drawn from a variety of ethnic groups.

CHAPTER 8

249
The Meaning
of Crime:
Social Structure
Perspective

Members of the Manitoba Warriors leave a courthouse in Winnipeg after being sentenced to time already served following their conviction on drug charges. Gangs have become a concern in today's society. What social structure theories might explain the proliferation of gangs and gang-related activity in Canada?
CP/Phil Hossack.

- One-third of gang members report that they have been able to conceal their gang membership from their parents.
- Most gangs (83 percent) report having female members, but few allow female members to assume leadership roles.
- Many gang members (40 percent) report knowing male members of their gangs who had raped females.

Contemporary researchers, however, are drawing some new distinctions between gangs and violence. Some years ago, G. David Curry and Irving A. Spergel, in a study of Chicago communities, distinguished between juvenile delinquency and gang-related homicide.[70] They found that communities characterized by high rates of delinquency do not necessarily experience exceptionally high rates of crime or of gang-related homicides. They concluded that although gang activity may be associated with homicide, "gang homicide rates and delinquency rates are ecologically distinct community problems." Gang-related homicide, they found, seems to be well explained by classical theories of social disorganization and is especially prevalent in areas of the city characterized by in-migration and by the "settlement of new immigrant groups." In their study, high rates of juvenile delinquency seemed to correlate more with poverty, which the researchers defined as "social adaptation to chronic deprivation." According to Curry and Spergel, "[s]ocial disorganization and poverty rather than criminal organization and conspiracy may better explain the recent growth and spread of youth gangs to many parts of the country. Moreover, community organization and social opportunity in conjunction with suppression, rather than simply suppression and incapacitation, may be more effective policies in dealing with the social problem."[71] In devising strategies to counter gang activity, policy makers must remember that many gang members are delinquent before they become associated with gangs and that merely suppressing gangs should not replace other youth crime intervention and prevention strategies.[72]

Box 8.3

Definition of Criminal Organization

As stated in the *Criminal Code*, section 467.1(1), a "criminal organization" means a group, however organized, that
* is composed of three or more persons in or outside Canada; and,
* has as one of its main purposes or main activities the facilitation or commission of one or more serious offences, that, if committed, would likely result in the direct or indirect receipt of a material benefit, including a financial benefit, by the group or by any one of the persons who constitute the group.

It does not include a group of persons that form randomly for the immediate commission of a single offence.

In determining whether an individual participates in OR actively contributes to any activity of a criminal organization, the Court may look at the following:

* If they use a name, word, symbol, or other representation that identifies, or is associated with, that criminal organization;
* If they frequently associate with any of the persons who constitute the criminal organization;
* If they receive any benefit from the criminal organization;
* If they repeatedly engage in activities at the instruction of any of the persons who constitute the criminal organization.

Source: Edmonton Police Service, www.police.edmonton.ab.ca/Pages/gangs/legislation.asp (Accessed March 24, 2007).

Policy Implications of Social Structure Theories

Theoretical approaches that look to the social environment as the root cause of crime point in the direction of social action as a panacea. In the 1930s, for example, Clifford Shaw, in an effort to put his theories into practice, established the Chicago Area Project. The Chicago Area Project attempted to reduce social disorganization in transient neighbourhoods through the creation of community committees. Shaw staffed committees with local residents rather than professional social workers. The project had three broad objectives: (1) improving the physical appearance of poor neighbourhoods, (2) providing recreational opportunities for youth, and (3) involving project members directly in the lives of troubled youth through school and courtroom mediation. The program also made use of "curbside counsellors," streetwise workers who could serve as positive role models for inner-city youth. Although no effective assessment programs were established to evaluate the Chicago Area Project during the program's tenure, reviewers in 1984 provided a 50-year review of the program, declaring it "effective in reducing rates of juvenile delinquency."[73]

Similarly, Mobilization for Youth (MFY), cited earlier in this chapter as an outgrowth of Cloward and Ohlin's theory of differential opportunity, provides a bold example of the treatment implications of social structure theories. Mobilization for Youth sought not only to provide new opportunities, but also to change the fundamental arrangements of society through direct social action and thereby address the root causes of crime and deviance. Leaders of Mobilization for Youth decided that "[w]hat was needed to overcome ... formidable barriers to opportunity ... was not community organization but community action" that attacked entrenched political interests. Accordingly, MFY promoted "boycotts

CHAPTER 8

251

**The Meaning
of Crime:
Social Structure
Perspective**

Street Gang Activity in Canada by Province

Box 8.4

Yukon Territory, Northwest Territories, and Nunavut

There are no identified street gangs or gang activity in the Yukon or Nunavut. Members of Alberta-based street gangs are involved in the street-level trafficking of various drugs in the Yellowknife area of the Northwest Territories.

British Columbia

Most of the 20 street gangs identified in British Columbia are concentrated in the Lower Mainland with little gang-related activity in rural areas. Most of these gangs are involved in the illicit drug trade, obtaining their supply of illicit drugs from Hells Angels chapters and from Asian and independent organized crime groups. A limited number of street gangs are able to create their own supply of drugs through the cultivation of marijuana, production of methamphetamine, and the importation of cocaine. Street gangs primarily distribute crack cocaine, cocaine, marijuana, heroin and, to a lesser extent, methamphetamine. There is tension between some street gangs and other organized crime groups such as the Hells Angels, creating the potential for violent conflict.

Alberta

Approximately 30 street gangs have been identified in Alberta and most are primarily involved in trafficking crack cocaine. They obtain illicit drugs from Asian criminal groups and outlaw motorcycle gangs. To a lesser extent, some street gangs receive illicit drugs from other crime groups based in British Columbia. Aboriginal street gangs are also prevalent in the province, trafficking street-level quantities of drugs between Edmonton and various Aboriginal reserves where gang members and associates may have family or personal ties.

Saskatchewan

A total of 21 street gangs have been identified in this province. Street gangs in Saskatchewan are active in urban and rural areas with gang associations and criminal activities extending to many Aboriginal reserve areas. Family and personal ties between gang members and communities facilitate gang-related interests and activities. However, conflict has emerged between street gangs and other organized crime groups over criminal market share and gang expansion into new territory. Currently, street gangs operate independently of each other and consequently operate locally.

Manitoba

Of the 25 street gangs identified in Manitoba, most are concentrated in the Winnipeg area with some gangs active in rural areas and Aboriginal reserves. Gang members tend to use personal and family associations within their respective communities in order to cultivate and maintain criminal markets, such as supplying illicit drugs. Similarly, gangs with Aboriginal members or associates that have links to rural and reserve areas capitalize upon those ties to recruit new members as well as further their criminal activities.

Ontario

There are approximately 80 street gangs currently active in Toronto with an additional 95 identified in the regions outside Toronto. As in other parts of the country, street-level drug trafficking is the major criminal activity, particularly involving cocaine or crack cocaine, as well as marijuana and ecstasy. In addition, a number of street gangs are reported to be involved in street-level prostitution, with a few also linked to the production of pornography. In Toronto,

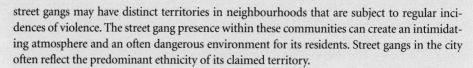

street gangs may have distinct territories in neighbourhoods that are subject to regular incidences of violence. The street gang presence within these communities can create an intimidating atmosphere and an often dangerous environment for its residents. Street gangs in the city often reflect the predominant ethnicity of its claimed territory.

Quebec

There are approximately 50 established and emerging street gangs identified in this province, most of which are ethnically homogenous, such as those of Caribbean or Hispanic composition. Several gangs are considered to have a higher level of criminal capability and primarily operate in the greater Montreal region and other urban areas. Quebec street gangs are often divided by broad alliances that can potentially increase gang-related violence as these alliances create even further opportunities for violent chance encounters or retaliatory events involving rivals. Some have associations with other organized crime groups within the province, particularly involving Italian criminal groups or the Hells Angels. Many street gangs are involved in the sex trade, in conjunction with the illicit drug trade. These gangs will often concentrate their efforts within either escort agencies and exotic dancing establishments or street-level prostitution.

Atlantic Provinces

Existing and emerging street gangs have been identified in Nova Scotia (10) and New Brunswick (7), with none identified in Prince Edward Island or Newfoundland and Labrador. They are typically involved in street-level drug trafficking of cocaine and crack cocaine. Some street gangs in Atlantic Canada are involved in the procuring of adult and underage females for exotic dancing and street-level prostitution.

Source: 2006 CISC Annual Report on Organized Crime in Canada. Reproduced with the permission of the Minister of Government Works and Public Services Canada, 2007.

against schools, protests against welfare policies, rent strikes against 'slum landlords', lawsuits to ensure poor people's rights, and voter registration."[74] A truly unusual government-sponsored program for its time, Mobilization for Youth was eventually disbanded in the face of protests that its mandate was to reduce delinquency, not reform society or test sociological theories.[75]

A contemporary example of social intervention efforts based on sociological theories can be had in the Youth Violence Project: A Community-Based Violence Prevention Project, recently introduced in a Vancouver Island school district. It is a community-based initiative designed to address the problem of youth violence and involves teachers, counsellors, parents, students, and representatives from health and social-service agencies. Consisting of 13 individual anti-violence initiatives, it is intended to educate and train students and community members in a preventative approach to violence by helping individuals change their behaviour and acquire skills that enable them to use non-violent responses in circumstances where violence might previously have been used.[76]

Mobilization for Youth and the Youth Violence Project both stand as examples of the kinds of programs that theorists who focus on the social environment typically seek to implement. Social programs of this sort are intended to change the cultural conditions and societal arrangements that are thought to lead people into crime.

CHAPTER 8

253

**The Meaning
of Crime:
Social Structure
Perspective**

Critique of Social Structure Theories

Social structure theories suffer from one general shortcoming that similarly affects most other perspectives on crime causation. In the words of Canadian criminologist Gwynn Nettler,

> *the conceptual bias of social scientists emphasizes environments—cultures and struc-tures—as the powerful causes of differential conduct. This bias places an intellectual taboo on looking elsewhere for possible causes as, for example, in physiologies. This taboo is … strongly applied against the possibility that ethnic groups may have genetically transmitted differential physiologies that have relevance for social behavior.*[77]

Nettler is telling us that social scientists downplay the causative role of non-sociological factors. Many believe that such factors are important. But, since sociological theorizing has captured most of the academic attention over the past few decades, the role of other causative factors in the etiology of criminal behaviour stands in danger of being shortchanged.

Social-structural approaches also suffer from a seeming inability to explain the behav-iour of many, even though they may appear applicable to a few. Moreover, some see the inability of social structure theories to predict which individuals—or at least what pro-portion of a given population—will turn to crime, as a crucial failure of such perspectives. Although the large majority of persons growing up in inner-city, poverty-ridden areas, for example, probably experiences an inequitable opportunity structure firsthand, only a rel-atively small number of those people become criminal. It is true that substantially more people living under such conditions may become criminal than those living in other types of social environments. Nonetheless, a large proportion of persons experiencing strain, as well as a large number of persons raised in deviant subcultures, will still embrace non-criminal lifestyles.

In his book, *The Moral Sense*, James Q. Wilson suggests that most people—regardless of socialization experiences and the structural aspects of their social circumstances—may still carry within themselves an inherent sense of fairness and interpersonal morality.[78] If what Wilson suggests is even partially true, then the explanatory power of social structure theories may be limited by human nature itself.

Summary

Sociological theories explore relationships between and among groups and institutions and see crime as the result of social processes, the consequence of aspects of social struc-ture, or the result of economic and class struggle. A number of the social structure theo-ries that have been examined in this chapter foreground lack of education, absence of marketable skills, blocked opportunities for achieving success, socio-economic disparity, and subcultural values as fundamental causes of crime. Because these theories look to the organization of society for their explanatory power, intervention strategies based on them typically argue for the modification of formal or informal group processes—including the educational process and familial and work arrangements—and to the increased availabil-ity of legitimate opportunity structures. Social programs may be created under the umbrella of particular sociological theories, as were the Youth Violence Project and Mobilization for Youth.

Discussion Questions

1. This book emphasizes a social problems versus social responsibility theme. Which of the theoretical perspectives discussed in this chapter best support the social problems approach? Which support the social responsibility approach? Why?

2. Do you believe that ecological theories have a valid place in contemporary criminological thinking? Why or why not?

3. How, if at all, does the notion of a "criminology of place" differ from more traditional ecological theories? Do you see the criminology of place approach as capable of offering anything new over traditional approaches? If so, what?

4. What is a violent subculture? Why do some subcultures stress violence? How might participants in a subculture of violence be turned toward less aggressive ways?

5. Compare and contrast the theories discussed in this chapter, citing differences and similarities between and among them. How, for example, does Miller's notion of strain differ from Cloward and Ohlin's idea of opportunity structures? How is it similar?

6. What policy implications do you think the theories discussed in this chapter hold? What kinds of changes in society and in government policy might be based on the theories discussed here? Would they be likely to bring about a reduction in crime?

Weblinks

www.publicsafety.gc.ca/prg/cp/ncps-en.asp
National Crime Prevention Strategy. A Public Safety Canada site that provides information on federal government crime-prevention projects.

www.childfind.ca
Child Find Canada. Child Find is a volunteer network of registered charitable organizations that provides public education and services related to missing children.

www.childcybersearch.org
Child Crisis Network. Child Crisis Network is Canada's first internet-based missing children agency. Provides links to police forces across Canada as well as a listing of related missing children sites. Lots of interesting links including one to gangs and gang related material at www.childcybersearch.org/gangs.shtml.

www.police.edmonton.ab.ca/Pages/Gangs
Edmonton Police Service. This site provides general information about street gangs including gang traits and activity.

www.iir.com/nygc
National Youth Gang Center. Under the auspices of the US federal government's Office of Juvenile Justice and Delinquency Prevention, the NYGC provides comprehensive statistical and legislative information about American gang activity.

The Meaning of Crime:
Social Process Perspective

Deviation is criminal only if effectively reacted to and symbolized as such.

—EDWIN M. LEMERT[1]

Children learn to become delinquents by becoming members of groups in which delinquent conduct is already established.

—ALBERT K. COHEN[2]

LEARNING OUTCOMES

After reading this chapter, you should be able to

- recognize how the process of social interaction between people contributes to criminal behaviour

- identify and distinguish between a number of social process theories

- appreciate the importance of an understanding of the victim in the study of crime and criminality

- identify current social policy initiatives reflecting the social process approach

- assess the shortcomings of the social process perspective

IMPORTANT NAMES

Edwin Sutherland	Howard Becker	Sheldon and Eleanor Glueck
Gresham Sykes	John Braithwaite	John Laub
David Matza	Walter C. Reckless	Robert Sampson
Frank Tannenbaum	Travis Hirschi	Lawrence E. Cohen
Edwin M. Lemert	Michael R. Gottfredson	Richard Machalek

IMPORTANT TERMS

social process theories	secondary deviance	social bond
interactionist perspectives	labelling	social development
social learning theory	moral enterprise	perspective
differential association	stigmatic shaming	life course theories
techniques of neutralization	reintegrative shaming	social capital
tagging	social control theories	cohort analysis
primary deviance	containment theory	cohort
	containment	evolutionary ecology

Introduction

In 2001, Andrew Leyshon-Hughes found himself at the centre of a vicious controversy. Leyshon-Hughes had been found not guilty by reason of insanity for the brutal stabbing murder and sexual assault of Nancy Eaton in 1985. Eaton, the great-great-granddaughter of Timothy Eaton, founder of Eaton's department store empire, had befriended Leyshon-Hughes, himself a member of an established Toronto family of lawyers. The murder shocked high society as did the court's ruling. Leyshon-Hughes' lawyer argued that his client, who was 17 at the time, suffered from brain damage at birth and that only the primitive part of his brain was functioning when he killed Nancy Eaton. Leyshon-Hughes was sentenced to treatment in the Ontario psychiatric hospital system and remained in psychiatric custody for the next 15 years.

In 2001, the community was shocked to learn that Leyshon-Hughes had been granted a number of privileges since 1999, including the right to leave the grounds of the psychiatric hospital to attend college or to socialize. His request for longer, overnight visits to stay with family in northern Ontario and British Columbia had the community asking questions about their safety, especially since, a few years earlier, Leyshon-Hughes had been considered too dangerous to leave hospital grounds.

His psychiatrist believed that Leyshon-Hughes wanted to eventually have a normal life and raise a family. Forensic psychiatrist John Bradford argued that his patient is not a sexual deviant or psychopath, testifying that the risk is manageable: "A manageable risk means that a person is in the community and we have procedures and treatment in place that reduces that level of risk," he says. "I don't think there's ever such a thing as a zero-risk. That's not feasible."[3]

Marlys Edward, who had been Leyshon-Hughes' lawyer since he was 17, said that her client was misdiagnosed. Once he was locked up, no one took into consideration that he could be treated and rehabilitated.[4]

The case of Andrew Leyshon-Hughes provides an example of how society's continued reaction to what it identifies as criminal behaviour can change the course of an offender's life. As some would say, while there are plenty of ex-cons, there is no such thing as an "ex–ex-con." Or "once a con, always a con."

CHAPTER 9

257
**The Meaning
of Crime:
Social Process
Perspective**

The Social Process Perspective

The theories discussed in the first part of this chapter are typically called **social process theories**, or **interactionist perspectives**, because they emphasize the process of interaction between individuals and society. Social process theories of crime causation assume that everyone has the potential to violate the law and that criminality is not an innate human characteristic. According to social process theories, criminal behaviour is learned in interaction with others, and the socialization process that occurs as the result of group membership is seen as the primary route through which learning occurs. Among the most important groups contributing to the process of socialization are family, peers, work groups, and reference groups with which one identifies. Such groups instill values and norms in their members and communicate what are (for their members) acceptable world views and patterns of behaviour.

Social process perspectives hold that the process through which criminality is acquired, deviant self-concepts are established, and criminal behaviour results is active, open-ended, and ongoing throughout a person's life. They suggest that individuals who have weak ties to conformity are more likely to be influenced by the social processes and experiences that lead to crime. Further, they believe that criminal choices, once made, tend to persist because they are reinforced by the reaction of society to those whom it has identified as deviant.

Most social process theories of crime causation make the following fundamental assumptions:

- The nature of social reality is in flux; what we think of as social reality is a construction—specifically, an artifact of socialization and social interaction. In short, human beings are seen as co-producers of their social worlds.
- The meaning of events and experiences is conferred upon them by the participants in any interaction. Social actors define the situations in which they are involved.
- Meaning is derived from previous learned experiences and is conferred upon experiences in typical and recurring ways.
- Behaviour is criminal insofar as others define it as such and agree to its meaning.
- Criminal behaviour is variously interpreted by the offender, the victim, agents of social control, and society.
- Deviant individuals and criminal offenders achieve their status by virtue of social definition, rather than because of inborn traits.
- Continued criminal activity may be a consequence of limited opportunities for acceptable behaviour, which follow from the negative responses of society to those defined as criminal.
- Career offenders participate in a world view that differs from the world view of the conformist and that grants legitimacy to non-conformist activity.

Types of Social Process Theories

A number of theories can be classified under the social process umbrella. This chapter describes a number of them, including social learning theory, labelling theory, reintegrative shaming, social control theory, and social development theories. Social learning theory

Social process theories, also known as **interactionist perspectives**, assert that criminal behaviour is learned in interaction with others, and the socialization processes that occur as a result of group membership are the primary route through which learning occurs.

Theory in Perspective
Types of Social Process Theories

**SOCIAL PROCESS THEORIES, ALSO KNOWN AS INTERACTIONIST
PERSPECTIVES**

Emphasize the process of interaction between individuals and society. According to social process
theories, criminal behaviour is learned in interaction with others, and the socialization process that
occurs as the result of group membership is seen as the primary route through which learning occurs.

Social Learning Theory. Maintains that all behaviour is learned in much the same way and
that crime, like other forms of behaviour, is also learned.
Period: 1930s–1960s
Theorists: Edwin Sutherland, Gresham Sykes, David Matza, others
Concepts: Differential association; crime as learned; neutralization techniques of crime;
            commission, frequency, duration, priority, and intensity of association

Labelling Theory. Points to the special significance of society's response to the offender,
and sees continued crime as a consequence of limited opportunities for acceptable
behaviour that follow from the negative responses of society to those defined as offenders.
Period: 1938–1940 and 1960s–1980s, 1990s revival
Theorists: Frank Tannenbaum, Edwin M. Lemert, Howard Becker, John Braithwaite, others
Concepts: Tagging, labelling, outsiders, moral enterprise, primary and secondary deviance,
            reintegrative shaming, stigmatic shaming

Social Control Theory. Focuses on the strength of the social bond that people share with
the institutions and individuals around them, especially as those relationships shape their
behaviour. Seeks to identify those features of personality and of the environment that keep
people from committing crimes.
Period: 1950s–present
Theorists: Walter C. Reckless, Travis Hirschi, Michael R. Gottfredson, others
Concepts: Inner and outer containment, social bond

Social Development Theories. Integrated theories of human development that examine
many different levels simultaneously, including psychological, biological, familial,
interpersonal, cultural, societal, and ecological aspects of development.
Period: 1980s–present
Theorists: Sheldon and Eleanor Glueck, John Laub, Robert Sampson, Lawrence E. Cohen,
            Richard Machalek, others
Concepts: Criminal career, life course, social capital, cohort analysis, evolutionary ecology

places primary emphasis upon the role of communication and socialization in the acquisition of earned patterns of criminal behaviour and the values that support that behaviour.
Labelling theory points to the special significance of society's response to the criminal. It
sees the process through which a person becomes defined as criminal, along with society's

CHAPTER 9

259
**The Meaning
of Crime:
Social Process
Perspective**

formal imposition of the label "criminal" upon that person, as a significant contributory factor in determining future criminality. Reintegrative shaming, a contemporary offshoot of labelling theory, emphasizes possible positive outcomes of the labelling process. Social control theory focuses on the strength of the bond that people share with institutions and individuals around them, especially as those relationships shape their behaviour. Finally, social development theories integrate theories of human development that examine psychological, biological, familial, interpersonal, cultural, societal, and ecological aspects of that development.

Social Learning Theory

Social learning theory says that all behaviour is learned in much the same way and that crime, like other forms of behaviour, is also learned. People learn to commit crimes from others, and such learning includes the acquisition of norms, values, and patterns of behaviour conducive to crime. Hence, according to social learning theory, criminal behaviour is a product of the social environment and not an innate characteristic of particular people.

Social learning theory a perspective that places primary emphasis upon the role of communication and socialization in the acquisition of learned patterns of criminal behaviour and the values that support that behaviour.

Differential Association

One of the earliest and most influential forms of social learning theories was advanced by **Edwin Sutherland** in 1939. Sutherland's thesis was that criminality is learned through a process of **differential association** with others who communicate criminal values and who advocate the commission of crimes.[5] Sutherland emphasized the role of social learning as an explanation for crime because he believed that many of the concepts popular in the field of criminology at the time—including social pathology, genetic inheritance, biological characteristics, and personality flaws—were inadequate to explain the process by which an otherwise normal individual turns to crime. Sutherland was the first well-known criminologist to suggest that all significant human behaviour is learned behaviour, and crime, therefore, is not substantively different from any other form of behaviour.

Differential association the sociological thesis that criminality, like any other form of behaviour, is learned through a process of association with others who communicate criminal values.

Although Sutherland died in 1950, the tenth edition of his famous book, *Criminology*, was published in 1978 under the authorship of Donald R. Cressey, a professor at the University of California at Santa Barbara. The 1978 edition of *Criminology* contained the finalized principles of differential association (which, for all practical purposes, were complete as early as 1947). Nine in number, the principles are as follows:[6]

1. *Criminal behaviour is learned.* Sutherland believed that criminal behaviour is learned in the same manner as learning how to read or write. In other words, criminal behaviour is not seen as an inherent character trait.
2. *Criminal behaviour is learned in interaction with other persons in a process of communication.* The learning of criminal behaviour is very much dependent on the association between individuals. Those who are already criminal serve as "teachers" to others.
3. *The principal part of the learning of criminal behaviour occurs within intimate personal groups.* Individuals are influenced by those closest to them—family members, peers, and friends. Relationships with these individuals will control the way one sees the world. For example, studies have shown that children who grow up in households

where parents abuse alcohol tend to develop the attitudes that support such behaviour.[7] The belief that many young people are pressured by peers to commit illegal acts is inherent in this third principle of Sutherland's. It is the intimate peer group that most significantly influences youth.

4. *When criminal behaviour is learned, the learning includes (a) techniques of committing the crime, which are sometimes very complicated, sometimes very simple, and (b) the specific direction of motives, drives, rationalizations, and attitudes.* Since learning criminal behaviour is like learning any other kind of behaviour, the actual techniques of committing the crime must be taught and learned. Offenders learn from others how to pick locks, get involved in prostitution, obtain and use illicit drugs, or shoplift, for example. In addition to learning the actual techniques of criminal behaviour, Sutherland contended that offenders also learn the attitudes necessary to justify the behaviour. Some of these justifications are discussed in the "Neutralization Techniques" section later in this chapter.

5. *The specific direction of motives and drives is learned from definitions of the legal codes as favourable or unfavourable.* Sutherland believed that there are a variety of attitudes toward both the legal code and notions of right and wrong behaviour. The attitudes toward criminal behaviour held by the significant people in an individual's life have the greatest impact on the attitudes developed by the individual, through differential association.

6. *A person becomes delinquent because of an excess of definitions favourable to violation of law over definitions unfavourable to violation of law.* Interaction with those people or events that promote a disregard for the law will serve to strengthen and solidify those attitudes in another. For example, if a person spends more time in the company of someone who is constantly stealing CDs from music stores than with parents who extol the virtues of honesty and respect for the property of others, then disregard for the law becomes reinforced.

7. *Differential associations may vary in frequency, duration, priority, and intensity.* Whether a person learns to disobey the law depends upon the quality of the social interactions experienced. The more often one interacts with a deviant group, the greater the likelihood of learning the behaviour. The length of the interaction also influences the likelihood of learning a given behaviour. Priority has been interpreted to mean the age at which a person first encounters criminality. It is believed that contacts made at an earlier age are likely to have a more significant impact on that person's behaviour than those made later in life. Sutherland referred to intensity as the importance attributed to the people or groups from whom the behaviour is being learned. For example, for many youth at a certain stage of development, peer groups take priority over parents and can significantly influence a young person's behaviour.

8. *The process of learning criminal behaviour by association with criminal and anti-criminal patterns involves all of the mechanisms that are involved in any other learning.* Sutherland believed that learning criminal behaviour occurs the same way as learning any other behaviour and does not simply involve imitation.

9. *While criminal behaviour is an expression of general needs and values, it is not explained by those general needs and values, since non-criminal behaviour is an expression of the same needs and values.* This final principle holds that the motive for criminal behaviour is not the same as that for non-criminal behaviour. In other words, the desire for a leather jacket in and of itself does not foster criminal behaviour. Why one person will work to earn money to buy the jacket and someone else will steal it is largely

CHAPTER 9
261
**The Meaning
of Crime:
Social Process
Perspective**

determined by the different norms learned through associations with various groups. The learning of deviant norms from deviant groups produces criminal behaviour, according to Sutherland.

Differential association found considerable acceptance among theorists of the mid-20th century because it combined then prevalent psychological and sociological principles into a coherent perspective on criminality. Crime as a form of learned behaviour became the catchword of mid-century criminology, and those involved in the process of theory testing essentially abandoned biological and other perspectives.

Critique of Differential Association   Differential association is not without its critics. Perhaps the most potent criticism is the claim that differential association, because of the way in which Sutherland presented it, is virtually untestable, even though much use has been made of the insights the perspective appears to offer. Other critics also suggest that differential association alone is not a sufficient explanation for crime. If it were, then we might expect correctional officers, for example, to become criminals by virtue of their constant and continued association with prison inmates. Similarly, wrongly imprisoned persons might be expected to turn to crime upon release from confinement. Little evidence suggests that either of these scenarios actually occurs. In effect, differential association does not seem to provide for free choice in individual circumstances, nor for the fact that some individuals, even when surrounded by associates who are committed to lives of crime, are still able to hold onto other, non-criminal, values.

Neutralization Techniques

Of particular interest to some proponents of differential association is the manner in which various rationalizations are employed by those involved in criminal behaviour. Those who disobey the law are, at least to some degree, participants in the larger culture that surrounds them. How is it, then, that they may choose behavioural alternatives that seemingly negate the norms and values of the larger society? While social learning theorists such as Sutherland and Cressey contend that criminal behaviour is learned through the mastery of techniques, values, and attitudes needed to commit deviant acts, neutralization theory holds that most offenders learn **techniques of neutralization** to allow them to go against conventional values and attitudes. **Gresham Sykes** and **David Matza** put forth this notion in their 1957 article, "Techniques of Neutralization."[8] Sykes and Matza suggest that offenders can overcome feelings of responsibility when involved in crime commission through the use of the following five types of justifications:

Techniques of neutralization learned justifications that can provide criminal offenders with the means to disavow responsibility for their behaviour.

• *Denial of responsibility*, by pointing to one's background of poverty, abuse, lack of opportunity, and so on. Example: "The trouble I get into is not my fault," or "They made me do it."
• *Denial of injury*, by explaining how insurance companies, for example, cover losses. Claims that "everyone does it" or that the specific victim could "afford it" fall into this category. Example: "They're so rich, they'll never miss it."
• *Denial of the victim*, or justifying the harm done by claiming that the victim, for whatever reason, deserved the victimization. Example: "I only beat up drunks," or, "She had it coming."

- *Condemning the condemners*, by asserting that authorities are corrupt or responsible for their own victimization. Offenders may also claim that society has made them into what they are, and must now suffer the consequences. Example: "They're worse than we are. They're all on the take," or "If I don't do it to him, he'll do it to me."
- *An appeal to higher loyalties*, as in defence of one's family honour, gang, girlfriend, or neighbourhood. Example: "We have to protect ourselves."

In the words of Sykes and Matza, "[i]t is our argument that much delinquency is based on what is essentially an unrecognized extension of defenses to crimes, in the form of justifications for deviance that are seen as valid by the delinquent but not by the legal system or society at large."9

A few years later, Matza went on to suggest that delinquents tended to drift into crime when available techniques of neutralization combined with weak or ineffective values espoused by the controlling elements in society. In effect, said Matza, the delinquent "drifts between criminal and conventional action," choosing whichever is the more expedient at the time. By employing techniques of neutralization, delinquents need not be fully alienated from the larger society. When opportunities for crime present themselves, such techniques provide an effective way of overcoming feelings of guilt and allowing for ease of action. Matza used the phrase "soft determinism" to describe drift, saying that delinquents were neither forced to make choices because of fateful experiences early in life, nor were they entirely free to make choices unencumbered by the realities of their situation.

More recent studies have found that whereas "only a small percentage of adolescents generally approve of violence or express indifference to violence … [a] large percentage of adolescents … accept neutralizations justifying the use of violence in particular situations."10 The acceptance of such justifications by many young people today is seen as supportive of high levels of youth violence. Studies have also found that young people who disapprove of violence but associate with delinquent peers will often use neutralization techniques as justifications for violence in which they personally engage.11

Labelling Theory

Another social process perspective is based on the study of societal reactions to deviance. Society's response to known or suspected offenders is important not only because it determines the individual futures of those who are labelled as offenders, but also because it may contribute to a heightened incidence of criminality by reducing options available to labelled offenders.

An early description of lasting societal reaction to deviance can be found in the work of **Frank Tannenbaum**. Tannenbaum's book, *Crime and the Community*, was published in 1938 and popularized the term **tagging** to explain what happens to offenders following arrest, conviction, and sentencing. Tannenbaum told his readers that crime was essentially the result of "two opposing definitions of the situation" between the delinquent and the community at large. "This conflict over the situation," he said,

Tagging the process whereby an individual is negatively defined by agencies of justice.

> *is one that arises out of a divergence of values. As the problem develops, the situation gradually becomes redefined. The attitude of the community hardens definitely into a demand for suppression. There is a gradual shift from the definition of the specific acts as evil to a definition of the individual as evil, so that all his acts come to be looked upon*

CHAPTER 9
263
The Meaning
of Crime:
Social Process
Perspective

with suspicion .... From the community's point of view, the individual who used to do bad and mischievous things has now become a bad and unredeemable human being .... The young delinquent becomes bad because he is defined as bad and because he is not believed if he is good. There is a persistent demand for consistency in character. The community cannot deal with people whom it cannot define.[12]

Tannenbaum used the phrase *dramatization of evil* to explain the process whereby an offender comes to be seen as ultimately and irrevocably "bad." After the process has been completed, Tannenbaum said, the offender "now lives in a different world. He has been tagged .... The process of making the criminal, therefore, is a process of tagging ...." Once a person has been defined as bad, few legitimate opportunities remain open to her. As a consequence, the offender finds that only other people who have been similarly defined by society as bad are available to associate with him. This continued association with negatively defined people leads to continued crime.

Using terminology developed by **Edwin M. Lemert**, it became fashionable to call an offender's initial acts of deviance *primary deviance* and continued acts of deviance, especially those resulting from forced association with other offenders, *secondary deviance*. **Primary deviance**, Lemert pointed out, may be undertaken to solve some immediate problem or to meet the expectations of one's subcultural group. Hence, the robbery of a convenience store by a college student temporarily desperate for tuition money, although not a wise undertaking, may be the first serious criminal offence ever committed by the student. The student may well intend for it to be the last, but if arrest ensues and the student is "tagged" with the status of a criminal, then secondary deviance may occur as a means of adjustment to the negative status. In Lemert's words, "[w]hen a person begins to employ his deviant behavior or a role based upon it as a means of defense, attack, or adjustment to the overt and covert problems created by the consequent societal reaction to him, his deviation is secondary."[13]

Primary deviance initial deviance often undertaken to deal with transient problems in living.

Secondary deviance becomes especially important because of the forceful role it plays in causing tagged individuals to internalize the negative labels that have been applied to them. Through such a process, labelled individuals assume the role of the deviant. According to Lemert, "[o]bjective evidences of this change will be found in the symbolic appurtenances of the new role, in clothes, speech, posture, and mannerisms, which in some cases heighten social visibility, and which in some cases serve as symbolic cues to professionalization."[14]

Secondary deviance that which results from official labelling and from association with others who have been so labelled.

The name most often associated with labelling theory is that of **Howard Becker**. In 1963, Becker published *Outsiders: Studies in the Sociology of Deviance*, a work in which the **labelling** perspective found its fullest development.[15] In *Outsiders*, Becker described, among other things, the deviant subculture of jazz musicians and the process by which an individual becomes a marijuana user. His primary focus, however, was to explain how a person becomes labelled an outsider, as "a special kind of person, one who cannot be trusted to live by the rules agreed on by the group."[16] The central fact about deviance, says Becker, is that it is a social product, that "it is created by society." Society creates both deviance and the deviant person by responding to circumscribed behaviours. The person who engages in sanctioned behaviour is, as part of the process, labelled a deviant. In Becker's words,

Labelling an interactionist perspective that sees continued crime as a consequence of limited opportunities for acceptable behaviour which follow from the negative responses of society to those defined as offenders. Also, the process by which a negative or deviant label is imposed.

social groups create deviance by making the rules whose infraction constitutes deviance, and by applying those rules to particular people and labeling them as outsiders. From this point of view, deviance is not a quality of the act the person commits, but rather a consequence of the application by others of rules and sanctions. ... The deviant is one to whom that label has been successfully applied.[17]

For Becker, as for other labelling theorists, no act is intrinsically deviant or criminal but must be defined as such by others. Becoming deviant, Becker noted, involves a sequence of steps that eventually lead to commitment to a deviant identity and participation in a deviant career.

In developing labelling theory, Becker attempted to explain how some rules come to carry the force of law, while others have less weight or apply only within the context of marginal subcultures. His explanation centred on the concept of **moral enterprise**, a term that he used to encompass all the efforts a particular interest group makes to have its sense of propriety embodied in law. "Rules are the products of someone's initiative," said Becker, "and we can think of the people who exhibit such enterprise as moral entrepreneurs."[18]

An early example of moral enterprise can be found in the Women's Christian Temperance Union (WCTU), a group devoted to the idea of prohibition. From 1881 to 1919, the WCTU was highly visible in its widespread fight against alcohol—holding marches and demonstrations, closing drinking establishments, and lobbying legislators. Press coverage of the WCTU's activities swayed many politicians into believing that lawful prohibition of alcoholic beverages was inevitable, and an amendment to the US Constitution soon followed, ushering in the era of Prohibition.

While the United States had national Prohibition, the situation in Canada was somewhat different. In 1878, the government passed the *Dominion Temperance Act*, which relegated the decision concerning prohibition to local jurisdictions. In 1901, Prince Edward Island became the first province to vote "dry," but the issue remained a hotly debated one in many other areas of the country. World War I brought a virtual national prohibition, and many provinces, including Nova Scotia, Ontario, Alberta, Saskatchewan, and Manitoba, continued to enforce bans on liquor following the war.[19]

Becker claimed that moral enterprise is used similarly to prohibition by other groups seeking to support their own interests with the weight of law. Often the group that is successful at moral enterprise does not represent a popular point of view. The group is simply more effective than others at manoeuvring through the formal bureaucracy that attends the creation of legislation.

Becker was especially interested in describing deviant careers—the processes by which individuals become members of deviant subcultures and take on the attributes associated with the deviant role. Becker argued that most deviance, when it first occurs, is likely to be transitory. That is, it is unlikely to occur again. For example, a youth who shoplifts a candy bar from a convenience store will probably not make a habit out of this behaviour. However, transitory deviance can be effectively stabilized in a person's behavioural repertoire through the labelling process. If that youth is caught and charged by the police, then he or she becomes known as a shoplifter or young offender. Once a person is labelled as deviant, opportunities for conforming behaviour are seriously reduced. Behavioural opportunities that remain open are primarily deviant ones. Hence, throughout the person's career, the budding deviant increasingly exhibits deviant behaviour, not so much out of choice, but rather because her choices are restricted by society. Additionally, successful deviants must acquire the techniques and resources necessary to undertake the deviant act (be it shoplifting larger items or breaking and entering), and develop the mindset characteristic of others like them. Near the completion of a deviant career, the person who has been labelled a deviant becomes stigmatized by society. He internalizes society's

Moral enterprise efforts of a particular interest group to have its sense of propriety enacted into law.

CHAPTER 9

265

**The Meaning
of Crime:
Social Process
Perspective**

negative label, assumes a deviant self-concept, and is likely to become a member of a deviant subgroup. Becker says, "[a] drug addict once told me that the moment she felt she was really 'hooked' was when she realized she no longer had any friends who were not drug addicts."[20] In this way, says Becker, deviance finally becomes a "self-fulfilling prophecy." Labelling, then, is a cause of crime insofar as the actions of society in defining the rule breaker as deviant push the person further in the direction of continued deviance.

Labelling theory contributed a number of unique ideas to the criminological literature, including the following:

- Deviance is the result of social processes involving the imposition of definitions, rather than the consequence of any quality inherent in human activity itself. In other words, it is society's definition of a given behaviour at a given time and place in history that determines whether or not that behaviour is acceptable.
- Deviant individuals achieve their status by virtue of social definition rather than because of inborn traits.
- The reaction of society to deviant behaviour and to actors who engage in such behaviour is the major element in determining the criminality of the person and of the behaviour in question.
- Negative self-images follow from processing by the formal criminal justice system, rather than preceding delinquency.
- Labelling by society and handling by the justice system tend to perpetuate crime and delinquency rather than reduce it. Those labelled "ex-cons" or "drug addicts" or "young offenders" may experience difficulty finding and holding a job, for example.

Becker's typology of delinquents helped explain the labelling approach. It consisted of those whom he called (1) the pure deviant, (2) the falsely accused deviant, and (3) the secret deviant. The pure deviant is one who commits norm-breaking behaviour and whose behaviour is accurately appraised as such by society. An example might be the burglar who is caught in the act of burglary, then tried and convicted. Such a person, we might say, has gotten what she deserves. The falsely accused individual is one who, in fact, is not guilty, but is labelled deviant nonetheless. The falsely accused category in Becker's typology demonstrates the power of social definition. Innocent people sometimes end up in prison, and one can imagine that the impact of conviction and of the experiences that attend prison life can leave the falsely accused with a negative self-concept and with group associations practically indistinguishable from those of the true deviant. In effect, the life of the falsely accused is changed just as thoroughly as is the life of the pure deviant by the process of labelling. Finally, the secret deviant violates social norms, but his behaviour is not noticed, and negative societal reactions do not follow. The secret deviant again demonstrates the power of societal reaction—in this case by the very lack of consequences.

Although labelling theory fell into disregard during the late 1970s and early 1980s due to allegations that it was vague and ambiguous, contemporary criminologists now see the theory as one that points out the cumulative effects over time of official intervention on future life chances and opportunities. For example, Mike S. Adams recently proposed a general social learning theory of crime and deviance incorporating components of labelling theory and differential association.[21] Adams contends that "labeling effects are mediated by associations with delinquent peers." He concludes that labelling is not a direct cause of delinquency and crime but "appears to cause delinquency indirectly via the effects of associations with delinquent peer groups." In other words, "the causal chain linking primary to secondary deviance must incorporate links that account for the effects of associations with delinquent [peers]."[22] The transition from primary to secondary deviance is outlined in Box 9.1. Box 9.2 provides an example of the stigmatizing effects of labelling.

Critique of Labelling Theory The labelling approach, although it delineates how a person might have reasons for continuing in deviance and suffering a stabilization in deviant identities, does little to explain the origin of crime and deviance. Likewise, few, if any, studies seem to support the basic tenets of the theory. Critics of labelling have pointed to its "lack of firm empirical support for the notion of secondary deviance," and observed that "many studies have not found that delinquents or criminals have a delinquent or criminal self-image."[23]

In addition, there is a lack of unequivocal empirical support for the claim that contact with the justice system is fundamentally detrimental to the personal lives of criminal perpetrators. Although labelling theory suggests that official processing makes a significant contribution to continued criminality, it is questionable whether offenders untouched by the system would forego the rewards of future criminality. Rather, it is the *type* of contact with the criminal justice system that many feel influences the future behaviour of an offender.

Reintegrative Shaming

In a contemporary offshoot of labelling theory, **John Braithwaite** and colleagues at the Australian National University (ANU) reported initial results of their studies on reintegrative shaming in 1997.[24] In contrast to traditional labelling theory, which emphasizes stigmatization and the resulting amplification of deviance, reintegrative shaming describes processes by which an individual is labelled deviant and sanctioned but then brought back into a community of conformity through words, gestures, or rituals.

The Deviance Process   Box 9.1

1. A person commits a deviant/criminal act (if undetected, the act remains primary deviance).
2. Society reacts in a retributive or punitive way.
3. The individual responds by committing more infractions (secondary deviation), which in turn draws additional attention to the criminal. The deviant cycle begins to escalate (e.g., in frequency and/or intensity), a self-fulfilling process.
4. The labelled individual develops more hostility and resentment toward criminal justice agents.
5. Society and the legal system respond by further labelling and stigmatizing the offender.
6. As the individual's options become increasingly restricted, the criminal justice system sees the offender as a problem and the offender sees him- or herself as deviant.
7. The probability for future acts of deviance increases—deviance amplification. Therefore, once labelled and stigmatized, the offender's identity and self-concept evolve around deviance.

General Model of Labelling Process

Primary deviance → information reaction → continuance of deviance → escalation of response (e.g., stereotyping, rejection, alienation of tagged actor) → more delinquency (secondary deviance) → formal intervention → individual begins to see self as delinquent → self-fulfilling process.

Source: J.A. Winterdyk, *Canadian Criminology* (Toronto: Prentice Hall, 2000), p. 241. Reprinted with permission of Pearson Education Canada.

CHAPTER 9

267

**The Meaning
of Crime:
Social Process
Perspective**

Braithwaite compared the effectiveness of traditional court processing of criminal offenders with a restorative justice approach operating in Canberra, Australia, known as "diversionary conferencing." The diversionary conferencing approach

> *consists of an emotionally intense meeting, led by a police officer, between admitted offenders and their supporters, usually family and friends, and the victim of the offence, together with their supporters. In the absence of a direct victim, a representative of the community in which the offence occurred expresses the victim perspective on the events. The group discusses the consequences of the offence for all the parties and then determines what restitution the offenders must comply with to repair the harm for which they are responsible and so avoid going to court.*[25]

Called RISE, for Reintegrative Shaming Experiments, the project assessed the efficacy of each approach using criteria such as (1) prevalence and frequency of repeat offending, (2) victim satisfaction with the process, (3) estimated cost savings within the justice

Living in Shame

Box 9.2

Labelling theory says that people who commit deviant acts may continue down aberrant pathways because of labels society applies to them. The label of "pedophile" is one of the most stigmatizing and affects more than just the offender, as the following article shows.

When her son was sent to prison for pedophilia, Sheila was plunged into a world of secrecy and loneliness.

Lance, 21, was convicted last year of sexually assaulting an eight-year-old girl and a ten-year-old boy. He was sentenced to 20 months in jail.

"When I first found out he was charged, I was horrified, and immediately thought, 'What have I done wrong?'" says Sheila, who prefers to be identified only as a Lower Mainland teacher.

"I didn't know what to do. It was a nightmare. And because I didn't know what was going on, I wasn't in any kind of position to offer support to my son—who was terrified."

The experience left Sheila feeling isolated and abandoned. She still hasn't told other members of Lance's family—including her ex-husband—about his crime.

"I was feeling so alone. I mean, who could I talk to about this?

"You have a sense of isolation because you cut off all your friends.

"I was worried that everyone would find out. I was worried it would reflect on me and put my job in jeopardy. I have shared with only a few friends.

"Even some of my friends who do understand ... their attitude has changed and they stay away. It's like we're all tarred with the same brush.

"People say he's not really a pedophile, and I have to say, 'Yes he is.'"

The system, Sheila says, is just as mystifying to the families of offenders as it is to the victims. For one thing, there are few if any support groups.

"I went to court with my son time after time. I would sit in that courtroom ... and I was alone."

Lance, she says, was totally unprepared for the prison system.

"When he was taken into jail you would not believe the harassment from staff, and the filthy comments they made.

"This is a first-time offender, a young kid. He was so frightened.

"The day he was pronounced guilty he wrapped piano wire around his top button. He was afraid he'd end up getting raped because of the hatred towards pedophiles."

It was Lance's first conviction. Sheila believes he had never sexually molested children before.

But she admits he was a difficult child. Being expelled from kindergarten was only the start.

When she divorced Lance's father, things got worse. The next man she married was an alcoholic.

By the time he reached his teens, Lance was stealing and doing drugs.

Finally, in desperation, Sheila had him placed in a foster home.

"It was the hardest thing I've ever done, signing those papers. ..."

The papers she signed declared that she was legally "abandoning" him. That's the official language of B.C.'s *Family Child Services Act*, but Sheila insists that was never her intention.

Within weeks, Sheila says, Lance was sexually molested by his foster mother.

Within months he was sexually molesting two other kids in the home, resulting in the two charges of sexual assault.

"She (the foster mother) has admitted it to me," say Sheila.

"We have not pressed charges because my son did not want me to go through any more trauma.

"I have a lot of anger toward her (the foster mom). But I have a lot of guilt because I feel that if I hadn't been with an alcoholic husband, I would have been more aware.

"But Lance himself said, 'Mom, I made those choices, I did those things.'"

That admission, and confrontation with his past, came after months of therapy at Stave Lake, a minimum-security institution near Maple Ridge for sex offenders.

Sheila has nothing but praise for the staff and program. Now she does volunteer work with sex offenders, helping them upgrade their education, and with victims, helping them understand offenders.

Lance was released from prison after six months and has moved away from Lower Mainland.

He lives with a family, Sheila says, which is aware of his conviction, and he is supervised at all times.

She's anxious for him to get back into counselling, but she says his probation officer won't let him because of his living arrangements.

"They want him to move to a family apartment building where there would be no supervision."

Sheila wonders what kind of life Lance will have.

"I look down the road and I really wonder what chance my son has for having a good, wholesome, healthy life—like having a family.

"I just have to turn it over to God."

DISCUSSION QUESTIONS

1. How can a label such as "pedophile" affect others associated with the offender? Is there a danger in using such labels?
2. Do you feel any differently about the offender in this story once you know a little about his background and what led him to commit the sexual assaults? Is it possible to separate the offender from the offence?
3. Do you think the names of sexual offenders should be made known to the public? Defend your position.

Source: S. Jiwa and C. Ogilvie, "Living in Shame," *The Province*, February 21, 1993, p. 58.

CHAPTER 9

269

**The Meaning
of Crime:
Social Process
Perspective**

process, (4) changes in drinking or drug use behaviour among offenders, and (5) perceptions of procedural justice, fairness, and protection of rights.[26]

At the core of the study is Braithwaite's belief that two different kinds of shame exist. One he calls *stigmatic shaming*. **Stigmatic shaming** is thought to destroy the moral bond between the offender and the community. According to Braithwaite,

> *stigmatic shaming is what American judges employ when they make an offender post a sign on his property saying "a violent felon lives here"'or a bumper sticker on his car saying "I am a drunk driver." Stigmatic shaming sets the offender apart as an outcast—often for the rest of the offender's life. By labeling him or her as someone who cannot be trusted to obey the law, stigmatic shaming says the offender is expected to commit more crimes.[27]*

The other type of shame, **reintegrative shaming**, is thought to strengthen the moral bond between the offender and the community. This alternative to stigmatic humiliation is meant "to condemn the crime, not the criminal."[28] Through carefully monitored diversionary conferences, Braithwaite hopes to give offenders the opportunity to rejoin the community as law-abiding citizens. To earn the right to a fresh start, says Braithwaite, offenders must express remorse for their past conduct, apologize to any victims, and repair the harm caused by the crimes.

Preliminary results from the RISE study support the claimed value of reintegrative shaming. To date, however, most such results are being measured through interviews with offenders following diversionary conferences. Findings show that offenders are far more likely to feel ashamed of their crimes if handled through conferences rather than through formal court processing. Moreover, both offenders and victims report finding conferences fairer than official court proceedings. See the discussion on the related topic of restorative justice in Chapter 10.

Social Control Theories

Social control theories seek to identify those features of the personality and the environment that keep people from committing crimes. Controlling features of personality and the physical environment were identified in Chapters 7 and 8 respectively. Social control theories, however, take a step beyond static aspects of the personality and physical features of the environment in order to focus on the *process* through which social integration develops. It is the extent of a person's integration with positive social institutions and with significant others that determines that person's resistance to deviant and criminal temptations. Social control theories focus on the process through which such integration develops. Rather than stressing causal factors in criminal behaviour, social control theories tend to ask why people actually obey rules instead of breaking them.[29]

Containment Theory

In the 1950s, **Walter C. Reckless**, a student of the Chicago School of Criminology, wrote *The Crime Problem*.[30] Reckless tackled head-on the realization that most sociological theories, although conceptually enlightening, offered less than perfect predictability. That is, they did not provide the researcher with the ability to predict precisely which individuals, even those exposed to various "causes" of crime, would become criminal. Reckless thought

Stigmatic shaming a form of shaming, imposed as a sanction by the criminal justice system, that is thought to destroy the moral bond between the offender and the community.

Reintegrative shaming a form of shaming, imposed as a sanction by the criminal justice system, that is thought to strengthen the moral bond between the offender and the community.

Social control theories perspectives predicting that when social constraints on anti-social behaviour are weakened or absent, delinquent behaviour emerges. Rather than stressing causative factors in criminal behaviour, control theory asks why people actually obey rules instead of breaking them.

that the sociological perspectives prevalent at the time offered only half of a comprehensive theoretical framework. Crime, Reckless wrote, was the consequence of social pressures to involve oneself in violations of the law, as well as of one's failure to resist such pressures. Reckless called his approach **containment theory**, and he compared it with a biological immune response, saying that only some people exposed to a disease actually come down with it. Sickness, like crime, Reckless avowed, results from the failure of control mechanisms—some internal to the person and others external. In the case of sickness, external failures might include unsanitary conditions, the failure of the public health service, the lack of availability of preventative medicine, or the lack of knowledge necessary to make such medicine effective. Still, disease would not result unless the individual's resistance to disease-causing organisms was low or unless the individual was in some other way weak or susceptible to the disease.

In the case of crime, Reckless wrote, *external containment* consists of "the holding power of the group." Under most circumstances, Reckless wrote, "[t]he society, the state, the tribe, the village, the family, and other nuclear groups are able to hold the individual within the bounds of the accepted norms and expectations." In addition to setting limits, Reckless saw society as providing individuals with meaningful roles and activities. Such roles were seen as an important factor of external containment.

Inner containment, said Reckless, "represents the ability of the person to follow the expected norms, to direct himself." Such ability was said to be enhanced by a positive self-image, a focus on socially approved goals, personal aspirations that are in line with reality, a good tolerance of frustration, and a general adherence to the norms and values of society. A person with a positive self-concept can avoid the temptations of crime simply by thinking, "I'm not that kind of person." A focus on approved goals helps keep one on the proverbial straight and narrow path. "Aspirations in line with reality" are simply realistic desires. In other words, if one seriously desires to be the richest person in the world, disappointment will probably result. Even when aspirations are reasonable, however, disappointments will occur—hence the need for a tolerance for frustration. Adherence to the norms and values of the larger society are a basic component of inner containment.

Reckless's containment theory is diagrammed in Figure 9.1. "Pushes toward Crime" represents those factors in an individual's background that might propel him or her into criminal behaviour. They include a criminogenic background or upbringing that involves participation in a delinquent subculture, deprivation, biological propensities toward deviant behaviour, and psychological maladjustment. "Pulls toward Crime" signifies all the perceived rewards crime may offer, including financial gain, sexual satisfaction, and higher status. **Containment** is a stabilizing force and, if effective, blocks such pushes and pulls from leading the individual toward crime.

Reckless believed that inner containment was far more effective than external containment in preventing law violations. In his words, "[a]s social relations become more impersonal, as society becomes more diverse and alienated, as people participate more and more for longer periods of time away from a home base, the self becomes more and more important as a controlling agent."[31]

Containment theory was one of the first social control theories to be proposed. Social control approaches argue that social institutions exercise considerable control over individuals, either directly (as in the case of external containment) or indirectly, perhaps through socialization (as in the case of inner containment).

CHAPTER 9
271
**The Meaning
of Crime:
Social Process
Perspective**

Figure 9.1

A Diagrammatic Representation of Containment Theory

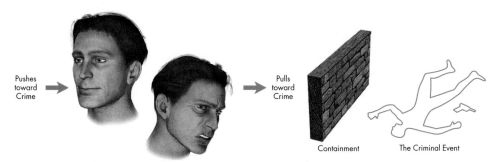

Pushes
toward
Crime

Pulls
toward
Crime

Containment   The Criminal Event

Social Bond Theory

An important form of social control theory was popularized by **Travis Hirschi** in his 1969 book *Causes of Delinquency*.[32] Hirschi argued that, through successful socialization, a bond forms between individuals and the social group. When that bond is weakened or broken, deviance and crime may result. Hirschi described four components of the **social bond**: attachment (a person's shared interests with others), commitment (the amount of energy and effort put into activities with others), involvement (the amount of time spent with others in shared activities), and belief (a shared system of values and morals).

In his writings, Hirschi cites the psychopath as an example of a person whose attachment to society is nearly non-existent.[33] Other relatively normal individuals may find their attachment to society loosened through "[t]he process of becoming alienated from others [which] often involves or is based on active interpersonal conflict. Such conflict could easily supply," says Hirschi, "a reservoir of socially derived hostility sufficient to account for the aggressiveness of those whose attachments to others have been weakened."[34]

The second component of the social bond—commitment—reflects a person's investment of time and energies into conforming behaviour and the potential loss of rewards that she has already gained from that behaviour. In Hirschi's words,

> [t]he idea, then, is that the person invests time, energy, himself, in a certain line of activity—say, getting an education, building up a business, acquiring a reputation for virtue. Whenever he considers deviant behavior, he must consider the costs of this deviant behavior, the risk he runs of losing the investment he has made in conventional behavior.[35]

For such a traditionally successful person, says Hirschi, "a ten-dollar-holdup is stupidity," because the potential for losing what has already been acquired through commitment to social norms far exceeds what stands to be gained. Recognizing that his approach applies primarily to individuals who have been successfully socialized into conventional society, Hirschi adds, "[t]he concept of commitment assumes that the organization of society is

Social bond the intangible link between individuals and the society of which they are a part, created through the process of socialization.

such that the interests of most persons would be endangered if they were to engage in criminal acts."[36]

Involvement, for Hirschi, means "engrossment in conventional activities" and is similar to Reckless's concept of meaningful roles.[37] In explaining the importance of involvement in determining conformity, Hirschi cites the colloquial saying that "idle hands are the devil's workshop." Time and energy, he says, are limited, and, if a person is busy at legitimate pursuits, he or she will have little opportunity for crime and deviance.

Belief is the last of Hirschi's four aspects of the social bond. Hirschi writes that "control theory assumes the existence of a common value system within the society or group whose norms are being violated …. We not only assume the deviant has believed the rules, we assume he believes the rules even as he violates them." How can a person simultaneously believe it is wrong to commit a crime and still commit it? Hirschi's answer is that "[m]any persons do not have an attitude of respect toward the rules of society."[38] That is, although they know the rules exist, they basically do not care. They invest little of their sense of self in moral standards.

In 1990, Hirschi, in collaboration with **Michael R. Gottfredson**, proposed a general theory of crime based on the concepts advanced earlier in control theory.[39] Gottfredson and Hirschi began by asking, "What is crime?" Nearly all crimes, they concluded, are mundane, simple, trivial, easy acts aimed at satisfying desires of the moment. Hence, their general theory built on a classical or rational choice perspective—that is, the belief that crime is a natural consequence of unrestrained human tendencies to seek pleasure and avoid pain. Crime, said Gottfredson and Hirschi, is little more than a subset of general deviant behaviour. Hence, they concluded, crime bears little resemblance to the explanations offered in the media, by law enforcement officials, or by most academic thinkers on the subject.

According to Gottfredson and Hirschi, the offender is neither the diabolical genius of fiction nor the ambitious seeker of the American Dream often portrayed by other social scientists. On the contrary, offenders appear to have little control over their own desires. When personal desires conflict with long-term interests, those who lack self-control often opt for the desires of the moment, thus contravening legal restrictions and becoming involved in crime.[40] Central to Gottfredson and Hirschi's thesis is the belief that a well-developed social bond will result in the creation of effective mechanisms of self-control. As others have noted, "for Gottfredson and Hirschi, self-control is the key concept in the explanation of all forms of crime as well as other types of behavior. Indeed, they believe that all current differences in rates of crime between groups and categories may be explained by differences in the management of self-control."[41] An overview of other integrated theories of crime follows.

Social Development Theories

Social development perspective an integrated view of human development that examines multiple levels of maturation simultaneously, including the psychological, biological, familial, interpersonal, cultural, societal, and ecological levels.

Over the past 25 years, an emerging appreciation for the process of human development has played an increasingly important role in helping us understand criminality.[42] *Human development* refers to the relationship between the maturing individual and his or her changing environment and to the social processes that relationship entails. The **social development perspective** understands that development, which begins at birth (and perhaps even earlier), occurs primarily within a social context. Unlike social learning theory (discussed earlier in this chapter), however, social development theories see socialization as only one feature of that context. If socialization were the primary determinant

CHAPTER 9

273

**The Meaning
of Crime:
Social Process
Perspective**

of criminality, development theorists point out, then we might expect that all problem children would become criminals as adults. Since that doesn't happen, there must be other aspects to the development process that social learning theories don't fully appreciate.

According to the social development perspective, human development occurs on many levels simultaneously, including psychological, biological, familial, interpersonal, cultural, societal, and ecological. Hence, social development theories tend to be integrated theories, or theories that combine various points of view on the process of development. The rest of this chapter looks briefly at the social development perspective.

Traditional explanations for crime and delinquency often lack a developmental perspective. They can ignore developmental changes throughout the life course and frequently fail to distinguish between different phases of criminal careers. In contrast, most theories of social development recognize that a critical transitional period occurs as a person moves from childhood to adulthood. In contrast, criminal careers and life course theory draw attention to the fact that criminal behaviour tends to follow a distinct pattern across the life cycle. Criminality is relatively uncommon during childhood; it tends to begin as sporadic instances of delinquency during late adolescence and early adulthood; and then it diminishes and sometimes completely disappears from a person's behaviour by age 30 or 40. Of course, some people never commit crimes or do so only rarely, while others become career criminals and persist in lives of crime.

Career criminality is frequently explained by **life course theories**, which provide a kind of summary approach incorporating many other sociological perspectives. Most life course theories recognize that criminogenic influences have their greatest impact during the early stages of life. Hence, such perspectives agree with the widely held belief that children are more impressionable than older people, and that the experiences children go through shape them for the rest of their lives.

Life course theorists have identified at least seven developmental tasks that adolescents must confront: (1) establishing identity, (2) cultivating symbiotic relationships, (3) defining physical attractiveness, (4) investing in a value system, (5) obtaining an education, (6) separating from family and achieving independence, and (7) obtaining and maintaining gainful employment.[43] It is generally recognized that youths are confronted with many obstacles, or risks, in their attempts to resolve these issues as they work to make a successful transition to adulthood. Figure 9.2 provides a conceptual model of the developmental processes that a maturing child experiences during adolescence.

Life course theories are supported by research dating back more than half a century. During the 1930s, for example, **Sheldon and Eleanor Glueck** studied the life cycles of delinquent boys. The Gluecks followed the careers of known delinquents in an effort to identify the causes of delinquency. Data were originally collected through psychiatric interviews with subjects, parent and teacher reports, and official records obtained from police, court, and correctional files. Surviving subjects were again interviewed between 1949 and 1965. The Gluecks found that family dynamics played an especially significant role in the development of criminality and observed that "the deeper the roots of childhood maladjustment, the smaller the chance of adult adjustment."[44] Delinquent careers, said the Gluecks, tend to carry over into adulthood and frequently lead to criminal careers.

Several years ago, **John Laub** and **Robert Sampson**[45] reanalyzed the data originally gathered by the Gluecks, and found that children who turn to delinquency are frequently those who have trouble at school and at home, and who have friends already involved in delinquency. Using a sophisticated computerized analysis of the Gluecks' original data, Laub and Sampson identified "turning points" in a criminal career.

Life course theories
explanations for criminality that recognize criminogenic influences as having their greatest impact during the early stages of life and that see formative childhood experiences as catalysts in shaping children for the rest of their lives.

Figure 9.2

A Conceptual Model of Adolescent Development

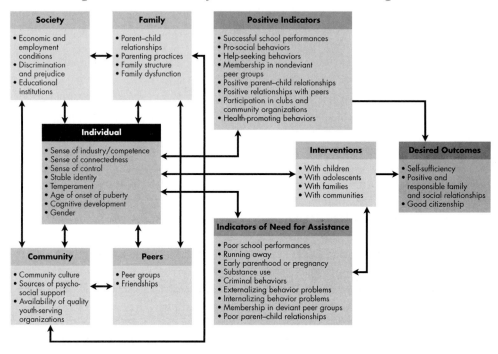

Source: Family and Youth Services Bureau, *Understanding Youth Development: Promoting Positive Pathways of Growth* (Washington, DC: U.S. Department of Health and Human Services, 2000).

Social capital the number of positive relationships with other persons and social institutions that individuals build up over the course of their lives.

Cohort analysis a social scientific technique that studies a population that shares common characteristics over time. Cohort analysis usually begins at birth and traces the development of cohort members until they reach a certain age.

Cohort a group of individuals sharing certain significant social characteristics, such as gender and time and place of birth.

Turning points, they found, may occur at any time in such a career, although two especially significant turning points centre on the choice of employment and marriage. Employers who are willing to give "troublemakers" a chance and marriage partners who insist on conventional lifestyles can successfully redirect the course of a budding offender's life, according to these authors. Laub and Sampson also developed the concept of **social capital** in reference to the number of positive relationships with other persons and social institutions that individuals build up over the course of their lives. The greater one's social capital, the less the chance of criminal activity.[46]

Life course theory uses a developmental perspective in the study of criminal careers. As a consequence, life course researchers frequently use cohort analysis. **Cohort analysis** usually begins at birth and traces the development of a population whose members share common characteristics until they reach a certain age. One well-known analysis of a birth **cohort**, undertaken by Marvin Wolfgang during the 1960s, found that a small nucleus of chronic juvenile offenders accounted for a disproportionately large share of all juvenile arrests.[47] Wolfgang studied male individuals born in Philadelphia in 1945, following them until they reached age 18. He concluded that a relatively small number of violent offenders were responsible for most of the crimes committed by the cohort. Eighteen percent of cohort members accounted for 52 percent of all arrests. A follow-up study found that the seriousness of offences among the cohort increased in adulthood, but that the actual

CHAPTER 9

275

**The Meaning
of Crime:
Social Process
Perspective**

number of offences decreased as the cohort aged.[48] Wolfgang's analysis has since been criticized for its lack of a second cohort, or control group, against which the experiences of the cohort under study could be compared.[49] More recently, Wolfgang published a cohort analysis of 5000 individuals born in the Wuchang district of the city of Wuhan in China. The study, from which preliminary results were published in 1996, utilized Chinese-supplied data to compare delinquents with non-delinquents. It found "striking differences in school deportment, achieved level of education, school dropout rate, type of employment, and unemployment rate ..."[50] between the two groups.

The ecological perspective on crime control, pioneered by **Lawrence E. Cohen** and **Richard Machalek**, provides a contemporary example of a life course approach.[51] Like other life course theories, **evolutionary ecology** blends elements of previous perspectives—in this case building upon the approach of social ecology—while emphasizing developmental pathways encountered early in life. According to Bryan Vila, "the evolutionary ecological approach ... draws attention to the ways people develop over the course of their lives. Experiences and environment early in life," says Vila, "especially those that affect child development and the transmission of biological traits and family management practices across generations, seem particularly important."[52] According to Vila, evolutionary ecology "attempts to explain how people acquire criminality—a predisposition that disproportionately favors criminal behavior—when and why they express it as crime, how individuals and groups respond to those crimes, and how all these phenomena interact as a dynamic self-reinforcing system that evolves over time."[53]

One of the most comprehensive studies to date that has attempted to detail life pathways leading to criminality began in 1986. The study, a cohort analysis, compiled data on 4500 youths from three distinct but coordinated projects throughout the United States.[54] A survey sampled youngsters at high risk for serious delinquency and drug use and found that (1) "the more seriously involved in drugs a youth was, the more seriously that juvenile was involved in delinquency," (2) "greater risks exist for violent offending when a child is physically abused or neglected early in life," (3) students who are not highly committed to school have higher rates of delinquency, (4) "poor family life exacerbates delinquency and drug use," and (5) affiliation with street gangs and illegal gun ownership are both predictive of delinquency. The study also found that "peers who were delinquent or used drugs had a great impact on [other] youth." Perhaps the most significant result of the study was the finding that three separate developmental pathways to delinquency exist. The pathways identified by the study are[55]

- the *authority conflict pathway*, down which subjects appear to begin quite young (as early as 3 or 4 years of age). "The first step," said the study authors, "was stubborn behavior, followed by defiance around age 11, and authority avoidance—truancy, staying out late at night, or running away."
- the *covert pathway*, which begins with "minor covert acts such as frequent lying and shoplifting, usually around age 10." Delinquents following this path quickly progress "to acts of property damage, such as firestarting or vandalism, around age 11 or 12, followed by moderate and serious forms of delinquency."
- the *overt pathway*, in which the first step is marked by minor aggression such as "annoying others and bullying—around age 11 or 12." Bullying was found to escalate into "physical fighting and violence as the juvenile progressed along this pathway."

Evolutionary ecology
an approach to understanding crime that draws attention to the ways people develop over the course of their lives.

Another recent study that could potentially produce substantially significant results began in 1990.[56] Project directors describe their ongoing research as "the major criminologic investigation of this century." The study consists of a longitudinal analysis of how individuals, families, institutions, and communities evolve together. It is now "tracing how criminal behavior develops from birth to age 32." Researchers are planning to follow a total of 11 000 individuals in 9 different age groups for 8 years. There are a variety of study methodologies being utilized, including self-reports, individualized tests and examinations, direct observation, the examination of existing records, and reports by informants. Researchers hope to provide answers to the following questions: (1) "How and why do anti-social and criminal behaviours originate?" (2) "What causes some individuals to continue those behaviours?" and (3) "How and why do some individuals cease law-violating behaviours while others continue?"

Life course theories often point to the need for early intervention through nurturant strategies that build self-control through positive socialization. As Vila points out, "[t]here are two main types of nurturant strategies: those that improve early life experiences to forestall the development of strategic styles based on criminality, and those that channel child and adolescent development in an effort to improve the match between individuals and their environment."[57]

Policy Implications of Social Process Theories

As has been noted throughout this chapter, both offenders and victims are stigmatized through social processes involving the formal and informal imposition of labels. Removal of the stigma would, at least theoretically, restore both to their pre-crime state.

Labelling theory, in particular, cautions against too much intervention, since it is often through contact with various types of rehabilitative programs that individuals become even further labelled. Even well-intentioned programs such as special education programs or support groups for released offenders can serve to label participants as "stupid" or "ex-con." Current restitution and court diversion programs are examples of policy initiatives that recognize the principles of labelling theory. Adult diversion projects or alternative measures for youth are designed to divert the offender away from formal contact with the criminal justice system, thereby avoiding the imposition of a label. For example, a man who is arrested for seeking the services of a prostitute but who has no previous criminal convictions may be ordered to attend "john school." Successful attendance means the offender has no further contact with the criminal justice system and is free of a criminal record. Diversion programs are usually joint initiatives involving the Crown's office and the local police service. Likewise, restitution initiatives are attempts to prevent the stigmatization of the offender. In lieu of the trial and court process, the offender is required to compensate either the victim or the community for the loss or for harm done. Since their inception, diversion programs have been surrounded by controversy. Whether they actually prevent the imposition of a negative label and thereby prevent future criminal activity is open to debate.[58]

Social learning perspectives have also had an impact on program initiatives dealing with offenders and those at risk of becoming offenders. Social learning is based on the principle that since criminal behaviour and attitudes can be learned through association with criminal types, so can conventional values be learned by interaction with those holding them. Well-known programs such as "Night Hoops" or "After-4 Drop-ins" are aimed at

CHAPTER 9

277

**The Meaning
of Crime:
Social Process
Perspective**

"at-risk" youth and provide an opportunity for them to associate with positive role models. Well-known sports figures will often participate and deliver positive messages telling kids to "Stay in school" or "Say no to drugs." In Ottawa, Ontario, the Ottawa Police Service runs a youth centre in a neighbourhood once ridden with youth crime. They have reported a significant decrease in illegal activity in the neighbourhood since the centre's opening.

Closely linked to the notion of learned behaviour are the notions of commitment and attachment put forth by social control theorists. Not only do recreation programs run by such organizations as the Boys and Girls Club and the YM/YWCA promote positive learning, they help to develop a positive bond between individual participants and the program. Individuals, in turn, will not want to risk losing the privilege of being a member of the program if they break the rules. Similarly, educational programs such as Head Start work to socialize children at the preschool stage to help make their school experiences more enjoyable and thereby decrease the chances of early withdrawal. Social control theorists believe that a strong commitment to school, family, employment, and recreation—assuming these environments are all positive ones—can help decrease an individual's likelihood of succumbing to a criminal lifestyle.

Life course theories have been widely applied to develop programs aimed at youth at conflict with the law. Most of these programs centre around a number of principles which include strengthening the role of the family in providing guidance and discipline, supporting core social institutions such as schools and community organizations, promoting prevention strategies, and intervening immediately and consistently when delinquent behaviour first occurs. Examples of programs that reflect these principles are found in Chapter 4 in the discussion of nurturant crime control policies.

Critique of Social Process Theories

Social process theories share some of the limitations of social structure theories, discussed in Chapter 8. Most notable of these is the disregard for biological and/or psychological contributions to criminal behaviour; indeed, all these theories are concerned with the social reality surrounding individuals and their interaction with all or some segments of it. In addition, like social structure theories, the social process perspective fails to fully explain why some individuals who are surrounded by negative environments and poor role models manage to avoid becoming involved in criminal behaviour. How is it that some manage to resist the peer pressure to get involved in deviant activity? How are they able to desist from "learning" from what they see all around them? If socialization is so crucial to an understanding of criminal behaviour, how is it that crime rates fluctuate from region to region in Canada? Are youth, for example, in the western provinces, where crime rates are generally higher, socialized differently than those in the eastern parts of the country, where crime rates are generally lower?

Summary

This chapter discussed a wide variety of perspectives, from social learning, social control, and labelling theories to social development theories. We have used both the terms *social process theory* and *interactionist perspective* to classify the theories found here. More fundamental to each of this chapter's perspectives, however, is the concept of social meaning; this chapter might be appropriately titled "the search for social meaning."

When individuals interact with others, they naturally learn certain behaviours and the justifications for them. Social learning theories contend that excessive interaction with those who promote a criminal lifestyle rather than a law-abiding one will result, for most, in the pursuit of a similar way of life. In addition to engaging in anti-social behaviour, individuals can also learn the rationalizations needed to ignore conventional societal norms in favour of deviant ones. Similarly, social control theory holds that the bonds individuals form with positive role models or institutions prevent them from engaging in criminal behaviour. When these bonds become weak or break, individuals have "nothing to lose" by turning to anti-social behaviour.

When individual offenders are labelled criminal or deviant, the meaning that their presence holds for the group of which they are a part, as well as the personal significance of their own lives, has been inexorably changed. They will rarely be seen in the same way (in the pre-deviant state) again. In like fashion, when offenders internalize an acquired or imposed deviant self-conception, the meaning of their own lives changes and any future decisions they will make take on a new significance in light of the new self-image.

Finally, life course theory evaluates all aspects of the life experience, from birth through adolescence and into adulthood, for clues to the social conditions, individual circumstances, and life experiences that lead to crime and deviance.

Discussion Questions

1. This book emphasizes a social problems versus social responsibility theme. Which of the theoretical perspectives discussed in this chapter (if any) best support the social problems approach? Which (if any) support the social responsibility approach? Why?

2. This chapter includes a discussion of the labelling process. Give a few examples of the everyday imposition of positive, rather than negative, labels. Why is it so difficult to successfully impose positive labels on individuals previously labelled negatively?

3. Compare and contrast the theories discussed in this chapter, citing differences and similarities between and among them. How, for example, does Reckless's notion of containment differ from Hirschi's idea of a social bond?

4. Do you believe that Sutherland's differential association approach, which contends that criminality is learned behaviour, provides any valuable insight into an explanation of deviant behaviour? If so, what is it? Do you believe that Sykes and Matza's techniques of neutralization can also be learned? Can deviant behaviour be "un-learned"?

5. What kinds of social policy initiatives might be suggested by social process theories?

6. What are the shortcomings of the social process perspective?

Weblinks

www.voicesforchildren.ca

Voices for Children. This group works with organizations and individuals to strengthen public commitment to the healthy development of children and youth.

www.cfc-efc.ca

Child and Family Canada. Public education site sponsored by 50 non-profit organizations to provide resources on children and families. Extensive library of research papers.

The Meaning of Crime: Social Conflict Perspective

Laws are like spiders' webs, which, if anything small falls into them, they ensnare it, but large things break through and escape.

—SOLON [1]

Our actions were not oriented toward intensive, wanton destruction but rather were carefully selected and carried out with great concern for political, economic, and human consequences.

—ANNE HANSEN [2]

LEARNING OUTCOMES

After reading this chapter, you should be able to

- recognize the ways in which power conflict between social groups contributes to crime and criminal activity

- understand the distinctions between a number of social conflict theories

- identify those policy initiatives that reflect the social conflict approach

- assess the shortcomings of the social conflict perspective

IMPORTANT NAMES

Karl Marx	Jeffrey H. Reiman	Harold E. Pepinsky
Ralf Dahrendorf	Freda Adler	Ezzat Fattah
George Vold	Rita J. Simon	Walter DeKeseredy
Austin Turk	Kathleen Daly	Jock Young
William J. Chambliss	Meda Chesney-Lind	
Richard Quinney	John Hagan	

IMPORTANT TERMS

social conflict perspective	feminist criminology	circle sentencing conferences
radical criminology	patriarchy	Victim–Offender Reconciliation
Marxist criminology	radical feminism	Program (VORP)
proletariat	liberal feminism	family group conferencing
bourgeoisie	socialist feminism	community sentencing panels
social class	power-control theory	community policing
structural Marxism	peacemaking criminology	participatory justice
instrumental Marxism	peace model	left-realist criminology
critical criminology	restorative justice	left realism

Introduction

On March 11, 1990, a small Mohawk Aboriginal band erected a barricade along the border of the Mohawk Nation reserve of Kanesatake. The nearby city of Oka, Quebec, was proceeding with plans to enlarge a golf course on 22 hectares of land known as "The Pines" that had been given to the city but was claimed by the Mohawks as a sacred native ancestral burial ground. Since the courts had rejected the Mohawks' claim to the land, the band concluded that their only option was to hold a standoff. It lasted 78 days.

Initially, the barricade was guarded mostly by women and children. The standoff intensified, however, as the Mohawks of Kanesatake were joined by Mohawk natives from other reserves in Canada and the United States, some of whom belonged to a society of heavily armed Mohawk Warriors. The introduction of high-powered firearms and other weapons increased the tension between the Mohawks and authorities, represented largely by the Quebec provincial police force, known as the Sûreté du Québec (SQ). The city of Oka was successful in obtaining a court order to evict the Mohawks, and on July 10, 1990, about 100 SQ personnel attempted to enforce this injunction on behalf of the municipality. Armed Mohawks were positioned to one side in the woods while police equipped with gas masks and assault rifles advanced on the barricade. An armed conflict erupted, and hundreds of rounds of ammunition were fired from both sides, resulting in the wounding and eventual death of a 31-year-old SQ corporal. The standoff had reached crisis proportions, and each side blamed the other for the death of the police officer.

Thirty kilometres to the south of the Kanesatake reserve, Mohawks from the Kahnawake reserve were outraged by the actions of the police. In a show of support, they blocked off all roads into the reserve. These included two major highways, one of which led to the Mercier Bridge linking the city of Montreal to the residential neighbourhood of

CHAPTER 10
281
**The Meaning
of Crime:
Social Conflict
Perspective**

Châteauguay, which forced thousands of commuters to take a two-hour daily detour. Threatening to "bring down the bridge" if there was another police assault at Oka, the Mohawks dug in. Over 100 chiefs from across Canada met at Kahnawake in a show of solidarity.

The crisis captured national attention, and throngs of media personnel transmitted interviews and pictures across the country. As the standoff continued throughout the summer of 1990, both sides in the conflict became more entrenched. Arms and ammunition were smuggled from native communities in the United States to bolster the Mohawk cause. Mohawk Warriors with monikers such as "Lasagna" and "Kadahfi" appeared before television cameras in army fatigues, with bandanas covering their faces. Two hundred or so Royal Canadian Mounted Police officers bolstered the 1400 to 1800 SQ forces throughout the duration of the crisis. As the standoff dragged on through the summer, with no progress made toward negotiating a settlement, then Prime Minister Mulroney called in the Canadian Armed Forces at the request of Premier Bourassa and the Quebec government. Approximately 1000 military personnel took over police positions established at Kanesatake and Kahnawake. Numerous violent clashes erupted as each side stood its ground. Canadians witnessed scenes of armoured personnel carriers, barbed-wire barricades, and shouting matches between the two sides as the group of Mohawk Warriors resisted advances by the authorities. Eventually, on September 6, 1990, the Kahnawake Mohawks ended their occupation of the Mercier Bridge. On September 26, after often heated negotiations, the standoff ended when the Mohawk Warriors agreed to lift the barricade. The golf course has not since been expanded.

In a standoff at the Kanesatake reserve in Oka, Quebec, on September 1, 1990, a Canadian soldier comes face to face with a Mohawk warrior.
The Canadian Press/Shaney Komulainen.

The Oka crisis cost the Canadian people $200 million, including the expense of extra policing and army intervention. The incident at Oka ended relatively peacefully; however, in the ensuing years there have been numerous similar standoffs: April 1995—members of the Adams Lake band in British Columbia stopped equipment from reaching a planned park near Chase, British Columbia, on an ancient burial site; June 1995—Micmacs from Nova Scotia set gill nets in New Brunswick's Miramichi River and blockaded the road to the native-run fishing camp; September 1995—members of the Stoney Point Ojibway band occupied Ipperwash Provincial Park in southwestern Ontario, saying it is a sacred burial ground, during which three Aboriginal protesters were shot by police in a gunfight and one protester, Dudley George, died; October 2005—a seven-hour standoff by the Stoney First Nations group prevented the planned construction of a $27-million casino project on land west of Calgary; and April 2006—protesters from the Six Nations of the Grand River Territory occupied a new subdivision construction site in Caledonia, in southwestern Ontario, claming that the land belongs to them.

The Social Conflict Perspective

Social conflict perspective an analytical perspective on social organization which holds that conflict is a fundamental aspect of social life itself and can never fully be resolved.

Social conflict theories emphasize social, economic, and political realities and place crime within this context. As with social process theories, the **social conflict perspective** focuses on the interaction between groups but views this interaction as one of conflict. Various groups within society, defined in terms of their political, economic, or social standing, are seen to compete with one another to promote their own best interests.

Crime and criminal activity are the outcome of this struggle, according to social conflict theories. The creation and application of criminal laws is crucial to determining who becomes criminalized; social conflict criminologists see these roles largely filled by that segment of society holding the economic and political power. This segment uses the law as a means of controlling the dissatisfied and less powerful groups within society while maintaining its position of power. As various groups struggle for power, conflict ensues, which promotes crime. Social conflict theories are also concerned with the role of government and the state in producing crime, since what is considered acceptable and unacceptable behaviour is determined by state-sanctioned laws designed to set boundaries governing such behaviour.

Most social conflict theories of crime causation make the following fundamental assumptions:

- Society is divided by conflict rather than integrated by consensus.
- Society is made up of groups based on political and economic power.
- Differences in social class, and in particular those arrangements within society that maintain class differences, are the focus for criminological study.
- Powerful groups make laws that reflect and protect their interests.
- Crime is an outcome of conflict between those who have and those who have not.

Types of Social Conflict Theories

Various theories found under the rubric of the social conflict perspective emphasize different root causes of the conflict. This chapter considers a number of these theories including radical and critical criminology, feminist criminology, the peacemaking model,

CHAPTER 10

283

**The Meaning
of Crime:
Social Conflict
Perspective**

Theory in Perspective
Social Conflict Approaches

SOCIAL CONFLICT THEORIES
Emphasize the power of conflict within society, based largely on inequalities between social classes.

Radical Criminology. Holds that the causes of crime are rooted in social conditions that empower the wealthy and the politically well organized, but disenfranchise those less fortunate.
Period: 1960s–present
Theorists: Karl Marx, Ralf Dahrendorf, Richard Quinney, William Chambliss, Raymond Michalowski, George B. Vold, Austin Turk, Jeffrey H. Reiman
Concepts: Social class, bourgeoisie, proletariat

Feminist Criminology. A radical criminological approach to the explanation of crime that sees the conflict and inequality present in society as based primarily on gender.
Period: 1970s–present
Theorists: Freda Adler, Rita J. Simon, Kathleen Daly, Meda Chesney-Lind, John Hagan
Concepts: Power-control, gender socialization, empowerment

Peacemaking Criminology. Holds that crime control agencies and citizens must work together to alleviate social problems including crime.
Period: 1980s–present
Theorists: Harold E. Pepinsky, Richard Quinney
Concepts: Compassionate criminology, restorative justice

Left-Realist Criminology. A branch of radical criminology that holds that crime is a "real" social problem experienced by the lower classes.
Period: 1980s–present
Theorists: Walter DeKeseredy, Jock Young
Concepts: Radical realism, critical realism, street crime, social justice, crime control

including restorative justice, and the left-realist perspective. Radical criminology is based on Marxist political thought and contends that current inequities in social standing and economic power are the main contributors to the reality of crime. Critical criminology is distinguished from radical criminology by its emphasis on a critique of the relationship between social classes; it is generally viewed as more reactive than the proactive approach taken by the radical criminological outlook. Feminist criminology sees the inequities that exist within society as drawn along gender lines. Peacemaking criminology advocates the reduction of crime through the cooperative efforts of criminal justice agencies and the citizens they serve. Restorative justice and alternative dispute resolution models have their roots in this perspective. Finally, the left-realist perspective moves away from a political-ideological explanation of crime and criminality toward the contention that crime is very "real," especially for marginalized segments of society.

"Cruel and Unusual": The Law and Latimer

Box 10.1

The social conflict perspective seems better suited to an understanding of many contemporary social issues, among them the heated debate around euthanasia and mercy killing, as the following article in this box shows.

Robert Latimer, a farmer working a spread in Saskatchewan northwest of Saskatoon, killed his 12-year-old daughter Tracy on October 24, 1993. There has never been any doubt about this.

Latimer told police he did it. He said he loved his daughter and could not bear to watch her suffer from a severe form of cerebral palsy. So he placed her in the cab of his Chevy pickup, ran a hose from the exhaust to the cab, climbed into the box of the truck, sat on a tire, and watched her die.

Tracy was a 40-pound quadriplegic, a 12-year-old who functioned at the level of a three-month-old. She had been repeatedly operated on and at the time of her murder was due for more surgery, this time to remove a thigh bone. She could not walk, talk, or feed herself, though she responded to affection and occasionally smiled. Tracy was in constant, excruciating pain yet, for reasons not entirely clear, could not be treated with a pain-killer stronger than Tylenol.

On November 4, 1993, Latimer was charged with first-degree murder. A year later, he was convicted of second-degree murder.

End of story?

No.

Over seven years later, January 18th 2001, the Supreme Court of Canada eventually upheld his conviction and life sentence.

The issues arising from the Latimer case are momentous. Should courts abide by the letter or the spirit of the law? Would a decision favourable to Latimer legalize euthanasia, mercy killing? Would it put the disabled in danger? Would it mean the end of mandatory minimum sentences for convicted persons?

The killing of Tracy Latimer has been called an act of "compassionate homicide." Others warn that leniency for Latimer, by means of a constitutional exception, would have shown that the disabled are regarded as second-class citizens.

Following his first conviction, the Latimer case became horrendously complex. The Supreme Court ordered a new trial when it was learned that the RCMP, acting on orders from the Crown, had possibly tainted the case by questioning potential jurors on their views on religion, abortion, and mercy killing.

Latimer stood trial again in October, 1997. A month later he was convicted, again, of second-degree murder.

The jury recommended he be eligible for parole after a year, even though the minimum sentence for second-degree murder is 25 years with no chance of parole for 10 years. (Automatic minimum sentences for first- and second-degree murder have been mandatory since 1976, as a trade-off for the abolition of capital punishment.)

New legal ground was broken in December, 1997, when Justice Ted Noble—trying to distinguish between mercy killing and cold-blooded murder—granted Latimer a constitutional exemption from the minimum sentence for second-degree murder. He explained that, for Latimer, the minimum sentence would constitute "cruel and unusual punishment."

Noble carefully detailed the reasons for his decision, anticipating the controversy it would provoke—and the likelihood it would be appealed. He said the law "recognizes that the moral culpability or the moral blameworthiness of murder can vary

CHAPTER 10

285

**The Meaning
of Crime:
Social Conflict
Perspective**

from one convicted offender to another." He called Tracy Latimer's murder a "rare act of homicide that was committed for caring and altruistic reasons. That is why for want of a better term this is called compassionate homicide."

Noble also described Latimer's relationship with Tracy as "that of a loving and protective parent" who wanted to end his daughter's suffering. Noble said Latimer "is not a threat to society, nor does he require any rehabilitation."

The Crown argued that Tracy was a relatively cheerful child, and her rights were violated by being killed by her father. According to the Crown brief presented at Latimer's second trial:

"Tracy enjoyed outings, one of which was to the circus, where she smiled when the horses went by. She also responded to visits by her family, smiling and looking happy to see them.

"There is no dispute that through her life, Tracy at times suffered considerable pain. As well, the quality of her life was limited by her severe disability. But the pain she suffered was not unremitting, and her life had value and quality."

Nearly a year later, in November, 1998, the Saskatchewan Court of Appeal overturned Noble's ruling, imposing the mandatory minimum sentence: 25 years, with no parole before 10 years.

Critics of leniency for Latimer worried that a Supreme Court decision soft on Latimer would send a signal to many convicted murderers that they, too, may be victims of "cruel and unusual punishment" and are eligible for constitutional exceptions

Robert Latimer
CP Photo/Kevin Frayer.

to reduce their mandatory minimum sentences.

"I think the (Supreme Court) could be opening a Pandora's box," University of Saskatchewan law professor Sanjeev Anand told Kirk Makin, justice reporter for *The Globe and Mail.* "If the court is very lax … and says you can make constitutional exemptions whenever you want to, it would also encourage Parliament to never create another mandatory minimum sentence."

After the Supreme Court ruling, Latimer's only remaining option is a plea to Ottawa for a rare federal pardon.

Unusual as the Latimer case is, there are related cases, such as battered women who have killed their batterers—often their husbands—and received leniency from the courts. Special legislation is being considered for victims who kill their oppressors, based on self-defence. It's more difficult when the victim, like Tracy Latimer, is so clearly blameless.

An old legal maxim is—"Hard cases make bad law." Whether this applies to the case of Robert Latimer remains to be seen.

DISCUSSION QUESTIONS

1. How is it that some people view Robert Latimer as a common criminal, while others see him as a hero? How can otherwise law-abiding citizens condone the killing of a handicapped child?
2. What does the debate over euthanasia have to tell us about the role of law in society and about how laws are made and enforced?
3. What other issues can you identify that are officially law violations, but that have numerous proponents?

Source: Martin O'Malley and Owen Wood, "'Cruel & Unusual': The Law and Latimer," *CBC News Online*, December 17, 2004, http://www.cbc.ca (Accessed May 19, 2007).

Radical Criminology

The conflict perspective is thoroughly entrenched in **radical criminology**, which is also diversely known as, or related to, schools of thought referred to as "new," "critical," or **Marxist criminology**. Radical criminology, which appeared on the criminology scene in the 1970s, has its roots in the writings of 19th-century social utopian thinkers. Primary among them is **Karl Marx**, whose writings on the conflicts inherent in capitalism led to the formulation of communist ideals and, many would say, to the rise of communist societies the world over.

According to Marx, two fundamental social classes exist within any capitalistic society: the "haves" and the "have-nots." Marx termed these two groups the *bourgeoisie* and the *proletariat*. The **proletariat** encompasses the large mass of people, those who are relatively uneducated and without power. In short, the proletariat are the workers, whereas the **bourgeoisie** are the capitalists—the wealthy owners of the means of production (i.e., the factories, businesses, and other elements of a society's organizational infrastructure). Although Marx was German, the terms *proletariat* and *bourgeoisie* were taken from Marx's knowledge of the French language, and are in turn derived from Latin. In ancient Rome, for example, that city's lowest class was propertyless and its members were individually referred to as *proletarius*.

According to Marx, the proletariat, since they possessed neither capital nor the means of production, such as factories, land, or natural resources, must earn their living by continuously selling their labour. The bourgeoisie, on the other hand, are the capitalist class who, by nature of their very position within society, stand opposed to the proletariat in an ongoing class struggle. Marx saw such struggle between classes as inevitable to the evolution of any capitalistic society and believed that the natural outcome of such struggle would be the overthrow of capitalistic social order and the birth of a truly classless, or communistic, society.

Early Radical Criminology

Radical criminology is the intellectual child of three important historical circumstances: (1) the ruminations of 19th-century social utopian thinkers, including Friedrich Engels, Georg Wilhelm, Friedrich Hegel, Karl Marx, George Simmel, and Max Weber; (2) the rise of conflict theory in the social sciences; and (3) the dramatic radicalization of North American academia in the 1960s and 1970s.

Central to the perspective of radical criminology is the notion of social class. Some authors maintain that "class is nothing but an abbreviation to describe a way of living, thinking, and feeling."[3] For most sociologists, however, the concept of **social class** entails distinctions made between individuals on the basis of significant defining characteristics such as race, religion, education, profession, income, wealth, family background, housing, artistic tastes, aspirations, cultural pursuits, child-rearing habits, speech, accent, and so forth. Individuals are assigned to classes by others and by themselves on the basis of characteristics that are both ascribed and achieved. Ascribed attributes are those with which a person is born, such as race or gender, while achieved characteristics are acquired through personal effort or chance over the course of one's life and include such things as level of education, income, place of residence, and profession.

CHAPTER 10

287

**The Meaning
of Crime:
Social Conflict
Perspective**

Although Marx concerned himself with only two social classes, most social scientists today talk in terms of at least three groups: upper, middle, and lower class. Some have distinguished between five hierarchically arranged classes (the real upper, semi-upper, limited-success, working, and real lower) while further subdividing classes "horizontally" according to ascribed characteristics such as race and religion.[4]

Conflict theorists of the early and middle 20th century saw in the concept of social class the rudimentary ingredients of other important concepts such as authority, power, and conflict. **Ralf Dahrendorf**, for example, wrote that "classes are social conflict groups the determinant of which can be found in the participation in or exclusion from the exercise of authority."[5] For Dahrendorf, conflict was ubiquitous, a fundamental part of and coextensive with any society. "Not the presence but the absence of conflict is surprising and abnormal," he wrote,

and we have good reason to be suspicious if we find a society or social organization that displays no evidence of conflict. To be sure, we do not have to assume that conflict is always violent and uncontrolled . . . [and] we must never lose sight of the underlying assumption that conflict can be temporarily suppressed, regulated, channeled, and controlled but that neither a philosopher-king nor a modern dictator can abolish it once and for all.[6]

From Dahrendorf's perspective, it was power and authority that were most at issue between groups and over which class conflicts arose. Dahrendorf also recognized that situations characterized by conflict are rarely static, and that it is out of conflict that change arises. For Dahrendorf, change could be either destructive or constructive. Destructive change brings about a lessening of social order, whereas constructive change increases cohesiveness within society. Dahrendorf's 1959 book, *Class and Class Conflict in Industrial Society*, set the stage for the radical writers of the 1960s and 1970s.

Within the discipline of criminology, **George Vold** helped to create the field of radical criminology. In his 1958 work entitled *Theoretical Criminology*, Vold described crime as the product of political conflict between groups, seeing it as a natural expression of the ongoing struggle for power, control, and material well-being.[7] According to Vold, conflict is "a universal form of interaction," and groups are naturally in conflict as their interests and purposes "overlap, encroach on one another and (tend to) be competitive."[8] Vold also addressed the issue of social cohesion, noting that as intergroup conflict intensifies, the loyalty of individual members to their respective groups increases. "It has long been realized that conflict between groups tends to develop and intensify the loyalty of group members to their respective groups," Vold wrote.[9] Vold's most succinct observation of the role conflict plays in contributing to crime was expressed in these words: "The whole political process of law making, law breaking, and law enforcement becomes a direct reflection of deep-seated and fundamental conflicts between interest groups. . . . Those who produce legislative majorities win control over the power, and dominate the policies that decide who is likely to be involved in violation of the law."[10]

From Vold's point of view, powerful groups make laws, and those laws express and protect their interests. Hence, the body of laws that characterizes any society is a political statement, and crime is a political definition imposed largely upon those whose interests lie outside of that which the powerful, through the law, define as acceptable. In his writings about conflict, Vold went so far as to compare the criminal with a soldier, fighting, through crime commission, for the very survival of the group whose values he or she represents. In

Vold's words, "[t]he individual criminal is then viewed as essentially a soldier under conditions of warfare: his behavior may not be 'normal' or 'happy' or 'adjusted'—it is the behavior of the soldier doing what is to be done in wartime."[11] Vold's analogy, probably influenced by the fact that he wrote in the wake of World War II, was meant to express the idea that crime was a manifestation of denied needs and values, that is, the cultural heritage of disenfranchised groups who were powerless to enact their interests in legitimate fashion. Hence, theft becomes necessary for many poor people, especially those left unemployed or unemployable by the socially acceptable forms of wealth distribution defined by law.

Another mid-20th-century conflict theorist, **Austin Turk**, said that in the search for an explanation of criminality, "one is led to investigate the tendency of laws to penalize persons whose behavior is more characteristic of the less powerful than of the more powerful and the extent to which some persons and groups can and do use legal processes and agencies to maintain and enhance their power position vis-à-vis other persons and groups."[12] In his 1969 seminal work, *Criminality and Legal Order*, Turk wrote that in any attempt to explain criminality, "it is more useful to view the social order as mainly a pattern of conflict" rather than to offer explanations for crime based on behavioural or psychological approaches.[13] Turk, like most other conflict criminologists, saw the law as a powerful tool in the service of prominent social groups seeking continued control over others. Crime was the natural consequence of such intergroup struggle because it resulted from the definitions imposed by the laws of the powerful upon the disapproved strivings of the unempowered.

Radical Criminology Today

Radical criminologists of today are considerably more sophisticated than their Marxist forebears. Contemporary radical criminology holds that the causes of crime are rooted in social conditions that empower the wealthy and the politically well organized, but disenfranchise those less fortunate. **William J. Chambliss**, a well-known spokesperson for radical thinkers, summarizes the modern perspective in these words: "What makes the behavior of some criminal is the coercive power of the state to enforce the will of the ruling class."[14]

In 1971, Chambliss, along with Robert T. Seidman, published a critically acclaimed volume entitled *Law, Order, and Power*. Their work represented something of a bridge between earlier conflict theorists and the more radical approach of Marxists. Through its emphasis on social class, class interests, and class conflict, *Law, Order, and Power* presented a Marxist perspective stripped of any overt references to capitalism as the root cause of crime. "The more economically stratified a society becomes," Chambliss and Seidman wrote, "the more it becomes necessary for the dominant groups in the society to enforce through coercion the norms of conduct which guarantee their supremacy."[15] Chambliss and Seidman outlined their position in four propositions:[16]

- The conditions of one's life affect one's values and norms. Complex societies are composed of groups with widely different life conditions.
- Complex societies are therefore composed of highly disparate and conflicting sets of norms.

CHAPTER 10

289

**The Meaning
of Crime:
Social Conflict
Perspective**

- The probability of a given group's having its particular normative system embodied in law is not distributed equally but is closely related to the political and economic position of that group.
- The higher a group's political or economic position, the greater the probability that its views will be reflected in laws.

Chambliss also believed that middle- and upper-class criminals are more apt to escape apprehension and punishment by the criminal justice system, not because they are any smarter or more capable of hiding their crimes than are lower class offenders, but because of a "very rational choice on the part of the legal system to pursue those violators that the community will reward them for pursuing and to ignore those violators who have the capability for causing trouble for the agencies."[17]

By the 1970s, however, Chambliss's writings assumed a much more Marxist flavour. In an article published in 1975, Chambliss once again recognized the huge power gap separating the "haves" from the "have-nots."[18] Crime, he said, is created by actions of the ruling class that define as criminal those undertakings and activities that contravene the interests of the rulers. At the same time, he said, members of the ruling class will inevitably be able to continue to violate the criminal law with impunity, because it is their own creation.

Soon the Marxist flavour of Chambliss's writing had become undeniable. He began using Marxist terminology. "[A]s capitalist societies industrialize and the gap between the bourgeoisie and the proletariat widens," he wrote, "penal law will expand in an effort to coerce the proletariat into submission."[19] For Chambliss, the economic consequences of crime within a capitalistic society were partially what perpetuated it. "[C]rime reduces surplus labor," he wrote, "by creating employment not only for the criminals but for law enforcers, welfare workers, professors of criminology, and a horde of people who live off the fact that crime exists. . . ."[20] Socialist societies, claimed Chambliss, should reflect much lower crime rates than capitalist societies because a "less intense class struggle should reduce the forces leading to and the functions of crime."[21]

Although Chambliss provides much of the intellectual bedrock of contemporary radical criminology, that school of thought found its most eloquent expression in the writings of **Richard Quinney**. In 1974, Quinney, in an attempt to challenge and change social life for the better, set forth his six Marxist propositions for an understanding of crime:[22]

- American society is based on an advanced capitalist economy.
- The state is organized to serve the interests of the dominant economic class, the capitalist ruling class.
- Criminal law is an instrument of the state and ruling class to maintain and perpetuate the existing social and economic order.
- Crime control in capitalist society is accomplished through a variety of institutions and agencies established and administered by a governmental elite, representing ruling class interests, for the purpose of establishing domestic order.
- The contradictions of advanced capitalism—the disjunction between existence and essence—require that the subordinate classes remain oppressed by whatever means necessary, especially through the coercion and violence of the legal system.
- Only with the collapse of capitalist society and the creation of a new society, based on socialist principles, will there be a solution to the crime problem.

A few years later, Quinney published *Class, State, and Crime,* in which he argued that almost all crimes committed by members of the lower classes are necessary for the survival of individual members of those classes. Crimes, said Quinney—in fashion reminiscent of Vold's notion of the criminal as a soldier—are actually an attempt by the socially disenfranchised "to exist in a society where *survival* is not assured by other, collective means."[23] He concludes, "[c]rime is inevitable under capitalist conditions" because crime is "a response to the material conditions of life. Permanent unemployment—and the acceptance of that condition, can result in a form of life where criminality is an appropriate and consistent response."[24] The solution offered by Quinney to the problem of crime is the development of a socialist society. "The *ultimate meaning* of crime in the development of capitalism," he writes, "is the need for a socialist society."[25]

Contemporary radical criminology attributes much of the existing propensity toward criminality to differences in social class, and in particular to those arrangements within society that maintain class differences. As Quinney puts it, "Classes are an expression of the underlying forces of the capitalist mode of production."[26] "Within the class structure of advanced capitalism," he writes, "is the dialectic that increases class struggle and the movement for socialist revolution."[27] Table 10.1 depicts the class structure of the United States as Quinney portrayed it.

Table 10.1

Class Structure of the United States with Estimated Percentages of the Adult Population

Capitalist Class 1.5%	Those who own and control production and wield state power
Petty Bourgeoisie 18.5%	Professionals, middle management, bureaucrats

Working Class
80%
	Technical and skilled working class
	Technical
	    teachers
	    nurses
	    medical technicians
	Skilled
	    craftsmen
	    clerical workers
	    salespeople
	    transportation workers
	    industrial workers
	
	Reserve army
	
	Unskilled working class
	Unskilled
	    industrial labour
	    service workers
	    office workers
	    salespeople
	    clerical workers
	Unemployed
	Pauperized poor

Source: Adapted from Richard Quinney, *Class, State, and Crime: On the Theory and Practice of Criminal Justice* (New York: David McKay, 1977), p. 77. Reprinted with permission.

CHAPTER 10

291
The Meaning
of Crime:
Social Conflict
Perspective

Today's radical criminologies can be divided into two schools: structuralist and instrumentalist. **Structural Marxism** sees capitalism as a self-maintaining system in which the law and the justice system work together to perpetuate the existing system of power relationships. Hence, according to structural Marxism, even the rich are subject to certain laws designed to prevent them from engaging in forms of behaviour that might undermine the system of which they are a part. Laws regulating trade practices and monopolies, for example, regulate the behaviour of the powerful and serve to ensure the survival of the capitalist system. **Instrumental Marxism**, on the other hand, sees the criminal law and the justice system as tools that the powerful use to control the poor and to keep them disenfranchised. Hence, according to instrumental Marxism, the legal system serves not only to perpetuate the power relationships that exist within society, but also to keep control in the hands of those who are already powerful. A recently popular book by **Jeffrey H. Reiman** builds upon this premise. Entitled *The Rich Get Richer and the Poor Get Prison*, Reiman's work contends that the criminal justice system is biased against the poor from start to finish and that well-to-do members of society control the criminal justice system—from the definition of crime through the process of arrest, trial, and sentencing.[28] Reiman also claims that many of the actions taken by well-off people should be defined as criminal, but they aren't. Such actions include the refusal to make workplaces safe, the refusal to curtail deadly industrial pollution, the promotion of unnecessary surgery, and the prescription of unnecessary drugs. This kind of self-serving behaviour, says Reiman, creates occupational and environmental hazards for the poor and for those who are less well off than the rule makers themselves. These conditions, claims Reiman, produce as much death, destruction, and financial loss as the so-called crimes of the poor.

Critical Criminology

Some writers distinguish between critical criminology and radical criminology, claiming that the former is simply a way of critiquing social relationships leading to crime, while the latter constitutes a proactive call for a radical change in the social conditions crime springs from.

Gresham Sykes explains **critical criminology** this way: "It forces an inquiry into precisely how the normative content of the criminal law is internalized in different segments of society, and how norm-holding is actually related to behavior."[29] As David A. Jones states in his *History of Criminology,* however, "Sometimes, it may be difficult to distinguish 'critical' from a truly Marxist criminology. One basis, advanced by Marvin Wolfgang, is that 'critical' criminology is 'more reactive than proactive,' meaning that 'critical' criminology does not aim to overthrow the 'ruling class' so much as it may criticize the way it believes such a group dominates society."[30]

A cogent example of the critical perspective in contemporary criminology can be had in the work of Elliott Currie. Currie claims "'market societies'—those in which the pursuit of private gain becomes the dominant organizing principle of social and economic life—are especially likely to breed high levels of violent crime."[31] Market societies, says Currie, are characterized by more than free enterprise and a free market economy. They are societies in which the striving after personal economic gain runs rampant and becomes the hallmark of social life. The conditions endemic to market societies lead to high crime rates because they undercut and overwhelm more traditional principles that "have historically sustained individuals, families, and communities." North American society, and the

Structural Marxism a perspective that holds that the structural institutions of society influence the behaviour of individuals and groups by virtue of the type of relationships created. The criminal law, for example, reflects class relationships and serves to reinforce those relationships.

Instrumental Marxism a perspective that holds that those in power intentionally create laws and social institutions that serve their own interests and that keep others from becoming powerful.

Critical criminology a perspective focused on challenging traditional understandings and on uncovering false beliefs about crime and criminal justice.

United States in particular, is the world's premier market society, says Currie, and its culture provides "a particularly fertile breeding ground for serious violent crime." Similarly, the recent and dramatic rise in crime rates in former communist countries throughout Europe can be explained by the burgeoning development of new market societies in those nations. According to Currie, seven "profoundly criminogenic and closely intertwined mechanisms" operate in a market society to produce crime:

1. "The progressive destruction of livelihood," which results from the long-term absence of opportunities for stable and rewarding work—a consequence of the fact that market societies view labour "simply as a cost to be reduced" rather than as an asset with intrinsic value.
2. "The growth of extremes of economic inequality and material deprivation," which causes many children to spend their developmental years in poverty.
3. "The withdrawal of public services and supports, especially for families and children," resulting from the fact that "it is a basic operating principle of market society to keep the public sector small . . . "
4. "The erosion of informal and communal networks of mutual support, supervision, and care" brought about by the high mobility of the workforce characteristic of market societies.
5. "The spread of a materialistic, neglectful, and 'hard' culture" that exalts brutal forms of individualized competition.
6. "The unregulated marketing of the technology of violence," including the ready availability of guns, an emphasis on advancing technologies of destruction (such as the military), and mass-marketed violence on television and in the media.
7. "The weakening of social and political alternatives," leaving people unable to cope effectively with the forces of the market society that undermine their communities and destroy valuable interpersonal relationships.

Currie suggests that as more nations emulate the "market society" culture of the United States, crime rates throughout the world will rise. An increasing emphasis on punishment, and the growth of prison systems, says Currie, will consequently be seen throughout most of the world in the 21st century.

Critique of Radical-Critical Criminology

Radical-critical criminology has been criticized for its nearly exclusive emphasis on methods of social change at the expense of well-developed theory. As William Pelfrey explains, "[i]t is in the Radical School of Criminology that theory is almost totally disregarded, except as something to criticize, and radical *methods* are seen as optimum."[32]

Radical-critical criminology can also be criticized for failing to recognize what appears to be at least a fair degree of public consensus about the nature of crime, that is, that crime is undesirable and that criminal activity is to be controlled. Were criminal activity in fact a true expression of the sentiments of the politically and economically disenfranchised, as some radical criminologists claim, then public opinion might be expected to offer support for at least certain forms of crime. Even the sale and consumption of illicit drugs, however—a type of crime that may provide an alternative path to riches for the otherwise disenfranchised—is frequently condemned by residents of working-class communities.[33]

CHAPTER 10
293
**The Meaning
of Crime:
Social Conflict
Perspective**

In October 1970, the Front de libération du Québec (FLQ) kidnapped British diplomat James Cross and murdered Quebec cabinet minister Pierre Laporte to bring attention to its struggle for independence for French-speaking Quebec. The Canadian government responded by invoking the *War Measures Act*. How would the radical criminology perspective interpret the actions of the FLQ? The Canadian government?
The Canadian Press/Peter Bregg.

An effective criticism of Marxist criminology, in particular, centres on the fact that Marxist thinkers appear to confuse issues of personal politics with what could otherwise be social reality. As a consequence of allowing personal values and political leanings to enter the criminological arena, Marxist criminologists have frequently appeared to sacrifice their objectivity. Jackson Toby, for example, claims that Marxist and radical thinkers are simply building upon an "old tradition of sentimentality toward those who break social rules."[34] Such sentimentality can be easily discounted, he says, when we realize that "[c]olor television sets and automobiles are stolen more often than food and blankets."[35]

Marxist criminology has also been refuted by contemporary thinkers who find that it falls short in appreciating the multiplicity of problems that contribute to the problem of crime. Some years ago, for example, Hermann Mannheim critiqued Marxist assumptions by showing how "subsequent developments" have exposed that "Marx was wrong in thinking" (1) "that there could be only two classes in a capitalist society;" (2) that "class struggle was entirely concerned with the question of private property in the means of production;" (3) "that the only way in which fundamental social changes could be effected was by violent social revolution;" and (4) "that all conflicts were class conflicts and all social change could be explained in terms of class conflicts."[36]

Mannheim went on to point out that the development of a semi-skilled workforce along with the advent of highly skilled and well-educated workers has led to the creation of a multiplicity of classes within contemporary capitalistic societies. The growth of such classes, said Mannheim, effectively spreads the available wealth in those societies where such workers are employed and reduces the likelihood of revolution.

Marxist criminology has suffered a considerable loss of prestige among many would-be followers in the wake of the collapse of the former Soviet Union and its client states in

Eastern Europe and other parts of the world. With the death of Marxist political organizations and their agendas, Marxist criminology seems to have lost some of its impetus. Many would argue that, in fact, the work of writers such as Quinney and Chambliss presaged the decline of Soviet influence and had already moved Marxist and radical criminology into new areas, effectively shedding the reins of world communism and ending any association with its institutional embodiment in specific parts of the world. The work of Elliott Currie (discussed earlier in this chapter) and others is now leading in a post-Marxist direction, while retaining a critical emphasis on the principles out of which radical criminology was fashioned. Consequently, today's radical criminologists have largely rescinded calls for revolutionary change while simultaneously escalating their demands for the eradication of gender, racial, and other inequalities within the criminal justice system; for the elimination of prisons; for the abolition of capital punishment; and for an end to police misconduct.

Emerging Conflict Theories

The radical ideas associated with mid-20th-century Marxist criminology contributed to the formation of a number of new and innovative approaches to crime and criminology. Among them are feminist criminology, peacemaking criminology, including restorative jutice, and left-realist criminology.

Feminist Criminology

As some writers have observed, "women have been virtually invisible in criminological analysis until recently and much theorizing has proceeded as though criminality is restricted to men."[37] Others put it this way: "criminological theory assumes a woman is like a man."[38] Beginning in the 1970s, however, advances in feminist theory were applied to criminology, resulting in what has been called a **feminist criminology**. Other strands of feminist thought inform feminist criminology, including liberal feminism, radical feminism, socialist feminism, and Marxist feminism. Each of these perspectives argues that conflict in society is based on inequalities due primarily to gender, although they may vary on the degree to which this inequality exists.

Feminist criminology a self-conscious corrective model intended to redirect the thinking of mainstream criminologists to include gender awareness.

Feminist criminology is a self-conscious corrective model intended to redirect the thinking of mainstream criminologists to include gender awareness. It points out the inequities inherent in patriarchal forms of thought. **Patriarchy** refers to male dominance and can be defined as a "set of social relations of power in which the male gender appropriates the labour power of women and controls their sexuality."[39] Evidence of patriarchy can be found in different places. The fact that crime is often seen as an act of aggression, for example, contributes to the perpetuation of a male-centred criminology in which men are biologically characterized as having an aggressive nature that needs to be channelled and controlled. Society's acceptance of the belief that men are predisposed to aggression, however, led to the socialization of women as passive actors, which has excluded them from criminological study and made them more susceptible to continued victimization by men. In other words, traditional criminology, like the society of which it has been a part, has been male-centred and women have been largely ignored by criminologists.

Patriarchy the tradition of male dominance.

CHAPTER 10

295

**The Meaning
of Crime:
Social Conflict
Perspective**

Early works in the field included **Freda Adler's** *Sisters in Crime*[40] and **Rita J. Simon's** *Women and Crime*,[41] both published in 1975. In these books, the authors attempt to explain existing divergences in crime rates between men and women as due primarily to socialization rather than biology. Women, claim these authors, were taught to believe in personal limitations, faced reduced socio-economic opportunities, and, as a result, suffered from lower aspirations. As gender equality increased, they say, it could be expected that male and female criminality would take on similar characteristics. Although Adler and Simon were instrumental in bringing the feminist perspective into theoretical criminology, their approach has not been validated by observations surrounding increased gender equality over the past few decades. Another early work, *Women, Crime and Criminology*, was published in 1977 by British sociologist Carol Smart.[42] Smart's book did much to sensitize criminologists to sexist traditions within the field. Smart pointed out that men and women perceive and experience the world in different ways. She showed how important it is for women to have a voice in interpreting the behaviour of other women, as opposed to having the behaviour of other women interpreted from a male standpoint—a perspective that does not include women's experience.

Early feminist theorizing may not have borne the fruit that some researchers anticipated, but it has led to a heightened awareness of gender issues within criminology. Two of the most insightful contemporary proponents of the usefulness of applying feminist thinking to criminological analysis are **Kathleen Daly** and **Meda Chesney-Lind**. Daly and Chesney-Lind point out that "gender differences in crime suggest that crime may not be so normal after all."[43] In other words, traditional understandings about what is "typical" about crime are derived from a study of men only, or, more precisely, from that relatively small group of men who commit crimes. In general terms, Daly and Chesney-Lind have identified the following five elements of feminist thought that "distinguish it from other types of social and political thought:"[44]

- Gender is not a natural fact but a complex social, historical, and cultural product; it is related to, but not simply derived from, biological sex differences and differing reproductive capacities.
- Gender and gender relations order social life and social institutions in fundamental ways.
- Gender relations and constructs of masculinity and femininity are not symmetrical but are based on an organizing principle of men's superiority and their socio- and political-economic dominance over women.
- Systems of knowledge reflect men's views of the natural and social world; the production of knowledge is gendered.
- Women should be at the centre, not the periphery, of intellectual inquiry; they should not be invisible or treated as appendages to men.

In a similar, but more recent, analysis of feminist criminology, Susan Caulfield and Nancy Wonders describe "five major contributions that have been made to criminological thinking by feminist scholarship and practice":[45] (1) a focus on gender as a central organizing principle of contemporary life; (2) the importance of power in shaping social relationships; (3) a heightened sensitivity to the way in which social context helps shape human relationships; (4) the recognition that social reality must be understood as a process, and the development of research methods that take this into account; and (5) a commitment to social change as a crucial part of feminist scholarship and practice.[46] As is the case with most feminist writing in the area of criminology today, Caulfield and Wonders hold that these five contributions of feminist scholarship "can help to guide research and practice within criminology."[47]

Feminism is a way of seeing the world. It has nothing to do with sexual orientation. To be a feminist is to "combine a female mental perspective with a sensitivity for those social issues that influence primarily women."[48] Central to understanding feminist thought in its historical and contemporary modes is the realization that feminism views gender in terms of power relationships. In other words, according to feminist approaches, men have traditionally held much more power in society than have women. Male dominance has long been reflected in the patriarchal structure of Western society, a structure that has excluded women from much decision making in socially significant areas. Sexist attitudes—deeply ingrained notions of male superiority—have perpetuated inequality between the sexes. The consequences of sexism and of the unequal gender-based distribution of power have been far-reaching, affecting fundamental aspects of social roles and personal expectation at all levels.

Various schools of feminist thought exist, with liberal and radical feminism envisioning a power-based and traditional domination of women's bodies and minds by men throughout history. **Radical feminism** depicts men as fundamentally brutish, aggressive, and violent and sees men as controlling women through sexuality by taking advantage of women's biological dependency during child-bearing years and their inherent lack of physical strength relative to men. Radical feminists believe, for example, that the sexual victimization of girls is a learned behaviour, as young males are socialized to be aggressive, resulting in male domination over females. They view society as patriarchal and believe that it is because of male control of the law that women are defined as subjects. Those young women who are sexually and physically exploited may then run away or abuse substances, thereby becoming criminalized; exploitation triggers the deviant behaviour. The elimination of male domination should therefore reduce crime rates for women and "even precipitate a decrease in male violence against women."[49]

Liberal feminists, although they want the same gender equality as other feminists, lay the blame for present inequalities on the development within culture and society of "separate and distinct spheres of influence and traditional attitudes about the appropriate role of men and women."[50] A recent book by Alida V. Merlo and Joycelyn M. Pollock, for example, points out that feminists are often blamed in today's political atmosphere for the recent upsurge in crime because many, by entering or creating innovative family structures, have lowered what might otherwise be the positive effect of traditional family values on crime control.[51] Liberal feminists call for the removal of the division of power and labour between the sexes. This, in turn, would eliminate inequality and promote greater social harmony.

Socialist feminists, who provide a third perspective, see gender oppression as a consequence of the economic structure of society and as a natural outgrowth of capitalist forms of social organization. Egalitarian societies, from the socialist point of view, would be built around socialist or Marxist principles with the aim of creating a society free of gender and class divisions. The present, capitalist social structure sees men committing violent street crimes, with women more likely to commit property and vice crimes.[52]

A fourth and complementary feminist perspective has been identified by Sally Simpson. She identifies it as an alternative framework developed by "women of color." In Simpson's words, "[t]he alternative frameworks developed by women of color heighten feminism's sensitivity to the complex interplay of gender, class, and race oppression."[53]

Radical feminism a perspective that holds that any significant change in the status of women can be accomplished only through substantial changes in social institutions such as the family, law, medicine, and so on.

Liberal feminism a perspective that holds that the concerns of women can be incorporated within existing social institutions through conventional means and without the need to drastically restructure society.

Socialist feminism a perspective that examines social roles and the gender-based division of labour within the family, seeing both as a significant source of women's insubordination within society.

CHAPTER 10

297

**The Meaning
of Crime:
Social Conflict
Perspective**

John Hagan built upon defining features of power relationships in his book *Structural Criminology*, in which he explained that power relationships existing in the wider society are effectively "brought home" to domestic settings and are reflected in everyday relationships between men, women, and children within the context of family life.[54] Hagan writes: "work relations structure family relations, particularly relations between fathers and mothers and, in turn, relations between parents and their children, especially mothers and their daughters."[55] Hagan's approach, which has been termed **power-control theory**, suggests that "family class structure shapes the social reproduction of gender relations, and in turn the social distribution of delinquency."[56] In most middle- and upper-middle-class families, says Hagan, a paternalistic model, in which the father works and the mother supervises the children, is the norm. Under the paternalistic model, girls are controlled by both parents— through male domination and by female role modelling. Boys, however, are less closely controlled and are relatively free to deviate from social norms, resulting in higher levels of delinquency among males. In lower-middle- and lower-class families, however, the paternalistic model is frequently absent. Hence, in such families there is less "gender socialization and less maternal supervision of girls," resulting in higher levels of female delinquency.[57]

In a work supportive of Hagan's thesis, Evelyn K. Sommers recently conducted a series of four hour–long interviews with fourteen female inmates in a Canadian medium-security prison.[58] Focusing on what led to violations of the criminal law, Sommers identified four common themes to explain the criminality of the women she interviewed: (1) economic and financial need; (2) drug involvement; (3) personal anger rooted in sexual and physical abuse or a sense of loss; and (4) fear. Because "need" was identified as the cause of law-breaking behaviour by four of the five women interviewed, Sommers concluded that women's criminality is based on two underlying issues: the effort to maintain connection within relationships (such as between mother and child), and a personal quest for empowerment (as single mothers are expected to be independent and capable of providing for themselves and their children).

Power-control theory a perspective that holds that the distribution of crime and delinquency within society is to some degree founded upon the consequences power relationships within the wider society hold for domestic settings, and for the everyday relationships among men, women, and children within the context of family life.

Aileen Wuornos, convicted female serial killer. Although some women are moving into areas of traditional male criminality, the number of women committing most forms of crime is still far lower than that of men. How does the criminality of women appear to differ from that of men?

Daytona Beach News/Sygma.

In a cogent analysis that encompasses much of contemporary feminist theory, Daly and Chesney-Lind suggest that feminist thought is more important for the way it informs and challenges existing criminology than for the new theories it offers. Much current feminist thought within criminology emphasizes the need for gender awareness. Theories of crime causation and prevention, it is suggested, must include women, and more research on gender-related issues in the field is badly needed. Additionally, say Daly and Chesney-Lind, "criminologists should begin to appreciate that their discipline and its questions are a product of white, economically privileged men's experiences"[59] and that rates of female criminality, which are lower than those of males, may highlight the fact that criminal behaviour is not as "normal" as once thought. Because modern-day criminological perspectives were mostly developed by Caucasian, middle-class men, the propositions and theories they advance fail to take into consideration women's "ways of knowing."[60] Hence, the fundamental challenge posed by feminist criminology is: do existing theories of crime causation apply as well to women as they do to men? Or, as Daly and Chesney-Lind ask, given the current situation in theory development, "do theories of men's crime apply to women?"[61]

Other feminists have analyzed the process by which laws are created and legislation passed and concluded that modern-day statutes frequently represent characteristically masculine modes of thought. Such analysts have concluded that existing criminal laws are overly rational and hierarchically structured, reflecting traditionally male ways of organizing the social world.[62] Some would argue that legal definitions of such behaviours as prostitution, pornography, and sexual assault are defined primarily by men's understanding of the behaviour in question and not by the experiences of women. Consequently, some suggest, existing laws need to be replaced by, or complemented with, "a system of justice based upon . . . the specifically feminine principles of care, connection, and community."[63]

In the area of social policy, feminist thinkers have pointed to the need for increased controls over men's violence toward women, the creation of alternatives (to supplement the home and traditional family structures) for women facing abuse, and the protection of children. They have also questioned the role of government, culture, and the mass media in promulgating pornography, prostitution, and sexual assault and have generally portrayed ongoing crimes against women as characteristic of continuing traditions in which women are undervalued and controlled. Many radical feminists have suggested the replacement of men with women in positions of power, especially within the justice system and government organizations, while others have noted that such a replacement still would not address needed changes in the structure of the system itself, which is gender-biased due to years of male domination. Centrists, on the other hand, suggest a more balanced approach, believing that individuals of both genders have much to contribute to a workable justice system.[64]

Critique of Feminist Criminology Some would argue that in the area of theoretical development, feminist criminology has yet to live up to its promise. Throughout the late 1970s and 1980s, few comprehensive feminist theories of crime were proposed, as feminist criminology focused instead on descriptive studies of female involvement in crime.[65] Although such data gathering may have laid the groundwork for theory building that is yet to come, few descriptive studies attempted to link their findings to existing feminist theory in any comprehensive way. Theory development suffered again in the late 1980s and early 1990s as an increased concern with women's victimization, especially the victimization of women at the hands of men, led to further descriptive studies with a somewhat different focus. Male violence against women was seen as adding support to the central tenet of

CHAPTER 10

299
**The Meaning
of Crime:
Social Conflict
Perspective**

feminist criminology that the relationship between the sexes is primarily characterized by the exercise of power (or lack thereof). Such singularity of focus, however, did not make for broad theory building. As one writer explains the current state of feminist criminology, "[f]eminist theory is a theory in formation."[66] To date, feminist researchers have continued to amass descriptive studies, while feminist analysis has hardly advanced beyond a framework for the "deconstruction" of existing theories—that is, for their re-evaluation in light of feminist insights.[67] A fair assessment of the current situation would probably conclude that the greatest contributions of feminist thought to criminological theory building are yet to come.

Feminist criminology has faced criticism from many other directions. As mentioned previously, predicted increases in female crime rates have failed to materialize as social opportunities available to both genders have become more balanced. The gender gap in crime—with males accounting for much more law violation than females—continues to exist. Other critics have pointed to fundamental flaws in feminist thought, asking questions such as, "If men have more power than women, then why are so many more men arrested?"[68] Where studies do exist,[69] gender disparities in arrest are rarely found, nor do sentencing practices seem to favour women.[70] The chivalry hypothesis of many years ago, under which it was proposed that women are apt to be treated more leniently by the justice system because of their gender, does not appear to operate today.[71]

Some critics even argue that a feminist criminology is impossible. Daly and Chesney-Lind, for example, agree that although feminist thought may inform criminology, "a feminist criminology cannot exist because neither feminism nor criminology is a unified set of principles and practices."[72] In other words, according to these authors, a criminology built solely on feminist principles is unlikely because neither feminist thought nor criminology meet the strict requirements of formal theory building. Even with such a caveat in mind, however, it should still be possible to construct a gender-aware criminology that is informed by issues of gender and that takes into consideration the concerns of feminist writers. A "feminist-oriented criminology," say Caulfield and Wonders, is one that will transgress traditional criminology. "This transgression, or 'going beyond boundaries,'" they write, "must occur at a number of levels across a number of areas covered within criminology" and will eventually move us toward a more just world.[73]

Peacemaking Criminology

Throughout much of history, formal agencies of social control, especially the police, officials of the courts, and correctional personnel have been seen as pitted against criminal perpetrators and would-be wrongdoers. Crime control has been traditionally depicted in terms of a kind of epic struggle in which diametrically opposed antagonists continuously engage one another, but in which only one side can emerge as victorious. Recently, however, a new point of view, **peacemaking criminology**, has come to the fore. Criminology as peacemaking has its roots in Christian and Eastern philosophies and advances the notion that crime-control agencies and the citizens they serve should work together to alleviate social problems and human suffering and thus reduce crime.[74] Peacemaking criminology, which includes the notion of service, has also been called "compassionate criminology" and suggests that "[c]ompassion, wisdom, and love are essential for understanding the suffering of which we are all a part and for practising a criminology of nonviolence."[75]

Peacemaking criminology a perspective that holds that crime-control agencies and the citizens they serve should work together to alleviate social problems and human suffering and thus reduce crime.

Peacemaking criminology is a new undertaking, popularized by the works of **Harold E. Pepinsky**[76] and Richard Quinney[77] beginning in 1986. Both Pepinsky and Quinney restate the problem of crime control from one of "how to stop crime" to one of "how to make peace" within society and between citizens and criminal justice agencies. Peacemaking criminology draws attention to many issues, among them (1) the perpetuation of violence through the continuation of social policies based on dominant forms of criminological theory; (2) the role of education in peacemaking; (3) "commonsense theories of crime;" (4) crime control as human rights enforcement; and (5) conflict resolution within community settings.[78]

Common-sense theories of crime are derived from everyday experience and beliefs and are characteristic of the person-in-the-street. Unfortunately, say peacemaking criminologists, fanciful common-sense theories all too often provide the basis for criminological investigations, which in turn offer support for the naive theories themselves. One common-sense theory criticized by peacemaking criminologists is the "Black-male-as-savage theory,"[79] which holds that men of African descent are far more crime-prone than their Caucasian counterparts. Such a perspective, frequently given added credence by official interpretations of criminal-incidence data, only increases the crime-control problem by further distancing these males from government-sponsored crime-control policies. A genuine concern for the problems facing all citizens, say peacemaking criminologists, would more effectively serve the ends of crime control.

Richard Quinney and John Wildeman summarize well the underpinnings of peacemaking criminology with these words:

(1) thought of the Western rational mode is conditional, limiting knowledge primarily to what is already known; (2) each life is a spiritual journey into the unknown and the unknowable, beyond the ego-centered self; (3) human existence is characterized by suffering; crime is suffering; and the sources of suffering are within each of us; (4) through love and compassion, beyond the ego-centered self, we can end suffering and live in peace, personally and collectively; (5) crime can be ended only with the ending of suffering, only when there is peace and social justice; and (6) understanding, service, justice—all these—flow naturally from love and compassion, from mindful attention to the reality of all that is, here and now. A criminology of peacemaking—a nonviolent criminology of compassion and service—seeks to end suffering and thereby eliminate crime.[80]

Elsewhere Quinney writes,

A society of meanness, competition, greed, and injustice is created by minds that are greedy, selfish, fearful, hateful, and crave power over others. Suffering on the social level can be ended only with the ending of suffering on the personal level. Wisdom brings the awareness that divisions between people and groups are not between the bad and the good or between the criminal and the non-criminal. Wisdom teaches interbeing. We must become one with all who suffer from lives of crime and from the sources that produce crime. Public policy must then flow from this wisdom.[81]

Other recent contributors to the peacemaking movement include Bo Lozoff, Michael Braswell, and Clemmons Bartollas. In *Inner Corrections*, Lozoff and Braswell claim that "[w]e are fully aware by now that the criminal justice system in this country is founded on violence. It is a system that assumes that violence can be overcome by violence, evil by evil. Criminal justice at home and warfare abroad are of the same principle of violence. This

CHAPTER 10

301
**The Meaning
of Crime:
Social Conflict
Perspective**

principle sadly dominates much of our criminology."[82] *Inner Corrections*, which is primarily a compilation of previous works on compassion and prison experience, provides meditative techniques and prayers for those seeking to become more compassionate and includes a number of letters from inmates who demonstrate the book's philosophy.

In another recent work entitled "Correctional Treatment, Peacemaking, and the New Age Movement," Bartollas and Braswell apply New Age principles to correctional treatment.[83] "Most offenders suffered abusive and deprived childhoods," they write.

> *Treatment that focuses on the inner child and such qualities as forgiveness and self-esteem could benefit offenders. Some New Age teachings tempered by the ancient spiritual traditions may offer offenders the hope they can create a future that brings greater fulfillment than their past. This changed future may include growing out of the fear of victimization, becoming more positive and open to possibilities, viewing one's self with more confidence and humility, understanding the futility of violence, and attaining emotional and financial sufficiency.*[84]

In a fundamental sense, peacemaking criminologists exhort their colleagues to transcend personal dichotomies to end the political and ideological divisiveness that separates people. "If we ourselves cannot know peace . . . how will our acts disarm hatred and violence?" they ask.[85] Lozoff and Braswell express the same sentiments this way: "human transformation takes place as we change our social, economic, and political structure. And the message is clear: without peace within us and in our actions, there can be no peace in our results. Peace is the way."[86]

Restorative Justice

Peacemaking criminology suggests that effective crime control in any future heterogeneous society can best be achieved by the adoption of a peace model based on cooperation rather than on retribution. The **peace model** of crime control focuses on effective ways of developing a shared consensus on critical issues that have the potential to seriously affect the quality of life. These issues include major crimes like murder and sexual assault but may also extend to property rights, rights to the use of new technologies, the ownership of information, and so on. Relatively minor issues, such as sexual preference, non-violent sexual deviance, gambling, drug use, noise, simple custody claims, and publicly offensive behaviour can be dealt with in ways that require few resources beyond those immediately available in the community.

The concept of **restorative justice** stems from these notions of cooperation and reconciliation rather than from retribution and punishment. The Canadian criminologist **Ezzat Fattah** has been a proponent of alternative forms of justice for several decades. In an article entitled "Restorative and Retributive Justice Models: A Comparison," Fattah critically examines the ineffectiveness of the punishment model.[87] Citing per capita prison rates in the United States and punitive criminal justice practices in China and Singapore, Fattah asks whether the retributive approach really does effectively deter crime. He argues that the punishment model is a costly one, with incarceration being the most expensive sentencing option. Moreover, punishment serves only to treat human beings as a means to an end since it has little positive effect on those being punished. Even though the public and the victim may feel somewhat vindicated by a harsh punitive sentence, punishment, Fattah contends, does nothing to assist either in the healing process. It is toward the goal of healing that the restorative-justice approach reaches.

Peace model an approach to crime control that focuses on effective ways for developing a shared consensus on critical issues that have the potential to seriously affect the quality of life.

Restorative justice a perspective that stresses remedies and restoration rather than prison, punishment, and victim neglect.

The principles of restorative justice are reflected in community sentencing conferences such as the one shown here at the Aboriginal Ganootamaage Justice Service Centre in Winnipeg, Manitoba. Do you think this approach is more effective at controlling crime than the adversarial approach? Why or why not?
The Canadian Press/Winnipeg Free Press/Joe Bryksa.

Restorative justice is defined as an approach to justice that focuses on dealing with the harmful effects of crime by engaging victims, offenders, and the community in a process of reparation and healing. The pain and suffering of victims is central to defining the harm that has resulted from the crime and the manner in which it is to be resolved. The community is active in offering support to victims and in holding offenders accountable for their crimes while giving the offenders the opportunity to make amends.[88]

Whereas the traditional adversarial system of justice defines crime as a violation of rules and a harm to the state, the restorative-justice approach views crime as a harm done to the victim and the community. The adversarial system blames and punishes the offender and assumes a win–loss outcome; the restorative-justice approach looks to a win–win outcome by focusing on the process of problem solving, including the reintegration of the offender into the community and the preservation of his or her dignity.

Restorative-justice models are not new. In Canada, Australia, and the United States, Aboriginal groups have traditionally practised what is commonly referred to as **circle sentencing conferences**, which are based on traditional Aboriginal principles of peacemaking, mediation, and consensus-building. Sentencing circles involve participation by the judge, victim, offender, family or supporters, elders, and other justice and community representatives. Each has input, and the needs of each are considered equally important and worthy of representation. The conference results in sentencing recommendations, which are passed on to the judge with a view to ensuring the protection of the community, healing the victim, and rehabilitating the offender. The judge may accept or reject the recommendations, and community members are responsible for ensuring that the eventual sentence is carried out.

Circle sentencing conferences groups of community members who actively assist justice authorities by participating in discussions about available sentencing options and plans to reintegrate the offender back into the community.

CHAPTER 10

303

**The Meaning
of Crime:
Social Conflict
Perspective**

Circle sentencing conferences have been revived in many parts of Canada. Used extensively in the Yukon since the 1980s, they have become more widely used in other parts of the country, primarily in rural communities. The Peigan Nation Youth Traditional Justice Circle on the Peigan Reserve near Lethbridge, Alberta, was founded over a decade ago and continues to function in the traditional manner. Adult and youth criminals can access the circle through pre- or post-charge diversion or even after a guilty plea is entered. The recommendations of the circle are forwarded to the Crown prosecutor, who then endeavours to have the presiding judge incorporate them into the court's final decision. In this way, the circle works in conjunction with the existing criminal justice system. Crown prosecutors screen cases coming through the courts and select those that appear suitable for referral to the circle. It is ultimately the circle's decision whether it wishes to accept any case. Interestingly, in cases where the Crown feels that a sentence of incarceration is warranted, the circle is advised of this at the time of referral. If the circle decides to accept the referral, it will often make a recommendation to the court that will not contradict the Crown's position, thereby ensuring that the court will not have to make a decision contrary to the wishes of the circle.[89]

The principles of restorative justice can be seen in a number of other Canadian criminal justice initiatives. The first **Victim–Offender Reconciliation Program (VORP)** was established by the Mennonite Community in Kitchener, Ontario, in 1974, and the model spread rapidly, in various forms, throughout Canada, the United States, and Europe. There are now dozens of programs across Canada, over 120 in the United States, and more than 500 throughout Europe.[90] Based on mediation and alternative dispute resolution principles, the VORP involves face-to-face meetings between victim and offender, facilitated by a trained mediator, to discuss the events of the crime and its effects and reach an agreed-upon outcome. The program is usually used with young offenders, in the post-charge phase of the criminal justice process or as an alternative measure. The proliferation of community and neighbourhood justice centres has enabled expansion of VORPs and other similar mediation and dispute resolution programs that deal with both criminal and civil cases.

Since the inception of Victim–Offender Reconciliation Programs, restorative-justice principles have been manifest in a number of other criminal justice initiatives. **Family group conferencing** provides a forum for dealing with unanswered questions, emotions, and the victim's right to restitution and reparation resulting from a crime. These conferences involve participation of the victim, offender, and their family members and supporters. **Community sentencing panels** are composed of volunteers from the community and focus on restorative measures such as restitution, reparation, mediation, and victim involvement. These panels also consider crime prevention by addressing social factors that may contribute to crime. The principles of **community policing**, which emphasize a proactive approach to law enforcement through the establishment of partnerships with the community, can be seen to be compatible with much of the philosophy of restorative justice. The community policing approach has been formally adopted by the Royal Canadian Mounted Police and the Ontario Provincial Police and is practised by most police services across Canada.

The restorative-justice philosophy has been embraced and endorsed by all levels of government in Canada as well as by voluntary and community organizations. The federal Public Safety Canada and the Department of Justice Canada, along with the National Parole Board and Correctional Service Canada, are exploring the scope of restorative

Victim–Offender Reconciliation Program (VORP) a program that gives the offender the opportunity to meet face-to-face with the victim in the presence of a trained mediator in an attempt to reduce the victim's fears while establishing accountability and reparation for the crime.

Family group conferencing a forum for dealing with unanswered questions, emotions, and the victim's right to restitution and reparation resulting from a crime.

Community sentencing panels groups composed of volunteers from the community who focus on restorative measures such as restitution, reparation, mediation, and victim involvement.

Community policing a philosophy of policing involving proactive collaboration between the police and the community to prevent and respond to crime and other community problems.

approaches and developing strategies for implementing them. Restorative Resolutions, operated by the John Howard Society of Manitoba, provides community-based alternatives for offenders who are likely to be incarcerated. Located in Winnipeg, this project attempts to redress the harm done to victims and supervises offenders in the community. Offenders referred to the program must be facing a custodial sentence of at least six months, are required to enter a guilty plea, and are obliged to follow a community-based plan that includes meeting with the victim. Those charged with sexual assault or gang- or drug-related offences, or those who have been involved in incidents of domestic violence, are excluded. Once accepted into the program, Restorative Resolutions staff develops an individualized restorative plan that includes involvement of the victim and members of the community. If accepted by the judge, Restorative Resolutions staff implements the plan and provides the necessary services.

A recent evaluation of Restorative Resolutions found that offenders in the program were more likely to make amends with victims and to participate in some form of community service. These offenders had better success rates in completing their sentences without violation (95 percent) compared to those offenders who did not have the benefit of a restorative approach (84 percent).[91] The evaluation concluded that Restorative Resolutions had a significant impact on those involved.

One client of the program, reflecting on her experience in the program, stated,

Going to jail would have been easier for me because I would not have had to be accountable for what I'd done. Restorative Resolutions challenged me to be honest with myself and others for the first time in my life. They forced me to figure out the real reasons why I did what I did, whom I had hurt, what I needed to do to fix it, and most important, how not to fall back into that destructive pattern. My victims now receive money from me on a monthly basis.[92]

Alternative dispute-resolution is another example of the restorative-justice approach and peacemaking perspective. Mediation programs such as dispute-resolution centres are characterized by cooperative efforts to reach dispute resolution rather than by the adversarial proceedings characteristic of most Canadian courts. Dispute-resolution programs are based on the principle of **participatory justice**, in which all parties to a dispute accept a kind of binding arbitration by neutral parties.

Participatory justice a relatively informal type of justice case processing which makes use of local community resources rather than requiring traditional forms of official intervention.

The Ontario Mandatory Mediation Program, operating in a number of centres across Ontario since 1999, is designed to help parties involved in civil litigation and estates matters attempt to settle their cases before they get to trial. Under the Ontario Mandatory Mediation Program, cases are referred to a mediation session early in the litigation process to give parties an opportunity to discuss the issues in dispute. With the assistance of a trained mediator, the parties explore settlement options and may be able to avoid the pretrial and trial process. The benefits of the program include resolutions that are tailored to the needs of the parties, and a greater sense of satisfaction because participants play an active role in resolving their dispute rather than having a solution determined by a judge.

The restorative-justice approach has often been criticized for its vagueness of definition and direction. The term "community," for example, is an abstract one and has been used indiscriminately. Not all communities are clearly defined, nor are they all capable of engaging in partnerships that will sustain a restorative-justice approach; for some, involving the community in restorative justice is seen as a "quick fix" for a crime issue that may require

CHAPTER 10

305

**The Meaning
of Crime:
Social Conflict
Perspective**

a more traditional approach. Some critics claim that the lack of due process and unclear legal procedures all serve to render the restorative-justice approach ineffective. Concern around disparity of sentencing has been raised, especially if not all accused persons are afforded access to restorative-justice programs. Whether or not power imbalances between those in positions of authority and the accused can be rectified to allow for the true implementation of restorative-justice initiatives has been questioned as well. Finally, some critics charge that existing structural and legislative realities restrict or prevent widespread acceptance of the restorative-justice approach. Table 10.2 compares retributive and restorative justice approaches.

Critique of Peacemaking Criminology

Peacemaking criminology has been criticized as being naive and utopian, as well as for failing to recognize the realities of crime control and law enforcement. Many victims, for example, do not expect to gain much during the victimization process from attempting to make peace with their victimizers (although such strategies do occasionally work). Such criticisms, however, may be improperly directed at a level of analysis that peacemaking criminologists have not assumed. In other words, peacemaking criminology, while it involves work with individual offenders, envisions positive change on the societal and institutional level and does not suggest to victims that they attempt to effect personal changes in offenders.

Table 10.2

Differences between Retributive and Restorative Justice

Retributive Justice	Restorative Justice
Crime is an act against the state, a violation of a law, an abstract idea.	Crime is an act against another person or the community.
The criminal justice system controls crime.	Crime control lies primarily with the community.
Offender accountability is defined as taking punishment.	Offender accountability is defined as assuming responsibility and taking action to repair harm.
Crime is an individual act with individual responsibility.	Crime has both individual and social dimensions of responsibility.
Victims are peripheral to the process of resolving a crime.	Victims are central to the process of resolving a crime.
The offender is defined by deficits.	The offender is defined by the capacity to make reparation.
The emphasis is on adversarial relationships.	The emphasis is on dialogue and negotiation.
Pain is imposed to punish, deter, and prevent.	Restitution is a means of restoring both parties; the goal is reconciliation.
The community is on the sidelines, represented abstractly by the state.	The community is the facilitator in the restorative process.
The response is focused on the offender's past behaviour.	The response is focused on harmful consequences of the offender's behaviour; the emphasis is on the future and on reparation.
There is dependence on criminal justice professionals.	There is direct involvement by both the offender and the victim.

Source: Adapted from Gordon Bazemore and Mark S. Umbreit, *Balanced and Restorative Justice: Program Summary* (Washington, DC: Office of Juvenile Justice and Delinquency Prevention, 1984), p. 7.

Left-realist criminology
or **left realism** a conflict
perspective that insists
on a pragmatic
assessment of crime and
its associated problems.

Left-Realist Criminology

Left-realist criminology, a recent addition to the criminological landscape, is a natural outgrowth of practical concerns with street crime, the fear of crime, and everyday victimization. Realist criminology faults radical-critical criminologists for romanticizing street crime and the criminals who commit it. Radical-critical criminologists, they charge, falsely imagine street criminals as political resistors in an oppressive capitalist society. While realist criminology does not reject the conflict perspective inherent in radical-critical criminology, it shifts the centre of focus onto a pragmatic assessment of crime and the needs of crime victims. Realist criminology seeks to portray crime in terms understandable to those most often affected by it: victims and their families, offenders, and criminal justice personnel. The test insisted upon by realist criminology is not whether a particular perspective on crime control or an explanation of crime causation complies with rigorous academic criteria, but whether the perspective speaks meaningfully to those faced with crime on a daily basis. As one contemporary source states, "for realists crime is no less harmful to its victims because of its socially constructed origins."[93]

Realist criminology is generally considered synonymous with **left realism**. Left realism, also called "radical realism" or "critical realism," builds on many of the concepts inherent in radical and Marxist criminology, while simultaneously claiming greater relevancy than either of its two parent perspectives. Left realism also tends to distance itself from some of the more visionary claims of early radical and Marxist theory. Daniel J. Curran and Claire M. Renzetti portray left realism as a natural consequence of increasingly conservative attitudes toward crime and criminals in both Europe and North America. "Though not successful in converting many radicals to the right," they write, "this new conservatism did lead a number of radical criminologists to temper their views a bit and to take what some might call a less romanticized look at street crime."[94]

Some authors credit **Walter DeKeseredy**[95] with popularizing left-realist notions in North America, and **Jock Young**[96] is identified as a major source of left-realist writings in England. Prior to the writings of DeKeseredy and Young, radical criminology, with its emphasis upon the crime-inducing consequences of existing power structures, tended to portray the ruling class as the "real criminals" and saw street criminals as social rebels who were acting out of felt deprivation. In contrast, DeKeseredy and Young were successful in refocusing leftist theories onto the serious consequences of street crime and upon the crimes of the lower classes. Left realists argue that victims of crime are often the poor and disenfranchised who fall prey to criminals with similar backgrounds. They do not see the criminal justice system and its agents as pawns of the powerful but rather as institutions that could offer useful services if modifications were made to reduce their use of force and increase their sensitivity toward the public.

A central tenet of left realism is the claim that radical ideas must be translated into realistic social policies if contemporary criminology is to have any practical relevance. In a recent review of left realism in Australia and England, concrete suggestions with respect to community policing models, for example, are indicative of the direction left realists are headed. Instead of seeing the police as oppressors working on behalf of the state, left realists recommend that police work with, and answer to, the communities being policed.[97] The major goal of left realism is, therefore, to achieve "a fair and orderly society" through a practical emphasis on social justice.[98] Hence left realists are concerned with the reality of crime and the damage it does to the most vulnerable segments of the population.

CHAPTER 10

307
The Meaning
of Crime:
Social Conflict
Perspective

Critique of Left-Realist Criminology   Left-realist criminology has been convincingly criticized for representing more of an ideological emphasis than a theory. As Don C. Gibbons explains, "Left realism can best be described as a general perspective centered on injunctions to 'take crime seriously' and to 'take crime control seriously' rather than as a well-developed criminological perspective."[99] Realist criminologists appear to build upon pre-existing theoretical frameworks, but rarely offer new propositions or hypotheses that are testable. They do, however, frequently suggest crime-control approaches that are in keeping with the needs of the victimized; policies promulgated by left realists understandably include an emphasis on community policing, neighbourhood justice centres, and dispute-resolution mechanisms. Piers Beirne and James W. Messerschmidt summarize the situation this way: "what left realists have essentially accomplished is an attempt to theorize about conventional crime realistically while simultaneously developing a 'radical law and order' program for curbing such behavior."[100]

Policy Implications

The policy implications of the social conflict theory are fairly clear: Bring about social change and redistribute the wealth in society, and crime rates will fall. At one extreme, radical-Marxist criminologists argue that the only effective way of reducing conflict is through a total dismantling of the existing capitalist state and its replacement by a socialist economic structure. Most radical-critical criminologists recognize that this is highly unlikely. They have begun to focus, instead, on promoting a gradual transition to socialism and to socialized forms of government activity. These middle-range policy alternatives include "equal justice in the bail system, the abolition of mandatory sentences, prosecution of corporate crimes, increased employment opportunities, and promoting community alternatives to imprisonment."[101] Likewise, programs to reduce prison overcrowding, efforts to highlight injustices within the current system, the elimination of racism and other forms of inequality in the handling of both victims and offenders, growing equality in criminal justice system employment, and the like are all frequently mentioned as midrange strategies for bringing about a justice system that is more fair and closer to the radical ideal.

At the other extreme are the calls of the peacemaking criminologists for a practical application of the principles of conflict resolution. Between these two extremes lie left realism and feminist criminology; the solutions they offer vary from the reduction of paternalism to a practical recognition of the consequences of crime to victims.

Summary

This chapter has described social conflict theories. Conflict theories hold that social conflict is the root cause of crime. For some conflict theorists, social order rests upon the exercise of coercive power rather than an agreed-upon consensus. Radical criminologists hold that the ongoing battle between the haves and the have-nots in capitalist societies leads to crime and the definitions of crime that unfairly criminalize the activities of the disenfranchised. They believe that criminal law is a tool of the powerful, who use it to perpetuate their control over the less fortunate.

Radical criminology and its contemporary offshoots, including feminist criminology, critical criminology, and peacemaking criminology, seek to redress injustices in society as a way of ending the marginalization of the politically and economically disentitled. Feminist criminology believes that the consequences of sexism and of the traditionally unequal gender-based distribution of power within our patriarchal society have been far-reaching, affecting fundamental aspects of social roles and expectations at all levels, including crime and the field of criminology.

Discussion Questions

1. This book emphasizes a social problems versus social responsibility theme. Which of the theoretical perspectives discussed in this chapter (if any) best support the social problems approach? Which (if any) support the social responsibility approach? Why?

2. What is Marxist criminology? How, if at all, does it differ from radical criminology? From critical criminology?

3. Does the Marxist perspective hold any significance for contemporary Canadian society? Why or why not?

4. What are the fundamental propositions of feminist criminology? How would feminists change the study of crime?

5. Describe peacemaking criminology. What are its central tenets? Do you believe that peacemaking criminology is realistic? Why or why not?

6. How do the central tenets of peacemaking criminology translate into the practice of restorative justice? Do you think the restorative-justice approach is a practical alternative to the adversarial approach to justice? Why or why not?

Weblinks

www.crimetheory.com
Teaching and learning resource maintained by Ohio University. Follow the links to a good, albeit condensed, look at radical criminology.

www.ainc-inac.gc.ca/index.html
Indian and Northern Affairs Canada. Links to analysis of the Oka Crisis from the perspective of the federal government.

www.rcmp.ca/ccaps/compol_e.htm
Community, Contract, and Aboriginal Policing, RCMP. Provides an overview of the principles of community policing as well as several RCMP initiatives.

www.ledevoir.com
Le Devoir newspaper. Provides a good, historical French-language overview of the FLQ crisis.

www.amnesty.org
Amnesty International Canada. Amnesty International is a worldwide movement that campaigns to promote human rights.

CHAPTER 11

Criminology and Social Policy

While the justice system is necessary to hold offenders accountable for their actions, it is only part of the solution to crime. A better solution is to prevent crime in the first place.

—NATIONAL CRIME PREVENTION COUNCIL[1]

Young people face a bewildering number of choices, or pathways, some positive, some negative. With little guidance and even less experience, they're forced to make critical choices about countless issues. And, not surprisingly, they often make bad choices.

—BARBARA HALL, CHAIR, NATIONAL STRATEGY ON COMMUNITY SAFETY[2]

LEARNING OUTCOMES

After reading this chapter, you should be able to

- distinguish between the social problems approach and the social responsibilities approach to crime prevention

- recognize and understand the various types of crime-prevention strategies

- relate various crime-prevention strategies to recent Canadian crime-prevention policy initiatives

- discuss the strengths and weaknesses of these and other recent Canadian crime-prevention policies

PART 3
310
Crime in the
Modern World and
the Response to It

IMPORTANT TERMS

public policy	nurturant strategy	deterrence strategy
social epidemiology	protection/avoidance strategy	*Kriminalpolitik*

IMPORTANT LEGISLATION AND GROUPS

National Strategy on Community Safety and Crime Prevention	Crime Prevention Through Environmental Design (CPTED)	*Youth Criminal Justice Act (YCJA)*

Introduction

In the study of crime, as in many other areas, life often imitates art. On September 7, 1996, rapper Tupak Shakur, well known for his starring role in the movie *Poetic Justice*, was gunned down after leaving a Mike Tyson fight in Las Vegas. He died in hospital one week after being attacked. Shakur's violent past included a shooting that injured two off-duty police officers, a conviction on sexual abuse charges,[3] and a mugging, during which the rapper was shot four times. The mugging had occurred as Shakur was awaiting sentencing after being convicted of assault and battery in an attack on his former film director, Allen Hughes.[4] During his brief rise to stardom, Shakur's brand of "gangsta rap" was condemned by some, who charged that Shakur's violent lyrics had led a youth to kill a state trooper.

Six months after Shakur died, the Notorious B.I.G., or Biggie Smalls—another of gangsta rap's best-known entertainers—was killed in a hail of gunfire. The 24-year-old B.I.G., whose given name was Christopher Wallace, was shot shortly after midnight on March 9, 1997, as he sat in the passenger seat of a GMC Suburban at a red light in downtown Los Angeles. He died in hospital a short time later. B.I.G., a former drug dealer and street hustler from New York, had burst onto the gangsta rap scene in 1994 with his million-selling album *Ready to Die*.

About the time B.I.G. died, another infamous rapper, Snoop Doggy Dogg, and his bodyguard McKinley Lee were acquitted of murder charges in the 1993 slaying of Phillip Woldermariam. Woldermariam, a member of the Venice Shoreline Crips, had been shot twice in the back after meeting with Snoop (whose birth name is Calvin Broadus). Others like Snoop have profited by selling images of urban violence to mainstream youth. A $25 million wrongful death suit filed by Woldemariam's family was settled out of court in late 1996 for an undisclosed sum.

There are many more examples of violent exploits of gangsta rappers. A few years before Shakur died, Flavor Flav (William Drayton), a rapper with the group Public Enemy, was arrested for firing a .38-calibre pistol at a neighbour. By the time of Flav's arrest, Ice-T's song *Cop Killer* had been blamed in the 1992 shooting deaths of two police officers who were ambushed and killed by four juveniles. The juveniles continued to sing *Cop Killer* lyrics following their arrest.[5] *Body Count*, the Time-Warner album on which *Cop Killer* appears, was shipped to stores in a miniature body bag.

One year later, rapper Dr. Dre (Andre Young) directed an 18-minute video of a Snoop performance called *Murder Was the Case*. Dre said he wanted to package the video with Oliver Stone's *Natural Born Killers*.[6] *Murder* and *Killers* were both quickly criticized by law-enforcement organizations, parents' groups, and political leaders, who decried the lyrics of gangsta music.[7] Some radio stations began banning violent rap music soon after.

Gangsta rap and "hip-hop" music have been condemned by many who claim that the lyrics promote anti-social and violent behaviour. But it is less clear whether gangsta rap is indeed a cause of crime or merely a quasi-poetic rendering of the social conditions characteristic of many large urban communities today. The real problems, some claim, lie outside rap music, not within it. Gangsta rap supporters suggest that rap may be the wake-up call needed to raise public awareness, thereby doing more to reduce violence than any government-sponsored program.

It should be noted that there is a current trend toward seeing rap and hip-hop music as vehicles for social change. Groups such as Dead Prez, The Coup, and Public Enemy, for example, condemn sweatshops and the use of child labour. Whatever the verdict on gangsta rap will eventually turn out to be, the issue of media-fed violence is only one of the concerns facing today's crime-prevention policy makers. Illicit drug use, drug trafficking, gun violence, youth crime, and overcrowded prisons are among the topics occupying today's policy makers. This chapter reviews some of these issues but begins with an outline of current crime-prevention directions.

Crime Prevention and Public Policy

Pressure by some public groups to investigate the possible behavioural consequences of rap music, in the hope that lawmakers will enact some sort of legislative control over the airing of offensive lyrics, is one way that public policy can be influenced. Some understanding of how public policy—especially crime-prevention policy—is created is essential to the study of criminology. Before we consider a number of current public policies in the criminal justice area, a definition of the term *public policy* is in order. **Public policy**, also called *social policy*, can be defined as "those standing directives, formulated by public organizations, on behalf of the public good"[8] or "a course of action that government takes in an effort to solve a problem or to achieve an end."[9] Other definitions contend that public policy is an expression of meaning: "A policy statement in the criminal justice system constitutes a declaration of social value, and it is upon the basis of the declared value that subsequent decisions are shaped."[10] Social values, in turn, are defined as ideals, customs, or institutions that society regards either positively (such as freedom) or negatively (such as cruelty). There are various types of public policy. Descriptors such as "social," "fiscal," "housing," "health," and "economic" can all be attached to the word "policy." Generally, policy dealing with issues of crime and its prevention and control fall under the rubric of social policy, which can be defined as policy "concerned with the betterment of social life, the amelioration of social ills, and the allocation of public money to accomplish that end."[11]

Analysts of public policy have observed that policies undergo five stages in their development:[12]

1. identification of the problem;
2. agenda setting or the prioritization of problems;
3. policy formation;
4. program implementation; and
5. program evaluation and reassessment.

Compare these stages to those described in Box 11.1.

Public policy
government-formulated directives made on behalf of the public good to solve a problem or achieve an end.

PART 3
312
**Crime in the
Modern World and
the Response to It**

The issue of criminal justice policy making in Canada has only recently become an area of concentrated interest for the field of criminology, and there is debate within Canadian criminology circles as to the impact of criminological research on the development of pub-

The Birth of a Criminal Justice Policy in Canada

Box 11.1

Conception

*Behavioural Event
Example:* Increase in reported incidence of drinking and driving and associated costs

Gestation

Interested group (response from domain of public-at-large) critical mass established

Bureaucratic Response
• report
• control
• increase resources
• provide legal restraints

Media Response
• report
• sensationalize
• editorialize

Political Response
• reduce threat to political stability
• satisfy interests of public servants
• maintain equilibrium in government services (e.g., competition among ministries to obtain additional resources)
• respond to issue through media

Birth

*Public Policy
Example:* The government announces that it will establish a major initiative to combat drinking and driving. One million dollars will be committed through the Ministry of Health and the Attorney General. A director will be appointed to coordinate program development. Completion of "gestation" period requires

1. the interest of bureaucracy
2. continuing (and mounting) pressure from groups that are (or appear to be) representatives of the public-at-large
3. continuing attention of the media
4. perceived threat to political stability

Growth

Procedures for policy implementation established

Education
For example, good school programs on drinking and driving, including participation of law-enforcement and other agencies

Law
For example, increasing civil and criminal sanctions

Regulation
For example, "tightening up" on criteria to obtain a driver's licence

Enforcement
For example, breath-analysis testing, roadside checks; methods for monitoring of policy outcomes established

Research
Continuing data gathering and analysis of drinking and driving

Program Evaluation
Measuring cost-effectiveness and program efficiency in relation to program objectives

ENERGY SUSTAINED BEYOND INITIAL RESPONSE ⟶

ENERGY NOT SUSTAINED BEYOND INITIAL RESPONSE ⟶
No change in public policy or bureaucratic energy devoted to the issue

Source: From *Canadian Criminology: Perspectives on Crime and Criminality,* Second Edition by Jackson/Griffiths, 1995. Reprinted with permission of Nelson, a division of Thomson Learning: www.thomsonrights.com. Fax 800-730-2215.

lic crime policy. As John Ekstedt and Curt Griffiths have noted, "Public policy making in areas of critical social awareness has taken on the atmosphere of political 'campaigns' with all the attention to the marketing of ideas, the testing of public reaction, and the selling of policy positions normally associated with an election process. Governments seek to promote policies that can contribute to the common good without resulting in political disruption."[13] The outline in Box 11.1 illustrates this process by examining legislation introduced to address the public's concern with impaired driving. Others have made the comment, "As all criminologists know, criminality is decided as much by legal and political authorities, and by their strategies of criminalization, enforcement, and control, as by criminals themselves."[14]

Crime-Prevention Philosophies Today

Today's policy response to crime has two prongs. One prong defines crime as an issue of individual responsibility. The other sees crime and criminal behaviour as resulting from poor social conditions and dysfunctional social structures. In Chapter 1, the first prong was termed the "social responsibility perspective," and the second approach was called the "social problems perspective."

Each of these perspectives sees the root causes of crime very differently and dictates a different approach to its resolution. Our American neighbours, for example, appear to have embraced the social responsibility perspective, which is clearly reflected in their current criminal justice policies. The United States has been "waging a war" on crime, criminals and, most recently, terror since 1980, resulting in such legislation as the *Comprehensive Crime Control Act* (1984), the *Omnibus Anti-Drug Abuse Act* (1988), the *Violent Crime Control and Law Enforcement Act* (1994) and the *USA PATRIOT Act* (2001). The full name of the act is "Uniting and Strengthening America by Providing Appropriate Tools Required to Intercept and Obstruct Terrorism." All of these pieces of legislation have introduced harsher penalties and increased law enforcement powers. Currently, policies at both the state and federal levels are becoming more and more focused on strict enforcement of existing laws and on strict punishments.[15] Prisons are being built apace, while tough legislation that will fill even more prisons is being passed at a feverish pitch. Americans are pushing their political representatives for the creation of conservative policy tools to deal with crime and the fear it engenders. At recent count, there were some 1.8 million people incarcerated in the United States, or roughly 714 per 100 000 population (over 1100 per 100 000 adult males). In fact, the United States now imprisons more people per capita than any other country in the Western world as illustrated in Figure 11.1.

Detractors of such "get-tough" policies claim that they may not provide the solution sought by those advocating them. They argue that those crime-prevention strategies that attempt to resolve the root causes of crime are more effective in the long run. "We know full well that the most serious and intractable types of crime have their roots in the very child welfare problems that are neglected as we trash through one ineffective war on crime after another," says one American commentator. "Political support for nurturant programs might be obtainable," he argues, "if we could reverse the vicious cycle of media sensationalism, short-sighted policy, and public impatience that encourages ineffective 'quick fixes' for crime."[16]

By way of contrast, the history of criminal justice policy making in Canada is largely based on the social problems perspective. Traditionally, the federal government and others

PART 3
314
**Crime in the
Modern World and
the Response to It**

| Figure 11.1 |

Canada's Incarceration Rate Compared to Other Western European Countries

Number of Inmates per 100 000 Population (2003)

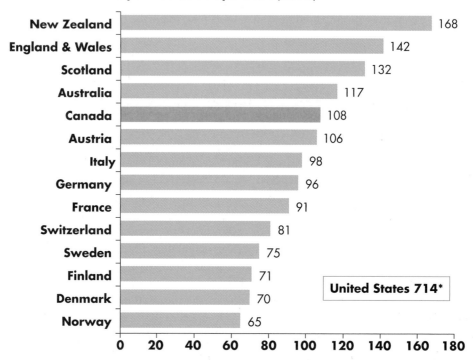

- Canada's incarceration rate is higher than the rates in most Western European countries but much lower than the United States, which had an incarceration rate of 714 per 100 000 general population in 2003.
- The incarceration rate in Canada has decreased 18.2% from 132 per 100 000 in 1995 to 108 per 100 000 in 2003, whereas most Western European rates have remained stable or increased during the same time period.

Note: *Figures for the United States are for incarcerated adults only (i.e. youths are excluded)
The incarceration rate, in this figure, is a measure of the number of people (i.e., adults and youth) in custody per 100 000 people in the general population. Different practice and variations in measurement in different countries limit the comparability of these figures.

Source: *Corrections and Conditional Release Statistical Overview*, p. 5, Solicitor General Canada, 2003. Reproduced with the permission of the Minister of Public Works and Government Services, 2007.

have decried the "get-tough" approach to crime prevention as being purely reactive and failing to address the underlying causes of crime and criminality. According to a former federal minister of justice,

> *We do not think for a moment that violent crime is going to be resolved in this society by tinkering with statutes or changing Acts. The fact of the matter is that the criminal justice system itself is not going to end violent crime. It only deals with the consequences of the underlying social problems. It is crime prevention that must have at least the equal focus of the House of Commons.*[17]

By addressing social problems and the need for improvements in the social infrastructure, the social problems perspective takes a *proactive* rather than *reactive* approach to the reality of crime. Within this context, Canadian crime policy initiatives overall have stressed strategies designed to prevent crime. The National Strategy on Community Safety and Crime Prevention (discussed in more detail later in this chapter) is anchored in the belief that crime prevention is best promoted through social development and that "[i]n order to prevent crime, action must take place at the community level. It is the people who live, work and play in a community who best understand their area's resources, problems, needs and capacities."[18]

Recently, a slight shift away from this social-problems-based approach to crime prevention has been apparent. The Conservative government of Stephen Harper has introduced proposed legislation that would appear closer to the "get-tough" approach to crime and criminality. In early 2006, the federal government announced plans to scrap previously proposed legislation to decriminalize the possession of small amounts of marijuana as well as to bring in tougher sentences for those convicted of a criminal offence. According to Harper, "We are going to hold criminals to account. This government will send a strong message to criminals: if you do a serious crime, you're going to start doing serious time."[19]

Later in 2006, the federal government introduced legislation designed to get tough with sex and high-risk offenders. The proposed reforms target *Criminal Code* provisions governing dangerous offenders, to make it easier for Crown prosecutors to obtain dangerous offender designations. A cornerstone of the reforms is that an offender found guilty of a third conviction of a designated violent or sexual offence must prove that he or she does not qualify as a dangerous offender. The reforms would also strengthen the peace bond provisions in the *Criminal Code* to allow for longer and more aggressive supervision after designated offenders are released back into communities. The Minister of Public Safety declared, "It is time to implement effective preventative measures to safeguard communities and children from individuals identified as dangerous or high-risk offenders, and at the same time, to strengthen the ability of law enforcement agencies to deal with these individuals. This government is serious about getting tough on crime."[20]

An interesting aspect of the social problems approach is its recasting in terms of social epidemiology. In terminology akin to the old social pathology approach of the Chicago school, some contemporary politicians and criminologists now view crime and the conditions that create it in terms of a disease model.[21] The word *epidemiology* refers to the study of epidemics and diseases, and the phrase **social epidemiology** has come to mean the study of social epidemics and diseases of the social order. Hence, the social epidemiological approach holds that crime arises from festering conditions that promote social ills, and that individuals caught in an environment within which crime may be communicated display symptoms of this disease and suffer from its maladies. Crime becomes an illness, a social malady, but one that can be cured if the necessary resources could be dedicated to its treatment and eradication. Such thinkers advance solutions based on what is, in effect, a public health model. In keeping with the old health adage that "an ounce of prevention is worth of pound of cure," crime as a disease becomes a new kind of social problem—one that shifts responsibility for law violations away from individuals "afflicted" with criminality and toward the society that is ultimately responsible for their control.

Advocates of this "public health" approach have developed programs to deal with a number of criminal behaviours, most notably violence. In the words of the Pacific Center for Violence Prevention, located in the United States,

> *Violence is a public health issue, and violence prevention is a public health mandate. Violence results in premature death, serious injury and disability in populations. These*

Social epidemiology
the study of social epidemics and diseases of the social order.

PART 3

316

**Crime in the
Modern World and
the Response to It**

are the concern of public health agencies and advocates. The public health model suggests that efforts to prevent violence, like those to prevent injury and infectious diseases, should consider the interaction between host, agent and environment. The host for violent injury is the person who is at risk of harming or being harmed by himself or herself or another person. The agent for violent injury is the weapon, be it a gun, knife, fist, foot, broken bottle or baseball bat. The environment for violent injury has three components: physical, economic, and social. Examples of the physical environment of violent injury are dark streets, abandoned buildings, bedrooms, bar rooms and work sites. The economic environment of violent injury includes limited social, recreational and educational activities, high levels of poverty and unemployment, particularly among young males. The social environment of violent injury includes fear, hopelessness, sexism and racism. Comprehensive programs to prevent violence cannot ignore the interaction among host, agent and environment. Within the public health approach, efforts to prevent violence necessitate identifying and addressing the root causes of violence . . .[22]

In Canada, the introduction of various pieces of legislation dealing with the registration and monitoring of firearms is an example of the public health model of crime prevention. Advocates of the gun control legislation believe that by more closely controlling the sale and use of firearms, violence using firearms can be controlled without first having to eradicate all the underlying social issues that contribute to gun violence. In other words, in the analogy of the public health approach, gun-related violence is symptomatic of a number of other issues, including socio-economic factors and substance abuse, just as tuberculosis has been linked to poverty. The public health approach has been successful in controlling tuberculosis without really affecting the underlying contributing factor—namely poverty. In the same way, it is believed that gun control legislation will address violence by "treating" the symptom—gun ownership—without addressing the causes.[23] Box 11.2 provides an overview of recent Canadian gun control legislation.

There is much debate surrounding the gun control legislation in Canada. Cost overruns in the administration of the registration system has many people questioning whether the current approach is worth the money being spent. Other concerns include the active resistance on the part of gun owners to the registration of their guns, citing an infringement on individual rights; the lack of buy-in by many provinces; and the reality that registration does not appear to reduce gun ownership levels. Supporters of the *Firearms Act* cite improvements in the ability to investigate offences involving firearms and the enhanced safety of officers, among others.

Detractors of the public health approach to crime contend that "Treating crime as a disease—the essence of the 'public health' approach to gun violence—is as illogical and ineffectual as the converse, treating disease as a crime. We would mock any criminologist who advocated criminalizing disease by measures such as fines for obesity or jail time for tobacco-related emphysema. We would condemn the police if they invaded bedrooms to ensure the use of condoms in the crusade against AIDS."[24]

Types of Crime-Prevention Strategies

The range of effective crime-prevention alternatives available to today's policy makers can be classified into three types of strategies. These three strategies differ in terms of

A Brief History of Gun Control Legislation in Canada

Box 11.2

1934:
- First real registration requirement for handguns is created.
- Records identifying the gun owner, the owner's address, and the firearm are required and are kept by the RCMP or police departments.

1938:
- Handguns have to be re-registered every five years.

1951:
- Registry system for handguns is centralized under the RCMP.
- Firearms are now required to have serial numbers.

1968–1969:
- Categories of "firearm," "restricted weapon," and "prohibited weapon" are created, allowing specific legislative controls for each category.

1977:
- Bill C-51 is enacted and comes into force in 1979.
- Bill C-51 includes requirements for Firearms Acquisition Certificates (FACs) and for Firearms and Ammunition Business Permits, both of which involve the screening of applicants and implementation of record-keeping systems.
- Provinces are given the option of requiring FAC applicants to take a firearms safety course.

1991–1994:
- Bill C-17 is enacted in 1991 and comes into force between 1992 and 1994.
- Bill C-17 makes changes to the FAC, including
  —applicants required to provide a photograph and two references;
  —mandatory 28-day waiting period for receiving an FAC imposed;
  —mandatory requirement for safety training imposed;
  —application form expanded to provide more background information; and
  —a more detailed screening check of FAC applicants required.
- New requirements in Bill C-17 include
  —regulations for firearms dealers; and
  —clearly defined regulations for the storage, handling, and transportation of firearms. By 1994, FAC applicants are required to demonstrate this by passing a firearms safety course test or receiving certification from a firearms officer.

1995:
- Bill C-68 is enacted and comes into force.
- Major changes include
  —the creation of the *Firearms Act*, which removes the administrative and regulatory aspects of the licensing and registration of firearms from the *Criminal Code*;
  —the *Firearms Act* regulates the manufacture, assembly, import, export, transfer, sale, lending, storage, transport, handling, possession, and registration of firearms in Canada;
  —the FAC is replaced with a new licensing system requiring licences for possession and acquisition of firearms and for buying ammunition; and
  —all firearms, including shotguns and rifles, must be registered.

PART 3

318

**Crime in the
Modern World and
the Response to It** ▶

1998:
- The amended *Firearms Act* is brought into force, to be phased in over the next five years.
- Regulations in the *Act* include
  —all gun owners require a licence to possess or acquire a firearm or to buy ammunition by January 1, 2001, and must renew this licence every five years;
  —all firearms must be registered by 2003, and to register, an applicant must first have a valid licence or valid FAC;
  —safety checks are done on all applicants before a licence is issued;
  —new applicants wanting to acquire firearms must take and pass the Firearms Safety Test;
  —safe storage regulations require that all firearms be stored unloaded and made inoperable; and
  —firearms brought into the country by visitors must be recorded at the point of entry.

2003:
- Bill C-10A is brought into force.
- Major changes include
  —simplifying the requirements for licence renewals;
  —staggering firearms licence renewals to avoid a surge of applications in five-year cycles;
  —establishing a pre-application process for temporary importation by non-resident visitors;
  —grandfathering additional handguns that were prohibited in 1995;
  —extending the terms of firearms business licences; and
  —clarifying the licensing requirements for the employees of firearms businesses.

2006:
- Bill C-21 is introduced.
- Major proposed changes will result in
  —the repeal of the requirement to register non-restricted long-guns;
  —the requirement that firearms retailers record all sales transactions of non-restricted firearms.

Source: Adapted from the Canada Firearms Centre website, www.cfc-cafc.gc.ca.

strategic focus.[25] That is, they are distinguishable from one another "by whether they attempt to block opportunities for crime, alter the outcome of conscious or unconscious decision making that precedes a criminal act, or alter the broad strategic style with which people approach many aspects of their lives."[26] The three strategies are

- Nurturant strategies
- Protection/avoidance strategies
- Deterrence strategies.

Nurturant strategy a crime-prevention strategy that attempts to forestall development of criminality by improving early life experiences and channelling child and adolescent development into desirable directions.

Nurturant strategies "attempt to forestall development of criminality by improving early life experiences and channelling child and adolescent development" into desirable directions. They "focus on prevention of criminality rather than its remediation or control."[27] Nurturant strategies include increased infant and maternal health care, child care for low-income families, training in parenting skills, enhanced public education, and stay-in-school programs.

Aboriginal sweat lodges within Canadian correctional facilities allow Aboriginal inmates to continue to practise traditional customs. What type of crime-prevention strategy does this represent?
www.justicebehindthewalls.net/book.asp?cid=23. Used with permission.

Protection/avoidance strategies "attempt to reduce criminal opportunities by changing people's routine activities, increasing guardianship, or incapacitating convicted offenders."[28] Incapacitating convicted offenders through incarceration or the use of electronic monitoring would be considered examples of protection/avoidance strategies. Target hardening or opportunity reduction through the use of architectural design, crime-prevention programs such as neighbourhood watch, and increased policing also fit into this category.

Deterrence strategies "attempt to diminish motivation for crime by increasing the perceived certainty, severity, or celerity of penalties."[29] New and tougher laws, quicker trial-court processing, harsher punishments, and faster imposition of sentences are all deterrence strategies.

A comprehensive crime-prevention strategy, say some criminologists, would be "a balanced mix of protection/avoidance, deterrence, and nurturant strategies."[30] Achieving the most effective balance in a politically sensitive world, however, is a difficult undertaking. In Canada, many crime-prevention initiatives emphasize the nurturant approach. Influential political constituencies, however, continue to press for crime-prevention measures that have protection/avoidance and deterrence strategies as their focus.

Protection/avoidance strategy a crime-prevention strategy that attempts to reduce criminal opportunities by changing people's routine activities, increasing guardianship, or incapacitating convicted offenders.

Deterrence strategy a crime-prevention strategy that attempts to diminish motivation for crime by increasing the perceived certainty, severity, or celerity of penalties.

Recent Crime-Prevention Policy Initiatives

The National Crime Prevention Strategy

Over the past decade, the Canadian federal and provincial governments have been paying greater attention to crime and community safety, targeting resources to understanding

PART 3

320

**Crime in the
Modern World and
the Response to It**

Nurturant crime-prevention strategies are largely aimed at improving the social conditions and experiences of youth such as these living in Toronto's Regent Park housing development prior to its redevelopment. Do you think the focus on preventing crime through social development is an effective crime-prevention approach?

Dick Hemingway.

and addressing risk factors associated with crime and victimization. In the 1990s, parliamentary committee reports called for a more concerted, national approach to crime prevention. In 1993, the Standing Committee on Justice and the Solicitor General tabled a report in Parliament that sent a clear message to the federal government about crime prevention. It advised that traditional "police, courts, and corrections" approaches to crime and community safety are limited in their scope and stated that "[i]t is time to translate the rhetoric of crime prevention into policies, legislation, and programs if we are to make real progress in our attempt to protect Canadians. . . ."[31]

National Strategy on Community Safety and Crime Prevention a federal crime-prevention initiative designed to create safer communities by supporting community-based crime-prevention efforts, enhancing communities' knowledge and experience with respect to crime prevention, and fostering partnerships and collaboration.

The federal government responded in 1994 by introducing the **National Strategy on Community Safety and Crime Prevention**.[32] A national council was created to develop a plan to coordinate national efforts in support of crime-prevention and community safety. The broad vision of the strategy was to encourage federal and provincial cooperation and the inclusion of citizens at the local level in a national crime-prevention initiative. The specific objectives of the National Strategy are as follows:

- to promote the integrated action of key governmental and non-governmental partners to reduce crime and victimization;
- to assist communities in developing and implementing community-based solutions that contribute to crime and victimization, particularly as they affect children, youth, women, and Aboriginal people; and
- to increase public awareness of and support for effective approaches to crime prevention.

Referred to as "crime prevention through social development," this initiative is emblematic of a nurturant strategy.

Phase I of the National Crime Prevention Strategy (NCPS) set the groundwork for its national implementation. The creation of the National Crime Prevention Council, made up of 25 volunteers including child development experts, community advocates, academics, social workers, lawyers, police officers, doctors, and business people, facilitated the development of a plan to deal with the underlying causes of crime. With a mission to "develop strategies to empower individuals and their communities to improve their safety, security and well-being," the council identified children and youth as its immediate focus for a national crime-prevention policy. It concluded that the failure of Canadians to invest in the social development of children and youth has had serious implications in the areas of criminal activity and victimization. The council identified a number of factors that place children and youth at risk of engaging in criminal activity, including child poverty, inadequate living conditions, inconsistent and uncaring parenting, childhood traumas such as physical and sexual abuse, family breakdown, racism and other forms of discrimination, difficulties in school, delinquent friends, and living situations where there is abuse of alcohol, drugs, and other kinds of substances. It concluded that what is needed in Canada is "a comprehensive approach to systemic crime prevention through social development" to best address "the combination of social, systemic, personal, and situational factors which place children and youth at risk and contribute to crime."

Building on the work of the National Crime Prevention Council, Phase II of the National Strategy was launched. Since its establishment in 1998, the National Crime Prevention Strategy has been mandated to promote activities between governmental and non-governmental partners, assist communities in developing and implementing community-based solutions, and increase public awareness of effective approaches to crime prevention. The National Crime Prevention Centre, under the auspices of Public Safety Canada, is currently responsible for this crime-prevention initiative.

Since 1998, the federal government has provided $32 million per year for crime-prevention initiatives across the country, targeting those initiatives that focus on children, youth, women, Aboriginal persons, and other at-risk groups, such as seniors, persons with disabilities, and ethno-cultural and other minority groups. The NCPS currently consists of four funding streams:

- The Community Mobilization Program supports community-based efforts to foster community partnerships to deal with crime and victimization, to increase public awareness and support for crime prevention, and to increase the capacity of communities to deal with crime and victimization.
- The Crime Prevention Partnership Program encourages non-governmental organizations to develop information, tools, and resources that facilitate community involvement in all phases of crime prevention.
- The Crime Prevention Investment Fund identifies, implements, and evaluates new social-development, community-based approaches to crime prevention by identifying crime risk factors and supports selected Canada-wide demonstration projects.
- The Business Action Program on Crime Prevention encourages the private sector to remain in crime prevention in their communities by expanding upon existing corporate efforts to prevent crime.

Since 1998, the National Crime Prevention Strategy has funded over 2500 projects in over 600 communities across Canada. Box 11.3 highlights several crime-prevention projects from across Canada that have received funding recently.

Canadian Crime-Prevention Projects

Box 11.3

BRITISH COLUMBIA

Silent and Invisible: What's Age Got to Do with It

British Columbia/Yukon Society of Transition Houses The goal of this initiative is to help decrease and prevent the incidence of domestic violence among older women and to raise public awareness about this issue. The first part of the project will create a curriculum for 2 days of specialized training for frontline workers and personnel working in the justice system. The second component of the project will produce a 12-minute docu-drama and study guide. The study guide will elaborate on each section in the video and offer solutions for healthy change, examples of what actions supportive people can do for abused older women, and other resources. Finally, the sponsor will implement a public awareness campaign to educate the public about the issue of domestic abuse involving older women. This will involve developing and distributing a safety tip card and an educational brochure to older women.

ONTARIO

Summer at Victory

Sudbury Better Beginnings Better Futures Parents in the Donovan and Flour Mill neighbourhoods of Sudbury have identified problems of violence, bullying, vandalism, drug use, gangs, criminal behaviour, and peer pressure amongst their pre-teen children. The goal of this project is to help these pre-teens become strong, positive leaders in the community. The young people, with the guidance of adult leaders, will decide on areas in the community that need cleaning and beautifying. They will clean and plant flowers in these designated areas. The children will also participate in outdoor sports and have the opportunity to participate on a camping trip. In addition, local police will provide educational workshops to the youth on different topics related to law. Overall, this project will help Sudbury pre-teens take control of their lives, build leadership, pro-social, and problem-solving skills, as well as respect for themselves, others, and the environment.

PRINCE EDWARD ISLAND

Virtues Language and Crime Prevention

Évangéline Community Consultative Group The goal of this initiative is to assist community members in forging better relationships with one another toward the strengthening of the community overall. This project will organize training workshops and present a program known as "The Virtues Project: Tools for Transformation." Designed to teach psycho-social skills, such as anger management, self-esteem, interpersonal relations and ways to communicate effectively and overcome difficulties, the program will target residents of the rural, francophone community of Évangéline, whose residents are largely employed seasonally. This program will attempt to attract youth, parents, educators, and community members from the private sector. Broadcasts of the Virtues Project video on the community television station will allow all members of the community to benefit from the training.

QUÉBEC

Jeunes anglophones et francophones se réconcilient

Maison des jeunes de Rawdon L'Excuse This project is aimed at anglophone and francophone youth, aged between 12 and 18, who feel in conflict with peers from a different language background, and who display their strife by committing acts of denigration and violence

▶

against those peers. The sponsoring organization will set out to facilitate and foster acceptance of differences by emphasizing things that are common to all youth despite different language backgrounds. It will achieve its objectives through various educational, cultural, and sporting activities organized by a round table made up of community partners. The sponsoring organization will organize discussion groups, stage a play, and offer weekly improvisation evenings in which the two language communities will be encouraged to use humour to demystify their conflicts. In addition, the project intends to train young mediators and to organize an exhibit and a meeting with police officers from the Sûreté du Québec dealing with crime in their community.

Source: Adapted from Department of Justice, "List of National Crime Prevention Centre (NCPC) Funded Projects for 2001/ 2002."

Crime Prevention Through Environmental Design

Indicative of the protection/avoidance approach to crime prevention is the notion of **Crime Prevention Through Environmental Design (CPTED)**. In 1971, C. Ray Jeffery's work entitled *Crime Prevention through Environmental Design* introduced the concept to North America.[33] It is based on the concept of *defensible space*, which holds that crime can be prevented through proper residential and commercial architectural design and the layout of the physical environment. The concept was introduced to Canada in the early 1980s by the Peel Regional Police Service and has since been endorsed by a great number of police services throughout Canada (including the RCMP), many of whom have trained CPTED officers.

The concept of CPTED has not been formally incorporated into any federal or provincial crime-prevention policies but has been widely incorporated into crime-prevention plans at the municipal level. Local governmental crime-prevention plans in Toronto and Edmonton include CPTED concepts, as does the mandate of the Peel Regional Police Service in Ontario. The municipalities of North York and Vancouver have both incorporated CPTED into their building codes and zoning bylaws. Its application is apparent in the design of various towns, shopping malls, schools, and public libraries. A CPTED analysis of the design and use of public parks is illustrated in Box 11.4.

Traditional "target hardening" crime-prevention approaches have employed physical or artificial barriers such as locks, alarms, fences, gates, etc., to deny access to a crime target. The CPTED model recognizes that these traditional methods often tend to place constraints on use, access, and enjoyment of the "hardened" environment. As an alternative, CPTED focuses on *natural surveillance* (keeping potential intruders under observation), natural access control (decreasing the opportunity for crime), and *territorial reinforcement* (creating or extending the sphere of influence through physical design to develop a sense of ownership). Further, the CPTED model insists upon an assessment of the physical environment to be protected. The designated purpose of the space, the social, cultural, legal, or physical definitions that suggest desired and acceptable behaviours for it, and the appropriateness of the design in the productive use of the space are included in this assessment.[34]

The Crime Prevention Association of New Brunswick identifies the following CPTED tactics that can be employed in a variety of settings:[35]

Crime Prevention Through Environmental Design (CPTED) a crime-prevention strategy based on the premise that the proper design and effective use of the built environment can lead to a reduction in the incidence and fear of crime.

PART 3

324

**Crime in the
Modern World and
the Response to It**

Making Parks Safer: A CPTED Analysis

Box 11.4

I use my experience as a police officer and Crime Prevention Through Environmental Design specialist to question everything, think like a criminal and never look at a property the same way again. This has led me to challenge three common practices found in the design and use of parks that negatively affects people's behaviour in unintended ways.

The Overuse of Lighting

The overuse of park lighting in parking lots and along walkways, whether isolated or not, can encourage the presence of people within the park at times when they're no longer desired. In the case of lighted parks, this routinely occurs after 11:00 p.m. when the park is supposed to be closed. Constant light sends a signal that the park is still open. This is a conditioned response that results from our day-to-day experiences whereby the presence of light is equated with a premise that is open and the dimming or absence of light is equated with a premise that is closed. It should therefore not be surprising that late night users of the park use this frame of reference when deciding whether to enter, exit, or stay in the park. It is my belief that the failure to signal the closing of a park through a conventional reduction in lighting results in several lost opportunities. They are the timely communication and reinforcement of the park closing time, the elimination of excuses by potential offenders found in the park and the natural withdrawal of users both to and from the park.

In order to achieve these and other advantages, such as a savings in hydro electricity costs and associated maintenance expenses, I strongly advocate creating an environment that is capable of sending environmental cues to park users. In particular I recommend the strategic use of timers and a "high/low" lighting system. High/low lighting systems were developed to provide a motion-activated capability for large-scale, commercial lighting applications that typically include high-pressure sodium (bronze-coloured) lights or other light sources that require an extended period of time prior to powering up. High/low lights that are activated by timers can send a clear signal that the park is closing. This is best accomplished by powering down the lights to a predetermined level then selectively turning off the lights to signal the park is closed.

With such a dynamic in place, we can reasonably expect both normal users and loiterers not engaged in disorderly conduct to head for better lit environments. The motivation for normal users to do this will be the perception of safety offered by the better lit environments. The motivation for loiterers not engaged in disorderly conduct to do this will be the desire to socialize in a lit setting. The intelligent use of lighting can create the conditions where people naturally use the park in the way that it was intended. It will also encourage police to increase their presence in the park as they will naturally be drawn to this environment once the lights are off.

Strategically Sited and Lit Playgrounds

Traditionally, there has never been a need to light children's playgrounds. They are, after all, intended to serve children's, and by extension parents', needs during the hours of light. Missing from this equation, however, is the real, yet unintended, use of these facilities by teenagers, loiterers, and other abnormal users during the hours of dark. This often results in damage to playground equipment, graffiti, and litter, some of which can be dangerous to children.

In order to address these problems, the playground must be fundamentally sited where there is reliable witness potential from nearby residents and passersby on the street. With this witness potential established, a strategic lighting application is once again recommended, only this time the recommendation is to add and maintain a constant level of light to the

▶ playground so that the witnesses now have the ability to see the actual structure. A strategically placed and lit playground that is capable of being seen by surrounding residents or passersby will tend to discourage loitering by such abnormal users as their prolonged behaviour is now more likely to be noticed.

Unrestricted Use of Natural Wood Lots

Natural wood lots are one of the most challenging environments within a park setting. They are by their nature fragile environments that favour the offender and defy traditional CPTED responses, such as establishing sightlines by trimming back shrubs or limbing up trees.

The night-time closure of the wood lot will accomplish a number of objectives. In the case of a typical wood lot with informal pathways, it will discourage abnormal traffic and activity that is otherwise drawn to the wood lot as a result of the cover provided by its foliage and the instinctive withdrawal of normal users during the hours of dark. It will also readily identify improper users of the wood lot to still-active residents, passersby, users of the adjacent green space, or law enforcement officers who, as a result of the recommended municipal by-law, will be given a viable means to address these problems before they get out of hand.

In the case of a wood lot with developed pathways, the solution is not so simple. The presence of walkways fundamentally alters the purpose of the wood lot. The wood lot now has a second objective that involves the safe movement of people. As I believe these objectives cannot be practically reconciled and are for all intents and purposes mutually exclusive, a choice must now be made.

In this regard, it is important to remember that the safest wood lots are those that naturally cue normal users to avoid them at night. These do not have formalized pathways. The presence of formal pathways confuses most people's instinct for safety. As a result, they should be removed.

While undoubtedly inconvenient and controversial, the re-establishment of the wood lot's primary purpose is the only practical and safe way to reconcile these conflicting objectives and, in the process, effectively reduce a considerable amount of criminal opportunity by getting people to instinctively bypass areas where there is substantial risk. This measure, along with a dusk-to-dawn closing, will go a considerable way toward preserving our wood lots, eliminating problems, and getting people to react in a manner that is consistent with street proofing advice.

Source: Constable Tom McKay is attached to the Peel Regional Police Crime Prevention Services where he implements CPTED Concepts. He is founding chair of CPTED Ontario.

Neighbourhoods
- Minimize the number of entry and exit points on a block.
- Design roadways to discourage through-traffic.
- Maximize residents' ability to view public spaces.
- Encourage residents' use of public spaces.
- Provide appropriate lighting for streets, paths, alleys, and parks.
- Encourage residents to watch over each other.

Houses
- Clearly delineate private property (e.g., yard, driveway) from public space (e.g., street, sidewalk) using shrubbery, alternate paving stone colour, and changes in grade.
- Use solid-core exterior doors.
- Use solid door frames with proper strike plates.

PART 3

326

**Crime in the
Modern World and
the Response to It**

Apartment Buildings
- Provide common spaces to ensure tenant interaction.
- Minimize the number of units sharing a common entrance.
- Equip shared entrances with an intercom.
- Ensure hallways are well lit.
- Provide a children's area that can be easily observed.
- Provide windows in laundry rooms that allow for surveillance in laundry rooms.

Parking Lots and Garages
- Avoid enclosed, underground, multi-storey garages.
- Install bright lights over driving lanes and parking spaces.
- Use paint to increase light levels.
- Control access and egress with automatic doors and gates.
- Avoid pillars and recesses that may hide offenders.

Public Spaces
- Encourage use by legitimate users.
- Avoid locating dark and/or hidden areas near activity nodes.
- Install appropriate lighting.
- Avoid locating covered outdoor areas where loitering may be a problem.

Advocates of CPTED stress that it should be considered only part of a comprehensive approach to crime prevention. Modifications to the physical environment will be effective only if they complement community-policing efforts and social programs that address some of the root causes of crime. One of CPTED's most ardent supporters, Greg Saville, claims, "On the one hand, a CPTED that pretends to solve problems with physical designs alone, while ignoring the psychological response of those living there, is doomed to failure.... On the other hand, also doomed is a socio-psychological CPTED that ignores all the advances we have learned in architecture and urban design since the 1970s."[36] Saville insists that there must be a balance struck between the physical aspects of CPTED, such as access control, natural surveillance, etc., with psycho-social crime-prevention strategies such as community-building, neighbourhood accords, school programs, and community policing. For Saville, initial analysis and diagnosis of the problem is crucial to striking that balance.[37]

Youth Criminal Justice Act

Youth Criminal Justice Act Canadian legislation that determines the way in which youth are prosecuted under the criminal justice system. It replaced the *Young Offenders Act* in 2003.

One example of a deterrence strategy, or an attempt to diminish crime by increasing the penalty, is the federal government's ***Youth Criminal Justice Act*** *(YCJA)*, which came into force in April 2003. Mounting public pressure on the government to deal with a perceived skyrocketing in the number of youths involved in crime, especially violent crime, precipitated the overhaul of the *Young Offenders Act*. Media stories of youth involved in violent incidents captured headlines across the country: an Anglican clergyman aged 75 and his 70-year-old wife were beaten to death with beer bottles and a baseball bat at their home near Montreal by three boys aged 13, 14, and 15; a group of Toronto youths aged 11 to 15 sexually assaulted a 13-year-old girl; a 13-year-old girl and her 15-year-old boyfriend were convicted of murdering the girl's mother in Lethbridge, Alberta. Growing incidents of school violence also have the public demanding harsher penalties for young people who commit adult offences: a 14-year-old boy and his 13-year-old friend were charged in Winnipeg with threatening to bring pipe bombs and weapons to their school to get back at a substitute teacher they didn't like; four students and one instructor were wounded in a knife attack at a high school on the outskirts of Ottawa.

In the year before the enactment of the *Youth Criminal Justice Act*, the Canadian Centre for Justice Statistics reported that the number of youths aged 12 to 17 charged with *Criminal Code* offences had reached 99 000, or a rate of 3956 offences per 100 000 youth. Of those, 24 percent were charged with violent crimes, 44 percent with property crimes, and 33 percent with other *Criminal Code* offences. While the rate of youths charged with violent crimes had fallen by 2.3 percent in 2002 from the previous year, the rate of youths charged with violent crimes remained 7 percent higher than it was a decade ago. Of those youths charged with violent offences, more than 73 percent of them were charged with assault, with the majority of these charges being laid for common assault. By comparison, less than 1 percent of the youths charged with violent crimes in 2002 were charged with homicide.[38]

By comparison, 2005 statistics indicate that the number of youths aged 12 to 17 charged with *Criminal Code* offences reached 169 462, a rate of 6603 offences per 100 000 youth. Of those, 22 percent were charged with violent crimes, 39 percent with property crimes, and 39 percent with other *Criminal Code* offences. Of those youths charged with violent offences, 78 percent were charged with assault and, again, the majority of these charges were laid for common assault. By comparison, less than 1 percent of the youths charged with violent crimes in 2005 were charged with homicide and attempted murder.[39]

The Declaration of Principle in the Preamble to the *YCJA* states that the protection of society is the primary objective of the youth justice system and is best achieved through prevention, meaningful consequences for youth crime, and rehabilitation. Moreover, youth are to be held accountable for their actions, and the consequences are designed to reinforce respect for social values and encourage reparation for harm done to the victim and community. Highlights of the *YCJA* include provisions that

- allow an adult sentence for any youth 14 years or older who is convicted of an offence punishable by more than 2 years in jail, if the Crown applies and the court finds it appropriate in the circumstances;
- expand the offences for which a young person convicted of an offence would be presumed to receive an adult sentence from murder, attempted murder, manslaughter, and aggravated sexual assault to include a new category of a pattern of repeat serious violent offences;
- lower the age for youth who are presumed to receive an adult sentence for the above offences to include 14- and 15-year-olds;
- permit the publication of names of all youth who receive an adult sentence. Publication of the names of 14- to 17-year-olds who receive a youth sentence for murder, attempted murder, manslaughter, aggravated sexual assault, or repeat serious violent offences will also be permitted;
- allow the Crown greater discretion in seeking adult sentences and publication of offenders' names;
- create a special intensive custody and supervision sentence for serious violent offenders who suffer from mental illness, psychological disorder, or emotional disturbance that includes an individualized plan for treatment and requires a court to make all decisions regarding release;

PART 3

328

**Crime in the
Modern World and
the Response to It**

- maintain sentence lengths for first-degree murder (10 years) and second-degree murder (7 years);
- promote a constructive role for victims and communities, including ensuring that they receive the information they need and that they have opportunities to be involved in the youth justice system (e.g., Victim Impact Statements permitted in youth court);
- give the courts more discretion to receive as evidence voluntary statements by youth to police;
- permit tougher penalties for adults who wilfully fail to comply with an undertaking made to the court to properly supervise youth who have been denied bail and placed in their care;
- permit the provinces to require young people or their parents to pay for legal counsel in cases where they are fully capable of paying;
- allow for and encourage the use of a full range of community-based sentences and effective alternatives to the justice system, such as victim compensation or retribution for youth who commit non-violent offences;
- require, in general, that youth be held in custody separately from adults to reduce the risk that they will be exposed to adult criminals; the maximum age for detention in youth custody is lowered from 21 to 20;
- require all periods of custody to be followed by a period of controlled supervision in the community that is equal to one-half of the period of custody imposed, to support safe and effective reintegration; and
- require police to consider all options outside the formal justice system before laying a charge in the case of minor youth offences. The range of options would include verbal warnings from police, informal police diversion programs, and formal programs requiring restitution.

Four years after the inception of the *Youth Criminal Justice Act*, analysis of its impact on the amounts and severity of crime committed by youth paints an interesting picture. Early studies examine a number of areas of impact of the *YCJA*; we will consider changes in patterns of charges laid by police, changes in the use of custodial sentences, and youth court judges' views of the youth system under the *YCJA*.[40]

Overall, it appears that there has been a significant reduction in the number of charges laid by police for less serious offences, but the rate of this reduction decreases as offences get more serious. There also seems to have been an increase in the use of extrajudicial measures by police, and law enforcement officials appear to be using the full range of measures set out in the *Act*, which includes options such as taking no further action, giving the youth an informal warning, giving the youth a formal police caution, referring the youth to a community program or agency, or referring the youth to an extrajudicial sanctions program. There are not sufficient data yet available, however, to determine the extent to which the use of these extrajudicial measures is proportionate to the seriousness of the offence. Interestingly, while preliminary national statistics do not indicate any significant increase in the number of youth being brought into the youth justice system, it does appear that there have been instances where police use of extrajudicial measures programs has served to "widen the net" by formally impacting youth who might otherwise have not been.[41]

While it remains unclear as to whether the pretrial detention of youth by police has increased or decreased under the *YCJA*, young persons who had previously breached a probation order or had three or more previous findings of guilt appear to be significantly more likely to be detained by the police under the new legislation. In addition, under the *YCJA*, police are more likely to impose conditions on young persons they release and the average number of conditions of release has been significantly higher.[42]

Early analysis indicates that the use of custodial sentences under the *YCJA* has decreased significantly for all major offence categories, and most notably for youth convicted of minor offences. This reduction in the use of custodial sentences appears to have been the result of two quite independent factors: the reduction in the overall youth court caseload and the reduction in the proportion of relatively comparable groupings of offences of those found guilty and sentenced to custody. Despite the latter reality, indications are that there has been an overall reduction in the proportion of guilty cases receiving custody, indicating that sentencing under the *YCJA* is being carried out in a manner that is different from that of earlier years. In particular, it seems that there is strong evidence that equivalent cases under the *YCJA* are less likely to be receiving a custodial sentence than they would have under the *Young Offenders Act*.[43] Finally, a recent survey of youth court judges' views of the current youth justice system indicates that judges vary on whether they think that large numbers of cases that come before them could be dealt with just as adequately outside of the youth justice system.[44] To some extent, this is dependent upon each judge's views about the adequacy of outside programs such as alternative measures in his or her community. Regardless, large numbers of judges expressed a lack of confidence that the "youth court experience" is beneficial to youths. Interestingly, however, more than half of the judges surveyed indicated that "public opinion" and the "prevalence of youth crime" in the community are factors often raised by Crown prosecutors and others at the time of sentencing. While research suggests that there is, in fact, very little that judges can do to affect the prevalence of crime in the community in which they sit, judges who hear a great deal of talk about the "prevalence" of crime indicate that they take it into account when sentencing, thereby accentuating the importance of "general deterrence" in the sentencing of youths.

Time will tell if the *Youth Criminal Justice Act* is having the desired effect on the prevention of youth crime. Controversy still surrounds the legislation—in March 2006, the Ontario Court of Appeal struck down sections of the *Act* that force some young offenders to prove that they should not receive adult sentences. Citing a breach of the *Charter of Rights and Freedoms*, the Appeal Court judges ruled that the onus lay with the Crown prosecutor to make the case that a serious youth crime should draw an adult sentence. They came to a similar conclusion on the issue of whether young offenders must persuade a court that their identity should be concealed after sentencing, ruling that the *Act* is wrong to place that onus on the defendant rather than the prosecution. In addition, the judges came out strongly in support of Canada's separate justice system for youth, a message welcomed by those concerned that the *YCJA* would have more young people tried and sentenced as adults. The ruling put Ontario in line with an earlier decision of the Quebec Court of Appeal; however when faced with a similar case, the Court of Appeal in British Columbia ruled the opposite way.[45]

Can We Solve the Problem of Crime?

In 1956, the European writer H. Bianchi emphasized what he saw as the difference between criminology and what he termed **Kriminalpolitik**.[46] Criminology, said Bianchi, should be considered a *metascience* or "a science of wider scope (than that of criminal law,

Kriminalpolitik the political handling of crime, or a criminology-based social policy.

PART 3

330

**Crime in the
Modern World and
the Response to It**

jurisprudence, criminal justice, or corrections) whose terminology can be used to clarify the conceptions of its subdisciplines. Far from being a mere auxiliary to the criminal law," said Bianchi, "it is therefore superior to it."[47]

For Bianchi and other writers of the time, the concept of *Kriminalpolitik* referred to the political handling of crime, or—as we might say today—a criminology-based social policy. Bianchi believed that if criminology were to remain pure, it could not afford to sully its hands, so to speak, with political concerns. Today, however, the image esteemed by criminologists and the expectations they hold for their discipline are quite different than they were in Bianchi's time. Many criminologists expect to work hand-in-hand with politicians and policy makers, forging crime-prevention agendas based on scientific knowledge and criminological theorizing. Some would say that this change in attitude represents a maturation of the discipline of criminology.

Whether effective crime-prevention policies can ever be implemented, however, is another question. Central to any discussion of public-policy development in Canada is the political reality of the country. Without going into a lot of detail on the impact of our decentralized, federalist political system, suffice it to say that the division of powers between the two levels of government in Canada—federal and provincial/territorial—has a profound impact on the creation and implementation of crime-prevention policy. Briefly, in criminal justice matters the federal government, through the Parliament of Canada, has exclusive jurisdiction to make criminal laws and set sanctions for their violation. The provinces and territories, on the other hand, are responsible for the implementation of the criminal laws, otherwise known as the administration of justice. There are a number of provincial/territorial statutes, such as those regulating liquor licensing and highway traffic, that are the sole responsibility of each individual provincial/territorial government. Needless to say, there is an overlap between the two governmental jurisdictions in the area of crime prevention, and, in many cases, joint decision-making mechanisms must be implemented before any policy can be developed—especially federal government initiatives with a national scope. Often referred to as federal/provincial/territorial conferences or task forces, these forums allow federal and provincial/territorial leaders to discuss issues of concern within the area of crime prevention and control. For example, a recent federal government initiative to explore strategies for managing offenders resulted in the creation of the Federal/Provincial/Territorial Task Force on High-Risk and Violent Offenders. The Task Force's work resulted in changes to legislation dealing with long-term dangerous offenders including a new long-term offender designation that targets sex offenders and adds a period of long-term supervision of up to ten years following release from prison as well as changes to the Dangerous Offender provisions of the *Criminal Code* to require that anyone classified as a dangerous offender must be given an indefinite sentence.

Matters of criminal justice are also dealt with at the municipal level of government. Essentially, municipalities are responsible for the enforcement of all laws and the creation of local bylaws.[48] In this way, a crime-prevention approach taken by a particular municipality through its police service may not necessarily dovetail neatly into crime-prevention approaches being taken at the provincial or federal levels.[49] In short, crime prevention and control is not as simple as implementing a federally developed policy across the country. Each level of government may interpret, implement, or challenge a policy, with the result that its uniform application from coast to coast often takes many years. What *is* known is that the costs of crime to society are significant. Box 11.5 presents the case of a fictitious,

The Costs to Society of a Young Person in Trouble

Box 11.5

Problems start early for many future offenders, especially those who will become chronic and persistent offenders. Patterns of troublesome behaviour are often apparent by the age of three. The costs to society start early as well, and increase as the years go by.

Identifying all the costs of a delinquent career would be an impossible task. But it is possible to identify some elements and make estimates or educated guesses of what they might cost in the life of a repeat young offender before he or she reaches the age of 18. Take the fictional, but typical, case of Jack. He is a troubled child who needs special help and preventive services early in his life—but the appropriate services are not available to him and his family.

Jack's First Three Years:

The child welfare authorities become aware of serious problems in Jack's home during his first year. His parents often have arguments, many of which end with the exchange of blows, especially after they have been drinking. Their parenting is affectionate, but erratic. Child welfare staff regularly visits Jack and his parents during his first three years of life. Social workers make a number of suggestions about his care and the special help he may need, but because of a lack of community resources, they are not able to refer Jack to appropriate support services.

Costs: Three years child welfare services at $2300 a year. Total = $6900

Jack Aged Three to Five:

Jack is showing a number of developmental problems, both physical and psychological. By the age of three he is difficult to manage. His parents do not know how to cope with his impulsive behaviour, and he shows no awareness of the consequences of his actions. The child welfare services, in conjunction with the family doctor and child psychiatric services, conclude that Jack would benefit from being placed in a subsidized child-care centre. Jack's mother qualifies for the subsidized service, but the staff at the centre is not trained to provide the remedial care he really needs. Jack tends to bully the other children, disrupt their play, and be insensitive to the needs of others.

Costs: Three years child welfare services at $2300 a year, child care at $12 000 a year, and health and psychiatric services at $2000 a year. Total = $48 900

Jack Aged Six to Ten:

Although Jack has benefited from the child-care services, and is better behaved in group settings, his home situation has gone from bad to worse. His parents have separated, and his mother is now living with a young man who appears jealous of the affection she shows towards Jack, and is abusive towards him. The child welfare services decide, reluctantly, that they have to take him into care; this requires an appearance in family court. Jack is placed in the first of a series of foster homes. Separation from his mother upsets him and reawakens his behaviour problems. He has difficulty relating to his foster parents and their children. In five years he lives in five foster homes. These moves disrupt his education and he has difficulty getting along with other children. Consequently, he is involved with school guidance counsellors and child psychiatric services.

Costs: Five years child welfare services at $2300 a year, foster care at $7300 a year, guidance counsellors and special education services at $2000 a year, health and child psychiatric services at $2000 a year, and court services for one appearance at $1000. Total = $69 000

PART 3

332

**Crime in the
Modern World and
the Response to It** ▶

Jack Aged 11 to 14:

By the age of 11, Jack is big for his age and precocious in his behaviour towards his peers, particularly girls. The child welfare services recognize that he has never settled down in the various foster homes he has lived in. In conjunction with the education and child health services, they conclude that a group home placement may be the only way to contain Jack's "acting-out."

The "acting-out" continues in the group home setting, however. He comes to the notice of the police several times before he turns 12, partly through misbehaviour at school and partly through various delinquent acts in the community.

Finally, at the age of 12 he is charged in relation to a number of incidents of shoplifting, vandalism, and rowdy behaviour in a local shopping mall. He goes to Youth Court for the first time, and is ordered to provide restitution services to make up for the damage he has done. He remains in the care of the child welfare services. Jack's contact with his mother is spasmodic after years of living away from her. When he does see her, it usually results in a period of disturbed behaviour in the group home and at school. At the age of 13, he gets involved with drugs at school, starts selling them to schoolmates, and becomes physically abusive in collecting his debts.

On one occasion, he hurts a boy seriously enough for the boy to receive in-patient care at a local hospital. Charges are laid, and Jack goes to Youth Court for a second time, where he is found guilty. The court is in a quandary over what sentence to give him. One possibility is to send him to a youth custodial facility, but this is seen as extreme for a boy of his age. Instead, he is placed on probation for a year, while continuing in the care of the child welfare services.

Jack is able to complete the year's probation without any further major incidents, with the help of the child welfare services, including the group home staff, the probation officer, and the school authorities. The probation ends when he has passed his 14th birthday. He is by now a physically mature young man, but he still has difficulty restraining his temper.

One weekend Jack leaves the group home without permission and meets some friends at a local mall. They obtain alcohol and drugs, and steal a car. Jack is the ringleader. They are caught after running the car off the road. On his third appearance in the Youth Court, Jack is remanded to the local detention facility for assessment reports. When he next returns to court, for his fourth appearance, the Youth Court sentences him to an open custodial placement followed by probation supervision of a year. He is sent to a youth centre for three months, and meets other youths with similar backgrounds. Jack receives some educational services, but is found to be backward for his age. The court had recommended psychological and psychiatric services, but no professional treatment other than assessments is provided in the open facility.

Costs: Four years of group home care at $36 500, special education services at $2000 a year, child welfare supervision at $2300 a year; probation supervision for one year at $1200; police contacts before age 12, $1000; three police investigations at $1500 each; four court sessions at $1000 each; four police attendances at court at $250 each; two psychological and psychiatric assessments at $2000 each; three months open custody $19 250. Total = $198 150.

Jack Aged 15 to 17:

When he leaves the open custody facility, Jack is 15 years old. He returns to the same group home, continues to have contact with the child welfare social worker, and attends school when he feels like it. He is again under probation supervision, but is very unsettled. He meets some of his former friends from the youth centre, and they decide to break into a local pharmacy to steal drugs. They trip the alarm and are apprehended. After a further remand in a detention

▶

facility, the Youth Court (where he has now made his fifth and sixth appearances) sends Jack to another open custody facility for six months, with supervision to follow. Halfway through his sentence, Jack escapes with some of his fellow inmates. They steal a car, but their erratic driving alerts a patrolling police car. In the subsequent chase with Jack at the wheel, they crash into another vehicle, killing the driver. It is now his seventh appearance. The Youth Court, without asking for further reports, sends him to a secure custody facility for two years with supervision to follow.

By the time Jack is released he is approaching the age of 18. He has a girlfriend, and their relationship is unstable and often violent. She soon becomes pregnant, and it is all too likely the cycle of Jack's early life is about to repeat itself.

Costs: Special education services, about $2000; two psychological and psychiatric assessments at $2000 each; three years for child welfare supervision at $2300 a year; one year for group home care at $36 500; three appearances in Youth Court at $1000; two police investigations at $1500 each and three police court attendances at $250 each; two years of probation supervision etc. at $1200; six months open custody at $38 500; one year closed custody at $91 500. Total = $188 550.
Grand Total for Jack's Career to Age 17 = $511 500.

The Moral of the Story

Jack's career as a repeat young offender illustrates some of the common features of how children and young people pass through the child welfare and young offender systems. Not only are these services expensive to provide, but also the offences themselves result in a cost to society in terms of the physical costs, personal injuries, and psychological harm experienced by victims.

Jack has a painful early life, and his offences cause pain to others. The cost of such pain is enormous and not easily calculated in dollar terms, which would require placing a figure on a lost life, or lost employment and lost enjoyment of life by victims and families. In addition, the costs of crime have to be calculated over time, because pain and suffering are not necessarily short-term in their effects.

Jack's story is not intended to suggest that the various services do not succeed in helping many young people. What it shows, in fact, is how important it is to invest early in helping young people and their families. Without this help, too many young people end up just like Jack, poised at the age of 18 to enter on a life of adult offending and to bring further costs to society and all who come in contact with them.

Source: Prevention, (Volume 1, Issue 1, p. 7), http://www.ps-sp.gc.ca/res/cp/nwslet/_fl/issue_1-en.pdf, National Crime Prevention Centre, 1999; Prevention, (Volume 1, Issue 2, p. 7), http://www.ps-sp.gc.ca/res/cp/nwslet/_fl/issue_2-en.pdf. National Crime Prevention Centre, 2000. Reproduced with the permission of the Minister of Public Works and Government Services, 2007.

yet typical, offender, and emphasizes the importance of investing in young people at the early stages of a delinquent lifestyle. The crime-prevention philosophy—be it a nurturant, protection/avoidance, or deterrence approach—will determine the tone and type of intervention policies adopted.

Summary

Efforts to reduce crime, although well intentioned, are fraught with political uncertainties resting largely upon fundamental disagreements within Canadian society itself as to the sources of crime and the most appropriate means of preventing and combatting it. One author summarizes the contemporary situation this way:

PART 3

334

**Crime in the
Modern World and
the Response to It**

Lack of a unified criminological framework has fostered short-sighted, inconsistent, and ineffective crime-control policies. Theoretical ambiguity made it easier for policymakers to base their decisions on politics rather than science. Lacking a reasonable complete and coherent explanation of the causes of crime, they have been free to shift the focus of crime-control efforts back and forth from individual-level to macro-level causes as the political pendulum swung from right to left. This erratic approach hindered crime-control efforts and fed the desperate belief that the problem of crime is intractable.[50]

Although answers to the crime problem appear to face formidable obstacles, all may not be lost. Fundamental social changes including the development of high moral values through education, the elimination (or significant reduction) of poverty, increased opportunities for success at all levels, and decriminalization of certain offences may all be combined some day into a workable strategy for the management of criminal activity.

Discussion Questions

1. This book emphasizes a social problems versus social responsibility theme. What types of crime-prevention social policies might be based on the social responsibility perspective? The social problems approach? Why?

2. What are the three types of crime-prevention strategies this chapter describes? Which comes closest to your own philosophy? Why?

3. What are the major differences between the social problems and social responsibilities approaches? Which one do you think would be most effective in responding to troubled youth such as Jack, whose story is found in Box 11.5. Why?

4. Explain the social epidemiological approach to reducing crime. In your opinion, is the approach worthwhile? Why or why not?

5. If you were in charge of government crime reduction and prevention efforts, what steps would you take to prevent and control crime in Canada? Why would you choose those particular approaches?

Weblinks

http://publicsafety.gc.ca/prg/cp/ncps_fundsindex-en.asp
National Crime Prevention Strategy. Information on Canada's crime-prevention strategy.

www.canada.justice.gc.ca/en/dept/pub/jc/index.html
Department of Justice Canada. Online newsletter, published quarterly. Good discussion of current issues within the criminal justice system.

www.crime-prevention-intl.org
International Centre for the Prevention of Crime. Information on crime-prevention initiatives worldwide.

http://www.peelpolice.on.ca/Crime%20Prevention.aspx
Peel Regional Police. Access to numerous crime-prevention articles, including many on CPTED.

www.cpted.net
International CPTED Association. This site is dedicated to creating a safe environment through the use of CPTED strategies. Links to the principles of CPTED.

http://www.cptedontario.ca
CPTED Ontario. Current information about CPTED initiatives, conferences, and news in Ontario.

www.canada.justice.gc.ca/en/index.html
Department of Justice Canada. Links to information about the Youth Justice Renewal Initiative and the *Youth Criminal Justice Act.*

Future Directions and Emerging Trends

As surely as the future will bring new forms of technology, it will bring new forms of crime.

—CYNTHIA MANSON AND CHARLES ARDAI [1]

Globalization will make it increasingly difficult for nation-states to ignore the criminal justice information of other countries.

—GREGORY HOWARD, GRAEME NEWMAN, WILLIAM PRIDEMORE [2]

LEARNING OUTCOMES

After reading this chapter, you should be able to

● discuss the concept of future criminology

● recognize the global and transnational nature of emerging trends

● realize the role of technology in emerging trends

● describe the advantages and challenges of a comparative approach to the study of criminology

Photofest.

IMPORTANT NAMES

Theodore Levitt
Richter H. Moore Jr.

IMPORTANT TERMS

futurists	migrant smuggling	phishing
globalization	human trafficking	computer virus
transnational crime	cyber-crime	comparative criminology
transnational organized crime	software piracy	
human smuggling	phone phreaking	

Introduction

Canadian criminologist Gwynn Nettler once told a story of two people passing on a street in New York City.[3] One carried a pint of whiskey; the other carried $100 in gold coins. In March 1933, near the end of the Prohibition era, the person with the alcohol would have been committing a crime, but the person carrying the gold would have been regarded as law-abiding. A year later, however, the same two people passing on the street would have occupied exactly the opposite legal positions. The repeal of Prohibition legalized carrying whiskey in most places, but gold hoarding became a federal crime in 1934, and remained so until 1974.

It is easy to look back in time and assess the legal standing of people like those in Nettler's story, but predicting what crimes the future will bring is far more difficult. Those who study the future are called **futurists**. Futurist criminologists try to imagine how crime will appear in both the near and distant future. Future criminology is the study of likely futures as they relate to crime and its control.

The future is an abstract concept through which human beings bring symbolic order to the "here and now" and meaning to past endeavours.[4] From our present point of view, multiple futures exist, each of which is probable and each of which may or may not come to pass. In other words, the future contains an almost limitless number of possibilities, any of which might unfold but only a few that actually will. The task of the futurist is to distinguish effectively between these impending possibilities, assessing the likelihood of each and making realistic forecasts based on such assessments.

Some assumptions about the future, such as estimates of future world populations, can be based on existing and highly credible public or private statistics and mathematical analyses of trends. Others, however, are more intuitive and result from the integration of a wide range of diverse materials derived from many different sources. As one futurist explains,

> before we can plan the future, we must make some assumptions about what that future will be like. . . . Assumptions about the future are not like assumptions in a geometry exercise. They are not abstract statements from which consequences can be derived with mathematical precision. But we need to make some assumptions about the future in order to plan it, prepare for it, and prevent undesired events from happening.[5]

International organizations such as the World Future Society bring ideas, people, and knowledge together to prepare for the future. Within criminology, the Society of Police Futurists International (PFI) concerns itself with research into future crime-prevention and crime-control policies.[6]

Futurists those who study the future; in the case of criminology, criminologists who try to imagine how crime will appear in both the near and distant future.

PART 3
338
**Crime in the
Modern World and
the Response to It**

Another group actively attempting to discern the future is the United Kingdom's government-led Foresight program, which "brings people, knowledge, and ideas together to look ahead and prepare for the future."[7] Foresight's Crime Prevention Panel released a report in 2001 entitled *Just around the Corner,* focusing on the year 2020.[8] The report provides a summation of the views of 60 experts given three tasks: to describe crimes of the near future, to identify methods to reduce and detect those crimes, and to decide what role science and technology will play in future criminality and crime prevention. According to Foresight's Crime Prevention Panel, a number of social characteristics will affect future crimes in Great Britain and throughout the world. One of these is what the panel calls "individuality and independence." The panel believes that greater individuality and personal independence will arise as traditional family forms decline over the next decade or two. Traditional limits on anti-social behaviour will erode, the panel predicts, as individuals gravitate toward membership in like-minded groups, many of which "may reinforce rather than challenge anti-social views."

A second social characteristic that will affect crime in the future, says the panel, is what it terms "Information Communication Technology (ICT) usage." The panel predicts that crimes like electronic theft and fraud will occur with increasing rapidity, reducing the likelihood that offenders can be caught. Websites are predicted to become highly targeted properties, and sites written in English will be the hardest hit. Such attacks will raise the need for increased acceptability of digital evidence in courts and will require jurors, judges, and attorneys to be educated in relevant technologies.

Technology is also leading to the growth of an impersonal society, says the panel, in which people meet and interact in virtual space rather than in physical society. As a consequence, the panel fears, physical space may become an increasingly hostile and dangerous place—"a dehumanized environment" in which "people may become less 'real' to one another leading to more extreme reactions, interactions, and the reluctance to intervene in conflicts."

A third social characteristic relevant to understanding and predicting future forms of criminality, according to the panel, is globalization. Globalization, which refers to the increasingly international character of social life, is having an impact on much of society, including technology, commerce, communication, and crime. "Already," says the panel, "crimes on the internet, drug dealing, and smuggling show the power of global crime and the difficulties it poses for local level law enforcement." Local crimes and small-time perpetrators will be replaced or supplemented by crimes and criminal groups with global scope, the panel predicts.

The panel notes that criminal organizations, like organizations everywhere, "are adapting to the opportunities offered by the flexibility of the internet." However, says the panel, modern technology offers individuals new opportunities to commit crimes that may be virtually unsolvable: "The clear danger is being at the mercy of a small technologically knowledgeable elite." At the same time, the panel warns, large numbers of people either won't have the opportunity to acquire advanced technological skills or will be unable to learn them. The consequence will be a technologically disenfranchised underclass whose existence will "further fuel crime and reduce the opportunities for access to mainstream society."

Globalization a complex series of economic, social, technological, cultural, and political changes seen as increasing interdependence, integration, and interaction between people and companies in disparate locations.

Globalization

Globalization is the term used to describe a complex series of economic, social, technological, cultural, and political changes seen as increasing, integration, and interaction between people and companies in disparate locations. **Theodore Levitt** is usually credited with coining the term "globalization" in an article he wrote in 1983 for the *Harvard Business Review* entitled "The Globalization of Markets."[9]

On a global scale, there appears to be a shared agreement that society is experiencing a period of unprecedented change. Both the substance and the pace of change are fundamentally different from what has occurred in past decades and centuries. No longer are sequences of events occurring in relative isolation or over longer spans of time. No longer are discrete groups of people affected by each change; rather, there is greater simultaneity of occurrence, swifter interpenetration, and increased feedback of one set of changes upon another.[10] Human societies across the globe have established progressively closer contacts. Jet airplanes, cheap telephone service, email, computers, huge oceangoing vessels, and instant capital flows have all made the world more interdependent than ever. Multinational corporations manufacture products in many countries and sell to consumers around the world. Money, technology, and raw materials move ever more swiftly across national borders. Along with products and finances, ideas and cultures circulate more freely. As a result, laws, economies, and social movements are forming at the international level.

The reality of globalization has been felt within the world of criminal activity as well. Indeed, globalization is making it impossible for Canadian policy makers to ignore criminal activity in other countries, especially where that crime is perpetrated by groups or organizations that cross national boundaries and borders. The globalization of crime has necessitated the enhanced coordination of law-enforcement efforts in different parts of the world. The recently ratified Council of Europe's *Convention on Cyber-Crime* binds the signatory countries to creating a minimum set of laws to deal with high-tech crimes. Signed by all members of the Council of Europe as well as Canada, the United States, Japan, and South Africa, it includes provisions that will ensure surveillance powers for governments and bind nations to helping each other gather evidence and enforce laws. Some are concerned that these new international powers will come at the expense of protection for citizens against government abuse. According to others, though, "globalization will make it increasingly difficult for nation-states to ignore the criminal justice information of other countries. Politicians and influential bureaucrats will be forced to answer as to why their country displays crime rates, prosecution rates, incarceration rates, or rates of violence or gun ownership that are strikingly different from similar countries."[11]

Transnational Crime

Transnational crime, or **transnational organized crime**, refers to unlawful activity undertaken and supported by organized criminal groups operating across national boundaries. At a recent summit meeting in Birmingham, England, G-8 leaders identified transnational criminal activity as one of the three major challenges facing the world in the 21st century. The leaders vowed to continue the fight against this worldwide problem which, they declared, threatens "to sap (economic) growth, undermine the rule of law, and damage the lives of individuals in all countries of the world."[12] In 2003, the United Nations (UN) made the issue of organized crime one of its priorities for the 21st century and ratified *The United Nations Convention against Transnational Organized Crime*. Supplementing the Convention are the *Protocol to Prevent, Suppress, and Punish Trafficking in Persons, Especially Women and Children*, the *Protocol against the Smuggling of Migrants by Land,*

Transnational crime or **transnational organized crime** refers to unlawful activity undertaken and supported by organized groups operating across national boundaries.

PART 3

340

Crime in the
Modern World and
the Response to It

Sea and Air, and the *Protocol against the Illicit Manufacture of and Trafficking in Firearms, Their Parts and Components and Ammunition.* The UN assists member states' governments in the efforts to ensure a comprehensive response to combatting transnational organized crime and drug trafficking include the monitoring and implementation of the Convention, the facilitation of information exchange, judicial cooperation and legal assistance between enforcement agencies, and leadership efforts in the collection, analysis, and dissemination of organized crime information at both the global and regional levels.[13]

As a signatory to the UN Convention and its protocols, Canada is a world partner in the effort to seek ways to prevent and control transnational organized crime. The Criminal Intelligence Service Canada (CISC) is an organization that provides the facilities to unite the criminal intelligence units of Canadian law enforcement agencies in the fight against organized crime and other serious crime in Canada. Its 2006 Annual Report contends that transnational criminal activity is a growing problem in Canada and that technological advances over the past 20 years have made national borders irrelevant to telecommunications and financial transactions, and have enabled the globalization of criminal activity.

Although statistics vary, CISC reports that there appear to be anywhere from five to eighteen active transnational criminal organizations represented in Canada. This includes Asian triads, Colombian cartels, Italian Mafia groups, (the most influential being the Sicilian Mafia), Russian/Eastern European *mafiyas*, Nigerian crime groups, and major outlaw motorcycle gangs.

Whereas crime syndicates of the past were involved in illegal street-level activities such as drug trafficking, prostitution, illegal gambling, loan sharking, and extortion, CISC reports that today's organized crime syndicates have become quasi-corporate in their activities and are now involved in arms dealing, large-scale insurance and financial fraud, environmental crime, the trafficking and smuggling of humans, money laundering, bank fraud, gasoline tax fraud, and corruption.[14]

Emerging Crimes

Murder, theft, sexual assault, and the other types of "everyday" crime that have become mainstays of contemporary criminological analysis will continue to occur in the future, to be sure, but other new and emergent forms of criminality will grow in frequency and number. One recent prediction, for example, contends that by the year 2025, "socially significant crime—that is, the crimes that have the widest negative effects—in the advanced nations will be increasingly economic and computer based. Examples include disruption of business, theft, introduction of maliciously false information, and tampering with medical records, air traffic control, or national-security systems."[15] Another futurist prediction states that "the top guns of twenty-first-century criminal organizations will be educated, highly sophisticated, computer-literate individuals who can wield state-of-the-art information technology to the best advantage—for themselves and for their organizations."[16]

In a wide-ranging overview of future crimes, **Richter H. Moore Jr.** painted a picture of future criminality that includes many dimensions. Already present are elements of what Moore predicted: "Computer hackers are changing bank records, credit accounts and reports, criminal-history files, and educational, medical, and even military records."[17] Identity manipulation, said Moore, will be a nexus of future criminality. "By the twenty-first century," he wrote, "genetic-based records will include a birth-to-death dossier of a person and will be the method of criminal identification." Already, the United States military is using genetic testing to assign unique identification codes to each of its soldiers. In the event of war, such codes will allow for the identification of human remains from as little as a single cell. DNA coding, unique to each of us, may soon form the basis for nearly foolproof identification technologies, which will take the science of personal identification far beyond fingerprinting, blood-type matching, or photography. The science of bioengineering, however, which is now undergoing clinical trials in the treatment of various forms of disease, may soon be clandestinely employed for the illegal modification of human DNA, with the goal of effectively altering a person's identity. It is but one more step by which the theft of computer-based genetic identification records could make it possible for one person to effectively imitate another in our future society.

Moore describes many other crimes of the future. Within a few decades, he says, "criminal organizations will be able to afford their own satellites." Drug trafficking and money laundering operations could be coordinated via satellite communications, couriers and shipments could be tracked, and satellite surveillance could provide alerts of enforcement activity. Likewise, says Moore, "prostitution rings will use modern technology to coordinate global activities," and children and fetuses may "become subject to unlawful trafficking." The illegal disposal of toxic materials, an activity that organized crime has already explored, may become even more profitable for criminal entrepreneurs as many more hazardous substances are produced in the face of ever-tighter controls. The supply of nuclear materials and military-quality armaments to "private armies ... terrorists, hate groups, questionable regimes, independent crime groups, and individual criminals" will be a fact of life in the 21st century, as will the infiltration of governments and financial institutions by sophisticated criminals whose activities are supported by large, illegally acquired fortunes.

Within Canada, increasing attention is being paid to these emerging realities of criminal activity. Of primary concern to government and law enforcement agencies is the transnational nature of more and more criminal activity, which is enhanced by the use and manipulation of a variety of types of technology. Within the borders of the nation, increased attention is being paid to the apparent strengthening and expansion of street gangs in all areas of the country. It is to some of these emerging criminal activities that we will now turn our attention.

Trafficking and Smuggling of Humans

The fact that slavery—in the form of human trafficking—still exists in the 21st century shames us all. Governments, international organizations and civil society are devoting considerable efforts to counter it, but there is still an information deficit about the extent of this tragedy. Only by understanding its depth, breadth and scope can we design policies to fight it. This understanding still eludes us: efforts to counter trafficking have so far been uncoordinated and inefficient.[18]

One of the most significant increases in organized transnational crime has been in the area of the smuggling and trafficking of human beings. According to the *United Nations Convention against Transnational Organized Crime,* **human smuggling** or **migrant smuggling** includes the "procurement of illegal entry of a person into a country of which the person is not a national or permanent resident in order to obtain direct or indirect financial or other material benefit."[19] **Human trafficking**, on the other hand, involves "the

Human smuggling or **migrant smuggling** the facilitation of illegal entry of a person into a country for financial gain.

Human trafficking the displacement of an individual by means of coercion, deceit, or violence for the purpose of exploitation.

PART 3

342

Crime in the
Modern World and
the Response to It

recruitment, transportation, transfer, harbouring or receipt of persons, by means of the threat or use of force or other forms of coercion, of abduction, of fraud, of deception, of the abuse of power or of a position of vulnerability or of the giving or receiving of payments or benefits to achieve the consent of a person having control over another person, for the purpose of exploitation. Exploitation shall include, at a minimum, the exploitation of the prostitution of others or other forms of sexual exploitation, forced labour or services, slavery or practices similar to slavery, servitude, or the removal of organs."[20] While it is often difficult to draw the distinction between these two illegal behaviours, smuggling of humans is usually limited to the transportation of individuals to the country of destination, after which the relationship between the smugglers and smuggled person ends. Trafficking, on the other hand, involves the delivery of persons to individuals or organizations who have paid for their delivery and the repayment of those debts to the traffickers by the trafficked persons, usually through prostitution or forced labour.[21] Finally, human smuggling is always transnational whereas human trafficking may not be; trafficking can occur regardless of whether victims are taken to another country or only moved from one place to another within the same country.

Reports estimate that anywhere between 700 000 and four million people are trafficked worldwide each year (See Box 12.1). The main targets are women and children in Third World countries who are recruited by criminals and promised a better life abroad. Instead, they are often sold into the sex trade and held against their wills. A comprehensive report released in 2006 by the United Nations Office on Drugs and Crime (UNODC) entitled *Trafficking in Persons: Global Patterns*, identifies countries of origin, transit, and destination as they pertain to the trafficking of human beings. It reports that Canada ranks high in terms of a destination country; however, the scope of these criminal activities in Canada remains a small percentage of the international (or even the North American) criminal market.[22] Canada is largely a destination and a transit country for women who are trafficked for the purposes of sexual exploitation. Most arrive from Asia, Latin America, Russia, and Eastern Europe. According to the latest strategic intelligence assessment on human trafficking produced by the Royal Canadian Mounted Police's Criminal Intelligence Directorate (CID), human trafficking has become "a global business that generates huge profits for traffickers and organized crime groups, rivaling those of drugs and weapons smuggling. [It] is one of the most acute international problems garnering tens of millions of dollars annually for organized crime."[23] Based on various reports, CID estimates that anywhere between 1500 and 2200 persons are trafficked from Canada into the United States each year.

Trafficking in human beings is a global issue, and illegal migrants and trafficking victims have become another commodity in a larger realm of criminal commerce involving other commodities, such as narcotic drugs, firearms or weapons, and money laundering, all of which generate illicit revenues or seek to reduce risks for traffickers. To date, the lack of systematic research in this area means that reliable data on the trafficking of human beings that would allow comparative analyses and the design of preventative measures is limited. The relatively low risks associated with trafficking and the potential for substantial profits have, in some cases, induced criminals to become involved as an alternative to other, riskier criminal pursuits. Furthermore, victims are intimidated by traffickers, both in destination countries, where they fear deportation or prosecution for offences such as prostitution or illegal immigration, and in their countries of origin, where they are often vulnerable to retaliation or re-victimization. As a result, many are reluctant to cooperate with criminal justice authorities, making detection and prosecution difficult. Supporting

Fact Sheet on Human Trafficking Box 12.1

Over the past decade, trafficking in human beings has reached epidemic proportions. No country is immune. The search for work abroad has been fuelled by economic disparity, high unemployment and the disruption of traditional livelihoods. Traffickers face few risks and can earn huge profits by taking advantage of large numbers of potential immigrants.

Trafficking in human beings is a crime in which victims are moved from poor environments to more affluent ones, with the profits flowing in the opposite direction, a pattern often repeated at the domestic, regional and global levels. It is believed to be growing fastest in Central and Eastern Europe and the former Soviet Union. In Asia, girls from villages in Nepal and Bangladesh—the majority of whom are under 18—are sold to brothels in India for $1000. Trafficked women from Thailand and the Philippines are increasingly being joined by women from other countries in Southeast Asia. Europol estimates that the industry is now worth several billion dollars a year.

Trafficking in human beings is not confined to the sex industry. Children are trafficked to work in sweatshops as bonded labour, and men work illegally in the "three D-jobs"—dirty, difficult and dangerous. A recent CIA report estimated that between 45 000 and 50 000 women and children are brought to the United States every year under false pretenses and are forced to work as prostitutes, abused labourers or servants. UNICEF estimates that more than 200 000 children are enslaved by cross-border smuggling in West and Central Africa. The children are often "sold" by unsuspecting parents who believe their children are going to be looked after, learn a trade or be educated.

In many cases, trafficking patterns are also related to conflict situations as combatants (or even peacekeepers) create a market for the services of victims and as the effects of conflict erode the capacity of law enforcement and other authorities to combat the problem. As a form of organized crime, trafficking can also threaten sustainable development and the rule of law, as illicit profits are used for corruption, other criminal activities and, in some cases, terrorism. The assistance, support and rehabilitation of victims are also a significant problem, particularly in source countries where resources are often limited and, in the case of trafficked children, where the need is most acute.

Additionally, the spread of HIV/AIDS among victims trafficked into prostitution makes victim support and repatriation a public health issue. The treatment of victims as a commodity is also a violation of their most basic rights to freedom, autonomy and human dignity. Although these violations are committed by traffickers, it is important for States to respond to alleviate the harm caused to victims by trafficking where possible and, at a minimum, to not cause further harm. Measures against trafficking should also respect the basic substantive and procedural rights of those accused of trafficking.

Trafficking is fostered, in part, by social and economic disparities that create a supply of victims seeking to migrate and a demand for sexual and other services that provide the economic impetus for trafficking. Deterrence and criminal punishments are important elements, but addressing the underlying conditions which drive both supply and demand are also necessary. Another important preventative measure is public information to mobilize support for effective laws, to raise the awareness of key law enforcement and other officials, and to make the socially marginalized groups from whom victims are often recruited more aware of the reality of trafficking and less likely to be deceived when approached by traffickers.

Source: United Nations Office on Drugs and Crime (UNODC).

PART 3

344

**Crime in the
Modern World and
the Response to It**

and protecting victims are critical elements in the fight against trafficking to increase their willingness to cooperate with authorities and as a necessary means of rehabilitation.[24]

The adoption of the UNODC *Protocol to Prevent, Suppress, and Punish Trafficking in Persons, especially Women and Children* in 2000 has initiated the cooperation of all countries to work together to produce and share greater information on the trafficking of humans, to enact domestic laws making human trafficking an offence, to ensure that such legislation applies to victims of all ages and both sexes, and to implement measures to provide for the physical, psychological, and social recovery of victims. In Canada, trafficking in humans wasn't recognized as an offence until November 2001, when Bill C-11 amended the former *Immigration Act* to include fines of up to $1 million and life imprisonment for the trafficking of people. The new *Immigration and Refugee Protection Act* (*IRPA*) was proclaimed in June 2002. Prior to the *IRPA*, police could lay *Criminal Code* charges only for such offences as kidnapping and forcible confinement in an attempt to combat trafficking activity.[25]

Nevertheless, even with the appropriate legislation, it is difficult to lay charges for human trafficking since these are not regular criminal cases. The lack of human trafficking charges speaks in large part to the very covert nature of these crimes, the reluctance of victims to come forward, and the complexity of human trafficking investigations that often span multiple international jurisdictions. In 2004, the RCMP established a new Human Trafficking Unit to provide guidance and analytical support for domestic investigations across Canada and to mount joint investigations with foreign law enforcement agencies. The unit shares information with the Canadian Security and Intelligence Service (CSIS) and works to coordinate domestic efforts of individual police services across the country and to link these efforts to the protocols, investigative standards, and training in the international arena.[26]

International Traffic in Human Organs

The Current Reality—Supply and Demand
Over the past 30 years, human organ transplantation has been transformed from an experimental procedure performed in highly developed Western countries to a medical intervention carried out in hospitals and clinics worldwide, saving lives around the globe. The extent to which and speed at which the technology has advanced have raised a number of critical concerns within the international law enforcement and human rights fields.

The most critical issue surrounds the reality that the supply of human organs has not kept pace with the demand. For example, despite a well-organized collection and distribution system, Canada has over 4000 people on organ donor waiting lists, and five people per week die while on the list.[27] The gap between demand and supply is even more acute in countries where religious or cultural considerations inhibit organ donation. The shortfall in available organs has generated a desperate search for them; many patients are prepared to travel outside of their home nations to secure a transplant, and many are prepared to put aside questions about how the organ was obtained.

The scarcity of human organs has also provided incentives to physicians, hospital administrators, and government officials in a number of countries to undertake ethically questionable strategies for obtaining them. They are motivated less by a desire to meet the needs of their country's patients than to secure payments from foreign patients. Countries such as India and China have been cited as among those whose readily accessible sale of organs and significantly lower cost ($15 000 to $20 000 for a kidney transplant, rather than

$40 000 to $70 000) have attracted patients from around the world. From the perspective of many patients, the availability of the organ outweighs the cost. But from the perspective of an Indian or Chinese health facility, the income that is earned through this traffic is substantial.[28]

Organs from Executed Prisoners
In a detailed report entitled *Report into Allegations of Organ Harvesting of Falun Gong Practitioners in China*, Canadian authors David Matas and David Kilgour contend that there is significant proof to allege that the organs of Falun Gong adherents who have been systematically arrested, imprisoned, tortured, and executed since the late 1990s have been harvested for transplant in Chinese hospitals.[29] Matas and Kilgour allege that the number of transplants performed in China far outnumbers the sources of the organs. Based on their research, they contend that there were about 30 000 transplants in China before the year 2000, but that the number of transplants between 2000 and 2005 has skyrocketed to 60 000.

They go on to contend that legitimate sources for organs (donations, brain dead patients) accounted for 18 500 transplants between 1994 and 1999, and they argue that this number is unlikely to be significantly different for the 2000 to 2005 period. They conclude that the organs for the remaining 41 500 transplants were illegally harvested from Falun Gong practitioners and sold.[30] China openly admits to the harvesting and transplant of organs from executed prisoners and has enacted legislation entitled *Rules Concerning the Utilization of Corpses or Organs from the Corpses of Executed Prisoners* to govern the practice. It provides that corpses or organs of executed prisoners can be harvested if no one claims the body, if the executed prisoner volunteers to have his/her corpse so used, or if the family consents.

The World Health Organization (WHO) has found the sale of organs to violate the *Universal Declaration of Human Rights* as well as its own constitution: "The human body and its parts cannot be the subject of commercial transactions. Accordingly, giving or receiving payment . . . for organs should be prohibited." It has condemned the practice and called upon national medical associations to "severely discipline the physicians involved." Along with organizations such as the World Medical Association and the International Council of the Transplantation Society, The WHO has unequivocally condemned the practice and has called upon physicians to refuse to transplant organs "if they have reason to believe that the organs concerned have been the subject of commercial transactions."[31]

Allegations of Kidnap and Murder for Organs
Questions and allegations about the kidnapping and murder of infants and babies for their organs have circulated within the international community for decades. Incidents are alleged to have occurred in Honduras, Guatemala, Argentina, and Brazil. In a Report of the Special Rapporteur to the United Nations Commission on Human Rights entitled *Sale of Children*, the question about the extent of the sale of children for the purposes of organ transplantation was raised while a Committee of European Parliament recently charged: "Organized trafficking in organs exists in the same way as trafficking in drugs. . . . It involved killing people to remove organs which can be sold at a profit. To deny the existence of such trafficking is comparable to denying the existence of the ovens and gas chambers during the last war."[32]

There is considerable evidence that infants and young children are kidnapped for the adoption market, and it is known that older boys and girls are sold or kidnapped for the sex trade. It would seem logical to conclude that infants and children are also abducted for their organs. To date, however, actual proof seems difficult to document.

PART 3

346

**Crime in the
Modern World and
the Response to It**

Cyber-crime

Technology and criminology have always been closely linked. The con artist who uses telephones in a financial scam, the robber who uses a firearm and drives a getaway car, even the murderer who wields a knife—all employ at least rudimentary forms of technology in the crimes they commit.

Technology, of course, can be employed by both crime fighters and lawbreakers. Early forms of technology, including the telegraph, the telephone, and the automobile, were embraced by agents of law enforcement as soon as they became available. Evidence derived from fingerprint and ballistics analysis is routinely employed by prosecutors, and emerging technologies promise to keep criminologists and law enforcement agents in step with high-tech offenders.

Technology that is taken for granted today was at one time almost unthinkable. Telephones, for example, were invented just over a century ago, and mass-produced automobiles are newer still. Even firearms are of relatively recent origin if one considers the entire history of humankind, and the manufacture of contemporary cutting instruments would be impossible were it not for an accumulation of technological expertise beginning with the progress in metallurgy during the Iron Age.

As technology advances, it facilitates new forms of behaviour. Just as we can be sure that everyday life in the future will be substantially different from life today, so, too, can we be certain that tomorrow's crimes will differ from those of today. In the future, personal crimes of violence and traditional property crimes will undoubtedly continue to occur, but advancing technology will create new and as yet unimaginable opportunities for criminals positioned to take advantage of it and of the power such technology will afford.

Cyber-crime a criminal offence involving a computer as the object of the crime, or the tool used to commit a material component of the offence.

Cyber-crime, also referred to as "computer crime," "computer-related crime," "net crime," "high-tech crime," and "internet crime," is generally defined as "a criminal offence involving a computer as the object of the crime, or the tool used to commit a material component of the offence."[33] The Canadian Police College recognizes two broad categories of cyber-crime—one in which the computer is the *tool* of the crime and one in which the computer is the *object* of the crime. Types of criminal behaviour in the first category include traditional crimes that are now being perpetrated more widely through the use of the internet. They include child pornography, criminal harassment, fraud, theft of intellectual property and information, and the sale of humans, illegal goods, and substances. The second category of cyber-crime speaks to relatively new crimes that are related more specifically to computer technology; it includes such activities as hacking or unauthorized use of computer systems, defacing of websites, and the creation and malicious dissemination of computer viruses.[34] The Federal Bureau of Investigation (FBI) in the United States recognizes five types of computer crime: (1) internal computer crimes, such as viruses, (2) internet and telecommunications crimes such as illegal hacking, (3) support of criminal enterprises such as databases supporting drug distribution, (4) computer manipulation crimes including embezzlement, and (5) hardware, software, and information theft.[35] (See Table 12.1 for a more detailed breakdown of the categories of computer crimes as defined by the FBI.)

A uniform definition of cyber-crime has not been established, however, either at the international or Canadian level. In fact, within Canada, only a handful of Canadian police services have a specialized unit responsible for the definition, policies, procedures, and

Table 12.1

Categories of Computer Crime

Internal Computer Crimes	**Support of Criminal Enterprises**
Trojan horses	Databases to support drug distribution
Logic bombs	Databases to support loan-sharking
Trapdoors	Databases to support illegal gambling
Viruses	Databases to keep records of illegal client transactions
	Electronic money laundering
Internet and Telecommunications Crimes	
Phone phreaking	**Computer-Manipulation Crimes**
Hacking	Embezzlement
Denial of service attacks	Electronic fund transfer fraud
Illegal websites	Other fraud/phishing
Dissemination of illegal material (i.e., child pornography)	Extortion threats/electronic terrorism
Misuse of telephone systems	
Theft of telecommunications services	**Hardware, Software, and Information Theft**
Illegal eavesdropping	Software piracy (warez)
Illegal intenet-based gambling	Thefts of computers
	Thefts of microprocessor chips
	Thefts of trade secrets and proprietary information
	Identify theft

investigation of cyber-crimes. Other countries around the world are looking for ways to ensure that these activities are properly investigated and reported. The Uniform Crime Reporting National Incident-Based Reporting System (NIBRS) in the United States includes a category that identifies computer-related crimes.[36] Currently, Canada does not have a uniform method of collecting data on cyber-crime activity.[37] Recent recommendations by Canadian officials have included the addition of a data element to the Uniform Crime Reporting Survey to identify *Criminal Code* offences involving computers/internet as the object or tool used to commit the crime.[38]

Computers as a Tool of Crime

The 21st century has been described by some as the epitome of the post-industrial information age. Information, as many now recognize, is vital to the success of any endeavour, and certain forms of information hold nearly incalculable value. Patents on new products, the chemical composition of innovative and effective drugs, corporate marketing strategies, and the financial resources of competing corporations are all forms of information whose illegitimate access might bestow unfair advantages upon unscrupulous competitors. Imagine, for example, the financial wealth and market share that would accrue to the first pharmaceutical company to patent an effective AIDS cure. Imagine, as well, the potential profitability inherent in the information describing the chemical composition of that drug—especially to a competitor who might beat the legitimate originator of the substance to the patent desk or who might use stolen information in a later bid to challenge patents already issued.

High-tech criminals seeking illegitimate access to computerized information and to the databases that contain it have taken a number of routes. One is the path of direct access, by which office workers or corporate spies, planted as seemingly innocuous employees, violate positions of trust and use otherwise legitimate work-related entry to a company's computer resources to acquire wanted information. Such interlopers typically steal data during business hours under the guise of normal work routines.

PART 3

348

**Crime in the
Modern World and
the Response to It**

Another path of illegal access, called "computer trespass," involves remote access to targeted machines. Anyone equipped with a home computer and a little bit of knowledge about computer modems, telecommunications, and log-on procedures has easy access to numerous computer systems across the country. Many such systems have few, if any, security procedures in place to thwart would-be invaders. In one case, for example, a Silicon Valley software company learned that a software developer who had been fired had been using her telephone to enter the company's computers.[39] By the time she was caught, she had copied several million dollars' worth of the company's programs. It was later learned that the stolen software had been slated for illicit transmission to collaborators in Taiwan. Had the scheme succeeded, many thousands of "pirated" copies of the software would have been distributed at great financial loss to the legitimate copyright owners.

Some criminal perpetrators intend simply to destroy or to alter data without otherwise accessing or copying the information. Disgruntled employees, mischievous computer hackers, business competitors, and others may all have varied degrees of interest in destroying a company's records or computer capabilities.

Software piracy the unauthorized and illegal copying of software programs.

Software piracy, or the unauthorized and illegal copying of software programs, is rampant. The Software and Information Industry Association (SIIA) distinguishes among various forms of software piracy:[40]

- Softlifting: purchasing a single licensed copy of software and loading the same copy onto several computers
- Internet piracy: making unauthorized copies of copyrighted software available to others electronically via the internet
- Software counterfeiting: illegally duplicating and distributing copyrighted software in a form designed to make it appear to be legitimate
- Original equipment manufacturer (OEM) unbundling: selling as stand-alone those software programs that were intended to be bundled with specific accompanying hardware
- Hard disk loading: installing unauthorized copies of software onto the hard disks of personal computers, often as an incentive for the end user to buy the hardware from that particular hardware vendor
- Renting: unauthorized renting of software for temporary installation, use, or copying

According to the Business Software Alliance, global losses from software piracy totalled $29 billion in 2003.[41] North America (at $7.23 billion), Asia ($7.55 billion), and Western Europe ($9.60 billion) accounted for the vast majority (83 percent) of worldwide revenue losses. Some countries have especially high rates of illegal use. Of all the computer software in use in China, for example, it is estimated that 92 percent has been illegally copied.

According to some experts, losses like these may be just the beginning. As one technological visionary observes, "Our society is about to feel the impact of the first generation of children who have grown up using computers. The increasing sophistication of hackers suggests that computer crime will soon soar, as members of this new generation are tempted to commit more serious offenses."[42]

While the theft or damage of information represents one area of illegitimate criminal activity, the use of technology in direct furtherance of criminal enterprise constitutes another. Illegal activity based on advanced technologies is as varied as the technologies themselves. Nuclear blackmail may represent the extreme technologically based criminal threat, whereas telephone fraud and phone "phreaking" are examples of low-end crimes that depend on modern technology for their commission.

One of the earliest forms of cyber-crime was **phone phreaking**. Phone phreaks use special dial-up access codes and other restricted technical information to avoid long-distance charges. Some are able to place calls from pay phones, while others fool telephone equipment into billing other callers. As a top telecommunications security expert explains, "Many organizations discover they have been victims of telephone fraud only after their telephone bill arrives in a carton instead of an envelope."[43]

A new form of phone phreaking emerged about 10 years ago. It involves the electronic theft of cellular telephone numbers and access codes. Thieves armed with simple mail-order scanners and low-end computers can "literally grab a caller's phone number and identification number out of the air."[44] Say experts, "Those numbers are [then] used to program computer chips, which are placed inside other cellular phones—or 'clones'—so the long-distance calls appear on the victim's bill."[45]

A relatively new form of high-technology fraud is phishing. **Phishing** is a scam that uses official-looking email messages to steal valuable information such as credit card numbers, social security numbers, user IDs, and passwords from victims. The email messages appear to come from a user's bank, credit card company, retail store, or ISP and generally inform the recipients that some vital information in their account urgently needs to be updated. Those who respond are provided with an official-looking Web form on which they can enter their private financial information. Once the information is submitted, it enters the phisher's database.

The Anti-Phishing Working Group—a coalition of banks and internet service providers—recently estimated that a typical phishing scheme reaches up to 1 million email inboxes. The watchdog group had identified more than 1000 different scams by 2004.[46] Some observers have noted that in addition to losses suffered by individuals and institutions, phishing has the potential to threaten the viability of e-commerce and to call into question the safety of all Web-based financial transactions.[47]

See Box 12.2 for the text of an online quiz, developed by Volunteer Toronto with the help of the RCMP and other Fraud Forum Council Partners, to educate the public about frauds and scams that victimize Canadians, many of which are perpetrated through the use of computers. You can complete the quiz at **www.abcfraud.ca**.

One form of cyber-crime that continues to challenge law enforcement officials and legal professionals alike is the commission of virtual crimes on the internet. For example, is it possible for authorities to criminalize and prosecute individuals who engage in virtual acts of pornography or sexual assault? The popular internet program *Second Life* allows users to interact in a virtual world and engage in individual and group activities, and create and trade items (virtual property) and services from one another. One such interaction, known as "ageplay," has users participating in virtual sexual activity between two adults, one of whom assumes the role, and the physical appearance, of a child. Should ageplay and other virtual versions of real crimes be against Canadian law?

If we assume that virtual sexual activity or sexual assault is *possible* in an online world like *Second Life*, the issue then becomes whether it inflicts a "harm" that the criminal law should address. A real online virtual sexual assault does inflict "harm" on the victims, but it is a psychic "harm." Canadian criminal law has historically dealt only with real, physical harm to persons and property. It did, however, begin to address a form of psychic harm a number of years ago with the introduction of the criminal harassment (stalking) laws. That trend has accelerated somewhat with the expanded use of this law to target those who use online communications such as email to inflict serious or substantial emotional distress on another person. Would virtual sexual assault be prosecutable under this statute? Is there an identified victim? What happens if the conduct is not repeated but occurs only once?

Phone phreaking use of special dial-up access codes and other restricted technical information to avoid long-distance charges.

Phishing use of official-looking email messages to steal valuable information such as credit card numbers, social security numbers, user IDs, and passwords from victims.

PART 3

350

**Crime in the
Modern World and
the Response to It**

Fraud ... Can You Recognize It? Report It? Stop It?

Box 12.2

ARE YOU A TARGET?

Question 1: Fraud is the number one crime against seniors.

Question 2: Con artists target people with lots of money to lose.

Question 3: Con artists give the impression that they are friendly, helpful, and trustworthy and won't usually use physical violence.

Question 4: If I lose only a small amount of money, then I am not a victim. I just made a mistake and should learn a lesson.

ONLINE SCAMS

Question 1: You need a loan and your credit is not the best. You go on the internet to see what you can find. Through your research, you find a company that has no complaints or negative feedback. You contact these friendly people and they will approve your loan after you have "secured" it with a small fee. This is a no-risk proposition, right?

Question 2: Only do business over the internet if the website you are looking at is professional looking and includes contact information.

Question 3: Promptly respond to any emails you receive, especially if your bank urgently needs your help to fix your account and asks you to confirm your identity.

Question 4: You have the latest computer with a current operating system, virus/spyware detection tools, and a firewall, and you check for and download updates on a daily basis. You know however that computers cannot be 100% safe. For that reason you are just a little extra careful when you use your personal information online.

Question 5: You have read and understood everything there is to read about online scams and you now have become an expert in your own right. You can check this item off your list and stop worrying because you are protected and aware.

CREDIT/DEBIT CARD FRAUD

Question 1: The number one way that con artists get people's identity is by stealing passports.

Question 2: The first thing to do if you think your credit card has been compromised is to cancel it.

Question 3: If you go to use your bank card at an ATM machine, and there are people loitering outside the machine, no problem, right?

Question 4: It is safe to give any caller the three-digit number from the back of your credit card.

Question 5: The people who benefit from credit and debit card theft are petty thieves looking to buy merchandise for themselves.

IDENTITY THEFT

Question 1: You think you are a victim of identity theft. The first thing you should do is call your financial institutions and local police.

Question 2: When you get rid of any documents with personal information, such as bank or credit card statements, transaction records, insurance forms, or even when you discard your computer hard drive, you should throw them directly in the garbage or recycling.

Question 3: When you get your bank account and credit card statements, you should read them and verify that the transactions listed are in fact ones you made.

Question 4: When you create an email password, you should use your date of birth or that of your spouse or children.

Question 5: The best place to keep your personal identification documents (Social Insurance Number (SIN), passport, birth certificate, citizenship papers) is in your wallet.

Source: Developed by Volunteer Toronto with the help of the RCMP and other Fraud Forum Council Partners. http://www. abcfraud.ca/ (Accessed Nov 19, 2006).

Law enforcement officials have also come to recognize the internet as a tool in their investigation of conventional crime. Recently, Sergeant Jorge Lasso of the Hamilton Police Service turned to the internet to help him do his job as a police detective. Specifically, he wanted to circulate a surveillance video while investigating an apparent murder near a hip-hop club. He thought of his own children, who are in their twenties, considered their main source of information, and concluded that the internet was the best way to communicate with youth who might be able to assist him. So rather than just showing on local television stations the video from the surveillance camera, which shows two men whom the police want to question, Sergeant Lasso also posted it on *YouTube*. Even though the *YouTube* post did not ultimately bring the police in Hamilton, Ontario, any closer to finding the culprits, Sergeant Lasso said the experiment was still worthwhile. It seems that other police services have followed suit; in London, England, the police have used the *YouTube* site as a means of distributing an appeal for help from the parents of a murder victim.[48]

Computers as an Object of Crime Not all computer crime is committed for financial gain. Some types of computer crime, including the creation and transmission of destructive computer viruses, "worms," and other malicious forms of programming code, might better be classified as "criminal mischief." Perhaps not surprisingly, these types of activities are typically associated with young, technologically sophisticated male miscreants seeking a kind of clandestine recognition from their computer-savvy peers. Computer crimes committed by youthful and idealistic offenders may represent a new form of juvenile delinquency—one aimed at expressing dissatisfaction with the status quo.

Viruses have already shown signs of becoming effective terrorist-like tools in the hands of young, disaffected "technonerds" intent on attacking or destroying existing social institutions. A **computer virus** is simply a computer program that is designed to secretly invade computer systems and either to modify the way in which they operate or to alter the information they store.[49] Other types of destructive programs are logic bombs, worms, and Trojan horse routines. Distinctions among these programs are based on either the way in which they infect targeted machines or the way in which they behave once they have managed to find their way into a computer.

Viruses may spread from one machine to another via modem or high-speed cable and DSL connections (when files are downloaded), through networks or direct links and through the exchange of floppy disks, CD-ROMs, or magnetic backup media. Most viruses hide inside executable computer software, or in the so-called boot sectors of floppy or hard disks. Recently, however, rogue codes known as "macro viruses" have been secreted into text documents. Viruses don't infect only desktop and laptop machines. Some viruses have been written that can interfere with the operation of popular handheld devices, including personal digital assistants (PDAs) and mobile phones.

Perhaps the most insidious forms of destructive programming making the rounds of the computer world today are polymorphic viruses. A polymorphic virus is one that uses advanced encryption techniques to assemble varied (yet entirely operational) clones of itself. Hence, polymorphic viruses have the ability to alter themselves once they have infected a computer. This strategy is effective in circumventing most security devices that depend on scanning techniques to recognize viral signatures. Simply put, when viruses change, they can no longer be recognized. Unfortunately, although many hardware devices and software products now on the market offer some degree of virus protection to individual and commercial users, new viruses are constantly being created that may soon have

Computer virus a computer program designed to secretly invade computer systems in order either to modify the way in which they operate or to alter the information they store.

PART 3
352
**Crime in the
Modern World and
the Response to It**

The Use of Biometric Technology

Box 12.3

People have always used individual traits for identification, whether a physical attribute such as a scar or birthmark or an assigned trait such as a signature or password. In today's world, many of these methods are no longer considered secure. The search for better means of identification and verification has led to the development of advancements in technologies that are being labelled *biometrics* because they apply statistical methods to biological observations and phenomena. The use of biometric technologies in the prevention of crime mostly involves identification, whereas verification is more common in commercial uses. When the police lift a fingerprint from a crime scene and match it against fingerprints in a database, they are *identifying* the culprit. The Automated Teller Machine (ATM) that uses a fingerprint instead of a number and then confirms your identity against an encoded "reference" fingerprint is *verifying* your identity.

FINGER SCANNING

The potential applications of using fingerprints are being made possible by the development of automated finger scanning. Optical finger-scanners, which work in a way similar to a photo scanner, have been in use for over a decade and are starting to be replaced by other methods. One of these methods is called *capacitive scanning*. It measures the electrical charge produced by the contact of the fingertip with an array of tiny capacitors mounted onto a silicon microchip. Because the ridges will make better contact with the capacitors than the valleys will, this technique generates an image of the fingerprint that can be processed in the same way as an image produced by optical scanning. Fingerprint verification is already being used to control access to personal computers, cell phones and ATMs. Some predict a time when it will be used to unlock car doors, open briefcases, verify identity over the internet, facilitate travel across international borders, and prevent voter fraud.

RETINA AND IRIS SCANNING

Retina and iris scanning seem to have considerable potential, especially since the patterns in both these parts of the eye are unique to the individual. The retina is the innermost layer of the eyeball "wall" and is criss-crossed by tiny blood vessels that form a unique pattern that does not change over an individual's lifetime. Retina scanning can map, code, and compare these blood vessel patterns. The iris, or coloured part of the eye, contains about 260 unchangeable characteristics (compared to fewer than 40 in fingerprints) that can be scanned by video camera, coded by algorithms, and then compared. Of the two eye-scanning technologies,

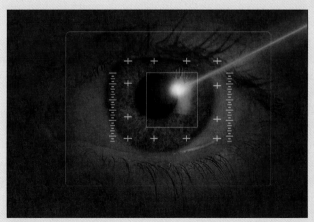

An iris scan
Jupiter Unlimited.

▶ iris-scanning is the more likely to gain in popularity for a number of reasons, one of which is that it can be done at a distance of a metre or so, in contrast to retina scanning, which must be done at close range.

OTHER BIOMETRIC TECHNOLOGIES

Hand geometry—Since the exact shape of the hand and the relative lengths of the fingers and thumb vary between individuals, hand geometry has been considered as a potentially useful biometric.

Typing patterns—Another kind of biometric technology looks at behavioural characteristics. Keyboard recognition technology assesses the typing style of the user. It determines "dwell time" (the time that each key is depressed), "flight time" (the time taken to move between keys), and a number of other characteristics, such as typing errors. An algorithm is used to code these patterns so that when the computer is used at a later time, the software compares the user's typing pattern against the template.

Other—Many other biometric technologies for identity verification are under development, including voice recognition, face recognition (systems are now being developed to assist police and security agencies to identify suspects in crowds), vein measurement, chemical odour analysis, signature identification and facial thermography (the measurement of the radiant heat from a person's face).

Source: Nova Science in the News, *Putting a Finger on it – The Loops and Whorls of Biometrics*, National Innovation Awareness Strategy, Australia, 2001, http://www.science.org.au/nova/064/064key.htm (Accessed May 20, 2007).

the ability to circumvent all security procedures now in place. The only fully effective technique for avoiding viral contamination is the complete and total isolation of computer equipment—a strategy as unlikely to be maintained as it is to be implemented.

The internet is now available in hundreds of countries and its borderless nature allows for crimes to be committed through a number of different countries. Challenges to the prevention and control of cyber-crime are that a criminal can commit a crime from any country in the world, target victims all over the world, hide his or her identity by using computer systems located in many different countries, and store evidence in remote locations. Given this transnational reality of cyber-crime, initiatives for combatting and preventing computer-based crime is largely reliant on international cooperation. The *Convention on Cyber-Crime* signed in 2001 by Canada and 29 other nations is the first international treaty on crimes that are committed via the internet and that involve the use of computer networks. It deals particularly with infringements on copyright, computer-related fraud, child pornography and violations of network security as well as containing a series of powers and procedures to oversee the search of computer networks and the interception of information. Critics of the Convention contend that the treaty fails to provide meaningful privacy and civil liberties protections, and that its scope is too broad and covers much more than computer-related crimes. Moreover, they argue, the treaty also lacks a "dual criminality" provision, under which an activity must be considered a crime in both countries before one nation could demand cooperation from another. Thus, the Convention would require Canadian law enforcement authorities, for example, to cooperate with foreign police forces even when such agencies are investigating an activity that, while constituting a crime in their territory, is perfectly legal in Canada.[50]

PART 3

354

**Crime in the
Modern World and
the Response to It**

One of the challenges within Canada in the battle against cyber-crime is the difficulty of applying existing legislation to criminal activities that involve new technologies. Nevertheless, Canada is well ahead of many nations in enacting laws to address cyber-crime. Amendments to the *Criminal Code of Canada* in 1985, 1997, and 2002 have addressed theft of telecommunications services, possession of a device to obtain computer services, computer fraud, and mischief in relation to data, among criminal acts. In many instances, revisions to legislation ensure that existing offences are defined in such a way as to address the new technological aspects of the crime. For example, revisions to legislation making the possession of child pornography illegal have now made it also illegal to download and view child pornography online.[51]

Comparative Criminology

The globalization of crime has also led to a resurgence in interest in **comparative criminology**, or the study of crime on a cross-national level. If crime patterns in one country are compared with those in another, theories and policies that have been taken for granted in one place can be re-evaluated in light of world experience. As some noted comparative criminologists have observed, "The challenge for comparative criminologists is to develop theories with increased specificity while managing to construct them in such a way that they can be applied across more than one culture or nation-state. This eventually must demand that theories be developed to conceptualize societies as totalities and that theories that manage to provide a world context in which total societies behave be further constructed.[52]

Some have used the term *globalization of knowledge* to describe the increase in understanding that results from a sharing of information between cultures. The globalization of knowledge is beginning to play a significant role in both the process of theory formation within criminology and the development of crime prevention policies. According to some, "Globalization will make it increasingly difficult for nation-states to ignore the criminal justice information of other countries. Politicians and influential bureaucrats increasingly will be forced to answer as to why their country displays crime rates, prosecution rates, incarceration rates, or rates of violence or gun ownership that are strikingly different from similar countries."[53] Only in recent years have students of criminology begun to closely examine crime in other cultures. Unfortunately, not all societies are equally open, and it is not always easy to explore them. In some societies, even the *study* of crime is taboo. As a result, data-gathering strategies taken for granted in Western culture may not be well received elsewhere. One author, for example, has observed that in China, "the seeking of criminal justice information through face-to-face questioning takes on a different meaning in Chinese officialdom than it does generally in the Western world. While we accept this method of inquiry because we prize thinking on our feet and quick answers, it is rather offensive in China because it shows lack of respect and appreciation for the information given through the preferred means of prepared questions and formal briefings."[54] Hence, most of the information available about Chinese crime rates comes by way of officialdom, and routine Western social science practices like door-to-door interviews, participant observation, and random surveys might produce substantial problems for researchers who attempt to use such techniques in China.

Similar difficulties arise in the comparison of crime rates from one country to another. The crime rates of different nations are difficult to compare because of (1) differences in the way a given crime is defined, (2) diverse crime-reporting practices, and (3) political, social, economic, and other influences on the reporting of statistics to international agencies.[55]

Definitional differences create what may be the biggest problem. For cross-national comparisons of crime data to be meaningful, the reported data must share conceptual similarities. Unfortunately, that is often not the case. Nations report offences according to the legal criteria by which arrests are made and under which prosecution can occur. Switzerland, for example, includes bicycle thefts in its reported data on what we call "auto theft" because Swiss data gathering focuses more on the concept of personal transportation than it does on the type of vehicle stolen. The Netherlands has no crime category for robberies, counting them as thefts. Japan classifies an assault that results in death as an assault or an aggravated assault, not as a homicide. Greek rape statistics include crimes of sodomy, "lewdness," seduction of a child, incest, and prostitution. Communist China reports only robberies and thefts that involve the property of citizens; crimes against state-owned property fall into a separate category.

Reporting practices vary substantially between nations. The International Criminal Police Organization (Interpol) and the United Nations are the only international organizations that regularly collect crime statistics from a large number of countries. Both agencies can only request data and have no way of checking on the accuracy of the data reported to them. Many countries do not disclose the requested information, and those that do sometimes make only partial reports. In general, small countries are more likely to report than are large ones, and non-socialist countries are more likely to report than are socialist nations.

International reports of crime are sometimes delayed, making comparisons even more difficult. Complete, up-to-date data are difficult to acquire, since the information made available to agencies like the United Nations and Interpol is reported at different times and according to schedules that vary from nation to nation. In addition, official United Nations world crime surveys are conducted infrequently. To date, only eight such surveys have been undertaken.[56]

Crime statistics also reflect social and political contexts. Some nations do not accurately admit to the frequency of certain kinds of culturally reprehensible crimes. Communist countries, for example, appear loathe to report crimes like theft, burglary, and robbery because the very existence of such offences might appear to demonstrate felt inequities within the Communist system. Likewise, the social norms in some societies may make it almost impossible for women to report cases of rape or sexual abuse, while in others, women are encouraged to come forward.

With all these caveats in mind, it may still be instructive to look at rates of crime in other countries and to attempt comparisons with rates of crime in Canada. One of the most useful tools for international crime rate comparisons is *The Ninth United Nations Survey on Crime Trends and the Operations of Criminal Justice Systems,* which covers the years 2003–2004. The survey questionnaire consists of four parts dealing with information, primarily statistical, on the main components of the criminal justice system (police, prosecution, courts, and prisons).[57]

PART 3

356

**Crime in the
Modern World and
the Response to It**

Summary

For all but the most astute, the future is difficult to predict. It is safe to assume, however, that the future will differ from the past. Crime and criminology are not exempt from the realities of globalization and the transnational nature of the world. Emerging theories of criminality and resultant policies of crime prevention and control will need to be international in scope to truly address the emerging realities within the world of criminology.

Discussion Questions

1. This book emphasizes a social problem versus social responsibility theme. Which perspective do you think will be dominant in 21st century crime-prevention planning? Why?
2. What is the difference between cyber-crime and traditional forms of criminal activity? Will the cyber-crimes of today continue to be the cyber-crimes of tomorrow? Why?
3. Do you believe that transnational crimes will eventually surpass the abilities of enforcement agencies to prevent or solve them? Why?
4. How might technology such as biometrics be used more extensively by law enforcement agencies to assist in the fight against crime?
5. What is comparative criminology? What are the advantages of a comparative perspective? Are there any disadvantages? If so, what are they?

Weblinks

www.crimsociety.wlu.ca
Canadian Society of Criminology. Active in looking at new directions in crime, law, and justice issues.

www.foresight.gov.uk
Foresight. British-based group active in providing challenging visions of the future including those in criminal justice.

www.ojp.usdoj.gov/bjs/abstract/wfcj.htm
The World Factbook of Criminal Justice Systems. Provides narrative descriptions of the criminal justice systems of 45 countries around the world.

www.policefuturists.org
Police Futurists International (PFI). PFI is an organization of law-enforcement practitioners, educators, researchers, private security specialists, technology experts, and other professionals dedicated to improving criminal and social justice through the professionalization of policing.

**http://conventions.coe.int/Treaty/Commun/QueVoulezVous.
asp?NT=185&CM=8&DF=5/24/2007&CL=ENG**
Convention on Cybercrime, Council of Europe. Ratified in 2004, this Convention binds the signatory countries to creating a minimum set of laws to deal with high-tech crimes.

Notes

Chapter 1

1. Thomas Gabor, *Everybody Does It! Crime by the Public* (Toronto: University of Toronto Press, 1994).

2. Hermann Mannheim, *Comparative Criminology* (Boston: Houghton Mifflin, 1967), p. 20.

3. Narrative materials in this section derive from Neal Hall, "All My Friends Betrayed Me" and "The Defence the Jurors Never Heard," *Ottawa Citizen*, March 20, 2000, p. A3; and Sandra Martin, "Murder in Victoria: Why Did Reena Virk Die?" *Chatelaine Magazine*, May 1998.

4. "Aborigine Cleared of Death Curse Extortion," Reuters wire service, February 20, 1997.

5. From the standpoint of the law, the proper word is *conduct* rather than *behaviour*, because the term *conduct* implies intentional and wilful activity, whereas *behaviour* refers to any human activity—even that which occurs while a person is unconscious, as well as that which is unintended.

6. Paul W. Tappan, "Who Is the Criminal?" in Gilbert Geis and Robert F. Meier, eds., *White Collar Crime* (New York: Free Press, 1947), p. 277.

7. Edwin Sutherland, *Principles of Criminology*, 4th ed. (New York: J. B. Lippincott, 1947).

8. "Decriminalizing Drugs," *Ottawa Citizen*, April 12, 1997, p. B5; and "Decriminalizing Drugs II," *Ottawa Citizen*, April 14, 1997, p. A10.

9. F. Schmalleger, *Criminology Today. An Integrative Introduction* (New Jersey: Prentice Hall, 1999), p. 11.

10. *The American Heritage Dictionary* on CD-ROM.

11. This list is not meant to be exclusive. There are many other journals in the field, too numerous to name here. See Box 1.3 for a more extensive list.

12. A paper entitled *Public Policing and Private Security: Canadian Jurisprudence in International Perspective* by Tom Quigley, Faculty of Law, University of Saskatchewan, contends that the ratio of private security personnel outnumbers police officers in Canada by 2 to 1. The 2003 statistics from Statistics Canada report that police officers in Canada number 59 494 (from www.statcan.ca/english/Pgdb/legal15.htm).

13. Integration and Analysis Program, "The Justice Factfinder 1997," *Juristat*, vol. 19, no. 7 (Ottawa: Minister of Industry, 1999).

14. Piers Beirne, *Inventing Criminology* (Albany: State University of New York Press, 1993).

15. See also Paul Topinard, *Anthropology* (London: Chapman and Hall, 1984).

16. Sutherland, 1947, p. 1.

17. Clarence Ray Jeffery, "The Historical Development of Criminology," in Herman Mannheim, ed., *Pioneers in Criminology* (Montclair, N.J.: Paterson Smith, 1972), p. 458.

18. Gregg Barak, *Integrating Criminologies* (Boston: Allyn and Bacon, 1998), p. 303.

19. Jack P. Gibbs, "The State of Criminological Theory," *Criminology*, vol. 25, no. 4 (November 1987), pp. 822–823.

20. Available through Sage Publications, Thousand Oaks, CA.

21. There are, however, those who deny that criminology is deserving of the name "discipline." See, for example, Don C. Gibbons, *Talking about Crime and Criminals: Problems and Issues in Theory Development in Criminology* (Englewood Cliffs, N.J.: Prentice Hall, 1994), p. 3.

22. Gibbons, 1994, p. 4.

23. Sutherland, 1947.

24. Don M. Gottfredson, "Criminological Theories: The Truth as Told by Mark Twain," in William S. Laufer and Freda Adler, eds., *Advances in Criminological Theory*, vol. 1 (New Brunswick, N.J.: Transaction, 1989), p. 1.

25. Barak, 1998, p. 5.

26. Don G. Gibbons, "Talking About Crime: Observations on the Prospects for Causal Theory in Criminology," *Criminal Justice Research Bulletin*, vol. 7, no. 6 (Sam Houston State University, 1992).

27. Gibbons, 1992.

28. Raymond J. Michalowski, "Perspectives and Paradigm: Structuring Criminological Thought," in Robert F. Meier, ed., *Theory in Criminology* (Beverly Hills, Calif.: Sage, 1977), pp. 17–39.

29. Adapted from Michalowski, 1977.

30. Adapted from Michalowski, 1977.

31. Hermann Mannheim, *Comparative Criminology* (Boston: Houghton Mifflin, 1967), p. 20.

32. Jim Crane, "Geo-Profiling: A Potent New Police Technique," APB News, December 3, 1998, http://apbnews.com/cjprofessionals/behindthebadge/1998/120310geoprofile1231_01.html.

33. Bernard P. Cohen, *Developing Sociological Knowledge: Theory and Method*, 2nd ed. (Chicago: Nelson-Hall, 1989), p. 71.

34. Susette M. Talarico, *Criminal Justice Research: Approaches, Problems and Policy* (Cincinnati: Anderson, 1980), p. 3.

35. For a good review of secondary research, see J. H. Laub, R. J. Sampson, and K. Kiger, "Assessing the Potential of Secondary Data Analysis:

A New Look at the Glueck's Unraveling Juvenile Delinquency Data," in Kimberly L. Kempf, ed., *Measurement Issues in Criminology* (New York: Springer-Verlag, 1990), pp. 241–257; and Robert J. Sampson and John H. Laub, *Crime in the Making* (Cambridge, Mass.: Harvard University Press, 1993).

36. Sampson and Laub, 1993, p. 3.

37. Frank E. Hagan, *Research Methods in Criminal Justice and Criminology* (New York: Macmillan, 1993), p. 103.

38. Canadian Centre for Justice Statistics, *The Juristat Reader. A Statistical Overview of the Criminal Justice System* (Toronto: Thompson Educational Publishing, Inc., 1999), p. v.

39. Of course, as with almost anything else, qualitative data can be assigned to categories and the categories numbered. Hence qualitative data can be quantified, although the worth of such effort is subject to debate.

40. Patrick J. Desroches, *Behind the Bars—Experiences in Crime* (Toronto: Canadian Scholars' Press, 1996), pp. 27–28.

41. Hagan, 1993, pp. 31–32, 42.

42. Alfred Blumstein, "Making Rationality Relevant: The American Society of Criminology 1992 Presidential Address," *Criminology*, vol. 31, no. 1 (February 1993), p. 1.

43. "Fanning the Fire over Beavis," *USA Today*, October 15, 1993, p. D1.

44. Department of Justice Canada and Solicitor General Canada, *Safer Communities. A Parliamentarian's Crime Prevention Guide* (Ottawa: Department of Justice Canada, Solicitor General Canada, 1996).

45. *Safer Communities*, 1996.

46. "Film Scene to Be Cut after Fatal Imitation," *USA Today*, October 20, 1993, p. 1A.

47. *Safer Communities*, 1996.

48. Carol La Prairie, "The Impact of Aboriginal Justice Research on Policy: A Marginal Past and an Even More Uncertain Future," *Canadian Journal of Criminology*, vol. 41, no. 2 (April 1999), p. 249.

49. La Prairie, 1999, p. 250.

50. The Campaign for an Effective Crime Policy, *The Impact of Three Strikes and You're Out Laws: What Have We Learned?* (Washington, D.C.: CECP, 1997).

51. Lawrence W. Sherman, Denise Gottfredson, Doris MacKenzie, John Eck, Peter Reuter, Shawn Bushway, et al., *Preventing Crime: What Works, What Doesn't, What's Promising* (Washington, D.C.: National Institute of Justice, 1997).

52. Fox Butterfield, no headline, *New York Times News Service* online, April 16, 1997, 7:06 EST.

53. Julian V. Roberts, *Fear of Crime and Attitudes to Criminal Justice: A Review of Recent Trends, 2001–02*, Report for the Ministry of the Solicitor General, 2001, pp. 24–26.

54. "Conservatives to Pitch 3-Strikes Crime Bill," www.cbc.ca/canada/story/2006/09/20/toews-bill.html, September 20, 2006 [Accessed October 15, 2006].

55. Paul Samyn, "Minister Hints Pedophile Case Inspired Law," *The Ottawa Citizen,* October 18, 2006, p. A8.

56. Roberts, 2001, p. 13.

57. Angus Reid Group Inc., "Crime and the Justice System," www.angusreid.com, 1997.

58. Karin Stein, *Public Perception of Crime and Justice in Canada: A Review of Opinion Polls*, Department of Justice, 2001.

59. For an especially good discussion of this issue, see Theodore Sasson, *Crime Talk: How Citizens Construct a Social Problem* (Hawthorne, N.Y.: Aldine de Gruyter, 1995).

60. Canada's National Strategy on Community Safety and Crime Prevention (now known as the National Crime Prevention Strategy), www.crime-prevention.org.

61. Environics, *Focus Canada 1999*, 1999.

62. Angus Reid Group Inc., "Crime and the Justice System," www.angusreid.com, 1997.

63. Nat Hentoff, "Justice Blackmun Reconsiders the Death Penalty," *Washington Post* wire service, December 11, 1993.

64. Megan's death led most states and the federal government to pass "Megan's Laws," requiring community notification when released sex offenders move into an area.

65. Melanie Burney, "Megan's Law," Associated Press wire service, June 21, 1997.

66. For a good overview of this issue, see Wesley G. Skogan, ed., *Reactions to Crime and Violence*, The Annals of the American Academy of Political and Social Science (Thousand Oaks, Calif.: Sage, 1995).

67. "Denny Beating," Associated Press wire service, December 8, 1993.

68. For an excellent discussion of crime as a social event, see Leslie W. Kennedy and Vincent F. Sacco, *Crime Counts: A Criminal Event Analysis* (Toronto: Nelson Canada, 1996).

69. For a good discussion of the social construction of crime, see Leslie T. Wilkins, "On Crime and its Social Construction: Observations on the Social Construction of Crime," *Social Pathology*, vol. 1, no. 1 (January 1995), pp. 1–11.

70. For a parallel approach, see Terance D. Miethe and Robert F. Meier, *Crime and Its Social Context: Toward an Integrated Theory of Offenders, Victims, and Situations* (Albany, N.Y.: State University of New York Press, 1995).

71. Joan McCord, "Family Relationships, Juvenile Delinquency, and Adult Criminality," *Criminology*, vol. 29, no. 3 (August 1991), pp. 397–417.

72. Elizabeth Candle and Sarnoff A. Mednick, "Perinatal Complications Predict Violent Offending," *Criminology*, vol. 29, no. 3 (August 1991), pp. 519–529.

73. Carol W. Kohfeld and John Sprague, "Demography, Police Behavior, and Deterrence," *Criminology*, vol. 28, no. 1 (February 1990). pp. 111–136.

74. Leslie W. Kennedy and David R. Forde, "Routine Activities and Crime: An Analysis of Victimization in Canada," *Criminology*, vol. 28, no. 1 (February 1990), pp. 137–152.

75. William G. Doerner, "The Impact of Medical Resources on Criminally Induced Lethality: A Further Examination," *Criminology*, vol. 26, no. 1 (February 1988), pp. 171–177.

76. Doerner, 1988, p. 177.

77. James F. Gilsinan, "They Is Clowning Tough: 911 and the Social Construction of Reality," *Criminology*, vol. 27, no. 2 (May 1989), pp. 329–344.

78. See, for example, Terance D. Miethe and Robert F. Meier, *Crime and Its Social Context: Toward an Integrated Theory of Offenders, Victims, and Situations* (Albany, N.Y.: State University of New York Press, 1995).

79. For a good discussion of the historical development of criminology, see Don C. Gibbons, *Talking About Crime and Criminals: Problems and Issues in Theory Development in Criminology* (Englewood Cliffs, N.J.: Prentice Hall, 1994); Don C. Gibbons, *The Criminological Enterprise* (Englewood Cliffs, N.J.: Prentice Hall, 1979); and Leon Radzinowicz, *In Search of Criminology* (Cambridge, Mass.: Harvard University Press, 1962).

Chapter 2

1. F. Schmalleger, D. MacAlister, P.F. McKenna, J. Winterdyk, *Canadian Criminal Justice Today. An Introduction for the Twenty-First Century* (Toronto: Prentice Hall Allyn and Bacon Canada, 2000), p. 29.

2. A number of contemporary criminologists continue to study the effect of weather on crime. See, for example, Ellen G. Cohn, "The Effect of Weather and Temporal Variations on Calls for Police Service," *American Journal of Police*, vol. 15, no. 1 (1996), pp. 23–43; Ellen G. Cohn, "The Prediction of Police Calls for Service: The Influence of Weather and Temporal Variables on Rape and Domestic Violence," *Environmental Psychology*, vol. 13 (1993), pp. 71–83; Ellen G. Cohn, "Weather and Crime," *British Journal of Criminology*, vol. 30, no. 1 (1990), pp. 51–64; and Derral Cheatwood, "Is There a Season for Homicide?" *Criminology*, vol. 26, no. 2 (May 1988), pp. 287–306.

3. B.J. Ennis and T.R. Litwack, "Psychiatry and the Presumption of Expertise: Flipping Coins in the Classroom," *California Law Review*, vol. 62 (1974), pp. 693–725.

4. Canadian Centre for Justice Statistics, *The Juristat Reader. A Statistical Overview of the Canadian Justice System* (Toronto: Thompson Educational Publishing, Inc., 1999), p. v.

5. R.A. Silverman, J.T. Teevan, and V.F. Sacco, eds., *Crime in Canadian Society* (Toronto: Harcourt Brace, 1996), p. 62.

6. Silverman et al., 1996, pp. 62–63.

7. M. Gannon, "Crime Statistics in Canada, 2005," *Juristat*, vol. 26, no. 4 (Ottawa: Minister of Industry, 2006).

8. Gannon, 2006.

9. Gannon, 2006

10. Gannon, 2006.

11. K. AuCoin, "Children and Youth as Victims of Violent Crime," *Juristat*, vol. 25, no. 1 (Ottawa: Minister of Industry, 2005).

12. Solicitor General of Canada, "Victims of Crime," *Canadian Urban Victimization Survey* (Ottawa: Solicitor General of Canada, 1983).

13. J. Short and F. Nye, "Extent of Unrecorded Juvenile Delinquency: Tentative Conclusions," *Journal of Criminal Law, Criminology and Police Science*, vol. 49 (1958), pp. 296–302.

14. M. LeBlanc and M. Fréchette, *Male Criminal Activity from Childhood through Youth: Multilevel and Developmental Perspectives* (New York: Springer-Verlag, 1989).

15. For an overview of the reliability of self-report studies, see M.J. Hindelang, T. Hirschi, and J.G. Weis, *Measuring Delinquency* (Beverly Hills: Sage, 1981).

16. For an excellent overview of the social dimensions of crime, see John Hagan and Ruth D. Peterson, *Crime and Inequality* (Stanford, Calif.: Stanford University Press, 1995); and James W. Messerschmidt, *Crime as Structured Action: Gender, Race, Class and Crime in the Making* (Thousand Oaks, Calif.: Sage, 1997).

17. V.P. Bunge, H. Johnson, T. Balde, "Exploring Crime Patterns in Canada," *Statistics Canada* (Ottawa: Minister of Industry, 2005).

18. Alfred Blumstein, "Violence by Young People: Why the Deadly Nexus?" *National Institute of Justice Journal*, no. 229 (August 1995).

19. John J. Dilulio, Jr., "The Question of Black Crime," *The Public Interest* (Fall 1994), pp. 3–12.

20. James Alan Fox, *Trends in Juvenile Violence: A Report to the United States Attorney General on Current and Future Rates of Juvenile Offending* (Washington, D.C.: Bureau of Justice Statistics, 1996); and Gary Fields, "Youth Violent Crime Falls 9.2%," *USA Today*, October 3–5, 1997, p. 1A (quoting James Fox).

21. James Q. Wilson and Joan Petersilia, *Crime* (San Francisco, Calif.: Institute of Contemporary Studies, 1995).

22. V.P. Bunge, H. Johnston, T. Balde, "Exploring Crime Patterns in Canada," Statistics Canada (Ottawa: Minister of Industry, 2005).

23. Marc Ouimet, "Explaining the American and Canadian Crime 'Drop' in the 1990s," *Canadian Journal of Criminology*, vol. 45, no. 2 (2002), pp. 33–50.

24. M. Gannon and K. Mihorean, "Criminal Victimization in Canada, 2004," *Juristat*, vol. 25, no. 7 (Ottawa: Minister of Industry, 2005).

25. K. AuCoin, "Children and Youth as Victims of Violent Crime," *Juristat*, vol. 25, no. 1 (Ottawa: Minister of Industry, 2005).

26. Stephen E. Brown, Finn-Aage Esbensen, and Gilbert Geis, *Criminology: Explaining Crime and Its Context*, 2nd ed. (Cincinnati, Ohio: Anderson, 1996), p. 198.

27. M. Wallace, "Crime Statistics in Canada, 2003," *Juristat*, vol. 24, no. 6 (Ottawa: Minister of Industry, 2004).

28. Elizabeth Cormack, "Women and Crime," in R. Linden, ed., *Criminology: A Canadian Perspective* (Toronto: Harcourt Brace Canada, 1996), pp. 139–175.

29. Leanne Fiftal Alarid, James W. Marquart, Velmer S. Burton, Jr., Francis T. Cullen, and Steven J. Cuvelier, "Women's Roles in Serious Offenses: A Study of Adult Felons," *Justice Quarterly*, vol. 13, no. 3 (September 1996), pp. 432–454.

30. M. Gannon and K. Mihorean, "Criminal Victimization in Canada, 2004," *Juristat*, vol. 25, no. 7 (Ottawa: Minister of Industry, 2005).

31. Statistics Canada, *Violence Against Women Survey. Survey Highlights* (Ottawa: Minister of Industry, 1993).

32. Public Safety and Emergency Preparedness Canada, *Corrections and Conditional Release Statistical Overview* (Ottawa: Public Works and Government Services Canada, 2005).

33. P. Havemann, K. Couse, L. Foster, and R. Matonovich, *Law and Order for Canada's Indigenous People* (Regina: Prairie Justice Research, School of Human Justice, University of Regina, 1985); and John Hagan, "Criminal Justice in Rural and Urban Communities," *Social Forces*, vol. 55(3), 1977, pp. 597–612; and D.F. Wayne, T.F. Hartnagel, "Race and Plea Negotiation," *Canadian Journal of Sociology*, vol. 1(2) (1975), pp. 147–155.

34. J.H. Hylton, "The Native Offender in Saskatchewan," *Canadian Journal of Criminology*, vol. 24(2) (1982), pp. 121–131; and Carol La Prairie, "Aboriginal Crime and Justice," *Canadian Journal of Criminology*, vol. 34 (1992), pp. 281–297.

35. Carol La Prairie, "Aboriginal Over-representation in the Criminal Justice System: A Tale of Nine Cities," *Canadian Journal of Criminology*, vol. 44, no. 2 (2002), pp. 181–208.

36. Havemann et al., 1985.

37. John Hagan, "Criminal Justice and Native People," *Canadian Review of Sociology and Anthropology, Special Issue* (August 1974), pp. 220–236.

38. J. Brzozowski, A. Taylor-Butts, and S. Johnson, "Victimization and Offending among the Aboriginal Population in Canada," *Juristat*, vol. 25, no. 3 (Ottawa: Minister of Industry, 2006).

39. For a good review of the issues involved, see John Hagan, *Structural Criminology* (New Brunswick, N.J.: Rutgers University Press, 1989).

40. Charles R. Tittle, Wayne Villemez, and Douglas Smith, "The Myth of Social Class and Criminality: An Empirical Assessment of the Empirical Evidence," *American Sociological Review*, vol. 43, no. 5 (1978), pp. 643–656; see also Charles R. Tittle, "Social Class and Criminality," *Social Forces*, vol. 56, no. 2 (1977), pp. 474–502.

41. John Braithwaite, "The Myth of Social Class and Criminality Reconsidered," *American Sociological Review*, vol. 46, no. 1 (1981), pp. 36–57.

42. Margaret Farnworth, Terence P. Thornberry, and Marvin D. Krohn, "Measurement in the Study of Class and Delinquency: Integrating Theory and Research," *Journal of Research in Crime and Delinquency*, vol. 31, no. 1 (1994), pp. 32–61.

43. J. Hagan and B. McCarthy, "Street Life and Delinquency," *British Journal of Sociology*, vol. 43(4) (1992), pp. 533–561.

44. V.P. Bunge, H. Johnson, and T. Balde, "Exploring Crime Patterns in Canada," *Statistics Canada* (Ottawa: Minister of Industry, 2005).

45. M. Gannon and K. Mihorean, "Criminal Victimization in Canada, 2004," *Juristat*, vol. 25, no. 7 (Ottawa: Minister of Industry, 2005).

Chapter 3

1. Peter Kent, as cited in Michele Mandel, "Crime Rate is Down: Violent Acts Are Changing Our Perspective," *Toronto Sun*, March 14, 1999, p. 32.

2. Michele Mandel, "Crime Rate Is Down: Violent Acts Are Changing Our Perspective," *Toronto Sun*, March 14, 1999, p. 32.

3. Jeremy Mercer, "'Locker Room Bandit' Benched," *Ottawa Citizen*, March 6, 1999, pp. A1–A2.

4. Maire Gannon, "Crime Statistics in Canada, 2005," *Juristat*, vol. 26, no. 4 (Ottawa: Minister of Industry, 2006).

5. Steve Cannon, "Grandson Gets Life in Prison for Murder of 90-Year-Old," *Ottawa Citizen*, January 10, 1998, p. E12.

6. Bureau of Justice Statistics, *Report to the Nation on Crime and Justice* (Washington, DC: U.S. Government Printing Office, 1988), p. 4.

7. Frank Schmalleger, *Criminology Today. An Integrated Introduction* (New Jersey: Prentice Hall, 1999), p. 63.

8. Bureau of Justice Statistics, *Report to the Nation on Crime and Justice* (1988), p. 4.

9. Detailed information about homicide in Canada in 2005 is from Mia Dauvergne and Geoffrey Li, "Homicide in Canada, 2005," *Juristat*, vol. 26, no. 6 (Ottawa: Minister of Industry, 2006).

10. Frank Schmalleger, *Criminology Today. An Integrative Introduction* (New Jersey: Pearson Prentice Hall, 2006), p. 51.

11. Schmalleger, 2006, p. 51.

12. See Elizabeth Cormack, "Women and Crime," in Rick Linden, ed., *Criminology: A Canadian Perspective* (Toronto: Harcourt Brace Canada, 1996), pp. 139–175.

13. Maire Gannon, "Canadian Crime Statistics, 2005," *Juristat*, vol. 26, no. 4 (Ottawa: Minister of Industry, 2006).

14. Frank Schmalleger and Ted Alleman, "The Collective Reality of Crime: An Integrative Approach to the Causes and Consequences of the Criminal Event," in Gregg Bank, *Varieties of Criminology: Readings from a Dynamic Discipline* (New York: Praeger Publishers, 1994).

15. David G. Curtis, "Perspectives on Acquaintance Rape," *American Academy of Experts in Traumatic Stress*, www.aaets.org (Accessed February 27, 2007).

16. Maire Gannon and Karen Mihorean, "Criminal Victimization in Canada, 2004," *Juristat*, vol. 25, no. 7 (Ottawa: Minister of Industry, 2005).

17. Gannon and Mihorean, 2005.

18. Gannon and Mihorean, 2005.

19. Rebecca Kong, Holly Johnston, Sara Beattie, and Andrea Cardillo, "Sexual Offences in Canada," *Juristat*, vol. 23, no. 6 (Ottawa: Minister of Industry, 2003).

20. Karen Hackett, "Criminal Harassment," *Juristat*, vol. 20, no. 11 (Ottawa: Minister of Industry, 2000).

21. The most recent data are from 1999. See Hackett, 2000.

22. Hackett, 2000.

23. One of the greatest difficulties in collecting official statistics on home invasions is a definitional one. There is yet to exist a single, agreed-upon definition. The most recent information on home invasions is found in Orest Fedorowycz, "Breaking and Entering in Canada, 2002," *Juristat*, vol. 24, no. 5 (Ottawa: Minister of Industry, 2004).

24. Frederick J. Desroches, *Force and Fear: Robbery in Canada* (Toronto: ITP Nelson, 1995).

25. Warren Silver, Karen Mihorean, Andrea Taylor-Butts, "Hate Crime in Canada," *Juristat*, vol. 24, no. 4 (Ottawa: Minister of Industry, 2004); Derek E. Janevich, "Hate Crime in Canada: An Overview of Issues and Data Sources," Canadian Centre for Justice Statistics (Ottawa: Minister of Industry, 2001).

26. All statistics taken from Warren Silver, Karen Mihorean, and Andrea Taylor-Butts, "Hate Crime in Canada," *Juristat*, vol. 24, no. 4 (Ottawa: Minister of Industry, 2004).

27. The twelve participating police services were Calgary, Edmonton, Toronto, Halton Regional, Montreal, Regina, Windsor, Winnipeg, Sudbury, Ottawa, Waterloo, and the RCMP. Combined, these police services represent about 45 percent of the national crime volume in Canada (W. Silver, K. Mihorean, A. Taylor-Butts, 2004).

28. Peter Hum, "Compassion for a Child Killer," *Ottawa Citizen*, December 28, 1999, p. B1.

29. Cathy S. Widom, "The Intergenerational Transmission of Violence," in Neil Warner and Marvin Wolfgang, eds., *Pathways to Criminal Violence* (Newbury Park, CA: Sage, 1989).

30. Fedorowycz, 2004.

31. Fedorowycz, 2004.

32. Sherrie Barnhorst and Richard Barnhorst, *Criminal Law and the Canadian Criminal Code* (Toronto: McGraw-Hill Ryerson Ltd., 2004), p. 314.

33. Julie Sauvé, "Motor Vehicle Theft in Canada, 1996," *Juristat*, vol. 18, no. 1 (Ottawa: Minister of Industry, 1997).

34. Paul McKay, "Hot Cars: Inside Ontario's Auto-Wreck Racket," *Ottawa Citizen*, March 7, 1998, pp. A1–A2, B1–B3.

35. For the most recent detailed information on impaired driving, see Derek Janhevich, Maire Gannon, and Nicolas Morisset, "Impaired Driving and Other Traffic Offences, 2002," *Juristat*, vol. 23, no. 9 (Ottawa: Minister of Industry, 2003).

36. Gannon, 2006.

37. Patrick Healy, "Counterfeit Canadian Bank Notes," April 2002, http://www.bankofcanada.ca/en/banknotes/pdf/healy_counterfeiting%20paper.pdf (Accessed February 27, 2007).

38. L.J. Siegel and C. McCormick, *Criminology in Canada* (Scarborough: ITP Nelson, 1999), p. 427.

39. Gannon, 2006.

40. Health Canada 2005 Fact Sheet – Methamphetamine, http://www.hc-sc.gc.ca/ahc-asc/media/nr-cp/2005/2005_58bk_e.html (Accessed February 28, 2007); D. McGhee, Crystal Meth, Centre for Addiction Research of British Columbia, University of Victoria, 2006, www.carbc.uvic.ca (Accessed February 28, 2007).

41. Gannon, 2006.

Chapter 4

1. Robert Reiff, *The Invisible Victim: The Criminal Justice System's Forgotten Responsibility* (New York: Basic Books, 1979), p. xi.

2. Alan Young, *Victims of Crime Research Series. The Role of the Victim in the Criminal Process: A Literature Review* (Department of Justice, 2001).

3. G. Dimmock and J. Rupert, "Student Dies Trying to Stop Bar Fight," *Ottawa Citizen*, December 24, 1998,http://andymoffitt.org/newspapers/ottawacitizen/sep152003/story.asp_modified.html (Accessed March 8, 2007).

4. Dimmock and Rupert, 1998.

5. D. Campbell, "Mother Haunted by Son's Dying Screams. Brockville Woman Speaks at Hearing into Killer's Sentencing," *Ottawa Citizen*, March 18, 2003, http://andymoffitt.org/newspapers/ottawacitizen/mar182003/story/story.asp_modified.html (Accessed March 8, 2007).

6. Hans von Hentig, *The Criminal and His Victim: Studies in the Sociobiology of Crime* (Archon Books, 1967), reprinted from the 1948 Yale University Press edition.

7. As noted by Stephen Schafer, *The Victim and His Criminal: A Study in Functional Responsibility* (New York: Random House, 1968).

8. Schafer, 1968, p. 384.

9. Benjamin Mendelsohn, "Method to Be Used by Counsel for the Defence in the Researches Made into the Personality of the Criminal," *Revue de Droit Pénal et de Criminologie* (Brussels, Fall 1937), p. 877.

10. See Henry Ellenberger, "Relations Psychologiques entre le Criminel et sa Victime," *Revue Internationale de Criminologie et de Police Technique*, no. 2 (Geneva, 1954).

11. Thorsten Sellin and Marvin E. Wolfgang, *The Measurement of Delinquency* (New York: John Wiley & Sons, 1964).

12. Ezzat Fattah, "Participation of the Public and Victims for More Fair Criminal Justice," paper delivered at the 112 International Training Course, www.unafei.or.jp/pdf/56-06.pdf (Tokyo, 2000), p. 63.

13. John A. Winterdyk, *Canadian Criminology* (Scarborough: Prentice Hall, 2000), p. 255.

14. Fattah, 2000, p. 64.

15. Fattah, 2000, p. 64.

16. Fattah, 2000, pp. 65–66.

17. Maire Gannon, Karen Mihorean, "Criminal Victimization in Canada, 2004," *Juristat*, vol. 25, no. 7 (Ottawa: Minister of Industry, 2005).

18. Rosa Casarez-Levison, "An Empirical Investigation of the Coping Strategies Used by Victims of Crime: Victimization Redefined," in Emilio Viano, ed., *Critical Issues in Victimology: International Perspectives* (New York: Springer Pub., 1992).

19. M. Bard and D. Sangrey, *The Crime Victim's Book*, 2nd ed. (New York: Brunner/Mazel, 1986).

20. Elizabeth Kübler-Ross, *On Death and Dying* (New York: Macmillan, 1969).

21. For an excellent review of many of these studies, see Alan Young, *Victims of Crime Research Series. The Role of the Victim in the Criminal Process: A Literature Review* (Department of Justice, 2001), pp. 57–59.

22. D. Kilpatrick and R. Otto, "Constitutionally Guaranteed Participation in Criminal Proceedings for Victims: Potential Effects on Psychological Functioning," *Wayne Law Review*, vol. 37, no. 7 (1987), p. 27.

23. Norris and M. Thomson, "The Victim in the System: The Influence of Police Responsiveness on Victim Alienation," *Journal of Traumatic Stress*, vol. 6 (1993), p. 515.

24. E. Erez, *Victim Impact Statements in South Australia: An Evaluation* (South Australia: Office of Crime Statistics, 1994).

25. J. Freedy, J. Resnick, D. Kilpatrick, B. Dansky, and R. Tidwell, "The Psychological Adjustment of Recent Crime Victims in the Criminal Justice System," in M. McShane and F. Williams, eds., *Victims of Crime and the Victimization Process* (New York: Garland Publishing, 1997).

26. Solicitor General of Canada, *The Psychological Impact of Crime: A Review* (Ottawa: Solicitor General of Canada, 1990–1991); and Solicitor General of Canada, *The Psychological Impact of Nonsexual Criminal Offences on Victims* (Ottawa: Solicitor General of Canada, 1992).

27. W. McDonald, "Towards a Bicentennial Revolution in Criminal Justice: The Return of the Victim," *American Criminal Law Review*, vol. 13 (1976); and S. Schafer, *Victimology: The Victim and His Criminal* (Reston: Reston Publishing, 1977).

28. Schafer, 1977.

29. Nils Christie, "Conflicts as Property," *British Journal of Criminology*, vol. 1, no. 1 (1977), pp. 3–4.

30. See D. Hall, "Victims' Voices in Criminal Court: The Need for Restraint," *American Criminal Law Review*, vol. 28 (1991); J Acker, "Social Sciences and the Criminal Law: Victims of Crime—Plight vs. Rights," *Criminal Law Bulletin*, vol. 28 (1992); and R. Black, "Forgotten Penological Purposes: A Critique of Victim Participation in Sentencing," *American Journal of Jurisprudence*, vol. 39 (1994).

31. Herbert Packer, *The Limits of the Criminal Process* (Stanford, CA: Stanford University Press, 1968).

32. Kent Roach, *Due Process and Victims' Rights. The New Law and Politics of Criminal Justice* (Toronto: University of Toronto Press, 1999).

33. Roach, 1999, pp. 30–31.

34. Roach, 1999, pp. 33–34.

35. Steven Rathgeb Smith and Susan Freinkel, *Adjusting the Balance: Federal Policy and Victim Services* (Westport, CT: Greenwood Press, 1988), p. 13.

36. V.F. Sacco and H. Johnson, *Patterns of Criminal Victimization in Canada* (Ottawa: Statistics Canada, 1990); and M. Baril, S. LaFlamme-Cusson, and S. Beauchemin, *Working Paper No. 12. Crime Victims Compensation: An Assessment of the Quebec IVAC Program* (Ottawa: Policy Planning and Development Branch, Department of Justice, 1984).

37. CTV.ca, "Ontario Crime Compensation System a 'Failure': Ombud," http://www.ctv.ca/servlet/ArticleNews/story/CTVNews/20070227/crime_victim_compensation_070227/20070227?hub=TopStories (Accessed March 8, 2007).

38. Keith Leslie, "Ontario Injuries Board Gets $20-Million," Globeandmail.com, http://www.theglobeandmail.com/servlet/story/RTGAM.20070302.winjuries0302/BNStory/National (Accessed March 8, 2007).

39. Fattah, 2000, p. 61.

40. I. Waller, "Victims, Safer Communities and Sentencing," *Canadian Journal of Criminology*, vol. 32, no. 2 (1990).

41. J. Moylan, *Victim Services and Canadian Police Agencies—A Source Book* (Ottawa: Canadian Association of Chiefs of Police and Solicitor General of Canada, 1990).

42. W. Jamieson and R.R. Ross, "An Evaluation of the Victim/Witness Assistance Programme, Ministry of the Attorney General of Ontario," *Canadian Journal of Program Evaluation*, vol. 6, no. 1 (1991), pp. 83–96.

43. A. Hatch Cunningham and C.T. Griffiths, *Canadian Criminal Justice, A Primer* (Toronto: Harcourt Brace Canada, 1997), p. 79.

44. M. Gannon, "General Social Survey on Victimization, 2004, Cycle 18: An Overview of Findings," *Statistics Canada* (Ottawa: Minister of Industry, 2005).

45. Ezzat Fatah, "Victims and Victimology: The Facts and the Rhetoric," *International Review of Victimology*, vol. 1 (1989), p. 43.

46. Ontario Legislative Assembly, *Report under Standing Order 125 on Victims of Crime* (1994).

47. Young, 2001, p. 29.

48. R. Elias, *Victims Still: The Political Manipulation of Crime Victims* (Thousand Oaks: Sage Publications, 1993), p. 26.

49. I. Waller, "Report on the Implementation of the Basic Principles Embodied in the United Nations Declaration on Victims," *International Review of Victimology*, vol. 2 (1991), p. 65.

Chapter 5

1. Jeremy Bentham, *An Introduction to the Principles of Morals and Legislation* (1789).

2. Cesare Beccaria, *Essay on Crimes and Punishments*, translated by Henry Paolucci (New York: Bobbs-Merrill, 1963).

3. William Graham Sumner, *Folkways* (New York: Dover, 1906).

4. L.J. Siegel and C. McCormick, *Criminology in Canada. Theories, Patterns and Typologies* (Toronto: ITP Nelson, 1999), pp. 447–448.

5. Marvin Wolfgang, "The Key Reporter," *Phi Beta Kappa*, vol. 52, no. 1.

6. Roman influence in England had ended by 442 AD, according to Crane Brinton, John B. Christopher, and Robert L. Wolff, *A History of Civilization*, 3rd ed., vol. 1 (Englewood Cliffs, N.J.: Prentice Hall, 1967), p. 180.

7. Howard Abadinsky, *Law and Justice* (Chicago: Nelson-Hall, 1988), p. 6.

8. Edward McNall Burns, *Western Civilization*, 7th ed. (New York: W. W. Norton, 1969), p. 339.

9. C. Brinton, J.B. Christopher, and R.L. Wolff, *A History of Civilization.* Vol. I (Englewood Cliffs, N.J.: Prentice-Hall Inc., 1955), p. 234.

10. Brinton et al., 1955, p. 274.

11. Referred to in official transcripts as Rudolf Franz Ferdinand Hoess.

12. International Military Tribunal, "One Hundred and Eighth Day, Monday, 4/15/1946, Part 03," in *Trial of the Major War Criminals before the International Military Tribunal, Volume XI. Proceedings: 4/8/1946–4/17/1946* (Nuremberg: IMT, 1943), pp. 398–400.

13. Beccaria, 1963.

14. Bentham, 1789.

15. R. Martinson, "What Works? Questions and Answers about Prison Reform," *Public Interest*, vol. 35 (1974), p. 25.

16. James Q. Wilson, *Thinking about Crime* (New York: Vintage, 1975).

17. Felton M. Earls and Albert J. Reiss, *Breaking the Cycle: Predicting and Preventing Crime* (Washington, D.C.: National Institute of Justice, 1994), p. 49.

18. L. E. Cohen and Marcus Felson, "Social Change and Crime Rate Trends: A Routine Activity Approach," *American Sociological Review*, vol. 44, no. 4 (August 1979), pp. 588–608. Also, see Marcus Felson and L.E. Cohen, "Human Ecology and Crime: A Routine Activity Approach," *Human Ecology*, vol. 8, no. 4 (1980), pp. 389–406; Marcus Felson, "Linking Criminal Choices, Routine Activities, Informal Control, and Criminal Outcomes," in Derek B. Cornish and Ronald V. Clarke, eds., *The Reasoning Criminal: Rational Choice Perspectives on*

Offending (New York: Springer-Verlag, 1986), pp. 119–128; and Ronald V. Clarke and Marcus Felson, eds., *Advances in Criminological Theory: Routine Activity and Rational Choice* (New Brunswick, N.J.: Transaction, 1993).

19. Cohen and Felson, 1979, p. 595.

20. For an analysis of the principles of routine activity theory in relation to crime prevention, see the January 1990 issue of the *Canadian Journal of Criminology*, entitled "Preventing Crime: Current Issues and Debates." For a test of routine activity theory as an explanation for victimization in the workplace, see John D. Wooldredge, Francis T. Cullen, and Edward J. Latessa, "Victimization in the Workplace: A Test of Routine Activities Theory," *Justice Quarterly,* vol. 9, no. 2 (June 1992), pp. 325–335.

21. Marcus Felson, *Crime and Everyday Life: Insight and Implications for Society* (Thousand Oaks, Calif.: Pine Forge Press, 1994).

22. Gary LaFree and Christopher Birkbeck, "The Neglected Situation: A Cross-National Study of the Situational Characteristics of Crime," *Criminology,* vol. 29, no. 1 (February 1991), p. 75.

23. Ronald V. Clarke and Derek B. Cornish, eds., *Crime Control in Britain: A Review of Police and Research* (Albany: State University of New York Press, 1983), p. 8.

24. See Derek B. Cornish and Ronald V. Clarke, "Understanding Crime Displacement: An Application of Rational Choice Theory," *Criminology,* vol. 25, no. 4 (November 1987), p. 933.

25. Clarke and Cornish, *Crime Control in Britain: A Review of Police and Research,* p. 48.

26. Werner Einstadter and Stuart Henry, *Criminological Theory: An Analysis of Its Underlying Assumptions* (Fort Worth: Harcourt Brace, 1995), p. 70.

27. Daniel J. Curran and Claire M. Renzetti, *Theories of Crime* (Boston: Allyn and Bacon, 1994), p. 18.

28. David Weisburd, "Reorienting Crime Prevention Research and Policy: From the Causes of Criminality to the Context of Crime," *NIJ Research Report* (Washington, D.C.: NIJ, June 1997).

29. Material in this section comes from Weisburd, 1997.

30. See P.J. Brantingham and P.L. Brantingham, "Situational Crime Prevention in Practice," *Canadian Journal of Criminology* (January 1990), pp. 17–40; and R.V. Clarke, "Situational Crime Prevention: Achievements and Challenges," in M. Tonry and D. Farrington, eds., *Building a Safer Society: Strategic Approaches to Crime Prevention, Crime and Justice: A Review of Research,* vol. 19 (Chicago: University of Chicago Press, 1995).

31. Weisburd, 1997.

32. See, for example, J.E. Eck and D. Weisburd, eds., *Crime and Place: Crime Prevention Studies,* vol. 4 (Monsey, N.Y.: Willow Tree Press, 1995).

33. See L. Sherman, "Hot Spots of Crime and Criminal Careers of Places," in J.E. Eck and D. Weisburd, eds., *Crime and Place: Crime Prevention Studies,* vol. 4 (Monsey, N.Y.: Willow Tree Press, 1995); and L. Sherman, P.R. Gartin, and M.E. Buerger, "Hot Spots of Predatory Crime: Routine Activities and the Criminology of Place," *Criminology,* vol. 27, no. 1 (1989), pp. 27–56.

34. Laura J. Moriarty and James E. Williams, "Examining the Relationship Between Routine Activities Theory and Social Disorganization: An Analysis of Property Crime Victimization," *American Journal of Criminal Justice,* vol. 21, no. 1 (1996), pp. 43–59.

35. Moriarty and Williams, 1996, p. 46.

36. Kenneth D. Tunnell, "Choosing Crime: Close Your Eyes and Take Your Chances," *Justice Quarterly,* vol. 7 (1990), pp. 673–690.

37. See R. Barr and K. Pease, "Crime Placement, Displacement and Deflection," in M. Tonry and N. Morris, eds., *Crime and Justice: A Review of Research,* vol. 12 (Chicago: University of Chicago Press, 1990).

38. For a good summation of target hardening, see Ronald V. Clarke, *Situational Crime Prevention* (New York: Harrow and Heston, 1992).

39. For a good summation of studies on displacement, see R. Hesseling, "Displacement: A Review of the Empirical Literature," in R.V. Clarke, ed., *Crime Prevention Studies,* vol. 3 (Monsey, N.Y.: Willow Tree Press, 1994).

40. Carol J. Castaneda, "Not All Urging Mercy for Teen Facing Flogging," *USA Today,* April 4, 1994, p. 3A.

41. The number of lashes Fay received was reduced to four, and he spent an additional month imprisoned in Singapore before he was released and returned to the United States.

42. Alberts, "Hanger's Cliffhanger," *Calgary Herald,* March 16, 1996, p. A3.

43. See Canadian Sentencing Commission, *Sentencing Reform: A Canadian Approach* (Ottawa: Supply and Services Canada, 1987).

44. J. Bonta, T. Rugge and M. Dauvergne, *The Reconviction Rate of Federal Offenders* (Ottawa: Solicitor General of Canada, 2003).

45. See, for example, W.C. Bailey, "Deterrence and the Death Penalty for Murders in Utah: A Time Series Analysis," *Journal of Contemporary Law,* vol. 5, no. 1 (1978), pp. 1–20; and "An Analysis of the Deterrent Effect of the Death Penalty for Murders in California," *Southern California Law Review,* vol. 52, no. 3 (1979), pp. 743–764.

46. See, for example, B.E. Forst, "The Deterrent Effect of Capital Punishment: A Cross-State

Analysis of the 1960s," *Minnesota Law Review*, vol. 61 (1977), pp. 743–764.

47. Scott H. Decker and Carol W. Kohfeld, "Capital Punishment and Executions in the Lone Star State: A Deterrence Study," *Criminal Justice Research Bulletin* (Criminal Justice Center, Sam Houston State University), vol. 3, no. 12 (1988).

48. *Ottawa Citizen*, December 4, 1996, p. A6.

49. J. Braithwaite, *Crime, Shame and Reintegration* (Melbourne: Cambridge University Press, 1989).

50. Donald T. Campbell and Julien C. Stanley, *Experimental and Quasi-Experimental Designs for Research* (Chicago: Rand McNally, 1996), p. 35.

51. K. Beattie, "Adult Correctional Services in Canada, 2004/2005," *Juristat*, vol. 26, no. 5 (Ottawa: Minister of Industry, 2006).

52. Beattie, 2006.

53. Randy Martin, Robert J. Mutchnick, and W. Timothy Austin, *Criminological Thought: Pioneers Past and Present* (New York: Macmillan, 1990), p. 17.

54. Martin et al., 1990, p. 18.

55. Colman McCarthy, "Give the Boot to Boot Camps," *Washington Post* wire service, March 26, 1994.

Chapter 6

1. Karen J. Winkler, "Criminals Are Born as Well as Made, Authors of Controversial Book Assert," *Chronicle of Higher Education*, January 16, 1986, p. 9.

2. Julian V. Roberts and Thomas Gabor, "Lombrosian Wine in a New Bottle: Research on Crime and Race," *Canadian Journal of Criminology*, vol. 32, no. 2 (April 1990), p. 309.

3. "Brain Tumour Causes Uncontrollable Paedophilia," *New Scientist*, October 21, 2002. www.newscientist.com/article/dn2943-brain-tumour-causes-uncontrollable-paedophilia.html (Accessed March 18, 2007).

4. C. Ray Jeffery, "Biological Perspectives," *Journal of Criminal Justice Education*, vol. 4, no. 2 (Fall 1993), pp. 292–293.

5. C. Ray Jeffery, "Genetics, Crime and the Canceled Conference," *The Criminologist*, vol. 18, no. 1 (January/February 1993), pp. 1–8.

6. Anastasia Toufexis, "Seeking the Roots of Violence," *Time*, April 19, 1993, p. 53. The leader of the opposition was Dr. Peter Breggin, director of the Center for the Study of Psychiatry in Bethesda, Maryland.

7. C. Ray Jeffery, "The Genetics and Crime Conference Revisited," *The Criminologist*, vol. 21, no. 2 (March/April 1996), p. 3.

8. Jeffery, "Biological Perspectives," 1993, p. 298.

9. Konrad Lorenz, *On Aggression* (New York: Harcourt, Brace & World, 1966).

10. Lorenz, 1966, p. 23.

11. Lorenz, 1966, p. 38.

12. Lorenz, 1966, p. 249.

13. Lorenz, 1966, p. 225.

14. Cesare Lombroso, "Introduction," in Gina Lombroso-Ferrero, *Criminal Man According to the Classification of Cesare Lombroso*, 1911; reprinted Montclair, N.J., 1972, by Patterson Smith, p. xiv.

15. Charles Darwin, *Descent of Man: And Selection in Relation to Sex*, rev. ed. (London: John Murray, 1874), p. 137.

16. Auguste Comte, *A System of Positive Polity*, translated by John Henry Bridges (New York: Franklin, 1875). Originally published in four volumes, 1851–1854.

17. See K.L. Henwood and N.F. Pidgeon, "Qualitative Research and Psychological Theorising," *British Journal of Psychology*, vol. 83 (1992), pp. 97–111.

18. Lombroso, "Introduction," p. xv.

19. *Della Fossetta Cerebellare Mediana in un Criminale*, Institute Lombardo di Scienze e Lettere, 1872, pp. 1058–1065, as cited and translated by Thorsten Sellin, "A New Phase of Criminal Anthropology in Italy," *The Annals of the American Academy of Political and Social Science, Modern Crime*, 525 (May 1926), p. 234.

20. The English language version appeared in 1895 as Cesare Lombroso, *The Female Offender* (New York: D. Appleton & Co., 1895).

21. Marvin Wolfgang, "Cesare Lombroso," in Hermann Mannheim, *Pioneers in Criminology*, 2nd ed. (Montclair, N.J.: Patterson Smith, 1972), p. 254.

22. Charles Goring, *The English Convict: A Statistical Study* (London: His Majesty's Stationary Office, 1913). Reprinted in 1972 by Patterson Smith, Montclair, N.J., p. 15.

23. Goring, 1913, p.15.

24. Earnest A. Hooton, *Crime and the Man* (Cambridge, Mass.: Harvard University Press, 1939). Reprinted by Greenwood Press, Westport, Conn., 1972.

25. Hooton, *Crime and the Man*, pp. 57–58.

26. Hooton, *Crime and the Man*, p. 72.

27. Hooton, *Crime and the Man*, p. 75.

28. Hooton, *Crime and the Man*, p. 388.

29. Ernest A. Hooton, *The American Criminal: An Anthropological Study* (Cambridge, Mass.: Harvard University Press, 1939).

30. Stephen Schafer, *Theories in Criminology: Past and Present Philosophies of the Crime Problem* (New York: Random House, 1969), p. 187.

31. L. Arseneault et al., "Minor Physical Anomalies and Family Adversity as Risk Factors for

Violent Delinquency in Adolescence," *American Journal of Psychiatry*, vol. 157, no. 6 (June 2000), pp. 917–923.

32. William H. Sheldon, *Varieties of Delinquent Youth* (New York: Harper & Brothers, 1949).

33. Sheldon Glueck and Eleanor Glueck, *Unraveling Juvenile Delinquency* (Cambridge, Mass.: Harvard University Press, 1950).

34. D. Hill and W. Sargent, "A Case of Matricide," *Lancet*, vol. 244 (1943), pp. 526–527.

35. William Dufty, *Sugar Blues* (Pandor, PA: Chilton, 1975).

36. Nanci Hellmich, "Sweets May Not Be Culprit in Hyper Kids," *USA Today*, February 3, 1994, p. 1A, reporting on a study reported in the *New England Journal of Medicine*.

37. Hellmich, 1994, p. 1A.

38. See, for example, A.R. Mawson and K.J. Jacobs, "Corn Consumption, Tryptophan, and Cross National Homicide Rates," *Journal of Orthomolecular Psychiatry*, vol. 7 (1978), pp. 227–230; and A. Hoffer, "The Relation of Crime to Nutrition," *Humanist in Canada*, vol. 8 (1975), p. 8.

39. See, for example, C. Hawley and R.E. Buckley, "Food Dyes and Hyperkinetic Children," *Academy Therapy*, vol. 10 (1974), pp. 27–32; and Alexander Schauss, *Diet, Crime & Delinquency* (Berkeley, Calif.: Parker House, 1980).

40. "Special Report: Measuring Your Life with Coffee Spoons," *Tufts University Diet & Nutrition Letter*, vol. 2, no. 2 (April 1984), pp. 3–6.

41. See, for example, "Special Report: Does What You Eat Affect Your Mood and Actions?" *Tufts University Diet & Nutrition Letter*, vol. 2, no. 12 (February 1985), pp. 4–6.

42. See *Tufts University Diet & Nutrition Newsletter*, vol. 2, no. 11 (January 1985), p. 2; and "Special Report: Why Sugar Continues to Concern Nutritionists," *Tufts University Diet & Nutrition Letter*, vol. 3, no. 3 (May 1985), pp. 3–6.

43. A. Hoffer, "Children with Learning and Behavioral Disorders," *Journal of Orthomolecular Psychiatry*, vol. 5 (1976), p. 229.

44. "Special Report: Does What You Eat Affect Your Mood and Actions?" *Tufts University Diet & Nutrition Letter*, vol. 2, no. 12 (February 1985), p. 4.

45. Roger D. Masters, Brian Hone, and Anil Doshi, "Environmental Pollution, Neurotoxicity, and Criminal Violence," in J. Rose, ed., *Environmental Toxicology* (London and New York: Gordon and Breach, 1997).

46. Peter Montague, "Toxics and Violent Crime," *Rachel's Environment & Health Weekly*, no. 551 (June 19, 1997).

47. Alison Motluck, "Pollution May Lead to a Life of Crime," *New Scientist*, vol. 154, no. 2084 (May 31, 1997), p. 4.

48. See Alexander G. Schauss, "Tranquilizing Effect of Color Reduces Aggressive Behavior and Potential Violence," *Journal of Orthomolecular Psychiatry*, vol. 8, no. 4 (1979), pp. 218–221; and David Johnston, "Is It Merely a Fad, Or Do Pastel Walls Stop Jail House Brawls?" *Corrections Magazine*, vol. 7, no. 3 (1981), pp. 28–32.

49. Questions were raised, however, about the long-term effects of confinement in pink cells, and some researchers suggested that extended exposure to the colour pink could generate suicidal impulses.

50. See, for example, R.T. Rada, D.R. Laws, and R. Kellner, "Plasma Testosterone Levels in the Rapist," *Psychomatic Medicine*, vol. 38 (1976), pp. 257–268.

51. "The Insanity of Steroid Abuse," *Newsweek*, May 23, 1988, p. 75.

52. Dan Olweus, Mattsson Ake, Daisy Schalling, and Hans Low, "Testosterone, Aggression, Physical and Personality Dimensions in Normal Adolescent Males," *Psychosomatic Medicine*, vol. 42 (1980), pp. 253–269.

53. Richard Udry, "Biosocial Models of Adolescent Problem Behaviors," *Social Biology*, vol. 37 (1990), pp. 1–10.

54. Dan Olweus, "Testosterone and Adrenaline: Aggressive Antisocial Behavior in Normal Adolescent Males," in Sarnoff A. Mednick, Terrie E. Moffitt, and Susan A. Stack, eds., *The Causes of Crime: New Biological Approaches* (Cambridge: Cambridge University Press, 1987), pp. 263–282.

55. Alan Booth and D. Wayne Osgood, "The Influence of Testosterone on Deviance in Adulthood: Assessing and Explaining the Relationship," *Criminology*, vol. 31, no. 1 (1993), pp. 93–117.

56. Booth and Osgood, 1993, p. 93.

57. Booth and Osgood, 1993, p. 93.

58. Richard Udry, Luther Talbert, and Naomi Morris, "Biosocial Foundations for Adolescent Female Sexuality," *Demography*, vol. 23 (1986), pp. 217–227.

59. "Drunk Driving Charge Dismissed: PMS Cited," *Fayetteville Observer-Times* (North Carolina), June 7, 1991, p. 3A.

60. See D. Asso, *The Real Menstrual Cycle* (Toronto: Wiley, 1984).

61. Anastasia Toufexis, "Seeking the Roots of Violence," *Time*, April 19, 1993, pp. 52–54.

62. Richard Louis Dugdale, *The Jukes: A Study in Crime, Pauperism, Disease, and Heredity*, 3rd ed. (New York: G.P. Putnam's Sons, 1895).

63. Arthur H. Estabrook, *The Jukes in 1915* (Washington, D.C.: Carnegie Institute of Washington, 1916).

64. Henry Herbert Goddard, *The Kallikak Family: A Study in the Heredity of Feeblemindedness* (New York: Macmillan, 1912).

65. Samuel Hopkins Adams, "The Juke Myth," *Saturday Review*, vol. 38, no. 13 (1960), pp. 48–49

66. T.L. Chapman, "The Early Eugenics Movement in Western Canada," *Alberta History*, vol. 25, (1977), pp. 9–17. See also A. McLaren, "The Creation of a Haven for Human Thoroughbreds," *Canadian Historical Review*, vol. 67 (1986), pp. 264–268.

67. P.A. Jacobs, M. Brunton, and M. Melville, "Aggressive Behavior, Mental Subnormality, and the XYY Male," *Nature*, vol. 208 (1965), p. 1351.

68. Biologists often define *karyotype* as "a photomicrograph of metaphase chromosomes in a standard array." The process of karyotyping typically involves drawing a small sample of blood.

69. See David A. Jones, *History of Criminology: A Philosophical Perspective* (Westport, Conn.: Greenwood Press, 1986), p. 124.

70. Many of which have been summarized in J. Katz and W. Chambliss, "Biology and Crime," in J.F. Sheley, ed., *Criminology* (Belmont, Calif.: Wadsworth, 1991), pp. 245–272.

71. As reported by S.A. Mednick and J. Volavka, "Biology and Crime," in N. Morris and M. Tonry, *Crime and Justice: An Annual Review of Research*, vol. 2 (Chicago: University of Chicago Press, 1980), pp. 85–158; and D.A. Andrews and James Bonta, *The Psychology of Criminal Conduct* (Cincinnati: Anderson, 1994), pp. 126–127.

72. T. Sarbin and J. Miller, "Demonism Revisited: The XYY Chromosomal Anomaly," *Issues in Criminology*, vol. 5 (1970), p. 199.

73. Geoffrey Cowley and Carol Hallin, "The Genetics of Bad Behavior: A Study Links Violence to Heredity," *Newsweek*, November 1, 1993, p. 57.

74. Johannes Lange, *Verbrechen als Schicksal* (Leipzig: Georg Thieme, 1929).

75. Karl O. Christiansen, "A Preliminary Study of Criminality among Twins," in Sarnoff Mednick and Karl Christiansen, eds., *Biosocial Bases of Criminal Behavior* (New York: Gardner Press, 1977).

76. S.A. Mednick, W.F. Gabrielli, Jr., and B. Hutchings, "Genetic Influences in Criminal Convictions: Evidence from an Adoption Cohort," *Science*, vol. 224 (1984), pp. 891–894.

77. Mednick et al., 1984, pp. 891–894.

78. S. Mednick and J. Volavka, "Biology and Crime," in N. Morris and M. Tonry, eds., *Crime and Justice* (Chicago: University of Chicago Press, 1980).

79. M. Bohman, R. Cloninger, S. Sigvardsson, and A.L. Von Knorring, "Predisposition to Petty Criminality in Swedish Adoptees: Genetic and Environmental Heterogeneity," *Archives of General Psychiatry*, vol. 39 (1982), pp. 1233–1241.

80. C. Ray Jeffery, "Biological Perspectives," *Journal of Criminal Justice Education*, vol. 4, no. 2 (Fall 1993), p. 300.

81. Diana Kendall, Jane L. Murray, and Rick Linden, *Sociology in Our Times. The Essentials* (Toronto: ITP Nelson, 2008).

82. Frank Schmalleger, *Criminology Today: An Integrative Introduction* (New Jersey: Prentice Hall, 2006), p. 166.

83. D. Thomas, *Criminality among the Foreign Born: Analysis of Federal Prison Population* (Ottawa: Immigration and Employment Canada, 1992).

84. Robert Silverman and Leslie Kennedy, *Deadly Deeds: Murder in Canada* (Scarborough, Ont.: Nelson Canada, 1993).

85. Mary Hyde and Carol La Prairie, *American Police Crime Prevention* (Working Paper) (Ottawa: Solicitor General of Canada, 1987).

86. Frank Schmalleger, *Criminology Today: An Integrative Introduction* (New Jersey: Prentice Hall, 2006), p. 166.

87. See, for example, D.H. Fishbein, "The Psychobiology of Female Aggression," *Criminal Justice and Behavior*, vol. 19 (1992), pp. 99–126.

88. Robbin S. Ogle, Daniel Maier-Katin, and Thomas J. Bernard, "A Theory of Homicidal Behavior among Women," *Criminology*, vol. 33, no. 2 (1995), pp. 173–193.

89. Ogle et al., 1995, p. 177.

90. Ogle et al., 1995, p. 179.

91. Arthur Fisher, "A New Synthesis Comes of Age," *Mosaic*, vol. 22, no. 1 (Spring 1991), pp. 2–9.

92. Edward O. Wilson, *Sociobiology: The New Synthesis* (Cambridge, Mass.: The Belknap Press of Harvard University Press, 1975).

93. Janet Zimmerman, "6 Held in Brutal Attack of Mich. Teens," *USA Today*, June 24, 1997, p. 3A.

94. Wilson, 1975, p. 327.

95. Sarah Blaffer Hrdy, *The Langurs of Abu: Female and Male Strategies of Reproduction* (Cambridge, Mass.: Harvard University Press, 1977).

96. Research by Martin Daly and Margo Wilson of McMaster University in Hamilton, Ontario, as reported in Arthur Fisher, "A New Synthesis II: How Different Are Humans?" *Mosaic*, vol. 22, no. 1 (Spring 1991), p. 14.

97. Arthur Fisher, "A New Synthesis II: How Different Are Humans?" *Mosaic*, vol. 22, no. 1 (Spring 1991), p. 11.

98. John H. Beckstrom, *Evolutionary Jurisprudence: Prospects and Limitations on the Youth of Modern Darwinism Throughout the Legal Process* (Urbana, Ill.: University of Illinois Press, 1989).

99. John Madison Memory, "Sociobiology and the Metamorphoses of Criminology: 1978– 2000," unpublished manuscript.

100. Memory, "Sociobiology," p. 33.

101. See also Arnold L. Lieber, *The Lunar Effect: Biological Tides and Human Emotions* (Garden City: Anchor Press, 1978).

102. James Q. Wilson and Richard J. Herrnstein, *Crime and Human Nature* (New York: Simon & Schuster, 1985).

103. Winkler, "Criminals Are Born," p. 5.

104. Winkler, "Criminals Are Born," p. 8.

105. Jeffery, "Biological Perspectives," p. 303.

106. Jeffery, "Biological Perspectives," p. 303.

107. Julian V. Roberts and Thomas Gabor, "Lombrosian Wine in a New Bottle: Research on Crime and Race," *Canadian Journal of Criminology*, vol. 32, no. 2 (April 1990), p. 309.

108. *Time*, April 19, 1993, p. 53.

109. Lee Ellis and Anthony Walsh, "Gene-Based Evolutionary Theories in Criminology," *Criminology*, vol. 35, no. 2 (1997), pp. 229–230.

110. Glenn D. Walters and Thomas W. White, "Heredity and Crime: Bad Genes or Bad Research?" *Criminology*, vol. 27, no. 3 (1989), pp. 455–485. See also P.A. Brennan and S.A. Mednick, "Reply to Walters and White: Heredity and Crime," *Criminology*, vol. 28, no. 4 (November 1990), pp. 657–661.

111. Walters and White, 1989, p. 478.

Chapter 7

1. William R. Doerner, "The Man Who Hated Women," *Time*, December 18, 1989, p. 34.

2. Robert D. Hare, *Without Conscience. The Disturbing World of the Psychopaths Among Us* (Pocket Books, 1993), p. xi.

3. R. Boyes, "On the Spot: The German Cannibal Verdict," *The Times*, January 30, 2004. http://www.timesonline.co.uk/tol/tools_and_services/specials/article1007718.ece.

4. R. Boyes, "Cannibal Reveals Man-Eater Network," *The Times*, January 7, 2004, www.news.com.au/common/printpage/0,6093,8340267,00.html.

5. Barry Came, "Montreal Massacre," *Maclean's Magazine*, December 18, 1989, p. 14.

6. Bruce Wallace, "The Making of a Mass Killer," *Maclean's Magazine*, December 18, 1989, p. 22.

7. D.A. Andrews and James Bonta, *The Psychology of Criminal Conduct* (Cincinnati: Anderson, 1998), p. 93.

8. See Adrian Raine, *The Psychopathology of Crime: Criminal Behavior as a Clinical Disorder* (Orlando: Academic Press, 1993).

9. Cathy Spatz Widom and Hans Toch, "The Contribution of Psychology to Criminal Justice Education," *Journal of Criminal Justice Education*, vol. 4, no. 2 (Fall 1993), p. 253.

10. Curt R. Bartol, *Criminal Behavior: A Psychosocial Approach*, 3rd ed. (Englewood Cliffs, N.J.: Prentice Hall, 1991), p. 16.

11. For additional information, see S. Giora Shoham and Mark C. Seis, *A Primer in the Psychology of Crime* (New York: Harrow and Heston, 1993); and Frederic L. Faust, "A Review of *A Primer in the Psychology of Crime*," in *Social Pathology*, vol. 1, no. 1 (January 1995), pp. 48–61.

12. Nicole Hahn Rafter, "Psychopathy and the Evolution of Criminological Knowledge," *Theoretical Criminology*, vol. 1, no. 2 (May 1997), pp. 235–259.

13. Nolan D.C. Lewis, "Foreword," in David Abrahamsen, *Crime and the Human Mind* (Montclair, N.J.: Patterson Smith, 1969), p. vii. Originally published in 1944.

14. David Abrahamsen, *Crime and the Human Mind* (Montclair, N.J.: Patterson Smith, 1969), p. vii. Originally published in 1944.

15. P.Q. Roche, *The Criminal Mind: A Study of Communications between Criminal Law and Psychiatry* (New York: Grove Press, 1958), p. 52.

16. *The American Heritage Dictionary and Electronic Thesaurus* (Boston: Houghton Mifflin, 1987).

17. *The American Heritage Dictionary and Electronic Thesaurus*, 1987.

18. *The American Heritage Dictionary and Electronic Thesaurus*, 1987.

19. *The American Heritage Dictionary and Electronic Thesaurus*, 1987.

20. "Nationline: Book Thief," *USA Today*, August 1, 1991, p. 3A.

21. Hans J. Eysenck, *Crime and Personality* (Boston: Houghton Mifflin, 1964).

22. Hans J. Eysenck, "Personality and Criminality: A Dispositional Analysis," in William S. Laufer and Freda Adler, eds., *Advances in Criminology Theory*, vol. 1 (New Brunswick, N.J.: Transaction, 1989), p. 90.

23. Eysenck, 1964, pp. 35–36.

24. Eysenck, 1964, p. 92.

25. Eysenck, 1964, p. 53, citing J.B.S. Haldane, "Foreword," to Johannes Lange, *Crime as Destiny, A Study of Criminal Twins* (London: G. Allen & Unwin, Ltd., 1931), p. 53.

26. J. Dollard, L. Doob, N. Miller, O. Mowrer, and R. Sears, *Frustration and Aggression* (New Haven, Conn.: Yale University Press, 1939).

27. Maria Bohuslawsky, "Troubled Killer Was Once Fired," *Ottawa Citizen*, April 7, 1999, p. C1.

28. Andrew F. Henry and James F. Short Jr., *Suicide and Homicide: Economic, Sociological, and Psychological Aspects of Aggression* (Glencoe, Ill.: Free Press, 1954).

29. Stewart Palmer, *A Study of Murder* (New York: Crowell, 1960).

30. Pauline Tam, "Not Criminally Responsible," *Ottawa Citizen*, October 29, 1996, p. C3.

31. Gwynn Nettler, *Killing One Another* (Cincinnati: Anderson, 1982), p. 159.

32. Nettler, 1982, p. 155.

33. Abrahamsen, 1969, p. 99.

34. Abrahamsen, 1969, p. 100.

35. As noted by Nicole Hahn Rafter in "Psychopathy and the Evolution of Criminological Knowledge." See Richard von Krafft-Ebing, *Psychopathia Sexualis* (New York: Stein and Day, 1965), reprint of the original 1886 edition; and *Text-Book of Insanity* (Philadelphia: F.A. Davis Company, 1904), first German edition, 1879.

36. Bernard H. Glueck, *Studies in Forensic Psychiatry* (Boston: Little, Brown, 1916).

37. William Healy, *The Individual Delinquent* (Boston: Little, Brown, 1915).

38. Early writings about the psychopath personality focused almost exclusively on men, and most psychiatrists appeared to believe that very few women (if any) possessed such traits.

39. Abrahamsen, 1969, p. 23.

40. Hervey M. Cleckley, *The Mask of Sanity*, 4th ed. (St. Louis: C.V. Mosby, 1964).

41. Nettler, 1982, p. 179.

42. Ralph Serin, "Can Criminal Psychopaths Be Identified?" Correctional Service of Canada, October 22, 1999.

43. Albert I. Rabin, "The Antisocial Personality—Psychopathy and Sociopathy," in Hans Toch, *Psychology of Crime and Criminal Justice* (Prospect Heights, Ill.: Waveland, 1979), p. 330.

44. M.F. Belmore and V.L. Quinsey, "Correlates of Psychopathy in a Noninstitutional Sample," *Journal of Interpersonal Violence*, vol. 9 (1994), pp. 339–349; and C.S. Widom, "A Methodology for Studying Non-Institutional Psychopaths," *Journal of Consulting and Clinical Psychology*, vol. 45 (1977), pp. 674–683.

45. A.A. Forth, S.D. Hart, and R.D. Hare, "Assessment of Psychopathy in Male Young Offenders," *Psychological Assessment: A Journal of Consulting and Clinical Psychology*, vol. 2 (1990), pp. 342–344.

46. R.H. Hare, "The Hare PCL-R: Some Issues Concerning Its Use and Misuse," *Legal and Criminological Psychology*, vol. 3 (1998), p. 99.

47. R.D. Hare, *Psychopathy: Theory and Research* (New York: John Wiley & Sons, 1970).

48. L.N. Robins, *Deviant Children Grow Up* (Baltimore: Williams and Wilkins, 1966).

49. S.B. Guze, *Criminality and Psychiatric Disorders* (New York: Oxford University Press, 1976).

50. R.D. Hare, "Psychopathy and Antisocial Personality Disorder: A Case of Diagnostic Confusion," *Psychiatric Times*, vol. 13, no. 2, February 1996.

51. Hare, 1996.

52. Hare, 1996.

53. A.L. Rabin, "The Antisocial Personality—Psychopathy and Sociopathy," in Hans Toch, *Psychology of Crime and Criminal Justice* (Prospect Heights, IL: Waveland, 1979), p. 330.

54. For recent research in this area, see A. Tengstrom et al., "Psychopathy as a Predictor of Violent Recidivism among Criminal Offenders with Schizophrenia in Sweden," *Law and Behavior*, vol. 23, no. 1 (2000), pp. 45–58. For additional information, see V.L. Quinsey et al., *Violent Offenders: Appraising and Managing Risk* (Washington, D.C.: American Psychological Association, 1998); and V.L. Quinsey, M.E. Rice, and G.T. Harris, "Actuarial Prediction of Sexual Recidivism," *Journal of Interpersonal Violence*, vol. 10, no. 1 (1995), pp. 85–105.

55. S. Hodgins and G. Cote, "The Prevalence of Mental Disorders Among Penitentiary Inmates in Quebec," *Canada's Mental Health*, vol. 38 (1990), pp. 1–4.

56. H. Prins, *Offenders, Deviants or Patients? An Introduction to the Study of Socio-Forensic Problems* (London: Tavistock, 1980).

57. Hare, 1996.

58. Hare, 1996.

59. Abrahamsen, 1969, p. 26.

60. Nancy Gibbs, "The Devil's Disciple," *Time*, January 11, 1993, p. 40.

61. Seymour L. Halleck, *Psychiatry and the Dilemmas of Crime: A Study of Causes, Punishment and Treatment* (Berkeley: University of California Press, 1971).

62. Halleck, 1971, p. 77.

63. Halleck, 1971, p. 78.

64. Halleck, 1971, p. 80.

65. Halleck, 1971, p. 80.

66. Halleck, 1971, p. 80.

67. Arnold S. Linsky, Ronet Bachman, and Murray A. Straus, *Stress, Culture, and Aggression* (New Haven: Yale University Press, 1995).

68. Linsky, Bachman, and Straus, 1995, p. 7.

69. Gabriel Tarde, *The Laws of Imitation*, trans. E. C. Parsons (1890; reprint, Gloucester, MA: Peter Smith, 1962).

70. Albert Bandura, "The Social Learning Perspective: Mechanisms of Aggression," in Toch, *Psychology of Crime and Criminal Justice*, pp. 198–236.

71. M.M. Lefkowitz, L.D. Eron, L.O. Walder, and L.R. Huesmann, "Television Violence and Child Aggression: A Follow-up Study," in G.A. Comstock and E.A. Rubinstein, eds., *Television and Social Behavior*, vol. 3 (Washington,

D.C.: U.S. Government Printing Office, 1972), pp. 35–135.

72. Jim Demers, "'I Am Gavin. How a Bright Kid with Excellent Self-Esteem Slaughtered His Whole Family," *Alberta Report*, December 6, 1993, pp. 18–22.

73. Demers, 1993, p. 19.

74. Demers, 1993, p. 22.

75. Widom and Toch, 1993.

76. Widom and Toch, 1993, p. 253.

77. C.R. Hollin, *Psychology and Crime: An Introduction to Criminological Psychology* (London: Routledge, 1989), p. 42.

78. Hollin, 1989, p. 254.

79. "15-Year-Old Killer Feared Being Called a 'Little Punk,'" *Fayetteville Observer-Times*, December 26, 1993, p. 1A.

80. *R. v. Parks* (1992), 75 C.C.C. (3d) 287 (S.C.C.).

81. S. Barnhorst and R. Barnhorst, *Criminal Law and the Canadian Criminal Code* (Toronto: McGraw-Hill Ryerson, 2004), p. 67.

82. Halleck, *Psychiatry and the Dilemmas of Crime*, p. 213.

83. *R. v. Swain* (1991), 63 C.C.C. (3d) 481 (S.C.C.).

84. Minister of Justice and Attorney General of Canada, *Justice Communiqué*, January 30, 1992, p. 2.

85. F. Schmalleger, *Criminology Today. An Integrated Introduction* (New Jersey: Prentice-Hall Inc., 1999), pp. 253–256.

86. *Martin's Annual Criminal Code* (Aurora: Canada Law Book Inc., 1999), s. 672.5(2).

87. M.A. Jackson and C.T. Griffiths, *Canadian Criminology. Perspectives on Crime and Criminality* (Toronto: Harcourt Brace and Co., 1995), p. 73.

88. Shirley Steller, Canadian Centre for Justice Statistics, *Special Study on Mentally Disordered Accused in the Criminal Justice System* (Ottawa: Minister of Industry, 2003).

89. Pauline Tam, *Ottawa Citizen*, October 29, 1996, p. C3.

90. See, for example, D.P. Farrington, "Childhood Aggression and Adult Violence: Early Precursors and Later Life Outcomes," in D.J. Pepler and K.H. Rubin, eds., *The Development and Treatment of Childhood Aggression* (Hillsdale, N.J.: Erlbaum, 1990), pp. 2–29; and R.E. Tremblay, B. Masse, D. Perron, M. LeBlanc, A.E. Schwartzman, and J.E. Ledingham, "Early Disruptive Behavior: Poor School Achievement, Delinquent Behavior and Delinquent Personality: Longitudinal Analyses," *Journal of Consulting and Clinical Psychology*, vol. 60, no. 1 (1992), pp. 64–72.

91. R. Loeber, "Questions and Advances in the Study of Developmental Pathways," in D. Cicchetti and S. Toth, eds., *Models and Integration: Rochester Symposium on Developmental Psychopathology* (Rochester, N.Y.: University of Rochester Press, 1991), pp. 97–115.

92. Joanne Laucius, "Pedophile's Trail of Destruction," *Ottawa Citizen*, April 28, 1999, p. B1.

93. Jennifer L. White, Terrie E. Moffitt, Felton Earls, Lee Robins, and Phil A. Silva, "How Early Can We Tell? Predictors of Childhood Conduct Disorder and Adolescent Delinquency," *Criminology*, vol. 28, no. 4 (1990), pp. 507–528.

94. Daniel S. Nagin and David P. Farrington, "The Stability of Criminal Potential from Childhood to Adulthood," *Criminology*, vol. 30, no. 2 (1992), pp. 235–260.

95. Paul Gendreau, Tracy Little, and Claire Goggin, "A Meta-Analysis of the Predictors of Adult Offender Recidivism: What Works!" *Criminology*, vol. 34, no. 4 (November 1996), pp. 575–607.

96. For one of the first and still definitive works in the area of selective incapacitation, see Peter Greenwood and Allan Abrahamsen, *Selective Incapacitation* (Santa Monica, CA: Rand Corporation, 1982).

97. M.A. Peterson, H.B. Braiker, and S.M. Polich, *Who Commits Crimes?* (Cambridge: Oelgeschlager, Gunn and Hain, 1981).

98. J. Monahan, *Predicting Violent Behavior: An Assessment of Clinical Techniques* (Beverly Hills, Calif.: Sage, 1981).

99. Canadian Press, *Number of Dangerous Offenders in Canada Growing*, May 16, 2004, http://www.ctv.ca/servlet/ArticleNews/story/CTVNews/20040516/dangerous040516?s_name=&no_ads (Accessed December 26, 2006).

100. J. Bonta, A. Harris, I. Zinger, and D. Carrière, "The Crown Files Research Project: A Study of Dangerous Offenders" (Ottawa: Solicitor General of Canada, 1996).

101. Jill Peay, "Dangerousness—Ascription or Description," in M.P. Feldman, ed., *Developments in the Study of Criminal Behavior*, vol. 2, *Violence* (New York: John Wiley & Sons, 1982), p. 211, citing N. Walker, "Dangerous People," *International Journal of Law and Psychiatry*, vol. 1 (1978), pp. 37–50.

102. See, for example, Michael Gottfredson and Travis Hirschi, *A General Theory of Crime* (Stanford, Calif.: Stanford University Press, 1990); and Travis Hirschi and Michael Gottfredson, "Age and the Explanation of Crime," *American Journal of Sociology*, vol. 89 (1983), pp. 552–584.

103. David F. Greenberg, "Modeling Criminal Careers," *Criminology*, vol. 29, no. 1 (1991), p. 39.

104. D.A. Andrews and James Bonta, *The Psychology of Criminal Conduct* (Cincinnati: Anderson, 1998).

105. Andrews and Bonta, 1998, p. 2.

106. Andrews and Bonta, 1998, p. 2.

107. Andrews and Bonta, 1998, p. 31.

108. Andrews and Bonta, 1998, p. 349.

109. Andrews and Bonta, 1998, p. 362.

110. Robert R. Hazelwood and John E. Douglas, "The Lust Murderer," *FBI Law Enforcement Bulletin* (Washington: U.S. Department of Justice, April 1980).

111. Hazelwood and Douglas, 1980.

112. Anastasia Toufexis, "Mind Games with Monsters," *Time*, May 6, 1991, pp. 68, 69.

Chapter 8

1. Frank Tannenbaum, *Crime and the Community* (Boston: Ginn and Company, 1938), p. 25.

2. William Faulkner, *As I Lay Dying* (New York: Random House, 1964).

3. P. Tam, "Driver in Battersby Killing Sent to Adult Jail," *Ottawa Citizen*, November 8, 1996, p. D1; and M. Blanchfield, "Crossed Paths," *Ottawa Citizen*, February 17, 1996, p. B2.

4. Peter Haggett, "Human Ecology," in Alan Bullock and Oliver Stallybrass, eds., *The Fontana Dictionary of Modern Social Thought* (London: Fontana, 1977), p. 187.

5. W.I. Thomas and Florian Znaniecki, *The Polish Peasant in Europe and America* (Boston: Gorham, 1920).

6. Clifford R. Shaw et al., *Delinquency Areas* (Chicago: University of Chicago Press, 1929).

7. David Matza, *Becoming Deviant* (Englewood Cliffs, N.J.: Prentice Hall, 1969).

8. C.P. La Prairie, "Community Types, Crime and Police Services on Canadian Indian Reserves," *Journal of Research in Crime and Delinquency*, vol. 25 (1987), pp. 375–391.

9. C.P. La Prairie, "Seen But Not Heard: Native People in the Inner City," in *City-By-City Differences: Inner Cities and the Criminal Justice System, Report 2, Aboriginal Justice Directorate* (Ottawa: Department of Justice, 1994).

10. W.S. Robinson, "Ecological Correlation and the Behavior of Individuals," *American Sociological Review*, vol. 15 (1950), pp. 351–357.

11. Robinson, 1950, pp. 351–357.

12. Robert J. Bursik, "Social Disorganization and Theories of Crime and Delinquency: Problems and Prospects," *Criminology*, vol. 26, no. 4 (1988), p. 519.

13. Stephen J. Pfohl, *Images of Deviance and Social Control* (New York: McGraw-Hill, 1985), p. 167.

14. Lawrence W. Sherman, Patrick R. Gartin, and Michael E. Buerger, "Hot Spots of Predatory Crime: Routine Activities and the Criminology of Place," *Criminology*, vol. 27, no. 1 (1989), pp. 27–55.

15. Rodney Stark, "Deviant Places: A Theory of the Ecology of Crime," *Criminology*, vol. 25, no. 4 (1987), p. 893.

16. Stark, 1987, pp. 895–899.

17. James Q. Wilson and George Kelling, "Broken Windows," *The Atlantic Monthly*, March 1982.

18. Oscar Newman, *Architectural Design for Crime Prevention* (Washington, D.C.: U.S. Department of Justice, 1973). See also Oscar Newman, *Defensible Space* (New York: Macmillan, 1972); and Oscar Newman, *Creating Defensible Space* (Washington, D.C.: Office of Housing and Urban Development, 1996).

19. Oscar Newman, *Defensible Space: Crime Prevention Through Urban Design* (New York: Macmillan, 1972), p. 3. See also Ralph B. Taylor and Adele V. Harrell, "Physical Environment and Crime" (National Institute of Justice, May 1996).

20. Sherman et al., 1989, p. 31.

21. Peel Regional Police Service, http://www.peelpolice.on.ca/Crime%20Prevention/CPTED.aspx (Accessed March 24, 2007).

22. Sherman et al., 1989, p. 49.

23. Émile Durkheim, *Suicide: A Study in Sociology* (New York: Free Press, 1897). Reprinted and translated in 1951.

24. Robert K. Merton, "Social Structure and Anomie," *American Sociological Review*, vol. 3 (October 1938), pp. 672–682; and Robert K. Merton, *Social Theory and Social Structure*, rev. ed. (New York: Free Press, 1957).

25. Robert K. Merton, *Social Theory and Social Structure* (New York: Glencoe, 1957), p. 190.

26. M. Beare, *Criminal Conspiracies: Organized Crime in Canada* (Toronto: McClelland & Stewart, 1996).

27. Robert Agnew, "Foundation for a General Strain Theory of Crime and Delinquency," *Criminology*, vol. 30, no. 1 (1992), pp. 47–87.

28. Agnew, 1992.

29. Agnew, 1992.

30. Raymond Paternoster and Paul Mazerolle, "General Strain Theory and Delinquency: A Replication and Extension," *Journal of Research in Crime and Delinquency*, vol. 31, no. 3 (1994), pp. 235–263.

31. Robert Agnew and Helene Raskin White, "An Empirical Test of General Strain Theory," *Criminology*, vol. 30, no. 4 (1992), pp. 475–499.

32. Agnew, 1992.

33. Travis Hirschi, "Review of Delbert S. Elliott, David Huizinga, and Suzanne S. Ageton,

Explaining Delinquency and Drug Use" (Beverly Hills, CA.: Sage, 1985), in *Criminology*, vol. 25, no. 1 (February 1987), p. 195.

34. Thorsten Sellin, *Culture Conflict and Crime* (New York: Social Science Research Council, 1938).

35. Rick Hampson, "Danish Mom Finds New York Doesn't Kid Around," *USA Today*, May 14, 1997, p. 3A.

36. Sellin, 1938, p. 68.

37. Frederick M. Thrasher, *The Gang* (Chicago: University of Chicago Press, 1927).

38. William F. Whyte, *Street Corner Society: The Social Structure of an Italian Slum* (Chicago: University of Chicago Press, 1943).

39. Walter Miller, "Lower Class Culture as a Generating Milieu of Gang Delinquency," *Journal of Social Issues*, vol. 14, no. 3 (1958), pp. 5–19.

40. Miller, 1958, p. 19.

41. Miller, 1958, p. 8.

42. Miller, 1958, p. 9.

43. Franco Ferracuti and Marvin Wolfgang, *The Subculture of Violence: Toward an Integrated Theory of Criminology* (London: Tavistock, 1967).

44. Frank P. Williams III and Marilyn D. McShane, *Criminological Theory* (Englewood Cliffs, N.J.: Prentice Hall, 1988), p. 79.

45. Ferracuti and Wolfgang, 1967, p. 151.

46. Ferracuti and Wolfgang, 1967, p. 151.

47. Jeffrey I. Ross, *Violence in Canada. Sociopolitical Perspectives* (Canada: Oxford University Press, 1995), pp. 195–196.

48. For an excellent review of the literature, see F. Frederick Hawley, "The Southern Violence Construct: A Skeleton in the Criminological Closet," paper presented at the annual meeting of the American Society of Criminology, 1988.

49. Bertram Wyatt-Brown, *Southern Honor: Ethics and Behavior in the Old South* (Oxford: Oxford University Press, 1983).

50. John Hagan, "Structural and Cultural Disinvestment and the New Ethnographies of Poverty and Culture," *Contemporary Sociology*, vol. 22, no. 3 (1993), pp. 327–31.

51. Richard A. Cloward and Lloyd E. Ohlin, *Delinquency and Opportunity: A Theory of Delinquent Gangs* (Glencoe, Ill.: Free Press, 1960).

52. Cloward and Ohlin, 1960, p. 7.

53. Cloward and Ohlin, 1960, p. 13.

54. Cloward and Ohlin, 1960, p. 16.

55. Cloward and Ohlin, 1960, p. 19.

56. Cloward and Ohlin, 1960, p. 3.

57. Cloward and Ohlin, 1960, p. 37.

58. Cloward and Ohlin, 1960, pp. 12–13.

59. Albert H. Cohen, *Delinquent Boys: The Culture of the Gang* (Glencoe, Ill.: Free Press, 1955).

60. Cohen, 1955, p. 13.

61. Donald J. Shoemaker, *Theories of Delinquency: An Examination of Explanations of Delinquent Behavior* (New York: Oxford University Press, 1984), p. 102, citing Cohen.

62. Cohen, 1955, p. 121.

63. Shoemaker, 1984, p. 105.

64. Gwynn Nettler, *Explaining Crime* (New York: McGraw-Hill, 1984).

65. Margaret Anderson, "Review Essay: Rape Theories, Myths, and Social Change," *Contemporary Crises*, vol. 5 (1983), p. 237.

66. Robert M. Gordon, "Criminal Business Organizations, Street Gangs and 'Wanna Be' Groups: A Vancouver Perspective," *Canadian Journal of Criminology*, vol. 42, no. 1 (January 2000), pp. 39–60.

67. Criminal Intelligence Service of Canada, *2006 Annual Report on Organized Crime*, http://www.cisc.gc.ca/annual_reports/annual_report2006/coverpage_2006_e.htm (Accessed March 14, 2007).

68. Arlen Egley Jr. and Aline K. Major, *Highlights of the 2002 National Youth Gang Survey* (Washington, D.C.: Office of Juvenile Justice and Delinquency Prevention, 2004).

69. National Gang Crime Research Center, *Achieving Justice and Reversing the Problem of Gang Crime and Gang Violence in America Today: Preliminary Results of the Project Gangfact Study* (Chicago: National Gang Crime Research Center, 1996).

70. G. David Curry and Irving A. Spergel, "Gang Homicide, Delinquency, and Community," *Criminology*, vol. 26, no. 3 (1988), pp. 381–405.

71. Curry and Spergel, 1988, p. 401.

72. See Mary H. Glazier, a review of J. Mitchell Miller and Jeffrey P. Rush, eds., *Gangs: A Criminal Justice Approach* (Cincinnati: Anderson, 1996), in *The Criminologist* (July/April 1996), p. 29.

73. Steven Schlossman et al., *Delinquency Prevention in South Chicago: A Fifty-Year Assessment of the Chicago Area Project* (Santa Monica, CA: Rand Corporation, 1984).

74. J. Robert Lilly, Francis T. Cullen, and Richard A. Ball, *Criminological Theory: Context and Consequences* (Newbury Park, CA: Sage, 1989), p. 80.

75. Lamar T. Empey, *American Delinquency: Its Meaning and Construction* (Homewood, IL: Dorsey, 1982), p. 243.

76. Sibylle Artz, *Sex, Power and the Violent School Girl* (Toronto: Trifolium Books Inc, 1998), p. 24.

77. Gwynn Nettler, *Killing One Another* (Cincinnati: Anderson, 1982), p. 54.

78. James Q. Wilson, *The Moral Sense* (New York: The Free Press, 1993).

Chapter 9

1. Edwin M. Lemert, *Social Pathology: A Systematic Approach to the Theory of Sociopathic Behavior* (New York: McGraw-Hill, 1951), p. 284.

2. Albert K. Cohen, *Delinquent Boys: The Culture of the Gang* (Glencoe, IL: Free Press, 1995), p. 11.

3. "Killer Seeks Family Visits," CBC news, cbc.ca, February 14, 2001, http://www.cbc.ca/news/story/2001/02/14/hearing010214.html (Accessed March 25, 2007).

4. "Freedom Weighed for Killer of Heiress," CBC news, cbc.ca, February 13, 2001, http://www.cbc.ca/news/story/2001/02/13/ott_eatonkiller010213.html (Accessed March 25, 2007).

5. Edwin Sutherland, *Principles of Criminology* (New York: Lippincott, 1939).

6. Edwin H. Sutherland and Donald R. Cressey, *Criminology* (New York: Lippincott, 1978).

7. S. Brown, V. Creamer, and B. Stetson, "Adolescent Alcohol Expectancies in Relation to Personal and Parental Drinking Patterns," *Journal of Abnormal Psychology*, vol. 96 (1987), pp. 117–121.

8. Gresham Sykes and David Matza, "Techniques of Neutralization: A Theory of Delinquency," *American Sociological Review*, vol. 22 (December 1957), pp. 664–670.

9. Sykes and Matza, 1957, pp. 664–670.

10. Robert Agnew, "The Techniques of Neutralization and Violence," *Criminology*, vol. 32, no. 4 (1994), pp. 555–580.

11. Agnew, 1994, pp. 555–580.

12. Frank Tannenbaum, *Crime and the Community* (New York: Atheneum Press, 1938), pp. 17–18.

13. Edwin M. Lemert, *Social Pathology: A Systematic Approach to the Theory of Sociopathic Behavior* (New York: McGraw-Hill, 1951), p. 76.

14. Lemert, 1951, p. 76.

15. Howard Becker, *Outsiders: Studies in the Sociology of Deviance* (New York: Free Press, 1963).

16. Becker, *Outsiders*, p. 1.

17. Becker, *Outsiders*, p. 9.

18. Becker, *Outsiders*, p. 147.

19. M.A. Jackson and C.T. Griffiths, *Canadian Criminology: Perspectives on Crime and Criminality* (Toronto: Harcourt Brace Canada, 1995), pp. 261–263.

20. Becker, *Outsiders*, pp. 37–38.

21. Mike S. Adams, "Labeling and Differential Association: Towards A General Social Learning Theory of Crime and Deviance," *American Journal of Criminal Justice*, vol. 20, no. 2 (1996), pp. 147–164.

22. Adams, 1996, p. 160.

23. Randy Martin, Robert J. Mutchnick, and W. Timothy Austin, *Criminological Thought: Pioneers Past and Present* (New York: Macmillan, 1990), p. 368.

24. A number of papers have been released in the Reintegrative Shaming Experiments (RISE) series to date: Lawrence W. Sherman and Heather Strang, *The Right Kind of Shame for Crime Prevention* (Canberra, Australia: Australian National University, 1997); Heather Strang and Lawrence W. Sherman, *The Victim's Perspective* (Canberra, Australia: Australian National University, 1997); Lawrence W. Sherman and Geoffrey C. Barnes, *Restorative Justice and Offenders' Respect for the Law* (Canberra, Australia: Australian National University, 1997); and Lawrence W. Sherman and Heather Strang, *Restorative Justice and Deterring Crime* (Canberra, Australia: Australian National University, 1997); Nathan Harris and Jamie B. Burton, *The Reliability of Observed Reintegrative Shaming, Shame, Defiance and Other Key Concepts in Diversionary Conferences* (Canberra, Australia: Australian National University, 1997).

25. RISE Working Papers: *Introduction* (Canberra, Australia: Australian National University, 1997).

26. See Chapter 9, endnote 24.

27. Cited in Lawrence W. Sherman and Heather Strang, *The Right Kind of Shame for Crime Prevention* (Canberra, Australia: Australian National University, 1997).

28. Cited in Lawrence W. Sherman and Heather Strang, *The Right Kind of Shame for Crime Prevention* (Canberra, Australia: Australian National University, 1997).

29. For a good overview of social control approaches, see George S. Bridges and Martha Myers, eds., *Inequality, Crime, and Social Control* (Boulder, CO: Westview Press, 1994).

30. Walter C. Reckless, *The Crime Problem*, 4th ed. (New York: Appleton-Century-Crofts, 1967).

31. Reckless, 1967, p. 475.

32. Travis Hirschi, *Causes of Delinquency* (Berkeley: University of California Press, 1969).

33. Hirschi, 1969.

34. Hirschi, 1969.

35. Hirschi, 1969.

36. Hirschi, 1969.

37. Hirschi, 1969.

38. Hirschi, 1969.

39. Michael Gottfredson and Travis Hirschi, *A General Theory of Crime* (Stanford, CA: Stanford University Press, 1990).

40. See also Michael R. Gottfredson and Travis Hirschi, "Criminality and Low Self-Control," in John E. Conklin, ed., *New Perspectives in Criminology* (Boston: Allyn and Bacon, 1996).

41. Werner Einstadter and Stuart Henry, *Criminological Theory: An Analysis of Its Underlying Assumptions* (Fort Worth: Harcourt Brace, 1995), p. 189.

42. For some influential writings of the period, see K.F. Riegel, "Toward a Dialectical Theory of Development," *Human Development,* vol. 18 (1975), pp. 50–64; and U. Bronfenbrenner, *The Ecology of Human Development* (Cambridge: Harvard University Press, 1979).

43. R.M. Lerner, "Early Adolescence: Towards an Agenda for the Integration of Research, Policy and Intervention," in R.M. Lerner, ed., *Early Adolescence: Perspectives on Research, Policy, and Intervention* (Hillsdale, NJ: Erlbaum, 1993), pp. 1–13.

44. Sheldon Glueck and Eleanor Glueck, *Delinquents and Nondelinquents in Perspective* (Cambridge, Mass.: Harvard University Press, 1968).

45. John H. Laub and Robert J. Sampson, "Turning Points in the Life Course: Why Change Matters to the Study of Crime," *Criminology,* vol. 31, no. 3 (1993), pp. 301–325. See also Robert J. Sampson and John H. Laub, "Crime and Deviance in the Life Course," *Annual Review of Sociology,* vol. 18 (1992), pp. 63–84.

46. Robert J. Sampson and John H. Laub, *Crime in the Making* (Cambridge, Mass.: Harvard University Press, 1993).

47. Marvin Wolfgang, Robert Figlio, and Thorsten Sellin, *Delinquency in a Birth Cohort* (Chicago: University of Chicago Press, 1972).

48. Marvin Wolfgang, Terence Thornberry, and Robert Figlio, *From Boy to Man, From Delinquency to Crime* (Chicago: University of Chicago Press, 1987).

49. Steven P. Lab, "Analyzing Change in Crime and Delinquency Rates: The Case for Cohort Analysis," *Criminal Justice Research Bulletin,* vol. 3, no. 10 (Huntsville, TX: Sam Houston State University, 1988), p. 2.

50. Marvin Wolfgang, "Delinquency in China: Study of a Birth Cohort," *National Institute of Justice Research Preview,* NIJ (May 1996).

51. Lawrence E. Cohen and Richard Machalek, "A General Theory of Expropriative Crime: An Evolutionary Ecological Approach," *American Journal of Sociology,* vol. 94, no. 3 (1988), pp. 465–501; and Lawrence E. Cohen and Richard Machalek, "The Normalcy of Crime: From Durkheim to Evolutionary Ecology," *Rationality and Society,* vol. 6 (1994), pp. 286–308.

52. Bryan Vila, "Human Nature and Crime Control: Improving the Feasibility of Nurturant Strategies," *Politics and the Life Sciences* (March 1997), pp. 3–21.

53. Vila, 1997, pp. 3–21.

54. See Stuart Greenbaum, "Drugs, Delinquency, and Other Data," in *Juvenile Justice,* vol. 2, no. 1 (Spring/Summer 1994), pp. 2–8.

55. For another interesting analysis, see Robert J. Sampson and John H. Laub, *Crime in the Making* (Cambridge, Mass.: Harvard University Press, 1993).

56. See Felton J. Earls and Albert J. Reiss, *Breaking the Cycle: Predicting and Preventing Crime* (Washington, D.C.: National Institute of Justice, 1994).

57. Vila, 1997, p. 10.

58. C.T. Griffiths and S. Verdun-Jones, *Canadian Criminal Justice* (Toronto: Harcourt Brace Canada, 1994), p. 559.

Chapter 10

1. Quoted in J.C. Hackler, *Canadian Criminology: Strategies and Perspectives* (Scarborough: Prentice Hall Allyn and Bacon Canada, 2000), p. 148. Solon, who lived from 640 to 559 BC, was known as one of the Seven Wise Men of Greece. He was a statesman, lawgiver, and poet, whose reforms included the end of slavery for debt, the replacement of the harsh draconian law code with a more humane one, and the end of exclusive aristocratic control of government. These, and other reforms, are considered to be the foundations of modern democracy.

2. Anne Hansen was leader of the Squamish Five and received a life sentence for her involvement in the bombing of a Toronto nuclear weapons system manufacturer. Ten people were critically injured in the bombing and $3.8 million damage was done.

3. Richard Quinney, *Class, State, and Class: On the Theory and Practice of Criminal Justice* (New York: David McKay, 1977), p. 145.

4. Vance Packard, *The Status Seekers* (London: Harmondsworth, 1961).

5. Ralf Dahrendorf, *Class and Class Conflict in Industrial Society* (Stanford, Calif.: Stanford University Press, 1959).

6. Ralf Dahrendorf, "Out of Utopia: Toward a Reorientation of Sociological Analysis," *American Journal of Sociology,* vol. 64 (1958), pp. 115–127.

7. George B. Vold, *Theoretical Criminology* (New York: Oxford University Press, 1958).

8. Vold, 1958, p. 205.

9. Vold, 1958, p. 206.

10. Vold, 1958, pp. 208–209.

11. Vold, 1958, p. 309.

12. Austin Turk, *Criminality and Legal Order* (Chicago: Rand McNally, 1969), p. vii.

13. Turk, 1969, p. vii.

14. William J. Chambliss, "Toward a Political Economy of Crime," in C. Reasons and R. Rich, eds., *The Sociology of Law* (Toronto: Butterworth, 1978), p. 193.

15. William Chambliss and Robert T. Seidman, *Law, Order, and Power* (Reading, Mass.: Addison-Wesley, 1971), p. 33.

16. Adapted from Chambliss and Seidman, 1971, pp. 473–474.

17. William J. Chambliss, *Crime and the Legal Process* (New York: McGraw-Hill, 1969), p. 88.

18. William J. Chambliss, "Toward a Political Economy of Crime," *Theory and Society*, vol. 2 (1975), pp. 152–153.

19. Chambliss, 1975, pp. 152–153.

20. Chambliss, 1975, p. 152.

21. Chambliss, 1975, p. 152.

22. Richard Quinney, *Critique of the Legal Order: Crime Control in Capitalist Society* (Boston: Little, Brown, 1974), p. 16.

23. Quinney, 1977, p. 58.

24. Quinney, 1977, p. 58.

25. Quinney, 1977, p. 61.

26. Quinney, 1977, p. 65.

27. Quinney, 1977, p. 77.

28. Jeffrey H. Reiman, *The Rich Get Richer and the Poor Get Prison: Ideology, Class and Criminal Justice* (Boston: Allyn and Bacon, 2000).

29. Gresham M. Sykes, "Critical Criminology," *Journal of Criminal Law and Criminology*, vol. 65 (1974), pp. 206–213.

30. David A. Jones, *History of Criminology: A Philosophical Perspective* (Westport, CT: Greenwood, 1986), p. 200.

31. Elliott Currie, "Market, Crime, and Community," *Theoretical Criminology*, vol. 1, no. 2 (May 1997), pp. 147–172.

32. William V. Pelfrey, *The Evolution of Criminology* (Cincinnati: Anderson Pub. Co., 1980), p. 86.

33. For a good overview of critiques of radical criminology, see J.F. Galliher, "Life and Death of Liberal Criminology," *Contemporary Crisis*, vol. 2, no. 3 (July 1978), pp. 245–263.

34. Jackson Toby, "The New Criminology Is the Old Sentimentality," *Criminology*, vol. 16 (1979), pp. 516–526.

35. Toby, 1979, pp. 516–526.

36. Hermann Mannheim, *Comparative Criminology* (Boston: Houghton Mifflin, 1965), p. 445.

37. Don C. Gibbons, *Talking About Crime and Criminals: Problems and Issues in Theory Development in Criminology* (Englewood Cliffs, N.J.: Prentice Hall, 1994), p. 165, citing Loraine Gelsthorpe and Alison Morris, "Feminism and Criminology in Britain," *British Journal of Criminology* (Spring 1988), pp. 93–110.

38. Sally S. Simpson, "Feminist Theory, Crime and Justice," *Criminology*, vol. 27, no. 4 (1989), p. 605.

39. James W. Messerschmidt, *Capitalism, Patriarchy, and Crime: Toward a Socialist Feminist Criminology* (Totowa, N.J.: Rowman and Littlefield, 1986).

40. Freda Adler, *Sisters in Crime: The Rise of the New Female Criminal* (New York: McGraw-Hill, 1975).

41. Rita J. Simon, *Women and Crime* (Lexington, Mass.: Lexington Books, 1975).

42. Carol Smart, *Women, Crime and Criminology: A Feminist Critique* (London: Routledge, 1977).

43. Rita J. Simon, *Women and Crime* (Lexington, MA: Lexington Books, 1975).

44. Kathleen Daly and Meda Chesney-Lind, "Feminism and Criminology," *Justice Quarterly*, vol. 5, no. 5 (December 1988), pp. 497–535.

45. Susan Caulfield and Nancy Wonders, "Gender and Justice: Feminist Contributions to Criminology," in Gregg Barak, ed., *Varieties of Criminology: Readings from a Dynamic Discipline* (Westport, Conn.: Praeger, 1994), pp. 213–229.

46. Caufield and Wonders, 1994, pp. 213–229.

47. Caufield and Wonders, 1994.

48. Roslyn Muraskin and Ted Alleman, eds., *It's a Crime: Women and Justice* (Englewood Cliffs, N.J.: Prentice Hall, 1993), p. 1.

49. F.P. Williams III, and M.D. McShane, *Criminological Theory* (Englewood Cliffs, N.J.: Prentice-Hall, 1994), p. 238.

50. Carol Pateman, "Feminist Critiques of the Public/Private Dichotomy," in Anne Phillips, ed., *Feminism and Equality* (Oxford: Basil Blackwell, 1987).

51. Alida V. Merlo and Joycelyn M. Pollock, eds., *Women, Law and Social Control* (Needham Heights, Mass.: Allyn and Bacon, 1995).

52. Williams and McShane, 1994, p. 238.

53. Simpson, 1989.

54. John Hagan, *Structural Criminology* (New Brunswick, N.J.: Rutgers University Press, 1989), p. 130.

55. Hagan, 1989.

56. Hagan, 1989.

57. Hagan, 1989.

58. Evelyn K. Sommers, *Voices from Within: Women Who Have Broken the Law* (Toronto: University of Toronto Press, 1995).

59. Daly and Chesney-Lind, 1988, p. 506.

60. Daly and Chesney-Lind, 1988, p. 506.

61. Daly and Chesney-Lind, 1988, p. 506.

62. For an intriguing analysis of how existing laws tend to criminalize women and their reproductive activities, see Susan O. Reed, "The Criminalization of Pregnancy: Drugs, Alcohol, and AIDS," in Muraskin and Alleman, eds., 1993, pp. 92–117; and Drew Humphries, "Mothers and Children, Drugs and Crack: Reactions to Maternal Drug Dependency," in Muraskin and Alleman, eds., 1993, pp. 131–145.

63. Dawn H. Currie, "Feminist Encounters with Postmodernism: Exploring the Impasse of the Debates on Patriarchy and Law," *Canadian Journal of Women and the Law*, vol. 5, no. 1 (1992), p. 10.

64. For an excellent overview of feminist theory in criminology, and for a comprehensive review of research regarding female offenders, see Joanne Belknap, *The Invisible Woman: Gender Crime and Justice* (Belmont, Calif.: Wadsworth, 1996).

65. Such studies are still ongoing and continue to add to the descriptive literature of feminist criminology. See, for example, Deborah R. Baskin and Ira Sommers, "Female Initiation into Violent Street Crime," *Justice Quarterly*, vol. 10, no. 4 (December 1993), pp. 559–583; Scott Decker, Richard Wright, Allison Redfern, and Dietrich Smith, "A Woman's Place Is In the Home: Females and Residential Burglary," *Justice Quarterly*, vol. 10, no. 1 (March 1993), pp. 143–162; and Jill L. Rosenbaum, "The Female Delinquent: Another Look at the Role of the Family," in Muraskin and Alleman, eds., 1993, pp. 399–420.

66. Ronald L. Akers, *Criminological Theories: Introduction and Evaluation* (Los Angeles: Roxbury, 1994), p. 39.

67. For additional insight into the notion of "deconstruction" as it applies to feminist thought within criminology, see Carol Smart, *Feminism and the Power of Law* (New York: Routledge, 1989).

68. Daly and Chesney-Lind, 1988, p. 512.

69. See, for example, Darrell J. Steffensmeier and Emile Andersen Allan, "Sex Disparities in Arrests by Residence, Race, and Age: An Assessment of the Gender Convergence/Crime Hypothesis," *Justice Quarterly*, vol. 5, no. 1 (March 1988), pp. 53–80.

70. Darrell Steffensmeier, John Kramer, and Cathy Streifel, "Gender and Imprisonment Decisions," *Criminology*, vol. 31, no. 3 (August 1993), pp. 411–446. Gender-based differences, however, have been discovered in some instances of probation- and parole-related decision making. See Edna Erez, "Gender, Rehabilitation, and Probation Decisions," *Criminology*, vol. 27, no. 2 (1989), pp. 307–327; and Edna Erez, "Dangerous Men, Evil Women: Gender and Parole Decision-Making," *Justice Quarterly*, vol. 9, no. 1 (March 1992), pp. 106–126.

71. See, for example, Kathleen Daly, "Neither Conflict nor Labeling nor Paternalism Will Suffice: Intersections of Race, Ethnicity, Gender, and Family in Criminal Court Decisions," *Crime and Delinquency*, vol. 35, no. 1 (January 1989), pp. 136–168.

72. Cited in Allison Morris, *Women, Crime and Criminal Justice* (New York: Blackwell, 1987).

73. Caulfield and Wonders, 1994, p. 229.

74. For examples of how this might be accomplished, see F.H. Knopp, "Community Solutions to Sexual Violence: Feminist/Abolitionist Perspectives," in Harold E. Pepinsky and Richard Quinney, eds., *Criminology as Peacemaking* (Bloomington: Indiana University Press, 1991), pp. 181–193; and S. Caringella-MacDonald and D. Humphries, "Sexual Assault, Women, and the Community: Organizing to Prevent Sexual Violence," in Harold E. Pepinsky and Richard Quinney, eds., *Criminology as Peacemaking* (Bloomington: Indiana University Press, 1991), pp. 98–113.

75. Richard Quinney, "Life of Crime: Criminology and Public Policy as Peacemaking," *Journal of Crime and Justice*, vol. 16, no. 2 (1993), pp. 3–9.

76. See, for example, Harold E. Pepinsky, "This Can't Be Peace: A Pessimist Looks at Punishment," in W.B. Groves and G. Newman, eds., *Punishment and Privilege* (Albany: Harrow and Heston, 1986); Harold E. Pepinsky, "Violence as Unresponsiveness: Toward a New Conception of Crime," *Justice Quarterly*, vol. 5 (1988), pp. 539–563; and Pepinsky and Quinney, eds., 1991.

77. See, for example, Richard Quinney, "Crime, Suffering, Service: Toward a Criminology of Peacemaking," *Quest*, vol. 1 (1988), pp. 66–75; Richard Quinney, "The Theory and Practice of Peacemaking in the Development of Radical Criminology," *Critical Criminologist*, vol. 1, no. 5 (1989), p. 5; and Richard Quinney and John Wildeman, *The Problem of Crime: A Peace and Social Justice Perspective*, 3rd ed. (Mayfield, Calif.: Mountain View Press, 1991)—originally published as *The Problem of Crime: A Critical Introduction to Criminology* (New York: Bantam, 1977).

78. All these themes are addressed, for example, in Pepinsky and Quinney, eds., 1991.

79. For a good discussion of this "theory," see John F. Galliher, "Willie Horton: Fact, Faith, and Commonsense Theory of Crime," in Pepinsky and Quinney, eds., 1991, pp. 245–250.

80. Quinney and Wildeman, 1991, pp. vii–viii.

81. Richard Quinney, "Life of Crime: Criminology and Public Policy as Peacemaking," *Journal of Crime and Justice*, vol. 16, no. 2 (1993), abstract.

82. Bo Lozoff and Michael Braswell, *Inner Corrections: Finding Peace and Peace Making* (Cincinnati: Anderson, 1989).

83. Clemmons Bartollas and Michael Braswell, "Correctional Treatment, Peacemaking, and the New Age Movement," *Journal of Crime and Justice*, vol. 16, no. 2 (1993), pp. 43–58.

84. Bartollas and Braswell, 1993.

85. Ram Dass and P. Gorman, *How Can I Help? Stories and Reflections on Service* (New York: Alfred A. Knopf, 1985), p. 165, as cited in Quinney and Wildeman, 1991, p. 116.

86. Lozoff and Braswell, 1989, p. vii.

87. E.A. Fattah, "Restorative and Retributive Justice Models. A Comparison," in H.H. Kuhne (ed.), *Festschrift fur Koichi Miyazawa* (Baden-Baden, Germany: Nomos Verlagsgesllschaft, 1995).

88. J. Bonta, S. Wallace-Capretta, and J. Rooney, *Restorative Justice: An Evaluation of the Restorative Justice Project, User Report 1998–05* (Ottawa: Solicitor General Canada, 1998).

89. Robin Dann, *Restorative Justice Initiatives in South Eastern Alberta* (unpublished paper, 2000).

90. Bonta et al., 1998.

91. Bonta et al., 1998.

92. The John Howard Society of Manitoba, Inc., http://www.johnhoward.mb.ca/pages/home.php (Accessed May 19, 2007).

93. Werner Einstadter and Stuart Henry, Criminological Theory: An Analysis of Its Underlying Assumptions (Fort Worth: Harcourt Brace, 1995), p. 233.

94. Daniel J. Curran and Claire M. Renzetti, *Theories of Crime* (Boston: Allyn & Bacon, 1994), p. 283.

95. See M.D. Schwartz and W.S. DeKeseredy, "Left Realist Criminology: Strengths, Weaknesses, and the Feminist Critique," *Crime, Law, and Social Change*, vol. 15, no. 1 (January 1991), pp. 51–72; W.S. DeKeseredy and B.D. MacLean, "Exploring the Gender, Race, and Class Dimensions of Victimization: A Left Realist Critique of the Canadian Urban Victimization Survey," *International Journal of Offender Therapy and Comparative Criminology*, vol. 35, no. 2 (Summer 1991), pp. 143–161; and W.S. DeKeseredy and M.D. Schwartz, "British and U.S. Left Realism: A Critical Comparison," *International Journal of Offender Therapy and Comparative Criminology*, vol. 35, no. 3 (Fall 1991), pp. 248–262.

96. See Jock Young, "The Failure of Criminology: The Need for a Radical Realism," in R. Matthews and J. Young, eds., *Confronting Crime* (Beverly Hills: Sage, 1986), pp. 4–30; Jock Young, "The Tasks of a Realist Criminology," *Contemporary Crisis*, vol. 11, no. 4 (1987) pp. 337–356; and "Radical Criminology in Britain: The Emergence of a Competing Paradigm," *British Journal of Criminology*, vol. 28 (1988), pp. 159–183.

97. D. Brown and R. Hogg, "Essentialism, Radical Criminology, and Left Realism," *Australian and New Zealand Journal of Criminology*, vol. 25 (1992), pp. 195–230.

98. Roger Matthews and Jock Young, "Reflections on Realism," in Jock Young and Roger Matthews, eds., *Rethinking Criminology: The Realist Debate* (Newbury Park, Calif.: Sage, 1992).

99. Don C. Gibbons, *Talking About Crime and Criminals: Problems and Issues in Theory Development in Criminology* (Englewood Cliffs, N.J.: Prentice Hall, 1994), p. 170.

100. Piers Beirne and James W. Messerschmidt, *Criminology* (New York: Harcourt Brace Jovanovich, 1991), p. 501.

101. Michael J. Lynch and W. Byron Groves, *A Primer in Radical Criminology*, 2nd ed. (Albany, N.Y.: Harrow and Heston, 1989), p. 128.

Chapter 11

1. National Crime Prevention Council (NCPC), "Working Together for Safer Communities," *National Crime Prevention Strategy* (Ottawa: NCPC, 1997).

2. Barbara Hall, "Let's Prevent Youth Crime, Not React to It," *Ottawa Citizen*, May 5, 2000, p. E4.

3. Although charged with sodomy, Shakur was convicted on three lesser counts of sexual abuse. See Samuel Maull, "Shakur Trial," Associated Press wire service, December 2, 1994.

4. James T. Jones IV, "Real-Life Woes Beset Actor/Rapper," *USA Today*, February 11, 1994, p. 2A.

5. Dennis R. Martin, "The Music of Murder," *ACJS Today*, November/December 1993, pp. 1, 3, 20.

6. Kendall Hamilton and Allison Samuels, "Dr. Dre's New 'Hood: Hollywood," *Newsweek*, August 22, 1994, p. 45.

7. See, for example, Elizabeth Snead, "Dogg's 'Murder' Video has Plenty of Bite," *USA Today*, October 13, 1994.

8. John Ekstedt, "Canadian Justice Policy," in Margaret A. Jackson and Curt T. Griffiths (eds.), *Canadian Criminology. Perspectives on Crime and Criminality* (Toronto: Harcourt Brace Canada, 1995), p. 311.

9. James E. Anderson, *Public Policymaking: An Introduction* (Boston: Houghton Mifflin, 1990).

10. Ekstedt, 1995, p. 308.

11. Ekstedt, 1995, p. 312.

12. Nancy E. Marion, *A History of Federal Crime Control Initiatives, 1960–1993* (Westport: Praeger, 1994), p. 3. For a more detailed analysis of the process by which crime control policies are created, see Paul Rock, "The Opening Stages of Criminal Justice Policy Making,"

British Journal of Criminology, vol. 35, no. 1 (Winter 1995).

13. Ekstedt, 1995, p. 308.

14. Jeff Ferrell, "Criminological *Verstehen*: Inside the Immediacy of Crime," *Justice Quarterly*, vol. 14, no. 1 (1997), p. 16.

15. For an excellent discussion of the policies associated with law, punishment, and social control, see Thomas G. Blomberg and Stanley Cohen, eds., *Punishment and Social Control: Essays in Honor of Sheldon L. Messinger* (Hawthorne, N.Y.: Aldine de Gruyter, 1995).

16. Bryan Vila, "Could We Break the Crime Control Paradox?" Paper presented at the annual meeting of the American Society of Criminology, Miami, Florida, November 1994 [abstract].

17. From an address to the Standing Committee on Justice and the Solicitor General, 1993.

18. Department of Justice Canada, *The National Strategy on Community Safety and Crime Prevention. Backgrounder.* http://www.justice.gc.ca/en/news/nr/1998/newsbckg.html (Accessed May 27, 2007).

19. CTV.ca Staff, *Harper's Crime Agenda Getting Mixed Reviews*, April 3, 2006, http://www.ctv.ca/servlet/ArticleNews/story/CTVNews/20060403marijuana_crime_harper_060403-20060403?hub=Canada (Accessed May 27, 2007).

20. Department of Justice Canada, *Minister of Justice Proposes Stringent New Rules to Protect Canadians from Dangerous and High-Risk Offenders*, October 17, 2006, http://www.justice.gc.ca/en/news/nr/2006/doc_31908.html (Accessed May 27, 2007).

21. See Arthur L. Kellermann, "Understanding and Prevention Violence: A Public Health Perspective," National Institute of Justice, June 1996.

22. Quoted in Frank Schmalleger, *Criminology Today. An Integrative Introduction* (New Jersey: Prentice-Hall Inc., 1999), p. 526.

23. Vincent F. Sacco and Leslie W. Kennedy, *The Criminal Event* (Toronto: ITP Nelson, 1998), p. 340.

24. E.A. Suter, W.C. Waters, G.B. Murray, et al., "Violence in America: Effective Solutions," *Journal of the Medical Association of Georgia*, vol. 85 (1995), pp. 253–263.

25. Bryan Vila, "A General Paradigm for Understanding Criminal Behavior: Extending Evolutionary Ecological Theory," *Criminology*, vol. 32, no. 3 (August 1994), pp. 311–359.

26. Vila, "Could We Break," 1994.

27. Bryan Vila, "Human Nature and Crime Control: Improving the Feasibility of Nurturant Strategies," *Politics and the Life Sciences*, March 1997, p. 10.

28. Vila, 1997, pp. 3–21.

29. Vila, "A General Paradigm," 1994.

30. Vila, 1997, p. 11

31. Canada, House of Commons, Standing Committee on Justice and the Solicitor General, "Crime Prevention in Canada: Toward a National Strategy," *Twelfth Report of the Standing Committee on Justice and the Solicitor General*, 1993.

32. Information for this section has been obtained from the Department of Justice Canada, http://www.justice.gc.ca/en/news/nr/1998/newsbckg.html (Accessed May 25, 2007).

33. C. Ray Jeffery, *Crime Control Through Environmental Design* (Beverley Hills, CA: Sage, 1971).

34. Peel Regional Police, "Fact Sheet: Crime Prevention Through Environmental Design," www.peelpolice.on.ca.

35. Crime Prevention Association of New Brunswick, http://jaba.net/cpanb/ (Accessed May 25, 2007).

36. Greg Saville, "Balancing the CPTED Response," www.cpted.net (Accessed May 25, 2007).

37. Saville, "Balancing the CPTED Response."

38. Marnie Wallace, "Crime Statistics in Canada, 2002" *Juristat*, vol. 23, no. 5 (Ottawa: Minister of Industry, 2003).

39. Marie Gagnon, "Crime Statistics in Canada, 2005", *Juristat*, vol. 26, no. 4 (Ottawa: Minister of Industry, 2006).

40. Department of Justice Canada, "*Youth Criminal Justice Act* 2005 Annual Statement," http://www.justice.gc.ca/en/ps/yj/ycja/statement/execsum.html (Accessed May 27, 2007).

41. Peter J. Carrington and Jennifer L. Schulenberg, *The Impact of the YCJA on Police Charging Practices with Young Persons: A Preliminary Statistical Analysis*, Report to the Department of Justice, 2005.

42. Department of Justice Canada, "*Youth Criminal Justice Act* 2005 Annual Statement," http://www.justice.gc.ca/en/ps/yj/ycja/statement/execsum.html (Accessed May 27, 2007).

43. Anthony N. Doob and Jane B. Sprott, *The Use of Custody under the Youth Criminal Justice Act*, A Paper Prepared for Department of Justice Canada, October 2005.

44. Anthony N. Doob, *Youth Court Judges' Views of the Youth Justice System; Results of a Survey*, Report to the Department of Justice Canada, 2004.

45. Richard Blackwell, "Court Strikes Down Part of Youth Justice Act," *The Globe and Mail*, March 26, 2006, http://www.canadiancrc.com/articles/Globe_and_Mail_Court_strikes_down_part_youth_justice_act_25MAR06.htm (Accessed May 27, 2007).

46. H. Bianchi, *Position and Subject-Matter of Criminology* (Amsterdam, 1956).

47. Hermann Mannheim, *Comparative Criminology* (New York: Houghton Mifflin, 1965), p. 18.

48. For an interesting look at jurisdictional complexities, see the discussion about the attempts to regulate lap dancing in Ontario in Alison Hatch Cunningham and Curt T. Griffiths, *Canadian Criminal Justice: A Primer* (Toronto: Harcourt Brace Canada, 1997), pp. 13–14.

49. Ekstedt, 1995, pp. 307–329.

50. Vila, "Could We Break," 1994, p. 3.

Chapter 12

1. Cynthia Manson and Charles Ardai, eds., *Future Crime: An Anthology of the Shape of Crime to Come* (New York: Donald I. Fine, 1992), p. ix.

2. Gregory J. Howard, Graeme Newman, and William Alex Pridemore, "Theory, Method, and Data in Comparative Criminology," in David Duffee, ed., *Criminal Justice 2000: Volume IV—Measurement and Analysis of Criminal Justice* (Washington, DC: National Institute of Justice, 2000), p. 189.

3. This story is adapted from Gary LaFree et al., "The Changing Nature of Crime in America," in Gary LaFree, ed., *Criminal Justice 2000: Volume III—the Nature of Crime—Continuity and Change* (Washington, DC: National Institute of Justice, 2000).

4. Darlene E. Weingand, "Futures Research Methodologies: Linking Today's Decisions with Tomorrow's Possibilities," paper presented at the Sixty-first International Federation of Library Associations and Institutions annual conference, August 20–25, 1995, www.ifla.org/IV/ifla61/61-weid.htm (Accessed November 12, 2006.)

5. Joseph F. Coates, "The Highly Probable Future: 83 Assumptions about the Year 2025," *The Futurist*, vol. 28, no. 4 (July/August 1994), p. 51.

6. Readers are referred to C.J. Swank, "Police in the Twenty-first Century: Hypotheses for the Future," *International Journal of Comparative and Applied Criminal Justice*, vol. 17, nos. 1 and 2 (spring/fall 1993), pp. 107–120, for an excellent analysis of policing in the future.

7. The Foresight Web Site, www.foresight.gov.uk (Accessed November 9, 2006.)

8. The quotations attributed to the panel in this section are from Foresight Crime Prevention Panel, *Just around the Corner: A Consultation Document*, www.foresight.gov.uk/servlet/DocViewer/docnoredirect5883 (Accessed November 9, 2006.)

9. Rawi Abdelal and Richard S. Tedlow, "Theodore Levitt's 'The Globalization of Markets': An Evaluation after Two Decades," 2003, *Social Science Research Network*, http://www.ssrn.com (Accessed November 9, 2006.)

10. Adapted from John McHale, "Futures Critical: A Review," in *Human Futures: Needs, Societies, Technologies* (Guildford, Surrey, UK: IPC Business Press Limited, 1974), p. 13.

11. Gregory J. Howard, Graeme Newman, and William Alex Pridemore, "Theory, Method, and Data in Comparative Criminology," in David Duffee, ed., *Criminal Justice 2000: Volume IV—Measurement and Analysis of Criminal Justice* (Washington, DC: National Institute of Justice, 2000).

12. Department of Justice, Canada, *G8 Recommendations on Transnational Crime*, http://www.justice.gc.ca/en/news/g8/doc1.html#preamble (Accessed November 10, 2006).

13. United Nations Office on Drugs and Crime, http://www.unodc.org/unodc/en/crime_prevention.html (Accessed November 15, 2006).

14. Criminal Intelligence Service Canada, *Annual Report, 2006*, http://www.cisc.gc.ca/annual_reports/annual_report2006/coverpage_2006_e.htm (Accessed November 15, 2006).

15. Joseph F. Coates et al., *2025: Scenarios of U.S. and Global Society Reshaped by Science and Technology* (Winchester, VA: Oakhill Press, 1997).

16. Richter H. Moore Jr., "Wiseguys: Smarter Criminals and Smarter Crime in the Twenty-First Century," *Futurist*, vol. 28, no. 5 (September/October 1994), p. 33.

17. The quotations attributed to Moore in this section are from Moore, 1994, pp. 33–37.

18. United Nations Office on Drugs and Crime (UNODC), *Trafficking in Persons: Global Patterns*, April 2006, p. 10, http://www.unodc.org/unodc/en/trafficking_persons_report_2006-04.html (Accessed May 25, 2007).

19. United Nations Office on Drugs and Crime (UNODC), http://www.unodc.org/unodc/en/crime_prevention.html (Accessed November 15, 2006).

20. Kristiina Kangaspunta, "Mapping the Inhuman Trade: Preliminary Findings of the Database on Trafficking in Human Beings," *Forum on Crime and Society*, vol. 3, nos. 1 and 2 (2003), pp. 82–83.

21. Kangaspunta, 2003, p. 83.

22. UNODC, 2006, p. 31

23. Royal Canadian Mounted Police, RCMP *Gazette*, vol. 66, no. 3 (2004), http://www.gazette.rcmp.gc.ca/ (Accessed November 19, 2006).

24. UNODC, http://www.unodc.org/unodc/en/trafficking_protocol.html (Accessed November 19, 2006).

25. RCMP, *Gazette*, vol. 66, no. 2 (2004), http://www.gazette.rcmp.gc.ca/archives-en.html (Accessed November 19, 2006).

26. RCMP, *Gazette*, vol. 66, no. 2 (2004), http://www.gazette.rcmp.gc.ca/archives-en.html (Accessed November 19, 2006).

27. Organ Donation and Transplant Association of Canada, http://www.organdonations.ca/ (Accessed May 20, 2007).

28. D.J. Rothman, E. Rose, T. Awaya, B. Cohen, A. Daar, S.L. Dzemeshkevich, C.J. Lee, R. Munro, H. Reyes, S.M. Rothman, K.F. Schoen, N. Scheper-Hughes, Z. Shapira, and H. Smit, *The Bellagio Task Force Report on Transplantation, Bodily Integrity, and the International Traffic in Organs* (Extract from Transplantation Proceedings, 29 (1997), pp. 2739–2745), http://www.icrc.org/Web/eng/siteeng0.nsf/html/57JNYK (Accessed May 20, 2007).

29. David Matas and David Kilgour, *Report into Allegations of Organ Harvesting of Falun Gong Practitioners in China*, Coalition to Investigate the Persecution of the Falun Gong in China (Washington, D.C., July 2006), http://www.david-kilgour.com/2006/Kilgour-Matas-organ-harvesting-rpt-July6-eng.pdf (Accessed May 20, 2007).

30. Matas and Kilgour, 2006.

31. Rothman et al., 1997.

32. Rothman et al., 1997.

33. Melanie Kowalski, "Cyber-Crime: Issues, Data Sources, and Feasibility of Collecting Police-Reported Statistics," *Juristat*, Canadian Centre for Justice Statistics, Minister of Industry, 2002, p. 6.

34. Kowalski, 2002, p. 6.

35. Catherine H. Conley and J. Thomas McEwen, "Computer Crime," *NIJ Reports,* (January/February, 1990), p. 3.

36. Kowalski, 2002, p. 5.

37. Kowalski, 2002, p. 15.

38. Kowalski, 2002, p. 25.

39. Adapted from John McHale, "Futures Critical: A Review," in *Human Futures: Needs, Societies, Technologies* (Guildford, Surrey, UK: IPC Business Press Limited, 1974), p. 13.

40. Society of Police Futurists International, *PFI: The Future of Policing* (brochure), no date.

41. William L. Tafoya, "Futures Research: Implications for Criminal Investigations," in James N. Gilbert, ed., *Criminal Investigation: Essays and Cases* (Columbus, OH: Charles E. Merrill, 1990), p. 214.

42. Frederick R. Brodzinski, "The Futurist Perspective and the Managerial Process," *Utilizing Futures Research*, no. 6 (1979), pp. 8–19.

43. Weingand, 2006.

44. Coates et al., 1997.

45. Moore, 1994, p. 33–40.

46. Georgette Bennett, *Crimewarps: The Future of Crime in America* (Garden City, NY: Anchor/Doubleday, 1987).

47. Technological devices described in this section are discussed in G. Gordon Liddy, "Rules of the Game," *Omni*, January 1989, pp. 43–47, 78–80.

48. Ian Austen, "Fighting Crime Uses Videos on YouTube," *The New York Times*, December 18, 2006, http://www.nytimes.com/2006/12/18/technology/18hamilton.html?ex=1179806400&en=946bd6af8594998b&ei=5070 (Accessed May 20, 2007).

49. CIA Directorate of Intelligence, *Terrorist CBRN: Materials and Effects* (Washington, DC: CIA, 2003).

50. "The Council of Europe's Convention on Cyber-Crime," Electronic Privacy Information Centre, 2005, http://www.epic.org/privacy/intl/ccc.html (Accessed November 29, 2006).

51. Kowalski, 2002, p. 7.

52. Gregory J. Howard, Graeme Newman, and William Alex Pridemore, "Theory, Method, and Data in Comparative Criminology," in David Duffee, ed., *Criminal Justice 2000: Volume IV—Measurement and Analysis of Criminal Justice* (Washington, DC: National Institute of Justice, 2000), p. 189.

53. Howard et al., 2000, p. 189.

54. Robert Lilly, "Forks and Chopsticks: Understanding Criminal Justice in the PRC," *Criminal Justice International,* March/April 1986, p. 15.

55. Frank Schmalleger, *Criminology Today. An Integrative Introduction* (New Jersey: Pearson Education Inc., 2006), p. 541.

56. For information about the latest survey, see *The Ninth United Nations Survey on Crime Trends and the Operations of Criminal Justice Systems* (New York: United Nations, 2005), http://www.unodc.org/unodc/en/crime_cicp_surveys.html (Accessed May 21, 2007).

57. *The Ninth United Nations Survey on Crime Trends and the Operations of Criminal Justice Systems* (2003–2004), http://www.unodc.org/unodc/en/crime_cicp_surveys.html (Accessed November 19, 2006).

Glossary

Administrative law regulates many daily business activities. Violation of such regulations generally results in warnings or fines, depending upon their adjudged severity.

Alloplastic adaptation that form of adjustment resulting from changes in the environment surrounding an individual.

Anomie a social condition in which norms are uncertain or lacking.

Anti-social personality disorder refers to individuals displaying a personality disorder that includes aggressive, impulsive behaviour and a general disregard for the rights of others.

Anti-social personality or **asocial personality** refers to individuals who are basically unsocialized and whose behaviour pattern can bring them into conflict with society.

Applied research scientific inquiry that is designed and carried out with practical application in mind.

Assault the intentional or threatened application of force on another person without consent. The categories of assault include level 1—assault or common assault; level 2—assault that involves the use of a weapon or that causes bodily harm; and level 3—assault that results in wounding or endangering the life of the victim.

Atavism a concept used by Cesare Lombroso to suggest that criminals are physiological throwbacks to earlier stages of human evolution. The term is derived from the Latin term *atavus*, which means "ancestor."

Autoplastic adaptation that form of adjustment resulting from changes within an individual.

Behavioural conditioning a psychological principle holding that the frequency of any behaviour can be increased or decreased through reward, punishment, and/or association with other stimuli.

Behaviour theory a psychological perspective positing that individual behaviour that is rewarded will increase in frequency, while that which is punished will decrease.

Biological theories (of criminology) maintain that the basic determinants of human behaviour, including criminality, are constitutionally or physiologically based and often inherited.

Born criminals individuals who are born with a genetic predilection toward criminality.

Bourgeoisie in Marxist theory, the class of people that owns the means of production.

Breaking and entering the unlawful entry of a place to commit an indictable offence.

Broken windows thesis a perspective on crime causation holding that physical deterioration in an area leads to increased concerns for personal safety among area residents and to higher crime rates in that area. The "broken windows" metaphor says that a broken window, left unattended, invites other windows to be broken, which leads to a sense of disorder that breeds fear and serious crime. Hence, by ignoring minor crimes we lose opportunities to repair the first signs of disorder and to hold offenders accountable.

Canadian Statement of Basic Principles of Justice for Victims of Crime a 1988 document promoting access to justice, fair treatment, and provision of assistance for victims of crime.

Capital punishment the legal imposition of a sentence of death upon a convicted offender. Another term for the death penalty.

Case study an investigation into an individual case.

Circle sentencing conferences groups of community members who actively assist justice authorities by participating in discussions about available sentencing options and plans to reintegrate the offender back into the community.

Civil law body of law that regulates arrangements between individuals, such as contracts and claims to property.

Classical school a criminological perspective operative in the late 18th and early 19th centuries that had its roots in the Enlightenment. It held that men and women are rational beings, that crime is the result of the exercise of free will, and that punishment can be effective in reducing the incidence of crime, as it negates the pleasure to be derived from crime commission.

Code of Hammurabi an early set of laws established by the Babylonian King Hammurabi, who ruled the ancient city from 1792 to 1750 BC.

Cohort a group of individuals sharing certain significant social characteristics, such as gender and time and place of birth.

Cohort analysis a social scientific technique that studies a population that shares common characteristics over time. Cohort analysis usually begins at birth and traces the development of cohort members until they reach a certain age.

Common law law originating from usage and custom rather than from written statutes. The term refers to non-statutory customs, traditions, and precedents that help guide judicial decision making.

Community policing a philosophy of policing involving proactive collaboration between the police and the community to prevent and respond to crime and other community problems.

Community sentencing panels groups composed of volunteers from the community who focus on restorative measures such as restitution, reparation, mediation, and victim involvement.

Comparative criminology the cross-national study of crime.

Computer virus a computer program designed to secretly invade computer systems in order either to modify the way in which they operate or to alter the information they store.

Conduct norms the shared expectations of a social group relative to personal conduct.

Confounding effects rival explanations, also called competing hypotheses, which are threats to the internal or external validity of any research design.

Consensus model an analytical perspective on social organization holding that most members of society agree as to what is right and wrong and that the various elements of society work together in unison toward a common and shared vision of the greater good.

Constitutional theories those that explain criminality by reference to offenders' body types, genetics, and/or external observable physical characteristics.

Containment aspects of the social bond that act to prevent individuals from committing crimes and that keep them from engaging in deviance.

Containment theory a form of control theory that suggests a series of both internal and external factors contributes to law-abiding behaviour.

Controlled experiments those that attempt to hold conditions (other than the intentionally introduced experimental intervention) constant.

Correctional psychology that aspect of forensic psychology that is concerned with the diagnosis and classification of offenders, the treatment of correctional populations, and the rehabilitation of inmates and other law violators.

Correlates of crime those variables observed to be related to criminal activity such as age, gender, ethnicity, and social class.

Correlation a causal, complementary, or reciprocal relationship between two measurable variables.

Counterfeiting any unauthorized reproduction of a thing with the intention that it be accepted as genuine. It can thus refer to any thing that is capable of reproduction, including things that are subjects of rights of private property. It also includes the reproduction of documents for identification, such as passports, or any paper that represents value (e.g., stamps, travellers' cheques, or negotiable instruments).

Crime human conduct in violation of the criminal laws of a jurisdiction that has the power to make such laws, and for which there is some form of authorized sanction.

Crime Prevention Through Environmental Design (CPTED) a crime-prevention strategy based on the premise that the proper design and effective use of the built environment can lead to a reduction in the incidence and fear of crime.

Crime rate crime per capita based on the number of recorded crimes calculated per 100 000 population.

Criminal anthropology the scientific study of the relationship between human physical characteristics and criminality.

Criminal harassment also known as stalking, is the repeated following, watching, or communicating with a person or someone known to that person in a way that causes the person to fear for his/her safety or for the safety of someone known to him/her.

Criminal justice the scientific study of crime, the criminal law, and components of the criminal justice system, including the police, courts, and corrections.

Criminal justice system the various agencies of justice, especially police, courts, and corrections, whose goal it is to apprehend, convict, sanction, and rehabilitate law violators.

Criminal law body of law that regulates actions that have the potential to harm interests of the state.

Criminality a behavioural predisposition that disproportionately favours criminal activity.

Criminalize to make illegal.

Criminaloids a term used by Cesare Lombroso to describe occasional criminals who were pulled into criminality primarily by environmental influences.

Criminologist one who is trained in the field of criminology; also, one who studies crime, criminals, and criminal behaviour.

Criminology an interdisciplinary profession built around the scientific study of crime and criminal behaviour, including their form, causes, legal aspects, and control.

Criminology of place or **environmental criminology** an emerging perspective that emphasizes the importance of geographic location and architectural features as they are associated with the prevalence of criminal victimization.

Critical criminology a perspective focused on challenging traditional understandings and on uncovering false beliefs about crime and criminal justice.

Culture conflict a sociological perspective on crime that suggests that the root cause of criminality can be found in a clash of values between variously socialized groups over what is acceptable or proper behaviour.

Cyber-crime a criminal offence involving a computer as the object of the crime, or the tool used to commit a material component of the offence.

Cycloid a term developed by Ernst Kretschmer to describe a particular relationship between body build and personality type. The cycloid personality, which was associated with a heavyset, soft type of body, was said to vacillate between normality and abnormality.

Dangerousness the likelihood that a given individual will later harm society; it is often measured in terms of recidivism, or the likelihood of new crime commission or rearrest for a new crime.

Dark figure of crime refers to that portion of criminal activity that goes unreported and/or undetected by official sources.

Data confidentiality an ethical requirement of social scientific research that stipulates that research data not be shared outside of the research environment.

Date rape sexual assault that occurs within the context of a dating relationship.

Defensible space the range of mechanisms that combine to bring an environment under the control of its residents.

Demographics the characteristics of population groups, usually expressed in statistical form.

Deterrence the prevention of crime.

Deterrence strategy a crime-prevention strategy that attempts to diminish motivation for crime by increasing the perceived certainty, severity, or celerity of penalties.

Deviance behaviour that violates social norms or is statistically different from the average.

Differential association the sociological thesis that criminality, like any other form of behaviour, is learned through a process of association with others who communicate criminal values.

Displacement a shift of criminal activity from one spatial location to another.

Displastics a mixed group of offenders described as highly emotional and often unable to control themselves.

Ecological theory, also called the **Chicago School of Criminology** a type of sociological approach that emphasizes demographics (the characteristics of population groups) and geographics (the mapped location of such groups relative to one another) and sees the social disorganization that characterizes delinquency areas as a major cause of criminality and victimization.

Ectomorph a body type originally described as thin and fragile, with long, slender, poorly muscled extremities, and delicate bones.

The Enlightenment, also known as the Age of Reason. A social movement that arose during the late 17th and 18th centuries and built upon ideas such as empiricism, rationality, free will, humanism, and natural law.

Ego the reality-testing part of the personality; also referred to as the reality principle. More formally, it is the personality component that is conscious, most immediately controls behaviour, and is most in touch with external reality.

Electroencephalogram (EEG) electrical measurements of brain wave activity.

Endomorph a body type originally described as soft and round, or overweight.

Eugenics the study of hereditary improvement by genetic control.

Evolutionary ecology an approach to understanding crime that draws attention to the ways people develop over the course of their lives.

Family group conferencing a forum for dealing with unanswered questions, emotions, and the victim's right to restitution and reparation resulting from a crime.

Feminist criminology a self-conscious corrective model intended to redirect the thinking of mainstream criminologists to include gender awareness.

First-degree murder culpable homicide that is planned and deliberate.

Focal concerns the key values of any culture, and especially the key values of a delinquent subculture.

Folkways time-honoured customs. Although folkways carry the force of tradition, their violation is unlikely to threaten the survival of the social group.

Forensic psychiatry that branch of psychiatry having to do with the study of crime and criminality.

Futurists those who study the future; in the case of criminology, criminologists who try to imagine how crime will appear in both the near and distant future.

General deterrence a goal of criminal sentencing that seeks to prevent others from committing crimes similar to the one for which a particular offender is being sentenced.

General theory one that attempts to explain all (or at least most) forms of criminal conduct through a single, overarching approach.

Globalization a complex series of economic, social, technological, cultural, and political changes seen as increasing interdependence, integration, and interaction between people and companies in disparate locations.

Hate crime a criminal act directed toward a person or group because of race, national or ethnic origin, religion, language, colour, sex, age, sexual orientation, or mental or physical disability. Also referred to as hate-motivated crime, or bias crime.

Hedonistic calculus or **utilitarianism** the belief, first proposed by Jeremy Bentham, that behaviour holds value to any individual undertaking it according to the amount of pleasure or pain that it can be expected to produce for that person.

Homicide when a person, directly or indirectly, by any means, causes the death of a human being. Homicide can be culpable or non-culpable.

Human smuggling or **migrant smuggling** the facilitation of illegal entry of a person into a country for financial gain.

Human trafficking the displacement of an individual by means of coercion, deceit, or violence for the purpose of exploitation.

Hybrid offence a criminal offence that can be classified as indictable or as a summary conviction; the classification is usually made by the Crown Attorney.

Hypoglycemia a condition characterized by low blood sugar.

Hypothesis 1. an explanation that accounts for a set of facts and that can be tested by further investigation. 2. something that is taken to be true for the purpose of argument or investigation.

Id the aspect of the personality from which drives, wishes, urges, and desires emanate. More formally, it is the division of the psyche associated with instinctual impulses and demands for immediate satisfaction of primitive needs.

Illegitimate opportunity structure subcultural pathways to success that are disapproved of by the wider society.

Impaired driving the operation of a motor vehicle by a person whose ability to operate it is impaired by alcohol or a drug. In the case of alcohol, impairment is said to occur when the concentration of alcohol in the person's blood exceeds 80 milligrams in 100 millilitres of blood.

Incapacitation the use of imprisonment or other means to reduce the likelihood that an offender will be capable of committing future offences.

Indictable offence a serious criminal offence; specifically, one that carries a prison sentence of 14 years or longer.

Individual-rights advocates those who seek to protect personal freedoms in the face of criminal prosecution.

Infanticide when a female considered disturbed from the effects of giving birth causes the death of her newborn child (under age 1).

Informed consent an ethical requirement of social scientific research that specifies that research subjects will be informed as to the nature of the research about to be conducted, their anticipated role in it, and the uses to which the data they provide will be put.

Instrumental Marxism a perspective that holds that those in power intentionally create laws and social institutions that serve their own interests and that keep others from becoming powerful.

Integrated theory an explanatory perspective that merges (or attempts to merge) concepts drawn from different sources.

Juke family a well-known "criminal family" studied by Richard L. Dugdale.

Just deserts model the notion that criminal offenders deserve the punishment they receive at the hands of the law and that punishments should be appropriate to the type and severity of the crime committed.

Kallikak family a well-known "criminal family" studied by Henry H. Goddard.

Kriminalpolitik the political handling of crime, or a criminology-based social policy.

Labelling an interactionist perspective that sees continued crime as a consequence of limited opportunities for acceptable behaviour which follow from the negative responses of society to those defined as offenders. Also, the process by which a negative or deviant label is imposed.

Law-and-order advocates those who suggest that, under certain circumstances involving criminal threats to public safety, the interests of society should take precedence over individual rights.

Left-realist criminology or **left realism** a conflict perspective that insists on a pragmatic assessment of crime and its associated problems.

Liberal feminism a perspective that holds that the concerns of women can be incorporated within existing social institutions through conventional means and without the need to drastically restructure society.

Life course theories explanations for criminality that recognize criminogenic influences as having their greatest impact during the early stages of life and that see formative childhood experiences as catalysts in shaping children for the rest of their lives.

Lifestyle model holds that the likelihood that an individual will suffer a personal victimization depends heavily on the concept of lifestyle.

Mala in se acts that are thought to be wrong in and of themselves.

Mala prohibita acts that are wrong only because they are prohibited.

Manslaughter all non-intentional homicide.

Mass murder the illegal killing of four or more victims at one location, within one event.

McNaughten rule a standard for judging legal insanity that requires that offenders did not know what they were doing, or if they did, that they did not know it was wrong.

Mental disorder (law) a legally established inability to understand right from wrong, or to conform one's behaviour to the requirements of the law. Also, a defence allowable in criminal courts.

Mental disorder (psychological) disease of the mind including schizophrenia, paranoia, senile dementia, melancholia, various types of epilepsy, and delirium tremens caused by alcohol abuse.

Mesomorph a body type originally described as athletic and muscular.

Modelling theory a psychological perspective that says people learn how to behave by modelling themselves after others whom they have the opportunity to observe.

Monozygotic (MZ) twins, as opposed to dizygotic (or DZ) twins, develop from the same egg and carry virtually the same genetic material.

Moral enterprise efforts of a particular interest group to have its sense of propriety enacted into law.

Mores behavioural proscriptions covering potentially serious violations of a group's values. Examples might include strictures against murder, sexual assault, and robbery.

Motor-vehicle theft the taking of a vehicle without the owner's authorization. A motor vehicle is defined as a car, truck, van, bus, recreational vehicle, semi-trailer truck, motorcycle, construction machinery, agricultural machinery, or other land-based motor vehicle (such as a go-kart, snowmobile, all-terrain vehicle, or dune buggy).

Murder when a person intentionally causes the death of another human being or intends to cause bodily harm likely to result in death.

National Strategy on Community Safety and Crime Prevention a federal crime-prevention initiative designed to create safer communities by supporting community-based crime-prevention efforts, enhancing communities' knowledge and experience with respect to crime prevention, and fostering partnerships and collaboration.

Natural law the philosophical perspective that certain immutable laws are fundamental to human nature and can be readily ascertained through reason. Human-made laws, in contrast, are said to derive from human experience and history—both of which are subject to continual change.

Natural rights the rights that, according to natural law theorists, individuals retain in the face of government action and interests.

Neo-classical criminology a contemporary version of classical criminology that emphasizes deterrence and retribution, with reduced emphasis on rehabilitation.

Neurosis functional disorders of the mind or of the emotions involving anxiety, phobia, or other abnormal behaviour.

Not criminally responsible by reason of mental disorder (NCRMD) a finding that offenders are responsible for committing the offence that they have committed but, because of their prevailing mental condition, should be sent to a psychiatric hospital for treatment rather than to prison. The maximum length of stay is predetermined.

Nurturant strategy a crime-prevention strategy that attempts to forestall development of criminality by improving early life experiences and channelling child and adolescent development into desirable directions.

Operant behaviour behaviour that affects the environment in such a way as to produce responses or further behavioural cues.

Opportunity model contends that the risk of criminal victimization depends largely on people's lifestyle and daily activities that bring them and their property into direct contact with potential offenders in the absence of capable guardians.

Opportunity structure a path to success. Opportunity structures may be of two types: legitimate and illegitimate.

Panopticon a prison designed by Jeremy Bentham that was to be a circular building with cells along the circumference, each clearly visible from a central location staffed by guards.

Paradigm an example, model, or theory.

Paranoid schizophrenics schizophrenic individuals who suffer from delusions and hallucinations.

Participant observation a variety of strategies in data gathering in which the researcher observes a group by participating, to varying degrees, in the activities of the group.

Participatory justice a relatively informal type of justice case processing which makes use of local community resources rather than requiring traditional forms of official intervention.

Patriarchy the tradition of male dominance.

Peace model an approach to crime control that focuses on effective ways for developing a shared consensus on critical issues that have the potential to seriously affect the quality of life.

Peacemaking criminology a perspective that holds that crime-control agencies and the citizens they serve should work together to alleviate social problems and human suffering and thus reduce crime.

Penal couple a term that describes the relationship between victim and criminal. Also, the two individuals most involved in the criminal act—the offender and the victim.

Phishing use of official-looking email messages to steal valuable information such as credit card numbers, social security numbers, user IDs, and passwords from victims.

Phone phreaking use of special dial-up access codes and other restricted technical information to avoid long-distance charges.

Phrenology the study of the shape of the head to determine anatomical correlates of human behaviour.

Pluralistic perspective an analytical approach to social organization holding that a multiplicity of values and beliefs exists in any complex society but that most social actors agree on the usefulness of law as a formal means of dispute resolution.

Positivism the application of scientific techniques to the study of crime and criminals.

Post-crime victimization or **secondary victimization** refers to problems in living that tend to follow from initial victimization, some of which may be related to the victim's interaction with the criminal justice system.

Power-control theory a perspective that holds that the distribution of crime and delinquency within society is to some degree founded upon the consequences power relationships within the wider society hold for domestic settings, and for the everyday relationships among men, women, and children within the context of family life.

Primary deviance initial deviance often undertaken to deal with transient problems in living.

Primary research research characterized by original and direct investigation.

Proletariat in Marxist theory, the working class.

Prostitution most commonly used to refer to the illegal activities of publicly communicating with another person for the purposes of buying or selling sexual services, running a bawdy house, or living on the avails of the prostitution of another person.

Protection/avoidance strategy a crime-prevention strategy that attempts to reduce criminal opportunities by changing people's routine activities, increasing guardianship, or incapacitating convicted offenders.

Psychiatric criminology theories derived from the medical sciences, including neurology, and which, like other psychological theories, focus on the individual as the unit of analysis. Psychiatric theories form the basis of psychiatric criminology.

Psychoanalysis the theory of human psychology founded by Freud and based on the concepts of the unconscious, resistance, repression, sexuality, and the Oedipus complex.

Psychological profiling the attempt to categorize, understand, and predict the behaviour of certain types of offenders based on behavioural clues they provide.

Psychological theories those that are derived from the behavioural sciences and that focus on the individual as the unit of analysis. Psychological theories place the locus of crime causation within the personality of the individual offender.

Psychopath or **sociopath** a person with a personality disorder, especially one manifested in aggressively anti-social behaviour, which is often said to be the result of a poorly developed superego.

Psychopathology the study of pathological mental conditions, that is, mental illness.

Psychosis a form of mental illness in which sufferers are said to be out of touch with reality.

Psychotherapy a form of psychiatric treatment based on psychoanalytical principles and techniques.

Public policy government-formulated directives made on behalf of the public good to solve a problem or achieve an end.

Punishments undesirable behavioural consequences likely to decrease the frequency of occurrence of that behaviour.

Pure research research undertaken simply for the sake of advancing scientific knowledge.

Qualitative methods research techniques that produce subjective results or results that are difficult to quantify.

Quantitative methods research techniques that produce measurable results.

Quasi-experimental designs approaches to research that, although less powerful than experimental designs, are deemed worthy of use when better designs are not feasible.

Radical criminology a perspective that holds that the causes of crime are rooted in social conditions that empower the wealthy and the politically well organized but disenfranchise those less fortunate. Radical criminology is sometimes called **Marxist criminology.**

Radical feminism a perspective that holds that any significant change in the status of women can be accomplished only through substantial changes in social institutions such as the family, law, medicine, and so on.

Rational choice theory a perspective that holds that criminality is the result of conscious choice and that predicts that individuals choose to commit crime when the benefits outweigh the costs of disobeying the law.

Reaction formation the process in which a person openly rejects that which he or she wants, or aspires to, but cannot obtain or achieve.

Recidivism the repetition of criminal behaviour.

Recidivism rate the percentage of convicted offenders who have been released from prison and who are later rearrested for a new crime.

Reintegrative shaming a form of shaming, imposed as a sanction by the criminal justice system, that is thought to strengthen the moral bond between the offender and the community.

Research the use of standardized, systematic procedures in the search for knowledge.

Research design the logic and structure inherent in an approach to data gathering.

Restitution a criminal sanction, in particular the payment of compensation by the offender to the victim.

Restorative justice a perspective that stresses remedies and restoration rather than prison, punishment, and victim neglect.

Retribution the act of taking revenge upon a criminal perpetrator.

Rewards desirable behavioural consequences likely to increase the frequency of occurrence of that behaviour.

Robbery the unlawful taking or attempted taking of property that is in the immediate possession of another, by threatened or actual use of force or violence.

Routine activity theory or **lifestyle theory** a brand of rational choice theory that suggests that lifestyles contribute significantly to both the volume and the type of crime found in any society.

Routine activity approach holds that occurrences of personal victimization are dependent upon the "routine" or "daily activities" of people and are the outcome of three elements: the motivated offender, a suitable target, and the absence of a capable guardian.

Schizoid a person characterized by a schizoid personality disorder. Such disordered personalities appear to be aloof, withdrawn, unresponsive, humourless, dull, and solitary to an abnormal degree.

Schizophrenics mentally ill individuals who are out of touch with reality and suffer from disjointed thinking.

Second-degree murder all murder that is not first-degree murder.

Secondary analysis the reanalysis of existing data.

Secondary deviance that which results from official labelling and from association with others who have been so labelled.

Secondary research new evaluations of existing information collected by other researchers.

Selective incapacitation a social policy that seeks to protect society by incarcerating those individuals deemed to be the most dangerous.

Self-report study a data collection method requiring subjects to reveal their own participation in criminal behaviour.

Self-reports research investigations of subjects in order to record and report their behaviours.

Serial murder culpable homicide that involves the killing of several victims in three or more separate events.

Sexual assault an assault committed in circumstances of a sexual nature such that the sexual integrity of the victim is violated. The degree of violence used determines whether the sexual assault is level 1, level 2, or level 3.

Situational choice theory a brand of rational choice theory that views criminal behaviour as a function of choices and decisions made within a context of situational constraints and opportunities.

Situational crime prevention a social policy approach that looks to develop greater understanding of crime and more effective crime prevention strategies through concern with the physical, organizational, and social environments that make crime possible.

Social bond the intangible link between individuals and the society of which they are a part, created through the process of socialization.

Social capital the number of positive relationships with other persons and social institutions that individuals build up over the course of their lives.

Social class distinctions made between individuals on the basis of important defining social characteristics.

Social conflict perspective an analytical perspective on social organization holding that conflict is a fundamental aspect of social life itself and can never be fully resolved.

Social contract the Enlightenment-era concept that human beings abandon their natural state of individual freedom to join together and form society. Although in the process of forming a social contract individuals surrender some freedoms to society as a whole, government, once formed, is obligated to assume responsibilities toward its citizens and to provide for their protection and welfare.

Social control theories perspectives predicting that when social constraints on antisocial behaviour are weakened or absent, delinquent behaviour emerges. Rather than stressing causative factors in criminal behaviour, social control theory asks why people actually obey rules instead of breaking them.

Social development perspective an integrated view of human development that examines multiple levels of maturation simultaneously, including the psychological, biological, familial, interpersonal, cultural, societal, and ecological levels.

Social ecology an approach to criminological theorizing that attempts to link the structure and organization of any human community to interactions with its localized environment.

Social epidemiology the study of social epidemics and diseases of the social order.

Social learning theory a perspective that places primary emphasis upon the role of communication and socialization in the acquisition of learned patterns of criminal behaviour and the values that support that behaviour.

Social policies government initiatives, programs, and plans intended to address problems in society. The National Crime Prevention Strategy (formerly known as the National Strategy on Community Safety and Crime Prevention), for example, is a kind of generic, large-scale social policy—one consisting of many smaller programs.

Social problems perspective the belief that crime is a manifestation of underlying social problems such as poverty, discrimination, pervasive family violence, inadequate socialization practices, and the breakdown of traditional social institutions.

Social process theories, also known as **interactionist perspectives**, assert that criminal behaviour is learned in interaction with others, and the socialization processes that occur as a result of group membership are the primary route through which learning occurs.

Social relativity the notion that social events are differently interpreted according to the cultural experiences and personal interests of the initiator, the observer, or the recipient of that behaviour.

Social responsibility perspective the belief that individuals are fundamentally responsible for their own behaviour and that they choose crime over other, more law-abiding courses of action.

Social structure theories explain crime by reference to various aspects of the social fabric. They emphasize relationships among social institutions and describe the types of behaviour that tend to characterize *groups* of people as opposed to *individuals*.

Socialist feminism a perspective that examines social roles and the gender-based division of labour within the family, seeing both as a significant source of women's insubordination within society.

Socialization the lifelong process of social experience whereby individuals acquire the cultural patterns of their society.

Sociobiology the systematic study of the biological basis of all social behaviour.

Software piracy the unauthorized and illegal copying of software programs.

Somatotyping the classification of human beings into types according to body build and other physical characteristics.

Specific deterrence a goal of criminal sentencing that seeks to prevent a particular offender from engaging in repeat criminality.

Statistical school a criminological perspective with roots in the early 19th century that seeks to uncover correlations between crime rates and other types of demographic data.

Statute a formal written enactment of a legislative body.

Statutory law law in the form of statutes or formal written strictures, made by a legislature or governing body with the power to make law.

Stigmatic shaming a form of shaming, imposed as a sanction by the criminal jus-

tice system, that is thought to destroy the moral bond between the offender and the community.

Strain or **anomie theory** a sociological approach that posits a disjuncture between socially and subculturally sanctioned means and goals as the cause of criminal behaviour.

Structural Marxism a perspective that holds that the structural institutions of society influence the behaviour of individuals and groups by virtue of the type of relationships created. The criminal law, for example, reflects class relationships and serves to reinforce those relationships.

Subcultural theory a sociological perspective that emphasizes the contribution made by variously socialized cultural groups to the phenomenon of crime.

Subculture a collection of values and preferences that is communicated to subcultural participants through a process of socialization.

Sublimation the psychological process whereby one aspect of consciousness comes to be symbolically substituted for another.

Summary conviction offence a criminal offence that is less serious than an indictable offence; one that carries a maximum penalty of six months in jail.

Superego the moral aspect of the personality; much like the conscience. More formally, it is the division of the psyche that develops by the incorporation of the perceived moral standards of the community, is mainly unconscious, and includes the conscience.

Supermale a male individual displaying the XYY chromosomal structure.

Survey research a social science data-gathering technique involving the use of questionnaires.

Tagging the process whereby an individual is negatively defined by agencies of justice.

Target hardening the reduction in criminal opportunity for a particular location, generally through the use of physical barriers, architectural design, and improved security measures.

Techniques of neutralization learned justifications that can provide criminal offenders with the means to disavow responsibility for their behaviour.

Testosterone the primary male sex hormone; produced in the testes, its function is to control secondary sex characteristics and sexual drive.

Thanatos a death wish.

Theft the act of dishonestly taking property belonging to another person with the intention of depriving its owner of it either permanently or temporarily.

Theory a series of interrelated propositions that attempt to describe, explain, predict, and ultimately to control some class of events. A theory gains explanatory power from inherent logical consistency and is "tested" by how well it describes and predicts reality.

Transnational crime or **transnational organized crime** refers to unlawful activity undertaken and supported by organized groups operating across national boundaries.

Trephination a form of surgery, typically involving bone and especially the skull. Early instances of cranial trephination have been taken as evidence for primitive beliefs in spirit possession.

Twelve Tables early Roman laws written circa 450 BC that regulated family, religious, and economic life.

Typologies of crime classifications of crime useful in identifying patterns of criminal activity and motivations for criminal behaviour.

Unicausal having one cause. Unicausal theories posit only one source for all that they attempt to explain.

Uniform Crime Report (UCR) a summation of crime statistics tallied annually by the Canadian Centre for Justice Statistics (CCJS) and consisting primarily of data on crimes reported to the police.

V-chip a device that enables viewers to program their televisions to block out content with a common rating. It is intended for use against violent or sexually explicit programming.

Variable a concept that can undergo measurable changes.

Victim-proneness the degree of an individual's likelihood of victimization.

Victim impact statement a written document that describes the losses, suffering, and trauma experienced by the crime victim or by the victim's survivors. Judges are expected to consider these effects in arriving at an appropriate sentence for the offender.

Victim–Offender Reconciliation Program (VORP) a program that gives the offender the opportunity to meet face-to-face with the victim in the presence of a trained mediator in an attempt to reduce the victim's fears while establishing accountability and reparation for the crime.

Victim surcharge a mandatory, judicial imposition of a monetary fine administered in addition to a criminal sentence and used to finance victim services.

Victim/Witness Assistance Program counsels victims, orients them to the justice process, and provides a variety of other services such as transportation to court, child care during court appearances, and referrals to social service agencies.

Victimization Survey first conducted as the Canadian Urban Victimization Survey in 1981 by Statistics Canada and then every five years since 1988 as part of the General Social Survey. It provides data on surveyed households reporting that they had been affected by crime.

Victimogenesis the contributory background of a victim as a result of which he or she becomes prone to victimization.

Victimology the study of victims and their contributory role, if any, in the criminal event.

Violent Crime Linkage Analysis System (ViCLAS) a centralized computer bank containing details of violent crimes that assists police in recognizing patterns among violent offences and offenders.

Youth Criminal Justice Act Canadian legislation that determines the way in which youth are prosecuted under the criminal justice system. It replaced the *Young Offenders Act* in 2003.

Name Index

Subject Index

Information Communication Technology (ICT)
    usage, 338
informed consent, 27
inner containment, 270
innovation, 234–235
insanity, 217
instrumental Marxism, 291
integrated theory, 16
integrative perspective, 41
interactionist perspective, 257
    see also social process theories
international crime rate comparisons, 355
International Crime Victimization Survey
    (ICVS), 59, 60
International Criminal Police Organization
    (Interpol), 355
International Review of Victimology, 108
international traffic in human organs, 344–345
Internet
    Convention on Cyber-Crime, 339
    crime. *See* cyber-crime
    and crime statistics, 51
    cyberstalking, 87
    geographical profiling, 146–148
    as investigative tool, 351
    piracy, 348
interpretations, 41
involvement decisions, 145, 272
iris scanning, 352–353

J
Jeffery, C. Ray, 164
Juke family, 179–180
Just around the Corner (Foresight), 338
just deserts model, 152
justifications, 261–262
Justinian Code, 135

K
Kallikak family, 180
karyotyping, 180–181
Kretschmer, Ernst, 173
Kriminalpolitik, 329–330

L
labelling theory
    critique, 266
    defined, 263
    described, 262–266
    general model of labelling process, 266
    moral enterprise, 264
    primary deviance, 263
    reintegrative shaming, 266–269
    secondary deviance, 263
    unique ideas of, 265
Laub, John, 273

law
    administrative law, 5
    changes in, 6
    civil law, 5
    common law, 6
    criminal law, 5
    and mental illness, 216–219
    re-evaluation of existing laws, 6–7
    statutory law, 6
    three-strikes laws, 30
law-and-order advocates, 157–158
left realism, 306
left-realist criminology, 306–307
legal insanity, 217
Lemert, Edwin M., 263
Levitt, Theodore, 339
liberal feminists, 296
life course theories, 273
life pathways, 275
lifestyle model, 109
lifestyle theory, 144–145
Locke, John, 137
Lombroso, Cesare, 169–170
long-term offenders, 221, 330
Lorenz, Konrad, 166–167
low blood sugar, 175
lower-class culture, 238–239

M
Machalek, Richard, 275
macho male figure, 213–214
Magna Carta, 136
Maison des jeunes de Rawdon L'Excuse, 322–323
mala in se, 133
mala prohibita, 133–134
maladaption
    anti-social personality disorder, 209–210
    frustration-aggression thesis, 203–204
    personality types, 202–203
    psychoanalytic perspective, 199–202
    psychopathy, 206–209
    psychotic offender, 204–205
male criminality
    gender differences in criminality, 183–186
    lower-class culture, 239
    psychopathy, 208
male-female differences, 183–186
Malthus, Thomas Robert, 47
manslaughter, 82
marijuana use, 7
Marx, Karl, 286
Marxist criminology, 286
    see also radical criminology
mass murder, 83
Matza, David, 261
McKay, Henry, 229–230